organizational context. The firm's incentive systems, group interaction and ethical culture drive the outcomes of organizational ethical decisions. It is important to note that organizational ethical decision making is very different from personal, individual ethical decisions in the home and family.

Fannie Mae and Freddie Mac Failed to Be Accountable

Fannie Mae is a stockholder-owned corporation chartered by Congress as a government-sponsored endeavor in 1968. The corporation's purpose is to purchase and securitize mortgages in order to ensure that funds are available to institutions that lend money to home buyers. Freddie Mac was created in 1970 as a way to expand the secondary market for mortgages in the United States. Freddie Mac buys mortgages on the secondary market, and then resells mortgage-backed securities to investors on the open market. This secondary market increases the money available for mortgage lending and new home purchases. On September 7, 2008, James Lockhart, the Director of the Federal Housing Finance Agency (FHFA), announced that Fannie Mae and Freddie Mac were being placed into conservatorship of the FHFA. The move was made to help save these institutions from potential failure due to their involvement in the subprime mortgage market.

Before their problems in 2008, Fannie Mae and Freddie Mac guaranteed about half of the $12 trillion mortgage market. The value of the corporations' common stock and preferred stock diminished greatly with the onset of the housing crisis, and all future dividends were suspended. The U.S. Treasury advanced funds for the purpose of stabilizing Fannie Mae and Freddie Mac.

The 2008 trouble did not come out of nowhere. Fannie Mae was already under investigation for its accounting practices and alleged widespread accounting errors in 2004. In 2006, U.S. regulators filed civil charges against the CEO, the CFO, and the former controller. They are accused of manipulating earnings to maximize bonuses. In 2003 Freddie Mac revealed that it underreported earnings by over $5 billion, one of the largest corporate restatements in history.

Throughout the years, Fannie Mae and Freddie Mac both donated large sum contributions to lawmakers currently sittcommittees that regulate their industry. Currently, Fannie Mae and Fre   by federal prosecutors and the SEC. Former C   ron had been accused of fraud in civil suits for   out their companies' capitalization levels, wh   . Many questions remain concerning ethical d   rnment-sponsored organizations and their oversight by the   ss. Both organizations were guilty of poor decision making that resulted in expanding subprime loans and collateralized debt obligations that created the financial disasters in 2008–2009.

The first step in understanding ethical issues is recognizing stakeholder interests and concerns. Stakeholders, obviously, are individuals, groups, and even communities that can directly or indirectly affect a firm's activities. Although most corporations have emphasized shareholders as the most important stakeholder group, the failure to consider all significant stakeholders can lead to ethical lapses. In the financial industry, stakeholders include employees, investors, regulators, suppliers of financial products, communities, clients, as well as shareholders. Some executives believe that if their companies adopt a market-orientation and focus only on customers and shareholders, everything else will take care of itself. Unfortunately, failure to recognize the needs and potential impact of employees, suppliers, regulators, special-interest groups, communities, and the media, can lead to regrettable consequences.

Therefore, organizations need to identify and prioritize stakeholders and their respective concerns about organizational activities, and gather information to respond to significant individuals, groups, and communities. These groups apply their own values and standards to their perception of many diverse issues. They supply resources—e.g., capital, labor, expertise, infrastructure, sales, etc.—that are more or less critical to a firm's long-term survival, and their ability to withdraw—or threaten to withdraw—these resources gives them power. The financial industry has a special responsibility because of the services it provides and the need to develop trust in intangible, complex financial instruments. Most investors have limited financial education and experience; and therefore trust financial institutions as they would a medical doctor or lawyer.

One approach to stakeholders is to deal proactively with their concerns and ethical issues and stimulate a sense of bonding with the firm. When an organization listens to their concerns and tries to resolve issues, the result is tangible benefits that can translate into customer loyalty, employee commitment, supplier partnerships, and improved corporate reputation. This requires going beyond basic regulatory requirements and making a difference by genuinely listening to stakeholders and addressing their concerns. In the financial industry, transparency and truthfulness about products is necessary. There is a requirement that top management or the board of directors exercise due diligence in managing their financial interests. When firms look only at the profits and financial incentives for employees to perform, they can lose sight of important stakeholder responsibilities. To achieve results, employees can be permitted to bend rules and the firm can limit transparency to manipulate decisions or use legal loopholes.

Although individuals must make ethical choices, they often do so in committees, group meetings, and through discussion with colleagues. It can be difficult to be sure you are making an ethical decision when you do not fully understand the details of a situation. In the financial industry, new, complex financial instruments that are sold to investors are provided by specialists in a specific area and approved as legitimate to lower-level traders. Ethical decisions in the workplace are guided by the organization's culture and the influence of coworkers, superiors, and subordinates. A significant element of organizational culture is a firm's ethical climate—its character or conscience. Whereas a firm's overall culture establishes ideals that guide a wide range of behaviors for members of the organization, its ethical climate focuses specifically on issues of right and wrong. Codes of conduct and ethics policies, top management's actions on

2009 Update
Understanding the Importance of Business Ethics in the 2008–2009 Financial Crisis

Business ethics continues to be one of the least understood and most poorly managed dimensions of corporate America. The failure to understand and manage ethical risks played a significant role in the financial crisis and recession of 2008–2009. While there is a difference between bad business decisions and business misconduct, there is also a thin red line between the ethics of using only financial incentives to gauge performance and the use of holistic measures that include ethics, transparency, and responsibility to stakeholders. From CEOs to traders and brokers lucrative financial incentives existed for performance in the financial industry.

This introduction highlights some of the developments that contributed to business failures and the worst financial meltdown since the 1930s Great Depression. Our purpose is to introduce you to some of the ethical issues that contributed to this crisis, to provide a background on the financial products and decisions that contributed to the crisis and we hope to motivate you to want to learn more about organizational ethical decision making. This overview will use terms and concepts that will be defined and discussed in much more depth in the following chapters and cases in this textbook. In addition, we have developed an appendix that provides a synthesis and expansion of some of the core financial concepts associated with the recent crisis. Our goal here is to provide an understanding about the complexities, risks, and failures in ethical decision making in the financial industry. This is a very dynamic crisis and the outcome remains uncertain.

THE 2008–2009 FINANCIAL CRISIS

While it may take many years for some firms to recover from the most recent financial crisis, others are already gone forever. The assets of over $4 trillion from Lehman Brothers, AIG, Washington Mutual, Bear Stearns, and a few other leading financial institutions, vanished between January 1 and December 31, 2008. Most banks, financial

Prepared by O. C. Ferrell, John Fraedrich, and Linda Ferrell for the 2009 edition of *Business Ethics* (Cengage).

institutions, and many businesses have lost billions and without a government intervention in the form of a bailout or rescue plan, the industry could have collapsed. By early 2009, the government had pumped $250 billion into U.S. banks as a part of the rescue plan. The U.S. government is now a major partner and investor in our largest banks, insurance companies, and mortgage lenders. Countrywide Financial, AIG, Wachovia, Fannie Mae, and Freddie Mac were all either rescued by the U.S. government or forced into a takeover by a more solvent financial institution. One of the country's oldest and most respected investment banks, Lehman Brothers, went bankrupt with top managers under investigation by the FBI. Britain-based Barclays Bank agreed to buy Lehman Brothers' assets for pennies on the dollar, wiping out shareholders' wealth.

The 2008–2009 global recession was caused in part by a failure of the financial industry to take appropriate responsibility for its decision to utilize risky and complex financial instruments. Loopholes in regulation and the failures of regulators were exploited. Corporate cultures were built on rewards for taking risks rather than rewards for creating value for stakeholders. Ethical decisions were based more on what is legal rather than what was the right thing to do. Unfortunately, most stakeholders, including the public, regulators, and the mass media, do not always understand the nature of the financial risks taken on by banks and other institutions to generate profits. The intangible nature of financial products makes it difficult to understand complex financial transactions. Problems in the subprime mortgage markets sounded the alarm in the most recent economic downturn.

Very simply, the subprime market was created by making loans to people who normally would not qualify based on their credit rating. The debt from these loans was often repackaged and sold to other financial institutions in order to take it off lenders' books and reduce their exposure. When the real estate market became overheated, many people were no longer able to make the payments on their variable rate mortgages. When consumers began to default on payments, prices in the housing market dropped, as well as the value of collateralized debt obligations, and credit default swaps (the insurance on repackaged mortgage debt) lost significant value.

The opposite was supposed to happen. Credit default swaps were sold as a method of insuring against loss on complex packages of subprime loans. These derivatives, investors were told, would act as an insurance policy to reduce the risk of loss. Unfortunately, losses in the financial industry were so widespread that even the derivative contracts that had been written to cover losses from unpaid subprime mortgages could not be covered by the financial institutions that had written the derivatives as insurance on debt. The financial industry and managers at all levels had become focused on the rewards for the transaction without concerns about how their actions could potentially damage others.

ETHICAL DECISION MAKING IN FINANCIAL ORGANIZATIONS

It is important to examine ethical decision making in organizations to understand some of the issues that caused the financial crisis. Ethical decision making involves understanding how decisions are made and the factors that are unique to ethics in an ethical issues, the values and philosophies of coworkers, and the opportunity for misconduct all contribute to an organization's ethical climate. In fact, the ethical climate actually determines whether certain dilemmas are perceived as having a level of ethical intensity that requires a decision. In providing financial incentives for performance, employees may only see the importance of the sale, not the consequences.

Organizational culture, especially the influence of managers and co-workers, may create conditions that limit or permit misconduct. If these conditions act to provide rewards—such as financial gain, recognition, promotion, or simply the good feeling from a job well done—for unethical conduct, the opportunity for further unethical conduct may exist. For example, a company policy that does not mandate punishment of employees who violate a rule (e.g., not to sell a flawed financial product) effectively provides an opportunity for that behavior because it allows individuals to break the rule without fear of consequences. Thus, organizational policies, processes, and other factors may contribute to the opportunity to act unethically.

Such opportunities often relate to employees' immediate job context—where they work, with whom they work, and the nature of the work. The specific work situation includes the motivational "carrots and sticks" that managers can use to influence employee behavior. Pay raises, bonuses, and public recognition are carrots, or positive reinforcement, whereas reprimands, pay penalties, demotions, and even firings act as sticks, the negative reinforcement. For example, a broker or trader who is publicly recognized and given a large bonus for making a valuable sale that he or she obtained through unethical tactics will probably be motivated to use unethical sales tactics in the future, even if such behavior goes against his or her personal value system.

THE PERFECT ETHICAL STORM: SUBPRIME LOANS

We will illustrate the complexity of ethical decision making in the financial industry by starting with subprime loans. A subprime loan is offered to borrowers who are often turned away by traditional lenders because they have a low credit rating. In other words, this group of borrowers has a higher probability of not being able to repay debt and represents a higher risk to the lender. Because of this increased risk level, the interest rate or loan costs are greater than to those with good credit ratings who qualify for prime rate loans. Making loans to subprime, if done correctly, is not unethical but does require a highly ethical approach to minimize or manage the risks. Communication about risks to borrowers, financial documents associated with these loans, and reported income necessary to support the loan need to be accurate and truthful for the system to work. There are many opportunities to engage in misconduct when making subprime loans. The two biggest risks would include lying to the borrower and helping the borrower falsify loan documents.

Subprime lending means lending at a rate higher than the prime rate, often a 1 percent higher interest rate, although how far above depends on factors like credit score, down payment, debt-to-income ratio, and recent payment delinquencies. However, a 2007 *Wall Street Journal* study revealed that from 2004–2006, the rate of middle- and upper-income subprime loan borrowers rose dramatically. During the early- to mid-2000s, when real estate prices were booming and confidence levels were high, even clients who could have qualified for regular loans chose to take out subprime loans to finance their real estate speculations. As real estate prices peaked, more well-to-do investors turned to subprime mortgages to finance their expensive, possibly overpriced, homes. In relation to the loan market as a whole, subprime loans comprise a relatively small part. In 2008, over 6 million U.S. homeowners had subprime loans with a combined value of over $600 billion. In comparison, all other U.S. loans amounted to over $10 trillion. Although they only make up a small chunk of the loan market, many consider subprime loans to be a key contributor to the 2008 financial crisis.

The Subprime Crisis

One of the tools of the subprime loan was the adjustable rate mortgage (ARM) that allowed borrowers to pay low introductory payments for three to five years that would then be adjusted annually as the prime interest rate increased or decreased. Another type of ARM was to pay interest for a set number of years with balloon payments, meaning that people would only make interest payments for the life of the loan, and then would be expected to pay the entire principal at once upon maturity of the loan. These tools worked as long as the housing market remained on an upward trajectory, but when housing prices fell or interest rates increased people found themselves unable to pay. Many financial experts contributed to the problem by telling clients that in the future they would certainly have more income because of the increases in their property's value. They assured home buyers that even if payments increased, they would be able to afford them because the value of their home would have increased so much. Even consumers with good credit looking to refinance were attracted to the low interest rates without fully recognizing the possible consequences.

Ethics issues emerged early in subprime lending with loan officers receiving commission on securing a loan from a borrower with no consequences if the borrower defaulted on the loan. "Liar loans" soon developed to create more sales for lenders and higher personal compensation. Lenders would encourage subprime borrowers to provide false information on their loan applications to clear the threshold and qualify the loan. Sometimes appraisers were used who provided inflated home values in order to secure the loan. In other instances, consumers were asked to falsify their income to make the loan more attractive to the lending organization. The opportunity for misconduct was widespread. Top managers and even CEOs thought nothing could go wrong and were complacent about the wrongdoing. Congress and President Clinton encouraged Fannie Mae and Freddie Mac, which agreed to purchase subprime loans from banks that make such loans, to support homeownership among low-income families. In an economy with home values rapidly increasing, this culture of unethical behavior was less transparent. When home values started to decline and individuals were "upside down" on their loans (owing more than the equity in the home) the failure of responsible lending and borrowing and unethical behavior became obvious.

When introduced on a trial basis in 1999, the new financial tool of subprime loans was praised for lowering barriers to homeownership. But then something happened that no one had considered. The U.S. economy began to slow. People started working more and earning less money. Jobs started moving abroad, health insurance became more expensive, gas prices increased, and the baby boomers began to sell their homes to fund their retirement. In spite of this, builders kept on building, and the financial industry continued to lend to increasingly risky buyers. Homeowners found that they had less disposable income to make housing payments.

The result was a surplus of housing that homeowners could no longer afford. Banks began to foreclose on houses when the homeowners could not pay. As the demand for housing decreased, banks lost significant amounts of money. Many other industries, like the automobile industry and insurance companies, were also negatively affected as struggling citizens tried to cope with the economic downturn. With plummeting stock prices, the United States began experiencing a financial crisis that had a rippling effect across the world. Economist Alan Greenspan said the crisis could be "the most wrenching since the end of the Second World War."

Starting late in 2007 and continuing into 2008 marked the tipping-point for the burgeoning mortgage crisis. Foreclosure rates skyrocketed and borrowers and investors began to feel the full ramifications of taking the subprime risk. Mortgage defaults played a part in triggering a string of serious bank and financial institution failures as well. In 2007, investors began to abandon their mortgage-backed securities, causing huge institutions such as Morgan Stanley, Merrill Lynch, and Citigroup to lose large sums of money. Morgan Stanley, for example, lost over $265 billion internationally. Bear Stearns required government assistance to help JP Morgan buy the firm for $10 a share. Analysts have attributed the banks' failings to poor intra-bank communication and a lack of effective risk management.

Although the Chief Financial Officer (CFO) is supposed to be in charge of risk management, it appears that many institutions viewed the role as merely advisory. It was highly risky for these firms to downplay the importance of the CFO. Not only did many of these banks fail at risk management, they may have been in violation of the Sarbanes–Oxley Act—which requires that a company verify its ability to internally control its financial reporting. A CFO not directly in charge of a company's finances is signing off on something that he or she actually knows little about. The extent of the 2008–2009 financial crisis has made it clear to many that a massive overhaul of the financial industry's regulatory system is needed.

DERIVATIVES CONTRIBUTE TO ETHICAL RISKS

Derivatives are financial instruments with values that change relative to underlying variables, such as assets, events, or prices. In other words, the value of derivatives is based on the change in value of something else, called the *underlying* trade or exchange. The main types of derivatives are futures, forwards, options, and swaps. Swaps live up to their name in that financial risks are exchanged between two parties. A swap can occur when two parties agree to exchange responsibility for a debt for cash flows to the insurer. Swaps can be used to hedge risks such as changes in interest rates, or to speculate on the changing prices of commodities or currencies. Swaps can be difficult to understand, so here is an example. JP Morgan developed credit default swaps (CDSs) that bundled together as many as 300 different assets, including subprime loans. Credit default swaps were meant as a form of insurance. In other words, securities were bundled into one financial package and companies such as JP Morgan were essentially paying insurance premiums to the investors who purchased them, who were now on the hook if payments of any of the securities defaulted.

Credit default swaps (CDSs) essentially insure the value of the underlying debt that the investor has purchased. Selling insurance against bond defaults allows the insurer to receive regular payments from securities owned by banks or hedge funds. In return for the payments the owner of the CDS agreed to repay the owner of the bonds or other securities in the highly unlikely event of a wave of corporate or bank defaults. By 2007, there were $57 trillion in these credit default swap contracts globally. Derivatives (in this case CDSs) were supposed to act as a "shock absorber" when one industry, or part of the world, gets into financial trouble. Many investors in CDSs included public sector and nonprofit organizations that did not understand the risks they were taking if there was a financial meltdown like the one that occurred in 2008–2009.

Derivatives pose high amounts of risk for the small or inexperienced investors. Because derivatives offer the possibility of large rewards, they offer an attraction to individual investors. But the basic premise of derivatives is to transfer risk among parties based on their willingness to assume additional risk, or hedge against it. Many smaller investors don't comprehend this until they lose. Sometimes investment advisors place small investors or even nonprofit organizations in these speculative investments without their knowledge. Warren Buffett, a well-known investor, has stated that he regards derivatives as "financial weapons of mass destruction." Derivatives have been used to leverage the debt in an economy, sometimes to a massive degree. When something unexpected happens, an economy will find it very difficult to pay its debts, thus causing a recession or even depression. Marriner S. Eccles, U.S. Federal Reserve Chairman from 1934 to 1948, stated that an excessively high level of debt was one of the primary causes of the Great Depression.

Finally, the ethical issues in using derivatives rest with managers and traders who use this highly complex and risky financial instrument. Derivatives soon became too complex for the average person to understand, and Wall Street turned to mathematicians and physicists to create models and computer programs that could analyze these exotic instruments. Derivatives were used in sales transactions where there is an opportunity of great financial rewards that does not take into account the level of risk for investors or other stakeholders. If the risk associated with a derivative is not communicated to the investor, this could result in deception or even fraud. It has become apparent that the use of derivatives such as credit default swaps became so profitable that traders and managers lost sight of anything but their incentives for selling these instruments. In other words, financial institutions were selling what could be called defective products because a true risk of these financial instruments was not understood or disclosed to the customer. In some cases these defective products were given to traders to sell without any due diligence from the company as to the level of risk.

While derivatives, including *credit default swaps*, were not the only cause of the failure of the banks and other financial institutions, the use of these instruments by decision makers resulted in taking enormous risks. In hindsight, these actions seem to be unwise and unfair to stakeholders. An ethical issue relates to the level of transparency that exists in using complex financial instruments to create profits. Irresponsible derivatives trading with limited regulatory oversight gave traders almost unlimited opportunities to manipulate the use of derivatives. In many financial institutions, there is no doubt that a number of key decision makers not only pushed the limits of legitimate risk-taking, but also engaged in manipulation, and in some cases fraud, to deceive shareholders by lying about the company's true financial condition.

INCENTIVES FOR FINANCIAL MISCONDUCT

The credit default swap (CDS) appears to have been the cause of the downfall of major investment banks. Enron also had built a number of its business areas on derivatives. The question remains: was there misconduct, or just bad business decisions related to the dependence of high-risk financial instruments? No doubt, greed and manipulation played a role in the widespread implementation of these new financial instruments. Complicated derivatives have certainly made the world of finance a more convoluted and opaque place.

Before 2008, very few people discussed the pros and cons of credit default swaps, even though they proved powerful enough to help bring down Bear Stearns, Lehman Brothers, AIG, Washington Mutual, and others. Credit default swaps were pioneered less than a decade ago by a young team of math whizzes at JP Morgan. This innovative instrument, which was supposed to help hedge risk, became responsible for integrating the global financial world. The regulatory system did not act to provide rules and oversight for these new financial instruments. Money managers around the world owned credit default swaps without understanding how they could fail and create a financial crisis.

Similar to the off-the-balance-sheet partnerships employed by Enron, credit default swaps are considered a legal approach to business. Unfortunately, with no regulatory oversight the model failed many companies, just as off-the-balance-sheet partnerships contributed to Enron's fall. Using credit default swaps, companies like JP Morgan created a means of keeping debt off of its balance sheet and sharing exposure through selling tranches of a combination of loans or bonds with underlying derivative contracts that essentially insured the buyer. Investment banks sold billions of dollars in securities that were mostly backed by loans made to consumers with shaky credit histories. These loans were packaged and sold as debt obligations. Most of these measurements carried embedded credit default derivatives. When AIG's trading partners demanded collateral from the insurer, AIG did not have enough money to cover its obligations. Similar to Enron, the entire global banking system had constructed veritable houses of cards. The CEOs of these companies, similar to Ken Lay, in most cases never anticipated the risk they were taking and the toxic nature of the products they were selling. The lesson learned here is that without a degree of transparency and critical analysis the regulatory system and other stakeholders cannot determine systemic flaws in business decision making.

The 2008–2009 financial crises have shown us a roadmap of companies failing to protect themselves against the unexpected. In the case of AIG, the toxic financial instruments were hidden deep in the credit default swap market. Credit default swaps were supposed to provide insurance against defaults. If AIG understood the complexity of the financial products they were employing, it is possible they would have better understood the extent of their risk. An excessively heavy reliance on complicated computer models that were flawed and did not adequately weigh risk caused many financial companies to cavalierly make risky investments. AIG relied on these computer models to help figure out which credit swap deals were supposedly safe. However, the model was not built to anticipate how market forces would turn these contracts into huge financial liabilities.

Financial dealings have become more complex with computer trading models, exotic derivative products, and extreme risk-taking that does not consider the ethical dimensions of decision making or the ramifications of high-risk financial instruments on stakeholders. All of these factors have made running a business more difficult; and the importance of ethics more important. The focus has become excessively fixed on the bottom line. The role of human beings utilizing experience and creative skills to predict consequences beyond the reach of quantitative models has diminished in recent decades. Questions remain as we experience a new financial meltdown that dwarfs the severity of the Enron scandal. This crisis involves the entire global financial industry. Paul Volcker stated, "For all its talented participants, for all its rich rewards . . . the bright new financial system has failed the test of the marketplace."

Enron, a Precursor to the Current Crisis?

Only eight years ago, Enron experienced a financial collapse very similar to AIG, Washington Mutual, Lehman Brothers, and Wachovia Banks. Enron also engaged in a type of high-risk gambling in its electronic trading models. Because of its convoluted system and accounting methods like mark-to-market, it became difficult for even company insiders to evaluate the true revenue stream and the value of assets. Moving assets off the balance sheet complicated issues and made financial reports opaque to analysts. Like an iceberg, the real structure and problems with companies like Enron and AIG lay out of sight, below the surface. The mass media and legal system, as well as the public, blamed Enron's failure on top executives Ken Lay and Jeff Skilling. It is easier to isolate blame and target top, highly compensated CEOs than to try and unwind the complex series of relationships that resulted in the misconduct.

Prosecutors often look for intentional wrongdoing that relates to very simple matters such as lying, cheating, or deception. Because juries often do not understand complex financial matters, the simpler the explanation the more likely a prosecutor is to get a conviction. Ken Lay returned as Enron's CEO after its business model had failed. Less than four months before Enron filed for bankruptcy, Lay remained highly positive about the company's financial health. He was undoubtedly convicted for what he said. Statements such as "the balance sheet is strong," "the third quarter is looking great," and "Enron stock is an incredible bargain at current prices" were where the jury found that Lay crossed the line and lied about Enron's financial condition. CEOs and CFOs of the financial companies that failed in 2008 will be similarly scrutinized for statements they made on "Investor Day" gatherings or on-camera statements as to their companies' financial health. Because the most recent meltdown occurred in the post-SOX era, these CFOs and CEOs will be held to even higher standards than Lay. Did these managers know they had flawed business models, or were they truly naïve about the goings-on at their own companies? The prosecutors are about to start forming their judgments.

Failed financial institutions and Enron share a common cause: a profound failure of corporate governance that supported a culture of financial incentives and inadequate monitoring of risk. Enron's board of directors ratified incentives and compensation packages that encouraged reckless speculation of shareholder money—the same scenario that has caused many of the United States' largest financial institutions to collapse. Enron's bonus system gave business developers and commodity traders the incentive to inflate future profitability estimates in order to earn bonuses, even before the outcomes of transactions were known. Convicting CEOs and passage of Sarbanes–Oxley regulation did not resolve the problems and organizational wrongdoing. The legalization of business ethics through such legislation appears to have failed.

THE ROLE OF BUSINESS ETHICS IN PREVENTING FINANCIAL MISCONDUCT

The 2008–2009 global financial crisis as well as the failures of Enron, WorldCom, Health South, Arthur Andersen, and other global firms in 2001–2002 illustrates the vital importance of an ethical organizational culture. Ethics is a key part of building relationships and providing value to customers and other key stakeholders. Most firms that failed were not the victims of one rogue employee or a CEO who developed an unethical scheme to deceive customers. If fact, if there had been only a few unethical employees in firms such as Bear Stearns, Fannie Mae, Freddie Mac, and Lehman Brothers then the misconduct would have been detected and the damage could have been contained and would have been much more minor. Unfortunately, the misconduct was systemic—not isolated and cultural—not individual. The regulatory system was reactive and did not anticipate how unregulated financial instruments and hedge funds could inflict so much damage on the economy. Many CEOs and other top executives did not understand derivatives or CDSs, but, trusted the operatives in middle-level positions to advance plans for helping the organization to achieve its objectives. The appropriate level of oversight and understanding was missing or not functioning as the ultimate check and balance of behavior, which supports an ethical organizational culture. The organization as a whole was focused on achieving short-term objectives. Whether it was interest-only loans or "liar loans," the mortgage and banking industries found ways to let an unprecedented number of people purchase the home of their choice. Wall Street compounded this mistake by packaging the mortgages into complex financial products and selling them to investors who mostly did not understand what they were buying or the risk they were taking. They trusted the sellers and insurers to have their interests protected. Investment banks made billions of dollars in fees giving mortgage underwriters the incentive to originate and sell even the most unscrupulous of loans.

The bottom line for organizations is that there must be a culture of ethical conduct that is developed by the CEO and top-level managers and implemented, embraced, and understood by all employees within the organization. Sidestepping regulations and best practices by creating new income-generating opportunities that had never been anticipated by regulators could be assumed to have an element of risk. The whole purpose of a due diligence ethics program is that it anticipates and manages current and emerging risks. It is not enough for top executives to say that they did not understand or that there was not the appropriate level of oversight or regulation of their industry. The top executives and CEOs are ultimately responsible for the destiny and decisions of their employees. Top executives at Merrill Lynch awarded $3.6 billion in bonuses to more than 39,000 employees shortly before its merger with Bank of America Corp. in 2008, with a combined $121 million going to four top executives. This was done in spite of the fact that Merrill Lynch had to be rescued by the government and Bank of America to save it from bankruptcy. Two ethics issues were first, paying the bonuses, and second, speeding up the timetable to distribute the payment of the bonuses before Bank of America's takeover at the beginning of the year. Risk management in the financial industry is a key top management concern, including the ethical risk associated with new products and market penetration, including paying bonuses to executives who failed in their duties. Unfortunately, at the same time the industry was only looking at their own interests and the bottom line, regulatory agencies and Congress were not proactive in investigating early cases of financial misconduct and the systemic issues that led to the crisis. The legal and regulatory systems focused more on individual misconduct rather than systemic ethical failure. Like Ken Lay and Jeff Skilling at Enron, CEOs will be scrutinized by prosecutors to see if they engaged in lies and deception to investors. In the case of Enron, Lay and Skilling were convicted because they allegedly lied about the financial condition of Enron. Did CEOs in the current financial disaster lie about their firms' financial condition? In conjunction, and partially in response to the misconduct, the economy slowed so dramatically that it became our most difficult economic times since the Depression of the 1930s.

THE IMPORTANCE OF BUSINESS ETHICS AND THIS COURSE

There are many aspects of life that are intuitive. You should be honest and truthful with others. This is relatively easy to do and commit to in your personal life because you control your environment. In an organization or business, you do not control your environment. You are given a title, position description, responsibilities for outcomes, evaluations which shape your behavior and influence your income, supervisors who provide leadership and guidance, and coworkers who influence your decision making. Very often, ethical issues are deeply embedded in daily decision making and unless you have anticipated the potential ramifications, risks, and consequences it is possible to engage in behavior with negative outcomes that you could not or did not anticipate. The purpose of this course is to prepare you for the challenges that you will face as an employee, manager, and potentially a business owner yourself. There is nothing commonsensical or easy about organizational ethical decision making. The companies who successfully navigate these challenges spend considerable time, effort, training, investment, and collaboration with others to discover risks and prevent misconduct. Currently, we are sending an ambiguous message to those in the financial industry who did the right thing in managing their risks. If you engaged in misconduct, you could benefit from government financial rescue funds. If you operated an ethical and high-integrity financial organization and are going through difficult financial times because of the economy, you do not qualify for government support. Ultimately, the outcome of this financial and ethics crisis will be determined by the survivors.

Business ethics from an organizational perspective is not merely about changing individuals' philosophies about ethics one person at a time and then assuming there will be no misconduct. Firms have to establish principles, develop shared values, and develop compliance standards to control misconduct. While many individuals think they have good ethics and want to do the right thing, they often have to trust others including managers, lawyers, and accountants when selling complex financial instruments. This means that unless there is transparency with critical ethical evaluations by those providing oversight, the individual can be a part of systemic ethical misconduct. To some extent, this is what happened in the 2008–2009 financial crisis. Many well-meaning individuals helped implement an ethically flawed financial model. This model inflicted major damage on the world economy and resulted in widespread government, nonprofit, business, and individual financial loss. Some of the social damage occurred from families losing their homes, millions losing their jobs, and charitable giving being forever impacted by investor misconduct.

Hopefully the regulatory system will become more proactive and provide incentives for more cooperation and transparency to discover risks. The financial industry needs to make ethics an enterprise-wide concern and a part of performance evaluations. Complacency and overreliance on complex computer models to determine decisions based only on formulas to maximize profits have failed the financial industry. The defense that subprime loans, credit default swaps, and computer models were not unethical approaches ignored the fact that decision makers misused their instruments to damage others. Concern for others and the avoidance of harm is a key principle of business ethics.

SOURCES: Chad Bray, "Cuomo Blasts Merrill Over Bonuses," *Wall Street Journal,* February 11, 2009, http://online.wsj.com/article/SB123436012776372943.html (accessed February 11, 2009); Jesse Eisinger, "First, Fire the Regulators," *Conde Nast Portfolio,* February 2009, 45–47; O. C. Ferrell, John Fraedrich, and Jennifer Jackson, "Countrywide Financial: The Subprime Meltdown," case in *Business Ethics: Ethical Decision Making and Cases* (7th edition); O. C. Ferrell, John Fraedrich, and Jennifer Jackson, "Banking Industry Meltdown: The Ethical and Financial Risks of Derivatives," case in *Business Ethics: Ethical Decision Making and Cases* (7th edition); O. C. Ferrell, John Fraedrich, and Jennifer Jackson, "Coping with Financial and Ethical Risks at American International Group," case in *Business Ethics: Ethical Decision Making and Cases* (7th edition); Matthew Malone, "The Usual Suspects," *Conde Nast Portfolio,* February 2009, 85–87; Roger Parloff, "Wall Street: It's Payback Time," *Fortune,* January 19, 2009, 57–69.

BUSINESS ETHICS
Ethical Decision Making and Cases
2009 Update

BUSINESS ETHICS
Ethical Decision Making and Cases
2009 Update

SEVENTH EDITION

O. C. FERRELL
University of New Mexico

JOHN FRAEDRICH
University of Wyoming

LINDA FERRELL
University of New Mexico

SOUTH-WESTERN
CENGAGE Learning™

Business Ethics
Ethical Decision Making and Cases
2009 Update, 7e
O. C. Ferrell
John Fraedrich
Linda Ferrell

Vice President of Editorial, Business:
  Jack W. Calhoun
Vice President/Editor-in-Chief:
  Melissa S. Acuna
Acquisitions Editor: Michele Rhodes
Developmental Editor: Joanne Dauksewicz
Marketing Manager: Nathan Anderson
Content Project Manager: Corey Geissler
Media Editor: Rob Ellington
Sr. Frontlist Buyer, Manufacturing:
  Kevin Kluck
Production Service: S4 Carlisle Publishing
  Services
Sr. Art Director: Tippy McIntosh
Cover Image: Michael Melford/Getty Images

For product information and technology assistance, contact us at **Cengage Learning Customer & Sales Support, 1-800-354-9706**
For permission to use material from this text or product, submit all requests online at
www.cengage.com/permissions
Further permissions questions can be emailed to
permissionrequest@cengage.com

Library of Congress Control Number: 2009923349
ISBN-13: 978-1-4390-4281-6
ISBN-10: 1-4390-4281-0

South-Western Cengage Learning
5191 Natorp Boulevard
Mason, OH 45040
USA

Cengage Learning products are represented in Canada by Nelson Education, Ltd.

For your course and learning solutions, visit www.cengage.com Purchase any of our products at your local college store or at our preferred online store
www.ichapters.com

Printed in the United States of America
1 2 3 4 5 6 7 13 12 11 10 09

This book is dedicated to
My son, James Collins Ferrell
— O. C. Ferrell
My wife, Debbie, and the mob Anna, Jacob,
Joseph, Joshua, Lael, Sam, Emma, and
Matthew,
as well as my parents, Gerhard and Bernice
— John Fraedrich
My parents, Norlan and Phyllis Nafziger
— Linda Ferrell

Brief Contents

Contents

PART THREE   **THE DECISION-MAKING PROCESS**   119

CHAPTER 5   **Ethical Decision Making and Ethical Leadership**   120

PART FOUR   IMPLEMENTING BUSINESS ETHICS IN A GLOBAL ECONOMY   203

Preface

In the last two years we have witnessed the most devastating financial crisis since the Great Depression. Not since the 1930s has the government assumed so much power over private industry in such a short period of time. In 2008 over $700 billion was injected into the economy to purchase failed debt obligations and keep the banking system and other financial institutions from collapsing. In 2009 a $787 million stimulus package was passed by Congress to hopefully avoid another Great Depression. As we try to understand what happened, it appears that greed, excessive risk-taking, and the financial industry culture of focusing on rewards and the bottom line helped to create their own demise. The failure to focus on ethical principles, values, and transparency in decision making was widespread. Wall Street was a highly interconnected system that thrived on finding loopholes in the regulatory system as well as ignoring the interests of stakeholders.

This update of the seventh edition of *Business Ethics* focuses on these recent events from an ethical perspective. We have developed a new introduction focused on understanding the importance of business ethics in the 2008–2009 financial crisis and an appendix that addresses foundational concepts in understanding ethical dimensions of the financial meltdown. This extensive update creates the most comprehensive and current business ethics text on the market. Our research indicated that you wanted updates in the teaching material and cases to address these new ethical dilemmas in our society. Therefore, we have updated content in each chapter and developed five new cases that address the current financial crisis from an ethical perspective. The issues associated with the financial crisis have caused us to look at ethics from a more systemic perspective. While individuals were often held accountable for lying, cheating, and deception we now have networks of organizations that created corrupt systems that severely damaged society.

Using a managerial framework, we explain how ethics can be integrated into strategic business decisions. This framework provides an *overview of the concepts, processes, mandatory, core, and voluntary business practices* associated with successful business ethics programs. Some approaches to business ethics are excellent as exercises in intellectual reasoning, but, do not deal with the actual issues and considerations that people in business organizations face. Our approach prepares students for ethical dilemmas that they will face in their business careers.

We have been diligent in this revision to provide the most relevant examples of how the lack of business ethics has challenged our economic viability and entangled countries and companies around the world. This book remains the market leader because it *addresses the complex environment of ethical decision making in organizations and pragmatic, actual business concerns.* Every individual has unique personal values and every organization has its own set of values, rules, and organizational ethical culture. Business ethics must consider the organizational culture and interdependent relationships between the individual and other significant persons involved in organizational decision making. Without effective guidance, a businessperson cannot make ethical decisions while facing a short-term orientation, feeling organizational pressure and rewards based on outcomes, and the challenges and changes caused by the competitive as well as external environment.

Employees cannot make the best, most ethical decisions in a vacuum devoid of the influence of organizational codes, policies, and culture. Most employees and all managers are responsible not only for their own ethical conduct, but for the conduct of co-workers and those who they supervise. Therefore, teaching business ethics as an exercise in independent, personal decision making fails to acknowledge the key influence upon (un)ethical conduct of co-workers and managers. Employees must know how to recognize and when to report and address ethical issues in the workplace. Students must also learn how to "fit in" the ethical culture of their organization and be responsible for their own decisions and upholding the standards of the organization.

By focusing on the issues and organizational environments, this book provides students the opportunity to see the roles and responsibilities they will face in business. The past decade has reinforced that business ethics is not a "fad" but a prevailing set of risks that organizations face on an ongoing basis. Our primary goal has always been to enhance the awareness and the ethical decision-making skills that students will need to make business ethics decisions that contribute to responsible business conduct. By focusing on these concerns and issues of today's challenging business environment, we demonstrate that the study of business ethics is imperative to the long-term well-being of not only businesses, but our economic system.

PHILOSOPHY OF THIS TEXT

Business ethics in organizations requires values-based leadership from top management and purposeful actions that include planning and implementation of standards of appropriate conduct, as well as openness and continuous effort to improve the organization's ethical performance. Although personal values are important in ethical decision making, they are just one of the components that guide the decisions, actions, and policies of organizations. The burden of ethical behavior relates to the organization's values and traditions, not just to the individuals who make the decisions and carry them out. A firm's ability to plan and implement ethical business standards depends in part on structuring resources and activities to achieve ethical objectives in an effective and efficient manner.

The purpose of this book is to help students improve their ability to make ethical decisions in business by providing them with a framework that they can use to identify, analyze, and resolve ethical issues in business decision making. Individual values and ethics are important in this process. By studying business ethics, students begin to understand how to cope with conflicts between their personal values and those of the organization.

Many ethical decisions in business are close calls. It often takes years of experience in a particular industry to know what is acceptable. We do not, in this book, provide ethical answers but instead attempt to prepare students to make informed ethical decisions. First, we do not moralize by indicating what to do in a specific situation. Second, although we provide an overview of moral philosophies and decision-making processes, we do not prescribe any one philosophy or process as best or most ethical. Third, by itself, this book will not make students more ethical nor will it tell them how to judge the ethical behavior of others. Rather, its goal is to help students understand and use their current values and convictions in making business decisions and to encourage everyone to think about the effects of their decisions on business and society.

Many people believe that business ethics cannot be taught. Although we do not claim to teach ethics, we suggest that by studying business ethics a person can improve ethical decision making by identifying ethical issues and recognizing the approaches available to resolve them. An organization's reward system can reinforce appropriate behavior and help shape attitudes and beliefs about important issues. For example, the success of some campaigns to end racial or gender discrimination in the workplace provides evidence that attitudes and behavior can be changed with new information, awareness, and shared values.

COMPLETE CONTENT COVERAGE

In writing *Business Ethics,* seventh edition, we have strived to be as informative, complete, accessible, and up to date as possible. Instead of focusing on one area of ethics, such as moral philosophy or social responsibility, we provide balanced coverage of all areas relevant to the current development and practice of ethical decision making. In short, we have tried to keep pace with new developments and current thinking in teaching and practices. The corporate governance and ethical compliance issues that resulted in the passage of the Sarbanes–Oxley Act of 2002 are appropriately addressed. The 2004 amendments of the Federal Sentencing Guidelines for Organizations provide directions for ethical leadership and oversight responsibilities for boards of directors. Specific ethical issues including abusive and intimidating behavior, lying, conflicts of interest, bribery, corporate intelligence, discrimination, sexual harassment, environmental issues, fraud, insider trading, intellectual-property rights, privacy, and other issues that may cause social or environmental damage are covered through dilemmas, examples, and cases. Additionally, we have added a new chapter on institutionalization of business ethics to reflect legal and societal pressures for required compliance, core practices, and voluntary activities to improve business ethics.

ORGANIZATION OF THE TEXT

The first half of the text consists of ten chapters, which provide a framework to identify, analyze, and understand how businesspeople make ethical decisions and deal with ethical issues. Several enhancements have been made to chapter content for this edition. Some of the most important are listed on pp. xxxiv–xxxv.

Part One, "An Overview of Business Ethics," includes two chapters that help provide a broader context for the study of business ethics. Chapter 1, "The Importance of Business Ethics," has been revised with many new examples and survey results to describe issues and concerns important to business ethics. Chapter 2, "Stakeholder Relationships, Social Responsibility, and Corporate Governance," has been significantly reorganized and updated with new examples and issues. This chapter was reorganized and expanded to develop an overall framework for the text.

Part Two, "Ethical Issues and the Institutionalization of Business Ethics," consists of two chapters that provide the background that students need to identify ethical issues and understand how society, through the legal system, has attempted to hold organizations responsible for managing these issues. Chapter 3, "Emerging Business Ethics Issues," has been significantly reorganized and updated and provides expanded coverage of business ethics issues. Reviewers requested more detail on key issues that create ethical decisions. Within this edition, we have increased the depth of ethical issues and have added the following new issues: abusive and intimidating behavior, lying, bribery, corporate intelligence, environmental issues, intellectual-property rights, and privacy. Chapter 4, "The Institutionalization of Business Ethics" examines key elements of core or best practices in corporate America today along with legislation and regulation requirements that support business ethics initiatives. The chapter is divided into three main areas: voluntary, mandated, and core boundaries.

Part Three, "The Decision-Making Process" consists of three chapters, which provide a framework to identify, analyze, and understand how businesspeople make ethical decisions and deal with ethical issues. Chapter 5, "Ethical Decision Making and Ethical Leadership," has been revised and updated to reflect current research and understanding of ethical decision making and contains a new section on ethical leadership. Chapter 6, "Individual Factors: Moral Philosophies and Values," has been updated and revised to explore the role of moral philosophies and moral development as individual factors in the ethical decision-making process. This chapter now includes a new section on white-collar crime. Chapter 7, "Organizational Factors: The Role of Ethical Culture and Relationships," considers organizational influences on business decisions, such as role relationships, differential association, and other organizational pressures, as well as whistle-blowing.

Part Four, "Implementing Business Ethics in a Global Economy," looks at specific measures that companies can take to build an effective ethics program, as well as how these programs may be affected by global issues. Chapter 8, "Developing an Effective Ethics Program," has been refined and updated with corporate best practices for developing effective ethics programs. Chapter 9, "Implementing and Auditing Ethics Programs," offers a framework for auditing ethics initiatives as well as the importance of doing so. Such audits can help companies pinpoint problem areas, measure their progress in improving conduct, and even provide a "debriefing" opportunity after a crisis. Finally, Chapter 10, "Business Ethics in a Global Economy," contains new examples of international business ethics issues, conflicts, and cooperative efforts to establish universal standards of conduct.

Part Five consists of eighteen cases that bring reality into the learning process. Nine of these cases are new to the seventh edition, and the remaining nine have been revised and updated. The companies and situations portrayed in these cases are real; names and other facts are not disguised; and all cases include developments up to 2009. By reading and analyzing these cases, students can gain insight into ethical decisions and the realities of making decisions in complex situations.

The seventh edition provides five behavioral simulation role-play cases developed for use in the business ethics course. The role-play cases and implementation methods can be found in the *Instructor's Resource Manual* and on the website. Role-play cases may be used as a culminating experience to help students integrate concepts covered in the text. Alternatively, the cases may be used as an ongoing exercise to provide students with extensive opportunities for interacting and making ethical decisions.

Role-play cases simulate a complex, realistic, and timely business ethics situation. Students form teams and make decisions based on an assigned role. The role-play case complements and enhances traditional approaches to business learning experiences because it (1) gives students the opportunity to practice making decisions that have business ethics consequences; (2) re-creates the power, pressures, and information that affect decision making at various levels of management; (3) provides students with a team-based experience that enriches their skills and understanding of group processes and dynamics; and (4) uses a feedback period to allow for the exploration of complex and controversial issues in business ethics decision making. The role play can be used with classes of any size.

STUDENT WEBSITE

The website developed for the seventh edition provides up-to-date examples, issues, and interactive learning devices to assist students in improving their decision-making skills. "The Business Ethics Learning Center" has been created to take advantage of information available on the Internet while providing new interactive skill-building exercises that can help students practice ethical decision making. The site contains links to companies and organizations highlighted in each chapter; Internet exercises; ACE (ACyber Evaluation) interactive quizzes, which help students master chapter content through multiple-choice questions; links to association, industry, and company codes of conduct; case website linkages; company and organizational examples; and academic resources, including links to business ethics centers throughout the world and the opportunity to sign up for weekly abstracts of relevant *Wall Street Journal* articles. Four Ethical Leadership Challenge scenarios are available for each chapter. Training devices, including Lockheed Martin's Gray Matters ethics game, are also available online. In addition, students have access to their own set of PowerPoint slides to help them review and master the text material.

To access the text's website

- Go to *www.cengage.com*
- Select "Higher Education" and then "Business and Economics"
- Select "Management" and then "Ethics"
- Select "Business Ethics: Ethical Decision Making and Cases, 7th Edition"

EFFECTIVE TOOLS FOR TEACHING AND LEARNING

Many tools are available in this text to help both students and instructors in the quest to improve students' ability to make ethical business decisions. Each chapter opens with an outline and a list of learning objectives. Immediately following is "An Ethical Dilemma" that should provoke discussion about ethical issues related to the chapter. The short vignette describes a hypothetical incident involving an ethical conflict. Questions at the end of the "Ethical Dilemma" section focus discussion on how the dilemma could be resolved. At the end of each chapter are a chapter summary and an important terms list, both of which are handy tools for review. Also included at the end of each chapter is a "Resolving Ethical Business Challenges" section. The vignette describes a realistic drama that helps students experience the process of ethical decision making. The "Resolving Ethical Business Challenges" minicases presented in this text are hypothetical; any resemblance to real persons, companies, or situations is coincidental. Keep in mind that there are no right or wrong solutions to the minicases. The ethical dilemmas and real-life situations provide an opportunity for students to use concepts in the chapter to resolve ethical issues. Each chapter concludes with a series of questions that allow students to test their EQ (Ethics Quotient).

In Part Five, following each real-world case are questions to guide students in recognizing and resolving ethical issues. For some cases, students can conduct additional research to determine recent developments because many ethical issues in companies take years to resolve.

The *Instructor's Resource Manual* contains a wealth of information. Teaching notes for every chapter include a brief chapter summary, detailed lecture outline, and notes for using the "Ethical Dilemma" and "Resolving Ethical Business Challenges" sections. Detailed case notes point out the key issues involved and offer suggested answers to the questions. A separate section provides guidelines for using case analysis in teaching business ethics. Detailed notes are provided to guide the instructor in analyzing or grading the cases. Simulation role-play cases, as well as implementation suggestions, are included. The *Test Bank* provides multiple-choice and essay questions for every chapter in the text. A computerized version of the test bank is also available. Password-protected PowerPoint slides are available at Cengage Learning's Instructor Companion site along with an online version of the *Instructor's Resource Manual*. Additional instructor resources can be found at www.e-businessethics.com including PowerPoint slides and an online *Teaching Business Ethics Resource Manual*. Finally, a selection of video segments is available to help bring real-world examples and skill-building scenarios into the classroom.

ACKNOWLEDGMENTS

A number of individuals provided reviews and suggestions that helped to improve this text. We sincerely appreciate their time and effort.

Donald Acker
Brown Mackie College

Donna Allen
Northwest Nazarene University

Suzanne Allen
Walsh University

Carolyn Ashe
University of Houston–Downtown

Laura Barelman
Wayne State College

Russell Bedard
Eastern Nazarene College

B. Barbara Boerner
Brevard College

Judie Bucholz
Guilford College

Greg Buntz
University of the Pacific

Julie Campbell
Adams State College

April Chatham-Carpenter
University of Northern Iowa

Peggy Cunningham
Queen's University

Carla Dando
Idaho State University

James E. Donovan
Detroit College of Business

Douglas Dow
University of Texas at Dallas

A. Charles Drubel
Muskingum College

Philip F. Esler
University of St. Andrews

Joseph M. Foster
*Indiana Vocational Technical
College–Evansville*

Terry Gable
Truman State University

Robert Giacalone
University of Richmond

Suresh Gopalan
West Texas A&M University

Mark Hammer
Northwest Nazarene University

Charles E. Harris, Jr.
Texas A&M University

Kenneth A. Heischmidt
Southeast Missouri State University

Neil Herndon
Educational Consultant

Walter Hill
Green River Community College

Jack Hires
Valparaiso University

David Jacobs
American University

R. J. Johansen
Montana State University–Bozeman

Edward Kimman
Vrije Universiteit

Janet Knight
Purdue North Central

Anita Leffel
University of Texas at San Antonio

Barbara Limbach
Chadron State College

Nick Lockard
Texas Lutheran College

Terry Loe
Kennesaw State University

Nick Maddox
Stetson University

Isabelle Maignan
ING Bank

Phylis Mansfield
Pennsylvania State University–Erie

Robert Markus
Babson College

Cynthia A. M. Simerly
Lakeland Community College

Randy McLeod
Harding University

Karen Smith
Columbia Southern University

Francy Milner
University of Colorado

Filiz Tabak
Towson University

Lester Myers
University of San Francisco

Debbie Thorne
Texas State University–San Marcos

Patrick E. Murphy
University of Notre Dame

Wanda V. Turner
Ferris State College

Cynthia Nicola
Carlow College

David Wasieleski
Duquesne University

Carol Nielsen
Bemidji State University

Jim Weber
Duquesne University

Lee Richardson
University of Baltimore

Ed Weiss
National-Louis University

Zachary Shank
*Albuquerque Technical
Vocational Institute*

Jan Zahrly
University of North Dakota

We wish to acknowledge the many people who assisted us in writing this book. We are deeply grateful to Melanie Drever and Jennifer Jackson for helping us organize and manage the revision process and for preparing the *Instructor's Resource Manual* and *Test Bank*. We are also indebted to Barbara Gilmer and Gwyneth V. Walters for their contributions to previous editions of this text. Debbie Thorne, Texas State University–San Marcos, provided advice and guidance on the text and cases. Thanks go to Matt Paproth, Katie Duncan, Raghu Kurthakoti, Deepa Pillai, Benjamin Siltman, Alexi Sherrill, and Rajendran Murthy in preparing and updating cases, test banks, and chapters in this edition. Finally, we express appreciation to the administration and to our colleagues at the University of New Mexico, Southern Illinois University at Carbondale, and the University of Wyoming for their support.

We invite your comments, questions, or criticisms. We want to do our best to provide teaching materials that enhance the study of business ethics. Your suggestions will be sincerely appreciated.

– O. C. Ferrell

– John Fraedrich

– Linda Ferrell

An Overview
of Business Ethics

CHAPTER 1

The Importance of Business Ethics

CHAPTER OBJECTIVES

- To explore conceptualizations of business ethics from an organizational perspective

- To examine the historical foundations and evolution of business ethics

- To provide evidence that ethical value systems support business performance

- To gain insight into the extent of ethical misconduct in the workplace and the pressures for unethical behavior

CHAPTER OUTLINE

John Peters had just arrived at the main offices of Dryer & Sons (D&S) from Midwest State University. A medium-size company, D&S manufactured components for several of the major defense contractors in the United States. Recently, D&S had started a specialized software division and had hired John as a salesperson for both the company's hardware and software.

A diligent student at Midwest State, John had earned degrees in engineering and management information systems (MIS). His minor was in marketing—specifically, sales. Because of his education as well as other activities, John was not only comfortable discussing numbers with engineers but also had the people skills to convey complex solutions in understandable terms. This was one of the main reasons Al Dryer had hired him. "You've got charisma, John, and you know your way around computers," Dryer explained.

D&S was established during World War II and had manufactured parts for military aircraft. During the Korean War and then the Vietnam War, D&S had become a stable subcontractor for specialized parts for aircraft and missiles. When Al Dryer and his father started the business, Al was the salesperson for the company. In time, D&S had grown to employ several hundred workers and five salespeople; John was the sixth salesperson.

During his first few months at the company, John got his bearings in the defense industry. For example, when Ed, his trainer, would take procurement people out to lunch, everyone would put money into a snifter at the table. The money collected was usually much less than the bill, and Ed would make up the difference. Golf was a skill that Ed required John to learn because often "that's where deals are really transacted." Again, Ed would indirectly pick up the golfing bill, which sometimes totaled several hundred dollars.

Another of Ed's requirements was that John read the Procurement Integrity Section of the Office of Federal Procurement Policy Act and the Federal Acquisition Regulation, which implements the act. In addition, John had to read the Certificate of Procurement Integrity, which procurement agents had to sign. As John read the documents, he noted the statement in Section 27(a)(2), forbidding agents to "offer, give, or promise to offer or give, directly or indirectly, any money, gratuity, or other thing of value to any procurement official of such agency; or (3) solicit or obtain, directly or indirectly, from any officer or employee of such agency, prior to the award of a contract any proprietary or source selection information regarding such procurement."

"Doesn't this relate to what we're doing, Ed?" John asked.

"Yes and no, my boy, yes and no," was Ed's only answer.

One Monday, when Ed and John had returned from sales calls in St. Louis and Washington, DC, Ed called John into his office and said, "John, you don't have the right numbers down for our expenses. You're 15 percent short because you forgot all of your tips." As John looked at his list of expenses, he realized that Ed was right, yet there was no item on his expense report for such things.

"Ed, where do I put the extra expenses? There's no line on the forms for this."

"Just add it into the cost of things as I've done," replied Ed, showing John his expense report.

As John looked at Ed's report, he noticed some numbers that seemed quite large. "Why don't we mention this problem to Mr. Dryer so that accounting can put the extra lines on the reports?" John suggested.

"Because this is the way we do things around here, and they don't like changes to the system. We have a saying in the company that a blind eye goes a long way to getting business done," Ed lectured John. John didn't quite grasp the problem and did as he was told.

On another trip, John learned the differences between working directly with the federal government procurement people and the companies with which D&S subcontracted. For example, certain conversations of the large defense contractors were relayed to D&S, and then Ed and John would visit certain government agencies and relay that information. In one case, Ed and John were told to relay a very large offer to an official who was entering the private sector the next year. In addition, Ed and John were used to obtaining information on requests for proposals, as well as other competitive information, from procurement agents. When John asked Ed about this, Ed said, "John, in order to excel in this business, you need to be an expert on knowing exactly where things become legal and illegal. Trust me, I've been doing this for fifteen years, and I've never had a problem. Why do you think I'm your trainer?"

John started reviewing more government documents and asking the other salespeople about Ed. Two replied that Ed was a smart operator and knew the ropes better than anyone at the company. The other two salespeople had a different story to tell. One asked, "Has he tried to explain away his padding of the expense reports to you yet?"

"But I thought that's what everyone does!" John exclaimed.

"Ed has been doing business with the Feds and the large defense companies for so long that he sometimes doesn't realize that the rules have changed. He's been lucky that he hasn't been caught. Watch your step, John, or you'll find yourself with dirty hands and nowhere to clean them," the second salesperson said.

At the end of another trip to Washington, DC, Ed called John into his office. "John, your numbers don't add up," he pointed out. "Didn't I tell you to add at least 15 percent to your totals for tips and miscellaneous items? Let's get with it. Do you want to be in training forever? You know that I have to sign off before you can go it alone, and I want to make sure you understand the ropes. Just between you and me, I think Dryer is finally going to make a vice president slot, which should go to me because of my seniority. So hurry up and learn this stuff because you're my last trainee. Now just sign the document with these revised numbers on them."

What should John do?

QUESTIONS • EXERCISES

1. What is Ed's ethical dilemma?
2. What are the ethical and legal considerations for John at D&S?
3. Identify the ethical conflict in this situation.
4. Discuss the implications of each decision John has made and will make.

*This case is strictly hypothetical; any resemblance to real persons, companies, or situations is coincidental.

The ability to recognize and deal with complex business ethics issues has become a significant priority in twenty-first-century companies. In recent years, a number of well-publicized scandals resulted in public outrage about deception and fraud in business and a demand for improved business ethics and greater corporate responsibility. The publicity and debate surrounding highly visible legal and ethical lapses at a number of well-known firms, including Enron, WorldCom, HealthSouth, and even Coca-Cola, highlight the need for businesses to integrate ethics and responsibility into all business decisions. Table 1–1 reflects increasing distrust of business among Americans as reported by a leading polling organization, Yankelovich Partners, Inc. A global opinion poll for the World Economic Forum concluded that public trust in companies has eroded and dropped significantly over the last few years. Public trust in national governments and the United Nations has fallen significantly too.[1] Largely in response to this crisis, business decisions and activities have come under greater scrutiny by many different constituents, including consumers, employees, investors, government regulators, and special-interest groups. Additionally, new legislation and regulations designed to encourage higher ethical standards in business have been put in place.

TABLE 1-1	American Distrust of Business	
80%	**70%**	**61%**
American business is too concerned about profits, not concerned about responsibilities to workers, consumers, and the environment.	If the opportunity arises, most businesses will take advantage of the public if they feel they are not likely to be found out.	Even long-established companies cannot be trusted to make safe, durable products without the government setting industry standards.

SOURCE: J. Walker Smith, Ann Clurman, and Craig Wood of Yankelovich Partners, Inc. *Point,* February 2005, www.racombooks.com; results from Yankelovich MONITOR.

The field of business ethics deals with questions about whether specific business practices are acceptable. For example, should a salesperson omit facts about a product's poor safety record in a sales presentation to a client? Should an accountant report inaccuracies that he or she discovered in an audit of a client, knowing the auditing company will probably be fired by the client for doing so? Should an automobile tire manufacturer intentionally conceal safety concerns to avoid a massive and costly tire recall? Regardless of their legality, others will certainly judge the actions taken in such situations as right or wrong, ethical or unethical. By its very nature, the field of business ethics is controversial, and there is no universally accepted approach for resolving its issues.

A Junior Achievement/Deloitte survey of teens showed that 71 percent feel prepared to make ethical decisions in the workplace. However, of those surveyed, 38 percent feel it is sometimes necessary to lie, cheat, plagiarize, or engage in violence to succeed. One-fourth think cheating on a test is acceptable and most can justify it saying that their desire to succeed is grounds for the behavior.[2] If today's students are tomorrow's leaders, there is likely to be a correlation between acceptable behavior today and tomorrow, adding to the argument that the leaders of today must be prepared for the ethical risks associated with this downward trend. According to another poll by Deloitte and Touche of teenagers aged 13 to 18 years old, when asked if people who practice good business ethics are more successful than those who don't, 69 percent of teenagers agreed.[3] On the other hand another survey indicated that many students do not define copying answers from another student's paper or downloading music or content for classroom work as cheating.[4]

Before we get started, it is important to state our philosophies regarding this book. First, we do not moralize by telling you what is right or wrong in a specific situation. Second, although we provide an overview of group and individual decision-making processes, we do not prescribe any one philosophy or process as best or most ethical. Third, by itself, this book will not make you more ethical, nor will it tell you how to judge the ethical behavior of others. Rather, its goal is to help you understand and use your current values and convictions when making business decisions so that you think about the effects of those decisions on business and society. In addition, this book will help you understand what businesses are doing to improve their ethical conduct. To this end, we aim to help you learn to recognize and resolve ethical issues within business organizations. As a manager, you will be responsible for your decisions and the ethical conduct of employees who you supervise. The framework we develop in this book therefore focuses on how organizational ethical decisions are made and on ways companies can improve their ethical conduct.

In this chapter, we first develop a definition of business ethics and discuss why it has become an important topic in business education. We also discuss why studying business ethics can be beneficial. Next, we examine the evolution of business ethics in North America. Then we explore the performance benefits of ethical decision making for businesses. Finally, we provide a brief overview of the framework we use for examining business ethics in this text.

BUSINESS ETHICS DEFINED

The term *ethics* has many nuances. It has been defined as "inquiry into the nature and grounds of morality where the term morality is taken to mean moral judgments, standards and rules of conduct."[5] Ethics has also been called the study and philosophy of human conduct, with an emphasis on determining right and wrong. *The American Heritage Dictionary* offers these definitions of ethics: "The study of the general nature of morals and of specific moral choices; moral philosophy; and the rules or standards governing the conduct of the members of a profession."[6] One difference between an ordinary decision and an ethical one lies in "the point where the accepted rules no longer serve, and the decision maker is faced with the responsibility for weighing values and reaching a judgment in a situation which is not quite the same as any he or she has faced before."[7] Another difference relates to the amount of emphasis that decision makers place on their own values and accepted practices within their company. Consequently, values and judgments play a critical role when we make ethical decisions.

Building on these definitions, we can begin to develop a concept of business ethics. Most people would agree that high ethical standards require both businesses and individuals to conform to sound moral principles. However, some special aspects must be considered when applying ethics to business. First, to survive, businesses must earn a profit. If profits are realized through misconduct, however, the life of the organization may be shortened. Many firms, including Arthur Andersen, Enron, WorldCom, and Sunbeam, that made headlines due to wrongdoing and scandal ultimately went bankrupt or failed because of the legal and financial repercussions of their misconduct. Second, businesses must balance their desires for profits against the needs and desires of society. Maintaining this balance often requires compromises or trade-offs. To address these unique aspects of the business world, society has developed rules—both legal and implicit—to guide businesses in their efforts to earn profits in ways that do not harm individuals or society as a whole.

Most definitions of business ethics relate to rules, standards, and moral principles regarding what is right or wrong in specific situations. For our purposes and in simple terms, **business ethics** comprises the principles and standards that guide behavior in the world of business. Investors, employees, customers, interest groups, the legal system, and the community often determine whether a specific action is right or wrong, ethical or unethical. Although these groups are not necessarily "right," their judgments influence society's acceptance or rejection of a business and its activities.

WHY STUDY BUSINESS ETHICS?

A Crisis in Business Ethics

As we've already mentioned, ethical misconduct has become a major concern in business today. The Ethics Resource Center conducted the National Business Ethics Survey (NBES) of about three thousand U.S. employees to gather reliable data on key ethics and compliance outcomes and to help identify and better understand the ethics issues that are important to employees. The NBES found that observed misconduct is higher in large organizations—those with more than five hundred employees—than in smaller ones and that there are also differences in observed misconduct across employee levels. Reporting of misconduct is most likely to come from upper-level management, as compared to lower-level supervisors and nonmanagement employees. Employees in lower-level positions have more of a tendency to not understand misconduct or be complacent about what misconduct they observe. Figure 1–1 shows the percentage of respondents who say that they trust a variety of business categories. Notice that the levels of consumer trust in most industries is declining. Among senior managers, 77 percent of employees report observed misconduct, while among nonmanagement, only 48 percent of employees report observed misconduct.[8]

SPECIFIC ISSUES Abusive behavior, harassment, accounting fraud, conflicts of interest, defective products, bribery, and employee theft are all problems cited as evidence of declining ethical standards. For example, Satyam Computer Services, an

---

FIGURE 1–1   Americans' Trust in Business (% of respondents who say they trust the following business categories a great deal or quite a lot)

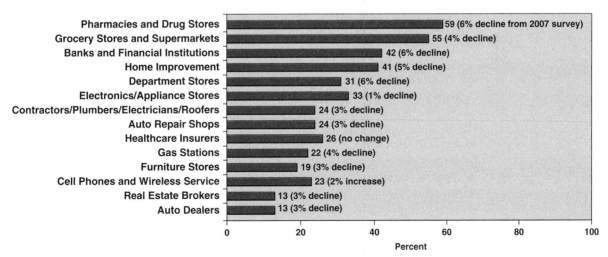

SOURCE: Better Business Bureau/Gallup Trust in Business Index, April 2008, http://www.bbb.org/us/sitepage.aspx?id=f36f50cc-8cb7-4507-9cfc-2f2d7aa2c3fc (accessed January 13, 2003).

outsourcing firm in India worked with more than one-third of Fortune 500 companies. The chairman of the company disclosed that $1.04 billion in cash and assets did not exist and that earnings and assets were inflated for years. The scandal was compared to Enron.[9] A poll by Harris Interactive found many scandal-plagued firms at the bottom of its annual survey of perceived corporate reputation, including Enron, Global Crossing, WorldCom, Andersen Worldwide, and Adelphia. The survey, which ranks companies according to how respondents rate them on twenty attributes, also found that public perceptions of trust had declined considerably as a result of the accounting scandals of the early twenty-first century. Joy Sever, a Harris vice president, reported, "The scandals cost many companies their emotional appeal, the strongest driver of reputation."[10]

A former Goldman Sachs executive was sentenced to almost five years in prison for a case of insider trading that yielded about $6.7 million. The Harvard graduate worked with a former Merrill Lynch analyst, a New Jersey postal worker, and two workers at a *Business Week* printing press. The former Merrill Lynch employee provided tips to Eugene Plotkin at Goldman on mergers and acquisitions. Another angle involved getting prepublication copies of *Business Week* and trading on that information. The third element involved working with a New Jersey postal worker who served on the Bristol-Myers Squibb grand jury investigation and shared inside information with Plotkin.[11]

Inflating earnings involves attempting to embellish or enhance a firm's profitability in a manner which is inconsistent with past practice, common regulatory guidelines, or industry practice. Many companies maintain a focus on making short-term profits and know that analysts and investors critique the company according to its ability to "make the numbers." PricewaterhouseCoopers (PWC) was forced to pay $97.5 million to settle a class action lawsuit for involvement with AIG in overstating their earnings. This settlement is a small part of a larger case against both AIG and its former CEO, Hank Greenberg. AIG's improper accounting for reinsurance and other dealings led to a restatement of earnings in the amount of $3.9 billion. The lawsuit normally proceeds against the company and personnel first with the related firms (such as PWC) paying a percentage of that settlement.[12] Such highly publicized cases strengthen the perception that ethical standards in business need to be raised.

In government, several politicians and some high-ranking officials have had to resign in disgrace over ethical indiscretions. For example, James Traficant of Ohio was expelled from Congress and sent to jail after being convicted of accepting bribes while serving in the U.S. House of Representatives.[13] Irv Lewis "Scooter" Libby, a White House advisor, was indicted on five counts of criminal charges:[14] one count of obstruction of justice, two counts of perjury, and two counts of making false statements. Each count carries a $250,000 fine and maximum prison term of thirty years.

Several scientists have been accused of falsifying research data, which could invalidate later research based on their data and jeopardize trust in all scientific research. Bell Labs, for example, fired a scientist for falsifying experiments on superconductivity and molecular electronics and for misrepresenting data in scientific publications. Jan Hendrik Schon's work on creating tiny, powerful microprocessors seemed poised to significantly advance microprocessor technology and potentially bring yet another Nobel Prize in physics to the award-winning laboratory, a subsidiary of Lucent Technologies.[15] Hwang Woo-Suk was found to have faked some of his famous stem-cell research in which he claimed to have created thirty cloned human embryos and made stem-cell lines from skin cells of eleven people, as well as producing the world's first cloned dog. He also apologized for using eggs from his own female researchers, which was in breach of guidelines, but still denies fabricating his research.[16]

Even sports can be subject to ethical lapses. Plaxico Burress, successful wide receiver for the 2008 Super Bowl Champion New York Giants, accidentally shot himself in the right thigh at a nightclub after midnight. Upon attempting to enter the nightclub, Burress was approached by security and disclosed that he had a handgun in his possession. He then stepped aside to unload the gun and accidentally shot himself, requiring hospitalization. Although Burress may have had a concealed weapons permit for Florida, New York and New Jersey do not recognize Florida permits. A full legal investigation followed as well as the Giants evaluating Plaxico's potential violation of the Personal Conduct Policy.[17]

Whether made in business, politics, science, or sports, most decisions are judged as either right or wrong, ethical or unethical. Regardless of what an individual believes about a particular action, if society judges it to be unethical or wrong, whether correctly or not, that judgment directly affects the organization's ability to achieve its business goals. For this reason alone, it is important to understand business ethics and recognize ethical issues.

The Reasons for Studying Business Ethics

Studying business ethics is valuable for several reasons. Business ethics is not merely an extension of an individual's own personal ethics. Many people believe that if a company hires good people with strong ethical values, then it will be a "good citizen" organization. But as we show throughout this text, an individual's personal values and moral philosophies are only one factor in the ethical decision-making process. True, moral rules can be applied to a variety of situations in life, and some people do not distinguish everyday ethical issues from business ones. Our concern, however, is with the application of rules and principles in the business context. Many important ethical issues do not arise very often in the business context although they remain complex moral dilemmas in one's own personal life. For example, although abortion and the possibility of human cloning are moral issues in many people's lives, they are usually not an issue in most business organizations.

Professionals in any field, including business, must deal with individuals' personal moral dilemmas because these issues affect everyone's ability to function on the job. Normally, a business does not establish rules or policies on personal ethical issues such as sex or the use of alcohol outside the workplace; indeed, in some cases, such policies would be illegal. Only when a person's preferences or values influence his or her performance on the job do an individual's ethics play a major role in the evaluation of business decisions.

Just being a good person and, in your own view, having sound personal ethics may not be sufficient to enable you to handle the ethical issues that arise in a business organization. It is important to recognize the relationship between legal and ethical decisions. Although abstract virtues linked to the high moral ground of truthfulness, honesty, fairness, and openness are often assumed to be self-evident and accepted by all employees, business-strategy decisions involve complex and detailed discussions. For example, there is considerable debate over what constitutes antitrust, deceptive advertising, and violations of the Foreign Corrupt Practices Act. A high level of personal moral development may not prevent an individual from violating the law in a complicated organizational context where even experienced lawyers debate the exact meaning of the law. Some approaches to business ethics assume that ethics training is for people whose personal moral development is unacceptable, but that is not the case. Because organizations are culturally diverse and personal values must be respected, ensuring collective agreement on organizational ethics (that is, codes reasonably capable of preventing misconduct) is as vital as any other effort an organization's management may undertake.

Many people who have limited business experience suddenly find themselves making decisions about product quality, advertising, pricing, sales techniques, hiring practices, and pollution control. The values they learned from family, religion, and school may not provide specific guidelines for these complex business decisions. In other words, a person's experiences and decisions at home, in school, and in the community may be quite different from his or her experiences and decisions at work. Many business ethics decisions are close calls. In addition managerial responsibility for the conduct of others requires knowledge of ethics and compliance processes and systems. Years of experience in a particular industry may be required to know what is acceptable. Consider the challenge faced by Harry Kraemer, the CEO of Baxter International, after fifty-three dialysis patients died during treatment in the United States, Spain, and five other countries. The dialysis filters used in each of the cases had come from a single lot manufactured by Althin Medical AB, a firm that Baxter had acquired the previous year. After investigating, Kraemer took responsibility, apologized, recalled all of Althin's dialysis filters, and ultimately decided to shut down Althin's operations, actions that cost Baxter $189 million. Kraemer later asked the company's board of directors to reduce his bonus because of the deaths. Kraemer could have made different decisions, but he put the situation in a broader context: "We have this situation. The financial people will assess the potential financial impact. The legal people will do the same. But at the end of the day, if we think it's a problem that a Baxter product was involved in the deaths of 53 people, then those other issues become pretty easy. If we don't do the right thing, then we won't be around to address those other issues."[18]

Studying business ethics will help you begin to identify ethical issues when they arise and recognize the approaches available for resolving them. You will also learn more about the ethical decision-making process and about ways to promote ethical behavior within your organization. By studying business ethics, you may begin to understand how to cope with conflicts between your own personal values and those of the organization in which you work.

THE DEVELOPMENT OF BUSINESS ETHICS

The study of business ethics in North America has evolved through five distinct stages— (1) before 1960, (2) the 1960s, (3) the 1970s, (4) the 1980s, and (5) the 1990s—and continues to evolve in the twenty-first century (see Table 1–2).

| TABLE 1-2 | A Timeline of Ethical and Socially Responsible Concerns | | | |

1960s	1970s	1980s	1990s	2000s
Environmental issues	Employee militancy	Bribes and illegal contracting practices	Sweatshops and unsafe working conditions in third-world countries	Cybercrime
Civil rights issues	Human rights issues	Influence peddling	Rising corporate liability for personal damages (for example, cigarette companies)	Financial management
Increased employee–employer tension	Covering up rather than correcting issues	Deceptive advertising	Financial mismanagement and fraud	International corruption
Honesty		Financial fraud (for example, savings and loan scandal)		Loss of employee privacy
Changing work ethic		Transparency issues		Intellectual-property theft
Rising drug use				

SOURCE: "Business Ethics Timeline," *Ethics Resource Center*, http://www.ethics.org/resources/business-ethics-timeline.asp (accessed March 29, 2006). Copyright © 2006, Ethics Resource Center (ERC). Used with permission of the ERC, 1747 Pennsylvania Ave., N.W., Suite 400, Washington, DC 2006, www.ethics.org.

Before 1960: Ethics in Business

Prior to 1960, the United States went through several agonizing phases of questioning the concept of capitalism. In the 1920s, the progressive movement attempted to provide citizens with a "living wage," defined as income sufficient for education, recreation, health, and retirement. Businesses were asked to check unwarranted price increases and any other practices that would hurt a family's "living wage." In the 1930s came the New Deal, which specifically blamed business for the country's economic woes. Business was asked to work more closely with the government to raise family income. By the 1950s, the New Deal had evolved into the Fair Deal by President Harry S. Truman; this program defined such matters as civil rights and environmental responsibility as ethical issues that businesses had to address.

Until 1960 ethical issues related to business were often discussed within the domain of theology or philosophy. Individual moral issues related to business were addressed in churches, synagogues, and mosques. Religious leaders raised questions about fair wages, labor practices, and the morality of capitalism. For example, Catholic social ethics, which were expressed in a series of papal encyclicals, included concern for morality in business, workers' rights, and living wages; for humanistic values rather than materialistic ones; and for improving the conditions of the poor. Some Catholic colleges and universities began to offer courses in social ethics. Protestants also developed ethics courses in their seminaries and schools of theology and addressed issues concerning morality and ethics in business. The Protestant work ethic encouraged individuals to be frugal, work hard, and attain success in the capitalistic system. Such religious traditions provided a foundation for the future field of business ethics. Each religion applied its moral concepts not only to business but also to government, politics, the family, personal life, and all other aspects of life.

The 1960s: The Rise of Social Issues in Business

During the 1960s, American society turned to causes. An antibusiness attitude developed as many critics attacked the vested interests that controlled the economic and political sides of society—the so-called military–industrial complex. The 1960s saw the decay of inner cities and the growth of ecological problems such as pollution and the disposal of toxic and nuclear wastes. This period also witnessed the rise of consumerism—activities undertaken by independent individuals, groups, and organizations to protect their rights as consumers. In 1962 President John F. Kennedy delivered a "Special Message on Protecting the Consumer Interest" in which he outlined four basic consumer rights: the right to safety, the right to be informed, the right to choose, and the right to be heard. These came to be known as the **Consumers' Bill of Rights.**

The modern consumer movement is generally considered to have begun in 1965 with the publication of Ralph Nader's *Unsafe at Any Speed,* which criticized the auto industry as a whole, and General Motors Corporation (GM) in particular, for putting profit and style ahead of lives and safety. GM's Corvair was the main target of Nader's criticism. His consumer protection organization, popularly known as Nader's Raiders, fought successfully for legislation that required automobile makers to equip cars with safety belts, padded dashboards, stronger door latches, head restraints, shatterproof windshields, and collapsible steering columns. Consumer activists also helped secure passage of several consumer protection laws such as the Wholesome Meat Act of 1967, the Radiation Control for Health and Safety Act of 1968, the Clean Water Act of 1972, and the Toxic Substance Act of 1976.[19]

After Kennedy came President Lyndon B. Johnson and the Great Society, which extended national capitalism and told the business community that the U.S. government's responsibility was to provide the citizen with some degree of economic stability, equality, and social justice. Activities that could destabilize the economy or discriminate against any class of citizens began to be viewed as unethical and unlawful.

The 1970s: Business Ethics as an Emerging Field

Business ethics began to develop as a field of study in the 1970s. Theologians and philosophers had laid the groundwork by suggesting that certain principles could be applied to business activities. Using this foundation, business professors began to teach and write about corporate **social responsibility,** an organization's obligation to maximize its positive impact on stakeholders and to minimize its negative impact. Philosophers increased their involvement, applying ethical theory and philosophical analysis to structure the discipline of business ethics. Companies became more concerned with their public images, and as social demands grew, many businesses realized that they had to address ethical issues more directly. The Nixon administration's Watergate scandal focused public interest on the importance of ethics in government. Conferences were held to discuss the social responsibilities and ethical issues of business. Centers dealing with issues of business ethics were established. Interdisciplinary meetings brought business professors, theologians, philosophers, and businesspeople together. President Jimmy Carter attempted to focus on personal and administrative efforts to uphold ethical principles in government.

The Foreign Corrupt Practices Act was passed during his administration, making it illegal for U.S. businesses to bribe government officials of other countries.

By the end of the 1970s, a number of major ethical issues had emerged, such as bribery, deceptive advertising, price collusion, product safety, and the environment. *Business ethics* became a common expression and was no longer considered an oxymoron. Academic researchers sought to identify ethical issues and describe how businesspeople might choose to act in particular situations. However, only limited efforts were made to describe how the ethical decision-making process worked and to identify the many variables that influence this process in organizations.

The 1980s: Consolidation

In the 1980s, business academics and practitioners acknowledged business ethics as a field of study. A growing and varied group of institutions with diverse interests promoted its study. Business ethics organizations grew to include thousands of members. Five hundred courses in business ethics were offered at colleges across the country, with more than forty thousand students enrolled. Centers for business ethics provided publications, courses, conferences, and seminars. Business ethics was also a prominent concern within such leading companies as General Electric, Chase Manhattan, General Motors, Atlantic Richfield, Caterpillar, and S. C. Johnson & Son, Inc. Many of these firms established ethics and social policy committees to address ethical issues.

In the 1980s, the **Defense Industry Initiative on Business Ethics and Conduct** (DII) was developed to guide corporate support for ethical conduct. In 1986 eighteen defense contractors drafted principles for guiding business ethics and conduct.[20] The organization has since grown to nearly fifty members. This effort established a method for discussing best practices and working tactics to link organizational practice and policy to successful ethical compliance. The DII includes six principles. First, DII supports codes of conduct and their widespread distribution. These codes of conduct must be understandable and provide details on more substantive areas. Second, member companies are expected to provide ethics training for their employees as well as continuous support between training periods. Third, defense contractors must create an open atmosphere in which employees feel comfortable reporting violations without fear of retribution. Fourth, companies need to perform extensive internal audits and develop effective internal reporting and voluntary disclosure plans. Fifth, DII insists that member companies preserve the integrity of the defense industry. Finally, member companies must adopt a philosophy of public accountability.[21]

The 1980s ushered in the Reagan–Bush eras, with the accompanying belief that self-regulation, rather than regulation by government, was in the public's interest. Many tariffs and trade barriers were lifted, and businesses merged and divested within an increasingly global atmosphere. Thus, while business schools were offering courses in business ethics, the rules of business were changing at a phenomenal rate because of less regulation. Corporations that once were nationally based began operating internationally and found themselves mired in value structures where accepted rules of business behavior no longer applied.

The 1990s: Institutionalization of Business Ethics

The administration of President Bill Clinton continued to support self-regulation and free trade. However, it also took unprecedented government action to deal with health-related social issues such as teenage smoking. Its proposals included restricting cigarette advertising, banning vending machine sales, and ending the use of cigarette logos in connection with sports events.[22] Clinton also appointed Arthur Levitt as chairman of the Securities and Exchange Commission in 1993. Levitt unsuccessfully pushed for many reforms that could have prevented the accounting ethics scandals exemplified by Enron and WorldCom.[23]

The **Federal Sentencing Guidelines for Organizations** (FSGO), approved by Congress in November 1991, set the tone for organizational ethical compliance programs in the 1990s. The guidelines, which were based on the six principles of the DII,[24] broke new ground by codifying into law incentives to reward organizations for taking action to prevent misconduct such as developing effective internal legal and ethical compliance programs.[25] Provisions in the guidelines mitigate penalties for businesses that strive to root out misconduct and establish high ethical and legal standards.[26] On the other hand, under FSGO, if a company lacks an effective ethical compliance program and its employees violate the law, it can incur severe penalties. The guidelines focus on firms taking action to prevent and detect business misconduct in cooperation with government regulation. At the heart of the FSGO is the carrot-and-stick approach: By taking preventive action against misconduct, a company may avoid onerous penalties should a violation occur. A mechanical approach using legalistic logic will not suffice to avert serious penalties. The company must develop corporate values, enforce its own code of ethics, and strive to prevent misconduct.

The Twenty-First Century: A New Focus on Business Ethics

Although business ethics appeared to become more institutionalized in the 1990s, new evidence emerged in the early 2000s that more than a few business executives and managers had not fully embraced the public's desire for high ethical standards. For example, Dennis Kozlowski, former CEO of Tyco, was indicted on thirty-eight counts of misappropriating $170 million of Tyco funds and netting $430 million from improper sales of stock. Kozlowski, who pleaded not guilty to the charges, allegedly used the funds to purchase many personal luxuries, including a $15 million vintage yacht and a $3.9 million Renoir painting and to throw a $2 million party for his wife's birthday.[27] Arthur Andersen, a "Big Five" accounting firm, was convicted of obstructing justice after shredding documents related to its role as Enron's auditor.[28] The reputation of the once venerable accounting firm disappeared over night, along with most of its clients, and the firm ultimately went out of business. Later the Supreme Court overruled the Arthur Andersen obstruction-of-justice conviction, but it was too late for the firm to recover. In addition to problems with its auditing of Enron, Arthur Andersen also faced questions surrounding its audits of other companies that were charged with employing questionable accounting practices, including Halliburton, WorldCom, Global Crossing, Dynegy, Qwest, and Sunbeam.[29] These accounting scandals made it evident that falsifying financial reports and reaping questionable benefits had become part of the culture of many companies. Firms outside the United States, such as Royal Ahold in the Netherlands and Parmalat in Italy, became major examples of accounting misconduct from a global perspective.

Such abuses increased public and political demands to improve ethical standards in business. In a survey of twenty thousand people across twenty countries, trust in global companies has declined significantly.[30] To address the loss of confidence in financial reporting and corporate ethics, Congress in 2002 passed the **Sarbanes–Oxley Act,** the most far-reaching change in organizational control and accounting regulations since the Securities and Exchange Act of 1934. The new law made securities fraud a criminal offense and stiffened penalties for corporate fraud. It also created an accounting oversight board that requires corporations to establish codes of ethics for financial reporting and to develop greater transparency in financial reports to investors and other interested parties. Additionally, the law requires top executives to sign off on their firms' financial reports, and they risk fines and long prison sentences if they misrepresent their companies' financial position. The legislation further requires company executives to disclose stock sales immediately and prohibits companies from giving loans to top managers.[31]

The 2004 amendment to the FSGO requires that a business's governing authority be well informed about its ethics program with respect to content, implementation, and effectiveness. This places the responsibility squarely on the shoulders of the firm's leadership, usually the board of directors. The board is required to oversee the discovery of risks and to design, implement, and modify approaches to deal with those risks.

The Sarbanes–Oxley Act and the FSGO have institutionalized the need to discover and address ethical and legal risk. Top management and the board of directors of a corporation are accountable for discovering risk associated with ethical conduct. Such specific industries as the public sector, energy and chemicals, health care, insurance, and retail have to discover the unique risk associated with their operations and develop an ethics program to prevent ethical misconduct before it creates a crisis. Most firms are developing formal and informal mechanisms to have interactive communication and transparency about issues associated with the risk of misconduct. Business leaders should view that their greatest danger is not discovering serious misconduct or illegal activities somewhere in the organization. Unfortunately most managers do not view the risk of an ethical disaster as important as risk associated with fires, natural disasters, or technology failure. Ethical disasters can be significantly more damaging to a company's reputation than risks that are managed through insurance and other methods. As Warren Buffett said in his interview in May of 2005 on Public Broadcasting Corporation's *Business Nightly News,* "We have 180,000 employees, we know there is somebody doing something wrong today, we just hope it's small and that we catch it. But that is going to happen in any large organization."

In the KPMG Forensic Integrity Survey, employees were asked whether they had "personally seen" or had "firsthand knowledge of" misconduct within their organizations over the prior twelve-month period. Roughly three-quarters of employees— 74 percent—reported that they had observed misconduct in the prior twelve-month period. Figure 1–2 shows the results of misconduct by industry; there are generally high levels of observed misconduct across all industries. Employees in highly regulated financial industries, such as banking, finance, and insurance, reported relatively lower rates of misconduct within their organizations compared with others. While

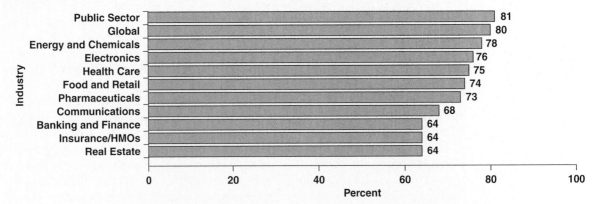

| FIGURE 1-2 | Prevalence of Misconduct by Industry during the Prior Twelve Months |

SOURCE: Copyright © 2006 KPMG International. KPMG International is a Swiss Cooperative that serves as a co-ordinating entity for a network of independent firms operating under the KPMG name. KPMG International provides no services to clients. All rights reserved. KPMG Forensic Integrity Survey 2005–2006 from http://www.kpmginsiders.com/display_analysis.asp?cs_id=148597 (accessed March 9, 2006).

employees working in the public sector, which has not been subject to many of the new regulatory mandates placed on its private-sector counterparts, reported relatively higher rates of misconduct compared with others.

DEVELOPING AN ORGANIZATIONAL AND GLOBAL ETHICAL CULTURE

The current trend is away from legally based compliance initiatives in organizations to cultural initiatives that make ethics a part of core organizational values. To develop more ethical corporate cultures, many businesses are communicating core values to their employees by creating ethics programs and appointing ethics officers to oversee them. The ethical component of a corporate culture relates to the values, beliefs, and established and enforced patterns of conduct that employees use to identify and respond to ethical issues. The term **ethical culture** can be viewed as the character or decision-making process that employees use to determine whether their responses to ethical issues are right or wrong. Ethical culture is used to describe the component of corporate culture that captures the rules and principles that an organization defines as appropriate conduct. The goal of an ethical culture is to minimize the need for enforced compliance of rules and maximize principles that contribute to ethical reasoning in difficult or new situations. An ethical culture creates shared values and support for ethical decisions and is driven by top management.

The New York Stock Exchange, for example, requires all member companies to have codes of ethics. Many firms now have ethics officers, and some firms, including UPS, Raytheon, and Baxter International, take ethics seriously enough to have their ethics officers report directly to senior management or boards of directors. The growth of the Ethics and Compliance Officer Association (ECOA) to over twelve hundred members, representing nearly every industry, to include more than 62 percent of the Fortune 100 and conducting business in over 160 countries, highlights the increasing importance of this position in business today.[32] The organization offers an intensive week-long course, Managing Ethics in Organizations, which provides practical knowledge, the fundamental theories, and general skills needed by prospective and recently appointed ethics and compliance officers and others who have responsibilities for their organization's ethics, compliance, or business conduct programs. They also offer a leadership seminar designed to examine the essential linkage between leadership, ethics, and corporate culture.[33] Most misconduct comes from employees trying to attain the performance objectives of the firm. Consider oil traders at Royal Dutch Shell who created fictitious sales that eliminated price competition and market risk for their companies. Houston-based Shell Trading U.S. Company and London-based Shell International Trading and Shipping Company trades violated futures trading rules on the New York Mercantile Exchange and resulted in a combined $300,000 in fines.[34]

Globally, businesses are working more closely together to establish standards of acceptable behavior. We are already seeing collaborative efforts by a range of organizations to establish goals and mandate minimum levels of ethical behavior, from the European Union, the North American Free Trade Agreement (NAFTA), the Common Market of the Southern Cone (MERCOSUR), and the World Trade Organization (WTO) to, more recently, the Council on Economic Priorities' Social Accountability 8000 (SA 8000), the Ethical Trading Initiative, and the U.S. Apparel Industry Partnership. Some companies will not do business with organizations that do not support and abide by these standards. The development of global codes of ethics, such as the Caux Round Table, highlights common ethical concerns for global firms. The Caux Round Table (www.cauxroundtable.org) is a group of businesses, political leaders, and concerned interest groups that desire responsible behavior in the global community.

THE BENEFITS OF BUSINESS ETHICS

The field of business ethics continues to change rapidly as more firms recognize the benefits of improving ethical conduct and the link between business ethics and financial performance. Both research and examples from the business world demonstrate that building an ethical reputation among employees, customers, and the general public pays off. Figure 1–3 provides an overview of the relationship between business ethics and organizational performance. Although we believe there are many practical benefits to being ethical, many businesspeople make decisions because they believe a particular course of action is simply the right thing to do as a responsible member of society. For example, after a small Massachusetts textile plant owned by Malden Mills burned to the ground, Malden Mills' CEO, Aaron Feuerstein, could have opted to close the plant in favor of moving the work to an overseas facility with lower wages, just as many of his competitors had already done. However, he recognized the negative impact that such a decision would have had on the plant's employees as well as the community. Thus, he chose not only to rebuild the plant but also to continue to pay its three thousand workers for ninety days while the plant was being rebuilt.[35]

FIGURE 1–3   The Role of Organizational Ethics in Performance

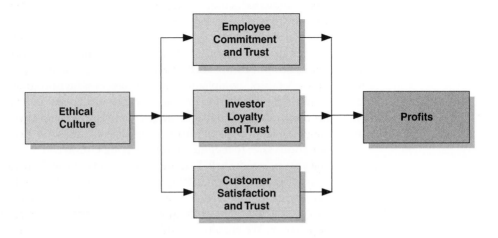

Texas Instruments, which has always been a company very concerned about ethics and ranked thirteenth on *Business Ethics* magazine's "100 Best Corporate Citizens" in 2007, proposed a challenge to its design team. If the team could find a way to build the new factory for $180 million less than the last Dallas factory built in the late 1990s, then Texas Instruments would locate in Dallas. The design team managed it by designing the new building with two floors, not three, and with a design that is expected to cut utility costs by 20 percent and water usage by 35 percent.[36]

Among the rewards for being more ethical and socially responsible in business are increased efficiency in daily operations, greater employee commitment, increased investor willingness to entrust funds, improved customer trust and satisfaction, and better financial performance. The reputation of a company has a major effect on its relationships with employees, investors, customers, and many other parties.

Ethics Contributes to Employee Commitment

Employee commitment comes from employees who believe their future is tied to that of the organization and their willingness to make personal sacrifices for the organization.[37] The more a company is dedicated to taking care of its employees, the more likely it is that the employees will take care of the organization. The NBES survey indicates that 79 percent of employees agree that ethics is important in continuing to work for their employer. It is also interesting to note that approximately 20 percent of employees are *not* concerned about the ethical environment of their organization.[38] This group is very complacent and has the potential for misconduct without guidance and ethical leadership. Issues that may foster the development of an ethical culture for employees include the absence of abusive behavior, a safe work environment, competitive salaries, and the fulfillment of all contractual obligations toward employees. An ethics and compliance program can support values and appropriate conduct. Social programs that may improve the ethical culture range from work–family programs and stock ownership plans to community service. Home Depot associates, for example, participate in disaster-relief efforts after hurricanes and tornadoes by rebuilding roofs, repairing water damage, planting trees, and clearing roads in their communities. Because employees spend a considerable amount of their waking time at work, a commitment by the organization to goodwill and respect for its employees usually increases the employees' loyalty to the organization and their support of its objectives. Companies like Wal-Mart responded in the wake of Hurricane Katrina not only to try to improve their image among customers and associates but also to help the community in which they operate. Wal-Mart also donated more than $15 million to relief efforts. They also established mini-Wal-Mart stores in areas impacted by the hurricane where such items as clothing, diapers, baby wipes, food, formula, toothbrushes, bedding, and water were given out free of charge to those with a demonstrated need.[39]

Employees' perception that their firm has an ethical culture leads to performance-enhancing outcomes within the organization.[40] For the sake of both productivity and teamwork, it is essential that employees both within and between departments throughout the organization share a common vision of trust. The influence of higher levels of trust is greatest on relationships within departments or work groups, but trust is a significant factor in relationships between departments as well. Consequently, programs that create a work environment that is trustworthy make individuals more willing to rely and act on the decisions and actions of their coworkers. In such a work environment, employees can reasonably expect to be treated with full respect and consideration by their coworkers and superiors. Trusting relationships between upper management and managers and their subordinates contribute to greater decision-making efficiencies. One survey found that when employees see values such as honesty, respect, and trust applied frequently in the workplace, they feel less pressure to compromise ethical standards, observe less misconduct, are more satisfied with their organizations overall, and feel more valued as employees.[41]

The ethical culture of a company seems to matter to employees. According to a report on employee loyalty and work practices, companies viewed as highly ethical by their employees were six times more likely to keep their workers.[42] Also, employees who view their company as having a strong community involvement feel more loyal to their employers and feel positive about themselves.

Ethics Contributes to Investor Loyalty

Employee commitment also helps a firm's reputation among other constituents. Companies perceived by their employees as having a high degree of honesty and integrity had an average three-year total return to shareholders of 101 percent, whereas companies perceived as having a low degree of honesty and integrity had a three-year total return to shareholders of just 69 percent.[43] Investors today are increasingly concerned about the ethics, social responsibility, and reputation of companies in which they invest, and various socially responsible mutual funds and asset management firms can help investors purchase stock in ethical companies. Investors are also recognizing that an ethical culture provides a foundation for efficiency, productivity, and profits. On the other hand, investors know too that negative publicity, lawsuits, and fines can lower stock prices, diminish customer loyalty, and threaten a company's long-term viability. Many companies accused of misconduct, including Global Crossing, Adelphia,

FreddieMac, and HealthSouth, have experienced dramatic declines in the value of their stock when concerned investors divested their stocks and bonds. TIAA-CREF investor participants were asked would they choose a financial services company with strong ethics or higher returns? Surprisingly 92 percent of respondents said they would choose ethics while only 5 percent chose higher returns.[44]

To be successful, relationships with investors must rest on dependability, trust, and commitment. Investors look at the bottom line for profits or the potential for increased stock prices or dividends. But they also look for any potential flaws in the company's performance, conduct, and financial reports. Thus, many executives spend considerable time communicating with investors about their firms' reputation and financial performance and trying to attract them to the company's stock. The issue of drawing and keeping investors is a critical one for CEOs because roughly 50 percent of investors sell their stock in companies within one year, and the average household replaces 80 percent of its common stock portfolio each year.[45] Therefore, gaining investors' trust and confidence is vital to sustaining the financial stability of the firm.

Ethics Contributes to Customer Satisfaction

It is generally accepted that customer satisfaction is one of the most important factors in successful business strategy. Although a company must continue to develop, alter, and adapt products to keep pace with customers' changing desires and preferences, it must also seek to develop long-term relationships with customers and its stakeholders. While Wal-Mart has focused on low prices for customers, today there are questions about who might be hurt by Wal-Mart's quest to maintain the lowest prices possible. Nearly four in ten Americans have an unfavorable opinion of Wal-Mart today. Wal-Mart's reputation has dropped rapidly as the mass media has reported low benefits to employees, environmental issues, and ethical issues in top management. In addition, there are concerns that Wal-Mart is outsourcing American jobs to China by forcing their suppliers to move manufacturing overseas.[46] For most businesses, both repeat purchases and an enduring relationship of mutual respect and cooperation with their customers are essential for success. By focusing on customer satisfaction, a company continually deepens the customer's dependence on the company, and as the customer's confidence grows, the firm gains a better understanding of how to serve the customer so the relationship may endure. Successful businesses provide an opportunity for customer feedback, which can engage the customer in cooperative problem solving. As is often pointed out, a happy customer will come back, but a disgruntled customer will tell others about his or her dissatisfaction with a company and discourage friends from dealing with it.

The public's trust is essential to maintaining a good long-term relationship between a business and consumers. The Millennium Poll of twenty-five thousand citizens in twenty-three countries found that almost 60 percent of people focus on social responsibility ahead of brand reputation or financial factors when forming impressions of companies.[47] As social responsibility becomes more important for companies, it has been suggested that corporate social responsibility is a sign of good management and that it may, according to one study, indicate good financial performance. However, another study indicates that the reverse may be true, that companies who have good financial performance are able to spend more money on social responsibility.[48] For example, after the *Exxon Valdez* oil spill, special-interest groups and individual citizens boycotted the company. Before Chicken of the Sea and many of its competitors adopted dolphin-friendly nets to catch tuna, many consumers refused to buy tuna. Moreover, consumers may avoid the products of companies that are perceived as treating their employees unfairly. For example, Wal-Mart has been facing increasing pressure from customers and employees regarding how it treats its employees. As a direct result, it has increased the health-care benefits that it offers its part-time workers.[49] Companies that subcontract manufacturing operations abroad have had to confront the ethical issues associated with supporting facilities that abuse or underpay their workforce—sometimes called "sweatshops." The Gap, the number-one U.S. clothing chain, and Nike, the world's largest maker of athletic shoes, suspended orders at June Textiles Company, a Cambodian garment factory, after learning that the British Broadcasting Corporation planned to air a program alleging use of child labor at the factory.[50] Because of a large amount of negative publicity about how they operated abroad, Nike completely changed the way that it operated. Nike now has a complete website devoted to responsibility, which includes a section on workers and factories and their evolving approach, as well as the code of conduct for their factories and employees. They also have improved their monitoring and assessment of factories abroad.[51] New industry codes of conduct, such as SA 8000 (www.sa-intl.org) mentioned earlier, have been established to help companies identify and address these ethical issues. When consumers learn about abuses in subcontracting, they may boycott the companies' products.

When an organization has a strong ethical environment, it usually focuses on the core value of placing customers' interests first.[52] Putting customers first does not mean that the interests of employees, investors, and local communities should be ignored, however. An ethical culture that focuses on customers incorporates the interests of all employees, suppliers, and other interested parties in decisions and actions. Employees working in an ethical environment support and contribute to the process of understanding customers' demands and concerns. Ethical conduct toward customers builds a strong competitive position that has been shown to affect business performance and product innovation positively.[53]

Ethics Contributes to Profits

A company cannot nurture and develop an ethical culture unless it has achieved adequate financial performance in terms of profits. Businesses with greater resources—regardless of their staff size—have the means to practice social responsibility while serving their customers, valuing their employees, and establishing trust with the public. Many studies have found a positive relationship between corporate social responsibility and business performance.[54] Companies convicted of misconduct experience a significantly lower return on assets and on sales than firms that have not faced such charges. Research indicates that the negative effect on return on sales does not appear until the third year following the conviction, and multiple convictions are more harmful than a single one.[55]

There are many examples of companies that have experienced significant performance declines after the disclosure of their failure to act responsibly toward various stakeholders. Although HealthSouth Corporation's CEO Richard Scrushy was acquitted of participating in a $2.7 billion accounting fraud, but later convicted of bribery in a state court, many of his executives plea-bargained deals with the government for more lenient sentences. Moreover, the resulting damage to the firm's reputation was a disaster, and their only means of distancing themselves from their former leader was to provide the following comment on the company's website:

> As HealthSouth continues its unprecedented recovery from a massive fraud that occurred during the tenure of Richard Scrushy as CEO and Chairman, it is astonishing that he would have the audacity and shamelessness to comment on the current operations or the dedication of our approximately 40,000 employees. As we have stated in the past, Scrushy will not be offered any position within the Company by this management team or this Board of Directors. Under no circumstances would we reach out to Scrushy, who by his own defense has claimed a complete lack of knowledge as to the financial workings of the Company during his tenure as CEO and Chairman, despite his claims of possessing valuable expertise.[56]

Another example is Columbia/HCA that experienced serious declines in stock prices and earnings after the revelation that it was systematically overcharging the government for Medicare services. Employees and customers also lodged complaints against the hospital chain for putting profits ahead of their interests. Employees alleged that they were forced to do jobs beyond their abilities, and many patients accused the company of charging them for services they did not need or transferring them to other facilities if questions arose about their ability to pay. Once Columbia/HCA's misconduct became public knowledge, its reputation was damaged within a few months.[57] Every day, business newspapers and magazines offer new examples of the consequences of business misconduct. It is also worth noting, however, that most of these companies have learned from their mistakes and recovered after they implemented programs to improve ethical and legal conduct. For example, Columbia/HCA, now renamed HCA—The Healthcare Company—has become a role model for organizational ethics programs in the health-care industry.

Ample evidence shows that being ethical pays off with better performance. As indicated earlier, companies that are perceived by their employees as having a high degree of honesty and integrity had a much higher average total return to shareholders than did companies perceived as having a low degree of honesty and integrity.[58] A study of the five hundred largest public corporations in the United States found that those that commit to ethical behavior or emphasize compliance with their code of conduct have better financial performance.[59] These results provide strong evidence that corporate concern for ethical conduct is becoming a part of strategic planning toward obtaining the outcome of higher profitability. Rather than being just a compliance program, ethics is becoming one of the management issues within the effort to achieve competitive advantage.

OUR FRAMEWORK FOR STUDYING BUSINESS ETHICS

We have developed a framework for this text to help you understand how people make ethical decisions and deal with ethical issues. Table 1–3 summarizes each element in the framework and describes where each topic is discussed in this book.

| **TABLE 1–3** | Our Framework for Studying Business Ethics |

Chapter	Highlights
1. The Importance of Business Ethics	• Definitions • Reasons for studying business ethics • History • Benefits of business ethics
2. Stakeholder Relationships, Social Responsibility, and Corporate Governance	• Stakeholder relationships • Stakeholder influences in social responsibility • Corporate governance
3. Emerging Business Ethics Issues	• Recognizing an ethical issue • Honesty, fairness, and integrity • Ethical issues and dilemmas in business: abusive and disruptive behavior, lying, conflicts of interest, bribery, corporate intelligence, discrimination, sexual harassment, environmental issues, fraud, insider trading, intellectual-property rights, and privacy • Determining an ethical issue in business
4. The Institutionalization of Business Ethics	• Mandatory requirements • Voluntary requirements • Core practices • Federal Sentencing Guidelines for Organizations • Sarbanes–Oxley Act
5. Ethical Decision Making and Ethical Leadership	• Ethical issue intensity • Individual factors in decision making • Organizational factors in decision making • Opportunity in decision making • Business ethics evaluations and intentions • The role of leadership in a corporate culture • Leadership styles influence ethical decisions • Habits of strong ethical leaders
6. Individual Factors: Moral Philosophies and Values	• Moral philosophies, including teleological development, philosophies; and cognitive moral deontological, relativist, virtue ethics, and justice philosophies • Stages of cognitive moral development
7. Organizational Factors: The Role of Ethical Culture and Relationships	• Corporate culture • Interpersonal relationships • Whistle-blowing • Opportunity and conflict
8. Developing an Effective Ethics Program	• Ethics programs • Codes of ethics • Program responsibility • Communication of ethical standards • Systems to monitor and enforce ethical standards • Continuous improvement of ethics programs
9. Implementing and Auditing Ethics Programs	• Implementation programs • Ethics audits
10. Business Ethics in a Global Economy	• Ethical perceptions economy • Culture and cultural relations • Multinational corporations • Universal ethics • Global ethics issues

In Part One, we provide an overview of business ethics. Chapter 1 defines the term *business ethics* and explores the development and importance of this critical business area. In Chapter 2, we explore the role of various stakeholder groups in social responsibility and corporate governance.

Part Two focuses on ethical issues and the institutionalization of business ethics. In Chapter 3, we examine business issues that create ethical decision making in organizations. In Chapter 4, we look at the institutionalization of business ethics including both mandatory and voluntary societal concerns.

In Part Three, we delineate the ethical decision-making process and then look at both individual factors and organizational factors that influence decisions. Chapter 5 describes the ethical decision-making process from an organizational perspective. Chapter 6 explores individual factors that may influence ethical decisions in business, including moral philosophies and cognitive moral development. Chapter 7 focuses on the organizational dimensions including corporate culture, relationships, and conflicts.

In Part Four, we explore systems and processes associated with implementing business ethics into global strategic planning. Chapter 8 discusses the development of an effective ethics program. In Chapter 9, we examine issues related to implementing and auditing ethics programs. And finally, Chapter 10 considers ethical issues in a global context.

We hope that this framework will help you to develop a balanced understanding of the various perspectives and alternatives available to you when making ethical business decisions. Regardless of your own personal values, the more you know about how individuals make decisions, the better prepared you will be to cope with difficult ethical decisions. Such knowledge will help you improve and control the ethical decision-making environment in which you work.

It is your job to make the final decision in an ethical situation that affects you. Sometimes that decision may be right; sometimes it may be wrong. It is always easy to look back with hindsight and know what one should have done in a particular situation. At the time, however, the choices might not have been so clear. To give you practice making ethical decisions, Part Five of this book contains a number of cases. In addition, each chapter begins with a vignette, "An Ethical Dilemma," and ends with a minicase, "Resolving Ethical Business Challenges," that involves ethical problems. We hope they will give you a better sense of the challenges of making ethical decisions in the real business world.

SUMMARY

This chapter provides an overview of the field of business ethics and introduces the framework for the discussion of business ethics. Business ethics comprises principles and standards that guide behavior in the world of business. Investors, employees, customers, interest groups, the legal system, and the community often determine whether a specific action is right or wrong, ethical or unethical.

Studying business ethics is important for many reasons. Recent incidents of unethical activity in business underscore the widespread need for a better understanding of the factors that contribute to ethical and unethical decisions. Individuals' personal moral philosophies and decision-making experience may not be sufficient to guide them in the business world. Studying business ethics will help you begin to identify ethical issues and recognize the approaches available to resolve them.

The study of business ethics evolved through five distinct stages. Before 1960, business ethics issues were discussed primarily from a religious perspective. The 1960s saw the emergence of many social issues involving business and the idea of social conscience as well as a rise in consumerism, which culminated with Kennedy's Consumers' Bill of Rights. Business ethics began to develop as an independent field of study in the 1970s, with academics and practitioners exploring ethical issues and attempting to understand how individuals and organizations make ethical decisions. These experts began to teach and write about the idea of corporate social responsibility, an organization's obligation to maximize its positive impact on stakeholders and to minimize its negative impact. In the 1980s, centers of business ethics provided publications, courses, conferences, and seminars, and many companies established ethics committees and social policy committees. The Defense Industry Initiative on Business Ethics and Conduct was developed to guide corporate support for ethical conduct; its principles had a major impact on corporate ethics.

However, less government regulation and an increase in businesses with international operations raised new ethical issues. In the 1990s, government continued to support self-regulation. The FSGO sets the tone for organizational ethics programs by providing incentives for companies to take action to prevent organizational misconduct. The twenty-first century ushered in a new set of ethics scandals, suggesting that many companies had not fully embraced the public's desire for higher ethical standards. The Sarbanes–Oxley Act therefore stiffened penalties for corporate fraud and established an accounting oversight board. The current trend is away from legally based ethical initiatives in organizations toward cultural initiatives that make ethics a part of core organizational values. The ethical component of a corporate culture relates to the values, beliefs, and established and enforced patterns of conduct that employees use to identify and respond to ethical issues. The term *ethical culture* describes the component of corporate culture that captures the rules and principles that an organization defines as appropriate conduct. It can be viewed as the character or decision-making process that employees use to determine whether their responses to ethical issues are right or wrong.

Research and anecdotes demonstrate that building an ethical reputation among employees, customers, and the general public provides benefits that include increased efficiency in daily operations, greater employee commitment, increased investor willingness to entrust funds, improved customer trust and satisfaction, and better financial performance. The reputation of a company has a major effect on its relationships with employees, investors, customers, and many other parties and thus has the potential to affect its bottom line.

Finally, this text introduces a framework for studying business ethics. Each chapter addresses some aspect of business ethics and decision making within a business context. The major concerns are ethical issues in business, stakeholder relationships, social responsibility and corporate governance, emerging business ethics issues, the institutionalization of business ethics, understanding the ethical decision-making process, moral philosophies and cognitive moral development, corporate culture, organizational relationships and conflicts, developing an effective ethics program, implementing and auditing the ethics program, and global business ethics.

IMPORTANT TERMS FOR REVIEW	business ethics
	Consumers' Bill of Rights
	social responsibility
	Defense Industry Initiative on Business
	    Ethics and Conduct
		Federal Sentencing Guidelines for
		    Organizations
		Sarbanes–Oxley Act
		ethical culture

RESOLVING ETHICAL BUSINESS CHALLENGES*

Frank Garcia was just starting out as a salesman with Acme Corporation. Acme's corporate culture was top-down, or hierarchical. Because of the competitive nature of the medical-supplies industry, few mistakes were tolerated. Otis Hillman was a buyer for Thermocare, a national hospital chain. Frank's first meeting with Otis was a success, resulting in a $500,000 contract. This sale represented a significant increase for Acme and an additional $1000 bonus for Frank.

Some months later, Frank called on Thermocare, seeking to increase the contract by $500,000. "Otis, I think you'll need the additional inventory. It looks as if you didn't have enough at the end of last quarter," said Frank.

"You may be right. Business has picked up. Maybe it's because of your product, but then again, maybe not. It's still not clear to me whether Acme is the best for us. Speaking of which, I heard that you have season tickets to the Cubs!" replied Otis.

Frank thought for a moment and said, "Otis, I know that part of your increases are due to our quality products. How about we discuss this over a ball game?"

"Well, OK," Otis agreed.

By the seventh-inning stretch, Frank had convinced Otis that the additional inventory was needed and offered to give Thermocare a pair of season tickets. When Frank's boss, Amber, heard of the sale, she was very pleased. "Frank, this is great. We've been trying to get Thermocare's business for a long time. You seem to have connected with their buyer." As a result of the Thermocare account, Frank received another large bonus check and a letter of achievement from the vice president of marketing.

Two quarters later, Frank had become one of the top producers in the division. At the beginning of the quarter, Frank had run the numbers on Thermocare's account and found that business was booming. The numbers showed that Otis's business could probably handle an additional $750,000 worth of goods without hurting return on assets. As Frank went over the figures with Otis, Otis's response was, "You know, Frank, I've really enjoyed the season tickets, but this is a big increase." As the conversation meandered, Frank soon found out that Otis and his wife had never been to Cancun, Mexico. Frank had never been in a situation like this before, so he excused himself to another room and called Amber about what he was thinking of doing.

"Are you kidding!" responded Amber. "Why are you even calling me on this? I'll find the money somewhere to pay for it."

"Is this OK with Acme?" asked Frank.

"You let me worry about that," Amber told him.

When Frank suggested that Otis and his wife be his guests in Cancun, the conversation seemed to go smoothly. In Cancun, Otis decided to purchase the additional goods, for which Frank received another bonus increase and another positive letter from headquarters.

Some time later, Amber announced to her division that they would be taking all of their best clients to Las Vegas for a thank-you party. One of those invited was Thermocare. When they arrived, Amber gave each person $500 and said, "I want you to know that Acme is very grateful for the business that you have provided us. As a result of your under-standing the qualitative differences of our products, we have doubled our production facilities. This trip and everything that goes with it for the next few days is our small way of saying thank you. Every one of you has your salesperson here. If there is anything that you need, please let him or her know, and we'll try to accommodate you. Have a good time!"

That night Otis had seen Frank at dinner and suggested to him that he was interested in attending an "adult entertainment" club. When Frank came to Amber about this, she said, "Is he asking you to go with him?"

"No, Amber, not me!"

"Well, then, if he's not asking you to go, I don't understand why you're talking to me. Didn't I say we'd take care of their needs?"

"But what will Acme say if this gets out?" asked Frank.

"Don't worry; it won't," said Amber.

QUESTIONS • EXERCISES

1. What are the potential ethical issues faced by the Acme Corporation?
2. What should Acme do if there is a desire to make ethics a part of its core organizational values?
3. Identify the ethical issues of which Frank needs to be aware.
4. Discuss the advantages and disadvantages of each decision that Frank could make.

*This case is strictly hypothetical; any resemblance to real persons, companies, or situations is coincidental.

CHECK YOUR EQ

Check your EQ, or Ethics Quotient, by completing the following. Assess your performance to evaluate your overall understanding of the chapter material.

1.	Business ethics focuses mostly on personal ethical issues.	Yes	No
2.	Business ethics deals with right or wrong behavior within a particular organization.	Yes	No
3.	The 1990s could be characterized as the period when ethics programs were greatly influenced by government legislation.	Yes	No
4.	Business ethics contributes to investor loyalty.	Yes	No
5.	The trend is away from cultural or ethically based initiatives to legal initiatives in organizations.	Yes	No

ANSWERS: 1. No. Business ethics focuses on organizational concerns (legal and ethical—employees, customers, suppliers, society). 2. Yes. That stems from the basic definition. 3. Yes. The impact of the FSGO means that the 1990s are seen as the period in which business ethics were institutionalized. 4. Yes. Many studies have shown that trust and ethical conduct contribute to investor loyalty. 5. No. Many businesses are communicating their core values to their employees by creating ethics programs and appointing ethics officers to oversee them.

CHAPTER 2

Stakeholder Relationships, Social Responsibility, and Corporate Governance

CHAPTER OBJECTIVES

- To identify stakeholders' roles in business ethics
- To define social responsibility
- To examine the relationship between stakeholder orientation and social responsibility
- To delineate a stakeholder orientation in creating corporate social responsibility
- To explore the role of corporate governance in structuring ethics and social responsibility in business
- To list the steps involved in implementing a stakeholder perspective in social responsibility and business ethics

CHAPTER OUTLINE

AN ETHICAL DILEMMA*

Carla knew something was wrong when Jack got back to his desk. He had been with Aker & Aker Accounting (A&A) for seventeen years, starting there right after graduation and progressing through the ranks. Jack was a strong supporter of the company, and that was why Carla had been assigned to him. Carla had been with A&A for two years. She had graduated in the top 10 percent of her class and passed the CPA exam on the first try. She had chosen A&A over one of the "Big Five" firms because A&A was the biggest and best firm in Smallville, Ohio, where her husband, Frank, managed a locally owned machine tools company. She and Frank had just purchased a new home when things started to turn strange with Jack, her boss.

"What's the matter, Jack?" Carla asked.

"Well, you'll hear about it sooner or later. I've been denied a partner's position. Can you imagine that? I have been working sixty- and seventy-hour weeks for the last ten years, and all that management can say to me is 'not at this time,'" complained Jack.

Carla asked, "So what else did they say?"

Jack turned red and blurted out, "They said maybe in a few more years. I've done all that they've asked me to do. I've sacrificed a lot, and now they say a few more years. It's not fair."

"What are you going to do?" Carla asked.

"I don't know," Jack said. "I just don't know."

Six months later, Carla noticed that Jack was behaving oddly. He came in late and left early. One Sunday Carla went into the office for some files and found Jack copying some of the software that A&A used in auditing and consulting. A couple of weeks later, at a dinner party, Carla overheard a conversation about Jack doing consulting work for some small firms. Monday morning, she asked him if what she had heard was true.

Jack responded, "Yes, Carla, it's true. I have a few clients that I do work for on occasion."

"Don't you think there's a conflict of interest between you and A&A?" asked Carla.

"No," said Jack. "You see, these clients are not technically within the market area of A&A. Besides, I was counting on that promotion to help pay some extra bills. My oldest son decided to go to a private university, which is an extra $25,000 each year. Plus our medical plan at A&A doesn't cover some of my medical problems. And you don't want to know the cost. The only way I can afford to pay for these things is to do some extra work on the side."

"But what if A&A finds out?" Carla asked. "Won't they terminate you?"

"I don't want to think about that. Besides, if they don't find out for another six months, I may be able to start my own company."

"How?" asked Carla.

"Don't be naive, Carla. You came in that Sunday. You know."

Carla realized that Jack had been using A&A software for his own gain. "That's stealing!" she said.

"Stealing?" Jack's voice grew calm. "Like when you use the office phones for personal long-distance calls? Like when you decided to volunteer to help out your church and copied all those things for them on the company machine? If I'm stealing, you're a thief as well. But let's not get into this discussion. I'm not hurting A&A and, who knows, maybe within the next year I'll become a partner and can quit my night job."

Carla backed off from the discussion and said nothing more. She couldn't afford to antagonize her boss and risk bad performance ratings. She and Frank had bills, too. She also knew that she wouldn't be able to get another job at the same pay if she quit. Moving to another town was not an option because of Frank's business. She had no physical evidence to take to the partners, which meant that it would be her word against Jack's, and he had seventeen years of experience with the company.

QUESTIONS • EXERCISES

1. Identify the ethical issues in this case.
2. Assume you are Carla. Discuss your options and what the consequences of each option might be.
3. Assume you are Jack. Discuss your options.
4. Discuss any additional information you feel you might need before making your decision.

*This case is strictly hypothetical; any resemblance to real persons, companies, or situations is coincidental.

Business ethics issues, conflicts, and successes revolve around relationships. Building effective relationships is considered one of the more important areas of business today. A business exists because of relationships between employees, customers, shareholders or investors, suppliers, and managers who develop strategies to attain success. In addition, an organization usually has a governing authority often called a board of directors that provides oversight and direction to make sure that the organization stays focused on objectives in an ethical, legal, and socially acceptable manner. When unethical acts are discovered in organizations, it is often found that in most instances there is knowing cooperation or compliancy that facilitates the acceptance and perpetuation of unethical conduct.[1] Therefore, relationships are not only associated with organizational success but also with organizational misconduct.

A stakeholder framework helps identify the internal stakeholders such as employees, boards of directors, and managers and external stakeholders such as customers, special-interest groups, regulators, and others who agree, collaborate, and have confrontations on ethical issues. Most ethical issues exist because of conflicts in values and belief patterns about right and wrong between and within stakeholder groups. This framework allows a firm to identify, monitor, and respond to the needs, values, and expectations of different stakeholder groups.

The formal system of accountability and control of ethical and socially responsible behavior is corporate governance. In theory, the board of directors provides oversight for all decisions and use of resources. Ethical issues relate to role of the board of directors, shareholder relationship, internal control, risk management, and executive compensation. Ethical leadership is associated with appropriate corporate governance.

In this chapter, we first focus on the concept of stakeholders and examine how a stakeholder framework can help understand organizational ethics. Then we identify stakeholders and the importance of a stakeholder orientation. Using the stakeholder framework, social responsibility is explored, including the various dimensions of social responsibility. Next, corporate governance as a dimension of social responsibility and ethical decision making is covered to provide an understanding of the importance of oversight in responding to stakeholders. Finally, we provide the steps for implementing a stakeholder perspective in creating social responsibility and ethical decisions in business.

STAKEHOLDERS DEFINE ETHICAL ISSUES IN BUSINESS

In a business context, customers, investors and shareholders, employees, suppliers, government agencies, communities, and many others who have a "stake" or claim in some aspect of a company's products, operations, markets, industry, and outcomes are known as **stakeholders.** These groups are influenced by business, but they also have the ability to influence businesses; thus, the relationship between companies and their stakeholders is a two-way street.[2]

The recent ethical/legal crisis in corporate America has demonstrated how employees and investors can suffer dire consequences as a result of unethical corporate practices. For example, with the collapse of Enron, many employees lost their jobs, Enron retirees and those near retirement saw their pension funds essentially erased, and Enron investors lost billions of dollars after the company's stock price plummeted.[3]

Many firms experienced conflicts with key stakeholders, and consequently damaged their reputations and shareholder confidence during the 2008–2009 financial crisis. While many threats to reputation stem from uncontrollable events and the environment, ethical misconduct is more difficult to overcome than poor financial performance. Stakeholders who are most directly affected by negative events will have a corresponding shift in their perceptions of a firm's reputation. On the other hand, firms such as financial institutions that receive negative publicity for misconduct destroy trust and tarnish their reputations, which will make it more difficult to retain existing customers or attract new ones.[4] Consider the decision made by Bear Stearns, at the time an investment bank, to allow managers to invest clients' money in high-risk, highly-leveraged portfolio instruments, which were backed in part by subprime mortgages. While losing money is not a crime, Ralph Cioffi and Matthew Tannin the founders and portfolio managers of two Bear Stearns hedge funds are charged with making false statements in the months leading to the funds' demise. These Bear Stearns managers made reassuring public statements to investors ("we are very comfortable with exactly where we are") on April 25, 2007. Although private e-mails days earlier stated ("if we believe the internal report is anywhere close to accurate, I think we should close the funds now"). The plaintiff's class action lawyers claimed that Bear Stearns' problems were compounded two months later when Bear Stearns CEO James E. Cayne assured investors that "the balance sheet, capital base, and liquidity profile have never been stronger. Bear Stearns' risk exposures to high-profile sectors are moderate and well-controlled."[5] Several months later the company sought emergency funding from the government and was sold to JP Morgan Chase.[6] Of course it's impossible to know if CEO Cayne knew the true state of the financial situation at the time he made his comment, but the damage to the reputation of the company from these events was fatal. Once the credibility of a firm's statements has been destroyed, the reputation of the company and trust with stakeholders is almost impossible to recover. While prosecutors asked questions after the firm's collapse, at this time there is no active criminal inquiry into the CEO's statements. To maintain trust and confidence with stakeholders, CEOs and other top managers are expected to tell the truth to prevent customers and investors from being damaged by the failure to receive timely and accurate information. Providing untruthful or deceptive information to stakeholders, if not illegal, is unethical.

The financial crisis was based on a failure to consider the ramifications of unethical decision making affecting all stakeholders, including society and the economic system. The foundation of the crisis was subprime loans, involving lending money to people who could not possibly repay their loans, and derivatives. Many companies engaged in providing fictitious financial information. For example, in California a Mexican strawberry picker with an income of $14,000 who spoke no English was lent all the money he needed to buy a house for $720,000.[7] This reckless disregard for the impact on financial organizations that purchased the loan obligations, which could never be repaid, was at the heart of the 2008–2009 financial crisis.

Ethical misconduct and decisions that damage stakeholders will generally impact the company's reputation both from investor confidence and consumer confidence. As investor perceptions and decisions begin to take their toll, shareholder value will drop, exposing the company to consumer scrutiny that can increase the damage. Reputation is a factor in the consumers' perceptions of product attributes and corporate image features that lead to consumer willingness to purchase goods and services at profitable prices. After Radio Shack's CEO resigned for lying on his résumé, the company was so concerned about its reputation and leadership that it brought in respected interim CEO Claire Babrowski, whose leadership was key in restructuring McDonald's; Radio Shack's stock rose 5 percent on news of her entry.[8] Some scandals may lead to boycotts and aggressive campaigns to dampen sales and earnings. Nike experienced such a backlash from its use of offshore subcontractors to manufacture its shoes and clothing. When Nike claimed no responsibility for the subcontractors' poor working conditions and extremely low wages, some consumers demanded greater accountability and responsibility by engaging in boycotts, letter-writing campaigns, and public-service announcements. Nike ultimately responded to the growing negative publicity by changing its practices and becoming a model company in managing offshore manufacturing.[9]

New reforms to improve corporate accountability and transparency also suggest that other stakeholders—including banks, attorneys, and public accounting firms—can play a major role in fostering responsible decision making.[10] Stakeholders apply their values and standards to many diverse issues—working conditions, consumer rights, environmental conservation, product safety, and proper information disclosure—that may or may not directly affect an individual stakeholder's own welfare. We can assess the level of social responsibility that an organization bears by scrutinizing its effects on the issues of concern to its stakeholders. Table 2–1 provides examples of common stakeholder issues along with indicators of businesses' impacts on those issues.[11]

Stakeholders provide resources that are more or less critical to a firm's long-term success. These resources may be both tangible and intangible. Shareholders, for example, supply capital; suppliers offer material resources or intangible knowledge; employees and managers grant expertise, leadership, and commitment; customers generate revenue and provide loyalty and positive word-of-mouth promotion; local communities provide infrastructure; and the media transmits positive corporate images. When individual stakeholders share similar expectations about desirable business conduct, they may choose to establish or join formal communities that are dedicated to better defining and advocating these values and expectations. Stakeholders' ability to withdraw—or to threaten to withdraw—these needed resources gives them power over businesses.[12]

Identifying Stakeholders

We can identify two different types of stakeholders. **Primary stakeholders** are those whose continued association is absolutely necessary for a firm's survival; these include employees, customers, investors, and shareholders, as well as the governments and communities that provide necessary infrastructure. Some firms take actions that can damage relationships with primary stakeholders. Figure 2–1 indicates that ethical culture in organizations is on the decline, in an age of ethical and financial scandals and continued examples of misconduct across many industries. Ethical corporate cultures are linked to positive relationships with stakeholders. Concern for stakeholders and their needs and expectations is necessary to avoid ethical conflicts.

Secondary stakeholders do not typically engage in transactions with a company and thus are not essential for its survival; these include the media, trade associations, and special-interest groups. The American Association of Retired People (AARP), a special-interest group, works to support retirees' rights such as health-care benefits.

TABLE 2-1	Examples of Stakeholder Issues and Associated Measures of Corporate Impacts
Stakeholder Groups and Issues	**Potential Indicators of Corporate Impact on These Issues**

Employees

1. Compensation and benefits	1. Ratio of lowest wage to national legal minimum or to local cost of living
2. Training and development	2. Changes in average years of training of employees
3. Employee diversity	3. Percentages of employees from different genders and races
4. Occupational health and safety	4. Standard injury rates and absentee rates
5. Communications with management	5. Availability of open-door policies or ombudsmen

Customers

1. Product safety and quality	1. Number of product recalls over time
2. Management of customer complaints	2. Number of customer complaints and availability of procedures to answer them
3. Services to disabled customers	3. Availability and nature of measures taken to ensure services to disabled customers

Investors

1. Transparency of shareholder communications	1. Availability of procedures to inform shareholders about corporate activities
2. Shareholder rights	2. Frequency and type of litigation involving violations of shareholder rights

Suppliers

1. Encouraging suppliers in developing countries	1. Prices offered to suppliers in developed countries in comparison to other suppliers
2. Encouraging minority suppliers	2. Percentage of minority suppliers

Community

1. Public health and safety protection	1. Availability of emergency-response plan
2. Conservation of energy and materials	2. Data on reduction of waste produced and comparison to industry
3. Donations and support of local organizations	3. Annual employee time spent in community service

Environmental Groups

1. Minimizing the use of energy	1. Amount of electricity purchased; percentage of "green" electricity
2. Minimizing emissions and waste	2. Type, amount, and designation of waste generated
3. Minimizing adverse environmental effects of goods and services	3. Percentage of product weight reclaimed after use

Both primary and secondary stakeholders embrace specific values and standards that dictate what constitutes acceptable or unacceptable corporate behaviors. It is important for managers to recognize that while primary groups may present more day-to-day concerns, secondary groups cannot be ignored or given less consideration in the ethical decision-making process.[13]

Figure 2–2 offers a conceptualization of the relationship between businesses and stakeholders. In this **stakeholder interaction model,** there are two-way relationships between the firm and a host of stakeholders. In addition to the fundamental input of investors, employees, and suppliers, this approach recognizes other stakeholders and explicitly acknowledges the dialogue that exists between a firm's internal and external environments.

FIGURE 2–1	Strength of Organizational Ethical Culture Is on the Decline

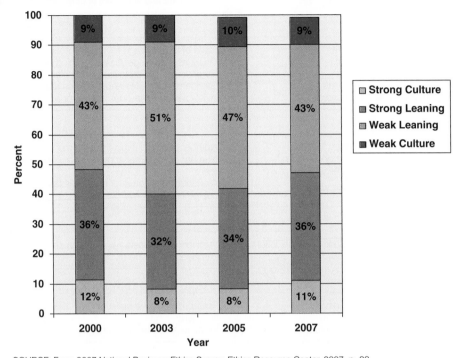

SOURCE: From *2007 National Business Ethics Survey*, Ethics Resource Center, 2007, p. 23.

A Stakeholder Orientation

The degree to which a firm understands and addresses stakeholder demands can be referred to as a **stakeholder orientation.** This orientation comprises three sets of activities: (1) the organization-wide generation of data about stakeholder groups and assessment of the firm's effects on these groups, (2) the distribution of this information throughout the firm, and (3) the organization's responsiveness as a whole to this intelligence.[14]

Generating data about stakeholders begins with identifying the stakeholders that are relevant to the firm. Relevant stakeholder communities should be analyzed on the basis of the power that each enjoys as well as by the ties between them. Next, the firm should characterize the concerns about the business's conduct that each relevant stakeholder group shares. This information can be derived from formal research, including surveys, focus groups, Internet searches, or press reviews. For example, Ford Motor Company obtains input on social and environmental responsibility issues from company representatives, suppliers, customers, and community leaders. Shell has an online discussion forum where website visitors are invited to express their opinions on the company's activities and their implications. Employees and managers can also generate this information informally as they carry out their daily activities. For example, purchasing managers know about suppliers' demands, public relations executives about the media, legal counselors about the regulatory environment, financial executives about investors, sales representatives about customers, and human resources advisers about

| **FIGURE 2–2** | Interactions between a Company and Its Primary and Secondary Stakeholders |

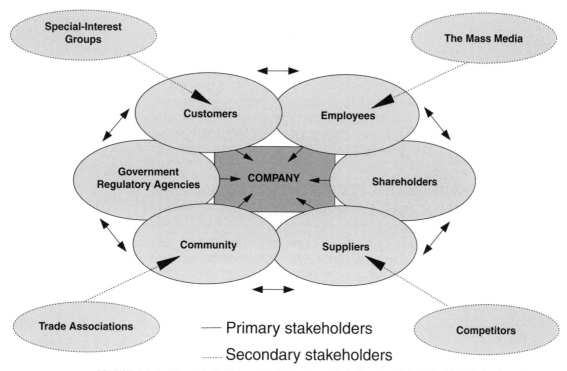

SOURCE: Adapted from Isabelle Maignan, O. C. Ferrell, and Linda Ferrell, "A Stakeholder Model for Implementing Social Responsibility in Marketing," *European Journal of Marketing* 39 (2005): 956–977. Used with permission.

employees. Finally, the company should evaluate its impact on the issues that are important to the various stakeholders it has identified.[15]

Given the variety of the employees involved in the generation of information about stakeholders, it is essential that this intelligence be circulated throughout the firm. This requires that the firm facilitate the communication of information about the nature of relevant stakeholder communities, stakeholder issues, and the current impact of the firm on these issues to all members of the organization. The dissemination of stakeholder intelligence can be organized formally through activities such as newsletters and internal information forums.[16]

A stakeholder orientation is not complete unless it includes activities that address stakeholder issues. For example Gap reported that although it is improving inspections it is still struggling to wipe out deep-seated problems such as discrimination and excessive overtime. In 2004 Gap revoked approval for seventy factories that violated its code of vendor conduct. Gap also realized that it sometimes contributes to problems by making unreasonable demands on factories; it is becoming more strict about its own deadlines to ensure that dumping rush jobs on factories does not occur.[17]

The responsiveness of the organization as a whole to stakeholder intelligence consists of the initiatives that the firm adopts to ensure that it abides by or exceeds stakeholder expectations and has a positive impact on stakeholder issues. Such activities are likely to be specific to a particular stakeholder group (for example, family-friendly work schedules) or to a particular stakeholder issue (for example, pollution-reduction programs). These responsiveness processes typically involve the participation of the concerned stakeholder groups. Kraft, for example, includes special-interest groups and university representatives in its programs to become sensitized to present and future ethical issues.

A stakeholder orientation can be viewed as a continuum in that firms are likely to adopt the concept to varying degrees. To gauge a given firm's stakeholder orientation, it is necessary to evaluate the extent to which the firm adopts behaviors that typify both the generation and dissemination of stakeholder intelligence and responsiveness to it. A given organization may generate and disseminate more intelligence about certain stakeholder communities than about others and, as a result, may respond to that intelligence differently.[18]

SOCIAL RESPONSIBILITY AND THE IMPORTANCE OF A STAKEHOLDER ORIENTATION

From the perspective of **social responsibility,** business ethics embodies standards, norms, and expectations that reflect a concern of major stakeholders, including consumers, employees, shareholders, suppliers, competitors, and the community. In other words, these stakeholders have concerns about what is fair, just, or in keeping with respect for stakeholders' rights.

Many businesspeople and scholars have questioned the role of ethics and social responsibility in business. Legal and economic responsibilities are generally accepted as the most important determinants of performance: "If this is well done," say classical theorists, "profits are maximized more or less continuously and firms carry out their major responsibilities to society."[19] Some economists believe that if companies address economic and legal issues, they are satisfying the demands of society and that trying to anticipate and meet additional needs would be almost impossible. Milton Friedman has been quoted as saying that "the basic mission of business [is] thus to produce goods and services at a profit, and in doing this, business [is] making its maximum contribution to society and, in fact, being socially responsible."[20] Even with the business ethics scandals of the twenty-first century, Friedman suggests that although those individuals guilty of wrongdoing should be held accountable, the market is a better deterrent than new laws and regulations at deterring firms from wrongdoing.[21] Thus, Friedman would diminish the role of stakeholders such as the government and employees in requiring that businesses demonstrate responsible and ethical behavior.

This Darwinian form of capitalism has been exported to many lesser and developing countries and is associated with a "Wild West" economy where anything goes in business. Friedman's capitalism is a far cry from Adam Smith's, one of the founders of capitalism. Smith created the concept of the invisible hand and spoke about self-interest; however, he went on to explain that "this common good is associated with six psychological motives and that each individual has to produce for the common good, with values such as Propriety, Prudence, Reason, Sentiment and promoting the happiness of mankind."[22] These values could be associated with the needs and concerns of stakeholders.

In the twenty-first century, Friedman's form of capitalism is being replaced by Smith's original concept of capitalism (or what is now called enlightened capitalism), a notion of capitalism that reemphasizes stakeholder concerns and issues. This shift may be occurring faster in developed countries than in those still being developed. Theodore Levitt, a renowned business professor, once wrote that although profits are required for business just like eating is required for living, profit is not the purpose of business any more than eating is the purpose of life.[23] Norman Bowie, a well-known philosopher, extended Levitt's sentiment by noting that focusing on profit alone can create an unfavorable paradox that causes a firm to fail to achieve its objective. Bowie contends that when a business also cares about the well-being of stakeholders, it earns trust and cooperation that ultimately reduce costs and increase productivity.[24]

Relationship between Social Responsibility and Profitability

Much evidence shows that social responsibility, including business ethics, is associated with increased profits. For example, one survey indicates that three out of four consumers refuse to buy from certain businesses, and a business's conduct was considered an important reason to avoid a business.[25] An important academic study found a direct relationship between social responsibility and profitability. The study also found that social responsibility contributes to employee commitment and customer loyalty—vital concerns of any firm trying to increase profits.[26]

It should be obvious from this discussion that ethics and social responsibility cannot be just a reactive approach to issues as they arise. Only if firms make ethical concerns a part of their foundation and incorporate ethics in their business strategy can social responsibility as a concept be embedded in daily decision making. A description of corporate ethical responsibility should include rights and duties, consequences and values, all of which refer to specific strategic decisions. The ethical component of

TABLE 2-2 *Fortune*'s Best and Worst Companies for Social Responsibility

Best Companies	Worst Companies
1. International Paper	1. Constellation Brands
2. United Parcel Service	2. WellCare Health Plans
3. Starbucks	3. Sears Holding*
4. Fortune Brands	3. Dana*
5. Walt Disney	5. Federal-Mogul
6. McDonald's	6. Beazer Homes USA*
7. Medco Health Solutions	6. S&C Holdco 3 (Swift & Co.)*
8. Herman Miller	8. Dollar General
9. Weyerhaeuser	9. Brown-Forman
10. Union Pacific	10. Delphi

*tied

SOURCE: From *Fortune*, "America's Most Admired Companies." Copyright © 2008 Time Inc. All rights reserved. March 3, 2008.

business strategy should be capable of providing an assessment of top-management, work-group, and individual behavior as it relates to ethical decisions. Table 2–2 lists *Fortune*'s best and worst companies in terms of social responsibility.

SOCIAL RESPONSIBILITY AND ETHICS

The concepts of ethics and social responsibility are often used interchangeably, although each has a distinct meaning. In Chapter 1, we defined the term *social responsibility* as an organization's obligation to maximize its positive impact on stakeholders and to minimize its negative impact. PNC Financial Services Group, for example, contributes $20 million in grants and corporate sponsorships to arts, community improvement, and educational causes. The company also supports employees with flexible work schedules and backup and holiday daycare, as well as a free daycare center for new parents. For its operations and technology center in Pittsburgh, the company built the nation's largest "green building" conforming to environmental guidelines on site planning, energy efficiency, water conservation, material conservation, and indoor environmental quality. It also built several "green" bank branches in New Jersey.[27]

Another example of a company being green is Whole Foods, which plans to become the largest buyer of wind-energy credits in North America by purchasing credits equal to 100 percent of its projected energy use.[28] General Electric also pledged to decrease pollution and double research-and-development spending on cleaner technologies.[29] Wal-Mart has also joined the growing ranks of green companies. In McKinney, Texas, and Aurora, Colorado, it has opened environmentally friendly stores, which should provide examples of the way they can work together to create stores that save energy, conserve natural resources, and reduce pollution. Wal-Mart hopes to take what it learns from the new stores and use it in all of the new stores that it builds.[30] Like Whole Foods and General Electric, many businesses have tried to determine what relationships, obligations, and duties are appropriate between the organization and various stakeholders. Social responsibility can be viewed as a contract with society, whereas business ethics involves carefully thought-out rules or heuristics of business conduct that guide decision making.

If social responsibility is considered an important corporate concern, then it does need quantitative credibility. Employee satisfaction, consumer loyalty, and other stakeholder concerns can be quantified to some extent, but some of the values and other dimensions are more qualitative. The International Organization for Standardization (ISO) has tried to establish a corporate responsibility standard, the ISO 26000; although the ISO 26000 has been demoted to a guideline rather than a standard, the discussion and debate surrounding the process is valuable. Whereas corporate responsibility needs quantitative credibility, significant aspects are more qualitative in nature: employee satisfaction, customer motivations, company values, and ethical decision-making processes, for instance. All to some extent can be broken down into quantitative data, but the essence of them cannot. However, they also shift constantly, which makes yesterday's survey an addition to today's recycle bin.[31]

Buildings are rarely considered major pollution sources. Yet 33 percent of major U.S. energy use, 33 percent of major greenhouse-gas emissions, and 30 percent of raw material use are the result of buildings.[32] Currently, there are two competitive certification groups that authorize schools, houses, and commercial buildings as green. These two rival groups, Green Globes and Leadership in Energy and Environmental Design (LEED), are vying for leadership in government adoption of environmental rules that determine whether a building can be called green. There is concern about stakeholder relationships between the two groups. Green Globes is led by a former timber-company executive and received much of its seed money from timber and wood-products companies. LEED is a nonprofit organization with less ties to business interest. Already two states, Maryland and Arkansas, have adopted Green Globes as an alternative to LEED, giving officials an alternative for government-funded construction. The Clinton Presidential Library in Little Rock as well as the 7 World Trade Center, the first tower rebuilt near Ground Zero in New York, was certified by Green Globes.[33]

There are four levels of social responsibility—economic, legal, ethical, and philanthropic—and they can be viewed as steps (see Figure 2–3).[34] At the most basic level, companies have an economic responsibility to be profitable so that they can provide a return on investment to their owners and investors, create jobs for the community, and contribute goods and services to the economy. Of course, businesses are also expected to obey all laws and regulations. Business ethics, as previously defined, comprises principles and standards that guide behavior in the world of business. Finally, philanthropic responsibility refers to activities that are not required of businesses but promote human welfare or goodwill. Ethics, then, is one dimension of social responsibility.

The term **corporate citizenship** is often used to express the extent to which businesses strategically meet the economic, legal, ethical, and philanthropic responsibilities placed on them by their various stakeholders.[35] Corporate citizenship has four interrelated dimensions: strong sustained economic performance, rigorous compliance, ethical actions beyond what the law requires, and voluntary contributions that advance the reputation and stakeholder commitment of the organization. A firm's commitment to corporate citizenship indicates a strategic focus on fulfilling the social responsibilities that its stakeholders expect of it. Corporate citizenship involves acting on the firm's commitment to the corporate citizenship philosophy and measuring the extent to which it follows through by actually implementing citizenship initiatives.

FIGURE 2-3   Steps of Social Responsibility

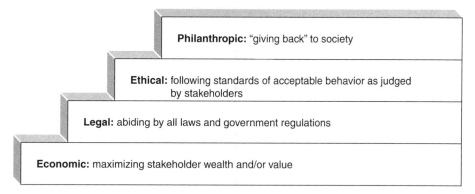

SOURCE: Adapted from Archie B. Carroll, "The Pyramid of Corporate Social Responsibility: Toward the Moral Management of Organizational Stakeholders," *Business Horizons* (July–August 1991): 42, Figure 3.

Rank	Company	Rank	Company
1	Green Mountain Coffee Roasters, Inc.	11	Salesforce.com, Inc.
2	Advanced Micro Devices	12	Applied Materials, Inc.
3	NIKE, Inc.	13	Texas Instruments, Inc.
4	Motorola, Inc.	14	Herman Miller, Inc.
5	Intel Corporation	15	Rockwell Collins
6	International Business Machines Corporation	16	Interface, Inc.
7	Agilent Technologies, Inc.	17	Steelcase, Inc.
8	The Timberland Company	18	Dell Inc.
9	Starbucks Corporation	19	Cisco Systems, Inc.
10	General Mills Incorporated	20	Lam Research Corporation

TABLE 2–3 The Top Twenty Best Corporate Citizens

SOURCE: Marjorie Kelly, Samuel Graves, and Sandra Waddock, "110 Best Corporate Citizens 2007," *Business Ethics Magazine*, http://www.business-ethics.com/BE100_all (accessed January 14, 2009).

Reputation is one of an organization's greatest intangible assets with tangible value. The value of a positive reputation is difficult to quantify, but it is very important. A single negative incident can influence perceptions of a corporation's image and reputation instantly and for years afterwards. Corporate reputation, image, and brands are more important than ever and are among the most critical aspects of sustaining relationships with constituents including investors, customers, financial analysts, media, and government watchdogs. It takes companies decades to build a great reputation, yet just one slip can cost a company dearly. Although an organization does not control its reputation in a direct sense, its actions, choices, behaviors, and consequences do influence the reputation that exists in perceptions of stakeholders. Companies such as Exxon Mobil, Chevron Corporation, and Royal Dutch Shell Plc. received low ratings from the public in a corporate reputation survey for what the public perceived as the "heartless" spike in prices at the pump while the companies were enjoying record profits. A recent Gallup survey found that consumer trust in industries declined by 14 percent between September 2007 and April 2008 alone.[36] Real estate brokers and auto dealers had the lowest levels of consumer trust. Table 2–3 lists the top twenty best corporate citizens, according to the spring 2008 issue of *Business Ethics.*

CORPORATE GOVERNANCE PROVIDES FORMALIZED RESPONSIBILITY TO STAKEHOLDERS

Most businesses, and often courses taught in colleges of business, operate under the belief that the purpose of business is to maximize profits for shareholders. In 1919 the Michigan Supreme Court in the case of *Dodge v. Ford Motor Co.*[37] ruled that a business exists for the profit of shareholders and the board of directors should focus on that objective. On the other hand, the stakeholder model places the board of directors in the central position to balance the interests and conflicts of the various constituencies. External control of the corporation includes not only government regulation but also key stakeholders including employees, consumers, and communities to exert pressures to responsible conduct. Many of the obligations to balance stakeholder interest have been institutionalized in legislation that provides incentives for responsible conduct. The Federal Sentencing Guidelines for Organizations (FSGO) provides incentives for developing an ethical culture and efforts to prevent misconduct.

Today, the failure to balance stakeholder interests can result in a failure to maximize shareholders' wealth. Wal-Mart may be failing to maximize the growth of its market value because investors are concerned about its ability to manage stakeholder interests. Wal-Mart's shareholders have seen almost no growth over the past few years as it battles employees, communities, and special-interest groups over ethical issues. Most firms are moving more toward a balanced stakeholder model as they see that this approach will sustain the relationships necessary for long-run success.

Both directors and officers of corporations are fiduciaries for the shareholders. Fiduciaries are persons placed in positions of trust who use due care and loyalty in acting on behalf of the best interests of the organization. There is a duty of care also called a *duty of diligence* to make informed and prudent decisions.[38] Directors have a duty to avoid ethical misconduct in their director role and to provide leadership in decisions to prevent ethical misconduct in the organization.

Directors are not held responsible for negative outcomes if they are informed and diligent in their decision making. This means they have an obligation to request information, research, use accountants and attorneys, and obtain the services of ethical compliance consultants.

The duty of loyalty means that all decisions should be in the interests of the corporation and its stakeholders. Conflicts of interest exist when a director uses the position to obtain personal gain usually at the expense of the organization. For example, before the Sarbanes–Oxley Act in 2002, directors could give themselves and officers interest-free loans. Scandals at Tyco, Kmart, and WorldCom are all associated with officers receiving personal loans that damaged the corporation.

Officer compensation packages challenge directors, especially those on the board and not independent. Directors have an opportunity to vote for others' compensation in return for their own increased compensation. Opportunities to know about the investments, business ventures, and stock-market information create issues that could violate the duty of loyalty. Insider trading of a firm's stock has very specific rules, and violations can result in serious punishment. The obligations of directors and officers for legal and ethical responsibility interface and fit together based on their fiduciary relationships. Ethical values should guide decisions and buffer the possibility of illegal conduct. With increased pressure on directors to provide oversight for organizational ethics, there is a trend toward directors receiving training to increase their competency in ethics program development, as well as other areas such as accounting.

To remove the opportunity for employees to make unethical decisions, most companies have developed formal systems of accountability, oversight, and control—known as **corporate governance.** *Accountability* refers to how closely workplace decisions are aligned with a firm's stated strategic direction and its compliance with ethical and legal considerations. *Oversight* provides a system of checks and balances that limit employees' and managers' opportunities to deviate from policies and strategies and that prevent unethical and illegal activities. *Control* is the process of auditing and improving organizational decisions and actions.

A clear delineation of accountability helps employees, customers, investors, government regulators, and other stakeholders understand why and how the organization chooses and achieves its goals. Corporate governance establishes fundamental systems and processes: for preventing and detecting misconduct, for investigating and disciplining, and for recovery and continuous improvement. Effective corporate governance creates a compliance and ethics culture so that employees feel that integrity is at the core of competitiveness.[39] Even if a company has adopted a consensus approach for decision making, there should be oversight and authority for delegating tasks, making difficult and sometimes controversial decisions, balancing power throughout the firm, and maintaining ethical compliance. Governance also provides mechanisms for identifying risks and for planning for recovery when mistakes or problems occur.

The development of stakeholder orientation should interface with the corporation's governance structure. Corporate governance is also part of a firm's corporate culture that establishes the integrity of all relationships. A governance system that does not provide checks and balances creates opportunities for top managers to put their own self-interests before those of important stakeholders. Consider the accounting scandal at Adelphia Communications. Founders John J. Rigas, Timothy J. Rigas, and Michael J. Rigas defrauded Adelphia's stockholders out of billions of dollars by falsifying the firm's financial reports because its corporate governance systems failed to prevent this type of fraud.[40]

Concerns about the need for greater corporate governance are not limited to the United States. Reforms in governance structures and issues are occurring all over the world.[41] In many nations, companies are being pressured to implement stronger corporate governance mechanisms by international investors, by the process of becoming privatized after years of unaccountability as state companies, or by the desire to imitate successful governance movements in the United States, Japan, and the European Union.[42]

Table 2–4 lists examples of major corporate governance issues. These issues normally involve strategic-level decisions and actions taken by boards of directors, business owners, top executives, and other managers with high levels of authority and accountability. Although these people have often been relatively free from scrutiny, changes in technology, consumer activism, government attention, recent ethical scandals, and other factors have brought new attention to such issues as transparency, executive pay, risk and control, resource accountability, strategic direction, stockholder rights, and other decisions made for the organization.

Views of Corporate Governance

To better understand the role of corporate governance in business today, it is important to consider how it relates to fundamental beliefs about the purpose of business. Some organizations take the view that as long as they are maximizing shareholder wealth and profitability, they are fulfilling their core responsibilities. Other firms,

TABLE 2-4	Corporate Governance Issues

Shareholder rights

Executive compensation

Composition and structure of the board of directors

Auditing and control

Risk management

CEO selection and termination decisions

Integrity of financial reporting

Stakeholder participation and input into decisions

Compliance with corporate governance reform

Role of the CEO in board decisions

Organizational ethics programs

however, believe that a business is an important member, even citizen, of society and therefore must assume broad responsibilities that include complying with social norms and expectations. From these assumptions, we can derive two major approaches to corporate governance: the shareholder model and the stakeholder model.[43]

The **shareholder model of corporate governance** is founded in classic economic precepts, including the goal of maximizing wealth for investors and owners. For publicly traded firms, corporate governance focuses on developing and improving the formal system for maintaining performance accountability between top management and the firms' shareholders.[44] Thus, a shareholder orientation should drive a firm's decisions toward serving the best interests of investors. Underlying these decisions is a classic agency problem, where ownership (that is, investors) and control (that is, managers) are separate. Managers act as agents for investors, whose primary goal is increasing the value of the stock they own. However, investors and managers are distinct parties with unique insights, goals, and values with respect to the business. Managers, for example, may have motivations beyond stockholder value, such as market share, personal compensation, or attachment to particular products and projects. For example, former Qwest Communications International Inc. CFO Robin Szeliga pleaded guilty to one count of insider trading. She was accused of improperly selling ten thousand shares of Qwest stock, earning a net profit of $125,000, in 2001 when she knew some business units would fail to meet revenue targets and that the company had improperly used nonrecurring revenue to meet those goals. Szeliga, former CEO Joseph Nacchio, and five other former executives were accused of orchestrating a massive financial fraud that forced Qwest Communications International Inc. to restate billions of dollars in revenue. The SEC wants repayment and civil penalties from all of the accused.[45] Because of these potential differences, corporate governance mechanisms are needed to align investor and management interests. The shareholder model has been criticized for its somewhat singular purpose and focus because there are other ways of "investing" in a business. Suppliers, creditors, customers, employees, business partners, the community, and others also invest their resources into the success of the firm.[46]

The **stakeholder model of corporate governance** adopts a broader view of the purpose of business. Although a company has a responsibility for economic success and viability to satisfy its stockholders, it also must answer to other stakeholders, including employees, suppliers, government regulators, communities, and special-interest groups with which it interacts. Due to limited resources, companies must determine which of their stakeholders are primary. Once the primary groups have been identified, managers must then implement the appropriate corporate governance mechanisms to promote the development of long-term relationships.[47] This approach entails creating governance systems that consider stakeholder welfare in tandem with corporate needs and interests.

Although these two approaches seem to represent the ends of a continuum, the reality is that the shareholder model is a more restrictive precursor to the stakeholder orientation. Many businesses have evolved into the stakeholder model as a result of government initiatives, consumer activism, industry activity, and other external forces.

The Role of Boards of Directors

For public corporations, boards of directors hold the ultimate responsibility for their firms' success or failure, as well as for the ethics of their actions. This governing authority is being held responsible by the 2004 amendments to the FSGO for creating an ethical culture that provides leadership, values, and compliance. The members of a company's board of directors assume legal responsibility for the firm's resources and decisions, and they appoint its top executive officers. Board members have a fiduciary duty, meaning they have assumed a position of trust and confidence that entails certain responsibilities, including acting in the best interests of those they serve. Thus, board membership is not intended as a vehicle for personal financial gain; rather, it provides the intangible benefit of ensuring the success of both the organization and people involved in the fiduciary arrangement. The role and expectations of boards of directors assumed greater significance after the accounting scandals of the early 2000s motivated many shareholders and other stakeholders to demand greater accountability from boards.[48] For example, after $9 billion in accounting irregularities led World-Com to declare the largest ever bankruptcy, the company replaced the board members who had failed to prevent the accounting scandal. The firm also fired many managers.[49]

The traditional approach to directorship assumed that board members managed the corporation's business. Research and practical observation have shown that boards of directors rarely, if ever, perform the management function.[50] First, boards meet only a few times a year, which precludes them from managing effectively. In addition, the complexity of modern organizations mandates full attention on a daily basis. Thus, boards of directors are concerned primarily with monitoring the decisions made by executives on behalf of the company. This includes choosing top executives, assessing their performance, helping set strategic direction, and ensuring that oversight, control, and accountability mechanisms are in place. In sum, board members assume ultimate authority for their organization's effectiveness and subsequent performance.

Many CEOs have lost their jobs because the board of directors was scared. Notable examples include Michael Eisner from Disney, Carly Fiorina from Hewlett-Packard, and Scott Livengood from Krispy Kreme. The main reason for this was that the boards feared losing all of their money. This fear came from two lawsuits by share-holders who sued the directors of Enron and WorldCom over their roles in the collapse of those firms. Both settlements called for the directors to pay large sums from their own pockets.[51]

GREATER DEMANDS FOR ACCOUNTABILITY AND TRANSPARENCY   Just as improved ethical decision making requires more of employees and executives, so too are boards of directors feeling greater demands for accountability and transparency. In the past, board members were often retired company executives or friends of current executives, but the trend today is toward "outside directors" who have little vested interest in the firm before assuming the director role. Inside directors are corporate officers, consultants, major shareholders, or others who benefit directly from the success of the organization. Directors today are increasingly chosen for their expertise, competence, and ability to bring diverse perspectives to strategic discussions. Outside directors are also thought to bring more independence to the monitoring function because they are not bound by past allegiances, friendships, a current role in the company, or some other issue that may create a conflict of interest.

Many of the corporate scandals uncovered in recent years might have been prevented if each of the companies' boards of directors had been better qualified, more knowledgeable, and less biased. Warren Buffett did not stand for reelection to Coca-Cola's board of directors, after serving for seventeen years. Buffett cited the need to focus his attention on Berkshire Hathaway and its subsidiaries.[52] Coca-Cola has struggled over the past ten years with involvement in ethical misconduct and high turnover of top managers. A survey by *USA Today* found that corporate boards have considerable overlap. More than one thousand corporate board members sit on four or more company boards, and of the nearly two thousand boards of directors in the United States, more than twenty-two thousand of their members are linked to boards of more than one company. For example, of the one thousand largest companies, one-fifth share at least one board member with another top one thousand firm. This overlap creates the opportunity for conflicts of interest in decision making and limits the independence of individual boards of directors. At Wal-Mart, questions have been raised by shareholders, who believe that recent reports of legal and regulatory noncompliance raise serious concerns about the adequacy of the company's controls. Such concerns involve the former Wal-Mart vice chairman Thomas Coughlin who pleaded guilty to fraud and tax charges or the charges that Wal-Mart knowingly hired contractors that furnished illegal immigrants to clean its floors. A group of institutional shareholders have called for Wal-Mart's board to form a special committee to conduct a "comprehensive review of the company's legal and regulatory controls, as well as its internal system for ensuring compliance with its own policies and standards."[53] In some cases, it seems that individuals have earned placement on multiple boards of directors because they have gained a reputation for going along with top management and never asking questions. This may foster a corporate culture that limits outside oversight of top managers' decisions.

Although labor and public pension-fund activities have waged hundreds of proxy battles in recent years, they rarely have much effect on the target companies. Now shareholder activists are attacking the process by which directors themselves are elected.

Shareholder resolutions at about 140 companies would require directors to gain a majority of votes cast to join the board. It is hoped that this new practice will make boards of directors more attentive.[54]

EXECUTIVE COMPENSATION   One of the biggest issues that corporate boards of directors face is **executive compensation.** In fact, most boards spend more time deciding how much to compensate top executives than they do ensuring the integrity of the company's financial reporting systems.[55] How executives are compensated for their leadership, organizational service, and performance has become a controversial topic. Indeed, 73 percent of respondents in a *BusinessWeek*/Harris poll indicated they believe that top officers of large U.S. companies receive too much compensation, while only 21 percent reported executive compensation as "just about the right amount."[56] Many executives have received large compensation and bonus packages regardless of the success of their companies. For example, Carly Fiorina, former CEO of Hewlett-Packard, received at least $14 million when she was terminated in early 2005, which represented 2.5 times her base salary and cash bonus, but not enough to require shareholder approval. However, two institutional shareholders are suing Hewlett-Packard over her severance package; they believe she received at least $21 million, more than 2.99 times her 2004 base salary and cash bonus of about $5.6 million. Stock options and other benefits raised her total exit package further to $42 million, which meant it should have received shareholder approval. It seems to be a growing trend by investors to sue over executive compensation.[57]

Many people believe that no executive is worth millions of dollars in annual salary and stock options, even if he or she has brought great financial return to investors. Their concerns often center on the relationship between the highest-paid executives and median employee wages in the company. If this ratio is perceived as too large, then critics believe that either employees are not being compensated fairly or high executive salaries represent an improper use of company resources. According to a recent report by United for a Fair Economy, the average executive now earns 431 times the average blue-collar worker. The average CEO pay is now $10.2 million, compared to worker pay that is now $27,460.[58] According to the report, if the minimum wage had risen as fast as CEO pay since 1990, the lowest paid workers in the United States would be earning $23.03 an hour today, not $5.15 an hour. Because of this enormous difference, the business press is now usually careful to support high levels of executive compensation only when it is directly linked to strong company performance.

Although the issue of executive compensation has received much attention in the media of late, some business owners have long recognized its potential ill effects. In the early twentieth century, for example, capitalist J. P. Morgan implemented a policy that limited the pay of top managers in businesses that he owned to no more than twenty times the pay of any other employee.[59]

Other people argue that because executives assume so much risk on behalf of the company, they deserve the rewards that follow from strong company performance. In addition, many executives' personal and professional lives meld to the point that they are "on call" twenty-four hours a day. Because not everyone has the skill, experience, and desire to become an executive, with the accompanying pressure and responsibility, market forces dictate a high level of compensation. When the pool of qualified individuals is limited, many corporate board members feel that offering large compensation packages is the only way to attract and retain top executives and so ensure that their firms are not left without strong leadership. In an era when top executives are increasingly willing to "jump ship" to other firms that offer higher pay, potentially lucrative stock options, bonuses, and other benefits, such thinking is not without merit.[60] The heads of the United States' 500 largest companies received an average of $14.2 million each in total compensation in 2007. This is up from $10.8 million in 2006, an increase of nearly 24 percent. While executive pay has increased at well over 20 percent annually for decades, revenues only increased 2.8 percent between 2006 and 2007.[61]

Executive compensation is a difficult but important issue for boards of directors and other stakeholders to consider because it receives much attention in the media, sparks shareholder concern, and is hotly debated in discussions of corporate governance. One area for board members to consider is the extent to which executive compensation is linked to company performance. Plans that base compensation on the achievement of several performance goals, including profits and revenues, are intended to align the interests of owners with management. Amid rising complaints about excessive executive compensation, an increasing number of corporate boards are imposing performance targets on the stock and stock options they include in their CEOs' pay package. In 2005 thirty companies based a portion of the equity granted to their CEOs on performance targets. The expanded emphasis on performance targets is designed to keep executives from reaping rich rewards for reasons unrelated to their leadership skills. Stock options, which became a popular form of compensation in the 1990s, can gain value in a rising stock market, enabling executives to pocket windfalls even if their own companies' earnings growth is modest.[62]

Another issue is whether performance-linked compensation encourages executives to focus on short-term performance at the expense of long-term growth.[63] Shareholders today, however, may be growing more concerned about transparency than short-term performance and executive compensation. One study determined that companies that divulge more details about their corporate governance practices generate higher shareholder returns than less transparent companies.[64]

IMPLEMENTING A STAKEHOLDER PERSPECTIVE[65]

An organization that develops effective corporate governance and understands the importance of business ethics and social responsibility in achieving success should develop some processes for managing these important concerns. Although there are many different approaches, we provide some steps that have been found effective to utilize the stakeholder framework in managing responsibility and business ethics. The steps include (1) assessing the corporate culture, (2) identifying stakeholder groups, (3) identifying stakeholder issues, (4) assessing organizational commitment to social responsibility, (5) identifying resources and determining urgency, and (6) gaining stakeholder feedback. The importance of these steps is to include feedback from relevant stakeholders in formulating organizational strategy and implementation.

Step 1: Assessing the Corporate Culture

To enhance organizational fit, a social responsibility program must align with the corporate culture of the organization. The purpose of this first step is to identify the organizational mission, values, and norms that are likely to have implications for social responsibility. In particular, relevant existing values and norms are those that specify the stakeholder groups and stakeholder issues that are deemed as most important by the organization. Very often, relevant organizational values and norms can be found in corporate documents such as the mission statement, annual reports, sales brochures, or websites. For example, Green Mountain Coffee is a pioneer in helping struggling coffee growers by paying them fair trade prices. The company also offers microloans to coffee-growing families, to underwrite business ventures that diversify agricultural economies. It has been on the *Business Ethics* "100 Best Corporate Citizens" since 2003 and climbed to the number-one position in 2006.[66]

Step 2: Identifying Stakeholder Groups

In managing this stage, it is important to recognize stakeholder needs, wants, and desires. Many important issues gain visibility because key constituencies such as consumer groups, regulators, or the media express an interest. When agreement, collaboration, or even confrontations exist on an issue, there is a need for a decision-making process. A model of collaboration to overcome the adversarial approaches to problem solving has been suggested. Managers can identify relevant stakeholders who may be affected by or may influence the development of organizational policy.

Stakeholders have some level of power over a business because they are in the position to withhold, or at least threaten to withhold, organizational resources. Stakeholders have most power when their own survival is not really affected by the success of the organization and when they have access to vital organizational resources. For example, most consumers of shoes do not need to buy Nike shoes. Therefore, if they decide to boycott Nike, they have to endure only minor inconveniences. Nevertheless, their loyalty to Nike is vital to the continued success of the sport apparel giant. The proper assessment of the power held by a given stakeholder community also requires an evaluation of the extent to which that community can collaborate with others to pressure the firm.

Step 3: Identifying Stakeholder Issues

Together, steps 1 and 2 lead to the identification of the stakeholders who are both the most powerful and legitimate. The level of power and legitimacy determines the degree of urgency in addressing their needs. Step 3 consists then in understanding the nature of the main issues of concern to these stakeholders. Conditions for collaboration exist when problems are so complex that multiple stakeholders are required to resolve the issue and the weaknesses of adversarial approaches are understood.

For example, obesity in children is becoming an issue across groups and stakeholders.[67] According to a recent survey of readers in the *Wall Street Journal,* most people (60 percent) believed that consumers should bear the main burden of health-care costs. Only 28 percent believed the government should bear the burden, and a small 13 percent believed the employers should foot the bill for rising costs associated with obesity and other problems.[68] The United States is the most obese nation with almost 40 percent of the population obese or overweight.

Step 4: Assessing Organizational Commitment to Social Responsibility

Steps 1 through 3 consist of generating information about social responsibility among a variety of influencers in and around the organization. Step 4 brings these three first stages together to arrive at an understanding of social responsibility that specifically matches the organization of interest. This general definition will then be used to evaluate current practices and to select concrete social responsibility initiatives. Firms such as Starbucks have selected activities that address stakeholder concerns. Starbucks has formalized its initiatives in official documents such as annual reports, webpages, and company brochures. Starbucks has a website devoted to social responsibility. Starbucks is concerned with the environment and integrates policies and programs throughout all aspects of operations to minimize their environmental impact. They also have many community-building programs that help them be good neighbors and contribute positively to the communities where their partners and customers live, work, and play.[69]

Step 5: Identifying Resources and Determining Urgency

The prioritization of stakeholders and issues, along with the assessment of past performance, provides for allocating resources. Two main criteria can be considered: First is the level of financial and organizational investments required by different actions; second is the urgency when prioritizing social responsibility challenges. When the challenge under consideration is viewed as significant and when stakeholder pressures on the issue could be expected, then the challenge can be considered as urgent. For example, Wal-Mart has been the focus of legislation in Maryland, which tried to make the retailer pay more for its employee health care. The legislation failed in its attempt to require employers with more than 10,000 workers to spend at least 8 percent of their payroll on employee health care.[70] Twenty-two other states are now considering this legislation. Wal-Mart has now offered to improve health-care benefits for its employees as a direct result of the pressure.[71]

Step 6: Gaining Stakeholder Feedback

Stakeholder feedback can be generated through a variety of means. First, stakeholders' general assessment of the firm and its practices can be obtained through satisfaction or reputation surveys. Second, gauge stakeholders' perceptions of the firm's contributions to specific issues, stakeholder-generated media such as blogs, websites, podcasts, and newsletters can be assessed. Third, more formal research may be conducted using focus groups, observation, and surveys. Websites can be both positive and negative; for example, www.wakeupwalmart.com launched by the United Food and Commercial Workers union has over 240,000 members, and another group called Wal-Mart Watch is also gaining members. Both groups have articles and stories about the retail giant on their websites that are not flattering for Wal-Mart. The pressure has forced the retail giant to listen to its consumers and change its ways. To counter the claims by these groups, Wal-Mart launched its own site, www.walmartfacts.com, to tell its side of the story.

SUMMARY

Business ethics, issues, and conflicts revolve around relationships. Customers, investors and shareholders, employees, suppliers, government agencies, communities, and many others who have a stake, or claim, in some aspect of a company's products, operations, markets, industry, and outcomes are known as stakeholders. They are both influenced by and have the ability to affect businesses. Stakeholders provide both tangible and intangible resources that are more or less critical to a firm's long-term success, and their ability to withdraw—or to threaten to withdraw—these resources gives them power. Stakeholders define significant ethical issues in business.

Primary stakeholders are those whose continued association is absolutely necessary for a firm's survival, whereas secondary stakeholders do not typically engage in transactions with a company and thus are not essential for its survival. The stakeholder interaction model suggests that there are two-way relationships between the firm and a host of stakeholders. The degree to which a firm understands and addresses stakeholder demands can be expressed as a stakeholder orientation, which includes three sets of activities: (1) the generation of data across the firm about its stakeholder groups and the assessment of the firm's effects on these groups, (2) the distribution of this information throughout the firm, and (3) the responsiveness of every level of the firm to this intelligence. A stakeholder orientation can be viewed as a continuum in that firms are likely to adopt the concept to varying degrees.

Although the concepts of business ethics and social responsibility are often used interchangeably, the two terms have distinct meanings. Social responsibility in business refers to an organization's obligation to maximize its positive impact and minimize its negative impact on society. There are four levels of social responsibility—economic, legal, ethical, and philanthropic—and they can be viewed as a pyramid. The term *corporate citizenship* is often used to communicate the extent to which businesses strategically meet the economic, legal, ethical, and philanthropic responsibilities placed on them by their various stakeholders.

From a social responsibility perspective, business ethics embodies standards, norms, and expectations that reflect a concern of major stakeholders including consumers, employees, shareholders, suppliers, competitors, and the community. Only if firms include ethical concerns in their foundational values and incorporate ethics in their business strategy can social responsibility as a value be embedded in daily decision making.

Most businesses operate under the assumption that the main purpose of business is to maximize profits for shareholders. The stakeholders model places the board of directors in the central position to balance the interests and conflicts of the various constituencies. Both directors and officers of corporations are fiduciaries for the shareholders. Fiduciaries are persons placed in positions of trust who use due care and loyalty in acting on behalf of the best interests of the organization. There is a duty of care (also called a duty of diligence) to make informed and prudent decisions. Directors have a duty to avoid ethical misconduct in their director role and to provide leadership in decisions to prevent ethical misconduct in the organization. To remove the opportunity for employees to make unethical decisions, most companies have developed formal systems of accountability, oversight, and control—known as corporate governance. Accountability refers to how closely workplace decisions are aligned with a firm's stated strategic direction and its compliance with ethical and legal considerations. Oversight provides a system of checks and balances that limit employees' and managers' opportunities to deviate from policies and strategies and that prevent unethical and illegal activities. Control is the process of auditing and improving organizational decisions and actions.

There are two perceptions of corporate governance, which can be viewed as a continuum. The shareholder model is founded in classic economic precepts, including the maximization of wealth for investors and owners. The stakeholder model adopts a broader view of the purpose of business that includes satisfying the concerns of other stakeholders, from employees, suppliers, and government regulators to communities and special-interest groups.

Two major elements of corporate governance that relate to ethical decision making are the role of the board of directors and executive compensation. The members of a public corporation's board of directors assume legal responsibility for the firm's resources and decisions. Important issues related to corporate boards of directors include accountability, transparency, and independence. Boards of directors are also responsible for appointing and setting the compensation for top executive officers, a controversial topic. Concerns about executive pay may center on the often disproportionate relationship between the highest-paid executives and median employee wages in the company.

IMPORTANT TERMS FOR REVIEW		
	stakeholder	reputation
	primary stakeholder	corporate governance
	secondary stakeholder	shareholder model of corporate
	stakeholder interaction model	governance
	stakeholder orientation	stakeholder model of corporate
	social responsibility	governance
	corporate citizenship	executive compensation

RESOLVING ETHICAL BUSINESS CHALLENGES*

Kent was getting pressure from his boss, parents, and wife about the marketing campaign for Broadway Corporation's new video game called "Lucky." He had been working for Broadway for about two years, and the Lucky game was his first big project. After Kent and his wife, Amy, had graduated from the same college, they decided to go back to their hometown of Las Cruces, New Mexico, near the Mexican border. Kent's father knew the president of Broadway, which enabled Kent to get a job in its marketing department. Broadway is a medium-size company with about five hundred employees, making it one of the largest employers in Las Cruces. Broadway develops, manufactures, and markets video arcade games.

Within the video arcade industry, competition is fierce. Games typically have a life cycle of only eighteen to twenty-four months. One of the key strategies in the industry is providing unique, visually stimulating games by using color graphics technology, fast action, and participant interaction. The target markets for Broadway's video products are children aged 5 to 12 and teenagers aged 13 to 19. Males constitute 75 percent of the market.

When Kent first started with Broadway, his task was to conduct market research on the types of games that players desired. His research showed that the market wanted more action (violence), quicker graphics, multiple levels of difficulty, and sound. Further research showed that certain tones and types of sound were more pleasing than others. As part of his research, Kent also observed people in video arcades, where he found that many became hypnotized by a game and would quickly put in quarters when told to do so. Research suggested that many target consumers exhibited the same symptoms as compulsive gamblers. Kent's research results were very well received by the company, which developed several new games using his information. The new games were instant hits with the market.

In his continuing research, Kent had found that the consumer's level of intensity increased as the game's intensity level increased. Several reports later, Kent suggested that target consumers might be willing, at strategic periods in a video game, to insert multiple coins. For example, a player who wanted to move to a higher level of difficulty would have to insert two coins; to play the final level, three coins would have to be inserted. When the idea was tested, Kent found it did increase game productivity.

Kent had also noticed that video games that gave positive reinforcements to the consumer, such as audio cues, were played much more frequently than others. He reported his findings to Brad, Broadway's president, who asked Kent to apply the information to the development of new games. Kent suggested having the machines give candy to the game players when they attained specific goals. For the teen market, the company modified the idea: The machines would give back coins at certain levels during the game. Players could then use the coins at strategic levels to play a "slot-type" chance opening of the next level. By inserting an element of chance, these games generated more coin input than output, and game productivity increased dramatically. These innovations were quite successful, giving Broadway a larger share of the market and Kent a promotion to product manager.

Kent's newest assignment was the Lucky game—a fast-action scenario in which the goal was to destroy the enemy before being destroyed. Kent expanded on the slot-type game for the older market, with two additions. First, the game employed virtual reality technology, which gives the player the sensation of actually being in the game. Second, keeping in mind that most of the teenage consumers were male, Kent incorporated a female character who, at each level, removed a piece of her clothing and taunted the player. A win at the highest level left her nude. Test market results suggested that the two additions increased profitability per game dramatically.

Several weeks later, Brad asked about the Lucky project. "I think we've got a real problem, Brad," Kent told him. "Maybe the nudity is a bad idea. Some people will be really upset about it." Brad was very displeased with Kent's response.

Word got around fast that the Lucky project had stalled. During dinner with his parents, Kent mentioned the Lucky project, and his dad said something that affected Kent. "You know, son, the Lucky project will bring in a great deal of revenue for Broadway, and jobs are at stake. Some of your coworkers are upset with your stand on this project. I'm not telling you what to do, but there's more at stake here than just a video game."

The next day Kent had a meeting with Brad about Lucky. "Well," Brad asked, "what have you decided?"

Kent answered, "I don't think we should go with the nudity idea."

Brad answered, "You know, Kent, you're right. The U.S. market just isn't ready to see full nudity as well as graphic violence in arcades in their local malls. That's why I've contacted an Internet provider who will take our game and put it on the Net as an adult product. I've also checked out the foreign markets and found that we can sell the machines to the Mexican market if we tone down the violence. The Taiwanese joint venture group has okayed the version we have now, but they would like you to develop something that is more graphic in both areas. You see, they already have similar versions of this type of game now, and their market is ready to go to the next level. I see the Internet market as secondary because we can't get the virtual reality equipment and software into an Internet mode. Maybe when PCs get faster, we'll be able to tap into it at that level, but not now. So, Kent, do you understand what you need to be doing on Lucky?"

QUESTIONS • EXERCISES

1. What are the ethical and legal issues?
2. What are Kent's options?
3. Discuss the acceptability and commercial use of sex, violence, and gambling in the United States.
4. Are marketing sex, violence, and gambling acceptable in other countries if they fit their culture?

*This case is strictly hypothetical; any resemblance to real persons, companies, or situations is coincidental.

Check Your EQ

Check your EQ, or Ethics Quotient, by completing the following. Assess your performance to evaluate your overall understanding of the chapter material.

	Yes	No
1. Social responsibility in business refers to maximizing the visibility of social involvement.	Yes	No
2. Stakeholders provide resources that are more or less critical to a firm's long-term success.	Yes	No
3. Three primary stakeholders are customers, special-interest groups, and the media.	Yes	No
4. The most significant influence on ethical behavior in the organization is the opportunity to engage in unethical behavior.	Yes	No
5. The stakeholder perspective is useful in managing social responsibility and business ethics.	Yes	No

ANSWERS: 1. No. Social responsibility refers to an organization's obligation to maximize its positive impact on society and minimize its negative impact. 2. Yes. These resources are both tangible and intangible. 3. No. Although customers are primary stakeholders, special-interest groups are usually considered secondary stakeholders. 4. No. Others have more impact on ethical decisions within the organization. 5. Yes. The six steps to implement this approach were provided in this chapter.

Ethical Issues and the Institutionalization of Business Ethics

CHAPTER 3

Emerging Business Ethics Issues

CHAPTER OBJECTIVES

- To define ethical issues in the context of organizational ethics

- To examine ethical issues as they relate to the basic values of honesty, fairness, and integrity

- To delineate abusive and intimidating behavior, lying, conflicts of interest, bribery, corporate intelligence, discrimination, sexual harassment, environmental issues, fraud, insider trading, intellectual-property rights, and privacy as business ethics issues

- To examine the challenge of determining an ethical issue in business

CHAPTER OUTLINE

As Lavonda sat in the Ethics Office of the vice president of Emma-Action Pharmaceuticals (EAP), she was worried. Because she was new in the company and didn't know the unwritten rules, the chain-of-command philosophy, and the employees and associates around her very well, her time in the soft leather chair of the office was very uncomfortable. Given how well things had started, it was painful for her to remember how she had gotten here.

Lavonda had been lured away from her last company because of her expertise in the pharmaceutical industry and her early success in management. Out of college just three and a half years, she had gotten out of the gate remarkably quickly. She had helpful mentors, challenging tasks that she excelled in, and came in below budget on each assignment. Lavonda was typically described as effective and efficient; in fact, at the last company, they even started to call her "E."

But the lure of a six-figure salary, the encounter with Allen (her future boss at EAP), and the chance to be close to her elderly mother made it nearly impossible for Lavonda to say no. She loved her mother and, being an only child, felt responsible for her. Her mother once said that she would prefer to take her own life rather than move to a nursing home.

In the beginning, Lavonda's immediate supervisor, Allen, had been very charming and taught her about the company, its products, the salespeople, and the politics. She knew from experience that she would have to earn the respect of the salespeople she would manage, all of whom were ten years her senior, and the fact that these men had never had a female boss was just another hurdle to overcome. Allen had helped her find a nice house in a good neighborhood, had assisted with the moving, and eventually had become more than her superior. The months slipped by, and their relationship had become "close," to the point where they began to discuss living arrangements. And then something strange happened—she heard a story about Allen and Karline.

Karline, who had come to EAP six months prior to Lavonda, worked in Human Resources, and in a few short months she had become head of the HR department at EAP amidst rumors of Allen "helping" her get the promotion. Six more months passed, and Lavonda had learned that the rumors about Karline and Allen were probably true. She heard the same type of scenario that she had experienced for herself: friend, helping with housing, possible intimacy, and so on. The rumors became so intense that Lavonda confronted Allen about them and discovered that they were true. Devastated, Lavonda ended the relationship with Allen in a heated confrontation, but it seemed as though Allen didn't understand that it was over.

Weeks went by with little contact between the two of them, and then one afternoon Allen stopped by her office. He apologized for his behavior, and Lavonda accepted his apology. But the next day he stopped by and began to touch and even grope Lavonda. She made a joke of it to defuse the situation, but several days later Allen repeated the same behavior, making several sexual remarks. He asked, "Honey, why can't it be like it was before?" and then he whispered some graphic sexual language.

Lavonda's face reddened and she said, "Allen, you are a pig. How dare you say such things to me! You've crossed the line. I've never heard such filth. Don't you ever say such things to me again, or I'll report you to Human Resources!"

Several weeks went by, and Lavonda got a phone call from Allen in which he described even more sexually suggestive things. Every few days, Allen would stop by or call and remind her of some "private" experience they had together, using vulgar sexual language. He would taunt her by saying, "Lavonda, you know you want this from me." It became almost a daily ritual. Allen never wrote any of the things down that he described to her, being sure not to leave tangible proof of his behavior, but occasionally he would grab or attempt to grab her sexually.

Eventually, Lavonda had had enough and went to the Human Resources Department to complain formally about Allen, his sexual advances, and the hostile environment that they had created. The person she met at HR was Karline. As Lavonda described the situation in detail, she finally said, "Karline, I need you to help me. What Allen is doing to me is wrong and illegal. I can't get my work done. He's undermining my position with my sales staff, he's giving me poor evaluations, and he's suggesting that I could change all that if I wanted to!"

Karline's response was, "Lavonda, I've heard what you've said, but I also have had people come to me with some very disturbing reports about you as well. For example, you and Allen were supposedly sleeping together, and he is your direct supervisor. If this was the case, then it should have been reported immediately; but it wasn't. You have no tangible evidence except for your word. Even if I believed you, the allegation that you had been sexually active with Allen can be construed as making all of what you've said mutual or consensual. If that's the case, then I would have to fire you because of the superior–employee ethics code, and a letter would go into your permanent file that would probably haunt your career for years to come. From my perspective, we can call this an informal and confidential meeting that was not to be repeated, or you can continue this formally and take your chances. It's your call, Lavonda, but you should know that I am disinclined to support your accusations."

In shock, Lavonda mumbled a thank you to Karline and left her office. The next day Allen stopped by, smiled, waved his finger at her and said, "Your next performance review is next week, and it doesn't look good. By the way, just so you know, the pharmaceutical industry is quite small, and I have friends at all the majors. Oh, I forgot to tell you how sorry I am for your mother and her cancer diagnosis. Chemo and the side effects are very draining. I'm glad that you're close by to help her through the ordeal. They say it takes months to fully recover. It would be horrible if you weren't here to help her and she had to go to a nursing home. Those places scare me."

Lavonda said, "Allen, why are you doing this to me? I'm not fond of you anymore. We have no future together. Doesn't that tell you something?"

Allen smiled and said, "It tells me that you're not interested in a permanent relationship, which is good, because neither am I. And you know that if you want to be promoted or go to another company with a good recommendation, it all starts with me. Lavonda, there might be another 'solution' to your perceived problem. You know that new sales rep you just hired out of school, Soo-Chin? Well, if you could have her assigned to me and maybe 'coax her in the right way,' I know of a position in the company that would be a promotion for you and you wouldn't be around me. But everything depends upon the success of your coaxing."

So now here Lavonda was, about to meet with the vice president of ethical affairs. As she got up from the wingback leather chair, she pondered her alternatives and what had led her there. In school she had learned that each company had its own individual code of ethics, but she didn't know the reality of the code at EAP until it was too late.

QUESTIONS • EXERCISES

1. Keeping in mind the facts and timeline of this situation, discuss Lavonda's situation in terms of legal and ethical issues.
2. Discuss Lavonda's alternatives and possible professional and private outcomes for her.
3. Is Allen in violation of sexual harassment and/or sexual discrimination laws in the United States?
4. Certainly Allen has damaged Lavonda's performance level; however, discuss whether he has created a legally hostile work environment.

*This case is strictly hypothetical; any resemblance to real persons, companies, or situations is coincidental.

Stakeholders' ethical concerns determine whether specific business actions and decisions are perceived as ethical or unethical. In the case of the government, community, and society, what was merely an ethical issue can soon become a legal debate and eventually law. Most ethical conflicts in which there are perceived dangers turn into litigation. Additionally, stakeholders often raise ethical issues when they exert pressure on businesses to make decisions that serve their particular agendas. For example, corporate shareholders often demand that managers make decisions that boost short-term earnings, thus maintaining or increasing the value of the shares of stock they own in that firm. Such pressure may have led managers at General Motors Corporation to overstate income by as much as $300–400 million, or approximately 50 percent of the profit it reported in one year. "It's not like that income shouldn't have been booked, it just shouldn't have been booked in all of [this year]." General Motors has denied any wrongdoing, and the Securities and Exchange Commission (SEC) is investigating General Motors and its relationship with one of its suppliers.[1]

Consumers also define the ethicality of actions relative to companies that can be in direct conflict with shareholders. For example, oil industry executives have told the U.S. Congress that legislation preventing gasoline price gouging could result in shortages and long lines, thus creating panic. Exxon Mobile's chairman and CEO has argued that higher prices would ensure less panic and that "shortage is a disaster and we don't want to go there." This initially sounds convincing, but recently Arizona's Attorney General explained that, although their gasoline comes from sources that have an adequate supply with no shortages, prices at the pumps have risen drastically. Additionally, Arizona's laws on price collusion and consumer fraud are very ineffective.[2]

People make ethical decisions only after they recognize that a particular issue or situation has an ethical component; thus, a first step toward understanding business ethics is to develop ethical-issue awareness. Ethical issues typically arise because of conflicts among individuals' personal moral philosophies and values, the values and culture of the organizations in which they work, and those of the society in which they live. The business environment presents many potential ethical conflicts. For example, a company's efforts to achieve its organizational objectives may collide with its employees' endeavors to fulfill their own personal goals. Similarly, consumers' desires for safe and quality products may conflict with a manufacturer's need to earn adequate profits. The ambition of top executives to secure sizable increases in compensation may conflict with the desires of shareholders to control costs and increase the value of the corporation. A manager's wish to hire specific employees that he or she likes may be at odds with the organization's intent to hire the best-qualified candidates, as well as with society's aim to offer equal opportunity to women and members of minority groups.

Characteristics of the job, the culture, and the organization of the society in which one does business can also create ethical issues. Gaining familiarity with the ethical issues that frequently arise in the business world will help you identify and resolve them when they occur.

In this chapter, we consider some of the ethical issues that are emerging in business today, including how these issues arise from the demands of specific stakeholder groups. In the first half of the chapter, we explain certain universal ethical concepts that pervade business ethics, such as honesty, fairness, and integrity. The second half of the chapter explores a number of emerging ethical issues, including abusive and intimidating behavior, lying, conflicts of interest, bribery, corporate intelligence, discrimination, sexual harassment, environmental issues, fraud, insider trading, intellectual-property rights, and privacy. We also examine the challenge of determining an ethical issue in business.

RECOGNIZING AN ETHICAL ISSUE

Although we have described a number of relationships and situations that may generate ethical issues, in practice it can be difficult to recognize specific ethical issues. Failure to acknowledge such ethical issues is a great danger in any organization, particularly if business is treated as a "game" in which ordinary rules of fairness do not apply. Sometimes, people who take this view are willing to do things that are not only unethical but also illegal so that they can maximize their own position or boost the profits of their organization. However, just because an unsettled situation or activity is an ethical issue does not mean the behavior is necessarily unethical. An ethical issue is simply a situation, a problem, or even an opportunity that requires thought, discussion, or investigation to make a decision. And because the business world is dynamic, new ethical issues are emerging all the time. Table 3–1 defines specific ethical issues identified by employees in the National Business Ethics Survey (NBES). Three types of misconduct make up 30 percent of the ethical problems within organizations. Putting one's own interests ahead of the organization, abusive behavior, and lying to employees are all personal in nature. Of the misconduct observed, 56.6 percent fall under the personal heading. Misreporting hours worked, safety violations, and provision of low quality goods and services are the top three issues that directly relate to the firm's agenda. Table 3–1 compares the percentage of employees who observed specific types of misconduct in 2005 and 2007.

Employees could select more than one form of misconduct; therefore, each type of misconduct represents the percentage of employees who saw that particular act. Although Table 3–1 documents many types of ethical issues that exist in organizations, due to the almost infinite number of ways that misconduct can occur, it is impossible in this chapter to list every conceivable ethical issue. Any type of manipulation, deceit, or even just the absence of transparency in decision making can create harm to others. For example, collusion is a secret agreement between two or more parties for a fraudulent, illegal, or deceitful purpose. "Deceitful purposes" is the relevant phrase in regard to business ethics, in that it suggests trickery, misrepresentation, or a strategy designed to lead others to believe one truth but not the entire truth.

Honesty

Honesty refers to truthfulness or trustworthiness. To be honest is to tell the truth to the best of your knowledge without hiding anything. Confucius defined several levels of honesty. The shallowest is called *Li,* and it relates to the superficial desires of a person. A key principle to *Li* is striving to convey feelings that outwardly are or appear to be honest but that are ultimately driven by self-interest. The second level is *Yi,* or righteousness, where a person does what is right based on reciprocity. The deepest level of honesty is called *Ren,* and it is based on understanding of and empathy toward others. The Confucian version of Kant's Golden Rule is to treat inferiors as you would

	TABLE 3-1	Specific Types of Observed Misconduct			
			2007	2005	Change
P	Putting own interests ahead of organization's interests		22%	18%	+4%
P	Abusive behavior		21%	21%	0%
P	Lying to employees		20%	19%	+1%
M	Misreporting hours worked		17%	16%	+1%
P	Internet abuse		16%	13%	+3%
M	Safety violations		15%	16%	−1%
P	Lying to stakeholders		14%	19%	−5%
P	Discrimination		13%	12%	+1%
P	Stealing		11%	11%	0%
P	Sexual harassment		10%	9%	+1%
M	Provision of low quality goods and services		10%	8%	+2%
P	Improper hiring practices		10%	NA	—
M	Environmental violations		7%	NA	—
M	Misuse of confidential organization information		6%	7%	−1%
M	Alteration of documents		5%	5%	0%
M	Alteration of financial records		5%	5%	0%
M	Bribes		4%	3%	+1%
M	Using competitors' inside information		4%	4%	0%

P denotes Personal Lapses, M denotes Misconduct that furthers the company's agenda.

SOURCE: From *2007 National Business Ethics Survey: An Inside View of Private Sector Ethics,* Copyright © 2007, Ethics Resource Center (ERC). Used with permission of the ERC, 1747 Pennsylvania Ave., N. W., Suite 400, Washington, DC 2006, www.ethics.org.

want superiors to treat you. As a result, virtues such as familial honor and reputation for honesty become paramount.

Issues related to honesty also arise because business is sometimes regarded as a "game" governed by its own rules rather than by those of society. Author Eric Beversluis suggests that honesty is a problem because people often reason along these lines:

1. Business relationships are a subset of human relationships that are governed by their own rules, which, in a market society, involve competition, profit maximization, and personal advancement within the organization.
2. Business can therefore be considered a game people play, comparable in certain respects to competitive sports such as basketball or boxing.
3. Ordinary rules and morality do not hold in games like basketball or boxing. (What if a basketball player did unto others as he would have them do unto him? What if a boxer decided it was wrong to try to injure another person?)
4. Logically, then, if business is a game like basketball or boxing, ordinary ethical rules do not apply.[3]

This type of reasoning leads many people to conclude that anything is acceptable in business. Indeed, several books have compared business to warfare—for example, *The Guerrilla Marketing Handbook* and *Sun Tsu: The Art of War for Managers.* The common theme in these books is that surprise attacks, guerrilla warfare, and other warlike tactics are necessary to win the battle for consumers' dollars. An example of this mentality at work is Larry Ellison, the CEO of Oracle. Ellison's warlike mentality is demonstrated by his decision to sell PeopleSoft's technology and let most of its eight thousand employees go. PeopleSoft CEO Craig Conway stated that "Ellison has followed a page straight out of Genghis Khan." Ellison has frequently recited phrases of the thirteenth century Mongol warlord such as "It's not enough that we win; everyone else must lose."[4] Recently Ellison was ordered to donate $100 million to charity and pay another $22 million to the attorneys who sued him for alleged stock-trading abuses. Ellison argues that he acted in good faith and in the best interests of Oracle and Oracle's shareholders.[5]

This business-as-war mentality may foster the idea that honesty is unnecessary in business. In addition, an intensely competitive environment creates the potential for companies to engage in questionable conduct. For example, as competition in the market for beer intensified, Miller, Coors, and Anheuser-Busch increasingly created advertising and offered products that appealed to younger consumers, even though marketing to minors under the age of 21 is illegal.

Many argue, however, that business is not a game like basketball or boxing; because people are not economically self-sufficient, they cannot withdraw from the game of business. Therefore, business ethics must not only make clear what rules apply in the "game" of business but must also develop rules appropriate to the involuntary nature of participation in it.[6]

Because of the economic motive, many in business can become confused with the opposite of honesty—dishonesty. *Dishonesty can be broadly defined as a lack of integrity, incomplete disclosure, and an unwillingness to tell the truth.* Dishonesty is also synonymous with lying, cheating, and stealing. Lying, cheating, and stealing are the actions usually associated with dishonest conduct. The causes of dishonesty are complex and relate to both individual and organizational pressures. Many employees lie to help achieve performance objectives. For example, they may be asked to lie about when a customer will receive a purchase. Lying can be segmented into (1) causing damage or harm; (2) a "white lie," which doesn't cause damage but can be called an excuse or something told to benefit someone else; and (3) statements that are obviously meant to engage or entertain with no malice. These definitions will become important to the remainder of this chapter.

Fairness

Fairness is the quality of being just, equitable, and impartial. Fairness clearly overlaps with other commonly used terms such as justice, equity, equality, and morality. There are three fundamental elements that seem to motivate people to be fair: equality, reciprocity and optimization. In business, **equality** is about how wealth or income is distributed between employees within a company, a country, or across the globe.

Reciprocity is an interchange of giving and receiving in social relationships. Reciprocity occurs when an action that has an effect upon another is reciprocated with an action that has an approximately equal effect upon the other. Reciprocity is the return of small favors that are approximately equal in value. For example, reciprocity implies that workers be compensated with wages that are approximately equal to their effort.

An ethical issue about reciprocity for business is the amount CEOs and other executives are paid in relation to their employees. Is a 431-to-1 pay ratio an example of ethical reciprocity? That is the average wage distance between a CEO and a production worker in the United States.

Optimization is the trade-off between equity (that is, equality or fairness) and efficiency (that is, maximum productivity). Discriminating on the basis of gender, race, or religion is generally considered to be unfair because these qualities have little bearing upon a person's ability to do a job. The optimal way is to choose the employee who is the most talented, most proficient, most educated, and most able. Ideas of fairness are sometimes shaped by vested interests. One or both parties in the relationship may view an action as unfair or unethical because the outcome was less beneficial than expected.

Integrity

Integrity is one of the most important and often-cited terms regarding virtue, and it refers to being whole, sound, and in an unimpaired condition. In an organization, it means uncompromising adherence to ethical values. Integrity is connected to acting ethically; in other words, there are substantive or normative constraints on what it means to act with integrity. This usually rests on an organization's enduring values and unwillingness to deviate from standards of behavior.

At a minimum, businesses are expected to follow all applicable laws and regulations. In addition, organizations should not knowingly harm customers, clients, employees, or even other competitors through deception, misrepresentation, or coercion. Although businesspeople often act in their own economic self-interest, ethical business relations should be grounded on honesty, integrity, fairness, justice, and trust. Buyers should be able to trust sellers; lenders should be able to trust borrowers. Failure to live up to these expectations or to abide by laws and standards destroys trust and makes it difficult, if not impossible, to continue business exchanges.[7] These virtues become the glue that holds business relationships together, making everything else more effective and efficient.

ETHICAL ISSUES AND DILEMMAS IN BUSINESS

As mentioned earlier, stakeholders define a business's ethical issues. An **ethical issue** is a problem, situation, or opportunity that requires an individual, group, or organization to choose among several actions that must be evaluated as right or wrong, ethical or unethical. An **ethical dilemma** is a problem, situation, or opportunity that requires an individual, group, or organization to choose among several wrong or unethical actions. There is not simply one right or ethical choice in a dilemma, only less unethical or illegal choices as perceived by any and all stakeholders.

A constructive next step toward identifying and resolving ethical issues is to classify the issues that are relevant to most business organizations. In this section, we classify ethical issues in relation to abusive or intimidating behavior, lying, conflicts of interest, bribery, corporate intelligence, discrimination, sexual harassment, environmental issues, fraud, insider trading, intellectual-property rights, and privacy issues.

Figure 3–1 reflects the ethical issues that are most likely to have impact on shareholder value for companies over the next five years. It is interesting to note that executives feel that their companies' shareholder value will be significantly affected by job loss and offshoring jobs when outsourcing to improve efficiency. Surprisingly, the ability to exert political influence or political involvement is also a major issue.

Abusive or Intimidating Behavior

Abusive or **intimidating behavior** is the most common ethical problem for employees, but what does it mean to be abusive or intimidating? The concepts can mean anything—physical threats, false accusations, being annoying, profanity, insults, yelling,

---

FIGURE 3–1 Issues That Affect Corporate Shareholder Value

Which three issues are likely to have the most impact, positive or negative, on shareholder value for companies in your industry over the next 5 years? (Percentage of respondents selecting given issues as one of top three. All data weighted by GDP of constituent countries to adjust for differences in response rates from various regions.)

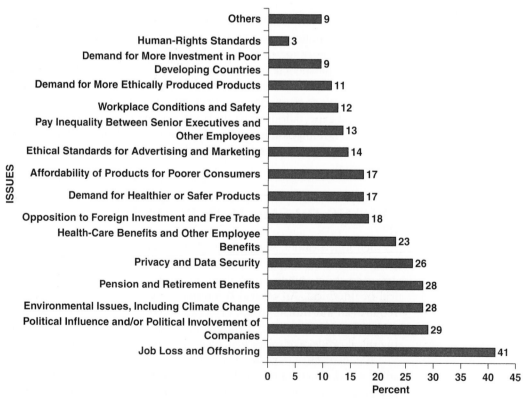

SOURCE: "The McKinsey Global Survey of Business Executives: Business and Society," *The McKinsey Quarterly: The Online Journal of McKinsey & Co.,* January 2006, http://www.mckinseyquarterly.com/The_McKinsey_Global_Survey_of_Business_Executives__Business_and_Society_1741 (accessed March 8, 2006).

harshness, ignoring someone, and unreasonableness—and the meaning of these words can differ by person. It is important to understand that with each term there is a continuum. For example, what one person may define as yelling might be another's definition of normal speech. Civility in our society has been a concern, and the workplace is no exception. The productivity level of many organizations has been damaged by the time spent unraveling abusive relationships.

Is it abusive behavior to ask an employee to complete a project rather than be with a family member or relative in a crisis situation? What does it mean to speak profanely? Is profanity only related to specific words or other such terms that are common in today's business world? If you are using words that are normal in your language but others consider profanity, have you just insulted, abused, or disrespected them?

Within the concept of abusive behavior or intimidation, intent should be a consideration. If the employee was trying to convey a compliment, then it was probably a mistake. What if a male manager asks his female subordinate if they have a date for tonight because they are dressed so nice? Does the way (voice inflection) a word is said become important? Add to this the fact that we now live in a multicultural environment doing business and working with many different cultural groups and the businessperson soon realizes the depth of the ethical and legal issues that may arise. Finally, you have the problem of word meanings by age and within cultures. Is it okay to say "honey" to an employee, fellow employee, employee friend, your superior, and does it depend on gender or location? For example, if you were to call a friend that worked with you "honey" in southern Illinois, Arkansas, or Kentucky, do you have the same acceptability factor in northern Illinois, Michigan, or Minnesota? Does abusive behavior vary by different genders? It is possible the term *honey* could be acceptable speech in some environments, or could it be construed as being abusive or intimidating in other situations?

Bullying is associated with a hostile workplace where someone (or a group) considered a target is threatened, harassed, belittled, or verbally abused or overly criticized. Bullying may create what some may call a hostile environment, but this term is generally associated with sexual harassment. Although sexual harassment has legal recourse, bullying has little legal recourse at this time. Bullying can cause psychological damage that can result in health-endangering consequences to the target. As Table 3–2 indicates, bullying can use a mix of verbal, nonverbal, and manipulative threatening expressions to damage workplace productivity. One may wonder why workers tolerate such activities; the problem is that 81 percent of workplace bullies are supervisors. Bullying happens more than people realize. For example, 37 percent (54 million) of American workers have been bullied at work and when witnesses are included it rises to 49 percent (71.5 million).[8]

Bullying can also occur between companies that are in intense competition. Even respected companies such as Intel have been accused of monopolistic bullying. A competitor, Advanced Micro Devices (AMD), claimed in a lawsuit that thirty-eight companies, including Dell and Sony, were strong-arming customers into buying Intel chips rather than those marketed by AMD. The AMD lawsuit seeks billions of dollars and will take years to litigate. In many cases, the alleged misconduct can not only have monetary and legal implications but also can threaten reputation, investor confidence, and customer loyalty. A front-cover *Forbes* headline stated "Intel to AMD: Drop Dead." An example of the intense competition and Intel's ability to use its large size won it

TABLE 3–2   Actions Associated with Bullies
1. Spreading rumors to damage others
2. Blocking others' communication in the workplace
3. Flaunting status or authority to take advantage of others
4. Discrediting others' ideas and opinions
5. Use of e-mails to demean others
6. Failing to communicate or return communication
7. Insults, yelling, and shouting
8. Using terminology to discriminate by gender, race, or age
9. Using eye or body language to hurt others or their reputation
10. Taking credit for others' work or ideas

SOURCE: Cathi McMahan, "Are You A Bully?," *Inside Seven*, California Department of Transportation Newsletter, June 1999, page 6.

the high-profile Apple account, displacing IBM and Freescale. ADM said it had no opportunity to bid because Intel offered to deploy six hundred Indian engineers to help Apple software run more smoothly on Intel chips.[9]

Lying

Earlier in this chapter, we discussed the definitions of **lying** and how it relates to distorting the truth. We mentioned three types of lies, one of which is joking without malice. The other two can become very troublesome for businesses. For example, one can lie by commission or omission. *Commission lying* is creating a perception or belief by words that intentionally deceive the receiver of the message. For example, lying about being at work, expense reports, or carrying out work assignments. Commission lying also entails intentionally creating "noise" within the communication that knowingly confuses or deceives the receiver. *Noise* can be defined as technical explanations that the communicator knows the receiver does not understand. It can be the intentional use of communication forms that make it difficult for the receiver to actually hear the true message. Using legal terms or relating to unfamiliar processes and systems to explain what was done in a work situation facilitate this type of lie.

Lying by commission can be complex forms, procedures, contracts, words that are spelled the same but have different meanings, or refuting the truth with a false statement. Forms of commission lying are puffery in advertising. For example saying that a product is "homemade" when it is made in a factory is lying. "Made from scratch" in cooking technically means that all ingredients within the product were distinct and separate and have not been combined prior to the beginning of the production process. One can lie by commission by showing a picture of the product that does not reflect the actual product. This happens frequently in business. For example, a national fast-food chain came out with a new product that had lettuce in it. There are many types of lettuce and the lettuce used in the national ad campaign both in print and TV used romaine lettuce. Yet this fast-food chain does not purchase that variety; they purchase iceberg lettuce. The obvious reason for the romaine is that it is prettier or more appealing than shredded iceberg lettuce. Another example is Schick's complaint against Gillette, alleging that the latter's claims for its Mach 3 Turbo Razor as "the world's best shave" and "the best a man can get" are false and misleading.

Omission lying is intentionally not informing the channel member of any differences, problems, safety warnings, or negative issues relating to the product, service, or company that significantly affects awareness, intention, or behavior. A classic example for decades was the tobacco manufacturers that did not allow negative research to appear on cigarettes and cigars. The drug Vioxx is being questioned because the manufacturer allegedly did not inform consumers as to the degree and occurrence of side effects, one of which is death. Finally, when lying damages others, it can be the focus of a lawsuit. For example, prosecutors and civil lawsuits often reduce misconduct to lying about a fact such as financial performance that has the potential to damage others. CEOs at AIG, Lehman Brothers, Fannie Mae, and Freddie Mac will be scrutinized to see if they told the truth about the financial conditions of their companies.

When a lie becomes unethical in business, it is based on the context and intent to distort the truth. A lie becomes illegal if it is determined by the judgment of courts to damage others. Some businesspeople may believe that one must lie a little or that the occasional lie is sanctioned by the organization. The question you need to ask is whether lies are distorting openness and transparency and other values that are associated with ethical behavior.

Conflicts of Interest

A **conflict of interest** exists when an individual must choose whether to advance his or her own interests, those of the organization, or those of some other group. For example, former Food and Drug Administration (FDA) head Lester Crawford and his wife owned stock in companies that were regulated by the FDA while he was at the federal agency. In one case, Crawford was on a company's board of directors that directly dealt with the FDA. While he was at the FDA, records show that ethics officials were purportedly concerned with Crawford's holdings and the appearance of a conflict of interest. One ethics official wrote "need more info" and called the broker who wrote "sending more info." But no ethics officer's signature appears on any form. Soon after, Crawford announced he was leaving the FDA. People knowledgeable of the matter said that the move occurred because of stock holdings that he might have failed to fully disclose. The inspector general at the Health and Human Services investigated the circumstances surrounding his departure.[10] Because his family interests conflicted with his position at the FDA, his actions constitute a conflict of interest.

To avoid conflicts of interest, employees must be able to separate their private interests from their business dealings. Organizations must also avoid potential conflicts of interest when providing products.[11] The U.S. General Accounting Office has found conflicts of interest when the government has awarded bids on defense contracts. The conflicts of interest usually relate to hiring friends, relatives, or retired military officers to enhance the probability of getting the contract.[12]

Bribery

Bribery is the practice of offering something (usually money) in order to gain an illicit advantage. The key issue regarding whether or not something is considered bribery is determining whether the act is illicit or contrary to accepted morality or convention. Bribery therefore is defined as an unlawful act, but it can be a business ethics issue. The reason is that bribery can be defined differently in varying situations and cultural environments.

Bribery can be defined many ways. For example, there is something called active corruption or **active bribery,** meaning that the person who promises or gives the bribe commits the offense. **Passive bribery** is an offense committed by the official who receives the bribe. It is not an offense, however, if the advantage was permitted or required by the written law or regulation of the foreign public official's country, including case law.

Small **facilitation payments** made to obtain or retain business or other improper advantages do not constitute bribery payments. In some countries, such payments are made to induce public officials to perform their functions such as issuing licenses or permits. However, criminalization by other countries does not seem a practical or effective complementary action. In many developed countries, it is generally recognized that employees should not accept bribes, personal payments, gifts, or special favors from people who hope to influence the outcome of a decision. However, bribery is an accepted way of doing business in many countries. Bribes have been associated with the downfall of many managers, legislators, and government officials. One source estimates that some $80 billion is paid out worldwide in the form of bribes or some other payoff every year.[13]

When a government official accepts a bribe, it is usually from a business that seeks some favor—perhaps a chance to influence legislation that affects it. Giving bribes to legislators or public officials, then, is a business ethics issue. For example, the Bataan nuclear power plant in the Philippines was built at a cost of more than $2 billion. The contractor, Westinghouse, admitted paying $17 million in commissions to a friend of former President Marcos.[14]

Corporate Intelligence

Many issues related to corporate intelligence have surfaced in the last few years. Defined broadly, **corporate intelligence** is the collection and analysis of information on markets, technologies, customers, and competitors, as well as on socioeconomic and external political trends. There are three distinct types of intelligence models: a passive monitoring system for early warning, tactical field support, and support dedicated to top-management strategy. Today, theft of trade secrets is estimated at $100 billion. One explanation is the increase in people with intelligence gathering competence and the proliferation of advanced technology.[15]

Corporate intelligence (CI) involves an in-depth discovery of information from corporate records, court documents, regulatory filings, and press releases, as well as any other background information that can be found about a company or its executives. Corporate intelligence is a legitimate inquiry into meaningful information that can be used in staying competitive. Corporate intelligence like other areas in business can be abused if due diligence is not taken to maintain legal and ethical methods of discovery. Computers, LANs (local-area networks), and the Internet have made the theft of trade secrets very easy. Proprietary information like secret formulas, manufacturing schematics, merger or acquisition plans, and marketing strategies all have tremendous value. A lack of security and proper training allows one to use a variety of techniques to gain access to a company's vital information. Some techniques for accessing valuable corporate information include physically removing the hard drive and copying the information to another machine, hacking, dumpster diving, social engineering, bribery, and hiring away key employees.

Hacking is considered one of the top three methods for obtaining trade secrets. Currently, there are over one hundred thousand websites that offer free downloadable and customizable hacking tools that require no in-depth knowledge of protocols or Internet protocol addressing. Hacking has three categories: system, remote, and physical. **System hacking** assumes that the attacker already has access to a low-level, privileged-user account. **Remote hacking** involves attempting to penetrate remotely a system across the Internet. A remote hacker usually begins with no special privileges and tries to obtain higher level or administrative access. Several forms of this type of hacking include unexpected input, buffer overflows, default configurations, and poor system administrator practices. **Physical hacking** requires that the CI agent enter a facility personally. Once inside, he or she can find a vacant or unsecured workstation with an employee's login name and password. Next, the CI agent searches for memos or unused letterheads and inserts the documents into the corporate mail system. Or the CI agent could gain physical access to a server or telephone room, look for remote-access equipment, note any telephone numbers written on wall jacks, and place a protocol analyzer in a wiring closet to capture data, user names, and passwords.

Social engineering is another popular method of obtaining valuable corporate information. The basic goals are the same as hacking. **Social engineering** is the tricking of individuals into revealing their passwords or other valuable corporate information. Tactics include casual conversations with relatives of company executives and sending e-mail claiming to be a system administrator that asks for passwords under the guise of "important system administration work." Another common social engineering trick is **shoulder surfing,** in which someone simply looks over an employee's shoulder while he or she types in a password. **Password guessing** is another easy social engineering technique. If a person can find out personal things about someone, he or she might be able to use that information to guess a password. For example, a child's name, birthdays and anniversaries, and Social Security numbers are all common passwords and are easily guessed or figured out by someone trying to do so.

Dumpster diving is messy but very successful for acquiring trade secrets. Once trash is discarded onto a public street or alley, it is considered fair game. Trash can provide a rich source of information for any CI agent. Phone books can give a hacker names and numbers of people to target and impersonate. Organizational charts contain information about people who are in positions of authority within the organization. Memos provide small amounts of useful information and assist in the creation of authentic-looking fake memos.

Whacking is wireless hacking. To eavesdrop on wireless networks, all a CI agent needs is the right kind of radio and to be within range of a wireless transmission. Once tapped into a wireless network, an intruder can easily access anything on both the wired and wireless networks because the data sent over networks is usually unencrypted. If a company is not using wireless networking, an attacker can pose as a janitor and insert a rogue wireless access node into a supposedly secure hard-wired network.

Phone eavesdropping is yet another tool in the game of CI agent. A person with a digital recording device can monitor and record a fax line. By playing the recording back an intruder can reproduce an exact copy of a message without anyone's knowledge. Even without monitoring a fax line, a fax sent to a "communal" fax machine can be read or copied. By picking up an extension or by tapping a telephone, it is possible to record the tones that represent someone's account number and password using a tape recorder. The tape recording can then be replayed over the telephone to gain access to someone else's account.

Discrimination

Although a person's racial and sexual prejudices belong to the domain of individual ethics, racial and sexual discrimination in the workplace creates ethical issues within the business world. **Discrimination** on the basis of race, color, religion, sex, marital status, sexual orientation, public assistance status, disability, age, national origin, or veteran status are illegal in the United States. Additionally, discrimination on the basis of political opinions or affiliation with a union is defined as harassment.

A company in the United States can be sued if it (1) refuses to hire an individual, (2) maintains a system of employment that unreasonably excludes an individual from employment, (3) discharges an individual, or (4) discriminates against an individual with respect to hiring, employment terms, promotion, or privileges of employment as it relates to the definition of discrimination.

Race, gender, and age discrimination are a major source of ethical and legal debate in the workplace. Between seventy-five thousand and eighty thousand charges of discrimination are filed annually with the **Equal Employment Opportunity Commission** (EEOC).[16] Discrimination remains a significant ethical issue in business despite nearly forty years of legislation attempting to outlaw it.

Once dominated by European American men, the U.S. workforce today includes significantly more women, African Americans, Hispanics, and other minorities, as well as disabled and older workers. Experts project that within the next fifty years, Hispanics will represent 24 percent of the population, and African Americans and Asian/Pacific Islanders will comprise 13 percent and 9 percent, respectively.[17] These groups have traditionally faced discrimination and higher unemployment rates and been denied opportunities to assume leadership roles in corporate America. For example, even today there are only three African Americans currently leading *Fortune* 100 companies: Richard Parsons, chairman and CEO of Time Warner Inc.; Kenneth Chenault, chairman and CEO of American Express Company; and Stanley O'Neal, chairman and CEO of Merrill Lynch. In the case of Merrill Lynch, even O'Neal is not immune to racial allegations. A complaint in federal court notes that only 2 percent of Merrill Lynch's 14,690 brokers are African American, although that percentage matches the industry standard. The ethical and potential illegal issue is Merrill Lynch's own claim of a higher, 6.5 percent, standard. George McReynolds, an African American broker for Merrill Lynch since 1983, contends that race is being used as a discrimination tool in the allocation of accounts, referrals, and leads. Although Merrill's African American broker trainee rate is approximately 7 percent, the argument is that those trainees will be discouraged to continue because of the discrimination.[18]

Another form of discrimination involves discriminating against individuals on the basis of age. The **Age Discrimination in Employment Act** specifically outlaws hiring practices that discriminate against people between the ages of 49 and 69, as well as those that require employees to retire before the age of 70. Despite this legislation, charges of age discrimination persist in the workplace. For example, the EEOC has charged Sidley Austin Brown & Wood, a Chicago-based international law firm with over fifteen hundred lawyers, with age discrimination when it selected "partners" for expulsion from the firm on account of their age. The act prohibits employers with twenty or more employees from making employment decisions, including decisions regarding the termination of employment, on the basis of age or from requiring retirement after the age of 40. EEOC trial attorney Deborah Hamilton stated that "having the power to fire an employee does not mean that a law firm or any other covered employer can do so because of the employee's age, if the employee is over 40. That is a violation of the ADEA and that the making of unlawful age-based selections for termination is precisely what EEOC is targeting in this lawsuit."[19] Sidley Austin Brown & Wood deny the charges, and at this point the case is still pending.

A survey by the American Association for Retired Persons (AARP), an advocacy organization for people ages 50 years and older, highlighted how little most companies value older workers. When the AARP mailed invitations to ten thousand companies for a chance to compete for a listing in *Modern Maturity* magazine as one of the "best employers for workers over 50," it received just fourteen applications. Given that nearly 20 percent of the nation's workers will be 55 years old or over by 2015, many companies need to change their approach toward older workers.[20]

To help build workforces that reflect their customer base, many companies have initiated **affirmative action programs,** which involve efforts to recruit, hire, train, and promote qualified individuals from groups that have traditionally been discriminated against on the basis of race, gender, or other characteristics. Such initiatives may be imposed by federal law on an employer that contracts or subcontracts for business with the federal government, as part of a settlement agreement with a state or federal agency, or by court order.[21] For example, Safeway, a chain of supermarkets, established a program to expand opportunities for women in middle- and upper-level management after settling a sex-discrimination lawsuit.[22] However, many companies voluntarily implement affirmative action plans in order to build a more diverse workforce.[23] For example, a Chicago real estate developer decided to help employers identify available female workers by launching the Female Employment Initiative, an outreach program designed to create opportunities for women in the construction industry through training programs, counseling and information services, and referral listings.[24]

Although many people believe that affirmative action requires that quotas be used to govern employment decisions, it is important to note that two decades of Supreme Court rulings have made it clear that affirmative action does not permit or require quotas, reverse discrimination, or favorable treatment of unqualified women or minorities. To ensure that affirmative action programs are fair, the Supreme Court has established a number of standards to guide their implementation: (1) There must be a strong reason for developing an affirmative action program; (2) affirmative action programs must apply only to qualified candidates; and (3) affirmative action programs must be limited and temporary and therefore cannot include "rigid and inflexible quotas."[25]

Discrimination can also be an ethical issue in business when companies use race or other personal factors to discriminate against specific groups of customers. Many companies have been accused of using race to deny service or charge higher prices to certain ethnic groups. For example, four airlines have settled lawsuits alleging discrimination against perceived Arab, Middle Eastern, or Southeast Asian descent passengers. United, American, Continental, and Delta have all denied any violations but agreed to spend as much as $1.5 million to train staff on respecting civil rights.[26]

Sexual Harassment

Sexual harassment is a form of sex discrimination that violates Title VII of the Civil Rights Act of 1964. Title VII applies to employers with fifteen or more employees, including state and local governments. To understand the magnitude of this volatile issue, in one year the EEOC received 13,136 charges of sexual harassment, over 15 percent of which were filed by men. In another recent year, the EEOC resolved 13,786 sexual harassment charges and recovered $37.1 million in penalties.[27] **Sexual harassment** can be defined as any repeated, unwanted behavior of a sexual nature perpetrated upon one individual by another. It may be verbal, visual, written, or physical and can occur between people of different genders or those of the same sex. "Workplace display of sexually explicit material—photos, magazines, or posters—may constitute a hostile work environment harassment, even though the private possession, reading, and consensual sharing of such materials is protected under the Constitution."[28]

To establish sexual harassment, an employee must understand the definition of a **hostile work environment,** for which three criteria must be met: the conduct was unwelcome; the conduct was severe, pervasive, and regarded by the claimant as so hostile or offensive as to alter his or her conditions of employment; and the conduct was such that a reasonable person would find it hostile or offensive. To assert a hostile work environment, an employee need not prove that it seriously affected his or her psychological well-being nor caused an injury; the decisive issue is whether the conduct interfered with the claimant's work performance.[29]

Sexual harassment includes unwanted sexual approaches (including touching, feeling, groping) and/or repeated unpleasant, degrading, or sexist remarks directed toward an employee with the implied suggestion that the target's employment status, promotion, or favorable treatment depend on a positive response and/or cooperation. It can be regarded as a private nuisance, unfair labor practice, or, in some states, a civil wrong (tort) that may be the basis for a lawsuit against the individual who made the advances and against the employer who did not take steps to halt the harassment. The law is primarily concerned with the impact of the behavior and not the intent. An important facet of sexual harassment law is its focus on the victim's reasonable behaviors and expectations.[30] However, the definition of reasonable varies from state to state, as does the concept of expectations. In addition, an argument used by some in defense of sexual harassment is the freedom of speech granted by the First Amendment.

The key ethical issue within sexual harassment is called dual relationships or unethically intimate relationships. A **dual relationship** is defined as a personal, loving, and/or sexual relationship with someone with whom you share professional responsibilities. Potentially, **unethical dual relationships** are those where the relationship causes either a direct or indirect conflict of interest or a risk of impairment to professional judgment.[31] Another important factor in these cases is intent. If the sexual advances in any form are considered mutual, then consent is created. The problem is that, unless the employee or employer gets something in writing before the romantic action, consent can always be questioned, and when it comes to sexual harassment, the alleged perpetrator must prove mutual consent.

For example, in a case in Illinois, a professor made advances to his office assistant, repeatedly asking her "Do you love me?" and "Would you ever marry a man like me?" He would also ask her for hugs, rub her shoulders, and tickle her. The assistant was troubled by these behaviors, and although she confided her distress to the proper authorities, nothing was done until she went to another institution and filed an official complaint. The university responded by directing the professor to undergo training in proper behavior toward female students and by placing a letter in his personnel file, outlining the actions to be taken and the method for evaluating their effectiveness. In this case, the university believed that there was no duality and the EEOC awarded no monetary damages to the assistant.

Three former female employees sued Florida-based Airguide Corporation and its parent company, Pioneer Metals, Inc., for sexual harassment. The courts awarded each of the three women $1 million, but the penalties for sexual harassment do not stop there. In addition, Airguide and Pioneer Metals must conduct annual training in nineteen facilities in Florida and undergo monitoring by the EEOC for three years.[32]

To avoid sexual misconduct or harassment charges a company should, at the minimum, take the following steps:

1. *A statement of policy* naming someone in the company as ultimately responsible for preventing harassment at the company.
2. *A definition of sexual harassment* that includes unwelcome advances, requests for sexual favors, and any other verbal, visual, or physical conduct of a sexual nature; that provides examples of each; and that reminds employees that the list of examples is not all inclusive.
3. *A nonretaliation policy* that protects complainants and witnesses.
4. *Specific procedures for prevention* of such practices at early stages. However, if a company puts these procedures in writing, they are expected by law to train, measure, and ensure that the policies are being enforced.
5. *Establish, enforce, and encourage* victims of sexual harassment to report the behavior to authorized individuals.
6. *Establish a reporting procedure.*
7. *Make sure that the company has timely reporting requirements to the proper authorities.* Usually, there is a time limitation to file the complaint for a formal administrative sexual charge, ranging from six months to a year. However, the

failure to meet a shorter complaint period (for example, sixty to ninety days) so that a "rapid response" and remediation may occur and to help to ensure a harassment-free environment could be a company's defense against the charge that it was negligent.

Once these steps have been taken, a training program should identify and describe forms of sexual harassment and give examples, outline the grievance procedure, explain how to use the procedures and discuss the importance of them, discuss the penalty for violation, and train employees for the essential need of a workplace that is free from harassment, offensive conduct, or intimidation. A corporation's training program should cover such items as how to spot sexual harassment; how to investigate complaints including proper documentation; what to do about observed sexual harassment, even when no complaint has been filed; how to keep the work environment as professional and nonhostile as possible; how to teach employees that the consequences can be dismissal; and how to train management to understand follow-up procedures on incidents.

Environmental Issues

Environmental issues are becoming the significant concerns within the business community. The **Kyoto Protocol,** one example of the world's growing concern about global warming, is an international treaty on climate change committed to reducing emissions of carbon dioxide and five other greenhouse gases and to engaging in emissions trading if they maintain or increase emissions of these gases. The objective is to stabilize greenhouse-gas concentrations in the atmosphere at a level that would prevent dangerous climate changes. Some current estimates indicate that, if these objectives are not successfully and completely implemented, the predicted global temperature increase could be between 1.4°C to 5.8°C. Possible massive tidal surges and extreme weather patterns are in store for our planet in the future if countries do not restrict specific gases emanating from business activities. The United States is one of the only countries not to sign the protocol.

Water pollution results from the dumping of raw sewage and toxic chemicals into rivers and oceans, from oil and gasoline spills, and from the burial of industrial wastes in the ground where they may filter into underground water supplies. Fertilizers and pesticides used in farming and grounds maintenance also drain into water supplies with each rainfall. When these chemicals reach the oceans, they encourage the growth of algae that use up all the nearby oxygen, thus killing the sea life. According to the Environmental Protection Agency (EPA), more than a third of the nation's rivers, lakes, and coastal waters are not safe for swimming or fishing as a result of contaminated runoff.

Waste management, or the green revolution, has flourished in Europe, especially in Germany, and appears to be growing globally. One green issue is plastic; in the United States alone, 30 million plastic bottles are thrown away daily for a total of nearly 11 billion a year. Those that are recycled use large amounts of energy in the recycling process. An even bigger problem for the future is that, as the world becomes more capitalistic, more people will buy more things using plastics that are made from oil and that do not degrade easily. In the twenty-first century, businesses must devise a solution to this ethical issue.

Fraud

When an individual engages in deceptive practices to advance his or her own interests over those of his or her organization or some other group, charges of fraud may result. In general, **fraud** is any purposeful communication that deceives, manipulates, or conceals facts in order to create a false impression. Fraud is a crime and convictions may result in fines, imprisonment, or both. Fraud costs U.S. organizations more than $400 billion a year; the average company loses about 6 percent of total revenues to fraud and abuses committed by its own employees.[33] Among the most common fraudulent activities employees report about their coworkers are stealing office supplies or shoplifting, claiming to have worked extra hours, and stealing money or products.[34] Table 3–3 indicates what fraud examiners view as the biggest risk to companies. In recent years, accounting fraud has become a major ethical issue, but as we will see, fraud can also relate to marketing and consumer issues as well.

Accounting fraud usually involves a corporation's financial reports in which companies provide important information on which investors and others base decisions that may involve millions of dollars. If the documents contain inaccurate information, whether intentionally or not, then lawsuits and criminal penalties may result. Thomas H. Lee Partners, a private-equity firm that invested in Refco Inc., sued to recover $245 million in losses that it allegedly sustained because of accounting fraud. After spending $10 million and thousands of accounting hours, Thomas H. Lee Partners invested $453 million in Refco. But former CEO Phillip R. Bennett, former CEO and President Santo C. Maggio, and former President Tone Grant are alleged to have "cooked the books." Bennett was indicted by a federal grand jury on charges of hiding as much as $720 million in bad debts from auditors and investors.[35] Such scrutiny of financial reporting increased dramatically in the wake of accounting scandals in the early twenty-first century. As a result of the negative publicity surrounding the allegations of accounting fraud at a number of companies, many firms were forced to take a second look at their financial documents. More than a few chose to restate their earnings to avoid being drawn into the scandal.[36] For example, Qwest Communications, which provides local and long-distance telephone service, announced that it overstated revenue by $1.9 billion during 2000 and was forced to restate about $1.5 billion in earnings for that year.[37]

The field of accounting has changed dramatically over the last decade. The profession used to have a club-type mentality: those who became certified public accountants (CPAs) were not concerned about competition. Now CPAs advertise their

TABLE 3–3	Greatest Fraud Risk for Companies
Conflicts of interest	56%
Fraudulent financial statements	57%
Billing schemes	22%
Expense and reimbursement schemes	41%
Bribery/economic extortions	35%

SOURCE: "The 2007 Oversight Systems Report on Corporate Fraud," Ethics World, http://www.ethicsworld.org/ethicsandemployees/PDF%20links/Oversight_2007_Fraud_Survey.pdf (accessed March 12, 2009).

skills and short-term results in an environment in which competition has increased and overall billable hours have significantly decreased because of technological innovations. Additionally, accountants are now permitted to charge performance-based fees rather than hourly rates, a rule change that encouraged some large accounting firms to promote tax-avoidance strategies for high-income individuals because the firms can charge 10 to 40 percent of the amount of taxes saved.[38]

Pressures on accountants today include time, reduced fees, client requests to alter opinions concerning financial conditions or lower tax payments, and increased competition. Other issues that accountants face daily involve compliance with complex rules and regulations, data overload, contingent fees, and commissions. An accountant's life is filled with rules and data that have to be interpreted correctly, and because of such pressures and the ethical predicaments they spawn, problems within the accounting industry are on the rise.

As a result, accountants must abide by a strict code of ethics that defines their responsibilities to their clients and the public interest. The code also discusses the concepts of integrity, objectivity, independence, and due care. Despite the standards the code provides, the accounting industry has been the source of numerous fraud investigations in recent years. Congress passed the Sarbanes–Oxley Act in 2002 to address many of the issues that could create conflicts of interest for accounting firms auditing public corporations. The law generally prohibits accounting firms from providing both auditing and consulting services to the same firm. Additionally, the law specifies that corporate boards of directors must include outside directors with financial knowledge on the company's audit committee.

Marketing fraud—the process of creating, distributing, promoting, and pricing products—is another business area that generates potential ethical issues. False or misleading marketing communications can destroy customers' trust in a company. Lying, a major ethical issue involving communications, is potentially a significant problem. In both external and internal communications, it causes ethical predicaments because it destroys trust. For example, former executives of WorldCom—Bernie Ebbers, Scott Sullivan, and David Myers—were arrested and charged with concealing $3.8 billion in expenses as well as lying to investors and regulators to hide their deception.[39] As a result of their lying and fraud, Ebbers was sentenced to twenty-five years in prison, Sullivan to five years, and Myers to a year and a day—for which they must serve a minimum of 80 percent.

False or deceptive advertising is a key issue in marketing communications. One set of laws that is common to many countries are laws concerning deceptive advertising—that is, advertisements that are not clearly labeled as advertisements. For example, in the United States, Section 5 of the Federal Trade Commission (FTC) Act addresses deceptive advertising. Abuses in advertising can range from exaggerated claims and concealed facts to outright lying, although improper categorization of advertising claims is the critical point. Courts place false or misleading advertisements into three categories: puffery, implied falsity, and literal falsity. **Puffery** can be defined as exaggerated advertising, blustering, and boasting upon which no reasonable buyer would rely and is not actionable under the Lanham Act. For example, in a Lanham Act suit between two shaving products companies, the defendant advertised that the moisturizing strip on its shaving razor was "six times smoother" than its competitors' strips, while showing a man rubbing his hand down his face. The court rejected the defendant's argument that "six times smoother" implied that only the moisturizing strip on the razor's head was smoother. Instead, the court found that the "six times smoother" advertising claim implied that the consumer would receive a smoother shave from the defendant's razor as a whole, a claim that was false.[40]

Implied falsity means that the message has a tendency to mislead, confuse, or deceive the public. The advertising claims that use implied falsity are those that are literally true but imply another message that is false. In most cases, this can be done only through a time-consuming and expensive consumer survey, whose results are often inconclusive.[41]

The characterization of an advertising claim as **literally false** can be divided into two subcategories: *tests prove* (*establishment claims*), in which the advertisement cites a study or test that establishes the claim; and *bald assertions* (*nonestablishment claims*), in which the advertisement makes a claim that cannot be substantiated, as when a commercial states that a certain product is superior to any other on the market. For example, the FTC filed formal complaints against Stock Value 1 Inc. and Comstar Communications Inc. for making unsubstantiated claims that their radiation-protection patches block the electromagnetic energy emitted by cellular telephones. The FTC's complaint charged that the companies "made false statements that their products had been scientifically 'proven' and tested," when in fact that was not the case.[42]

Another form of advertising abuse involves making ambiguous statements in which the words are so weak or general that the viewer, reader, or listener must infer the advertiser's intended message. These "weasel words" are inherently vague and enable the advertiser to deny any intent to deceive. The verb *help* is a good example (as in expressions such as "helps prevent," "helps fight," "helps make you feel").[43] Consumers may view such advertisements as unethical because they fail to communicate all the information needed to make a good purchasing decision or because they deceive the consumer outright.

Labeling issues are even murkier. For example, Netgear Inc. agreed to settle a class-action suit that claimed it exaggerated the data-transfer speeds of its wireless equipment. As part of the settlement, the company must pay $700,000 in legal fees, give a 15 percent discount to members of the class action, donate $25,000 of product to charity, and include disclaimers about the data-transfer speed of its products.[44]

Slamming, or changing a customer's phone service without authorization, is another important issue involving labeling that is specific to the telephone industry. AT&T sued Business Discount Plan (BDP), accusing it of using fraud and deception to routinely "slam" customers to its telecommunication service by suggesting that they were affiliated with AT&T. As part of the settlement, BDP had to send letters to consumers telling them that BDP was not affiliated with AT&T.[45] Such misleading behavior creates ethical issues because the communicated messages do not include all the information that consumers need to make good purchasing decisions, frustrating and angering customers who feel that they have been deceived. In addition, they damage the seller's credibility and reputation.

Advertising and direct sales communication can also mislead by concealing the facts within the message. For instance, a salesperson anxious to sell a medical insurance policy might list a large number of illnesses covered by the policy but fail to mention that it does not cover some commonly covered illnesses. Indeed, the fastest-growing area of fraudulent activity is in direct marketing, which employs the telephone and impersonal media to communicate information to customers, who then purchase products via mail, telephone, or the Internet.

Consumer Fraud

Consumer fraud is when consumers attempt to deceive businesses for their own gain. In 2006 the FTC estimated that 25 million consumers had engaged in consumer fraud.[46] Shoplifting, for example, accounts for nearly 32 percent of the losses of the 118 largest U.S. retail chains, although this figure is still far outweighed by the nearly 49 percent of losses perpetrated by store employees, according to the National Retail Security Survey. Together with vendor fraud and administrative error, these losses cost U.S. retailers more than $31 billion annually.[47]

Consumers engage in many other forms of fraud against businesses, including price-tag switching, item switching, lying to obtain age-related and other discounts, and taking advantage of generous return policies by returning used items, especially clothing that has been worn (with the price tags still attached). Such behavior by consumers affects retail stores as well as other consumers who, for example, may unwittingly purchase new clothing that has actually been worn.[48]

Consumer fraud involves intentional deception to derive an unfair economic advantage by an individual or group over an organization. Examples of fraudulent activities include shoplifting, collusion or duplicity, and guile. *Collusion* typically involves an employee who assists the consumer in fraud. For example, a cashier may not ring up all merchandise or may give an unwarranted discount. *Duplicity* may involve a consumer staging an accident in a grocery store and then seeking damages against the store for its lack of attention to safety. A consumer may purchase, wear, and then return an item of clothing for a full refund. In other situations, the consumer may ask for a refund by claiming a defect. *Guile* is associated with a person who is crafty or understands right/wrong behavior but uses tricks to obtain an unfair advantage. The advantage is unfair because the person has the intent to go against the right behavior or end. Although some of these acts warrant legal prosecution, they can be very difficult to prove, and many companies are reluctant to accuse patrons of a crime when there is no way to verify it. Businesses that operate with the "customer is always right" philosophy have found that some consumers will take advantage of this promise and have therefore modified return policies to curb unfair use.

Insider Trading

An insider is any officer, director, or owner of 10 percent or more of a class of a company's securities. There are two types of **insider trading:** illegal and legal. *Illegal insider trading* is the buying or selling of stocks by insiders who possess material that is still not public. The act, which puts insiders in breach of their fiduciary duty, can be committed by anyone who has access to nonpublic material, such as brokers, family, friends, and employees. In addition, someone caught "tipping" an outsider with material nonpublic information can also be found liable. To determine if an insider gave a tip illegally, the SEC uses the *Dirks test*, which states that if a tipster breaches his or her trust with the company and understands that this was a breach, he or she is liable for insider trading.

Legal insider trading involves legally buying and selling stock in an insider's own company, but not all the time. Insiders are required to report their insider transactions within two business days of the date the transaction occurred. For example, if an insider sold ten thousand shares on Monday, June 12, he or she would have to report this change to the SEC by Wednesday, June 14. To deter insider trading, insiders are prevented from buying and selling their company stock within a six-month period; therefore, insiders buy stock when they feel the company will perform well over the long term.

An example of insider trading occurred at Charter One Bank, where federal prosecutors accused an insider of failing to report several of her transactions. Wang, the insider, and her husband, Liu, invested personal funds in a hedge fund operated by a former coworker. After learning that Citizens Corporation coworkers were performing due diligence on a Charter One Bank, Wang passed on her insider information to the manager of a hedge fund, who then purchased a large quantity of Charter One stock. On the following day, when Citizens announced the Charter One acquisition, the hedge fund yielded a profit of about $700,000. As a result of their actions, the players in this scandal each face a maximum sentence of ten years in prison and a $1 million fine.[49]

Intellectual-Property Rights

Intellectual-property rights involve the legal protection of intellectual properties such as music, books, and movies. Laws such as the Copyright Act of 1976, the Digital Millennium Copyright Act, and the Digital Theft Deterrence and Copyright Damages Improvement Act of 1999 were designed to protect the creators of intellectual property. However, with the advance of technology, ethical issues still abound for websites. For example, until it was sued for copyright infringement, Napster.com allowed individuals to download copyrighted music for personal use without providing compensation to the artists.

A decision by the Federal Copyright Office (FCO) helped lay the groundwork for intellectual property rules in a digital world. The FCO decided to make it illegal for Web users to hack through barriers that copyright holders erect around material released online, allowing only two exceptions. The first exception was for software that blocks users from finding obscene or controversial material on the Web, and the second was for people who want to bypass malfunctioning security features of software or other copyrighted goods they have purchased. This decision reflects the fact that copyright owners are typically being favored in digital copyright issues.[50] There have been many lawsuits related to this issue, and some have had costly results. MP3.com paid Universal Music Group $53.4 million to end its dispute with major record labels over copyright infringement.[51]

Privacy Issues

Consumer advocates continue to warn consumers about new threats to their privacy especially within the health-care and Internet industries.[52] As the number of people using the Internet increases, the areas of concern related to its use increase as well.[53]

Some **privacy issues** that must be addressed by businesses include the monitoring of employees' use of available technology and consumer privacy. Current research suggests that, even if businesses use price discounts or personalized services, consumers remain suspicious. However, certain materialistic consumers are still willing to provide personal information, despite the potential risks.[54]

A challenge for companies today is meeting their business needs while protecting employees' desires for privacy. There are few legal protections of an employee's right to privacy, which allows businesses a great deal of flexibility in establishing policies regarding employees' privacy while they are on company property and using company equipment. The increased use of electronic communications in the workplace and technological advances that permit employee monitoring and surveillance have provided companies with new opportunities to obtain data about employees. From computer monitoring and telephone taping to video surveillance and GPS satellite tracking, employers are using technology to manage their productivity and protect their resources.

To motivate employee compliance, over 25 percent of 596 companies have fired workers for misusing the Internet, 6 percent have fired employees for misusing office telephones, 76 percent monitor their workers' website connections, and 65 percent use software to block connections to inappropriate websites. In addition, 36 percent of those employers track content, keystrokes, and time spent at keyboards and store the data in order to review it later. Employers are also notifying employees when they are being watched; of the organizations monitoring employees, 80 percent informed their workers.[55]

Because of the increased legal and regulatory investigations, employers have established policies governing personal e-mail use, personal Internet use, personal instant messenger use, personal blogs, and operation of personal websites on company time. Companies are also concerned about inappropriate telephone use, such as 1-900 lines or personal long-distance calls. Hence, some businesses routinely track phone numbers and, in selected job categories, record and review all employees' phone calls. More than half of the companies surveyed use video monitoring to counter theft, violence, and sabotage. The use of video surveillance to track employees' on-the-job performance has also increased, although companies that videotape workers usually notify them of the practice.

Concerns about employee privacy extend to Europe as well. In Finland an executive vice president and several employees of Sonera Corporation were arrested as part of an investigation into whether the wireless telecommunications company violated the privacy of its workers by monitoring their call records, a serious offense in Finland. The investigation was launched after a local newspaper reported that Sonera was tracing employees' phone calls in order to identify who may have leaked information about the company to the media. The company denied the accusations.[56]

Clearly conveying the organization's policy on workplace privacy should reduce the opportunity for employee lawsuits and the resulting costs of such actions. However, if a company fails to monitor employees' use of e-mail and the Internet, the costs can be huge. For example, Chevron Corporation agreed to pay $2.2 million to employees who claimed that unmonitored sexually harassing e-mail created a threatening environment for them.[57] Instituting practices that show respect for employee privacy but do not abdicate the employer's responsibility should help create a climate of trust that promotes opportunities for resolving employee–employer disputes without lawsuits.

Electronic monitoring allows a company to determine whether productivity is being reduced because employees are spending too much time on personal Web activities. Knowing this can then enable the company to take steps to remedy the situation. Internet filtering companies such as Cyber Patrol, Surfcontrol, Surfwatch, and Web-Sense provide products that block employee access to websites deemed distracting or objectionable. WebSense launched AfterWork.com, a personal homepage for each employee at a company that allows employees to visit nonwork-related websites during breaks and lunch, as well as before and after work hours.[58] One survey about this subject found that 58 percent of employees considered using company resources for personal Web surfing to be an "extremely serious" or "very serious" business ethics violation.[59]

There are two dimensions to consumer privacy: consumer awareness of information collection and a growing lack of consumer control over how companies use the personal information that they collect. For example, many are not aware that Google Inc. reserves the right to track every time you click on a link from one of its searches.[60] Online purchases and even random Web surfing can be tracked without a consumer's knowledge. A survey by the Progress and Freedom Foundation found that 96 percent of popular commercial websites collect personally identifying information from visitors.[61]

For example, the FTC asked a federal judge to shut down Odysseus Marketing Inc. on the grounds that it secretly installed spyware that could not be removed by the consumers whose computers it infected. The company offered a free software package to make peer-to-peer file sharing anonymous, but consumers ended up downloading a program called Clientman, a spyware program that altered search results, disseminated pop-up ads, and installed third-party ads without notice to consumers. The company denies any wrongdoing.[62]

A U.S. Department of Commerce study on e-commerce and privacy found that 81 percent of Internet users and 79 percent of consumers who buy products and services over the Web were concerned about online threats to privacy.[63] Another survey found that 38 percent of respondents felt that it is never ethical to track customers' Web activities, and 64 percent said that they do not trust websites that do.[64] These concerns have led some companies to cut back on the amount of information they collect: Of the sites surveyed by the Progress and Freedom Foundation, 84 percent indicated that they are collecting less data than before.[65] However, in a random survey of 1006 consumers on consumer fraud and privacy, only 13 percent believed that the problem of payment fraud would improve over the next six months, while 55 percent believed that it would worsen. In addition, nearly 35 percent expressed a low level of confidence in their ability to avoid becoming a victim of credit or debit card fraud.[66]

Companies are also working to find ways to improve consumers' trust in their websites. For example, an increasing number of websites display an online seal from BBBOnline, available only to sites that subscribe to certain standards. A similar seal is available through TRUSTe, a nonprofit global initiative that certifies those websites that adhere to its principles. (Visit e-businessethics.com for more on Internet privacy.)

THE CHALLENGE OF DETERMINING AN ETHICAL ISSUE IN BUSINESS

Most ethical issues will become visible through stakeholder concerns about an event, activity, or the results of a business decision. The mass media, special-interest groups, and individuals, through the use of blogs, podcasts, or other individual-generated media, often generate discussion about the ethicalness of a decision. Another way to determine whether a specific behavior or situation has an ethical component is to ask other individuals in the business how they feel about it and whether they view it as ethically challenging. Trade associations and business self-regulatory groups such as the Better Business Bureau often provide direction for companies in defining ethical issues. Finally, it is important to determine whether the organization has adopted specific policies on the activity. An activity approved of by most members of an organization, if it is also customary in the industry, is probably ethical. An issue, activity, or situation that can withstand open discussion between many stakeholders, both inside and outside the organization, probably does not pose ethical problems.

Over half (52 percent) of the national sample of employees observed some type of misconduct. Figure 3–2 provides a view of many different forms of misconduct.

However, over time, problems can become ethical issues as a result of changing societal values. For instance, for decades Kraft Foods Inc. has been a staple in almost every home in the United States, with products such as Kraft Macaroni and Cheese, Chips Ahoy! cookies, Lunchables, Kool-Aid, Fruity Pebbles, and Oreos. Nothing was said about such foods until 2004. However, a problem was perceived first by parents, then schools, and then politicians who became aware that the United States has the most obese people in the world, with approximately 40 percent of the population overweight.

The fact is that since 1980 the rate of obesity in children (ages 6 to 11) has more than doubled, and it has tripled in adolescents. Children who are 10 years of age weigh ten pounds more than they did in the 1960s. As a result, Congress has proposed legislation relative to obesity and concerning the advertising of unhealthy food products to children. Kraft realized that they now have an ethical situation regarding the advertising of such items as hotdogs, cookies, and cereals with high-sugar levels. Some consumer groups might now perceive Kraft's $90 million annual advertising budget, which was primarily directed at children, as unethical. Because ignoring the situation could be potentially disastrous, Kraft instead devised a compromise: It would stop advertising some of its products to children under 12 years of age and instead market healthier foods. As a result of government recommendations, Kraft executives have continually revised their advertising guidelines regarding children and the advertisement of products containing large amounts of sugar, fat, and calories, knowing that their decisions would probably negatively affect their bottom line.[67]

Once stakeholders trigger ethical-issue awareness and individuals openly discuss it and ask for guidance and the opinions of others, one enters the ethical decision-making process, which we examine in Chapter 5.

| FIGURE 3-2 | Most Common Types of Misconduct |

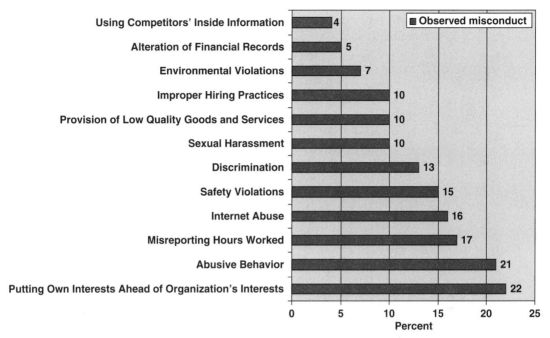

SOURCE: From *2007 National Business Ethics Survey: How Employees Perceive Ethics at Work,* 2007. Copyright © 2007, Ethics Resource Center (ERC).

SUMMARY

Stakeholders' concerns largely determine whether business actions and decisions are perceived as ethical or unethical. When government, communities, and society become involved, what was merely an ethical issue can quickly become a legal one. Shareholders can unwittingly complicate the issue of conducting business ethically by demanding that managers make decisions to boost short-term earnings to maintain or boost the value of their shares of stock.

A first step toward understanding business ethics is to develop ethical-issue awareness; that is, to learn to identify which stakeholder issues contain an ethical component. Characteristics of the job, the corporate or local culture, or the organization of the society in which one does business can all create ethical issues. Recognizing an ethical issue is essential to understanding business ethics and therefore to creating an effective ethics and compliance program that will seek to minimize unethical behavior. In order to do this, people must understand the universal moral constants of honesty, fairness, and integrity, which are accepted by businesspeople everywhere. Without embracing these concepts, running a business becomes very difficult. To be honest is to tell the truth to the best of your ability without hiding anything. Confucius defined several levels of honesty: *Li*, which relates to the superficial desires of a person; *Yi*, which relates to doing business based on reciprocity; and *Ren*, which is based on empathy and understanding others. Confucianism advocates treating inferiors as you would want superiors to treat you, an idea that is later reflected in Kant's Golden Rule. Virtues such as a family's honor and a person's reputation for honesty are of paramount importance.

Fairness is the quality of being just, equitable, and impartial, and it overlaps terms such as *justice, equity, equality*, and *morality*. The three fundamental elements that motivate people to be fair are equality, reciprocity, and optimization. Equality relates to how wealth is distributed between employees, within a company or a country, or globally; reciprocity relates to the return of small favors that are approximately equal in value; and integrity relates to a person's character and is made up of two basic parts: a formal relation that one has to oneself and a person's set of terminal, or enduring, values from which he or she does not deviate.

An ethical issue is a problem, situation, or opportunity that requires an individual, group, or organization to choose among several actions that must be evaluated as right or wrong, ethical or unethical, but an ethical dilemma has no right or ethical choice.

Bribery is the practice of offering something (usually money) in order to gain an illicit advantage. A conflict of interest is when an individual must choose whether to advance his or her own interests, those of the organization, or those of some other group. Corporate intelligence is the collection and analysis of information on markets, technologies, customers, and competitors, as well as on socioeconomic and external political trends. There are three intelligence models: passive, tactical, and top-management. The tools of corporate intelligence are many. One tool is hacking, which has three categories: system, remote, and physical; another is social engineering in which someone is tricked into revealing valuable corporate information; and other techniques include dumpster diving, whacking, and phone eavesdropping.

Another ethical/legal issue is discrimination, which is illegal in the United States when it occurs on the basis of race, color, religion, sex, marital status, sexual orientation, public-assistance status, disability, age, national origin, or veteran status. Additionally, discrimination on the basis of political opinions or affiliation with a union is defined as harassment. Sexual harassment is a form of sex discrimination. To help build workforces that reflect their customer base, many companies have initiated affirmative action programs. Environmental issues such as air, water, and waste are becoming an ethical concern within business. In general, fraud is any purposeful communication that deceives, manipulates, or conceals facts in order to create a false impression. There are several types of fraud: accounting, marketing, and consumer.

An insider is any officer, director, or owner of 10 percent or more of a class of a company's securities. There are two types of insider trading: legal and illegal. Intellectual-property rights involve the legal protection of intellectual properties such as music, books, and movies. Consumer advocates continue to warn consumers about new threats to their privacy.

IMPORTANT TERMS FOR REVIEW		
	honesty	phone eavesdropping
	fairness	discrimination
	equality	Equal Employment Opportunity Commission
	reciprocity	
	optimization	Age Discrimination in Employment Act
	integrity	affirmative action program
	ethical issue	sexual harassment
	ethical dilemma	hostile work environment
	abusive/intimidating behavior	dual relationship
	lying	unethical dual relationship
	conflict of interest	environmental issue
	bribery	Kyoto Protocol
	active bribery	water pollution
	passive bribery	fraud
	facilitation payment	accounting fraud
	corporate intelligence	marketing fraud
	hacking	puffery
	system hacking	implied falsity
	remote hacking	literally false
	physical hacking	labeling issue
	social engineering	slamming
	shoulder surfing	consumer fraud
	password guessing	insider trading
	dumpster diving	intellectual-property right
	whacking	privacy issue

RESOLVING ETHICAL BUSINESS CHALLENGES*

Joseph Freberg had been with Al-con for eighteen months. He had begun his career right out of college with a firm in the Southeast called Cala Industrial, which specialized in air compressors. Because of his work with Cala, he had been lured away to Alcon, in Omaha, as a sales manager. Joseph's first six months had been hard. Working with salespeople older than he, trying to get a handle on his people's sales territories, and settling into the corporate culture of a new firm took sixteen-hour days, six days a week. During those six months, he also bought a house, and his fiancé, Ellen, furnished it. Ellen had stepped right in and decided almost everything, from the color of the rugs to the style of the curtains.

Ellen had taken a brokerage job with Trout Brothers and seemed to be working even more hours than Joseph. But the long days were paying off. Ellen was now starting to handle some large accounts and was being noticed by the "right" crowd in the wealthier Omaha areas.

Costs for the new home had exceeded their anticipated spending limit, and the plans for their wedding seemed to be getting larger and larger. In addition, Ellen was commuting from her apartment to the new home and then to her job, and the commute killed her car. As a result, she decided to lease something that exuded success.

"Ellen, don't you think a Mercedes is a little out of our range? What are the payments?" inquired Joseph.

"Don't worry, darling. When my clients see me in this—as well as when we start entertaining at the new house once we're married—the payments on the car will seem small compared with the money I'll be making," Ellen mused as she ran her fingers through Joseph's hair and gave him a peck on the cheek.

By the time of the wedding and honeymoon, Joseph and Ellen's bank statement looked like a bullfighter's cape—red. "Don't worry, Joseph, everything will turn out okay. You've got a good job. I've got a good job. We're young and have drive. Things will straighten out after a while," said Ellen as she eyed a Rolex in a store window.

After the wedding, things did settle down—to a hectic pace, given their two careers and their two sets of parents two thousand miles in either direction. Joseph had realized that Alcon was a paternal type of organization, with good benefits and tremendous growth potential. He had identified whom to be friends with and whom to stay away from in the company. His salespeople seemed to tolerate him, sometimes calling him "Little Joe" or "Joey" because of his age, and his salespeople were producing—slowly climbing up the sales ladder to the number-one spot in the company.

While doing some regular checkup work on sales personnel, Joseph found out that Carl had been giving kickbacks to some of his buyers. Carl's sales volume accounted for a substantial amount of the company's existing clientele sales, and he had been a trainer for the company for several years. Carl also happened to be the vice president's son-in-law. Joseph started to check on the other reps more closely and discovered that, although Carl seemed to be the biggest offender, three of his ten people were doing the same thing. The next day, Joseph looked up Alcon's policy handbook and found this statement: "Our company stands for doing the right thing at all times and giving our customers the best product for the best prices." There was no specific mention of kickbacks, but everyone knew that kickbacks ultimately reduce fair competition, which eventually leads to reduced quality and increased prices for customers.

By talking to a few of the old-timers at Alcon, Joseph learned that there had been sporadic enforcement of the "no kickback" policy. It seemed that when times were good it became unacceptable and when times were bad it slipped into the acceptable range. And then there was his boss, Kathryn, the vice president. Joseph knew that Kathryn had a tendency to shoot the bearer of bad news. He remembered a story that he had heard about a sales manager coming in to see Kathryn to explain an error in a bid that one of his salespeople had made. Kathryn called in the entire sales staff and fired the salesman on the spot. Then, smiling, she told the sales manager: "This was your second mistake, so I hope that you can get a good recommendation from personnel. You have two weeks to find employment elsewhere." From then on, the office staff had a nickname for Kathryn—Jaws.

Trying to solve the problem that he was facing, Joseph broached the subject of kickbacks at his monthly meeting with Carl. Carl responded, "You've been in this business long enough to know that this happens all the time. I see nothing wrong with this practice if it increases sales. Besides, I take the money out of my commission. You know that right now I'm trying to pay off some big medical bills. I've also gotten tacit clearance from above, but I wouldn't mention that if I were you." Joseph knew that the chain-of-command structure in the company made it very dangerous to go directly to a vice president with this type of information.

As Joseph was pondering whether to do nothing, bring the matter into the open and state that it was wrong and that such practices were against policy, or talk to Kathryn about the situation, his cell phone rang. It was Ellen. "Honey, guess what just happened. Kathryn, your boss, has decided to use me as her new broker. Isn't that fantastic!"

What should Joseph do?

QUESTIONS • EXERCISES

1. What are Joseph's ethical problems?
2. Assume that you are Joseph and discuss your options.

3. What other information do you feel you need before making your decision?
4. Discuss in which business areas the ethical problems lie.

*This case is strictly hypothetical; any resemblance to real persons, companies, or situations is coincidental.

Check Your EQ

Check your EQ, or Ethics Quotient, by completing the following. Assess your performance to evaluate your overall understanding of the chapter material.

1. Business can be considered a game people play like basketball or boxing.   **Yes**   **No**
2. Key ethical issues in an organization relate to fraud, discrimination, honesty and fairness, conflicts of interest, and technology.   **Yes**   **No**
3. Only 10 percent of employees observe abusive behavior in the workplace.   **Yes**   **No**
4. Fraud occurs when a false impression exists, which conceals facts.   **Yes**   **No**
5. Putting one's own interests ahead of the organization is the most commonly observed type of misconduct.   **Yes**   **No**

ANSWERS: 1. No. People are not economically self-sufficient and cannot withdraw from the game of business. 2. Yes. See pages 64–82 regarding these key ethical issues and their implications for the organization. 3. No. According to Figure 3–2, 21 percent of employees observe abusive behavior in the workplace. 4. No. Fraud must be purposeful, rather than accidental, and exists when deception and manipulation of facts are concealed to create a false impression that causes harm. 5. Yes. The most observed form of misconduct in Table 3–1 is putting one's own interests ahead of the company.

CHAPTER 4

The Institutionalization of Business Ethics

CHAPTER OBJECTIVES

- To distinguish between the voluntary and mandated boundaries of ethical conduct

- To provide specific mandated requirements for legal compliance in specific subject matter areas related to competition, consumers, safety, and the environment

- To specifically address the requirements of the Sarbanes–Oxley legislation and implementation by the Securities and Exchange Commission

- To provide an overview of regulatory efforts to provide incentives for ethical behavior

- To provide an overview of the Federal Sentencing Guidelines for Organizations recommendations and incentives for developing an ethical corporate culture

- To provide an overview of voluntary boundaries and the relationship to social responsibility

CHAPTER OUTLINE

Myron had just graduated from West Coast University with both chemistry–pharmacy and business degrees and was excited to work for Producto International (PI). He loved having the opportunity to discover medicinal products around the world. His wife, Quan, was also enthusiastic about her job as an import–export agent for a subsidiary of PI.

Producto International was the industry leader, with headquarters in Paris. Worldwide, hundreds of small firms were competing with PI; however, only six had equivalent magnitude. These six had cornered 75 percent of world sales. So many interrelationships had developed that competition had become "managed." However, this did not constitute any illegal form of monopolistic behavior as defined by the European Union.

Myron's first assignment was in India and concerned exporting betel nuts to South and perhaps North America. It is estimated that more than 20 million people chew betel nuts in India alone. The betel nut is one of the world's most popular plants, and its leaf is used as a paper for rolling tobacco. The betel nut is also mashed or powdered with other ingredients and rolled up in a leaf and sold as candy. Myron quickly found that regular use of the betel nut will, in time, stain the mouth, gums, and teeth a deep red, which in Asia is a positive quality. As Myron was learning more about the betel nut, he came across the following report from the People's Republic of China: "Studies show that the chewing of the spiced betel nut can lead to oral cancer. According to research, 88 percent of China's oral cancer patients are betel nut chewers. Also, people who chew betel nuts and smoke are ninety times more likely to develop oral cancer than nonusers." Myron found that the betel nut primarily affects the central nervous system. It increases respiration while decreasing the workload on the heart (a mild high). Myron also found that demand for it was starting to emerge in the United States as well as in other developed countries.

While Myron was working on the betel nut, David, Myron's boss, also wanted him to work on introducing khat (pronounced "cot") into Asia. Khat is a natural stimulant from a plant grown in East Africa and southern Arabia. Fresh khat leaves, which are typically chewed like tobacco, produce a mild cocaine- or amphetamine-like euphoria. However, its effect is much less intense than that produced by either of those substances, with no reports of a rush sensation or paranoia, for example. Chewing khat produces a strong aroma and generates intense thirst. Casual users claim that khat lifts spirits, sharpens thinking, and, when its effects wear off, generates mild lapses into depression similar to those observed among cocaine users. The body appears to have a physical intolerance to khat due in part to limitations in how much can be ingested by chewing. As a result, reports suggest that there are no physical symptoms accompanying withdrawal. Advocates of khat use claim that it eases symptoms of diabetes, asthma, and disorders of the stomach and the intestinal tract. Opponents claim that khat damages health, suppresses appetite, and prevents sleep. In the United States, khat has been classified as a schedule IV substance by the Drug Enforcement Agency (DEA): freshly picked khat leaves (that is, within forty-eight hours of harvest) are classified as a schedule I narcotic, the most restrictive category used by the DEA.

After doing his research, Myron delivered his report to David and said, "I really think that, given the right marketing to some of the big pharmaceutical companies, we should have two huge revenue makers."

"That's great, Myron, but the pharmaceutical market is only secondary to our primary market—the two billion consumers to whom we can introduce these products."

"What do you mean, David?" Myron asked.

"I mean these products are grown legally around the world, and the countries that we are targeting have no restrictions on these substances," David explained. "Why not tailor the delivery of the product by country? For example, we find out which flavors people want the betel nut in, in North and South America or the Middle East. The packaging will have to change by country as well as branding. Pricing strategies will need to be developed relative to our branding decisions, and of course quantity usages will have to be calculated. For example, single, multiple, supervalue sizes, and the like need to be explored. The same can be done for khat. Because of your research and your business background, I'm putting you on the marketing team for both. Of course, this means that you're going to have to be promoted and at least for a while live in Hong Kong. I know Quan will be excited. In fact, I told her the news this morning that she would be working on the same project in Hong Kong. Producto International tries to be sensitive to the dual-career family problems that can occur. Plus you'll be closer to relatives. I told Quan that with living allowances and all of the other things that go with international placement, you two should almost triple your salaries! You don't have to thank me, Myron. You've worked hard on these projects, and now you deserve to have some of the benefits."

Myron went back to his office to think about his and Quan's future. He had heard of another employee who had rejected a similar offer, and that person's career had languished at PI. Eventually, that individual left the industry, never to be heard from again.

QUESTIONS • EXERCISES

1. Identify the social responsibility issues in this scenario.
2. Discuss the advantages and disadvantages of each decision that Myron could make.
3. Discuss the issue of marketing products that are legal but have addictive properties associated with them.

*This case is strictly hypothetical; any resemblance to real persons, companies, or situations is coincidental.

To understand the institutionalization of business ethics it is important to understand the voluntary and legally mandated dimensions of organizational practices. In addition, there are core practices sometimes called best practices that most responsible firms—trying to achieve acceptable conduct—embrace and implement. The effective organizational practice of business ethics requires all three dimensions to be integrated into an ethics and compliance program. This creates an ethical culture that can effectively manage the risks of misconduct. Institutionalization relates to legal and societal forces that provide both rewards and punishment to organizations based on the stakeholder evaluations of specific conduct. Institutionalization in business ethics relates to established laws, customs, and expected organizational programs that are considered normative in establishing reputation. Institutions provide requirements, structure, and societal expectations to reward and sanction ethical decision making.

MANAGING ETHICAL RISK THROUGH MANDATED AND VOLUNTARY PROGRAMS

Table 4–1 provides an overview of the three dimensions of institutionalization. **Voluntary practices** include the beliefs, values, and voluntary contractual obligations. All businesses engage in some level of commitment to voluntary activities to benefit both internal and external stakeholders. For example, Starbucks provides health benefits to

TABLE 4–1	Voluntary Boundary, Core Practices, and Mandated Boundaries of Ethical Decisions
Voluntary boundary	A management-initiated boundary of conduct (beliefs, values, voluntary policies, and voluntary contractual obligations)
Core practice	A highly appropriate and common practice that helps ensure compliance with legal requirements, industry self-regulation, and societal expectations
Mandated boundary	An externally imposed boundary of conduct (laws, rules, regulations, and other requirements)

SOURCE: Adapted from the "Open Compliance Ethics Group (OCEG) Foundation Guidelines," v1.0, Steering Committee Update, December 2005, Phoenix, AZ.

part-time employees. Under pressure from many states to require Wal-Mart to increase health care for employees, it developed voluntary contractual commitments to increase health-care benefits to part-time workers. Most firms engage in **philanthropy**—giving back to communities and causes.

Core practices are documented best practices, often encouraged by legal and regulatory forces as well as industry trade associations. The **Better Business Bureau** is a leading self-regulatory body that provides directions for managing customer disputes and reviews advertising cases. These practices are appropriate and common practices that help ensure compliance with legal requirements and societal expectations. Although these practices are not enforced, there are consequences for not engaging in these practices when there is misconduct. For example, the Federal Sentencing Guidelines for Organizations (FSGO) suggest that the governing authority (board of directors) be responsible for and assess an organization's ethical and compliance activities. There is no required reporting of investigations by government regulatory bodies, but there are incentives to the firm that effectively implement this recommendation. If misconduct occurs, there may be opportunities to avoid serious punishment. On the other hand, if there has been no effort by the board to oversee ethics and compliance, this could increase and compound the level of punishment. In this way, the government in institutionalizing core practices provides organizations the opportunity to take their own approach and only taking action if there are violations. **Mandated boundaries** are the externally imposed boundaries of conduct, such as laws, rules, regulations, and other requirements.

There is a need to maintain the values, ethical culture, and expectations for appropriate conduct in an organization. This is achieved through compliance, corporate governance, risk management, and voluntary activities. The development of these drivers of an ethical culture has been institutionally supported by government initiatives and the demands of stakeholders. The compliance element represents areas that must conform to existing legal and regulatory requirements. Established laws and regulatory decisions leave limited flexibility to organizations in adhering to these standards. Corporate governance (as discussed in Chapter 2) is structured by a governing authority providing oversight as well as checks and balances to make sure that the organization meets its goals and objectives for ethical performance. Risk management analyzes the probability or chance that misconduct could occur based on the nature of

---

FIGURE 4–1   Elements That Create an Ethical Culture

SOURCE: Based on the principles and framework of the "Open Compliance Ethics Group (OCEG) Foundation Guidelines," v1.0, Steering Committee Update, December 2005, Phoenix, AZ. Copyright © O.C. Ferrell 2007.

the business and the exposure to risky events. Voluntary activities often represent the values and responsibilities that firms accept in contributing to society.

Figure 4–1 depicts how these various elements of ethical culture shape the character of an organization. Corporate culture is created by corporate vision, values, principles, and rules. Vision and values provide aspirational guidance, whereas rules encourage mandatory compliance in activities. Principles provide a guiding sense of the right conduct in varying situations and dilemmas. Corporate governance, risk management, compliance, and voluntary activities, relate to formal structures in organizations that help shape and maintain the corporate culture.

In this chapter, we examine the boundaries of ethical conduct and focus on the voluntary, core practices, and mandated requirements for legal compliance—three important areas in developing an ethical culture. In particular, we concentrate on compliance in specific areas related to competition, consumers, safety, and the environment. We also consider the requirements of the Sarbanes–Oxley legislation and its implementation by the Securities and Exchange Commission (SEC) and how its implementation has affected companies. We also provide an overview of the FSGO for organizations and give recommendations and incentives for developing an ethical corporate culture. The FSGO, the Sarbanes–Oxley Act, industry trade associations, and societal expectations support core practices. Finally, we examine philanthropic contributions and how strategic philanthropy can be an important core competency to manage stakeholder relationships.

MANDATED REQUIREMENTS
FOR LEGAL COMPLIANCE

Laws and regulations are established by governments to set minimum standards for responsible behavior—society's codification of what is right and wrong. Laws regulating business conduct are passed because certain stakeholders believe that business cannot be trusted to do what is right in certain areas, such as consumer safety and environmental protection. Because public policy is dynamic and often changes in response to business abuses and consumer demands for safety and equality, many laws have been passed to resolve specific problems and issues. But the opinions of society, as expressed in legislation, can change over time, and different courts or state legislatures may take diverging views. For example, the thrust of most business legislation can be summed up as follows: Any practice is permitted that does not substantially lessen or reduce competition or harm consumers or society. Courts differ, however, in their interpretations of what constitutes a "substantial" reduction of competition. Laws can help businesspeople determine what society believes at a certain time, but what is legally wrong today may be perceived as acceptable tomorrow, and vice versa. The government lost $85 billion in the past decade because of illegal tax shelters. However, personal views on legal and illegal activity in this area vary tremendously and explain why accounting firms struggle to advise.[1] Instructions to employees to "just obey the law" are meaningless without effective training and experience in dealing with specific legal risk areas.

Laws are categorized as either civil or criminal. **Civil law** defines the rights and duties of individuals and organizations (including businesses). **Criminal law** not only prohibits specific actions—such as fraud, theft, or securities trading violations—but also imposes fines or imprisonment as punishment for breaking the law. The primary difference between criminal and civil law is that the state or nation enforces criminal laws, whereas individuals (generally, in court) enforce civil laws. Criminal and civil laws are derived from four sources: the U.S. Constitution (constitutional law), precedents established by judges (common law), federal and state laws or statutes (statutory law), and federal and state administrative agencies (administrative law). Federal administrative agencies established by Congress control and influence business by enforcing laws and regulations to encourage competition and to protect consumers, workers, and the environment. State laws and regulatory agencies also exist to achieve these objectives. The Department of Justice became concerned about antitrust issues in the online advertising business when Google and Microsoft attempted to engage in an advertising partnership.[2]

The primary method of resolving conflicts and serious business ethics disputes is through lawsuits in which one individual or organization uses civil laws to take another individual or organization to court. To avoid lawsuits and to maintain the standards necessary to reduce risk and create an ethical culture, it is necessary to have both legal and organizational standards enforced. When violations of organizational standards occur,

FIGURE 4–2   Only One in Four Companies Has a Well-Implemented Ethics Program

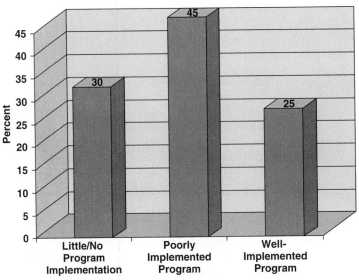

SOURCE: *2007 National Business Ethics Survey*, p. 20.

the National Business Ethics Survey (NBES) notes that many employees do not feel that their company has a strong ethics program. In fact, Figure 4–2 demonstrates that only 25 percent of companies in the United States have a well-implemented ethics program. A full 30 percent of companies do not have any ethics program at all to speak of, a serious problem in this age of misconduct and ethical violations. It is important for a company to have a functioning program in place long before an ethical disaster strikes.

The role of laws is not so much to distinguish what is ethical or unethical as to determine the appropriateness of specific activities or situations. In other words, laws establish the basic ground rules for responsible business activities. Most of the laws and regulations that govern business activities fall into one of five groups: (1) regulation of competition, (2) protection of consumers, (3) promotion of equity and safety, (4) protection of the natural environment, and (5) incentives to encourage organizational compliance programs to deter misconduct, which we examine later.

Laws Regulating Competition

The issues surrounding the impact of competition on business's social responsibility arise from the rivalry among businesses for customers and profits. When businesses compete unfairly, legal and social responsibility issues can result. Intense competition sometimes makes managers feel that their company's very survival is threatened. In these situations, managers may begin to see unacceptable alternatives as acceptable, and they may begin engaging in questionable practices to ensure the survival of their organizations. For example, Aventis SA and Andrx Corporation agreed to pay $80 million to settle charges that Aventis had paid Andrx nearly $100 million not to market a cheaper, generic version of Cardizem CD, a blood-pressure medication. Although both companies denied conspiring to manipulate the supply of the drug, pharmaceutical wholesalers also sued them over the same practice. Aventis claimed the agreement was necessary to protect its patent.[3] Because medications are necessary to so many people, ethical and social issues arise when a lower-price drug that should be available is not.

Size frequently gives some companies an advantage over others. For example, large firms can often generate economies of scale (for example, by forcing their suppliers to lower their prices) that allow them to put smaller firms out of business. Consequently, small companies and even whole communities may resist the efforts of firms like Wal-Mart, Home Depot, and Best Buy to open stores in their vicinity. These firms' sheer size enables them to operate at such low costs that small, local firms often cannot compete. In Austin, Texas, for example, many consumers threatened to boycott a new development that would have featured a Borders Books and Music superstore because it would have competed with popular locally owned book and music stores across the street from the new development.[4] Borders eventually withdrew from the project, citing "economic reasons."

Some companies' competitive strategies may focus on weakening or destroying a competitor, which can harm competition and ultimately reduce consumer choice. For example, Clear Channel Communications, which owns more than 10 percent of the nation's radio stations, was summoned before a U.S. Senate hearing to answer charges that it was using unfair competitive tactics. Small radio station owners and musicians charged that Clear Channel forces musicians to offer "payola" to promoters to get their songs played on the company's stations. They also charged that Clear Channel's ownership of so many stations in certain large markets represents a monopoly that limits consumer access to new music. Other critics accused the conglomerate of "blackballing" artists and promoters who refuse to use Clear Channel stations to promote their songs and concerts. Musician Don Henley argued that the firm's domination of the airwaves in some large cities had transformed the radio dial from a place where consumers had great choice in music to one where "everyone gets the same McDonald's hamburger." The Senate was considering whether to allow the modification of current regulations on the number of stations that one company can own in certain markets and strengthen punishment for anticompetitive tactics in radio and television. Despite the issues raised during the hearing, the Federal Communications Commission (FCC) further relaxed regulations to permit companies to operate even more media outlets within a single market.[5]

Other examples of anticompetitive strategies include sustained price cuts, discriminatory pricing, and price wars. The primary objective of U.S. antitrust laws is to distinguish competitive strategies that enhance consumer welfare from those that reduce it. The difficulty of this task lies in determining whether the intent of a company's pricing policy is to weaken or even destroy a competitor.[6] For example, concerns about anticompetitive behavior emerged in the software industry when the Department of Justice investigated Microsoft. Ken Wasch, president of the Software Publishers Association, stated that "justice clearly recognizes that the restoration of a level playing field in the computer software and technology industries is critical for ensuring consumer choice and ongoing innovation."[7] Microsoft's competitors complained that the company's practice of bundling its Internet Explorer Web browser into its Windows operating system stifled consumers' choice as to which Internet browser they would use. They also claimed that Microsoft's virtual monopoly on the market for operating system software reduced consumer choice and stifled innovation in the software industry.[8] After a year-long process, Microsoft settled the charges with the Justice Department and nine states. The company later settled a suit brought by the state of California, agreeing to repay consumers $1 billion in the form of vouchers.[9]

Intense competition may also lead companies to resort to corporate espionage. Corporate espionage is the act of illegally taking information from a corporation through computer hacking, theft, intimidation, sorting through trash, and through impersonation of organizational members. Estimates show corporate espionage may cost companies nearly $50 billion annually. Unauthorized information collected includes patents in development, intellectual property, pricing strategies, customer information, unique manufacturing and technological operations, as well as marketing plans, research and development, and future plans for market and customer expansion.[10] Determining an accurate amount for losses is difficult because most companies do not report such losses for fear that the publicity will harm their stock price or encourage further break-ins. Espionage may be carried out by outsiders or by employees—executives, programmers, network or computer auditors, engineers, or janitors who have legitimate reasons to access facilities, data, computers or networks. They may use a variety of techniques for obtaining valuable information such as dumpster diving, whacking, and hacking as discussed in Chapter 3.

Laws have been passed to prevent the establishment of monopolies, inequitable pricing practices, and other practices that reduce or restrict competition among businesses. These laws are sometimes called **procompetitive legislation** because they were enacted to encourage competition and prevent activities that restrain trade (Table 4–2). The Sherman Antitrust Act of 1890, for example, prohibits organizations from holding monopolies in their industry, and the Robinson–Patman Act of 1936 bans price discrimination between retailers and wholesalers.

In law, however, there are always exceptions. Under the McCarran–Ferguson Act of 1944, for example, Congress exempted the insurance industry from the Sherman Antitrust Act and other antitrust laws. Insurance companies were allowed to join together and set insurance premiums at specific industry-wide levels. However, this legal "permission" could still be viewed as irresponsible and unethical if it neutralizes competition and if prices no longer reflect the true costs of insurance protection. This illustrates the point that what is legal is not always considered ethical by some interest groups.

Laws Protecting Consumers

Laws that protect consumers require businesses to provide accurate information about products and services and to follow safety standards (Table 4–3). The first **consumer protection law** was passed in 1906, partly in response to a novel by Upton Sinclair. *The Jungle* describes, among other things, the atrocities and unsanitary conditions of the meatpacking industry in turn-of-the-century Chicago. The outraged public response to this book and other exposés of the industry resulted in the passage of the Pure Food and Drug Act. Likewise, Ralph Nader had a tremendous impact on consumer protection laws with his book *Unsafe at Any Speed*. His critique and attack of General Motors' Corvair had far-reaching effects on autos and other consumer products. Other consumer protection laws emerged from similar processes.

TABLE 4–2	Laws Regulating Competition
Sherman Antitrust Act, 1890	Prohibits monopolies.
Clayton Act, 1914	Prohibits price discrimination, exclusive dealing, and other efforts to restrict competition.
Federal Trade Commission Act, 1914	Created the Federal Trade Commission (FTC) to help enforce antitrust laws.
Robinson–Patman Act, 1936	Bans price discrimination between retailers and wholesalers.
Wheeler–Lea Act, 1938	Prohibits unfair and deceptive acts regardless of whether competition is injured.
McCarran–Ferguson Act, 1944	Exempts the insurance industry from antitrust laws.
Lanham Act, 1946	Protects and regulates brand names, brand marks, trade names, and trademarks.
Celler–Kefauver Act, 1950	Prohibits one corporation from controlling another where the effect is to lessen competition.
Consumer Goods Pricing Act, 1975	Prohibits price maintenance agreements among manufacturers and resellers in interstate commerce.
FTC Improvement Act, 1975	Gives the FTC more power to prohibit unfair industry practices.
Antitrust Improvements Act, 1976	Strengthens earlier antitrust laws—Justice Department has more investigative authority.
Trademark Counterfeiting Act, 1980	Provides penalties for individuals dealing in counterfeit goods.
Trademark Law Revision Act, 1988	Amends the Lanham Act to allow brands not yet introduced to be protected through patent and trademark registration.
Federal Trademark Dilution Act, 1995	Gives trademark owners the right to protect trademarks and requires them to relinquish those that match or parallel existing trademarks.
Digital Millennium Copyright Act, 1998	Refines copyright laws to protect digital versions of copyrighted materials, including music and movies.

In recent years, large groups of people with specific vulnerabilities have been granted special levels of legal protection relative to the general population. For example, the legal status of children and the elderly, defined according to age-related criteria, has received greater attention. American society has responded to research and documentation showing that young consumers and senior citizens encounter difficulties in the acquisition, consumption, and disposition of products. Special legal protection provided to vulnerable consumers is considered to be in the public interest.[11] For example, the Children's Online Privacy Protection Act (COPPA) requires commercial Internet sites to carry privacy policy statements, obtain parental consent before soliciting information from children under the age of 13, and provide an opportunity to remove any information provided by children using such sites. Simply uploading schoolchildren's drawings onto a website can be impacted by COPPA. Any identification through address, names, or license plates requires parental permission. The biggest fine for violating COPPA is $1 million.[12] Critics of COPPA argue that children age 13 and older should not be treated as adults on the Web. In a study of children ages 10 to 17, nearly half indicated that they would give their name, address, and other demographic information in exchange for a gift worth $100 or more. In addition, about half of the teens surveyed would provide information on family cars and their parents' favorite stores in exchange for a free gift. More than 20 percent would reveal their parents' number of sick days, alcohol consumption, weekend hobbies, church attendance—and whether they speed when driving.[13]

TABLE 4-3   Laws Protecting Consumers

Pure Food and Drug Act, 1906	Prohibits adulteration and mislabeling of foods and drugs sold in interstate commerce.
Wool Products Labeling Act, 1939	Prohibits mislabeling of wool products.
Fur Products Labeling Act, 1951	Requires proper identification of the fur content of all products.
Federal Hazardous Substances Labeling Act, 1960	Controls the labeling of hazardous substances for household use.
Truth in Lending Act, 1968	Requires full disclosure of credit terms to purchasers.
Consumer Product Safety Act, 1972	Created the Consumer Product Safety Commission to establish safety standards and regulations for consumer products.
Fair Credit Billing Act, 1974	Requires accurate, up-to-date consumer credit records.
Magnuson–Moss Warranty Act, 1975	Established standards for consumer product warranties.
Energy Policy and Conservation Act, 1975	Requires auto dealers to have "gas mileage guides" in their showrooms.
Consumer Goods Pricing Act, 1975	Prohibits price maintenance agreements.
Consumer Leasing Act, 1976	Requires accurate disclosure of leasing terms to consumers.
Fair Debt Collection Practices Act, 1978	Defines permissible debt collection practices.
Toy Safety Act, 1984	Gives the government the power to recall dangerous toys quickly.
Nutritional Labeling and Education Act, 1990	Prohibits exaggerated health claims and requires all processed foods to have labels showing nutritional information.
Telephone Consumer Protection Act, 1991	Establishes procedures for avoiding unwanted telephone solicitations.
Children's Online Privacy Protection Act, 1998	Requires the FTC to formulate rules for collecting online information from children under age thirteen.
Do Not Call Implementation Act, 2003	Directs the FCC and the FTC to coordinate so that their rules are consistent regarding telemarketing call practices including the Do Not Call Registry and other lists, as well as call abandonment.

The role of the FTC's Bureau of Consumer Protection is to protect consumers against unfair, deceptive, or fraudulent practices. The bureau, which enforces a variety of consumer protection laws, is divided into five divisions. The Division of Enforcement monitors compliance with and investigates violations of laws, including unfulfilled holiday delivery promises by online shopping sites, employment opportunities fraud, scholarship scams, misleading advertising for health-care products, and more.

Laws Promoting Equity and Safety

Laws promoting equity in the workplace were passed during the 1960s and 1970s to protect the rights of minorities, women, older persons, and persons with disabilities; other legislation has sought to protect the safety of all workers (Table 4–4). Of these laws, probably the most important to business is Title VII of the Civil Rights Act, originally passed in 1964 and amended several times since. Title VII specifically prohibits discrimination in employment on the basis of race, sex, religion, color, or national origin. The Civil Rights Act also created the Equal Employment Opportunity Commission (EEOC) to help enforce the provisions of Title VII. Among other things, the EEOC helps businesses design affirmative action programs. These programs aim to increase job

TABLE 4-4 Laws Promoting Equity and Safety	
Equal Pay Act of 1963	Prohibits discrimination in pay on the basis of sex.
Equal Pay Act of 1963 (amended)	Prohibits sex-based discrimination in the rate of pay to men and women working in the same or similar jobs.
Title VII of the Civil Rights Act of 1964 (amended in 1972)	Prohibits discrimination in employment on the basis of race, color, sex, religion, or national origin.
Age Discrimination in Employment Act, 1967	Prohibits discrimination in employment against persons between the ages of 40 and 70.
Occupational Safety and Health Act, 1970	Designed to ensure healthful and safe working conditions for all employees.
Title IX of Education Amendments of 1972	Prohibits discrimination based on sex in education programs or activities that receive federal financial assistance.
Vocational Rehabilitation Act, 1973	Prohibits discrimination in employment because of physical or mental handicaps.
Vietnam Era Veterans Readjustment Act, 1974	Prohibits discrimination against disabled veterans and Vietnam War veterans.
Pension Reform Act, 1974	Designed to prevent abuses in employee retirement, profit-sharing, thrift, and savings plans.
Equal Credit Opportunity Act, 1974	Prohibits discrimination in credit on the basis of sex or marital status.
Age Discrimination Act, 1975	Prohibits discrimination on age in federally assisted programs.
Pregnancy Discrimination Act, 1978	Prohibits discrimination on the basis of pregnancy, childbirth, or related medical conditions.
Immigration Reform and Control Act, 1986	Prohibits employers from knowingly hiring a person who is an unauthorized alien.
Americans with Disabilities Act, 1990	Prohibits discrimination against people with disabilities and requires that they be given the same opportunities as people without disabilities.
Civil Rights Act of 1991	Provides monetary damages in cases of intentional employment discrimination.

opportunities for women and minorities by analyzing the present pool of employees, identifying areas where women and minorities are underrepresented, and establishing specific hiring and promotion goals, along with target dates for meeting those goals.

Other legislation addresses more specific employment practices. The Equal Pay Act of 1963 mandates that women and men who do equal work must receive equal pay. Wage differences are allowed only if they can be attributed to seniority, performance, or qualifications. The Americans with Disabilities Act of 1990 prohibits discrimination against people with disabilities. Despite these laws, inequities in the workplace still exist. According to the U.S. Women's Bureau and National Committee on Pay Equity, women earn 77.8 percent of what men earn.[14] The disparity in wages is even higher for African American, Hispanic, and older women.

Congress has also passed laws that seek to improve safety in the workplace. By far the most significant of these is the Occupational Safety and Health Act of 1970, which mandates that employers provide safe and healthy working conditions for all workers. The **Occupational Safety and Health Administration** (OSHA), which enforces the act, makes regular surprise inspections to ensure that businesses maintain safe working environments.

Even with the passage and enforcement of safety laws, many employees still work in unhealthy or dangerous environments. Safety experts suspect that companies underreport industrial accidents to avoid state and federal inspection and regulation. The current emphasis on increased productivity has been cited as the main reason for the growing number of such accidents. Competitive pressures are also believed to lie behind the increases in manufacturing injuries. Greater turnover in organizations due to downsizing means that employees may have more responsibilities and less experience in their current positions, thus increasing the potential for accidents. They may also be required to work longer hours, perhaps in violation of the law. Wal-Mart, for example, was found guilty of illegally requiring some employees to work unpaid overtime. A class-action lawsuit filed seven years earlier resulted in four Minnesota women winning a class-action lawsuit against Wal-Mart claiming that they were forced to work through breaks without pay and denied meal and rest breaks. Over $54 million was awarded in the lawsuit that covers 100,000 current and past Wal-Mart employees in Minnesota over ten years.[15] An earlier ruling showed that Wal-Mart violated labor laws more than two million times over six years by forcing employees to work "off the clock." Lawsuits in Pennsylvania resulted in workers getting a $78.5 million judgment. In California, where law requires a thirty-minute meal break within the first five hours of a shift or an extra hour's pay, Wal-Mart had a $172 million verdict for denying lunch breaks. Although appealing many of these rulings, Wal-Mart also settled a Colorado lawsuit for $50 million. Some perceive the fines not severe enough for the world's largest retailer who makes roughly $35 million an hour.[16]

Laws Protecting the Environment

Environmental protection laws have been enacted largely in response to concerns over business's impact on the environment, which began to emerge in the 1960s. Many people have questioned the cost–benefit analyses often used in making business decisions. Such analyses try to take into account all factors in a situation, represent them with dollar figures, calculate the costs and benefits of the proposed action, and determine whether an action's benefits outweigh its costs. The problem, however, is that it is difficult to arrive at an accurate monetary valuation of environmental damage or physical pain and injury. In addition, people outside the business world often perceive such analyses as inhumane.

The **Environmental Protection Agency** (EPA) was created in 1970 to coordinate environmental agencies involved in enforcing the nation's environmental laws. The major area of environmental concern relates to air, water, and land pollution. Large corporations are being encouraged to establish pollution-control mechanisms and other policies favorable to the environment. Otherwise, these companies could deplete resources and damage the health and welfare of society by focusing only on their own economic interests. For example, 3M voluntarily stopped making Scotchguard, a successful product for forty years with $300 million in sales, after tests showed that it did not decompose in the environment.[17]

Increases in toxic waste in the air and water, as well as noise pollution, have prompted the passage of a number of laws (Table 4–5). Many environmental protection laws have resulted in the elimination or modification of goods and services. For instance, leaded gasoline was phased out during the 1990s by the EPA because catalytic converters, which reduce pollution caused by automobile emissions and are required by law on most vehicles, do not work properly with leaded gasoline.

TABLE 4-5	Laws Protecting the Environment
Clean Air Act, 1970	Established air-quality standards; requires approved state plans for implementation of the standards.
National Environmental Policy Act, 1970	Established broad policy goals for all federal agencies; created the Council on Environmental Quality as a monitoring agency.
Coastal Zone Management Act, 1972	Provides financial resources to the states to protect coastal zones from overpopulation.
Federal Water Pollution Control Act, 1972	Designed to prevent, reduce, or eliminate water pollution.
Endangered Species Act, 1973	Provides a program for the conservation of threatened and endangered plants and animals and the habitats in which they are found.
Noise Pollution Control Act, 1972	Designed to control the noise emission of certain manufactured items.
Federal Insecticide, Fungicide and Rodenticide Act, 1972	Provides federal control of pesticide distribution, sale, and use.
Safe Drinking Water Act, 1974	Established to protect the quality of drinking water in the United States; focused on all waters actually or potentially designed for drinking use, whether from aboveground or underground sources; established safe standards of purity and required all owners or operators of public water systems to comply with primary (health-related) standards.
Toxic Substances Control Act, 1976	Requires testing and restricts use of certain chemical substances, to protect human health and the environment.
Resource Conservation and Recovery Act, 1976	Gives the EPA authority to control hazardous waste from the "cradle to grave"; includes the generation, transportation, treatment, storage, and disposal of hazardous waste, as well as a framework for the management of nonhazardous waste.
Comprehensive Environmental Response, Compensation, and Liability Act, 1980	Created a tax on chemical and petroleum industries and provides broad federal authority to respond directly to releases or threatened releases of hazardous substances that may endanger public health or the environment.
Emergency Planning and Community Right-to-Know Act, 1986	The national legislation on community safety, designed to help local communities protect public health, safety, and the environment from chemical hazards.
Oil Pollution Act, 1990	Streamlined and strengthened the EPA's ability to prevent and respond to catastrophic oil spills; a trust fund financed by a tax on oil is available to clean up spills when the responsible party is incapable or unwilling to do so.
Pollution Prevention Act, 1990	Focuses industry, government, and public attention on reducing the amount of pollution through cost-effective changes in production, operation, and raw materials use.
Food Quality Protection Act, 1996	Amended the Federal Insecticide, Fungicide and Rodenticide Act and the Federal Food Drug and Cosmetic Act; the requirements included a new safety standard—reasonable certainty of no harm—that must be applied to all pesticides used on foods.

The harmful effects of toxic waste on water life and on leisure industries such as resorts and fishing have raised concerns about proper disposal of these wastes. Few disposal sites meet EPA standards, so businesses must decide what to do with their waste until disposal sites become available. Some firms have solved this problem by illegal or unethical measures: dumping toxic wastes along highways, improperly burying drums containing toxic chemicals, and discarding hazardous waste at sea. For example, a five-year investigation found that ships owned by Royal Caribbean Cruises Ltd.

used "secret bypass pipes" to dump waste oil and hazardous materials overboard, often at night. Justice Department officials accused the company of dumping to save the expense of properly disposing waste at the same time that the cruise line was promoting itself as environmentally friendly. The company ultimately pleaded guilty to twenty-one felony counts, paid $27 million in fines, spent as much as $90,000 per vessel to install new oily water–treatment systems and placed an environmental officer on board each vessel.[18] Congress regularly evaluates legislation to increase the penalties for disposing of toxic wastes in this way. Disposal issues remain controversial because, although everyone acknowledges that the wastes must go somewhere, no community wants them dumped in its own backyard.

One solid-waste problem is the result of rapid innovations in computer hardware, which render machines obsolete after just eighteen months. Today 350 million computers have reached obsolescence, and at least 55 million are expected to end up in landfills.[19] Computers contain such toxic substances as lead, mercury, and polyvinyl chloride, which can leach into the soil and contaminate groundwater when disposed of improperly. Dell Computer has come under increasing criticism from environmental groups for failing to adopt a leadership role in reducing the use of toxic materials in the manufacture of computers and in recycling used computer parts. The company has also encountered criticism for using prison labor to handle the recycling it does do. Several states are considering legislation that would require computers to be recycled at the same levels as in Europe.[20]

THE SARBANES–OXLEY ACT

In 2002, largely in response to widespread corporate accounting scandals, Congress passed the Sarbanes–Oxley Act to establish a system of federal oversight of corporate accounting practices. In addition to making fraudulent financial reporting a criminal offense and strengthening penalties for corporate fraud, the law requires corporations to establish codes of ethics for financial reporting and to develop greater transparency in financial reporting to investors and other stakeholders.[21]

Supported by both Republicans and Democrats, the Sarbanes–Oxley Act was enacted to restore stakeholder confidence after accounting fraud at Enron, WorldCom, and hundreds of other companies resulted in investors and employees losing much of their savings. During the resulting investigations, the public learned that hundreds of corporations had not reported their financial results accurately. Many stakeholders came to believe that accounting firms, lawyers, top executives, and boards of directors had developed a culture of deception to ensure investor approval and gain competitive advantage. Many boards failed to provide appropriate oversight of the decisions of their companies' top officers. At Adelphia Communications, for example, the Rigas family amassed $3.1 billion in off-balance-sheet loans backed by the company. Dennis Kozlowski, CEO of Tyco, was accused of improperly using corporate funds for personal use as well as fraudulent accounting practices.[22] At Kmart, CEO Charles Conaway allegedly hired unqualified executives and consultants for excessive fees. Kmart's board also approved $24 million in loans to various executives, just a month before the retailer filed for Chapter 11 bankruptcy protection. Conaway and the other executives have since left the company or were fired. Loans of this type are now illegal under the Sarbanes–Oxley Act.[23]

As a result of public outrage over the accounting scandals, the Sarbanes–Oxley Act garnered nearly unanimous support not only in Congress but also by government regulatory agencies, the president, and the general public. When President George W. Bush signed the Sarbanes–Oxley Act into law, he emphasized the need for new standards of ethical behavior in business, particularly among the top managers and boards of directors responsible for overseeing business decisions and activities.

At the heart of the Sarbanes–Oxley Act is the **Public Company Accounting Oversight Board,** which monitors accounting firms that audit public corporations and establishes standards and rules for auditors in accounting firms. The law gave the board investigatory and disciplinary power over auditors and securities analysts who issue reports about corporate performance and health. The law attempts to eliminate conflicts of interest by prohibiting accounting firms from providing both auditing and consulting services to the same client companies without special permission from the client firm's audit committee; it also places limits on the length of time lead auditors can serve a particular client. Table 4–6 summarizes the significant provisions of the new law.

TABLE 4–6 Major Provisions of the Sarbanes–Oxley Act

1. Requires the establishment of a Public Company Accounting Oversight Board in charge of regulations administered by the SEC.

2. Requires CEOs and CFOs to certify that their companies' financial statements are true and without misleading statements.

3. Requires that corporate board of directors' audit committees consist of independent members who have no material interests in the company.

4. Prohibits corporations from making or offering loans to officers and board members.

5. Requires codes of ethics for senior financial officers; code must be registered with the SEC.

6. Prohibits accounting firms from providing both auditing and consulting services to the same client without the approval of the client firm's audit committee.

7. Requires company attorneys to report wrongdoing to top managers and, if necessary, to the board of directors; if managers and directors fail to respond to reports of wrongdoing, the attorney should stop representing the company.

8. Mandates "whistle-blower protection" for persons who disclose wrongdoing to authorities.

9. Requires financial securities analysts to certify that their recommendations are based on objective reports.

10. Requires mutual fund managers to disclose how they vote shareholder proxies, giving investors information about how their shares influence decisions.

11. Establishes a ten-year penalty for mail/wire fraud.

12. Prohibits the two senior auditors from working on a corporation's account for more than five years; other auditors are prohibited from working on an account for more than seven years. In other words, accounting firms must rotate individual auditors from one account to another from time to time.

TABLE 4-7	Benefits of the Sarbanes–Oxley Act

1. Greater accountability of top managers and boards of directors to employees, investors, communities, and society

2. Renewed investor confidence

3. Clear explanations by CEOs as to why their compensation package is in the best interest of the company; the loss of some traditional senior-management perks such as company loans; greater disclosures by executives about their own stock trades

4. Greater protection of employee retirement plans

5. Improved information from stock analysts and rating agencies

6. Greater penalties for and accountability of senior managers, auditors, and board members

The Sarbanes–Oxley Act requires corporations to take greater responsibility for their decisions and to provide leadership based on ethical principles. For instance, the law requires top managers to certify that their firms' financial reports are complete and accurate, making CEOs and CFOs personally accountable for the credibility and accuracy of their companies' financial statements. Similar provisions are required of corporate boards of directors, especially audit committees, and senior financial officers are now subject to a code of ethics that addresses their specific areas of risk. Additionally, the law modifies the attorney–client relationship to require lawyers to report wrongdoing to top managers and/or the board of directors. It also provides protection for "whistle-blowing" employees who might report illegal activity to authorities. These provisions provide internal controls to make managers aware of and responsible for legal and ethical problems. Table 4–7 summarizes the benefits of the legislation.

On the other hand, the Sarbanes–Oxley Act has raised a number of concerns. The complex law may impose burdensome requirements on executives; the rules and regulations already run to thousands of pages. Some people also believe that the law will not be sufficient to stop those executives who want to lie, steal, manipulate, or deceive. They believe that a deep commitment to managerial integrity, rather than additional rules and regulations, are the key to solving the current crisis in business.[24] Additionally, the new act has caused many firms to restate their financial reports to avoid penalties. Big public companies spent thousands of hours and an average of $4.4 million each last year to make sure that someone was looking over the shoulder of key accounting personnel at every step of every business process, according to Financial Executives International. Section 404 is a core provision of the 2002 corporate reform law. The number of companies that disclosed serious chinks in their internal accounting controls jumped to more than 586 in 2005 compared to 313 for 2004.[25]

Public Company Accounting Oversight Board

The Sarbanes–Oxley Act establishes an oversight board to oversee the audit of public companies in order to protect the interests of investors and further the public interest in the preparation of informative, accurate, and independent audit reports for companies. Their duties include (1) registration of public accounting firms, (2) establishment of auditing, quality control, ethics, independence and other standards relating to preparation of audit reports, (3) inspection of accounting firms, (4) investigations, disciplinary proceedings, and imposition of sanctions, and (5) enforcement of compliance with accounting rules of the board, professional standards, and securities laws relating to the preparation and issuance of audit reports and obligations and liabilities of accountants.

The board reports to the SEC on an annual basis that includes any new established rules and any final disciplinary rulings. The board works with designated professional groups of accountants and other standard-setting advisory groups in establishing auditing, quality control, ethics, and independence rules.

Conflicts of Interest: Auditor and Analyst Independence

The Sarbanes–Oxley Act also seeks to eliminate conflicts of interest among auditors, security analysts, brokers, and dealers and the public companies they serve in order to ensure enhanced financial disclosures of public companies' true condition. To accomplish auditor independence, Section 201 of the act no longer allows registered public accounting firms to provide both nonaudit and audit services to a public company. National securities exchanges and registered securities associations have already adopted similar conflict-of-interest rules for security analysts, brokers, and dealers, who recommend equities in research reports. The face of Wall Street is experiencing major changes. In early 2003, ten of the nation's largest securities firms agreed to pay a record $1.4 billion to settle government charges involving abuse of investors during the stock market bubble of the late 1990s. Wall Street firms routinely issued overly optimistic stock research to investors in order to gain favor with corporate clients and win their lucrative investment–banking business.

Enhanced Financial Disclosures

With independence, the Sarbanes–Oxley Act is better able to ensure compliance with the enhanced financial disclosures of public companies' true condition. For example, registered public accounting firms are now required to identify all material correcting adjustments to reflect accurate financial statements. Also, all material off-balance-sheet transactions and other relationships with unconsolidated entities that affect current or future financial conditions of a public company must be disclosed in each annual and quarterly financial report. In addition, public companies must also report "on a rapid and current basis" material changes in the financial condition or operations.

Whistle-Blower Protection

Employees of public companies and accounting firms, in general, are also accountable to report unethical behavior. The Sarbanes–Oxley Act intends to motivate employees through whistle-blower protection that would prohibit the employer from taking certain actions against employees who lawfully disclose private employer information to, among others, parties in a judicial proceeding involving a fraud claim. Whistle-blowers are also granted a remedy of special damages and attorney's fees. Two years after the act, the SEC received approximately forty thousand whistle-blowing reports per month, compared with sixty-four hundred per month in 2001.[26] With only eleven thousand publicly-traded companies in the United States, it seems that even though 75 percent of the whistle-blowing reports have no validity, there are still more whistle-blowing reports every month than the number of companies listed.[27]

Also, any act of retaliation that harms informants, including interference with the lawful employment or livelihood of any person, for providing to a law enforcement officer any truthful information relating to the commission or possible commission of any federal offense, will be fined and/or imprisoned for ten years. (Whistle-blowers are discussed in more detail in Chapter 8.)

Corporate and Criminal Fraud Accountability

Title VIII of the Sarbanes–Oxley Act, Corporate and Criminal Fraud Accountability, makes the knowing destruction or creation of documents to "impede, obstruct or influence" any existing or contemplated federal investigation a felony. The White-Collar Crime Penalty Enhancements Act of 2002 increased the maximum penalty for mail and wire fraud from five to ten years in prison. It also makes record tampering or otherwise impeding with any official proceeding a crime. If necessary, the SEC could freeze extraordinary payments to directors, officers, partners, controlling persons, and agents of employees. The U.S. Sentencing Commission reviews sentencing guidelines for securities and accounting fraud.

The act may not prevent future Enron-type businesses from occurring. However, the act's uniqueness from past legislation is its perspective to mandate accountability from the many players in the "game of business," creating more explicit rules in playing fair. The act creates a foundation to strongly discourage wrongdoing and sets ethical standards of what's expected of American business.

Cost of Compliance

The national cost of compliance of the Sarbanes–Oxley Act is estimated at $1 million per $1 billion in revenues.[28] For many companies, this means the cost of compliance is in excess of $10 million annually.[29] The average total cost for only the first year of Section 404 compliance is $4.36 million. These costs come from internal costs, external costs, and auditor fees. In a survey by Financial Executives International, nearly all the respondents (94 percent) said that the costs of compliance exceeded the benefits.[30] This act has increased external auditing costs for mid- to large-size companies between 52 and 81 percent. The section that has caused the most cost for companies has been compliance with Section 404. Section 404 has three central issues: It requires that (1) management create reliable internal financial controls, (2) that management attest to the reliability of those controls and the accuracy of financial statements that result from those controls, and (3) an independent auditor to further attest to the statements made by management. Section 404 requires companies to document both the results of financial transactions and the processes they have used to generate them. A company may have thousands of processes that may work, but they have never been written down. Writing down the processes is time consuming and costly.[31] Also, because the cost of compliance is so high for many small companies, some publicly traded companies are even considering delisting themselves from the U.S. Stock Exchange. Companies based outside the United States have also been weighing the costs of compliance versus the savings of deregistration. Sweden-based Electrolux was among the first to delist from NASDAQ after the Sarbanes–Oxley Act was passed. Many new non-U.S. companies may be avoiding the U.S. market altogether. New listings with the SEC from companies outside the United States have dropped to almost zero since the act passed in 2002.[32]

However, there are some cases where companies are benefiting from the act's implementation. Apart from the obvious increase in books and materials to help people comply with the act, there is also a growing business for people teaching and implementing ethics programs and hot lines for organizations. Companies such as EthicsPoint and LRN have grown rapidly as companies rush to learn ethics virtually overnight; as they do, a vast new industry of consultants and suppliers has emerged.[33] Other benefits and savings have come in the form of increased efficiency as companies such as Pitney Bowes Inc. find that they can meld various units such as combining four accounts-receivable offices into one, saving more than $500,000 a year. At Genentech Inc., simply having detailed reports on financial controls sped up installation, by several months, of a new computer system that consolidates financial data, which meant that they were running months ahead of schedule. The new system allows managers to analyze data from customers rather than just collecting it. Cisco spent $50 million and two hundred and forty thousand hours on its first-year audit of internal controls. The mind-numbing effort revealed opportunities to streamline steps for ordering products and services, making it easier for customers to do business with Cisco. It forced them to make sure that sales and support were integrated when a customer called, resulting in one-stop shopping for their customers. Other companies have been able to streamline steps for ordering products and services, making it easier for customers to do business with them.[34]

LAWS THAT ENCOURAGE ETHICAL CONDUCT

Violations of the law usually begin when businesspeople stretch the limits of ethical standards, as defined by company or industry codes of conduct, and then choose to engage in schemes that knowingly or unwittingly violate the law. In recent years, new laws and regulations have been passed to discourage such decisions—and to foster programs designed to improve business ethics and social responsibility (Table 4–8). The most important of these are the FSGO and the Sarbanes–Oxley Act. One of the goals of both acts is to require employees to report observed misconduct. The development of reporting systems has advanced with most companies having some method for employees to report observed misconduct. While reported misconduct is up, a sizable percentage of employees still do not report misconduct, as Figure 4–3 shows.

TABLE 4–8	Institutionalization of Ethics Through Laws

1991   *Organizational Sentencing Guidelines created.* These guidelines, added to the FSGO, created organizational responsibility for employee conduct. Sentences and fines are lessened for organizations with ethics programs. Firms that fail to take due diligence actions to prevent misconduct are given stricter sentences or fines.

2002   *Sarbanes–Oxley Act passed.* Companies now must create an independent board audit committee, a code of conduct and ethics policies, whistle-blower hot lines, and annual reports on effectiveness of financial reporting systems. CEOs and CFOs must sign off on the accuracy of financial statements. The act directs that Organizational Sentencing Guidelines be reviewed and amended. Penalties: up to $5 million and twenty years in prison.

2004   *Organizational Sentencing Guidelines stiffened.* In accord with the Sarbanes–Oxley Act, guidelines are revised so that organizations are held to a stiffer definition of an effective ethics program in order to receive lenient treatment for offenses. Directors and executives must assume responsibility for such programs, identify areas of risk, train officials in ethics, create an ethics hot line, designate an individual to oversee ethics, and give that person sufficient authority and resources to do the job. Companies must also create a corporate culture that encourages ethics.

SOURCE: Adapted from James C. Hyatt, "Birth of the Ethics Industry," *Business Ethics,* Summer 2005, p. 27. Reprinted with permission of Business Ethics.

FIGURE 4–3	Percentage of Employees Who Still DO NOT Report Observed Misconduct

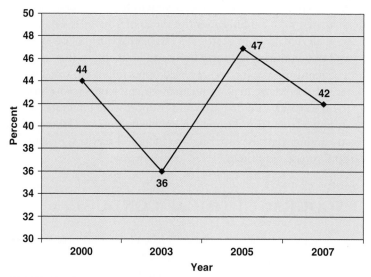

SOURCE: *2007 National Business Ethics Survey*, p. 17.

FEDERAL SENTENCING GUIDELINES FOR ORGANIZATIONS

As mentioned in Chapter 1, Congress passed the FSGO in 1991 to create an incentive for organizations to develop and implement programs designed to foster ethical and legal compliance. These guidelines, which were developed by the U.S. Sentencing Commission, apply to all felonies and class A misdemeanors committed by employees in association with their work. As an incentive, organizations that have demonstrated due diligence in developing effective compliance programs that discourage unethical and illegal conduct may be subject to reduced organizational penalties if an employee commits a crime.[35] Overall, the government philosophy is that legal violations can be prevented through organizational values and a commitment to ethical conduct.

The commission delineated seven steps that companies must implement to demonstrate due diligence:

1. A firm must develop and disseminate a code of conduct that communicates required standards and identifies key risk areas for the organization.
2. High-ranking personnel in the organization who are known to abide by the legal and ethical standards of the industry (such as an ethics officer, vice president of human resources, general counsel, and so forth) must have oversight over the program.
3. No one with a known propensity to engage in misconduct should be put in a position of authority.
4. A communications system for disseminating standards and procedures (ethics training) must also be put into place.
5. Organizational communications should include a way for employees to report misconduct without fearing retaliation, such as an anonymous toll-free hot line or an ombudsman. Monitoring and auditing systems designed to detect misconduct are also required.
6. If misconduct is detected, then the firm must take appropriate and fair disciplinary action. Individuals both directly and indirectly responsible for the offense should be disciplined. In addition, the sanctions should be appropriate for the offense.
7. After misconduct has been discovered, the organization must take steps to prevent similar offenses in the future. This usually involves making modifications to the ethical compliance program, additional employee training, and issuing communications about specific types of conduct.

The government expects these seven steps for compliance programs to undergo continuous improvement and refinement.[36]

These steps are based on the commission's determination to emphasize compliance programs and to provide guidance for both organizations and courts regarding program effectiveness. Organizations have flexibility about the type of program they develop; the seven steps are not a checklist requiring that legal procedures be followed to gain certification of an effective program. Organizations implement the guidelines through effective core practices that are appropriate for their firms. The program must be capable of reducing the opportunity that employees have to engage in misconduct.

A 2005 Supreme Court decision held that the sentences for violations of law were not mandatory but should serve only as recommendations for judges to use in their decisions. Some legal and business experts believe that this decision might weaken the implementation of the FSGO, but as shown in Table 4–9, most sentences have remained in the same range as before the Supreme Court decision. The guidelines remain an important consideration in developing an effective ethics and compliance program.

A 2004 amendment to the FSGO requires that a business's governing authority be well informed about its ethics program with respect to content, implementation, and

TABLE 4–9	Recent Changes in Organizational Sentencing

After the U.S. Supreme Court ruled that exact sentences were not mandatory and gave judges more latitude in 2005, most judges continued to use sentences within the range of the sentencing guidelines.

62%	Sentences within the range of the sentencing guidelines; compares with 68% in previous four years, when guidelines were mandatory
24%	Sentences cut below the guidelines at the government's request; unchanged from previous four years
7.8%	Sentences cut at least in part as a result of the Court's decision

SOURCE: U.S. Sentencing Commission Special Post-Booker Coding Project, as referenced in *Forbes,* January 30, 2006, 48.

effectiveness. This places the responsibility squarely on the shoulders of the firm's leadership, usually the board of directors. The board must ensure that there is a high-ranking manager accountable for the day-to-day operational oversight of the ethics program. The board must provide for adequate authority, resources, and access to the board or an appropriate subcommittee of the board. The board must ensure that there are confidential mechanisms available so that the organization's employees and agents may report or seek guidance about potential or actual misconduct without fear of retaliation. Finally, the board is required to oversee the discovery of risks and to design, implement, and modify approaches to deal with those risks. Figure 4–4 provides an overview from NBES about how well prepared employees are to respond to various ethical and legal risk. Over three-quarters of employees who encounter risk feel adequately prepared to respond. If board members do not understand the nature, purpose, and methods available to implement an ethics program, the firm is at risk of inadequate oversight in the event of ethical misconduct that escalates into a scandal.[37]

The Department of Justice, through the Thompson Memo (Larry Thompson, deputy attorney general, 2003 memo to U.S. Attorneys), advanced general principles

FIGURE 4–4	Employees Preparation to Respond to Risk

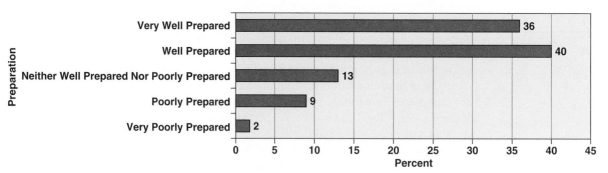

SOURCE: National Business Ethics Survey, *How Employees View Ethics in Their Organizations 1994–2005* (Washington, DC: Ethics Resource Center, 2005), 39.

to consider in cases involving corporate wrongdoing. This memo makes it clear that ethics and compliance programs are important to detect types of misconduct most likely to occur in a particular corporation's line of business. Without an effective ethics and compliance program to detect ethical and legal lapses, the firm should not be treated leniently. Also, the prosecutor generally has wide latitude in determining when, whom, and whether to prosecute violations of federal law. U.S. Attorneys are directed that charging for even minor misconduct may be appropriate when the wrongdoing was pervasive by a large number of employees in a particular role—for example, sales staff, procurement officers—or was condoned by upper management. Without an effective program to identify an isolated rogue employee involved in misconduct, serious consequences can be associated with regulatory issues, enforcement, and sentencing.[38] Therefore, there is general agreement both from laws and administrative policy that an effective ethics and compliance program is necessary to prevent conduct and reduce the legal consequences.

HIGHLY APPROPRIATE CORE PRACTICES

The FSGO and the Sarbanes–Oxley Act provide incentives for developing core practices that help ensure ethical and legal compliance. Core practices move the emphasis from a focus on individuals' moral capability to developing structurally sound organization core practices and developing structural integrity for both financial performance and nonfinancial performance. Although the Sarbanes–Oxley Act provides standards for financial performance, most ethical issues relate to nonfinancial issues such as marketing, human resource management, and customer relationships. Abusive behavior, lying, and conflict of interest are still the top three ethical issues.

The Integrity Institute has developed an integrated model to standardize the measurement of nonfinancial performance. Methodologies have been developed to assess communications, compensation, social responsibility, corporate culture, leadership, risk, and stakeholder perceptions, as well as more subjective aspects of earnings, corporate governance, technology, and other important nonfinancial areas. The model exists to establish a standard that can predict sustainability and success of an organization. The Integrity Institute uses the measurement to an established standard as the basis of certification of integrity.[39]

The majority of executives and board members want to measure nonfinancial performance, but no standards currently exist. The Open Compliance Ethics Group (oceg.org) has developed benchmarking studies available to organizations to conduct self-assessments to develop ethics program elements. Developing organizational systems and processes is a requirement of the regulatory environment, but organizations are given considerable freedom in developing ethics and compliance programs. Core practices do exist and can be identified in every industry. Trade associations self-regulatory groups and research studies often provide insights about the expected best core practices. The most important is for each firm to assess its legal and ethical risk areas and then develop structures to prevent, detect, and quickly correct any misconduct.

TABLE 4–10	Key Findings from the Open Compliance Ethics Group Benchmarking Survey
Crisis Can Help the Cause	Companies that have experienced reputation damage in the past see themselves as much further along in terms of program maturity and in relation to their peers—both today and in the future.
Pay Now or Pay Later	Companies that have experienced reputation damage invest *three* times more than their nondamaged peers in specific compliance and ethics processes.
Preference for Proactive and Values-Based Programs	Compliance and ethics programs are becoming more proactive and values based, allowing companies to prevent ethical and compliance violations before they become a crisis.
Proactive Skills Training May Need More Emphasis	To reach the objective of more proactive programs, companies must provide training to the people who are accountable for the compliance and ethics program—training that focuses on more proactive disciplines.
Set/Align Objectives for More Benefit	Companies that set explicit objectives for their compliance and ethics programs rate the benefits of their programs more highly and ascribe them more than companies that do not set explicit objectives.
Integrate/Cooperate for More Benefit	Additional benefits and performance can be realized when an organization integrates the compliance and ethics program with other aspects of the enterprise and when the program has a good working relationship with other business functions/processes.
Experience	Of the companies in this study, 54% have implemented a compliance and ethics program relatively recently (within the last five years). *Zero* companies in this study with a program in place for ten years or more experienced highly visible reputation damage in the last five years, a testament to the important impact these programs can have over time.

SOURCE: Open Compliance Ethics Group 2005 Benchmarking Study Key Findings, http://www.oceg.org/view/Benchmarking2005 (accessed January 14, 2009). Reprinted with permission.

Consider McDonald's approach to answering critics about nutritional guidance. It announced a move to provide nutritional information on its product packaging worldwide. Nutrient information will be featured on its packaging across 20,000 of its 31,561 restaurants around the world. Mike Roberts, the president and chief operating officer for McDonald's, said, "There is nothing more important to McDonald's than building customer trust and loyalty around the world. We know how important transparency is, which is what this initiative is all about." McDonald's also introduced a "Balanced Lifestyles" initiative for kids, which involved offering healthier menu options, promoting physical activity, and providing more nutritional information to its customers about its products. In 2004 it withdrew its supersize meals after a damaging portrayal of the company in the film *Super Size Me*. The product sizes available at McDonald's are small, medium, and large, but upgrading to a bigger-portion size remains cheap.[40]

Table 4–10 provides some general findings from the 2005 OCEG benchmarking survey that provides insights on effective core practices.

Philanthropic Contributions

Philanthropic issues are another dimension of voluntary social responsibility and relate to business's contributions to stakeholders. Philanthropy provides four major benefits to society:

1. Philanthropy improves the quality of life and helps make communities places where people want to do business, raise families, and enjoy life. Thus, improving the quality of life in a community makes it easier to attract and retain employees and customers.
2. Philanthropy reduces government involvement by providing assistance to stakeholders.
3. Philanthropy develops employee leadership skills. Many firms, for example, use campaigns by the United Way and other community service organizations as leadership- and skill-building exercises for their employees.
4. Philanthropy helps create an ethical culture and the values that can act as a buffer to organizational misconduct.[41]

The most common way that businesses demonstrate philanthropy is through donations to local and national charitable organizations. Corporations gave more than $12 billion to environmental and social causes in 2004.[42] Wells Fargo & Company, for example, contributed $93 million to fifteen thousand different organizations. It helped finance the construction of single-family homes on or near Native American reservations in seven states, bringing private mortgage capital to those historically denied access.[43] Indeed, many companies have become concerned about the quality of education in the United States after realizing that the current pool of prospective employees lacks many basic work skills. Recognizing that today's students are tomorrow's employees and customers, firms such as Kroger, Campbell Soup Company, Eastman Kodak, American Express, Apple Computer, Xerox, and Coca-Cola have donated money, equipment, and employee time to help improve schools in their communities and throughout the nation.

Wal-Mart donated more than $200 million in 2005 to help charities and organizations throughout the United States. More than 90 percent of the contributions were directed at the local level. The Chronicle of Philanthropy recognized Wal-Mart as the largest corporate cash contributor in America. They helped more than one hundred thousand charitable organizations around the country and gave back $547,945 each day. The money supported a variety of causes such as child development, education, the environment, and disaster relief. Wal-Mart feels that they can make the greatest impact on communities by supporting issues and causes that are important to their customers and associates in their own neighborhoods. Wal-Mart relies on their own associates to know which organizations are the most important to their hometowns, and they empower them to determine how money will be spent in their communities. Wal-Mart supports charities such as the American Cancer Society and The Salvation Army, as well as helping out soldiers wounded in Iraq and donating more than $2.5 million to tsunami relief efforts. After Hurricane Katrina, Wal-Mart donated more than $17 million in cash to help the victims of the hurricane, as well as donating much needed supplies right after the disaster. By supporting communities at the local level, it encourages customer loyalty and goodwill.[44]

Strategic Philanthropy

Tying philanthropic giving to overall strategy and objectives is also known as strategic philanthropy. **Strategic philanthropy** is the synergistic and mutually beneficial use of an organization's core competencies and resources to deal with key stakeholders so as to bring about organizational and societal benefits. For example, last year Bisto, a staple of Britain's meal tables since 1908 with its instant gravy, launched a new marketing campaign. The focus was on families trying to eat one meal together a week. Bisto called it "ahh nights" based on its long time marketing slogan of "ahh . . . Bisto." Families eat fewer and fewer meals together; this has been identified by social policy experts as playing a key role in a wide range of social problems such as teenage drug abuse, sexual promiscuity, teenage pregnancy, crime, antisocial behavior, truancy, and poor academic performance. Bisto used the new marketing slogan to extol the virtues of eating together as a family while explicitly recognizing the challenges of doing this in the modern world. It used a website www.aahnight.co.uk to make it easy for families to have a meal together at least once a week. It used three steps: (1) Download a contract that families can sign and stick on the refrigerator; (2) invite the family or friends by e-mail; (3) make a delicious meal with recipes provided using—you guessed it—Bisto.[45]

Founder's Week, McDonald's annual celebration of company founder Ray Kroc's birthday, focuses on giving back to local communities. Last year, McDonald's employees nationwide participated in twenty-five thousand hours of community service, including tutoring children, painting classrooms, planting trees and shrubs, constructing homes with Habitat for Humanity, and assisting families and children at Ronald McDonald Houses across the country.[46]

Home Depot directs much of the money it spends on philanthropy to affordable housing, at-risk youth, the environment, and disaster recovery. Through Team Depot, an organized volunteer force of Home Depot, more than 6 million hours of volunteer community service is contributed annually. Together with Habitat for Humanity, Home Depot and its associates have built more than 150 affordable homes across the country. Home Depot has been supporting Habitat for Humanity since 1989 with donations and volunteers to build affordable housing for people in need of adequate shelter, and in Canada, Home Depot donates its unsold merchandise to Habitat for Humanity.[47] Through its partnership with "Rebuilding Together with Christmas in April," they have helped renovate more than twenty thousand homes in over 230 communities nationwide.[48]

SUMMARY

To understand the institutionalization of business ethics, it is important to understand the voluntary and legally mandated dimensions of organizational practices. Core practices are documented best practices, often encouraged by legal and regulatory forces as well as industry trade associations. The effective organizational practice of business ethics requires all three dimensions to be integrated into an ethics and compliance program. This creates an ethical culture that can effectively manage the risks of misconduct. Institutionalization in business ethics relates to established laws, customs, and expected organizational programs that are considered normative in establishing reputation. Institutions provide requirements, structure, and societal expectations to reward and sanction ethical decision making. In this way, society is institutionalizing core practices and provides organizations the opportunity to take their own approach, only taking action if there are violations.

Laws and regulations are established by governments to set minimum standards for responsible behavior—society's codification of what is right and wrong. Civil and criminal laws regulating business conduct are passed because society—including consumers, interest groups, competitors, and legislators—believes that business must comply with society's standards. Such laws regulate competition, protect consumers, promote safety and equity in the workplace, protect the environment, and provide incentives for preventing misconduct.

In 2002, largely in response to widespread corporate accounting scandals, Congress passed the Sarbanes–Oxley Act to establish a system of federal oversight of corporate accounting practices. In addition to making fraudulent financial reporting a criminal offense and strengthening penalties for corporate fraud, the law requires corporations to establish codes of ethics for financial reporting and to develop greater transparency in financial reporting to investors and other stakeholders. The Sarbanes–Oxley Act requires corporations to take greater responsibility for their decisions and to provide leadership based on ethical principles. For instance, the law requires top managers to certify that their firms' financial reports are complete and accurate, making CEOs and CFOs personally accountable for the credibility and accuracy of their companies' financial statements. The act establishes an oversight board to oversee the audit of public companies in order to protect the interests of investors and further the public interest in the preparation of informative, accurate, and independent audit reports for companies.

Congress passed the Federal Sentencing Guidelines for Organizations (FSGO) in 1991 to create an incentive for organizations to develop and implement programs designed to foster ethical and legal compliance. These guidelines, which were developed by the U.S. Sentencing Commission, apply to all felonies and class A misdemeanors committed by employees in association with their work. As an incentive, organizations that have demonstrated due diligence in developing effective compliance programs that discourage unethical and illegal conduct may be subject to reduced organizational penalties if an employee commits a crime.[49] Overall, the government philosophy is that legal violations can be prevented through organizational values and a commitment to ethical conduct. A 2004 amendment to the FSGO requires that a business's governing authority be well informed about its ethics program with respect to content, implementation, and effectiveness. This places the responsibility squarely on the shoulders of the firm's leadership, usually the board of directors. The board must ensure that there is a high-ranking manager accountable for the day-to-day operational oversight of the ethics program. The board must provide for adequate authority, resources, and access to the board or an appropriate subcommittee of the board. The board must ensure that there are confidential mechanisms available so that the organization's employees and agents may report or seek guidance about potential or actual misconduct without fear of retaliation.

The FSGO and the Sarbanes–Oxley Act provide incentives for developing core practices that help ensure ethical and legal compliance. Core practices move the emphasis from a focus on the individual's moral capability to developing structurally sound organization core practices and develop structural integrity for both financial performance and nonfinancial performance. The Integrity Institute has developed an integrated model to standardize the measurement of nonfinancial performance.

Methodologies have been developed to assess communications, compensation, social responsibility, corporate culture, leadership, risk, and stakeholder perceptions, as well as more subjective aspects of earnings, corporate governance, technology, and other important non-financial areas.

Philanthropic issues touch on businesses' social responsibility insofar as businesses contribute to the local community and to society. Philanthropy provides four major benefits to society: improving the quality of life, reducing government involvement, developing staff leadership skills, and building staff morale. Companies contribute significant amounts of money to education, the arts, environmental causes, and the disadvantaged by supporting local and national charitable organizations. Strategic philanthropy involves linking core business competencies to societal and community needs.

IMPORTANT TERMS FOR REVIEW	voluntary practices
	philanthropy
	core practices
	Better Business Bureau
	mandated boundaries
	civil law
	criminal law
	procompetitive legislation
		consumer protection law
		Occupational Safety and Health
		    Administration
		Environmental Protection Agency
		Public Company Accounting Oversight
		    Board
		strategic philanthropy

RESOLVING ETHICAL BUSINESS CHALLENGES*

Albert Chen was sweating profusely in his Jaguar on the expressway as he thought about his options and the fact that Christmas and the Chinese New Year were at hand. He and his wife, Mary, who were on their way to meet Albert's parents at New York's John F. Kennedy Airport, seemed to be looking up from an abyss, with no daylight to be seen. Several visits and phone calls from various people had engulfed both him and Mary.

He had graduated with honors in finance and had married Mary in his senior year. They had both obtained prestigious brokerage jobs in the New York area, and both had been working killer hours to develop their accounts. Listening to other brokers, both had learned that there were some added expenses to their professions. For example, they were told that brokers need to "look" and "act" successful. So Albert and Mary bought the appropriate clothes and

cars, joined the right clubs, and ate at the right restaurants with the right people. They also took the advice of others, which was to identify the "players" of large corporations at parties and take mental notes. "You'd be surprised at what information you hear with a little alcohol in these people," said one broker. Both started using this strategy, and five months later their clients began to see significant profits in their portfolios.

Their good luck even came from strange places. For example, Albert had an uncle whose work as a janitor gave him access to many law offices that had information on a number of companies, especially those about to file for bankruptcy. Mary and Albert were able to use information provided by this uncle to benefit their clients' portfolios. The uncle even had some of his friends use Albert. To Albert's surprise, his uncle's friends often had nest eggs in excess of $200,000. Because some of these friends were quite elderly, Albert was given permission to buy and sell nonrisky stocks at will.

Because both of them were earning good salaries, the Chens soon managed to invest in the market themselves, and their investments included stock in the company for which Mary's father worked. After eighteen months, Albert decided to jump ship and start working for Jarvis, Sunni, Lamar & Morten (JSL&M). JSL&M's reputation was that of a fast mover in the business. "We go up to the line and then measure how wide the line is so that we know how far we can go into it," was a common remark at the brokerage firm.

About six months ago, Mary's father, who was with a major health-care company, commented that the management team was running the company into the ground. "If only someone could buy the company and put in a good management team," he mused. After the conversation, Mary investigated the company and discovered that the stock was grossly undervalued. She made a few phone calls and found a company that was interested in doing a hostile takeover. Mary also learned from her father that if a new management were acceptable to the union, the union would do everything in its power to oust the old management—by striking, if necessary—and welcome the new one. As things started to materialize, Mary told several of her best clients, who in turn did very well on the stock. This increased her status in the firm, which kept drawing bigger clients.

Albert soon became a player in initial public stock offerings (IPOs) of new companies. Occasionally, when Albert saw a very hot IPO, he would talk to some of his best venture-capital friends, who then bought the IPOs and gained some very good returns. This strategy helped attract some larger players in the market. By this point in his young career, Albert had made a great many friends.

One of those friends was Barry, who worked on the stock floor. As they were talking, Barry mentioned that if Albert wanted to, he, as a favor, when placing orders to buy shares, would occasionally put Albert's or Mary's trade before the client order.

The first sign of trouble came when Mary told Albert about what was happening at her office. "I'm getting e-mail from some of the brokers with off-color jokes and even some nude photos of women and men. I just don't care for it."

"So what are you doing about it?" Albert asked.

"Well, I've just started not even opening my messages if they come from these people," Mary replied.

"What about messages that request that you send them on? What do you do with those?" queried Albert.

"I just e-mail them along without looking at them," was her response.

"This isn't good, Mary. A couple of analysts were just fired for doing that at a big firm last week," said Albert.

Several weeks later the people who were sending Mary the obnoxious messages were fired. Mary was also asked to see the head of her division. When she came to his office, he said, "Please shut the door, Mary. I have some bad news. I know that you weren't involved with what was happening with the e-mail scandal; however, you did forward messages that contained such material. As a result, I have no alternative but to give you your two weeks' notice. I know this is unfair, but I have my orders. Because of this mess, the SEC wants to check all your trades for the last eight months. It seems to be a formality, but it will take time, and as you well know, the chances of going to another firm with that hanging over your head are slim. I'm sorry that it's only two months until the holidays." That night Mary fell into a depression.

To exacerbate the situation, Albert's parents were flying in from the People's Republic of China. They were not happy with Albert's marriage to a white woman, but they had consoled themselves that Mary had a good job. They had also said that if things should go badly for them in New York, they could always come to the parents' retirement home in Taiwan. However, the idea of leaving the United States, attempting to learn Mandarin, and raising children in an unfamiliar culture did not appeal to Mary.

Albert was also having some problems. Because their income was cut in half, Albert tried to make up for the loss by trading in some high-risk markets, such as commodities and precious metals. However, many of these investments turned sour, and he found himself buying and selling more and more to pull his own portfolio, as well as those of his clients, into the black. He was getting worried because some of his uncle's friends' portfolios were losing significant value. Other matters, however, were causing him even more anxiety. The previous week, Barry had called him, asking for some inside information on several companies that he was working with for an IPO. Albert knew that this could be construed as insider information and had said no.

Today, Barry called again and said, "Look, Al, I've been doing you favors for a while. I need to score big because of the holidays. You probably don't know, but what I've been doing for you could be construed as spinning, which is not looked upon favorably. I'm not asking for the IPO information—I'm demanding it. Is that clear enough for you, Al? E-mail it over by tomorrow morning." Then Barry hung up.

An hour later Albert's supervisor came in and said, "Al, I need a favor from you. I want you to buy some stock for a few friends and me. When it goes to $112, I want you to sell it. We'll pay the taxes and give you a little bonus for Christmas as well. I want you to buy tomorrow as soon as the market opens. Here are the account numbers for the transaction. I must run. See you tomorrow."

QUESTIONS • EXERCISES

1. Identify the ethical and legal issues of which Albert needs to be aware.
2. Discuss the advantages and disadvantages of each decision that Albert could make and has made.
3. Identify the pressures that have brought about these issues.

*This case is strictly hypothetical; any resemblance to real persons, companies, or situations is coincidental.

Check Your EQ

Check your EQ, or Ethics Quotient, by completing the following. Assess your performance to evaluate your overall understanding of the chapter material.

1.	Voluntary practices include documented best practices.	**Yes**	**No**
2.	The primary method for resolving business ethics disputes is through the criminal court system.	**Yes**	**No**
3.	The FSGO provides an incentive for organizations to conscientiously develop and implement ethics programs.	**Yes**	**No**
4.	The Sarbanes–Oxley Act encourages CEOs and CFOs to report their financial statements accurately.	**Yes**	**No**
5.	Strategic philanthropy represents a new direction in corporate giving that maximizes the benefit to societal or community needs and relates to business objectives.	**Yes**	**No**

ANSWERS: 1. No. Core practices are documented best practices. 2. No. Lawsuits and civil litigation are the primary way in which business ethics disputes are resolved. 3. Yes. Well-designed ethics and compliance programs can minimize legal liability when organizational misconduct is detected. 4. No. The Sarbanes–Oxley Act *requires* CEOs and CFOs to accurately report their financial statements to a federal oversight committee; they must sign the document and are held personally liable for any inaccuracies. 5. Yes. Strategic philanthropy helps society both the organization.

The Decision-Making Process

CHAPTER 5

Ethical Decision Making and Ethical Leadership

Bill Church was in a bind. A recent graduate of a prestigious business school, he had taken a job in the auditing division of Greenspan & Company, a fast-growing leader in the accounting industry. Greenspan relocated Bill, his wife, and their 1-year-old daughter from the Midwest to the East Coast. On arriving, they bought their first home and a second car. Bill was told that the company had big plans for him. Thus, he did not worry about being financially overextended.

Several months into the job, Bill found that he was working late into the night to complete his auditing assignments. He realized that the company did not want its clients billed for excessive hours and that he needed to become more efficient if he wanted to move up in the company. He asked one of his friends, Ann, how she managed to be so efficient in auditing client records.

Ann quietly explained: "Bill, there are times when being efficient isn't enough. You need to do what is required to get ahead. The partners just want results—they don't care how you get them."

"I don't understand," said Bill.

"Look," Ann explained, "I had the same problem you have a few years ago, but Mr. Reed [the manager of the auditing department] explained that everyone 'eats time' so that the group shows top results and looks good. And when the group looks good, everyone in it looks good. No one cares if a little time gets lost in the shuffle."

Bill realized that "eating time" meant not reporting all the hours required to complete a project. He also remembered one of Reed's classic catch phrases, "results, results, results." He thanked Ann for her input and went back to work. Bill thought of going over Reed's head and asking for advice from the division manager, but he had met her only once and did not know anything about her.

QUESTIONS • EXERCISES

1. What should Bill do?
2. Describe the process through which Bill might attempt to resolve his dilemma.
3. Consider the impact of this company's approach on young accountants. How could working long hours be an ethical problem?

*This case is strictly hypothetical; any resemblance to real persons, companies, or situations is coincidental.

To improve ethical decision making in business, one must first understand how individuals make ethical decisions in an organizational environment. Too often it is assumed that individuals in organizations make ethical decisions in the same way that they make ethical decisions at home, in their family, or in their personal lives. Within the context of an organizational work group, however, few individuals have the freedom to decide ethical issues independent of organizational pressures.

This chapter summarizes our current knowledge of ethical decision making in business and provides insights into ethical decision making in organizations. Although it is impossible to describe exactly how any one individual or work group might make ethical decisions, we can offer generalizations about average or typical behavior patterns within organizations. These generalizations are based on many studies and at least six ethical decision models that have been widely accepted by academics and practitioners.[1] Based on these models, we present a framework for understanding ethical decision making in the context of business organizations. In addition to business, this framework integrates concepts from philosophy, psychology, and sociology, and organizational behavior.

A FRAMEWORK FOR ETHICAL DECISION MAKING IN BUSINESS

As Figure 5–1 shows, our model of the ethical decision-making process in business includes ethical-issue intensity, individual factors, and organizational factors such as corporate culture and opportunity. All of these interrelated factors influence the evaluations of and intentions behind the decisions that produce ethical or unethical behavior.

Ethical-Issue Intensity

The first step in ethical decision making is to recognize that an ethical issue requires an individual or work group to choose among several actions that various stakeholders inside or outside the firm will ultimately evaluate as right or wrong. The intensity of an ethical issue relates to its perceived importance to the decision maker.[2] **Ethical-issue intensity,** then, can be defined as the relevance or importance of an ethical issue in the eyes of the individual, work group, and/or organization. It is personal and temporal in character to accommodate values, beliefs, needs, perceptions, the special characteristics of the situation, and the personal pressures prevailing at a particular place and time.[3] Senior employees and those with administrative authority contribute significantly to intensity because they typically dictate an organization's stance on ethical issues. In fact, under current law, managers can be held liable for the unethical and illegal

---

FIGURE 5–1   Framework for Understanding Ethical Decision Making in Business

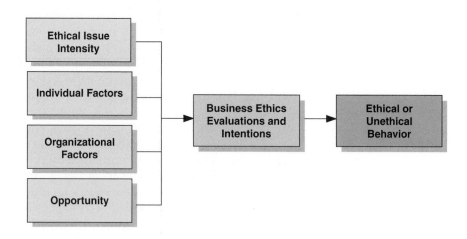

actions of subordinates. In the United States, the Federal Sentencing Guidelines for Organizations have a liability formula that judges those who are in positions of authority in regard to their action or inaction regarding the unethical and illegal activities of those around them. For example, many of the Enron employees and managers who were aware of the firm's use of off-balance-sheet partnerships—which turned out to be the major cause of the energy firm's collapse—were advised that these partnerships were legal, so they did not perceive them as an ethical issue. Although such partnerships were in fact legal at that time, the way that some Enron officials designed them and the methods they used to provide collateral (that is, Enron stock) created a scheme that brought about the collapse of the company.[4] Thus, ethical-issue intensity involves individuals' cognitive state of concern about an issue, whether or not they have knowledge that an issue is unethical, which indicates their involvement in making choices.

Ethical-issue intensity reflects the ethical sensitivity of the individual or work group that faces the ethical decision-making process. Research suggests that individuals are subject to six "spheres of influence" when confronted with ethical choices—the workplace, family, religion, legal system, community, and profession—and that the level of importance of each of these influences will vary depending on how important the decision maker perceives the issue to be.[5] Additionally, the individual's sense of the situation's moral intensity increases the individual's perceptiveness regarding ethical problems, which in turn reduces his or her intention to act unethically.[6] **Moral intensity** relates to a person's perception of social pressure and the harm the decision will have on others.[7] All other factors in Figure 5–1, including individual factors, organizational factors, and intentions, determine why different individuals perceive ethical issues differently. Unless individuals in an organization share common concerns about ethical issues, the stage is set for ethical conflict. The perception of ethical-issue intensity can be influenced by management's use of rewards and punishments, corporate policies, and corporate values to sensitize employees. In other words, managers can affect the degree to which employees perceive the importance of an ethical issue through positive and/or negative incentives.[8]

For some employees, ethical issues may not reach the critical awareness level if managers fail to identify and educate employees about specific problem areas. Organizations that consist of employees with diverse values and backgrounds must train them in the way the firm wants specific ethical issues handled. Identifying the ethical issues that employees might encounter is a significant step toward developing their ability to make ethical decisions. Many ethical issues are identified by industry groups or through general information available to a firm. Companies must assess areas of ethical and legal risk that are in reality ethical issues. Issues that are communicated as being high in ethical importance could trigger increases in employees' ethical-issue intensity. The perceived importance of an ethical issue has been found to have a strong influence on both employees' ethical judgment and their behavioral intention. In other words, the more likely individuals are to perceive an ethical issue as important, the less likely they are to engage in questionable or unethical behavior.[9] Therefore, ethical-issue intensity should be considered a key factor in the ethical decision-making process.

Individual Factors

When people need to resolve ethical issues in their daily lives, they often base their decisions on their own values and principles of right or wrong. They generally learn these values and principles through the socialization process with family members, social groups, and religion and in their formal education. The actions of specific individuals in scandal-plagued companies such as Enron, WorldCom, Halliburton, Qwest, Arthur Andersen, and Adelphia often raise questions about those individuals' personal character and integrity. They appear to operate in their own self-interest or in total disregard of the law and interests of society. At Adelphia Communications, for example, the Rigas family members who founded the firm had forgotten about general societal values. As a result, U.S. Attorney General Alberto Gonzales stated:

> As many of you know, on July 8, 2004, Adelphia's founder, Chairman and CEO, John J. Rigas, and his son, CFO Timothy J. Rigas, were convicted on conspiracy, securities fraud and bank fraud charges. . . . John and Timothy Rigas each face up to 215 years in prison for their actions.
>
> The Justice Department has reached an agreement with John Rigas that obligates all members of the Rigas family to forfeit to the United States in excess of 95 percent of all the family's assets. These assets include privately owned cable systems worth between 700 and 900 million dollars; all Adelphia securities owned by the Rigas family and its affiliated entities, valued at approximately 567 million dollars; and real estate holdings valued at approximately ten million dollars. In total, this represents the largest forfeiture ever made by individuals in a corporate fraud matter.
>
> Second, today I am announcing the creation of the Adelphia Victim Compensation Fund to compensate the victims who lost money as the result of fraud at Adelphia. Under the terms of a second agreement reached in this matter, Adelphia Corporation will not be prosecuted for the actions of its executives but will incur two obligations: To continue to cooperate with the government—and to contribute 715 million dollars to this new fund.[10]

In the workplace, personal ethical issues typically involve honesty, conflicts of interest, discrimination, nepotism, and theft of organizational resources. For example, many individuals make personal phone calls on company time. Most employees limit personal calls to a few minutes, and most companies probably overlook these as reasonable. Some employees, however, make personal calls in excess of thirty minutes, which companies are likely to view as an excessive use of company time for personal reasons. The decision to use company time to make a personal phone call is an example of a personal ethical decision. It illustrates the fine line between what may be acceptable or unacceptable in a business environment. It also reflects how well an individual will assume responsibilities in the work environment. Often this decision will depend on company policy and the corporate environment.

The way the public perceives individual ethics generally varies according to the profession in question. Telemarketers, car salespersons, advertising practitioners, stockbrokers, and real estate brokers are often perceived as having the lowest ethics. Research regarding individual factors that affect ethical awareness, judgment, intent, and behavior include gender, education, work experience, nationality, age, and locus of control.

Extensive research has been done regarding the link between gender and ethical decision making. The research shows that in many aspects there are no differences between men and women, but when differences are found, women are generally more ethical than men.[11] By "more ethical," we mean that women seem to be more sensitive to ethical scenarios and less tolerant of unethical actions. As more and more women work in managerial positions, these findings may become increasingly significant.

Education, the number of years spent in pursuit of academic knowledge, is also a significant factor in the ethical decision-making process. The important thing to remember about education is that it does not reflect experience. Work experience is defined as the number of years within a specific job, occupation, and/or industry. Generally, the more education or work experience that one has, the better he or she is at ethical decision making. The type of education has little or no effect on ethics. For example, it doesn't matter if you are a business student or a liberal arts student—you're pretty much the same in terms of ethical decision making. Lest you assume that the higher the education level the less likely one is to commit unethical acts, Seton Hall University has created Halls of Shame. There's Kozlowski Hall, named after Tyco's ex-CEO Dennis Kozlowski, who looted more than $600 million from shareholders. Near the library there is a green area named after Frank Walsh Jr., a former Tyco board member being sued by the company for breach of fiduciary responsibility for receiving a $20 million bonus from Kozlowski without the board's approval. Next to the library is the recreation center named for First Jersey Securities founder Robert Brennan, who was convicted of bankruptcy fraud and money laundering. Current research, however, does show that students are less ethical than businesspeople, which is likely because businesspeople have been exposed to more ethically challenging situations than students.[12]

Nationality is the legal relationship between a person and the country in which he or she is born. Within the twenty-first century, nationality is being redefined by such things as the European Union (EU). When European students are asked their nationality, they are less likely to state where they were born than where they currently live. The same thing is happening in the United States, as someone born in Florida who lives in New York might consider him- or herself to be a New Yorker. Research about nationality and ethics appears to be significant in that it affects ethical decision making; however, the true effect is somewhat hard to interpret.[13] Because of cultural differences, it is impossible to state, for example, whether Belgians are more ethical than Nigerians. The fact is that the concept of nationality is in flux. The reality of today is that multinational companies look for businesspeople who can make decisions regardless of nationality. Perhaps in twenty years, nationality will no longer be an issue in that the multinational's culture will replace the national status, a fact that can be seen in the number of young people in the European Union who are less likely to align themselves with a country and more open to the multinational EU concept.

Age is another individual factor that has been researched within business ethics. Several decades ago, we believed that age was positively correlated with ethical decision making. In other words, the older you are, the more ethical you are. However, recent research suggests that there is probably a more complex relationship between ethics and age. As a result, we can no longer say "the older, the wiser."[14]

Locus of control relates to individual differences in relation to a generalized belief about how one is affected by internal versus external events or reinforcements. In other words, the concept relates to where people view themselves in relation to power. Those who believe in **external control** (that is, externals) see themselves as going with the flow because that's all they can do. They believe that the events in their lives are due to uncontrollable forces. They consider what they want to achieve depends on luck, chance, and powerful people in their company. In addition, they believe that the probability of being able to control their lives by their own actions and efforts is low. Conversely, those who believe in **internal control** (that is, internals) believe that they control the events in their lives by their own effort and skill, viewing themselves as masters of their destinies and trusting in their capacity to influence their environment.

Current research suggests that we still can't be sure how significant locus of control is in terms of ethical decision making. One study that found a relationship between locus of control and ethical decision making concluded that internals were positively related whereas externals were negative.[15] In other words, those who believe that their fate is in the hands of others were more ethical than those who believed that they formed their own destiny.

Organizational Factors

Although people can and do make individual ethical choices in business situations, no one operates in a vacuum. Indeed, research has established that in the workplace the organization's values often have greater influence on decisions than a person's own values.[16] Ethical choices in business are most often made jointly, in work groups and committees, or in conversations and discussions with coworkers. Employees approach ethical issues on the basis of what they have learned not only from their own backgrounds but also from others in the organization. The outcome of this learning process depends on the strength of each person's personal values, the opportunities he or she has to behave unethically, and the exposure he or she has to others who behave ethically or unethically. Although people outside the organization, such as family members and friends, also influence decision makers, an organization's culture and structure operate through the relationships of its members to influence their ethical decisions.

A **corporate culture** can be defined as a set of values, beliefs, goals, norms, and ways of solving problems that members (employees) of an organization share. As time passes, stakeholders come to view the company or organization as a living organism, with a mind and will of its own. The Walt Disney Company, for example, requires all new employees to take a course in the traditions and history of Disneyland and Walt Disney, including the ethical dimensions of the company. The corporate culture at American Express Company stresses that employees help customers out of difficult situations whenever possible. This attitude is reinforced through numerous company legends of employees who have gone above and beyond the call of duty to help customers. This strong tradition of customer loyalty thus might encourage an American Express employee to take unorthodox steps to help a customer who encounters a problem while traveling overseas. Employees learn that they can take some risks in helping customers. Saturn is a division of General Motors, but it has developed its own corporate culture, including values related to product quality, customer service, and fairness in pricing. Such strong traditions and values have become a driving force in many companies, including McDonald's, IBM, Procter & Gamble, Southwest Airlines, and Hershey Foods.

An important component of corporate, or organizational, culture is the company's ethical culture. Whereas corporate culture involves values and rules that prescribe a wide range of behavior for organizational members, the **ethical culture** reflects whether the firm also has an ethical conscience. Ethical culture is a function of many factors, including corporate policies on ethics, top management's leadership on ethical issues, the influence of coworkers, and the opportunity for unethical behavior. Within the organization as a whole, subclimates can develop within individual departments or work groups, but they are influenced by the strength of the firm's overall ethical culture, as well as the function of the department and the stakeholders it serves.[17]

The more ethical employees perceive an organization's culture to be, the less likely they are to make unethical decisions. Corporate culture and ethical culture are closely associated with the idea that significant others within the organization help determine ethical decisions within that organization. Research also indicates that the ethical values embodied in an organization's culture are positively related to employees' commitment to the firm and their sense that they fit into the company. These findings suggest that companies should develop and promote ethical values to enhance employees' experiences in the workplace.[18]

Those who have influence in a work group, including peers, managers, coworkers, and subordinates, are referred to as **significant others.** They help workers on a daily basis with unfamiliar tasks and provide advice and information in both formal and informal ways. Coworkers, for instance, can offer help in the comments they make in discussions over lunch or when the boss is away. Likewise, a manager may provide directives about certain types of activities that employees perform on the job. Indeed, an employee's supervisor can play a central role in helping employees develop and fit in socially in the workplace.[19] Numerous studies conducted over the years confirm that significant others within an organization may have more impact on a worker's decisions on a daily basis than any other factor.[20]

Obedience to authority is another aspect of the influence that significant others can exercise. Obedience to authority helps to explain why many employees resolve business ethics issues by simply following the directives of a superior. In organizations that emphasize respect for superiors, for example, employees may feel that they are expected to carry out orders by a supervisor even if those orders are contrary to the employees' sense of right and wrong. Later, if the employee's decision is judged to have been wrong, he or she is likely to say, "I was only carrying out orders" or "My boss told me to do it this way." In addition, the type of industry and the size of organization have also been researched and found to be relevant factors; the bigger the company, the more unethical it has the potential to become.[21]

Opportunity

Opportunity describes the conditions in an organization that limit or permit ethical or unethical behavior. Opportunity results from conditions that either provide rewards, whether internal or external, or fail to erect barriers against unethical behavior.

Examples of internal rewards include feelings of goodness and personal worth generated by performing altruistic acts. External rewards refer to what an individual expects to receive from others in the social environment. Rewards are external to the individual to the degree that they bring social approval, status, and esteem.

An example of a condition that fails to erect barriers against unethical behavior is a company policy that does not punish employees who accept large gifts from clients. The absence of punishment essentially provides an opportunity for unethical behavior because it allows individuals to engage in such behavior without fear of consequences. The prospect of a reward for unethical behavior can also create an opportunity for questionable decisions. For example, a salesperson who is given public recognition and a large bonus for making a valuable sale that he or she obtained through unethical tactics will probably be motivated to use such tactics in the future, even if such behavior goes against the salesperson's personal value system. If 10 percent of employees report observing others at the workplace abusing drugs or alcohol, then the opportunity to engage in these activities exists if there is a failure to report and respond to this conduct.[22]

Opportunity relates to individuals' **immediate job context**—where they work, whom they work with, and the nature of the work. The immediate job context includes the motivational "carrots and sticks" that superiors use to influence employee behavior. Pay raises, bonuses, and public recognition act as carrots, or positive reinforcements, whereas demotions, firings, reprimands, and pay penalties act as sticks, the negative reinforcements. The United States Chamber of Commerce reports that 75 percent of employees steal from their workplaces, and most do so repeatedly.[23] As Figure 5–2 shows, many employees pilfer office-supply rooms for matters unrelated to the job. It is possible that the opportunity is provided, and in some cases, there are no concerns if employees take pens, Post-its, envelopes, notepads, and paper. Respondents to the survey by Vault.com indicated that 25 percent felt that no one cared if they

FIGURE 5–2   Items That Employees Pilfer in the Workplace

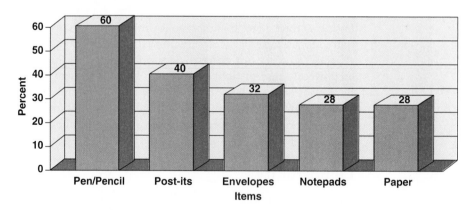

SOURCE: "Top Items Employees Pilfer." The most popular items that employees take from office-supply rooms for matters unrelated to the job. Vault's office survey of 1152 respondents. In Snapshots, *USA Today,* March 29, 2006, B1.

took office supplies, 34 percent said that they never got caught, and 1 percent said that they were caught and got in trouble. If there is no policy against this practice, one concern is that employees will not learn where to draw the line and will get into the habit of taking even more expensive items for personal use.

The opportunity that employees have for unethical behavior in an organization can be eliminated through formal codes, policies, and rules that are adequately enforced by management. For example, financial companies—such as banks, savings and loan associations, and securities companies—have developed elaborate sets of rules and procedures to avoid the opportunity for individual employees to manipulate or take advantage of their trusted position. In banks, one such rule requires most employees to take a vacation and stay out of the bank a certain number of days every year so that they cannot be physically present to cover up embezzlement or other diversion of funds. This rule prevents the opportunity for inappropriate conduct. Even after audits by prestigious accounting firm PricewaterhouseCoopers, the founder and Chairman of one of India's largest technology companies, Satyam Computer Services Ltd., admitted he invented financial results, including a fictitious cash balance of more than $1 billion. He was able to overstate profits and understate liabilities. This was allowed to happen, even though Satyam had independent directors, including a Harvard business school professor, on its board. The question is: how did the CEO manage to blatantly manipulate financial information without anyone catching on? There had to be loopholes in the oversight of the company's accounting, audits, and corporate governance that allowed this fraud. In addition, government regulation of financial reporting allowed the opportunity for misconduct. To avoid situations like this in the future, there must be checks and balances that create transparency.[24]

Opportunity also comes from knowledge. Major misconduct observed among employees in the workplace include lying to employees, customers, vendors, or the public or withholding needed information from them.[25] A person who has an information base, expertise, or information about competition has the opportunity to exploit this knowledge. An individual can be a source of information because he or she is familiar with the organization. Individuals who have been employed by one organization for many years become "gatekeepers" of its culture and often have the opportunity to make decisions related to unwritten traditions and rules. They help socialize newer employees to abide by the rules and norms of the company's internal and external ways of doing business, as well as understanding when the opportunity exists to cross the line. They may function as mentors or supervise managers in training. Like drill sergeants in the army, these trainers mold the new recruits into what the company wants. This can contribute to either ethical or unethical conduct.

The opportunity for unethical behavior cannot be eliminated without aggressive enforcement of codes and rules. A national jewelry store–chain president explained to us how he dealt with a jewelry buyer in one of his stores who had taken a bribe from a supplier. There was an explicit company policy against taking incentive payments in order to deal with a specific supplier. When the president of the firm learned that one of his buyers had taken a bribe, he immediately traveled to that buyer's office and terminated his employment. He then traveled to the supplier (manufacturer) selling jewelry to his stores and terminated his relationship with the firm. The message was clear: Taking a bribe is unacceptable for the store's buyers, and salespeople from supplying companies could cost their firm significant sales by offering bribes. This type of policy enforcement illustrates how the opportunity to commit unethical acts can be eliminated.

Business Ethics Evaluations and Intentions

Ethical dilemmas involve problem-solving situations in which decision rules are often vague or in conflict. The results of an ethical decision are often uncertain; no one can always tell us whether we have made the right decision. There are no magic formulas, nor is there computer software that ethical dilemmas can be plugged into for a solution. Even if they mean well, most businesspeople will make ethical mistakes. Thus, there is no substitute for critical thinking and the ability to take responsibility for our own decisions.

An individual's intentions and the final decision regarding what action he or she will take are the last steps in the ethical decision-making process. When the individual's intentions and behavior are inconsistent with his or her ethical judgment, the person may feel guilty. For example, when an advertising account executive is asked by her client to create an advertisement that she perceives as misleading, she has two alternatives: to comply or to refuse. If she refuses, she stands to lose business from that client and possibly her job. Other factors—such as pressure from the client, the need to keep her job to pay her debts and living expenses, and the possibility of a raise if she develops the advertisement successfully—may influence her resolution of this ethical dilemma. Because of these other factors, she may decide to act unethically and develop the advertisement even though she believes it to be inaccurate. Because her actions are inconsistent with her ethical judgment, she will probably feel guilty about her decision.

Guilt or an uneasiness is the first sign that an unethical decision has occurred. The next step is changing one's behavior to reduce such feelings. This change can reflect a person's values shifting to fit the decision or the person changing his or her decision type the next time a similar situation occurs. Finally, one can eliminate some of the situational factors by quitting. For those who begin the value shift, the following are the usual justifications that will reduce and finally eliminate guilt:

1. I need the paycheck and can't afford to quit right now.
2. Those around me are doing it so why shouldn't I? They believe it's okay.
3. If I hadn't have done this, I may not be able to get a good reference from my boss or company when I leave.
4. This is not such a big deal, given the potential benefits.
5. Business is business with a different set of rules.
6. If not me, someone else would do it and get rewarded.

The road to success depends on how the businessperson defines *success*. The success concept drives intentions and behavior in business either implicitly or explicitly. Money, security, family, power, wealth, and personal or group gratification are all types of success measures that people use. The list described is not comprehensive, and in the next chapter, you will understand more about how success can be defined. Another concept that affects behavior is the probability of rewards and punishments. That too will be explained further in Chapter 6.

USING THE ETHICAL DECISION-MAKING FRAMEWORK TO IMPROVE ETHICAL DECISIONS

The ethical decision-making framework presented in this chapter cannot tell you if a business decision is ethical or unethical. It bears repeating that it is impossible to tell you what is right or wrong; instead, we are attempting to prepare you to make informed ethical decisions. Although this chapter does not moralize by telling you what to do in a specific situation, it does provide an overview of typical decision-making processes and factors that influence ethical decisions. The framework is not a guide for how to make decisions but is intended to provide you with insights and knowledge about typical ethical decision-making processes in business organizations.

Because it is impossible to agree on normative judgments about what is ethical, business ethics scholars developing descriptive models have instead focused on regularities in decision making and the various phenomena that interact in a dynamic environment to produce predictable behavioral patterns. Furthermore, it is unlikely that an organization's ethical problems will be solved strictly by having a thorough knowledge about how ethical decisions are made. By its very nature, business ethics involves value judgments and collective agreement about acceptable patterns of behavior.

We propose that gaining an understanding of typical ethical decision making in business organizations will reveal several ways that such decision making could be improved. With more knowledge about how the decision process works, you will be better prepared to analyze critical ethical dilemmas and to provide ethical leadership regardless of your role in the organization. One important conclusion that should be taken from our framework is that ethical decision making within an organization does not rely strictly on the personal values and morals of individuals. Organizations take on a culture of their own, which, when combined with corporate governance mechanisms, have a significant influence on business ethics.

THE ROLE OF LEADERSHIP IN A CORPORATE CULTURE

Top managers provide a blueprint for what a firm's corporate culture should be.[26] If these leaders fail to express desired behaviors and goals, a corporate culture will evolve on its own but will still reflect the goals and values of the company. **Leadership,** the ability or authority to guide and direct others toward achievement of a goal, has a significant impact on ethical decision making because leaders have the power to motivate others and enforce the organization's rules and policies as well as their own viewpoints. Leaders are key to influencing an organization's corporate culture and ethical posture. However, one poll found that less than half (47 percent) of employees in large (twenty-five hundred employees or more) organizations think that their senior leadership is highly ethical.[27]

Although we often think of CEOs and other top managers as the most important leaders in an organization, the corporate governance reforms discussed in Chapter 4 make it clear that a firm's board of directors is also an important leadership component.

TABLE 5-1	The Role of Leadership in Developing an Ethics Program

1. Conduct a rigorous self-assessment of the firm's values and its existing ethics and compliance program.

2. Maintain commitment from top managers.

3. Publish, post, and make codes of ethics available and understandable.

4. Communicate ethical standards through multiple channels (for example, paper documents and webpages).

5. Provide timely training to reinforce knowledge.

6. Provide confidential resources to whom employees can go for advice or to report their concerns.

7. Ensure consistent implementation.

8. Respond and enforce consistently, promptly, and fairly.

9. Monitor and assess using appropriate methods.

10. Revise and reform to ensure continuous improvement.

SOURCE: Adapted from Jane E. Dubinsky, "Business Ethics: A Set of Practical Tools," *Internal Auditing,* July/August 2002.

Indeed, directors have a legal obligation to manage companies "for the best interests of the corporation." To determine what is in the best interest of the firm, directors can consider the effects that a decision may have on not only shareholders and employees but also other important stakeholders.[28] Therefore, when we discuss leadership, we include the corporate directors as well as top executives.

In the long run, if stakeholders are not reasonably satisfied with a company's leader, he or she will not retain a leadership position. A leader must have not only his or her followers' respect but also provide a standard of ethical conduct to them. Sunbeam, for example, fired CEO Al Dunlap after the Securities and Exchange Commission (SEC) initiated an investigation into whether the firm had fraudulently manipulated its financial reports (see Case 8). Dunlap, nicknamed "Chainsaw Al" for his track record of aggressive downsizing, wrote a book entitled *Mean Business,* which took a somewhat questionable approach to achieving organizational profitability.[29] He ultimately paid $500,000 to settle the SEC's charges that he had defrauded investors by inflating the small-appliance maker's sales. He also paid $15 million to shareholders who filed a class-action suit on similar charges.[30] Table 5–1 summarizes the steps executives should take to demonstrate that they understand the importance of ethics in doing business.

LEADERSHIP STYLES INFLUENCE ETHICAL DECISIONS

Leadership styles influence many aspects of organizational behavior, including employees' acceptance of and adherence to organizational norms and values. Styles that focus on building strong organizational values among employees contribute to shared standards of conduct. They also influence the organization's transmittal and monitoring of values, norms, and codes of ethics.[31] In short, the leadership style of an organization influences how its employees act. For example, the management philosophy of Mike Armstrong, former CEO of AT&T, is characterized by the observations of its lab's chief, David Nagel: "Most bosses hate conflict. Mike is delighted when he sees us getting at each other." Armstrong has been characterized as scary, demanding, a taskmaster, and a maniac—in an affectionate way. The fast-paced, intensely competitive telecommunications industry requires a "nontraditional" leadership style to achieve success.[32] Studying a firm's leadership styles and attitudes can also help pinpoint where future ethical issues may arise. Even for actions that may be against the law, employees often look to their organizational leaders to determine how to resolve the issue.

Although we often think of CEOs and other top managers as the most important leaders in an organization, a firm's board of directors is also a required leadership and an oversight component. The ethical leadership concept is not only for CEOs, boards of directors, and managers but can also be fellow employees. Ethical leadership by the CEO requires an understanding of the firm's vision and values, as well as the challenges of responsibility and the risk in achieving organizational objectives. Lapses in ethical leadership do occur even in people who possess strong ethical character, especially if they view the organization's ethical culture as being outside the realm of decision making that exists in the home, family, and community. This phenomenon has been observed in countless cases of so-called good community citizens engaging in unethical business activities. For example, Robin Szeliga, former CFO of Qwest, who pleaded guilty for insider trading, was an excellent community leader, even serving on a college-of-business advisory board.

Ethical leaders need both knowledge and experience to make decisions. Strong ethical leaders must have the right kind of moral integrity. Such integrity must be transparent or, in other words, do in private as if it were always public. This type of integrity relates to values and is discussed in later chapters. They must be proactive and be ready to leave the organization if its corporate governance system makes it impossible to make the right choice. Such right choices are complex by definition. The ethical leader must choose a balance of all involved today as well as in the future. Such a person must be concerned with shareholders as well as the lowest-paid employee. Experience shows that no leader can always be right or judged ethical by stakeholders in every case. The acknowledgment of this may be perceived as a weakness, but in reality it supports integrity and increases the debate exchange of views on ethics and openness.

Six leadership styles that are based on emotional intelligence—the ability to manage ourselves and our relationships effectively—have been identified by Daniel Goleman.[33]

1. The coercive leader demands instantaneous obedience and focuses on achievement, initiative, and self-control. Although this style can be very effective during times of crisis or during a turnaround, it otherwise creates a negative climate for organizational performance.
2. The authoritative leader—considered to be one of the most effective styles—inspires employees to follow a vision, facilitates change, and creates a strongly positive performance climate.

3. The affiliative leader values people, their emotions, and their needs and relies on friendship and trust to promote flexibility, innovation, and risk taking.
4. The democratic leader relies on participation and teamwork to reach collaborative decisions. This style focuses on communication and creates a positive climate for achieving results.
5. The pacesetting leader can create a negative climate because of the high standards that he or she sets. This style works best for attaining quick results from highly motivated individuals who value achievement and take the initiative.
6. The coaching leader builds a positive climate by developing skills to foster long-term success, delegates responsibility, and is skillful in issuing challenging assignments.

The most successful leaders do not rely on one style but alter their techniques based on the characteristics of the situation. Different styles can be effective in developing an ethical culture depending on the leader's assessment of risks and desire to achieve a positive climate for organizational performance.

Another way to consider leadership styles is to classify them as transactional or transformational. **Transactional leaders** attempt to create employee satisfaction through negotiating, or "bartering," for desired behaviors or levels of performance. **Transformational leaders** strive to raise employees' level of commitment and to foster trust and motivation.[34] Both transformational and transactional leaders can positively influence the corporate culture.

Transformational leaders communicate a sense of mission, stimulate new ways of thinking, and enhance as well as generate new learning experiences. They consider employee needs and aspirations in conjunction with organizational needs. They also build commitment and respect for values that provide agreement on how to deal with ethical issues.

Thus, transformational leaders strive to promote activities and behavior through a shared vision and common learning experience. As a result, they have a stronger influence on coworker support for ethical decisions and building an ethical culture than do transactional leaders. Transformational ethical leadership is best suited for organizations that have higher levels of ethical commitment among employees and strong stakeholder support for an ethical culture. A number of industry trade associations—including the American Institute of Certified Public Accountants, Defense Industry Initiative on Business Ethics and Conduct, Ethics and Compliance Officer Association, and Mortgage Bankers Association of America—are helping companies provide transformational leadership.[35]

In contrast, transactional leaders focus on ensuring that required conduct and procedures are implemented. Their negotiations to achieve desired outcomes result in a dynamic relationship with subordinates in which reactions, conflict, and crisis influence the relationship more than ethical concerns. Transactional leaders produce employees who achieve a negotiated level of performance, including compliance with ethical and legal standards. As long as employees and leaders both find this exchange mutually rewarding, the relationship is likely to be successful. However, transactional leadership is best suited for rapidly changing situations, including those that require responses to ethical problems or issues. When Michael Capellas took over as CEO and chairman of WorldCom, he used transactional leadership to change the firm's culture and ethical conduct after an accounting scandal had forced the company into bankruptcy proceedings. Capellas sought to restore WorldCom's credibility in the marketplace by bringing in a new board of directors, creating a corporate ethics office, enhancing the code of ethics, and launching new employee financial-reporting and ethics-training initiatives.[36]

HABITS OF STRONG ETHICAL LEADERS

Archie Carroll, University of Georgia business professor, crafted "7 Habits of Highly Moral Leaders" based on the idea of Stephen Covey's *The 7 Habits of Highly Effective People*.[37] We have adapted Carroll's "7 Habits of Highly Moral Leaders"[38] to create our own "Seven Habits of Strong Ethical Leaders" (Table 5–2). In particular, we believe that ethical leadership is based on holistic thinking that embraces the complex and challenging issues that companies face on a daily basis. Ethical leaders need both knowledge and experience to make the right decision. Strong ethical leaders have both the courage and the most complete information to make decisions that will be the best in the long run. Strong ethical leaders must stick to their principles and, if necessary, be ready to leave the organization if its corporate governance system is so flawed that it is impossible to make the right choice.

Founders of many corporations—such as Sam Walton, Bill Gates, Milton Hershey, Martha Stewart, Michael Dell, and Steve Jobs, as well as Ben Cohen and Jerry Greenfield—left their ethical stamp on their companies. Their conduct set the tone, making them role models for desired conduct in the early growth of their respective corporations. In the case of Milton Hershey, his legacy endures, and Hershey Foods continues to be a role model for ethical corporate culture. In the case of Sam Walton, Wal-Mart embarked on a course of rapid growth after his death and became involved in numerous conflicts with various stakeholder groups, especially employees, regulators, competitors, and communities. Despite the ethical foundation left by Sam Walton,

---

TABLE 5–2	Seven Habits of Strong Ethical Leaders

1. Ethical leaders have strong personal character.
2. Ethical leaders have a passion to do right.
3. Ethical leaders are proactive.
4. Ethical leaders consider stakeholders' interests.
5. Ethical leaders are role models for the organization's values.
6. Ethical leaders are transparent and actively involved in organizational decision making.
7. Ethical leaders are competent managers who take a holistic view of the firm's ethical culture.

Wal-Mart, as well as most large corporations, deals with hundreds of reported ethical lapses every month.[39] (See Case 1.)

Ethical Leaders Have Strong Personal Character

There is general agreement that ethical leadership is highly unlikely without a strong personal character. The question is how to teach or develop a moral person in a corporate environment. Thomas I. White, a leading authority on character development, believes the focus should be on "ethical reasoning" rather than on being a "moral person." According to White, the ability to resolve the complex ethical dilemmas encountered in a corporate culture requires intellectual skills.[40] For example, when Lawrence S. Benjamin took over as president of U.S. Food Service after a major ethical disaster, he initiated an ethics and compliance program to promote transparency and to teach employees how to make difficult ethical choices. A fundamental problem in traditional character development is that specific values and virtues are used to teach a belief or philosophy. This approach may be inappropriate for a business environment where cultural diversity and privacy must be respected. On the other hand, teaching individuals who want to do the right thing regarding corporate values and ethical codes, and equipping them with the intellectual skills to address the complexities of ethical issues, is the correct approach.

Ethical Leaders Have a Passion to Do Right

The passion to do right is "the glue that holds ethical concepts together." Some leaders develop this trait early in life, whereas others develop it over time through experience, reason, or spiritual growth. They often cite familiar arguments for doing right—to keep society from disintegrating, to alleviate human suffering, to advance human prosperity, to resolve conflicts of interest fairly and logically, to praise the good and punish the guilty, or just because something "is the right thing to do."[41] Having a passion to do right indicates a personal characteristic of not only recognizing the importance of ethical behavior but also the willingness to face challenges and make tough choices. Consider the crisis faced by Harry Kraemer, the CEO of Baxter International, after fifty-three dialysis patients died during treatment. "We have this situation. The financial people will assess the potential financial impact. The legal people will do the same. But at the end of the day, if we think it's a problem that a Baxter product was involved in the deaths of 53 people, then those other issues become pretty easy. If we don't do the right thing, then we won't be around to address those other issues."[42]

Ethical Leaders Are Proactive

Ethical leaders do not hang around waiting for ethical problems to arise. They anticipate, plan, and act proactively to avoid potential ethical crises.[43] One way to be proactive is to take a leadership role in developing effective programs that provide employees with guidance and support for making more ethical choices even in the face of considerable pressure to do otherwise. Ethical leaders who are proactive understand social needs and apply or even develop "the best practices" of ethical leadership that exist in their industry. PepsiCo has made diversity a high priority to make its workforce better reflect its customer demographics and to channel those diverse perspectives into innovative marketing and products, like Mountain Dew Code Red. To enforce the importance of that goal, CEO Steve Reinemund made eight members of his senior-management team executive sponsors, each for a specific group of employees: African Americans, Latinos, women, women of color, white males, the disabled, gays and lesbians, and the transgendered. Reinemund expects each executive to understand his or her group members' unique needs, discover new talent, and personally mentor at least three people from within the group. Reinemund's directive exemplifies the proactive approach that PepsiCo has adopted toward diversity in recent years and illustrates why the company was recently named the best workplace for Latinos and African Americans.[44]

Ethical Leaders Consider Stakeholders' Interests

Ethical leaders consider the interests of and implications for all stakeholders, not just those that have an economic impact on the firm. This requires acknowledging and monitoring the concerns of all legitimate stakeholders, actively communicating and cooperating with them, employing processes that are respectful of them, recognizing interdependencies among them, avoiding activities that would harm their human rights, and recognizing the potential conflicts between leaders' "own role as corporate stakeholders and their legal and moral responsibilities for the interests of other stakeholders."[45]

Ethical leaders have the responsibility to balance stakeholder interests to ensure that the organization maximizes its role as a responsible corporate citizen. Wal-Mart, for example, opened a 206,000-square-foot "green" store in McKinney, Texas, that features a 120-foot-tall wind turbine to generate electricity, a rain water–harvesting pond that provides 95 percent of the water needed for irrigation, and many other environmentally friendly and energy-saving features. One such effort is reclaiming used motor oil from the auto center to help heat the building. Long criticized by environmentalists, consumer activists, and neighborhood groups, Wal-Mart says the new store is evidence that the retail giant is listening to stakeholders' desires for it to support sustainability, be more economical, and be more environmentally responsible. Although the store is a prototype, the store manager says many of its features may one day be standard in all new Wal-Mart stores.[46]

Ethical Leaders Are Role Models for the Organization's Values

If leaders do not actively serve as role models for the organization's core values, then those values become nothing more than lip service. According to behavioral scientist Brent Smith, as role models, leaders are the primary influence on individual ethical behavior. Leaders whose decisions and actions are contrary to the firm's values send a signal that the firm's values are trivial or irrelevant.[47] Firms such as Enron and WorldCom articulated core values that were only used as window dressing. On the other hand, when leaders model the firm's core values at every turn, the results can be powerful.

Consider New Belgium Brewing Company, the third-largest craft brewer in the United States. Early in the firm's history, founders Jeff Lebesch and Kim Jordan wrestled with defining New Belgium's core purpose above and beyond profitability (see Case 18). The values they developed (see Table 5–3) have changed little over the years despite mostly double-digit growth. Indeed, those values dictated a more controlled pace of growth to ensure quality, even when so-called experts believed the firm could have grown much faster. Those values were also behind the company's state-of-the-art, wind-powered brew house with numerous award-winning environmentally friendly and waste-minimizing features. They are also behind the firm's generous donations to many charitable causes and event sponsorships. New Belgium also gives employees a piece of the company (and a fat-tire bicycle) after one year's tenure. The owners believe that employee ownership and open-book management policy translate into a community of trust and mutual responsibility. This proactive approach and devotion to core values have helped New Belgium gain a cultlike customer base, devoted employee-owners, and numerous awards for environmental stewardship, ethics, entrepreneurship, and beer making.[48]

Ethical Leaders Are Transparent and Actively Involved in Organizational Decision Making

Being transparent fosters openness, freedom to express ideas, and the ability to question conduct, and it encourages stakeholders to learn about and comment on what a firm is doing. Transparent leaders will not be effective unless they are

---

TABLE 5-3   New Belgium Brewing Company's Core Values

- Producing world-class beers
- Promoting beer culture and the responsible enjoyment of beer
- Seeking continuous, innovative quality and efficiency improvements
- Transcending customers' expectations
- Practicing environmental stewardship: minimizing resource consumption, maximizing energy efficiency, and recycling
- Kindling social, environmental, and cultural change as a business role model
- Cultivating potential through learning, participative management, and the pursuit of opportunities
- Balancing the myriad needs of the company, staff and their families
- Committing ourselves to authentic relationships, communications, and promises
- Having fun

---

personally involved in the key decisions that have ethical ramifications. Transformational leaders are collaborative, which opens the door for transparency through interpersonal exchange. Earlier we said that transformational leaders instill commitment and respect for values that provide guidance on how to deal with ethical issues. Herb Baum, former CEO of the Dial Corporation, says, "In today's business environment, if you're a leader—or want to be—and you aren't contributing to a values based business culture that encourages your entire organization to operate with integrity, your company is as vulnerable as a baby chick in a pit of rattlesnakes." Baum's three remarkably simple principles of transparency are (1) tell the whole truth, (2) build a values-based culture, and (3) hire "people people."[49]

Ethical Leaders Are Competent Managers Who Take a Holistic View of the Firm's Ethical Culture

Ethical leaders can see a holistic view of their organization and therefore view ethics as a strategic component of decision making, much like marketing, information systems, production, and so on. When Charles O. Prince took over as chairman of Citigroup, Inc., he sought to not only placate regulators and other stakeholders but also reshape the troubled company from the inside out. He viewed Citigroup not just as a profit-seeking business but also as a "quasi-public institution." Prince instituted numerous internal controls, slashed costs, and slowed the huge company's pace of expansion, and he spent a major portion of his time addressing issues related to the company's culture and values. Although his inward focus and management style resulted in the exodus of a number of executives and the first earnings drop in years, Prince says, "You can never sacrifice your long-term growth, your long-term reputation, to the short term."[50] The challenge of being an effective leader is illustrated in Table 5–4. Most senior executives believe that it is much more challenging to be a leader in today's business environment compared to five years ago. Leadership continues to be one of the most important drivers of ethical conduct in organizations.

TABLE 5–4   Leadership Is More Challenging in Today's Business Environment

Do you think it is more or less challenging to be a company leader in today's business environment compared with five years ago?

• More challenging	89%
• No change	9%
• Less challenging	1%
• Don't know	1%

SOURCE: Robert Half Management Resources poll of 150 senior executives at companies with revenue of $1 billion to $40 billion. In *USA Today,* March 6, 2006, B1.

SUMMARY

The key components of the ethical decision-making framework include ethical-issue intensity, individual factors, organizational factors, and opportunity. These factors are interrelated and influence business ethics evaluations and intentions, which result in ethical or unethical behavior.

The first step in ethical decision making is to recognize that an ethical issue requires that an individual or work group choose among several actions that will ultimately be evaluated as ethical or unethical by various stakeholders. Ethical-issue intensity is the perceived relevance or importance of an ethical issue to the individual or work group. It reflects the ethical sensitivity of the individual or work group that triggers the ethical decision process. Other factors in our ethical decision-making framework influence this sensitivity, thus determining why different individuals often perceive ethical issues differently.

Individual factors such as gender, education, nationality, age, and locus of control can affect the ethical decision-making process, with some factors being more important than others. Organizational factors such as an organization's values often have greater influence on an individual's decisions than that person's own values. In addition, decisions in business are most often made jointly, in work groups and committees, or in conversations and discussions with coworkers. Corporate cultures and structures operate through the individual relationships of the organization's members to influence those members' ethical decisions. A corporate culture can be defined as a set of values, beliefs, goals, norms, and ways of solving problems that members (employees) of an organization share. Corporate culture involves norms that prescribe a wide range of behavior for the organization's members. The ethical culture of an organization indicates whether it has an ethical conscience. Significant others—including peers, managers, coworkers, and subordinates—who influence the work group have more daily impact on an employee's decisions than any other factor in the decision-making framework. Obedience to authority may explain why many business ethics issues are resolved simply by following the directives of a superior.

Ethical opportunity results from conditions that either provide rewards, whether internal or external, or limit barriers to ethical or unethical behavior. Included in opportunity is a person's immediate job context, which includes the motivational techniques superiors use to influence employee behavior. The opportunity employees have for unethical behavior in an organization can be eliminated through formal codes, policies, and rules that are adequately enforced by management.

The ethical decision-making framework is not a guide for making decisions. It is intended to provide insights and knowledge about typical ethical decision-making processes in business organizations. Ethical decision making within organizations does not rely strictly on the personal values and morals of employees. Organizations have a culture of their own, which when combined with corporate governance mechanisms, may significantly influence business ethics.

Leadership styles and habits promote an organizational ethical climate. Leadership styles include coercive, authoritative, affiliative, democratic, and coaching elements. Transactional leaders negotiate or barter with employees. Transformational leaders strive for a shared vision and common learning experience. Strong ethical leaders have a strong personal character, have a passion to do the right thing, are proactive, focus on stakeholders' interests, are role models for the organization's values, make transparent decisions, and take a holistic view of the firm's ethical culture.

IMPORTANT TERMS FOR REVIEW		
ethical-issue intensity		ethical culture
moral intensity		significant other
education		obedience to authority
nationality		opportunity
locus of control		immediate job context
external control		leadership
internal control		transactional leader
corporate culture		transformational leader

RESOLVING ETHICAL BUSINESS CHALLENGES*

Peter had been a human resource (HR) manager for eighteen years and vice president for two more years for Zyedego Corporation, a small company in New Orleans. In the last decade, there have been many changes to what potential/actual employees can be asked and what constitutes fair and equitable treatment. Frankly, the situation Peter was in was partly his own fault.

The first issue began with a hurricane. After Hurricane Katrina, Zyedego employees had been working around the clock to get the company up and running. The company had been calling all former employees (if they could locate them) to rehire them. Gwyn, one of Peter's HR managers, was planning on rehiring Dana Gonzales but found out that Dana was pregnant. Because of the "rough" condition of the workplace, Gwyn was concerned for Dana's safety. Gwyn feels that if Dana is rehired, her hourly wages should be decreased by 25 percent because, as she said, "the entire group had exceeded their budget." Gwyn had asked some difficult questions, and Dana stated that if not rehired she would go to a competitor and expected the company to pay severance of two weeks' wages. In addition, Gwyn is concerned that Dana may not really be a U.S. citizen because some of her documents appear to be

questionable and possibly fake. The flooding destroyed the original documents, and although Gwyn has requested new documents, Dana has been slow in providing them.

Another issue is the hiring of truck drivers. Zyedego hires many truck drivers and routinely requests driving records as part of the preemployment process. Several of the potential new hires have past DWI records, but in all cases, it was over five years ago. All have stated that they would never do it again, have maintained a clean record for at least five years, and understand the consequences of another infraction. Gwyn has been hiring some drivers with infractions, including DWI, to secure the number of drivers needed for the company. Gwyn is beginning to wonder if she is creating a potential risk for the company if any of these drivers are involved in an accident that relates to a repeat violation. From Peter, Gwyn needs guidance related to continuing these hiring practices.

If it were only these issues, Peter would not be so concerned, but he is. The problem really started when Peter was still an HR manager, and it revolves around one "family." Guy Martin started working for Zyedego twenty years ago. He was married, with two children, and had a mortgage. The family has had its ups and downs. On several occasions, Guy separated from his wife, and last year they divorced.

But six months later, they remarried one another. When Guy was hired, Peter had made sure that Guy's son who had asthma would be covered instead of being listed as a preexisting condition. Peter also helped out the family several times when money was tight and provided Guy with overtime work.

"I know how it is, Guy, to have kids and a stay-at-home wife. It can be really hard to make ends meet, but in the long run, your children have a better chance of turning out okay."

"I know what you mean, Pete. If Martha had been working, I'm afraid the boys would have gotten into real trouble. But she was always there, making sure that homework was done, meals prepared, and just all the things a mother has to do to keep a house going."

"You know, Guy," said Peter, "we in HR calculated that a mother at home is equal to about $80,000 to $100,000 a year."

"Wow!" said Guy. "I'm glad Martha hasn't heard she's worth that much. She'll want a pay increase."

Peter said, "Don't worry about overtime. When you need it, it will always be there for you."

But tragedy struck the Martins when Guy was killed in the hurricane. He had gone to the Zyedego warehouses to help evacuate machinery and products when a gust of wind tore off the roof and the levee broke with massive flooding. Police and rescue workers hunted for his body, but it was never found. It was a strong possibility that he could have been taken away by the floodwaters that were infested with alligators and venomous snakes. Because Martha, Guy's wife, was a stay-at-home mother, their only income had been from Zyedego. Death benefits from his retirement program only provide 50 percent benefits for a surviving spouse. Also, because the body had not been found, there was the legal question of death. Usually, it takes seven years before one can claim any type of insurance or death-benefit payments, as well as medical insurance, for the family. Even with Social Security benefits, Martha would probably lose the house and could be forced to seek employment.

Zyedego has been sustaining substantial losses since the hurricane. Insurance companies were extremely slow concerning payments to all the small businesses, arguing about wind versus water damage. Impeding the process of obtaining benefits was the lack of many documents destroyed in the storm.

The storm really began for Peter late last week when he met with the insurance company about medical reimbursements, death benefits, and the pension plans. Darrell Lambert was the chief adjuster for Zyedego's insurance and pension provider.

"Here's another case that we will not cover," said Darrell as he flipped the file to Peter. "We can't help the Martins for a variety of reasons. First, there's no body. No body, no payment until after a judge declares him legally dead. That will take at least a year. While that is being settled, Mrs. Martin and her family will not be eligible for medical coverage unless Zyedego is going to pay their amount. Finally, and I know this may sound heartless, but Mrs. Martin will only get a maximum of half of Mr. Martin's pension."

"But he was killed on the job!" exclaimed Peter.

"Did you require him to work that day? Did he punch in or out? Is there any record that he was called in from Zyedego to help? The answer is no to all of the above. He helped because he felt obligated to Zyedego. But I am not Zyedego, and I do not have any obligation to the Martins," Darrell said with a smile.

"Peter," exclaimed Darrell, "I know that Zyedego is under intense financial pressure, but we are too. You have approximately one hundred families that we will have to pay something to. You and I can spend the next twelve months going over every case, bit by bit, item by item, but if that's what you want, Zyedego will go into bankruptcy. We don't want that to happen. But we also are not going to pay for everything that you claim you are due. Our lawyers will stall the system until you go broke, and your one hundred families will get nothing. Well, maybe something in five to seven years. What I am proposing is a way for you to stay in business and for my company to reduce its financial payouts. Remember, we have hundreds of small businesses like you to deal with."

Darrell then calmly said, "My proposal is that you look over these files and reduce your total reimbursements to us by 40 percent. To help you out, I'll start with this case [Martin's]. You decide whether we pay out 40 percent or nothing. Tomorrow at 9:00 A.M., I want you to have twenty-five cases, including this one, pared down by forty percent. If not, well, I'm sure my superiors have informed your superiors about this arrangement by now. You should be getting a call within the hour. So, I'll see you here at 9:00," and Darrell walked out the door.

Several hours later, Peter received a phone call from upper management about the deal he was to implement to save the company.

QUESTIONS • EXERCISES

1. What are the legal and ethical risks associated with the decision about hiring truck drivers at Zyedego?
2. What should Peter recommend to Gwyn about Dana's case?
3. Do you think Peter is too emotionally attached to the Martin case to make an objective decision?

*This case is strictly hypothetical; any resemblance to real persons, companies, or situations is coincidental.

Check Your EQ

Check your EQ, or Ethics Quotient, by completing the following. Assess your performance to evaluate your overall understanding of the chapter material.

		Yes	No
1.	The first step in ethical decision making is to understand the individual factors that influence the process.	Yes	No
2.	Opportunity describes the conditions within an organization that limit or permit ethical or unethical behavior.	Yes	No
3.	Transactional leaders negotiate compliance and ethics.	Yes	No
4.	The most significant influence on ethical behavior in the organization is the opportunity to engage in (un)ethical behavior.	Yes	No
5.	Obedience to authority relates to the influence of corporate culture.	Yes	No

ANSWERS 1. No. The first step is to become more aware that an ethical issue exists and to consider its relevance to the individual or work group. 2. Yes. Opportunity results from conditions that provide rewards or fail to erect barriers against unethical behavior. 3. Yes. Transactional leaders barter or negotiate with employees. 4. No. Significant others have more impact on ethical decisions within an organization. 5. No. Obedience to authority relates to the influence of significant others and supervisors.

CHAPTER 6

Individual Factors: Moral Philosophies and Values

CHAPTER OBJECTIVES

- To understand how moral philosophies and values influence individual and group ethical decision making in business

- To compare and contrast the teleological, deontological, virtue, and justice perspectives of moral philosophy

- To discuss the impact of philosophies on business ethics

- To recognize the stages of cognitive moral development and its shortcomings

- To introduce white-collar crime as it relates to moral philosophies, values, and corporate culture

CHAPTER OUTLINE

One of the problems that Lael Matthews has had to deal with in trying to climb the corporate ladder is the "glass ceiling" faced by minorities and women. In her current position, she must decide which of three managers to promote, a decision that, as her superior has informed her, could have serious repercussions for her future. These people are the candidates.

Liz is a 34-year-old African American, divorced with one child, who graduated in the lower half of her college class at Northwest State. She has been with the company for four years and in the industry for eight years, with mediocre performance ratings but a high-energy level. She has had, however, some difficulties in managing her staff. In addition, her child has had various medical problems, and so higher pay would be helpful. If promoted, Liz would be the first African American female manager at this level. Although Lael has known Liz only a short time, they seem to have hit it off; in fact, Lael once babysat Liz's daughter, Janeen, in an emergency. The downside to promoting Liz, though, might be a perception that Lael is playing favorites.

Roy is a white 57-year-old, married with three children, who graduated from a private university in the top half of his class. Roy has been with the company for twenty years and in the industry for thirty, and he has always been a steady performer, with mostly average ratings. The reason why Roy had been passed over before was his refusal to relocate, but that is no longer a problem. Roy's energy level is average to low; however, he has produced many of the company's top sales performers in the past. This promotion would be his last before retirement, and many in the company feel that he has earned it. In fact, one senior manager stopped Lael in the hall and said, "You know, Lael, Roy has been with us for a long time. He has done many good things for the company, sacrificing not only himself but also his family. I really hope that you can see your way to promoting him. It would be a favor to me that I wouldn't forget."

Quang Yeh, a single, 27-year-old Asian American, graduated from State University in the top 3 percent of her class and has been with the company for three years. She is known for putting in sixty-hour weeks and for her meticulous management style, which has generated some criticism from her sales staff. The last area that she managed showed record increases, despite the loss of some older accounts that for some reason did not like dealing with Quang. Moreover, Quang sued her previous employer for discrimination and won. A comment that Lael had heard from that company was that Quang was intense and that nothing would stop her from reaching her goals. As Lael was going over some of her notes, another upper-management individual came to her office and said, "You know, Lael, Quang is engaged to my son. I've looked over her personnel files, and she looks very good. She looks like a rising star, which would indicate that she should be promoted as quickly as possible. I realize that you're not in my division, but the way people get transferred, you never know. I would really like to see Quang get this promotion."

As she was considering the choices, Lael's immediate supervisor came to her to talk about Liz. "You know, Lael, Liz is one of a very few people in the company who is both an African American woman and qualified for this position. I've been going over the company's hiring and promotion figures, and it would be very advantageous for me personally and for the company to promote her. I've also spoken to public relations, and they believe that this would be a tremendous boost for the company."

As Lael pondered her decision, she mentally went through each candidate's records and found that each had advantages and disadvantages. While she was considering her problem, the phone rang. It was Liz, sounding frantic. "Lael, I'm sorry to disturb you at this late hour, but I need you to come to the hospital. Janeen has been in an accident, and I don't know who to turn to." When Lael got to the hospital, she found that Janeen's injuries were fairly serious and that Liz would have to miss some work to help with the recuperation process. Lael also realized that this accident would create a financial problem for Liz, which a promotion could help solve.

The next day seemed very long and was punctuated by the announcement that Roy's son was getting married to the vice president's daughter. The wedding would be in June, and it sounded as though it would be a company affair. By 4:30 that afternoon, Lael had gone through four aspirins and two antacids. Her decision was due in two days. What should she do?

QUESTIONS • EXERCISES

1. Discuss the advantages and disadvantages of each candidate.

2. What are the ethical and legal considerations for Lael?

3. Identify the pressures that have made her promotion decision an ethical and legal issue.

4. Discuss the implications of each decision that Lael could make.

*This case is strictly hypothetical; any resemblance to real persons, companies, or situations is coincidental.

M ost discussions of business ethics address the role of the individual in ethical decision making. The ethical decision-making model that was described in Chapter 5 placed the individual moral perspectives as a central component in making an ethical decision. In this chapter, we provide a detailed description and analysis of how individuals' background and philosophies influence their decisions. It is important to determine when one action is right and when another is viewed as wrong, and individual moral philosophies are often used to justify decisions or explain actions. To understand how people make ethical decisions, it is useful to have a grasp of the major types of moral philosophies. In this chapter, a discussion of the stages of cognitive development as it relates to these moral philosophies and its shortcomings is addressed. Finally, we examine white-collar crime as it relates to moral philosophies and values.

MORAL PHILOSOPHY DEFINED

When people talk about philosophy, they usually mean the general system of values by which they live. **Moral philosophy,** on the other hand, refers in particular to the specific principles or rules that people use to decide what is right or wrong. For example, a production manager may be guided by a general philosophy of management that emphasizes encouraging workers to know as much as possible about the product that they are manufacturing. However, his moral philosophy comes into play when he must make decisions such as whether to notify employees in advance of upcoming layoffs. Although workers would prefer advance warning, giving it might adversely affect the quality and quantity of production. Such decisions require a person to evaluate the "rightness," or morality, of choices in terms of his or her own principles and values.

Moral philosophies present guidelines for "determining how conflicts in human interests are to be settled and for optimizing mutual benefit of people living together in groups," guiding businesspeople as they formulate business strategies and resolve specific ethical issues.[1] However, there is no single moral philosophy that everyone accepts. Some managers, for example, view profit as the ultimate goal of an enterprise and therefore may not be concerned about the impact of their firms' decisions on society. As we have seen, the economist Milton Friedman supports this viewpoint, contending that the market will reward or punish companies for unethical conduct without the need for government regulation.[2] The emergence of this Friedman-type capitalism as the dominant and most widely accepted economic system has created market-driven societies around the world. However, economic systems not only allocate resources and products within a society but also affect individuals and society as a whole. Thus, the success of an economic system depends both on its philosophical framework and on the individuals within the system who maintain moral philosophies that bring people together in a cooperative, efficient, and productive marketplace. Going back to Aristotle, there is a long Western tradition of questioning whether a market economy and individual moral behavior are compatible. In reality, individuals in today's society exist within the framework of social, political, and economic institutions.

People who face ethical issues often base their decisions on their own values and principles of right or wrong, most of which are learned through the socialization process with the help of family members, social groups, church, and formal education. Individual factors that influence decision making include personal moral philosophies. Ethical dilemmas arise in problem-solving situations in which the rules governing decision making are often vague or in conflict. In real-life situations, there is no substitute for an individual's own critical thinking and ability to accept responsibility for his or her decision.

Moral philosophies are ideal moral perspectives that provide individuals with abstract principles for guiding their social existence. For example, individuals' decisions to recycle waste or to purchase or sell recycled or recyclable products are influenced by moral philosophies and attitudes toward recycling.[3] Thus, it is often difficult to implement an individual moral philosophy within the complex environment of a business organization. On the other hand, the functioning of our economic system depends on individuals coming together and sharing philosophies that create the moral values, trust, and expectations that allow the system to work. Most employees within a business organization do not think about what particular moral philosophy they are using when they are confronted with an ethical issue. Individuals learn decision-making approaches or philosophies through their cultural and social development.

Many theories associated with moral philosophies refer to a value orientation and such things as economics, idealism, and relativism. The concept of the **economic value orientation** is associated with values that can be quantified by monetary means; thus, according to this theory, if an act produces more value than its effort, then it should be accepted as ethical. **Idealism,** on the other hand, is a moral philosophy that places special value on ideas and ideals as products of the mind, in comparison with the world's view. The term refers to efforts to account for all objects in nature and experience and assign to such representations a higher order of existence. Studies have found that there is a positive correlation between idealistic thinking and ethical decision making. **Realism** is the view that an external world exists independent of our perception of it. Realists work under the assumption that humankind is not inherently benevolent and kind but instead is inherently self-centered and competitive. According to realists, each person is always ultimately guided by his or her own self-interest. Research shows a negative correlation between realistic thinking and ethical decision making. Thus, the belief that all actions are ultimately self-motivated leads to a tendency toward negative ethical decision making.

MORAL PHILOSOPHIES

There are many moral philosophies, but because a detailed study of all moral philosophies is beyond the scope of this book, we limit our discussion to those that are most applicable to the study of business ethics. Our approach focuses on the most basic concepts needed to help you understand the ethical decision-making process in business. We do not prescribe the use of any particular moral philosophy, for there is no one "correct" way to resolve ethical issues in business.

To help you understand how the moral philosophies discussed in this chapter may be applied in decision making, we use a hypothetical situation as an illustration. Suppose that Sam Colt, a sales representative, is preparing a sales presentation for his firm Midwest Hardware, which manufactures nuts and bolts. Sam hopes to obtain a large sale from a construction firm that is building a bridge across the Mississippi River near St. Louis. The bolts manufactured by Midwest Hardware have a 3 percent defect rate, which, although acceptable in the industry, makes them unsuitable for use in certain types of projects, such as those that may be subject to sudden, severe stress. The new bridge will be located near the New Madrid Fault line, the source of the United States' greatest earthquake in 1811. The epicenter of that earthquake, which caused extensive damage and altered the flow of the Mississippi, is less than two hundred miles from the new bridge site. Earthquake experts believe there is a 50 percent chance that an earthquake with a magnitude greater than 7 on the Richter scale will occur somewhere along the New Madrid Fault by the year 2015. Bridge construction in the area is not regulated by earthquake codes, however. If Sam wins the sale, he will earn a commission of $25,000 on top of his regular salary. But if he tells the contractor about the defect rate, Midwest may lose the sale to a competitor that markets bolts with a lower defect rate. Thus, Sam's ethical issue is whether to point out to the bridge contractor that, in the event of an earthquake, some Midwest bolts could fail, possibly resulting in the collapse of the bridge.

We will come back to this illustration as we discuss particular moral philosophies, asking how Sam Colt might use each philosophy to resolve his ethical issue. We don't judge the quality of Sam's decision, nor do we advocate any one moral philosophy; in fact, this illustration and Sam's decision rationales are necessarily simplistic as well as hypothetical. In reality, the decision maker would probably have many more factors to consider in making his or her choice and thus might reach a different decision. With that note of caution, we introduce the concept of goodness and several types of moral philosophy: teleology, deontology, the relativist perspective, virtue ethics, and justice theories (Table 6–1).

Goodness—Instrumental and Intrinsic

To appreciate moral philosophy, one must understand the differing perspectives of goodness. Are there clearly defined goods and bads, and if so, what is the relationship between the ends and the means of bringing them about? Is there some intrinsic way of determining if the ends can be identified independently as good or bad? Aristotle, for example, argued that happiness is an intrinsically good end—in other words, its goodness is natural and universal, without relativity. On the other hand, the philosopher

TABLE 6-1	A Comparison of the Philosophies Used in Business Decisions
Teleology	Stipulates that acts are morally right or acceptable if they produce some desired result, such as realization of self-interest or utility.
Egoism	Defines right or acceptable actions as those that maximize a particular person's self-interest as defined by the individual.
Utilitarianism	Defines right or acceptable actions as those that maximize total utility, or the greatest good for the greatest number of people.
Deontology	Focuses on the preservation of individual rights and on the intentions associated with a particular behavior rather than on its consequences.
Relativist	Evaluates ethicalness subjectively on the basis of individual and group experiences.
Virtue ethics	Assumes that what is moral in a given situation is not only what conventional morality requires but also what the mature person with a "good" moral character would deem appropriate.
Justice	Evaluates ethicalness on the basis of fairness: distributive, procedural, and interactional.

Immanuel Kant emphasized means and motivations to argue that goodwill, seriously applied toward accomplishment, is the only thing good in itself.

Two basic concepts of goodness are monism and pluralism. **Monists** believe that only one thing is intrinsically good, and the pluralists believe that two or more things are intrinsically good. Monists are often exemplified by **hedonism**—that one's pleasure is the ultimate intrinsic good or that the moral end, or goodness, is the greatest balance of pleasure over pain. Hedonism defines right or acceptable behavior as that which maximizes personal pleasure. Moral philosophers describe those who believe that more pleasure is better as **quantitative hedonists** and those who believe that it is possible to get too much of a good thing (such as pleasure) as **qualitative hedonists.**

Pluralists, often referred to as nonhedonists, take the opposite position that no *one* thing is intrinsically good. For example, a pluralist might view other ultimate goods as beauty, aesthetic experience, knowledge, and personal affection. Plato argued that the good life is a mixture of (1) moderation and fitness, (2) proportion and beauty, (3) intelligence and wisdom, (4) sciences and arts, and (5) pure pleasures of the soul.

Although all pluralists are nonhedonists, it is important to note that all monists are not necessarily hedonists. An individual can believe in a single intrinsic good other than pleasure; Machiavelli and Nietzsche, for example, each held power to be the sole good, and Kant's belief in the single virtue of goodwill classifies him as a monistic nonhedonist.

A more modern view is expressed in the instrumentalist position. Sometimes called pragmatists, **instrumentalists** reject the idea that (1) ends can be separated from the means that produce them and (2) ends, purposes, or outcomes are intrinsically good in and of themselves. The philosopher John Dewey argued that the ends–means perspective is a relative distinction, that the difference between ends and means is no difference at all but merely a matter of the individual's perspective; thus, almost any action can be an end or a means. Dewey gives the example that people eat in order to be able to work, and they work in order to eat. From a practical standpoint, an end is only a remote means, and a means is but a series of acts viewed from an earlier stage. From this it follows that there is no such thing as a single, universal end.

So how does this discussion equate to business? Isn't business about shareholder wealth and the wealth of executives? To measure success in business is to measure monetary wealth . . . right? To answer this question, let's go back to 1923 when a meeting was held at the Edgewater Beach Hotel in Chicago. Attending this meeting were nine of the richest men in the world: (1) Charles Schwab, president of the world's largest independent steel company; (2) Samuel Insull, president of the world's largest utility company; (3) Howard Hopson, president of the world's largest gas firm; (4) Arthur Cutten, the greatest wheat speculator; (5) Richard Whitney, president of the New York Stock Exchange; (6) Albert Fall, member of the president's cabinet; (7) Leon Fraizer, president of the Bank of International Settlements; (8) Jessie Livermore, the greatest speculator in the stock market; and (9) Ivar Kreuger, head of the company with the most widely distributed securities in the world. Twenty-five years later, (1) Charles Schwab had died having lived on borrowed money for the last five years of his life, (2) Samuel Insull had died a penniless fugitive, (3) Howard Hopson had gone insane, (4) Arthur Cutten had died bankrupt, (5) Richard Whitney had spent time in prison, (6) Albert Fall had been pardoned from prison so that he could die at home, and (7) Leon Fraizer, (8) Jessie Livermore, and (9) Ivar Kreuger had committed suicide. Measured by wealth and power, these men had achieved success, at least temporarily. So this begs the question of whether money guarantees happiness; in other words, do the ends always justify the means?

A discussion of moral value often revolves around the nature of goodness—instrumental or intrinsic. Theories of moral obligation, by contrast, change the question to "What makes a given action right or obligatory?" **Goodness theories** typically focus on the *end result* of actions and the goodness or happiness created by them, whereas **obligation theories** emphasize the *means* and *motives* by which actions are justified. These obligation theories are teleology and deontology, respectively.

Teleology

Teleology (from the Greek word for "end" or "purpose") refers to moral philosophies in which an act is considered morally right or acceptable if it produces some desired result such as pleasure, knowledge, career growth, the realization of self-interest, utility, wealth, or even fame. In other words, teleological philosophies assess the moral worth of a behavior by looking at its consequences, and thus moral philosophers today often refer to these theories as **consequentialist.** Two important teleological philosophies that often guide decision making in individual business decisions are egoism and utilitarianism.

Egoism defines right or acceptable behavior in terms of its consequences for the individual. Egoists believe that they should make decisions that maximize their own self-interest, which is defined differently by each individual. Depending on the egoist, self-interest may be construed as physical well-being, power, pleasure, fame, a satisfying career, a good family life, wealth, or something else. In an ethical decision-making situation, an egoist will probably choose the alternative that contributes most to his or her self-interest. The egoist's creed can be generally stated as "Do the act that promotes the greatest good for oneself." Many believe that egoistic people and companies are inherently unethical, are short-term oriented, and will take advantage of any opportunity. For example, some telemarketers demonstrate this negative tendency when they prey on elderly consumers who may be vulnerable because of loneliness or fear of losing their financial independence. Thousands of senior citizens fall victim to fraudulent telemarketers every year, in many cases losing all of their savings and sometimes their homes.

However, there is also **enlightened egoism.** Enlightened egoists take a long-range perspective and allow for the well-being of others although their own self-interest remains paramount. Enlightened egoists may, for example, abide by professional codes of ethics, control pollution, avoid cheating on taxes, help create jobs, and support community projects. Yet they do so not because these actions benefit others but because they help achieve some ultimate goal for the egoist, such as advancement within the firm. An enlightened egoist might call management's attention to a coworker who is making false accounting reports but only to safeguard the company's reputation and thus the egoist's own job security. In addition, some enlightened egoists may become whistle-blowers and report misconduct to a government regulatory agency to keep their job and receive a reward for exposing misconduct. When businesses donate money, resources, or time to specific causes and institutions, their motives may not be purely altruistic either. For example, International Business Machines (IBM) has a policy of donating or reducing the cost of computers to educational institutions; in exchange, the company receives tax breaks for donations of equipment, which reduces the cost of its philanthropy. In addition, IBM hopes to build future sales by placing its products on campuses. When students enter the workforce, they may request the IBM products with which they have become familiar. Although the company's actions benefit society in general, in the long run they also benefit IBM.

Let's return to the hypothetical case of Sam Colt, who must decide whether to warn the bridge contractor that 3 percent of Midwest Hardware's bolts are likely to be defective. If he is an egoist, he will probably choose the alternative that maximizes his own self-interest. If he defines self-interest in terms of personal wealth, his personal moral philosophy may lead him to value a $25,000 commission more than a chance to reduce the risk of a bridge collapse. As a result, an egoist might well resolve this ethical dilemma by keeping quiet about the bolts' defect rate, hoping to win the sale and the $25,000 commission, rationalizing that there is a slim chance of an earthquake, that bolts would not be a factor in a major earthquake, and that, even if they were, no one would be able to prove that defective bolts caused the bridge to collapse.

Like egoism, **utilitarianism** is concerned with consequences, but the utilitarian seeks the greatest good for the greatest number of people. Utilitarians believe that they should make decisions that result in the greatest total *utility,* that achieve the greatest benefit for all those affected by a decision.

Utilitarian decision making relies on a systematic comparison of the costs and benefits to all affected parties. Using such a cost–benefit analysis, a utilitarian decision maker calculates the utility of the consequences of all possible alternatives and then selects the one that results in the greatest benefit. For example, the U.S. Supreme Court has ruled that supervisors are responsible for the sexual misconduct of employees, even if the employers knew nothing about the behavior, establishing a strict standard for harassment on the job. One of the justices indicated in the ruling that the employer's burden to prevent harassment is "one of the costs of doing business."[4] Apparently, the Court has decided that the greatest utility to society will result from forcing businesses to prevent harassment.

In evaluating an action's consequences, some utilitarians consider the effects on animals as well as on human beings. This perspective is especially significant in the controversy surrounding the use of animals for research purposes by cosmetics and pharmaceutical companies. Animal rights groups have protested that such testing is unethical because it harms and even kills the animals, depriving them of their rights. Researchers for pharmaceutical and cosmetics manufacturers, however, defend animal testing on utilitarian grounds. The consequences of the research (such as new or improved drugs to treat disease, or safer cosmetics) create more benefit for society, they argue, than would be achieved by halting the research and preserving the animals' rights. Nonetheless, many cosmetics firms have responded to the controversy by agreeing to stop animal research.

Now suppose that Sam Colt, the bolt salesperson, is a utilitarian. Before making his decision, he would conduct a cost–benefit analysis to assess which alternative would create the greatest utility. On one hand, building the bridge would improve roadways and allow more people to cross the Mississippi River to reach jobs in St. Louis. The project would create hundreds of jobs, enhance the local economy, and unite communities on both sides of the river. Additionally, it would increase the revenues of Midwest Hardware, allowing the firm to invest more in research to lower the defect rate of bolts it produced in the future. On the other hand, a bridge collapse could kill or injure as many as one hundred people. But the bolts have only a 3 percent defect rate, there is only a 50 percent probability of an earthquake *somewhere* along the fault line, and there might be only a few cars on the bridge at the time of a disaster.

After analyzing the costs and benefits of the situation, Sam might rationalize that building the bridge with his company's bolts would create more utility (jobs, unity, economic growth, and company growth) than would result from telling the bridge contractor that the bolts might fail in an earthquake. If so, a utilitarian would probably not alert the bridge contractor to the defect rate of the bolts.

Utilitarians use various criteria to judge the morality of an action. Some utilitarian philosophers have argued that general rules should be followed to decide which action is best.[5] These **rule utilitarians** determine behavior on the basis of principles, or rules, designed to promote the greatest utility rather than on an examination of each particular situation. One such rule might be "Bribery is wrong." If people felt free to offer bribes whenever they might be useful, the world would become chaotic; therefore, a rule prohibiting bribery would increase utility. A rule utilitarian would not bribe an official, even to preserve workers' jobs, but would adhere strictly to the rule. Rule utilitarians do not automatically accept conventional moral rules, however; thus, if they determined that an alternative rule would promote greater utility, they would advocate changing it.

Other utilitarian philosophers have argued that the rightness of each individual action must be evaluated to determine whether it produces the greatest utility for the greatest number of people.[6] These **act utilitarians** examine a specific action itself, rather than the general rules governing it, to assess whether it will result in the greatest utility. Rules such as "Bribery is wrong" serve only as general guidelines for act utilitarians. They would likely agree that bribery is generally wrong, not because there is anything inherently wrong with bribery, but because the total amount of utility decreases when one person's interests are placed ahead of those of society.[7] In a particular case, however, an act utilitarian might argue that bribery is acceptable.

For example, a sales manager might believe that his or her firm will not win a construction contract unless a local government official gets a bribe; moreover, if the firm does not obtain the contract, it will have to lay off one hundred workers. The manager might therefore argue that bribery is justified because saving a hundred jobs creates more utility than obeying a law. Another example may be found in the actions of farmers in China who use toxic melamine to increase milk quality. Melamine's chemical properties boost the apparent presence of protein in food. Manufacturers of melamine, an industrial chemical used in plastics, say they had noticed a rising demand for their factories' scrap. Actual protein powders are also prohibited from being added to raw milk. They are made from ground animal parts, soy, and other sources. China's biggest local seller of liquid milk, Nestlé SA, said they were aware that Chinese farmers and traders added unauthorized substances to raw milk, but that they didn't know melamine was among them. Among other common milk additives: a viscous yellow liquid containing fat and a combination of preservatives and antibiotics, known as "fresh-keeping liquid" is "very common" and hard to detect. It can be argued that everyone within the milk supply chain saw their actions as helping more people financially rather than the unknown dangers of the additives.[8]

Deontology

Deontology (from the Greek word for "ethics") refers to moral philosophies that focus on the rights of individuals and on the intentions associated with a particular behavior rather than on its consequences. Fundamental to deontological theory is the idea that equal respect must be given to all persons. Unlike utilitarians, deontologists argue that there are some things that we should *not* do, even to maximize utility. For example, deontologists would consider it wrong to kill an innocent person or commit a serious injustice against a person, no matter how much greater social utility might result from doing so, because such an action would infringe on that person's rights as an individual. The utilitarian, however, might consider as acceptable an action that resulted in a person's death if that action created some greater benefit. Deontological philosophies regard certain behaviors as inherently right, and the determination of this rightness focuses on the individual actor, not society. Thus, these perspectives are sometimes referred to as **nonconsequentialist,** an ethics based on *respect for persons.*

Contemporary deontology has been greatly influenced by the German philosopher Immanuel Kant, who developed the so-called categorical imperative: "Act as if the maxim of thy action were to become by thy will a universal law of nature."[9] Simply put, if you feel comfortable allowing everyone in the world to see you commit an act and if your rationale for acting in a particular manner is suitable to become a universal principle guiding behavior, then committing that act is ethical. For example, if a person borrows money, promising to return it but with no intention of keeping that promise, he or she cannot "universalize" that act. If everyone were to borrow money without the intention of returning it, no one would take such promises seriously, and all lending would cease.[10] Therefore, the rationale for the action would not be a suitable universal principle, and the act could not be considered ethical.

The term *nature* is crucial for deontologists. In general, deontologists regard the nature of moral principles as permanent and stable, and they believe that compliance with these principles defines ethicalness. Deontologists believe that individuals have certain absolute rights:

- Freedom of conscience
- Freedom of consent
- Freedom of privacy
- Freedom of speech
- Due process[11]

To decide whether a behavior is ethical, deontologists look for conformity to moral principles. For example, if a manufacturing worker becomes ill or dies as a result of conditions in the workplace, a deontologist might argue that the company must modify its production processes to correct the condition, no matter what the cost—even if it means bankrupting the company and thus causing all workers to lose their jobs. In contrast, a utilitarian would analyze all the costs and benefits of modifying production processes and make a decision on that basis. This example is greatly oversimplified, of course, but it helps clarify the difference between teleology and deontology. In short, teleological philosophies consider the *ends* associated with an action whereas deontological philosophies consider the *means*.

Returning again to our bolt salesman, let's consider a deontological Sam Colt. He would probably feel obliged to tell the bridge contractor about the defect rate because of the potential loss of life that might result from an earthquake-caused bridge collapse. Even though constructing the bridge would benefit residents and earn the salesman a substantial commission, the failure of the bolts during an earthquake would infringe on the rights of any person crossing the bridge at the time of the collapse. Thus, the deontological Colt would likely inform the bridge contractor of the defect rate and point out the earthquake risk, even though, by doing so, he would probably lose the sale.

As with utilitarians, deontologists may be divided into those who focus on moral rules and those who focus on the nature of the acts themselves. **Rule deontologists** believe that conformity to general moral principles determines ethicalness. Deontological philosophies use reason and logic to formulate rules for behavior. Examples include Kant's categorical imperative and the Golden Rule of the Judeo-Christian tradition: Do unto others as you would have them do unto you. Such rules, or principles, guiding ethical behavior override the imperatives that emerge from a specific context. One could argue that Jeffery Wigand—who exposed the underside of the tobacco industry when he blew the whistle on his employer, Brown & Williamson Tobacco—was such a rule deontologist. Although it cost him both financially and socially, Wigand testified to Congress about the realities of marketing cigarettes and their effects on society.[12]

Rule deontology is determined by the relationship between the basic rights of the individual and a set of rules governing conduct. For example, a video store owner accused of distributing obscene materials could argue from a rule deontological perspective that the basic right to freedom of speech overrides the other indecency or pornography aspects of his business. Indeed, the free-speech argument has held up in many courts. Kant and rule deontologists would support a process of discovery to identify the moral issues relevant to a firm's mission and objectives. Then, they would follow a process of justifying that mission or those objectives based on rules.[13]

Act deontologists, in contrast, hold that actions are the proper basis on which to judge morality or ethicalness. Act deontology requires that a person use equity, fairness, and impartiality when making and enforcing decisions.[14] For act deontologists, as for act utilitarians, rules serve only as guidelines, with past experiences weighing more heavily than rules upon the decision-making process. In effect, act deontologists suggest that people simply *know* that certain acts are right or wrong, regardless of the consequences or any appeal to deontological rules. In addition, act deontologists regard the particular act or moment in time as taking precedence over any rule. For example, many people view data collection by Internet sites as a violation of personal privacy in itself. Regardless of any website's stated rules or policies, many Internet users want to be left alone unless they provide permission to be tracked while online.[15] Current research suggests that rule and act deontological principles play a larger role in a person's decision than teleological philosophies.[16]

As we have seen, ethical issues can be evaluated from many different perspectives. Each type of philosophy discussed here would have a distinct basis for deciding whether a particular action is right or wrong. Adherents of different personal moral philosophies may disagree in their evaluations of a given action, yet all are behaving ethically *according to their own standards*. All would agree that there is no one "right" way to make ethical decisions and no best moral philosophy except their own. The relativist perspective may be helpful in understanding how people make such decisions in practice.

Relativist Perspective

From the **relativist perspective,** definitions of ethical behavior are derived subjectively from the experiences of individuals and groups. Relativists use themselves or the people around them as their basis for defining ethical standards, and the various forms of relativism include descriptive, metaethical, or normative.[17] **Descriptive relativism** relates to observing cultures. We may observe that different cultures exhibit different norms, customs, and values and, in so doing, arrive at a factual description of a culture. These observations say nothing about the higher questions of ethical justification, however. At this point metaethical relativism comes into play.

Metaethical relativists understand that people naturally see situations from their own perspectives and argue that, as a result, there is no objective way of resolving ethical disputes between value systems and individuals. Simply put, one culture's moral philosophy cannot logically be preferred to another because there exists no meaningful basis for comparison. Because ethical rules are relative to a specific culture, the values and behaviors of people in one culture need not influence the behaviors of people in another culture.[18] At the individual level of reasoning, we have **normative relativism.** Normative relativists assume that one person's opinion is as good as another's.[19]

Basic relativism acknowledges that we live in a society in which people have many different views and bases from which to justify decisions as right or wrong. The relativist looks to the interacting groups and tries to determine probable solutions based on group consensus. When formulating business strategies and plans, for example, a relativist would try to anticipate the conflicts that might arise between the different philosophies held by members of the organization, its suppliers, its customers, and the community at large.

The relativist observes the actions of members of an involved group and attempts to determine that group's consensus on a given behavior. A positive consensus, for example, would signify that the group considers the action to be right or ethical. However, such judgments may not remain valid forever. As circumstances evolve or the makeup of the group changes, a formerly accepted behavior may come to be viewed as wrong or unethical, or vice versa. Within the accounting profession, for example, it was traditionally considered unethical to advertise. However, advertising has been gaining acceptance among accountants. This shift in ethical views may have come about as a result of the steady increase in the number of accountants, which has led to greater competition. Moreover, the federal government investigated the restrictions that accounting groups placed on their members and concluded that they inhibited free competition. Consequently, an informal consensus has emerged in the accounting industry that advertising is now acceptable. A problem with relativism is that it places too much emphasis on peoples' differences while ignoring their basic similarities. Similarities within different people and cultures—such as beliefs against incest, murder, and theft or promoting reciprocity and respect for the elderly—are hard to argue away and hard to explain from the relativist perspective.

In the case of the Midwest Hardware salesperson, if he were a relativist, he would attempt to determine the group consensus before deciding whether to tell his prospective customer about the bolts' defect rate. The relativist Sam Colt would look at both his own company's policy and at the general industry practice. He might also informally survey his colleagues and superiors as well as consulting industry trade journals and codes of ethics. Such investigations would help him determine the group consensus, which should reflect a variety of moral philosophies. If he learns that general company policy, as well as industry practice, is to discuss defect rates with those customers for whom faulty bolts may cause serious problems, he may infer that there is a consensus on the matter. As a relativist, he would probably then inform the bridge contractor that some of the bolts may fail, perhaps leading to a bridge collapse in the event of an earthquake. Conversely, if Sam determines that the normal practice in his company and the industry is to not inform customers about defect rates, he would probably not raise the subject with the bridge contractor.

Empirical research into the general concept of relativism suggests that it is negatively related to a person's ethical sensitivity to issues. Thus, if someone scores high on relativism, he or she will probably be less likely to detect or be sensitive to issues that are defined by others as having an ethical component.[20]

Virtue Ethics

A moral virtue represents an acquired disposition that is valued as a part of an individual's character. As an individual develops socially, he or she may become disposed to behave in the same way (in terms of reasons, feelings, and desires) as what he considers to be moral.[21] A person who has the character trait of honesty will be disposed to tell the truth because it is considered to be right and comfortable. This individual will always try to tell the truth because of its importance in human communication.

A virtue is considered praiseworthy because it is an achievement that an individual develops through practice and commitment.[22]

This philosophy is called **virtue ethics,** and it posits that what is moral in a given situation is not only what conventional morality or moral rules (current societal definitions) require but also what the mature person with a "good" moral character would deem appropriate.

Proponents of virtue ethics frequently discuss lists of basic goods and virtues, which are generally presented as positive and useful mental habits or cultivated character traits. Aristotle named, among others, standards of loyalty, courage, wit, community, and judgment as the "excellences" that society requires. While listing the important virtues is a popular theoretical task, the philosopher Dewey cautions that virtues should not be looked at separately. The pluralism of virtues gives the businessperson a positive character and constitutes the very best idea of integrity of character. The virtue ethics approach to business can be summarized as follows:

1. Individual virtue and integrity count, but good corporate ethics programs encourage individual virtue and integrity.
2. By the employee's role in the community (organization), these virtues associated with appropriate conduct form a good person.
3. The ultimate purpose is to serve society's demands and the public good and to be rewarded in one's career.
4. The well-being of the community goes together with individual excellence because of the social consciousness and public spirit of every individual.[23]

The difference between deontology, teleology, and virtue ethics is that the first two are applied *deductively* to problems whereas virtue ethics is applied *inductively*. Virtue ethics assumes that what current societal moral rules require may indeed be the moral minimum for the beginning of virtue. The viability of our political, social, and economic systems depends on the presence of certain virtues among the citizenry that are vital for the proper functioning of a market economy.[24]

Indeed, virtue theory could be thought of as a dynamic theory of how to conduct business activities. The virtue ethicist believes that to have a successful market economy, society must be capable of carving out sanctuaries such as family, school, church, and community, where virtues can be nurtured. These virtues, including truth, trust, tolerance, and restraint, can play a role in the functioning of an individualistic, contractual economy and create obligations that make social cooperation possible. The operation of a market economy based on virtues provides a traditional existence where individuals in the economic system have powerful inducements to conform to prevailing standards of behavior. Some philosophers think that virtues may be weakened by the operation of the market, but virtue ethicists believe that institutions and society must maintain a balance and constantly add to their stock of virtues.[25] Some of the virtues that could drive a market economy are listed in Table 6–2; the list, although not comprehensive, provides examples of the types of virtues that support the business environment.

The elements of virtue that are important to business transactions have been defined as trust, self-control, empathy, fairness, and truthfulness. Attributes in contrast to virtue would include lying, cheating, fraud, and corruption. In their broadest sense, these concepts appear to be accepted within all cultures. The problem of virtue ethics

---

TABLE 6-2	Virtues That Support Business Transactions

Trust: The predisposition to place confidence in the behavior of others while taking the risk that the expected behavior will not be performed	Trust eliminates the need for and associated cost of monitoring compliance with agreements, contracts, and reciprocal agreements. There is the expectation that a promise or agreement can be relied on.
Self-control: The disposition to pass up an immediate advantage or gratification. It indicates the ability to avoid exploiting a known opportunity for self-interest	The tradeoff is between short-term self-interest and long-term benefits.
Empathy: The ability to share the feelings or emotions of others	Empathy promotes civility because success in the market depends on the courteous treatment of people who have the option of going to competitors. The ability to anticipate needs and satisfy customers and employees contributes to a firm's economic success.
Fairness: The disposition to deal equitably with the perceived injustices of others	Fairness often relates to doing the right thing with respect to small matters in order to cultivate a long-term business relationship.
Truthfulness: The disposition to provide the facts or correct information as known to the individual	Telling the truth involves avoiding deception and contributes to trust in business relationships.
Learning: The disposition to constantly acquire knowledge internal and external to the firm, whether of an industry, culture, or other societies	Learning involves gaining knowledge to make better, more informed decisions.
Gratitude: A sign of maturity that is the beginning of civility and decency	Gratitude is the recognition that people do not succeed alone.
Civility: The disposition or essence of courtesy, politeness, respect, and consideration for others	Civility relates to the process of doing business in a culturally correct way, thus decreasing communication errors and increasing trust.
Moral leadership: Strength of character, peace of mind, heart, and happiness in life	Moral leadership is a trait of those leaders who follow a consistent pattern of behavior based on virtues.

SOURCE: Adapted from Ian Maitland, "Virtuous Markets: The Market as School of the Virtues," *Business Ethics Quarterly* (January 1997): 97; and Gordon B. Hinckley, *Standing for Something: 10 Neglected Virtues That Will Heal Our Hearts and Homes* (New York: Three Rivers Press, 2001).

comes in its implementation within and between cultures, as those who practice virtue ethics go beyond social norms. For example, if a company tacitly approves of corruption, the employee who adheres to the virtues of trust and truthfulness would consider it wrong to sell unneeded repair parts despite the organization's approval of such acts. Some employees might view this truthful employee as highly ethical but, in order to rationalize their own behavior, judge his or her ethics as going beyond what is required by their job or society. They might argue that virtue is an unattainable goal and thus one should not be obliged to live up to its standards. However, to those who espouse virtue ethics, this relativistic argument is meaningless because they believe in the universal reality of the elements of virtue.

If our salesman Sam Colt were a virtue ethicist, he would consider the elements of virtue and then tell the prospective customer about the defect rate and about his concerns regarding the building of the bridge. He would not resort to puffery to explain the product or its risks and, indeed, might suggest alternative products or companies that would lower the probability of the bridge collapsing.

Justice

Justice as it is applied in business ethics involves evaluations of fairness or the disposition to deal with perceived injustices of others. Justice is fair treatment and due reward in accordance with ethical or legal standards. In business, this means that the decision rules used by an individual to determine the justice of a situation could be based on the perceived rights of individuals and on the intentions of the people involved in a given business interaction. For that reason, justice is more likely to be based on deontological moral philosophies than on teleological or utilitarian philosophies. In other words, justice deals more with the issue of what individuals feel they are due based on their rights and performance in the workplace. For example, the U.S. Equal Employment Opportunity Commission exists to help employees who suspect they have been unjustly discriminated against in the workplace.

Three types of justice provide a framework for evaluating the fairness of different situations (Table 6–3). **Distributive justice** is based on the evaluation of the outcomes or results of the business relationship. If some employees feel that they are paid less than their coworkers for the same work, then they have concerns about distributive justice. Distributive justice is difficult to develop when one member of the business exchange intends to take advantage of the relationship. A boss who forces his employees to do more work so that he can take more time off would be seen as unjust because he is taking advantage of his position to redistribute the workers under him. Situations such as this cause an imbalance in distributive justice.

Procedural justice is based on the processes and activities that produce the outcome or results. Evaluations of performance that are not consistently developed and applied can lead to problems with procedural justice. For instance, employees' concerns about inequitable compensation would relate to their perception that the processes of fairness or justice in their company were inconsistent. A climate that emphasizes procedural justice is expected to positively influence employees' attitudes and behaviors toward work-group cohesion. The visibility of supervisors and the work group's perceptions of its own cohesiveness are products of a climate of procedural justice.[26] When there is strong employee support for decisions, decision makers, organizations, and outcomes, procedural justice is less important to the individual. In contrast, when employees' support for decisions, decision makers, organizations, or outcomes is not very

TABLE 6-3	Types of Justice

Justice Type	Evaluations of Fairness
Distributive justice: Based on the evaluation of outcomes or results of the business relationship	Benefits derived Equity in rewards
Procedural justice: Based on the processes and activities that produce the outcome or results	Decision-making process Level of access, openness, and participation
Interactional justice: Based on an evaluation of the communication process used in the business relationship	Accuracy of information Truthfulness, respect, and courtesy in the process

strong, then procedural justice becomes more important.[27] For example, Wainwright Bank and Trust Corporation in Boston has made a commitment to promoting justice to all stakeholders by providing a "sense of inclusion and diversity that extends from the boardroom to the mail room."[28] The bank, in other words, uses methods of procedural justice to establish positive stakeholder relationships by promoting understanding and inclusion in the decision-making process.

Interactional justice is based on evaluating the communication processes used in the business relationship. Because interactional justice is linked to fairness in communication, it often involves the individual's relationship with the business organization through the accuracy of the information the organization provides. Employees can also be guilty in interactional justice disputes. For example, many employees admit that they stay home when they are not really sick if they feel they can get away with it. Such workplace absenteeism costs businesses millions of dollars each year. Being untruthful about the reasons for missing work is an example of an interactional justice issue.

All three types of justice—distributive, procedural, and interactional—could be used to evaluate a single business situation and the fairness of the organization involved. In the example of Sam Colt, Sam's decision to implement a justice perspective would be identical to using a deontological moral philosophy. That is, he would feel obligated to tell all affected parties about the bolt defect rate and the possible consequences of it. In general, justice evaluations result in restitution seeking, relationship building, and evaluations of fairness in business relationships.

APPLYING MORAL PHILOSOPHY TO ETHICAL DECISION MAKING

Strong evidence shows that individuals use different moral philosophies depending on whether they are making a personal decision outside the work environment or making a work-related decision on the job.[29] Two possible reasons may explain this. First, in the business arena, some goals and pressures for success differ from the goals and pressures in a person's life outside of work. As a result, an employee might view a specific action as "good" in the business sector but "unacceptable" in the nonwork environment. The second reason people change moral philosophies could be the corporate culture where they work. When a child enters school, for example, he or she learns certain rules such as raising your hand to speak or asking permission to use the restroom. So it is with a new employee. Rules, personalities, and historical precedence exert pressure on the employee to conform to the new firm's culture. As this occurs, the individual's moral philosophy may change to be compatible with the work environment. The employee may alter some or all of the values within his or her moral philosophy as he or she shifts into the firm's different moral philosophy.

Obviously, the concept of a moral philosophy is inexact. For that reason, moral philosophies must be assessed on a continuum rather than as static entities. Simply put, when examining moral philosophies, we must remember that each philosophy states an ideal perspective and that most individuals seem to shift to other moral philosophies in their individual interpretation of and experiencing of ethical dilemmas. In other words, implementing moral philosophies from an individual perspective is not an exact science. It requires individuals to apply their own accepted value systems to real-world situations. Individuals make judgments about what they believe to be right or wrong, but in their business lives they make decisions that may be based not only on perceived right or wrong but also on producing the greatest benefits with the least harm. Such decisions should respect fundamental moral rights as well as perspectives on fairness, justice, and the common good, but these issues become complicated in the real world.

The virtue approach to business ethics, as discussed earlier, assumes that there are certain ideals and values that everyone should strive for in order to achieve the maximum welfare and happiness of society.[30] Aspects of these ideals and values are expressed through individuals' specific moral philosophies. Every day in the workplace, employees must decide what is right or wrong and act accordingly. At the same time, as a member of a larger organization, an employee cannot simply enforce his or her own personal perspective, especially if he or she adheres narrowly to a single moral philosophy. Because individuals cannot control most of the decisions in their work environment, though they are always responsible for their own actions, they rarely have the power (especially in entry-level and middle-management positions) to impose their own personal moral perspective on others. In fact, the idea that a new employee has the freedom to make independent decisions on a variety of job responsibilities is not realistic.

Sometimes a company makes decisions that could be questionable according to individual customers' values and moral philosophies. For example, a brewery or a distributor of sexually explicit movies could be considered unethical to some stakeholders based on a personal perspective. A company's core values will determine how decisions that bring moral philosophies into conflict are made. Most businesses have developed a mission statement, a corporate culture, and a set of core values that express how they want to relate to their stakeholders, including customers, employees, the legal system, and society. It is usually impossible to please all stakeholders.

Problems arise when employees encounter ethical situations that they cannot resolve. Sometimes gaining a better understanding of the basic premise of their decision rationale can help them choose the "right" solution. For instance, to decide whether they should offer bribes to customers to secure a large contract, salespeople need to understand their own personal moral philosophies as well as their firm's core values. If complying with company policy or legal requirements is an important motivation to the individual, he or she is less likely to offer a bribe. On the other hand, if the salesperson's ultimate goal is a "successful" career and if offering a bribe seems likely to result in a promotion, then bribery might not be inconsistent with that person's moral philosophy of acceptable business behavior. Even though bribery is illegal under U.S. law, the employee may rationalize that bribery is necessary "because everyone else does it."

COGNITIVE MORAL DEVELOPMENT

Many people believe that individuals advance through stages of moral development as their knowledge and socialization continue over time. In this section, we examine a model that describes this cognitive moral development process—that is, the stages through which people may progress in their development of moral thought. Many models, developed to explain, predict, and control individuals' ethical behavior within business organizations, have proposed that cognitive moral processing is an element in ethical decision making. Cognitive moral processing is based on a body of literature in psychology that focuses on studying children and their cognitive development.[31] Psychologist Lawrence Kohlberg adapted Piaget's theory and developed the six-stage model of cognitive development, which, although not specifically designed for business contexts, provides an interesting perspective on the question of moral philosophy in business. According to **Kohlberg's model of cognitive moral development,** people make different decisions in similar ethical situations because they are in different stages of six cognitive moral development stages:

1. *The stage of punishment and obedience.* An individual in Kohlberg's first stage defines *right* as literal obedience to rules and authority. A person in this stage will respond to rules and labels of "good" and "bad" in terms of the physical power of those who determine such rules. Right and wrong are not associated with any higher order or philosophy but rather with a person who has power. Stage 1 is usually associated with small children, but signs of stage 1 development are also evident in adult behavior. For example, some companies forbid their buyers to accept gifts from salespeople. A buyer in stage 1 might justify a refusal to accept gifts from salespeople by referring to the company's rule that defines accepting gifts as an unethical practice, or the buyer may accept the gift if he or she believes that there is no chance of being caught and punished.

2. *The stage of individual instrumental purpose and exchange.* An individual in stage 2 defines *right* as that which serves his or her own needs. In this stage, the individual no longer makes moral decisions solely on the basis of specific rules or authority figures; he or she now evaluates behavior on the basis of its fairness to him or her. For example, a sales representative in stage 2 doing business for the first time in a foreign country may be expected by custom to give customers "gifts." Although gift giving may be against company policy in the United States, the salesperson may decide that certain company rules designed for operating in the United States do not apply overseas. In the culture of some foreign countries, gifts may be considered part of a person's pay. So, in this instance, not giving a gift might put the salesperson at a disadvantage. Some refer to stage 2 as the stage of reciprocity because, from a practical standpoint, ethical decisions are based on an agreement that "you scratch my back and I'll scratch yours" instead of on principles of loyalty, gratitude, or justice.

3. *The stage of mutual interpersonal expectations, relationships, and conformity.* An individual in stage 3 emphasizes others rather than him- or herself. Although ethical motivation is still derived from obedience to rules, the individual considers the well-being of others. A production manager in this stage might obey upper management's order to speed up an assembly line if he or she believed that this would generate more profit for the company and thus save employee jobs. This manager not only considers his or her own well-being in deciding to follow the order but also tries to put him- or herself in upper management's and fellow employees' shoes. Thus, stage 3 differs from stage 2 in that fairness to others is one of the individual's ethical motives.

4. *The stage of social system and conscience maintenance.* An individual in stage 4 determines what is right by considering his or her duty to society, not just to other

specific people. Duty, respect for authority, and maintaining the social order become the focal points. For example, some managers consider it a duty to society to protect privacy and therefore refrain from monitoring employee conversations.

5. *The stage of prior rights, social contract, or utility.* In stage 5, an individual is concerned with upholding the basic rights, values, and legal contracts of society. Individuals in this stage feel a sense of obligation or commitment, a "social contract," to other groups and recognize that in some cases legal and moral points of view may conflict. To reduce such conflict, stage 5 individuals base their decisions on a rational calculation of overall utilities. The president of a firm may decide to establish an ethics program because it will provide a buffer against legal problems and the firm will be perceived as a responsible contributor to society.

6. *The stage of universal ethical principles.* A person in this stage believes that right is determined by universal ethical principles that everyone should follow. Stage 6 individuals believe that there are inalienable rights, which are universal in nature and consequence. These rights, laws, or social agreements are valid, not because of a particular society's laws or customs, but because they rest on the premise of universality. Justice and equality are examples of principles that are deemed universal in nature. A person in this stage may be more concerned with social ethical issues and thus not rely on the business organization for ethical direction. For example, a businessperson at this stage might argue for discontinuing a product that has caused death and injury because the inalienable right to life makes killing wrong, regardless of the reason. Therefore, company profits would not be a justification for the continued sale of the product.[32]

Kohlberg's six stages can be reduced to three different levels of ethical concern. At the first level, a person is concerned with his or her own immediate interests and with external rewards and punishments. At the second level, an individual equates *right* with conformity to the expectations of good behavior of the larger society or some significant reference group. Finally, at the third, or "principled," level, an individual sees beyond the norms, laws, and authority of groups or individuals. Employees at this level make ethical decisions regardless of negative external pressures. However, research has shown that most workers' abilities to identify and resolve moral dilemmas do not reside at this third level and that their motives are often a mixture of selflessness, self-interest, and selfishness.

Kohlberg suggests that people continue to change their decision-making priorities after their formative years, and as a result of time, education, and experience, they may change their values and ethical behavior. In the context of business, an individual's moral development can be influenced by corporate culture, especially ethics training. Ethics training and education have been shown to improve managers' cognitive development scores.[33] Because of corporate reform, most employees in *Fortune* 1000 companies today receive some type of ethics training.

Some feel that experience in resolving moral conflicts accelerates an individual's progress in moral development. A manager who relies on a specific set of values or rules may eventually come across a situation in which the rules do not apply. For example, suppose Sarah is a manager whose policy is to fire any employee whose productivity declines for four consecutive months. Sarah has an employee, George, whose productivity has suffered because of depression, but George's coworkers tell Sarah that George will recover and soon be a top performer again. Because of the circumstances and the perceived value of the employee, Sarah may bend the rule and keep George. Managers in the highest stages of the moral development process seem to be more democratic than autocratic, more likely to consider the ethical views of the other people involved in an ethical decision-making situation.

Once thought to be critical, the theory of cognitive moral development and the empirical research for the last ten years has been mixed, suggesting both a positive and negative relationship between it and ethical decision making. The consensus appears to be that cognitive moral development is difficult at best to measure and connect with ethical decision making.[34]

WHITE-COLLAR CRIME

The terms *crime* and *criminal* normally conjures up thoughts of rape, arson, armed robbery, or murder. The news constantly reports on the damages that occur as a result of these types of crimes. But, although the devastation caused by these "crimes of the street" is more appealing to the evening news, it is no less destructive than the crimes perpetrated every year by seemingly nonviolent white-collar criminals. Referred to as **white-collar crimes** (WCCs), these "crimes of the suite" do more damage in monetary and emotional loss in one year than the crimes of the street over several years combined.[35]

WCC creates victims by establishing trust and respectability. WCCs are often considered to be different than crimes of the street. It is interesting to note in Figure 6–1 that deceptive pricing, unnecessary repairs, and credit card fraud are the three victim categories that were found in the national public household survey of consumers reporting over their lifetime. The victims of WCC are often trusting consumers who

| **FIGURE 6-1** | Individual Victimization Trends (Lifetime Consumer Experiences) |

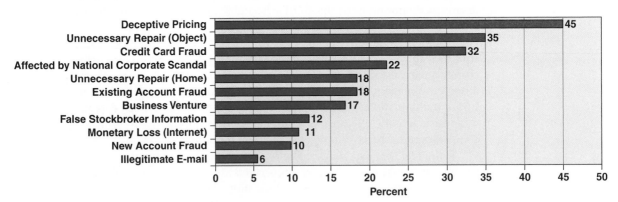

SOURCE: "The 2005 National Public Survey on White Collar Crime," National White Collar Crime Center, http://www.nw3c.org/research/national_public_survey.cfm (accessed March 9, 2006).

believe that businesses are legitimate. Unfortunately, senior citizens and other disadvantaged consumers fall prey to WCC perpetrators. In the White Collar Crime Center's survey nearly one in two households was victimized by WCC in 2005, and well over half of the individuals surveyed had been victimized by WCC over their lifetimes. WCC cost the United States more than $300 billion annually.[36]

From various proposed definitions of WCC, the following appears to be inclusive of the main criminology literature yet parsimonious and exacting enough to be understood:

> An individual or group committing an illegal act in relation to his/her employment, who is highly educated (college), in a position of power, trust, respectability and responsibility, within a profit/nonprofit business or government organization and who abuses the trust and authority normally associated with the position for personal and/or organizational gains.

The presence of technology also seems to be giving a whole new generation of criminals the opportunity to score big. WCCs that previously originated at the top of organizations are now able to be committed at lower levels. Because of these advanced technology systems and corporate culture's increased reliance on them, anyone with the ability to hack into a system now can access the highly sensitive information necessary to commit WCC.

A classic example of WCC is the fraud perpetrated by Bernard Madoff, which was discovered in December 2008. Madoff's scam was based upon a Ponzi scheme, in which the operating principle is that you must constantly attract new investors to pay off old investors the "gains" they were promised. Most Ponzi schemes self-destruct fairly quickly as the ability to keep attracting new investors dwindles.

However, Madoff kept his scheme going for many years. The business that started with a small circle of friends and relatives was built on the promise of modest and steady returns in spite of market swings. With Madoff's social and business connections, and remarkably steady returns of 10 percent to 12 percent, investors were willing to spend billions of dollars. Part of the appeal was the aura that this investment opportunity was highly exclusive, although it later came out that thousands had given their money to Madoff.

When investors questioned Madoff about their investments, he refused to provide them online access to their accounts. Nonetheless, Madoff's well-dressed, multilingual sales representatives continued to convince European buyers to invest. With the large financial portfolio.

Many people indicate that one red flag would have been the fact that he would have overtaken the market had he traded the options in the volumes necessary to meet his financial goals. Madoff ultimately admitted to running a 4,800-client Ponzi scheme for more than a decade. While investors thought they had nearly $65 billion invested with Madoff, his financial advisement firm never had anywhere near that much money. Incredibly, he had not invested a single penny. Instead, Madoff deposited the money in a bank account, which he then used to pay investors when they asked for their money back. The only way he sustained the operation for as long as he did was through attracting new clients. Madoff will spend the rest of his life in prison for his crime.[37]

The focus of criminology is often the behavior of the individual and discovery of the reasons why people commit such crimes. Advocates of the organizational deviance perspective argue that a corporation is a living, breathing organism that can collectively become deviant; that companies have a life of their own, separate and distinct from biological persons; that the ultimate "actors" in an organization are individuals; and that the corporate culture of the company transcends the individuals who occupy these positions. With time, patterns of activities become institutionalized within the organization that live on after those who established them have left the firm.

Another common cause of WCC is peer influence, the result of an individual's circle of acquaintances within an organization, with their accompanying views and behaviors. Employees, at least in part, self-select the people with whom they associate within an organization. For companies with a high number of ethical employees, there is a higher probability that a fence sitter (the 40 percent of businesspeople who could be persuaded to be ethical or unethical) will go along with their coworkers.

Finally, there is an argument to be made that some businesspeople may have personalities that are inherently criminal.[38] Personality tests have been used to predict behavior in individuals working within an organization, but such tests presuppose that values and philosophies are constant; thus, they seem to be ineffective as an approach to understanding the subtleties of white-collar criminals.[39] We also know that businesspeople and companies must make a profit on revenue to exist, slanting their orientation toward teleology and making them increasingly likely to commit white-collar crimes. The answer to the increase in WCC is not easy to pinpoint because many variables cause good people to make bad decisions.

As Figure 6–2 shows, the National White Collar Crime Center survey indicates that over half the respondents disagree that the government is devoting enough resources to combat WCC. The current focus of the Federal Sentencing Guidelines for Organizations is that all organizations should develop effective ethics and compliance programs to prevent WCC.

FIGURE 6–2   Does the Government Devote Enough Resources to Combat White-Collar Crime?

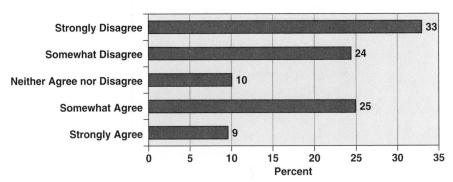

SOURCE: "The 2005 National Public Survey on White Collar Crime," National White Collar Crime Center, http://www.nw3c.org/research/national_public_survey.cfm (accessed March 9, 2006).

THE ROLE OF INDIVIDUAL FACTORS IN BUSINESS ETHICS

Of course, not everyone agrees on what the role of traditional moral philosophies in ethical decision making in an organization is. Some types such as Machiavellianism, which comes from the writing of Machiavelli, an Italian political theorist, have been found to influence ethical decisions. *The Prince* (a letter that Machiavelli wrote from exile to an Italian prince) argues against the relevance of morality in political affairs and holds that craft and deceit are justified in pursuing and maintaining political power. Machiavelli is famous for the idea that, for a leader, it is better to be feared than to be loved, and this type of thinking abounds within *The Prince* because Machiavelli presents basically a guidebook for obtaining and maintaining power without the need for morality. Most business managers do not embrace this extreme philosophy, and most managers cannot communicate the exact moral philosophy that they use to make ethical decisions.

According to ethics consultant David Gebler, "Most unethical behavior is not done for personal gain, it's done to meet performance goals."[40] Unfortunately, many people believe that individual moral philosophies are the main driver of ethical behavior in business. This belief can be a stumbling block in assessing ethical risk and preventing misconduct in an organizational context. The moral values learned within the family and through religion and education are key factors that do influence decision making, but as indicated in the models in Chapter 5, it is only one major factor. The fact that many companies and business schools focus on personal character or moral development in their training programs as the main consideration reinforces the idea that employees can control the work environment. Although a personal moral compass is important, it is not sufficient to prevent ethical misconduct in an organizational context. The rewards for meeting performance goals and the corporate culture, especially for coworkers and managers, have been found to be the most important drivers of ethical decision making.[41]

Strong abilities in ethical reasoning will probably lead to more ethical business decisions in the future than trying to provide detached character education for each employee.[42] Equipping employees with intellectual skills that will allow them to understand and resolve complex ethical dilemmas that they encounter in complex corporate cultures will help them make the right decisions. This approach will hopefully keep them from being carried along by peer pressure and lulled by unethical managers to engage in misconduct.[43] The West Point model for character development focuses on the fact that competence and character must be developed simultaneously. This model assumes that ethical reasoning has to be approached in the context of a specific profession. The military has been effective in teaching skills and developing principles and values that can be used in most situations that a soldier will encounter. In a similar manner, accountants, managers, or marketers need to develop ethical reasoning in the context of their jobs.

SUMMARY

Moral philosophy refers to the set of principles, or rules, that people use to decide what is right or wrong. These principles, rules, or philosophies present guidelines for resolving conflicts and for optimizing the mutual benefit of people living in groups.

Businesspeople are somewhat guided by moral philosophies as they formulate business strategies and resolve specific ethical issues.

Teleological, or consequentialist, philosophies stipulate that acts are morally right or acceptable if they produce some desired result, such as realization of self-interest or utility. Egoism defines right or acceptable behavior in terms of the consequences for the individual. In an ethical decision-making situation, the egoist will choose the alternative that contributes most to his or her own self-interest. Egoism can be further classified into hedonism and enlightened egoism. Utilitarianism is concerned with maximizing total utility, or providing the greatest benefit for the greatest number of people. In making ethical decisions, utilitarians often conduct a cost-benefit analysis, which considers the costs and benefits to all affected parties. Rule utilitarians determine behavior on the basis of rules designed to promote the greatest utility rather than by examining particular situations. Act utilitarians examine the action itself, rather than the rules governing the action, to determine whether it will result in the greatest utility.

Deontological, or nonconsequentialist, philosophies focus on the rights of individuals and on the intentions behind an individual's particular behavior rather than on its consequences. In general, deontologists regard the nature of moral principles as permanent and stable, and they believe that compliance with these principles defines ethicalness. Deontologists believe that individuals have certain absolute rights that must be respected. Rule deontologists believe that conformity to general moral principles determines ethicalness. Act deontologists hold that actions are the proper basis on which to judge morality or ethicalness and that rules serve only as guidelines.

According to the relativist perspective, definitions of ethical behavior are derived subjectively from the experiences of individuals and groups. The relativist observes behavior within a relevant group and attempts to determine what consensus group members have reached on the issue in question.

Virtue ethics posits that what is moral in a given situation is not only what is required by conventional morality or current social definitions, however justified, but also what a person with a "good" moral character would deem appropriate. Those who profess virtue ethics do not believe that the end justifies the means in any situation.

Ideas of justice as applied in business relate to evaluations of fairness. Justice relates to the fair treatment and due reward in accordance with ethical or legal standards. Distributive justice is based on the evaluation of the outcome or results of a business relationship. Procedural justice is based on the processes and activities that produce the outcomes or results. Interactional justice is based on an evaluation of the communication process in business.

The concept of a moral philosophy is not exact; moral philosophies can only be assessed on a continuum. Individuals use different moral philosophies depending on whether they are making a personal or a workplace decision.

According to Kohlberg's model of cognitive moral development, individuals make different decisions in similar ethical situations because they are in different stages of moral development. In Kohlberg's model, people progress through six stages of moral development: (1) punishment and obedience; (2) individual instrumental purpose and exchange; (3) mutual interpersonal expectations, relationships, and conformity; (4) social system and conscience maintenance; (5) prior rights, social contract, or utility;

and (6) universal ethical principles. Kohlberg's six stages can be further reduced to three levels of ethical concern: immediate self-interest, social expectations, and general ethical principles. Cognitive moral development may not explain as much as was once believed.

White-collar crime can be defined as an individual committing an illegal act in relation to his or her employment, who is highly educated; in a position of power, trust, respectability and responsibility; and abuses the trust and authority normally associated with the position for personal and/or organizational gains. Some reasons why white-collar crime is not being heavily researched are that it doesn't come to mind when people think of crime, the offender (or organization) is in a position of trust and respectability, criminology or criminal justice systems look at white-collar crime differently, and many researchers have not moved past the definitional issues. The increase in technology use seems to be increasing the opportunity to commit white-collar crime with less risk.

Individual factors such as religion, moral intensity, and a person's professional affiliations can affect a person's values and decision-making process. Other factors such as ethical awareness, biases, conflict, personality type, and intelligence have been studied, but no definitive conclusions can be made at this time about their relationship to ethical behavior. One thing we do know is that moral philosophies, values, and business are more complex than merely giving people honesty tests or value profiles that are not business oriented. Paper-and-pencil techniques do not yield accurate profiles for companies.

IMPORTANT TERMS FOR REVIEW

moral philosophy	act utilitarian
economic value orientation	deontology
idealism	nonconsequentialist
realism	rule deontologist
monist	act deontologist
hedonism	relativist perspective
quantitative hedonist	descriptive relativism
qualitative hedonist	metaethical relativist
pluralist	normative relativism
instrumentalist	virtue ethics
goodness theory	justice
obligation theory	distributive justice
teleology	procedural justice
consequentialism	interactional justice
egoism	Kohlberg's model of cognitive moral
enlightened egoism	development
utilitarianism	white-collar crime
rule utilitarian	

RESOLVING ETHICAL BUSINESS CHALLENGES*

Twenty-eight-year-old Elaine Hunt, who is married and has one child, has been with United Banc Corporation (UBC) for several years. During that time, she has seen it grow from a relatively small-size to a medium-size company with domestic and international customers. Elaine's husband, Dennis, has been involved in the import–export business.

The situation that precipitated their current problem began six months ago. Elaine had just been promoted to senior financial manager, which put her in charge of ten branch-office loan managers, each of whom had five loan officers who reported to him or her. For the most part, the branch loan officers would go through the numbers of their loan people, as well as sign off on loans under $250,000. However, recently this limit had been increased to $500,000. For any loan over this amount and up to $40 million, Elaine had to sign off. For larger loans, a vice president would have to be involved.

Recently, Graphco Inc. requested a $10 million loan, which Elaine had been hesitant to approve. Graphco was a subsidiary of a tobacco firm embroiled in litigation concerning the promotion of its products to children. When reviewing the numbers, Elaine could not find any glaring problems, yet she had decided against the loan even when Graphco had offered to pay an additional interest point. Some at UBC applauded her moral stance while others did not, arguing that it was not a good financial business decision. The next prospective loan was for a Canadian company that was exporting cigars from Cuba. Elaine cited the U.S. policy against Cuba as the reason for not approving that loan. "The Helms-Burton Amendment gives us clear guidance as to what we shouldn't be doing with Cuba," she said to others in the company, even though the loan was to a Canadian firm. The third loan application she was unwilling to approve had come from Electrode International, which sought $50 million. The numbers had been marginal, but the sticking point for Elaine was Electrode's unusually high profits during the last two years. During dinner with Dennis, she had learned about a meeting in Zurich during which Electrode and others had allegedly fixed the prices on their products. Because only a handful of companies manufactured these particular products, the price increases were very successful. When Elaine suggested denying the loan on the basis of this information, she was overruled. At the same time, a company in Brazil was asking for an agricultural loan to harvest parts of the rain forest. The Brazilian company was willing to pay almost 2 points over the going rate for a $40 million loan. Because of her stand on environmental issues, Elaine rejected this application as well. The company obtained the loan from one of UBC's competitors.

Recently, Elaine's husband's decision making had fallen short of his superior's expectations. First, there was the problem of an American firm wanting to export nicotine and caffeine patches to Southeast Asia. With new research showing both these drugs to be more problematic than previously thought, the manufacturing firm had decided to attempt a rapid-penetration marketing strategy—that is, to price the products very low or at cost in order to gain market share and then over time slightly increase the margin. With 2 billion potential customers, a 1-cent markup could result in millions of dollars in profits. Dennis had rejected the deal, and the firm had gone to another company. One person in Dennis's division had said, "Do you realize that you had the perfect product—one that was low cost and both physically and psychologically addictive? You could have serviced that one account for years and would have had enough for early retirement. Are you nuts for turning it down?!"

Soon afterward, an area financial bank manager wanted Elaine to sign off on a revolving loan for ABCO. ABCO's debt/equity ratio had increased significantly and did not conform to company regulations. However, Elaine was the one who had written the standards for UBC. Some in the company felt that Elaine was not quite up with the times. For example, several very good bank staff members had left in the past year because they found her regulations too provincial for the emerging global marketplace. As Elaine reviewed ABCO's credit report, she found many danger signals; however, the loan was relatively large, $30 million, and the company had been in a credit sales slump. As she questioned ABCO, Elaine learned that the loan was to develop a new business venture within the People's Republic of China, which rumor had it was also working with the Democratic People's Republic of Korea. The biotech venture was for fetal tissue research and harvesting. Recently, attention had focused on the economic benefits of such tissue in helping a host of ailments. Anticipated global market sales for such products were being estimated at $10 billion for the next decade. ABCO was also willing to go almost 2 points above the standard interest equation for such a revolving loan. Elaine realized that if she signed off on this sale, it would signal an end to her standards. However, if she did not and ABCO went to another company for the loan and paid off the debt, she would have made a gross error, and everyone in the company would know it.

As Elaine was wrestling with this problem, Dennis's commissions began to slip, putting a crimp in their cash-flow projections. If things did not turn around quickly for him, they would lose their new home, fall behind in other payments, and reduce the number of educational options for their child. Elaine had also had a frank discussion with senior management about her loan standards as well as her stand on tobacco, which had lost UBC precious income. The response was, "Elaine, we applaud your moral outrage about such products, but your morals are negatively impacting the bottom line. We can't have that all the time."

QUESTIONS • EXERCISES

1. Discuss the advantages and disadvantages of each decision that Elaine has made.
2. What are the ethical and legal considerations facing Elaine, Dennis, and UBC?
3. Discuss the moral philosophies that may be relevant to this situation.
4. Discuss the implications of each decision that Elaine could make.

*This case is strictly hypothetical; any resemblance to real persons, companies, or situations is coincidental.

Check Your EQ

Check your EQ, or Ethics Quotient, by completing the following. Assess your performance to evaluate your overall understanding of the chapter material.

1. Teleology defines right or acceptable behavior in terms of consequences for the individual.   **Yes**   **No**
2. A relativist looks at an ethical situation and considers the individuals and groups involved.   **Yes**   **No**
3. A utilitarian is most concerned with the bottom-line benefits.   **Yes**   **No**
4. Act deontology requires that a person use equity, fairness, and impartiality in making decisions and evaluating actions.   **Yes**   **No**
5. Virtues that support business transactions include trust, fairness, truthfulness, competitiveness, and focus.   **Yes**   **No**

ANSWERS: 1. No. That's egoism. 2. Yes. Relativists look at themselves and those around them to determine ethical standards. 3. Yes. Utilitarians look for the greatest good for the greatest number of people and use a cost–benefit approach. 4. Yes. The rules serve only as guidelines, and past experience weighs more heavily than the rules. 5. No. The characteristics include trust, self-control, empathy, fairness, and truthfulness—not competitiveness and focus.

CHAPTER 7

Organizational Factors: The Role of Ethical Culture and Relationships

CHAPTER OBJECTIVES

- To examine the influence of corporate culture on business ethics
- To determine how leadership, power, and motivation relate to ethical decision making in organizations
- To assess organizational structure and its relationship to business ethics
- To explore how the work group influences ethical decisions
- To discuss the relationship between individual and group ethical decision making

CHAPTER OUTLINE

Dawn Prarie had been with PCA Health Care Hospitals for three years and had been promoted to marketing director in the Miami area. She had a staff of ten and a fairly healthy budget. Dawn's job was to attract more patients into the HMO while helping keep costs down. At a meeting with Dawn, Nancy Belle, the vice president, had explained the ramifications of the Balanced Budget Act and how it was affecting all HMOs. "Being here in Miami does not help our division," she told Dawn. "Because of this Balanced Budget Act, we have been losing money on many of our elderly patients. For example, we used to receive $600 or more a month, per patient, from Medicare, but now our minimum reimbursement is just $367 a month! I need solutions, and that's where you come in. By the end of the month, I want a list of things that will help us show a profit. Anything less than a positive balance sheet will be unacceptable."

It was obvious that Nancy was serious about cutting costs and increasing revenues within the elderly market. That's why Dawn had been promoted to marketing director. The first thing Dawn did after the meeting with Nancy was to fire four key people. She then gave their duties to six who were at lower salaries and put the hospital staff on notice that changes would be occurring at the hospital over the next several months. In about three weeks, Dawn presented Nancy with an extensive list of ideas. It included these suggestions:

1. Trimming some prescription drug benefits
2. Reducing redundant tests for terminal patients
3. Hiring physician assistants to see patients but billing patients at the physician rate
4. Allowing physicians to buy shares in PCA, thus providing an incentive for bringing in more patients
5. Sterilizing and reusing cardiac catheters
6. Instituting a one-vendor policy on hospital products to gain quantity discounts
7. Prescreening "insurance" patients for probability of payment

Dawn's assistants felt that some of the hospital staff could be more aggressive in the marketing area. They urged using more promotional materials, offering incentives for physicians who suggested PCA or required their patients to be hospitalized, and prescreening potential clients into categories. "You see," said Ron, one of Dawn's staff, "we feel that there are four types of elderly patients. There are the healthy elderly, whose life expectancies are ten or more years. There are the fragile elderly, with life expectancies of two to seven years. Then there are the demented and dying elderly, who usually have one to three years. Finally, we have the high-cost or uninsured elderly. Patients who are designated healthy would get the most care, including mammograms, prostate-cancer screening, and cholesterol checks. Patients in the other categories would get less."

As she implemented some of the recommendations on Dawn's list, Nancy also launched an aggressive plan to destabilize the nurses' union. As a result, many nurses began a work slowdown and were filing internal petitions to upper management. Headquarters told Nancy to give the nurses and other hospital staff as much overtime as they wanted but not to hire anyone new. One floor manager suggested splitting up the staff into work teams, with built-in incentives for those who worked smarter and/or faster. Nancy approved the plan, and in three months productivity jumped 50 percent, with many of the hospital workers making more money. The downside for Nancy was an increase in worker-related accidents.

When Dawn toured the hospital around this time, she found that some of the most productive workers were using substandard procedures and poorly made products. One nurse said, "Yes, the surgical gloves are somewhat of a problem, but we were told that the quality met the minimum requirements and so we have to use them." Dawn brought this to Nancy's attention, whereupon Nancy drafted the following memo:

ATTENTION HOSPITAL STAFF

It has come to management's attention that minor injuries to staff and patients are on the rise.

Please review the Occupational Safety and Health Administration guidelines, as well as the standard procedures handbook, to make sure you are in compliance. I also want to thank all those teams that have been keeping costs down. We have finally gone into the plus side as far as profitability. Hang on and we'll be able to stabilize the hospital to make it a better place to care for patients and to work.

At Nancy's latest meeting with Dawn, she told Dawn, "We've decided on your staff's segmentation strategy for the elderly market. We want you to develop a questionnaire to prescreen incoming HMO patients, as well as existing clients, into one of the four categories so that we can tag their charts and alert the HMO physicians to the new protocols. Also, because the recommendations that we've put into practice have worked so well, we've decided to use the rest of your suggestions. The implementation

phase will start next month. I want you, Dawn, to be the lead person in developing a long-term strategy to break the unions in the hospital. Do whatever it takes. We just need to do more with less. I'm firm on this—so you're either on board or you're not. Which is it going to be?"

QUESTIONS • EXERCISES

1. Discuss PCA Health Care Hospitals' corporate culture and its ethical implications.
2. What factors are affecting Dawn's options?
3. Discuss the issue of for-profit versus nonprofit health-care facilities.
4. If you were Dawn, what information would you like to have to make your decisions?

*This case is strictly hypothetical; any resemblance to real persons, companies, or situations is coincidental.

Organizations are much more than structures in which we work. Although they are not alive, we attribute human characteristics to them. When times are good, we say the company is "well"; when times are not so good, we may try to "save" the company. Understandably, people have feelings toward the place that provides them with income and benefits; challenge, satisfaction, self-esteem, and often lifelong friendships. In fact, excluding the time spent sleeping, we spend almost 50 percent of our lives in this second home with our second "family." It is important, then, to examine how the culture and structure of these organizations influence the ethical decisions made within them.

In the ethical decision-making framework described in Chapter 5, we introduced the idea that organizational factors such as corporate culture and interpersonal relationships influence the ethical decision-making process. In this chapter, we take a closer look at corporate culture and the way a company's values and traditions can affect employees' ethical behavior. We also discuss the role of leadership in influencing ethical behavior within the organization. Next we describe two organizational structures and examine how they may influence ethical decisions. Then we consider the impact of groups within organizations. Finally, we examine the implications of organizational relationships for ethical decisions.

THE ROLE OF CORPORATE CULTURE IN ETHICAL DECISION MAKING

Chapter 5 defined the term *corporate culture* as a set of values, beliefs, goals, norms, and ways of solving problems shared by the members (employees) of an organization of any size (for profit or nonprofit). A founder and his or her values and expectations can create corporate culture, as in the case of McDonald's. The fast-food giant's support of and reputation for quality, service, cleanliness, and value derive from founder Ray Kroc. However, McDonald's faces problems with customer satisfaction. Over 10 percent of McDonald's customers are dissatisfied with their visit and share their complaint with the restaurant. The top-five customer complaints at McDonald's include (1) rude employees, (2) being out of Happy Meal toys, (3) slow service, (4) missing product/wrong order, and (5) unclean restaurants.[1] Corporate culture includes the behavioral patterns, concepts, values, ceremonies, and rituals that take place in the organization.[2] It gives the members of the organization meaning as well as the internal rules of behavior.[3] When these values, beliefs, customs, rules, and ceremonies are accepted, shared, and circulated throughout the organization, they represent its culture. All organizations, not just corporations, have some sort of culture, and thus we use the terms *organizational culture* and *corporate culture* interchangeably.

Although corporate culture is a broad and widely used concept, the term has a multitude of definitions, none of which has achieved universal acceptance. These range from highly specific to generically broad. For example, *culture* has been defined as "the way we do things around here,"[4] "the collective programming of the mind,"[5] and "the social fiber that holds the organization together."[6] Culture is also viewed as "the shared beliefs top managers in a company have about how they should manage themselves and other employees, and how they should conduct their business(es)."[7] Mutual of Omaha defines corporate culture as the "personality of the organization, the shared beliefs that determine how its people behave and solve business problems."[8] Mutual of Omaha executives believe that its corporate culture provides the foundation for the company's work and objectives, and the company has adopted a set of core values called "Values for Success" (Table 7–1). The company believes that these values form the foundation for a corporate culture that will help the organization realize its vision and achieve its goals.

A company's history and unwritten rules are a part of its culture. Thus, for many years, IBM salespeople adhered to a series of unwritten standards for dealing with clients. The history or stories passed down from generation to generation within an organization are like the traditions that are propagated within society. Henry Ford, the founder of Ford Motor Company, left a legacy that emphasized the importance of the individual employee and the natural environment. Just as Henry Ford pioneered the then-unheard-of high wage of $5 a day in the early years of the twentieth century, current chairman William Clay Ford, Jr., continues to affirm that employees represent the only sustainable advantage of a company. William Ford has maintained his grandfather's legacy by taking a leadership role in improving vehicle fuel efficiency while reducing emissions. Ford faces many financial challenges, especially with the financial meltdown. Although it is not one of the companies that took government monies, Ford's recovery plan is to shut down sixteen North American plants and cut forty thousand jobs. William Ford is committed to successfully restructuring Ford to more successfully compete in the future.[9]

Some cultures are so strong that to outsiders they come to represent the character of the entire organization. For example, Levi Strauss, Ben & Jerry's Homemade (the ice cream company), and Hershey Foods are widely perceived as casual organizations with strong ethical cultures, whereas Lockheed Martin, Procter & Gamble, and Texas

TABLE 7-1	Mutual of Omaha's "Values for Success"

Openness and Trust—We encourage an open sharing of ideas and information, displaying a fundamental respect for each other as well as our cultural diversity.

Teamwork (Win/Win)—We work together to find solutions that carry positive results for others as well as ourselves, creating an environment that brings out the best in everyone.

Accountability/Ownership—We take ownership and accept accountability for achieving end results, and empower team members to do the same.

Sense of Urgency—We set priorities and handle all tasks and assignments in a timely manner.

Honesty and Integrity—We are honest and ethical with others, maintaining the highest standards of personal and professional conduct.

Customer-Focus—We never lose sight of our customers, and constantly challenge ourselves to meet their requirements even better.

Innovation and Risk—We question "the old way of doing things" and take prudent risks that can lead to innovative performance and process improvements.

Caring/Attentive (Be Here Now)—We take time to clear our minds to focus on the present moment, listening to our teammates and customers, and caring enough to hear their concerns.

Leadership—We provide direction, purpose, support, encouragement, and recognition to achieve our vision, meet our objectives and our values.

Personal and Professional Growth—We challenge ourselves and look for ways to be even more effective as a team and as individuals.

SOURCE: "Transforming Our Culture: The Values for Success," Mutual of Omaha, www.careerlink.org/emp/mut/corp.htm (accessed March 30, 2006). Reprinted with permission.

Instruments are perceived as more formal, ethical ones. The culture of an organization may be explicitly articulated or left unspoken.

Explicit statements of values, beliefs, and customs usually come from upper management. Memos, written codes of conduct, handbooks, manuals, forms, and ceremonies are all formal expressions of an organization's culture. Many of these statements can be found on company websites, like Mutual of Omaha's "Values for Success."

Corporate culture is often expressed informally—for example, through comments, both direct and indirect, that communicate the wishes of management. In some companies, shared values are expressed through informal dress codes, working late, and participation in extracurricular activities. Corporate culture can even be expressed through gestures, looks, labels, promotions, programs, and legends (or the lack of these). Southwest Airlines is involved with more than thirty thousand students nationwide as part of their "Adopt-a-Pilot" educational program. The program encourages students to research careers, set personal goals, and realize the importance of succeeding in school. During the four-week mentorship program, pilots volunteer their time and correspond with their student, mentor while on the road, and speak in their classes.[10] This program reinforces Southwest's commitment to its communities and caring organizational culture. The press generated by community involvement reinforces organizational values and priorities.

The "tone at the top" is often cited as a determining factor in creating a high-integrity organization. Employees were asked, in a KPMG Forensic Integrity Survey

FIGURE 7-1 Perceived Tone and Culture, Tone at the Top, and Perceptions of the CEO and Other Senior Executives

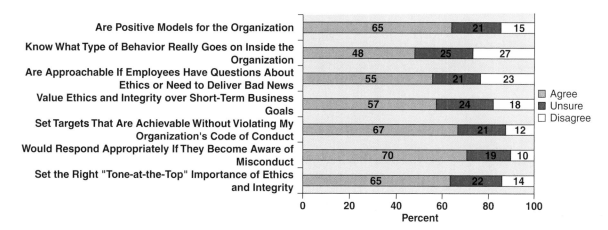

SOURCE: "KPMG Forensic Integrity Survey 2005–2006,"
http://www.kpmginsiders.com/display_analysis.asp?cs_id=148597 (accessed March 9, 2006).

(Figure 7–1) whether their CEO and other senior executives exhibited characteristics attributable to personal integrity and ethical leadership. Nearly two-thirds of employees believed that their leaders served as positive role models for their organizations. However, roughly half suggested a lack of confidence (based on "unsure" and "disagree" responses) that their CEOs knew about behaviors further down in the organization. Nearly half suggested a lack of confidence that their leaders would be approachable if employees had ethics concerns, and 70 percent agreed that their CEOs would respond appropriately to matters brought to their attention. Overall, nearly two-thirds of employees agreed their leaders set the right tone at the top, leaving one-third unsure or in disagreement.

Ethical Framework and Audit for Corporate Culture

Corporate culture has been conceptualized in many ways. Authors N. K. Sethia and Mary Ann Von Glinow have proposed two basic dimensions to describe an organization's culture: (1) concern for people—the organization's efforts to care for its employees' well-being; and (2) concern for performance—the organization's efforts to focus on output and employee productivity. A two-by-two matrix represents the four general types of organizational cultures (Figure 7–2).[11]

As Figure 7–2 shows, the four organizational cultures can be classified as apathetic, caring, exacting, and integrative. The *apathetic culture* shows minimal concern for either people or performance. In this culture, individuals focus on their own self-interests. Apathetic tendencies can occur in almost any organization. Steel companies

| FIGURE 7-2 | A Framework of Organizational Culture Typologies |

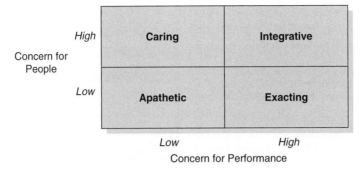

SOURCE: From *Gaining Control of the Corporate Culture*, by N. K. Sethia and M. A. Von Glinow, 1985, Jossey-Bass, Inc. Reprinted with permission of John Wiley & Sons, Inc.

and airlines were among the first to freeze employee pensions to keep their businesses operating, now *Fortune* 500 companies such as Sears, IBM, and Verizon are engaging in the same behaviors. Workers can still keep their pensions, but the payout will not be based on their final, higher paying salary years. A study by Hewitt Associates found that 21 percent of the nation's companies plan to freeze employee benefits at their current levels, and 17 percent will omit them completely for new employees.[12] Sweeping changes in corporate America are impacting employee compensation and retirement plans. Simple gestures of appreciation, such as anniversary watches, rings, dinners, or birthday cards for family members, are being dropped. Many companies view long-serving employees as deadwood and do not take into account past performance. This attitude demonstrates the companies' apathetic culture.

The *caring culture* exhibits high concern for people but minimal concern for performance issues. From an ethical standpoint, the caring culture seems to be very appealing. Southwest Airlines, for example, has a long-standing reputation of concern for its employees. CEO Herb Kelleher is the purveyor of wit, wisdom, and continuity in Southwest's culture. Employees "love the company" because they believe it cares for and is concerned about them. Employee loyalty and commitment at Southwest are very high. Kelleher has been known to go into the cargo hold of a plane attired in a dress and feather boa to assist employees with baggage. Southwest feels that if employees are well cared for, then customers will be taken care of and the competition will be surpassed. But as of late Southwest no longer holds the number-one spot, AirTran does, and the rate of consumer complaints reported to the Department of Transportation rose to 1.42 per 100,000 passengers, versus 0.88. US Airways drew the most complaints, followed by United and Delta.[13]

In contrast, the *exacting culture* shows little concern for people but a high concern for performance; it focuses on the interests of the organization. United Parcel Service (UPS) has always been very exacting. It knows precisely how many workers it needs to deliver its 14.8 million packages a day. To combat the uncaring, unsympathetic attitude of many of its managers, UPS developed a community service program for its employees. Global Volunteer Week gives UPS employees around the world the opportunity to help paint schools, renovate shelters, and assist with many other needed projects within their communities. Recently UPS has started to go "green" with the deployment of 167 compressed natural gas (CNG) delivery vehicles in Texas, Georgia, and California. The trucks are expected to reduce emissions by 20 percent and improve fuel economy by 10 percent compared to the cleanest diesel engines available today.[14]

The *integrative culture* combines high concern for people and for performance. An organization becomes integrative when superiors recognize that employees are more than interchangeable parts—that employees have an ineffable quality that helps the firm meet its performance criteria. Many companies, such as U.S. Foodservice, have such a culture. U.S. Foodservice is the number-two food service distributor, behind Sysco, serving over two hundred and fifty thousand customers, including restaurants, hotels, schools, and other institutions. The company was involved in improper revenue recognition resulting in an $800 million revenue overstatement. Today, U.S. Foodservice operates a comprehensive ethics and compliance program including training videos featuring Ben Stein (actor and comedian) and the company's president and CEO Lawrence Benjamin.[15]

Companies can classify their corporate culture and identify its specific values, norms, beliefs, and customs by conducting a cultural audit. A *cultural audit* is an assessment of the organization's values. It is usually conducted by outside consultants but may be performed internally as well. Table 7–2 illustrates some of the issues that an ethics

TABLE 7–2 Ethics Related Actions Among Levels of Employees	
Statement Describing Ethics Related Actions	**Percentage of Employees Strongly Agreeing or Agreeing (2005)**
Top management provides information	80
Top management keeps commitments	81
Top management communicates ethics	89
Top management sets a good example of ethics	87
Middle management keeps commitments	85
Middle management communicates ethics	89
Middle management sets good example of ethics	89
Supervisor sets good example of ethics	91
Supervisor keeps commitments	88
Supervisor talks about ethics	90
Supervisor supports standards	93
Coworkers consider ethics in decisions	91
Coworkers support standards	94
Coworkers set good example of ethics	92
Coworkers talk about ethics	80

SOURCE: From *2005 National Business Ethics Survey: How Employees Perceive Ethics at Work*, p. 20.
Copyright © 2006, Ethics Resource Center (ERC). Used with permission of the ERC, 1747 Pennsylvania Ave., N.W., Suite 400, Washington, DC 2006, www.ethics.org.

audit of a corporate culture should address. The table identifies components of an organizational ethical culture, with the percentage of those employees who strongly agreed or agreed that the specific action was being displayed in their organizations. There has been little change since 2000–2005 in the figures. These issues can help identify a corporate culture that creates ethical conflict.

Ethics as a Component of Corporate Culture

As indicated in the framework presented in Chapter 5, ethical culture, the ethical component of corporate culture, is a significant factor in ethical decision making. If a firm's culture encourages or rewards unethical behavior, its employees may well act unethically. If the culture dictates hiring people who have specific, similar values and if those values are perceived as unethical by society, society will view the organization and its members as unethical. Such a pattern often occurs in certain areas of marketing. For instance, salespeople may be seen as unethical because they sometimes use aggressive selling tactics to get customers to buy things they do not need or want. If a company's primary objective is to make as much profit as possible, through whatever means, its culture may foster behavior that conflicts with stakeholders' ethical values. For example, Boeing general counsel, Doug Bain, noted in an annual leadership meeting that Boeing operated with a culture of winning at any cost. He continued noting that fifteen company vice presidents have been removed for a variety of ethical lapses. Boeing is under investigation by the Justice Department and could face heavy fines.[16] The interests of diverse Boeing stakeholders (shareholders, suppliers, and employees) may have been ignored in their efforts to boost profits.

On the other hand, if the organization values ethical behaviors, it will reward them. Green Mountain Coffee Roasters, Inc., was ranked as the most socially responsible company in 2008 by *Business Ethics* magazine. The company integrates their values to achieve success because "the more profitable we are, the more good we can do in the world."[17] They have focused on eradicating extreme poverty and hunger and on ensuring environmental sustainability because they believe Green Mountain Coffee Roasters has the most potential for ongoing positive change in these areas.[18]

An organization's failure to monitor or manage its culture may foster questionable behavior. In a patent infringement case brought against Gateway in Utah, a federal judge reprimanded the company for destroying or losing evidence in "bad faith." A former IBM engineer brought the suit against Gateway, indicating that they infringed upon his patents for addressing defects in floppy-disk drives. The engineer also added that Gateway lost or destroyed documents that would have helped prove his case. Attempts to cover up wrongdoing by destroying documents should not be tolerated.[19]

Management's sense of the organization's culture may be quite different from the values and ethical beliefs that are actually guiding the firm's employees. Table 7–3 provides an example of a corporate culture ethics audit. Companies interested in assessing their culture can use this tool and benchmark against previous years' results to measure for organizational improvements. Ethical issues may arise because of conflicts between the cultural values perceived by management and those actually at work in the organization. For example, managers may believe that the culture encourages respect for peers and subordinates. On the basis of the rewards or sanctions associated with

TABLE 7-3	Corporate Culture Ethics Audit

Answer Yes or No to each of the following questions.*

Yes	No	Has the founder or top management of the company left an ethical legacy to the organization?
Yes	No	Does the company have methods for detecting ethical concerns within the organization and outside it?
Yes	No	Is there a shared value system and understanding of what constitutes appropriate behavior within the organization?
Yes	No	Are stories and myths embedded in daily conversations about appropriate ethical conduct when confronting ethical situations?
Yes	No	Are codes of ethics or ethical policies communicated to employees?
Yes	No	Are there ethical rules or procedures in training manuals or other company publications?
Yes	No	Are there penalties that are publicly discussed for ethical transgressions?
Yes	No	Are there rewards for good ethical decisions even if they don't always result in a profit?
Yes	No	Does the company recognize the importance of creating a culture that is concerned about people and their self-development as members of the business?
Yes	No	Does the company have a value system of fair play and honesty toward customers?
Yes	No	Do employees treat each other with respect, honesty, and fairness?
Yes	No	Do employees spend their time working in a cohesive way on what is valued by the organization?
Yes	No	Are there ethically based beliefs and values about how to succeed in the company?
Yes	No	Are there heroes or stars in the organization who communicate a common understanding about what positive ethical values are important?
Yes	No	Are there day-to-day rituals or behavior patterns that create direction and prevent confusion or mixed signals on ethics matters?
Yes	No	Is the firm more focused on the long run than on the short run?
Yes	No	Are employees satisfied or happy, and is employee turnover low?
Yes	No	Do the dress, speech, and physical work setting prevent an environment of fragmentation or inconsistency about what is right?
Yes	No	Are emotional outbursts about role conflict and ambiguity very rare?
Yes	No	Has discrimination and/or sexual harassment been eliminated?
Yes	No	Is there an absence of open hostility and severe conflict?
Yes	No	Do people act on the job in a way that is consistent with what they say is ethical?
Yes	No	Is the firm more externally focused on customers, the environment, and the welfare of society than on its own profits?
Yes	No	Is there open communication between superiors and subordinates on ethical dilemmas?
Yes	No	Have employees ever received advice on how to improve ethical behavior or been disciplined for committing unethical acts?

*Add the number of Yes answers. The greater the number of Yes answers, the less ethical conflict is likely in your organization.

various behaviors, however, the firm's employees may believe that the company encourages competition among organizational members. A competitive orientation may result in a less ethical corporate culture. On the other hand, employees appreciate working in an environment that is designed to enhance workplace experiences through goals that encompass more than just maximizing profits.[20] Thus, it is very important for top managers to determine what the organization's culture is and to monitor its values, traditions, and beliefs to ensure that they represent the desired culture. However, the rewards and punishments imposed by an organization need to be consistent with the actual corporate culture. As two business ethics experts have observed, "Employees will value and use as guidelines those activities for which they will be rewarded. When a behavior that is rewarded comes into conflict with an unstated and unmonitored ethical value, usually the rewarded behavior wins out."[21]

Differential Association

Differential association refers to the idea that people learn ethical or unethical behavior while interacting with others who are part of their role-sets or belong to other intimate personal groups.[22] The learning process is more likely to result in unethical behavior if the individual associates primarily with persons who behave unethically. Associating with others who are unethical, combined with the opportunity to act unethically, is a major influence on ethical decision making, as described in the decision-making framework in Chapter 5.[23]

Consider two cashiers working different shifts at the same supermarket. Kevin, who works in the evenings, has seen his cashier friends take money from the bag containing the soft-drink machine change, which is collected every afternoon but not counted until closing time. Although Kevin personally believes that stealing is wrong, he has often heard his friends rationalize that the company owes them free beverages while they work. During his break one evening, Kevin discovers that he has no money to buy a soda. Because he has seen his friends take money from the bag and has heard them justify the practice, Kevin does not feel guilty about taking four quarters. However, Sally, who works the day shift, has never seen her friends take money from the bag. When she discovers that she does not have enough money to purchase a beverage for her break, it does not occur to her to take money from the change bag. Instead, she borrows from a friend. Although both Sally and Kevin view stealing as wrong, Kevin has associated with others who say the practice is justified. When the opportunity arose, Kevin used his friends' rationalization to justify his theft.

A variety of studies have supported the notion that such differential association influences ethical decision making. In particular, superiors have a strong influence on the ethics of their subordinates. Consider the actions of Mark Hernandez, who worked at NASA's Michoud Assembly Facility applying insulating foam to the space shuttles' external fuel tanks. Within a few weeks on the job, coworkers taught him to repair scratches in the insulation without reporting the repairs. Supervisors encouraged the workers not to bother filling out the required paperwork on the repairs so they could meet the space shuttle program's tight production schedules. After the shuttle *Columbia* broke up on reentry, killing all seven astronauts on board, investigators focused on whether a piece of foam falling off a fuel tank during liftoff may have irreparably damaged the shuttle. The final determination of the cause of the disaster may require years of investigation.[24]

Several research studies have found that employees, especially young managers, tend to go along with their superiors' moral judgments to demonstrate loyalty.[25] Hopefully, we have made it clear that *how* people typically make ethical decisions is not necessarily the way they *should* make ethical decisions. But we believe that you will be able to improve your own ethical decision making once you understand the potential influence of your interaction with others in your intimate work groups.

Whistle-Blowing

Interpersonal conflict ensues when employees think they know the right course of action in a situation, yet their work group or company promotes or requires a different, unethical decision. In such cases, employees may choose to follow their own values and refuse to participate in the unethical or illegal conduct. If they conclude that they cannot discuss what they are doing or what should be done with their coworkers or immediate supervisors, these employees may go outside the organization to publicize and correct the unethical situation.

Whistle-blowing means exposing an employer's wrongdoing to outsiders (external to the company) such as the media or government regulatory agencies. The term *whistle-blowing* is also used for internal reporting of misconduct to management, especially through anonymous reporting mechanisms, often called hot lines. The Sarbanes–Oxley Act and the Federal Sentencing Guidelines for Organizations (FSGO) has institutionalized internal whistle-blowing to encourage discovery of internal misconduct.

Whistle-blowers have provided pivotal evidence documenting corporate malfeasance at a number of companies. The importance of their role was highlighted when *Time* magazine named three whistle-blowers a few years ago as "Persons of the Year": Sherron Watkins of Enron, Cynthia Cooper of WorldCom, and Coleen Rowley of the FBI. Watkins, an Enron vice president, warned Kenneth Lay, the firm's CEO, that the company was using improper accounting procedures. "I am incredibly nervous that we will implode in a wave of accounting scandals," she told him, and the energy firm did exactly that within a few short months. Lay seemed skeptical of her concerns because of approval of Arthur Andersen, their external auditor, and Vinson and Elkins (their law firm). Lay turned over the case to their law and accounting firms for investigation, an activity that Watkins referred to as "whitewash" with these firms reviewing their own work. Soon after, Watkins became an external whistle-blower testifying before Congress that Enron had concealed billions of dollars in debt through a complex scheme of off-balance-sheet partnerships.[26]

Historically, the fortunes of external whistle-blowers have not been as positive: Most were labeled traitors, and many lost their jobs. Even Watkins was a potential candidate for firing as the Enron investigation unfolded with law firms assessing the implications of terminating her in light of her ethical and legal concerns about Enron.[27]

A study of three hundred whistle-blowers by researchers at the University of Pennsylvania found that 69 percent lost their jobs or were forced to retire after exposing their companies' misdeeds.[28] For example, the whistle-blower who exposed Wal-Mart chairman Thomas Coughlin of defrauding the company was terminated about a week after Coughlin resigned. Jared Bowen, a former vice president for Wal-Mart Stores, Inc., claims that he was terminated for his exposure of Coughlin, in violation of a provision of the Sarbanes–Oxley Act protecting whistle-blowers.[29] If an employee provides information to the government about their company's wrongdoing, under the Federal False Claims Act, the whistle-blower is known as a *qui tam relator*. Upon investigation

TABLE 7-4	Questions to Ask Before Engaging in External Whistle-Blowing

1. Have I exhausted internal anonymous reporting opportunities within the organization?
2. Have I examined company policies and codes that outline acceptable behavior and violations of standards?
3. Is this a personal issue that should be resolved through other means?
4. Can I manage the stress that may evolve from exposing potential wrongdoing in the organization?
5. Can I deal with the consequences of resolving an ethical or legal conflict within the organization?

by the U.S. Department of Justice, the whistle-blower can receive between 15 and 25 percent of the recovered funds, depending upon how instrumental their claims were in holding the firm accountable for their wrongdoing.[30] Although most whistle-blowers do not receive positive recognition for pointing out corporate misconduct, some have turned to the courts and obtained substantial settlements. Table 7–4 provides a checklist of questions an employee should ask before blowing the whistle externally. Figure 7–3 shows that nearly one in four employees experience retaliation after reporting misconduct. Nearly half of all employees who report misconduct received positive feedback for having done so.

If whistle-blowers present an accurate picture of organizational misconduct, they should not fear for their jobs. Indeed, the Sarbanes–Oxley Act makes it illegal to "discharge, demote, suspend, threaten, harass, or in any manner discriminate against" a whistle-blower and sets penalties of up to ten years in jail for executives who retaliate against whistle-blowers. The law also requires publicly traded companies to implement an anonymous reporting mechanism that allows employees to question actions that they

FIGURE 7-3	Outcome for Internal Whistle-Blowers Reporting Misconduct

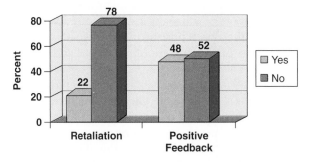

SOURCE: National Business Ethics Survey, *How Employees View Ethics in Their Organizations 1994–2005* (Washington, DC: Ethics Resource Center, 2005), 32.

| FIGURE 7-4 | Reasons Why Employees Do Not Report Observed Misconduct |

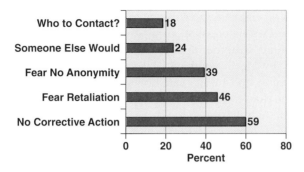

SOURCE: National Business Ethics Survey, *How Employees View Ethics in Their Organizations 1994–2005* (Washington, DC: Ethics Resource Center, 2005), 29.

believe may indicate fraud or other misconduct.[31] Additionally, the FSGO provides rewards for companies that systematically detect and address unethical or illegal activities.

Some U.S. companies are setting up computer systems that encourage internal whistle-blowing. With over fifty-five hundred employees, Marvin Windows (one of the world's largest custom manufacturers of wood windows and doors) is concerned about employees feeling comfortable reporting violations of safety conditions, bad management, fraud, or theft. The system is anonymous and allows for reporting in native-country languages. This system is used to alert management to potential problems in the organization and facilitate an investigation.[32]

Even before the passage of the Sarbanes–Oxley Act, an increasing number of companies were setting up anonymous reporting services, normally toll-free numbers, through which employees can report suspected violations or seek input on how to proceed when encountering ambiguous situations. These internal reporting services are perceived to be most effective when they are managed by an outside organization that specializes in maintaining ethics hot lines.

Figure 7–4 indicates the reasons why employees do not report misconduct in the organization. The extent to which employees feel there will be no corrective action or there will be retaliation are leading factors influencing their decisions not to report observed misconduct.

LEADERS INFLUENCE CORPORATE CULTURE

Organizational leaders use their power and influence to shape corporate culture. *Power* refers to the influence that leaders and managers have over the behavior and decisions of subordinates. An individual has power over others when his or her presence causes them to behave differently. Exerting power is one way to influence the ethical decision-making framework described in Chapter 5 (especially significant others and opportunity).

The status and power of leaders is directly related to the amount of pressure that they can exert on employees to conform to their expectations. A superior in an authority position can put strong pressure on employees to comply, even when their personal ethical values conflict with the superior's wishes. For example, a manager might say to a subordinate, "I want the confidential data about our competitor's sales on my desk by Monday morning, and I don't care how you get it." A subordinate who values his or her job or who does not realize the ethical questions involved may feel pressure to do something unethical to obtain the data.

There are five power bases from which one person may influence another: (1) reward power, (2) coercive power, (3) legitimate power, (4) expert power, and (5) referent power.[33] These five bases of power can be used to motivate individuals either ethically or unethically.

REWARD POWER   **Reward power** refers to a person's ability to influence the behavior of others by offering them something desirable. Typical rewards might be money, status, or promotion. Consider, for example, a retail salesperson who has two watches (a Timex and a Casio) for sale. Let's assume that the Timex is of higher quality than the Casio but is priced about the same. In the absence of any form of reward power, the salesperson would logically attempt to sell the Timex watch. However, if Casio gave him an extra 10 percent commission, he would probably focus his efforts on selling the Casio watch. This "carrot dangling" and incentives have been shown to be very effective in getting people to change their behavior in the long run. In the short run, however, it is not as effective as coercive power.

COERCIVE POWER   **Coercive power** is essentially the opposite of reward power. Instead of rewarding a person for doing something, coercive power penalizes actions or behavior. As an example, suppose a valuable client asks an industrial salesperson for a bribe and insinuates that he will take his business elsewhere if his demands are not met. Although the salesperson believes bribery is unethical, her boss has told her that she must keep the client happy or lose her chance at promotion. The boss is imposing a negative sanction if certain actions are not performed. Every year 20 percent of Enron's workforce was asked to leave as they were ranked as "needs improvement" or other issues were noted. Employees, not wanting to fall into the bottom 20 percent went along with the corporate culture, which might include complacency toward corruption.[34]

Coercive power relies on fear to change behavior. For this reason, it has been found to be more effective in changing behavior in the short run than in the long run. Coercion is often employed in situations where there is an extreme imbalance in power. However, people who are continually subjected to coercion may seek a counterbalance by aligning themselves with other, more powerful persons or by simply leaving the organization. In firms that use coercive power, relationships usually break down in the long run. Power is an ethical issue not only for individuals but also for work groups that establish policy for large corporations.

LEGITIMATE POWER **Legitimate power** stems from the belief that a certain person has the right to exert influence and that certain others have an obligation to accept it. The titles and positions of authority that organizations bestow on individuals appeal to this traditional view of power. Many people readily acquiesce to those who wield legitimate power, sometimes committing acts that are contrary to their beliefs and values. Betty Vinson, an accountant at WorldCom, objected to her supervisor's requests to produce improper accounting entries in an effort to conceal WorldCom's deteriorating financial condition. She finally gave in to their requests, being told this was the only way to save the company. She and other WorldCom accountants eventually plead guilty to conspiracy and fraud charges. She was sentenced to five months in prison and five months of house arrest.[35]

Such staunch loyalty to authority figures can also be seen in corporations that have strong charismatic leaders and centralized structures. In business, if a superior tells an employee to increase sales "no matter what it takes" and that employee has a strong affiliation to legitimate power, the employee may try anything to fulfill that order.

EXPERT POWER **Expert power** is derived from a person's knowledge (or the perception that the person possesses knowledge). Expert power usually stems from a superior's credibility with subordinates. Credibility, and thus expert power, is positively related to the number of years that a person has worked in a firm or industry, the person's education, or the honors that he or she has received for performance. Others who perceive a person to be an expert on a specific topic can also confer expert power on him or her. A relatively low-level secretary may have expert power because he or she knows specific details about how the business operates and can even make suggestions on how to inflate revenue through expense reimbursements.

Expert power may cause ethical problems when it is used to manipulate others or to gain an unfair advantage. Physicians, lawyers, or consultants can take unfair advantage of unknowing clients, for example. Accounting firms may gain extra income by ignoring concerns about the accuracy of financial data that they are provided in an audit.

REFERENT POWER **Referent power** may exist when one person perceives that his or her goals or objectives are similar to another's. The second person may attempt to influence the first to take actions that will lead both to achieve their objectives. Because they share the same objective, the person influenced by the other will perceive the other's use of referent power as beneficial. For this power relationship to be effective, however, some sort of empathy must exist between the individuals. Identification with others helps boost the decision maker's confidence when making a decision, thus increasing his or her referent power.

Consider the following situation: Lisa Jones, a manager in the accounting department of a manufacturing firm, has asked Michael Wong, a salesperson, to speed up the delivery of sales contracts, which usually take about one month to process after a deal is reached. Michael protests that he is not to blame for the slow process. Rather than threaten to slow delivery of Michael's commission checks (coercive power), Lisa makes use of referent power. She invites Michael to lunch, and they discuss some of their work concerns, including the problem of slow-moving documentation. They agree that if document processing cannot be speeded up, both will be hurt. Lisa then suggests that Michael start faxing contracts instead of mailing them. He agrees to give it a try, and within several weeks the contracts are moving faster. Lisa's job is made easier, and Michael gets his commission checks a little sooner.

The five bases of power are not mutually exclusive. People typically use several power bases to effect change in others. Although power in itself is neither ethical nor unethical, its use can raise ethical issues. Sometimes a leader uses power to manipulate a situation or a person's values in a way that creates a conflict with the person's value structure. For example, a manager who forces an employee to choose between staying home with his sick child and keeping his job is using coercive power, which creates a direct conflict with the employee's values.

MOTIVATING ETHICAL BEHAVIOR

A leader's ability to motivate subordinates plays a key role in maintaining an ethical organization. **Motivation** is a force within the individual that focuses his or her behavior toward achieving a goal. To create motivation, an organization offers incentives to encourage employees to work toward organizational objectives. Understanding motivation is important to the effective management of people, and it also helps explain their ethical behavior. For example, a person who aspires to higher positions in an organization may sabotage a coworker's project so as to make that person look bad. This unethical behavior is directly related to the first employee's ambition (motivation) to rise in the organization.

As businesspeople move into middle management and beyond, higher-order needs (social, esteem, and recognition) tend to become more important than lower-order needs (salary, safety, and job security).[36] Research has shown that an individual's career stage, age, organization size, and geographic location affect the relative priority that he or she gives to satisfying respect, self-esteem, and basic physiological needs.

From an ethics perspective, needs or goals may change as a person progresses through the ranks of the company. This shift may cause or help solve problems depending on that person's current ethical status relative to the company or society. For example, junior executives might inflate purchase or sales orders, overbill time worked on projects, or accept cash gratuities if they are worried about providing for their families' basic physical necessities. As they continue up the ladder and are able to fulfill these needs, such concerns may become less important. Consequently, these managers may go back to obeying company policy or culture and be more concerned with internal recognition and achievement than their families' physical needs.

An individual's hierarchy of needs may influence his or her motivation and ethical behavior. After basic needs such as food, working conditions (existence needs), and survival are satisfied, relatedness needs and growth needs become important. **Relatedness needs** are satisfied by social and interpersonal relationships, and **growth needs** are satisfied by creative or productive activities.[37] Consider what happens when a new employee, Jill Taylor, joins a company. At first Jill is concerned about working conditions, pay, and security (existence needs). After some time on the job, she feels she has satisfied these needs and begins to focus on developing good interpersonal relations with coworkers. When these relatedness needs have been satisfied, Jill wants to advance to a more challenging job. However, she learns that a higher-level job would require her to travel a lot. She greatly values her family life and feels that travel and nights away from home would not be good for her. She decides, therefore, not to work toward a promotion (resulting in a "need frustration"). Instead, she decides to focus on furthering good interpersonal relations with her coworkers. This is termed *frustration-regression* because, to reduce her anxiety, Jill is now focusing on an area (interpersonal relations) not related to her main problem: the need for a more challenging job. In this example, Jill's need for promotion has been modified by her values. To feel productive, she attempts to fill her needs by going back to an earlier stage in her hierarchy of needs. Whatever her present job is, Jill would continue to emphasize high performance in it. But this regression creates frustration that may lead Jill to seek other employment.

Examining the role that motivation plays in ethics offers a way to relate business ethics to the broader social context in which workers live and the deeper moral assumptions on which society depends. Workers are individuals and they will be motivated by a variety of personal interests. Although we keep emphasizing that managers are positioned to exert pressure and force individuals' compliance on ethically related issues, we also acknowledge that an individual's personal ethics and needs will significantly affect his or her ethical decisions.

ORGANIZATIONAL STRUCTURE AND BUSINESS ETHICS

An organization's structure is important to the study of business ethics because the various roles and job descriptions that comprise that structure may create opportunities for unethical behavior.[38] The structure of organizations can be described in many ways. For simplicity's sake, we discuss two broad categories of organizational structures—centralized and decentralized. Note that these are not mutually exclusive structures; in the real world, organizational structures exist on a continuum. Table 7–5 compares some strengths and weaknesses of centralized and decentralized structures.

In a **centralized organization,** decision-making authority is concentrated in the hands of top-level managers, and little authority is delegated to lower levels. Responsibility, both internal and external, rests with top-level managers. This structure is especially suited for organizations that make high-risk decisions and whose lower-level managers are not highly skilled in decision making. It is also suitable for organizations in which production processes are routine and efficiency is of primary importance. These organizations are usually extremely bureaucratic, and the division of labor is typically very well defined. Each worker knows his or her job and what is specifically expected, and each has a clear understanding of how to carry out assigned tasks. Centralized organizations stress formal rules, policies, and procedures, backed up with elaborate control systems. Their codes of ethics may specify the techniques to be used for decision making. General Motors, the Internal Revenue Service, and the U.S. Army are examples of centralized organizations.

TABLE 7–5	Structural Comparison of Organizational Types	
	Emphasis	
Characteristic	**Decentralized**	**Centralized**
Hierarchy of authority	Decentralized	Centralized
Flexibility	High	Low
Adaptability	High	Low
Problem recognition	High	Low
Implementation	Low	High
Dealing with changes in environmental complexity	Good	Poor
Rules and procedures	Few and informal	Many and formal
Division of labor	Ambiguous	Clear-cut
Span of control	Few employees	Many employees
Use of managerial techniques	Minimal	Extensive
Coordination and control	Informal and personal	Formal and impersonal

Because of their top-down approach and the distance between employee and decision maker, centralized organizational structures can lead to unethical acts. If the centralized organization is very bureaucratic, some employees may behave according to "the letter of the law" rather than the spirit. For example, a centralized organization can have a policy about bribes that does not include wording about donating to a client's favorite charity before or after a sale. Such donations or gifts can, in some cases, be construed as a tacit bribe because the employee buyer could be swayed by the donation, or gift, to act in a less than favorable way or not to act in the best interests of his or her firm.

Other ethical concerns may arise in centralized structures because they typically have very little upward communication. Top-level managers may not be aware of problems and unethical activity. Some companies' use of sweatshop labor may be one manifestation of this lack of upward communication. Sweatshops produce products such as garments by employing laborers, sometimes forced immigrant labor, who often work twelve- to sixteen-hour shifts for little or no pay. Many illegal immigrants in Europe become indentured slaves or earn little more than the food they eat. By outsourcing production to such sweatshops, small- and mid-size suppliers are able to offer products to retailers that beat or match the lowest global market prices. Many of these products end up in leading retailers' stores because their suppliers' top managers claim they were not aware of how their products were made.[39]

Another ethical issue that may arise in centralized organizations is blame shifting, or scapegoating. People may try to transfer blame for their actions to others who are not responsible. The specialization and significant division of labor in centralized organizations can also create ethical problems. Employees may not understand how their actions can affect the overall organization because they work on one piece of a much larger puzzle. This lack of connectedness can lead employees to engage in unethical behavior because they fail to understand the overall ramifications of their behavior.

In a **decentralized organization,** decision-making authority is delegated as far down the chain of command as possible. Such organizations have relatively few formal rules, and coordination and control are usually informal and personal. They focus instead on increasing the flow of information. As a result, one of the main strengths of decentralized organizations is their adaptability and early recognition of external change. With greater flexibility, managers can react quickly to changes in their ethical environment. A parallel weakness of decentralized organizations is the difficulty that they have in responding quickly to changes in policy and procedures established by top management. In addition, independent profit centers within a decentralized organization may deviate from organizational objectives. Other decentralized firms may look no further than the local community for their ethical standards. For example, if a firm that produces toxic wastes leaves decisions on disposal to lower-level operating units, the managers of those units may feel that they have solved their waste-disposal problem as long as they find a way to dump wastes outside their immediate community. Table 7–6 gives examples of centralized versus decentralized organizations and describes their corporate culture.

Due to the strict formalization and implementation of ethics policies and procedures in centralized organizations, they tend to be more ethical in their practices than decentralized organizations. Centralized organizations may also exert more influence on their employees because they have a central core of policies and codes of ethical conduct. Decentralized organizations give employees extensive decision-making autonomy because management empowers the employees. However, it is also true that decentralized organizations may be able to avoid ethical dilemmas by tailoring their decisions to the specific situations, laws, and values of a particular community. If widely shared values are in place in decentralized organizations, there may be no need for excessive compliance programs. However, different units in the company may evolve diverse value systems and approaches to ethical decision making. For example, a high-tech defense firm like Lockheed Martin, which employs more than two hundred thousand people, might have to cope with many different decisions on the same ethical issue if it did not have a centralized ethics program. Boeing has become more centralized since the entrance of CEO W. James McNerney, Jr., and exit of previous CEO

TABLE 7–6	Examples of Centralized and Decentralized Corporate Cultures	
Company	**Organizational Culture**	**Characterized by**
Nike	Decentralized	Creativity, freedom, informality
Southwest Airlines	Decentralized	Fun, teamwork orientation, loyalty
General Motors	Centralized	Unions, adherence to task assignments, structured
Microsoft	Decentralized	Creative, investigative, fast paced
Procter & Gamble	Centralized	Experienced, dependable, a rich history and tradition of products, powerful

Harry Stonecipher who carried on a relationship with a female vice president of the company, resulting in his exit. Boeing had gone through several years of ethics and legal difficulties including the jailing of the former CFO for illegal job negotiations with Pentagon officials, indictment of a manager for stealing twenty-five thousand pages of proprietary documents, abuse of attorney–client privilege to cover up internal studies showing pay inequities, and other scandals.[40]

Unethical behavior is possible in either centralized or decentralized structures when specific corporate cultures permit or encourage workers to deviate from accepted standards or ignore corporate legal and ethical responsibilities. Centralized firms may have a more difficult time uprooting unethical activity than decentralized organizations. The latter may have a more fluid history in which changes affect only a small portion of the company. Often, when a centralized firm uncovers unethical activity and it appears to be pervasive, the leadership is removed so that the old unethical culture can be uprooted and replaced with a more ethical one. For example, Mitsubishi Motors suggested significant management changes after it was discovered that a cover-up of auto defects had been going on for more than two decades.

Some centralized organizations are seeking to restructure to become more decentralized, flexible, and adaptive to the needs of employees and customers. In other cases, entire industries are being impacted by a trend of decentralization. For example, many software companies, such as Citrix Systems, can cut their employee costs by decentralizing and operating development centers in Florida, Washington, and California.[41] Decentralized decisions about ethics and social responsibility allow regional or local operators to set policy and establish conduct requirements.

GROUP DIMENSIONS OF CORPORATE STRUCTURE AND CULTURE

When discussing corporate culture, we tend to focus on the organization as a whole. But corporate values, beliefs, patterns, and rules are often expressed through smaller groups within the organization. Moreover, individual groups within organizations often adopt their own rules and values.

Types of Groups

Two main categories of groups affect ethical behavior in business. A **formal group** is defined as an assembly of individuals that has an organized structure accepted explicitly by the group. An **informal group** is defined as two or more individuals with a common interest but without an explicit organizational structure.

FORMAL GROUPS   Formal groups can be divided into committees and work groups and teams.

Committees A *committee* is a formal group of individuals assigned to a specific task. Often a single manager could not complete the task, or management may believe that a committee can better represent different constituencies and improve the coordination and implementation of decisions. Committees may meet regularly to review performance, develop plans, or make decisions. Most formal committees in organizations operate on an ongoing basis, but their membership may change over time. A committee is an excellent example of a situation in which coworkers and significant others within the organization can influence ethical decisions. Committee decisions are to some extent legitimized because of agreement or majority rule. In this respect, minority views on issues such as ethics can be pushed aside through the majority's authority. Committees bring diverse personal moral values into the ethical decision-making process, which may expand the number of alternatives considered.

The main disadvantage of committees is that they typically take longer to reach a decision than an individual would. Committee decisions are also generally more conservative than those made by individuals and may be based on unnecessary compromise rather than on identifying the best alternative. Also inherent in the committee structure is a lack of individual responsibility. Because of the diverse composition of the group, members may not be committed or willing to assume responsibility for the group decision. Groupthink may emerge and the majority can explain ethical considerations away.

Although many organizations have financial, diversity, personnel, or social responsibility committees, only a very few organizations have committees that are devoted exclusively to ethics. An ethics committee might raise ethical concerns, resolve ethical dilemmas in the organization, and create or update the company's code of ethics. Motorola, for example, maintains a Business Ethics Compliance Committee, which interprets, classifies, communicates, and enforces the company's code and ethics initiatives. An ethics committee can gather information on functional areas of the business and examine manufacturing practices, personnel policies, dealings with suppliers, financial reporting, and sales techniques to find out whether the company's practices are ethical. Though much of a corporation's culture operates informally, an ethics committee would be a highly formalized approach for dealing with ethical issues.

Ethics committees can be misused if they are established for the purpose of legitimizing management's ethical standards on some issue. For example, ethics committees may be quickly assembled for political purposes—that is, to make a symbolic decision on some event that has occurred within the company. If the CEO or manager in charge selects committee members who will produce a predetermined outcome, the ethics committee may not help the organization resolve its ethical issues in the long run. For example, organizations have been known to quickly assemble an ethics committee to fire someone for a minor infraction because they wanted him or her out of the organization and needed an excuse for termination.

Ethics committee members may also fail to understand their role or function. If they attempt to apply their own personal ethics to complex business issues, resolving ethical issues may be difficult. Because most people's personal ethical perspectives differ, the committee may experience conflict. Even if the committee members reach a consensus, they may enforce their personal beliefs rather than the organization's standards on certain ethical issues.

Ethics committees should be organized around professional, business-related issues that occur internally. In general, the ethics committee should formulate policy, develop ethical standards, and then assess the organization's compliance with these requirements. Ethics committees should be aware of their industries' codes of ethics, community standards, and the organizational culture in which they work. Although ethics committees do not always succeed, they can provide one of the best organizational approaches to resolving internal ethical issues fairly. As one of many examples in the corporate world, Sunstrand Corporation, a *Fortune* 500 company, has established employee-managed ethics committees at each of its facilities to stimulate employees' "ownership" of their ethical conduct and to distribute accountability throughout the organization.

Work Groups and Teams *Work groups* are used to subdivide duties within specific functional areas of a company. For example, on an automotive assembly line, one work group might install the seats and interior design elements of the vehicle while another group installs all the dashboard instruments. This enables production supervisors to specialize in a specific area and provide expert advice to work groups.

Whereas work groups operate within a single functional area, *teams* bring together the functional expertise of employees from several different areas of the organization—for example, finance, marketing, and production—on a single project, such as developing a new product. Many manufacturing firms, including General Motors, Westinghouse, and Procter & Gamble, are using the team concept to improve participative management. Ethical conflicts may arise because team members come from different functional areas. Each member of the team has a particular role to play and has probably had limited interaction with other members of the team. Members may have encountered different ethical issues in their own functional areas and may therefore bring different viewpoints when the team faces an ethical issue. For example, a production quality-control employee might believe that side-impact air bags should be standard equipment on all automobiles for safety reasons. A marketing member of the team may reply that the cost of adding the air bags would force the company to raise prices beyond the reach of some consumers. The production employee might then argue that it is unethical for an automobile maker to fail to include a safety feature that could save hundreds of lives. Such conflicts often occur when members of different organizational groups must interact. However, airing viewpoints representative of all the functional areas helps provide more options from which to choose.

Work groups and teams provide the organizational structure for group decision making. One of the reasons why individuals cannot implement their personal ethical beliefs in organizations is that so many decisions are reached collectively by work groups. However, those who have legitimate power are in a position to influence ethics-related activities. The work group and team often sanction certain activities as ethical or define others as unethical.

INFORMAL GROUPS In addition to the groups that businesses formally organize and recognize—such as committees, work groups, and teams—most organizations have a number of informal groups. These groups are usually composed of individuals, often from the same department, who have similar interests and band together for companionship or for purposes that may or may not be relevant to the goals of the organization. For example, four or five people who have similar tastes in outdoor activities and music may discuss their interests while working, and they may meet outside work for dinner, concerts, sports events, or other activities. Other informal groups may evolve to form a union, improve working conditions or benefits, get a manager fired, or protest work practices that they view as unfair. Informal groups may generate disagreement and conflict, or they may enhance morale and job satisfaction.

Informal groups help develop informal channels of communication, sometimes called the "grapevine," which are important in every organization. Informal communication flows up, down, diagonally, and horizontally, not necessarily following the communication lines on a company's organization chart. Information passed along the grapevine may relate to the job, the organization, or an ethical issue, or it may simply be gossip and rumors. The grapevine can act as an early warning system for employees. If employees learn informally that their company may be sold or that a particular action will be condemned as unethical by top management or the community, they have time to think about what they will do. Because gossip is not uncommon in an organization, the information passed along the grapevine is not always accurate. Managers who understand how the grapevine works can use it to reinforce acceptable values and beliefs.

The grapevine is also an important source of information for individuals to assess ethical behavior within their organization. One way an employee can determine acceptable behavior is to ask friends and peers in informal groups about the consequences of certain actions such as lying to a customer about a product-safety issue. The corporate culture may provide employees with a general understanding of the patterns and rules that govern behavior, but informal groups make this culture come alive and provide direction for employees' daily choices. For example, if a new employee learns anecdotally through the grapevine that the organization does not punish ethical violations, he or she may seize the next opportunity for unethical behavior if it accomplishes the organization's objectives. There is a general tendency to discipline top sales performers more leniently than poor sales performers for engaging in identical forms of unethical selling behavior. A superior sales record appears to induce more lenient forms of discipline, despite organizational policies that state otherwise.[42] In this case, the grapevine has clearly communicated that the organization rewards those who break the ethical rules to achieve desirable objectives.

Group Norms

Group norms are standards of behavior that groups expect of their members. Just as corporate culture establishes behavior guidelines for an organization's members, so group norms help define acceptable and unacceptable behavior within a group. In particular, group norms define the limit allowed on deviations from group expectations.

Most work organizations, for example, develop norms that govern groups' rates of production and communication with management as well as providing a general understanding of behavior considered right or wrong, ethical or unethical, within the group. For example, an employee who reports to a supervisor that a coworker has covered up a serious production error may be punished by other group members for this breach of confidence. Other members of the group may glare at the informant, who has violated a group norm, and refuse to talk to or sit by him or her.

Norms have the power to enforce a strong degree of conformity among group members. At the same time, norms define the different roles for various positions within the organization. Thus, a low-ranking member of a group may be expected to carry out an unpleasant task such as accepting responsibility for someone else's ethical mistake. Abusive behavior toward new or lower-ranking employees could be a norm in an informal group.

Sometimes group norms conflict with the values and rules prescribed by the organization's culture. For example, the organization may have policies about the personal use of computers during work hours and may use rewards and punishments to encourage this culture. In a particular informal group, however, norms may encourage using computers for personal use during work hours and avoiding management's attention. Issues of equity may arise in this situation if other groups believe they are unfairly forced to follow policies that are not enforced. These other employees may complain to management or to the offending group. If they believe management is not taking corrective action, they, too, may use computers for personal use, thus hurting the whole organization's productivity. For this reason, management must carefully monitor not only the corporate culture but also the norms of all the various groups within the organization. Sanctions may be necessary to bring in line a group whose norms deviate sharply from the overall culture.

VARIATION IN EMPLOYEE CONDUCT

Although the corporation is required to take responsibility for conducting its business ethically, a substantial amount of research indicates that significant differences exist in the values and philosophies that influence how the individuals that comprise corporations make ethical decisions.[43] In other words, because people are culturally diverse and have different values, they interpret situations differently and will vary in the ethical decisions they make on the same ethical issue.

Table 7–7 shows that approximately 10 percent of employees take advantage of situations to further their own personal interests. These individuals are more likely to manipulate, cheat, or be self-serving when the benefits gained from doing so are greater than the penalties for the misconduct. Such employees may choose to take office

TABLE 7-7	Variation in Employee Conduct*		
10%	**40%**	**40%**	**10%**
Follow their own values and beliefs; believe that their values are superior to those of others in the company.	Always try to follow company policies.	Go along with the work group.	Take advantage of situations if the penalty is less than the benefit and the risk of being caught is low.

*These percentages are based on a number of studies in the popular press and data gathered by the authors. These percentages are not exact and represent a general typology that may vary by organization.

SOURCE: From John Fraedrich and O.C. Ferrell, "Cognitive Consistency of Marketing Managers in Ethical Situations," *Journal of the Academy of Marketing Science*, Summer 1992, Vol. 20, pp. 243–252. Copyright © 1992 by Sage Publications, Inc. Reprinted by permission of Sage Publications, Inc.

supplies from work for personal use if the only penalty they may suffer if caught is having to pay for the supplies. The lower the risk of being caught, the higher is the likelihood that the 10 percent most likely to take advantage will be involved in unethical activities.

Another 40 percent of workers go along with the work group on most matters. These employees are most concerned about the social implications of their actions and want to fit into the organization. Although they have their own personal opinions, they are easily influenced by what people around them are doing. These individuals may know that using office supplies for personal use is improper, yet they view it as acceptable because their coworkers do so. These employees rationalize their action by saying that the use of office supplies is one of the benefits of working at their particular business and it must be acceptable because the company does not enforce a policy precluding the behavior. Coupled with this philosophy is the belief that no one will get into trouble for doing what everybody else is doing, for there is safety in numbers.

About 40 percent of a company's employees, as shown in Table 7–7, always try to follow company policies and rules. These workers not only have a strong grasp of their corporate culture's definition of acceptable behavior but also attempt to comply with codes of ethics, ethics training, and other communications about appropriate conduct. If the company has a policy prohibiting taking office supplies from work, these employees probably would observe it. However, they likely would not speak out about the 40 percent who choose to go along with the work group, for these employees prefer to focus on their jobs and steer clear of any organizational misconduct. If the company fails to communicate standards of appropriate behavior, members of this group will devise their own.

The final 10 percent of employees try to maintain formal ethical standards that focus on rights, duties, and rules. They embrace values that assert certain inalienable rights and actions, which they perceive to be always ethically correct. In general, members of this group believe that their values are right and superior to the values of others in the company, or even to the company's value system, when an ethical conflict arises. These individuals have a tendency to report the misconduct of others or to speak out when they view activities within the company as unethical. Consequently, members of this group would probably report colleagues who take office supplies.

The significance of this variation in the way individuals behave ethically is simply this: Employees use different approaches when making ethical decisions. Because of the probability that a large percentage of any work group will either take advantage of a situation or at least go along with the work group, it is vital that companies provide communication and control mechanisms to maintain an ethical culture. Companies that fail to monitor activities and enforce ethics policies provide a low-risk environment for those employees who are inclined to take advantage of situations to accomplish their personal, and sometimes unethical, objectives.

Good business practice and concern for the law requires organizations to recognize this variation in employees' desire to be ethical. The percentages cited in Table 7–7 are only estimates, and the actual percentages of each type of employee may vary widely across organizations based on individuals and corporate culture. The specific percentages are less important than the fact that our research has identified these variations as existing within most organizations. Organizations should focus particular attention

TABLE 7-8	Penalties for Convictions of Organizational Wrongdoing

Executive/Company	Trial Outcome
Franklin Brown, former general counsel, Rite Aid	Convicted and sentenced to 10 years in prison.
Bernard Ebbers, former chairman and CEO, WorldCom	Convicted and sentenced to 25 years to life in prison.
Dennis Kozlowski, former CEO, Tyco	Mistrial in first trial; in second, convicted and sentenced to 8⅓ years to 25 years in prison.
Gregory L. Reyes, former CEO of Brocade Communication Systems	Convicted of ten counts of securities fraud, $15 million fine and 21 months in prison.
Joseph P. Nacchio, former CEO of Qwest Communications International	Convicted of insider trading, $19 million fine, forfeit of $52 million, and 6 years in prison.
Xujia Wang, Vice President of Finance, Morgan Stanley Company	Convicted of securities fraud and conspiracy to commit securities fraud, 18 months in prison and $611,248 fine.
Attorney Raymond Joseph Costanzo, Jr.	Provided false qualifying information and falsified down payments, 3 years, 5 months in prison to be followed by 4 years of supervised release and ordered to pay $7,843,184 in restitution.
Gandhi Ben Morka, real estate appraiser	Convicted of mortgage fraud, 60 months in prison and ordered to pay more than $2.3 million in restitution.

SOURCE: From *Wall Street Journal Online*, "White-Collar Defendants: Take the Stand, or Not?," April 2, 2006; FBI Report, http://www.fbi.gov/publications/financial/fcs_report2007/financial_crime_2007.htm corporate (accessed January 13, 2009).

on managers who oversee the day-to-day operations of employees within the company. They should also provide training and communication to ensure that the business operates ethically, that it does not become the victim of fraud or theft, and that employees, customers, and other stakeholders are not abused through the misconduct of people who have a pattern of unethical behavior.

As we have seen throughout this book, many examples can be cited of employees and managers who have no concern for ethical conduct but are nonetheless hired and placed in positions of trust. Some corporations continue to support executives who ignore environmental concerns, poor working conditions, or defective products, or who engage in accounting fraud. Executives who can get results, regardless of the consequences, are often admired and lauded, especially in the business press. When their unethical or even illegal actions become public knowledge, however, they risk more than the loss of their positions. Table 7–8 summarizes the penalties that corporate executives have experienced over the past several years.

CAN PEOPLE CONTROL THEIR OWN ACTIONS WITHIN A CORPORATE CULTURE?

Many people find it hard to believe that an organization's culture can exert so strong an influence on individuals' behavior within the organization. In our society, we want to believe that individuals control their own destiny. A popular way of viewing business ethics is therefore to see it as a reflection of the alternative moral philosophies that individuals use to resolve their personal moral dilemmas. As this chapter has shown, however, ethical decisions within organizations are often made by committees and formal and informal groups, not by individuals. Decisions related to financial reporting, advertising, product design, sales practices, and pollution-control issues are often beyond the influence of individuals alone. In addition, these decisions are frequently based on business rather than personal goals.

Most new employees in highly bureaucratic organizations have almost no input into the basic operating rules and procedures for getting things done. Along with learning sales tactics and accounting procedures, employees may be taught to ignore a design flaw in a product that could be dangerous to users. Although many personal ethics issues may seem straightforward and easy to resolve, individuals entering business will usually need several years of experience within a specific industry to understand how to resolve ethical close calls. For example, what constitutes misleading advertising? When Corvette introduced the new C-6 design, they wanted to reach a younger demographic. They hired Madonna's husband, Guy Richie, and used the Rolling Stones singing "Jumpin' Jack Flash" to create a memorable TV commercial showing a young boy fantasizing about being able to drive the Corvette. General Motors received complaints from parents and organizations indicating that it was inappropriate for GM to show a clearly underage driver, driving recklessly, even if it was a fantasy. GM responded quickly by withdrawing the commercial from the airwaves. How could this problem have been prevented? Perhaps, GM should have screened the ads to a variety of audiences, not just the target audience for the vehicle. The only thing that is certain is that one person's opinion or maybe even a work group's opinion is insufficient in dealing with complex decisions.

It is not our purpose to suggest that you ought to go along with management or the group on business ethics issues. Honesty and open discussion of ethical issues are important to successful ethical decision making. We believe that most companies and businesspeople try to make ethical decisions. However, because there is so much difference between individuals, ethical conflict is inevitable. If you manage and supervise others, it will be necessary to maintain ethical policies for your organization and report misconduct that occurs. This means that ethics is not just a personal matter.

Regardless of how a person or organization views the acceptability of a particular activity, if society judges it to be wrong or unethical, then this larger view directly affects the organization's ability to achieve its goals. Not all activities deemed unethical by society are illegal. But if public opinion decries or consumers protest against a particular activity, the result may be legislation that restricts or bans a specific business practice. For instance, concern about teen smoking prompted the government to regulate the placement of cigarette advertising and curb the use of characters and approaches designed to appeal to children. Public concern and outrage at the growth in cigarette smoking among minors spurred much of this intervention. Besieged by mounting negative opinion, numerous class-action lawsuits, and a landmark settlement with forty-six states, Philip Morris USA, producer of the world's best-selling cigarette, was forced to modify its marketing strategies, in particular to avoid marketing its products to minors. The company now uses the Internet, TV commercials, school publications, and print ads to encourage teenagers not to smoke. Philip Morris has spent over $600 million on youth smoking-prevention advertising, providing grants to youth-development organizations, producing tools and resources to help parents talk to their children about the hazards of smoking, and supporting youth access prevention initiatives to help keep cigarettes out of children's hands.[44]

If a person believes that his or her personal ethics severely conflict with the ethics of the work group and of superiors in an organization, that individual's only alternative may be to leave the organization. In the highly competitive employment market of the twenty-first century, quitting a job because of an ethical conflict requires courage and, possibly, the ability to survive without a job. Obviously, there are no easy answers for resolving ethical conflicts between the organization and the individual. Our goal is not to tell you what you should do. But we do believe that the more you know about how ethical decision making occurs within organizations, the more opportunity you will have to influence decisions positively and resolve ethical conflict more effectively.

SUMMARY

Corporate culture refers to the set of values, beliefs, goals, norms, and ways of solving problems that the members (employees) of an organization share. These shared values may be formally expressed or unspoken. Corporate cultures can be classified in several ways, and a cultural audit can be conducted to identify an organization's culture. If an organization's culture rewards unethical behavior, people within the company are more likely to act unethically. A company's failure to monitor or manage its culture may foster questionable behavior.

Leadership—the ability or authority to guide others toward achieving goals—has a significant impact on the ethical decision-making process because leaders have the power to motivate others and enforce both the organization's rules and policies and their own viewpoints. A leader must not only gain the respect of his or her followers but also provide a standard of ethical conduct. Leaders exert power to influence the behaviors and decisions of subordinates. There are five power bases from which a leader may influence ethical behavior: reward power, coercive power, legitimate power, expert power, and referent power. Leaders also attempt to motivate subordinates; motivation is an internal force that focuses an individual's behavior toward achieving a goal. It can be created by the incentives that an organization offers employees.

The structure of an organization may create opportunities to engage in unethical behavior. In a centralized organization, decision-making authority is concentrated in the hands of top managers, and little authority is delegated to lower levels. In a decentralized organization, decision-making authority is delegated as far down the chain of command as possible. Centralized organizations tend to be more ethical than decentralized ones because they enforce more rigid controls such as codes of ethics and corporate policies on ethical practices. However, unethical conduct can occur in both types of structures.

In addition to the values and customs that represent the culture of an organization, individual groups within the organization often adopt their own rules and values and even create subcultures. The main types of groups are formal groups—which include committees, work groups, and teams—and informal groups. Informal groups often feed an informal channel of communication called the "grapevine." Group norms are standards of behavior that groups expect of their members. They help define acceptable and unacceptable behavior within a group and especially define the limits on deviating from group expectations. Sometimes group norms conflict with the values and rules prescribed by the organization's culture.

Sometimes an employee's own personal ethical standards conflict with what is expected of him or her as a member of an organization and its corporate culture. This is especially true given that an organization's ethical decisions are often resolved by committees, formal groups, and informal groups rather than by individuals. When such ethical conflict is severe, the individual may have to decide whether to leave the organization.

IMPORTANT TERMS FOR REVIEW	differential association	relatedness needs
	whistle-blowing	growth needs
	reward power	centralized organization
	coercive power	decentralized organization
	legitimate power	formal group
	expert power	informal group
	referent power	group norm
	motivation	

RESOLVING ETHICAL BUSINESS CHALLENGES*

As Gerard sat down in his expensive new chair, he was worried. What had he gotten himself into? How could things have gone so wrong so fast? It was as if he'd been walking and some truck had blindsided him. Gerard had been with Trawlers Accounting, a medium-size firm, for several years. His wife, Vicky, had a job in the pharmaceutical industry, and their first child was due any day now. The doctor had told her that she would need to stop work early because hers was a high-risk pregnancy. So three months before her due date, she asked and received a four-month leave of absence. This was great, but the leave was without pay. Luckily, Gerard had received a promotion and now headed a department.

Some interesting activities were going on in the accounting industry. For example, Gerard's superior had decided that all CPAs would take exams to become registered investment advisers. The rationale for such a new development was simple. The firm could

use its relationships with clients to increase investment revenues. Because of the long-term nature of these relationships with many firms and individuals as well as the implicit sense of honesty that CPAs must bring to their jobs, clients understood that a violation of so high a trust was unlikely—or so Gerard's boss argued. Many of the people in Gerard's department didn't like this new policy; however, some who had passed the exams increased their pay by 15 percent. During lunch, one of Gerard's financial friends engaged him heatedly.

"What you're doing, Gerard, is called unfair competition," the friend accused him. "For example, your CPAs have exclusive access to confidential client taxpayer information, which could give you insight into people's financial needs. Besides, you could easily direct clients to mutual funds that you already own in order to keep your own personal investments afloat. Also, if your people start chasing commissions and fees on mutual funds that go bad, your credibility will become suspect, and you won't be trusted.

Plus, your people will now have to keep abreast of financial, tax, and accounting changes."

When Gerard got to his office, he found that some of his people had been recommending a group of mutual funds that Trawlers had been auditing. Then someone from another of his company's accounting clients, CENA Mutual Funds, telephoned.

"What's the idea of having your people suggest PPI Mutual Funds when they are in direct competition with us?" the caller yelled. "We pay you a lot, Gerard, to do our accounting procedures, and that's how you reward us? I want to know by the end of the day if you are going to continue to push our competitor's product. I don't have to tell you that this will directly affect your department and you. Also, things like this get around the business circles, if you know what I mean."

With these words, the caller hung up on Gerard.

QUESTIONS • EXERCISES

1. Identify any ethical and legal issues of which Gerard needs to be aware.
2. Discuss the advantages and disadvantages of each decision Gerard has made and could make.
3. Discuss the issue of accounting firms going into the financial services market.
4. Discuss the type of groups that are influencing Gerard.

*This case is strictly hypothetical; any resemblance to real persons, companies, or situations is coincidental.

Check Your EQ

Check your EQ, or Ethics Quotient, by completing the following. Assess your performance to evaluate your overall understanding of the chapter material.

1. Decentralized organizations tend to put the blame for unethical behavior on lower-level personnel.   **Yes**   **No**
2. Decentralized organizations give employees extensive decision-making autonomy.   **Yes**   **No**
3. Corporate culture provides rules for behaving within the organization.   **Yes**   **No**
4. An integrative culture shows high concern for performance and little concern for people.   **Yes**   **No**
5. Coercive power works in the same manner as reward power.   **Yes**   **No**

ANSWERS: 1. No. That's more likely to occur in centralized organizations. 2. Yes. This is known as empowerment. 3. Yes. Values, beliefs, customs, and ceremonies represent what is acceptable and unacceptable in the organization. 4. No. That's an exacting culture. An integrative culture combines high concern for people and production. 5. No. Coercive power is the opposite of reward power. One offers rewards and the other punishment to encourage appropriate behavior.

Implementing Business Ethics in a Global Economy

CHAPTER 8

Developing an Effective Ethics Program

CHAPTER OBJECTIVES

- To understand the responsibility of the corporation to be a moral agent

- To understand why businesses need to develop ethics programs

- To list the minimum requirements for an ethics program

- To describe the role of codes of ethics in identifying key risk areas for the organization

- To identify the keys to successful ethics training, including program types and goals

- To examine the ways that ethical standards are monitored, audited, and enforced and to understand the need for continuous improvement

CHAPTER OUTLINE

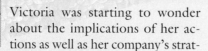

Victoria was starting to wonder about the implications of her actions as well as her company's strategy. She had begun working for Koke International (KI) after graduating from Pacific West University with degrees in both finance and marketing. KI was the leader in franchised home repair outlets in the United States. In twenty-five years, KI had grown from several stores in the Pacific Northwest to two hundred and fifty over much of the United States and Canada. Koke International came to dominate the markets that it entered by undercutting local competitors on price and quality. The lower prices were easy to charge because KI received large quantity discounts from its vendors. The franchise concept also helped create another barrier to entry for KI's competitors. By expanding rapidly, KI was able to spread the costs of marketing to many more stores, giving it still another differential advantage. This active nourishment of its brand image coupled with some technological advances such as just-in-time inventory, electronic scanners, and electronic market niching had sent KI's stock soaring. As a result, it had a 50 percent share of the market. Koke International had done such an excellent job of positioning itself in its field that articles in major business newspapers were calling it "the Microsoft of home improvements." The view was that "KI is going to continue to be a very profitable endeavor, with less expected direct competition in a slow-growth, high-margin market for the future."

Wendy, Victoria's boss, had brought her in on KI's next potential conquest: the New England states of Maine, Vermont, New Hampshire, Connecticut, and Massachusetts.

"This is the last big potential market," Wendy said at a planning session with her senior staff. "I want you to realize that when we launch into these states we're going to have to be ruthless. I'd like your suggestions as to how we're going to eliminate the competition."

One person spoke up: "We first need to recognize that there are only five major players (multiple-store chains), with Home Designs being the largest."

"The top corporate people want us to attack Maine, New Hampshire, and Vermont first and then make a secondary attack on the other two states," interjected Victoria.

"Our buildings are four months from completion," Wendy pointed out, "and the media blitz is due to start one month prior to the twenty-store grand opening. With that much exposed capital from our franchises, we need to make sure everything goes well. Vicky, have you completed your price analysis of all of the surrounding home repair stores?"

"Yes, and you're not going to like the news," Victoria replied. "Many of the stores are going to be extremely competitive relative to our normal pricing. In a few cases, they seem to have an edge."

Wendy turned to Ed. "Ed, how much cash flow/reserves have you been able to calculate from the five players?"

"Well, Wendy, it looks like if we slash our prices for about six months to a year, we could drive all but Home Designs into near bankruptcy, providing that our promotional campaign doesn't have a misstep."

"What about personnel, Frank?" Wendy cut in. "Have you done the usual research to see about hiring away the five players' key personnel?"

"Yes, but many won't go unless they get a 50 percent raise, which is way out of line with our other stores."

At this point, Wendy slammed her fist on the table and shouted, "I'm tired of hearing negative reports! It's our job to drive out the competition, so I want solutions!"

There was a long silence in the room. Wendy was noted for her quick temper and her quick firings when things didn't go as planned. She had been the first woman to make it this high in the company, and it wasn't the result of being overly pleasant.

"So this is what we're going to do," Wendy said softly. "Frank, you're going to hire those key people at a 50 percent increase. You're going to keep the unions away from the rest of the people. In eighteen months, when these overpriced employees have trained the others, we'll find some way of getting rid of them. Ed, you're going to lean on the players' bankers. See if we do business with them as well. See what other information you can squeeze out of them. Victoria, since you're the newest, I'm putting you in charge of breaking the pricing problem. I want you to come up with a unique pricing strategy for each of the twenty stores that will consistently undercut the competition for the next eighteen months, even if we have to lose money on everything in the stores! The franchisees will go with this once we explain the payout."

One of the newer staff asked, "If we're successful, doesn't that make us a monopoly in the area? Don't we have to worry about antitrust issues?"

Wendy raised her eyebrow a little and said, "We don't mention the word *monopoly* around here as if it were wrong. It took the Feds decades to break up AT&T. Microsoft was next on their list, and now it's MasterCard. We're in retail. No one has ever had problems with the Feds in this industry. By the time they deal with what we're doing, we will all be retired."

QUESTIONS • EXERCISES

1. Identify the issues of which Victoria needs to be aware.
2. Discuss the implications of each decision that Wendy made.
3. Discuss the issue of monopolies and whether they are right or wrong.

*This case is strictly hypothetical; any resemblance to real persons, companies, or situations is coincidental.

Programs that are designed to foster ethical decision making in business are controversial today because much unethical and illegal business conduct has continued to occur, even in organizations that have adopted such programs. Enron, for example, had a code of ethics and was a member of the Better Business Bureau, yet the company was ruined by unethical activities and corporate scandal. Many business leaders believe that ethics initiatives should arise naturally from a company's corporate culture and that hiring good employees will limit unethical conduct. Moreover, many business executives and board members often do not understand how organizational ethics can be systematically implemented. We believe, however, that a customized ethics and compliance program will help many businesses provide guidance so that employees from diverse backgrounds will understand what behaviors are acceptable (or unacceptable) within the organization. In business, many ethical issues are complex and require that organizations reach a consensus on appropriate action. Top executives and boards of directors must provide the leadership and a system to resolve these issues.

Business ethics programs have the potential to help top managers establish an ethical culture and eliminate the opportunity for unethical conduct. This chapter therefore provides a framework for developing an ethics program that is consistent with research, best practices, and the decision-making process described in Chapter 5, as well as the Federal Sentencing Guidelines for Organizations (FSGO) and the Sarbanes–Oxley Act in Chapter 4. These legislative reforms require both executives and boards of directors to assume responsibility and ensure that ethical standards are properly implemented on a daily basis.

In this chapter, we first provide an assessment of the corporation as an entity in society, and then we give an overview of why businesses need to develop an organizational ethics program. Next, we consider the factors that must be part of such a program: a code of conduct, an ethics officer and the appropriate delegation of authority, an effective ethics-training program, a system for monitoring and supporting ethical compliance, and continual efforts to improve the ethics program. Finally, we consider common mistakes made in designing and implementing ethics programs.

THE RESPONSIBILITY OF THE CORPORATION AS A MORAL AGENT

Increasingly, corporations are viewed not merely as profit-making entities but also as moral agents that are accountable for their conduct to their employees, investors, suppliers, and customers. Companies are more than the sum of their parts or participants. Because corporations are chartered as citizens of a state and/or nation, they generally have the same rights and responsibilities as individuals. Through legislation and court precedents, society holds companies accountable for the conduct of their employees as well as for their decisions and the consequences of those decisions. Publicity in the news media about specific issues such as employee benefits, executive compensation, defective products, competitive practices, and financial reporting contribute to a firm's reputation as a moral agent.

Viewed as moral agents, companies are required to obey the laws and regulations that define acceptable business conduct. However, it is important to acknowledge that they are not human beings who can think through moral issues. Because companies are not human, laws and regulations are necessary to provide formal structural restraints and guidance on ethical issues. Although individuals may attempt to abide by their own values and moral philosophy, as employees they are supposed to act in the company's best interests. Thus, the individual as a moral agent has a moral obligation beyond that of the corporation because it is the individual, not the company, who can think responsibly through complex ethical issues.[1] Figure 8–1 illustrates the basic causes of individual misconduct, the key reason why individuals engage in misconduct to do "whatever it takes to meet business targets."

Though obviously not a person, a corporation can be considered a societal moral agent that is created to perform specific functions in society and is therefore responsible to society for its actions. Because corporations have the characteristics of agents, responsibility for ethical behavior is assigned to them as legal entities as well as to individuals or work groups they employ. As Figure 8–1 indicates, a corporate culture without values and appropriate communication about ethics can facilitate individual misconduct. As such, companies may be punished for wrongdoing and rewarded for good business ethics. The FSGO holds corporations responsible for conduct they engage in as an entity. Some corporate outcomes cannot be tied to one individual or even a group, and misconduct can be the result of a collective pattern of decisions supported by a corporate culture. Therefore, corporations can be held accountable, fined, and even receive the death penalty when they are operating in a manner inconsistent with major legal requirements. Some organizations receive such large fines and negative publicity that they have to go out of business because there is no way to survive under these pressures. On the other hand, companies that have been selected as the top corporate citizens—such as Green Mountain Coffee Roasters, Hewlett-Packard,

| FIGURE 8-1 | Root Causes of Misconduct |

SOURCE: "KPMG Forensic Integrity Survey 2005–2006,"
http://www.us.kpmg.com/microsite/attachments/2006/ForIntegritySurv.pdf (accessed January 14, 2009).

Advanced Micro Devices, and Motorola—receive awards and positive publicity for being responsible moral agents in our society.[2]

One major misunderstanding in studying business ethics is to assume that a coherent ethical corporate culture will evolve through individual and interpersonal relationships. Because ethics is often viewed as an individual matter, many reason that the best way to develop an ethical corporate culture is to provide character education to employees or to hire individuals with good character and sensitize them to ethical issues. This assumes that ethical conduct will develop through company-wide agreement and consensus. Although these assumptions are laudable and have some truth, the companies that are responsible for most of the economic activity in the world employ thousands of culturally diverse individuals who will never reach agreement on all ethical issues. Many ethical business issues are complex close calls, and the only way to ensure consistent decisions that represent the interests of all stakeholders is to require ethical policies. This chapter provides support for the belief that implementing a centralized corporate ethics program can provide a cohesive, internally consistent set of statements and policies representing the corporation as a moral agent.

THE NEED FOR ORGANIZATIONAL ETHICS PROGRAMS

To understand why companies need to develop ethics programs, consider the following exercise and judge whether each of the described actions is unethical or illegal:

1. You want to skip work to go to a baseball game, but you need a doctor's excuse, so you make up some symptoms so that your insurance company pays for the doctor's visit. (unethical, illegal)

2. While having a latte at Starbucks, you run into an acquaintance who works as a salesperson at a competing firm. You wind up chatting about future product prices. When you get back to your office, you tell your supervisor what you heard. (unethical, illegal)
3. You get fired from your company, but before leaving to take a position with another company, you take a confidential list of client names and telephone numbers that you compiled for your former employer. (unethical, illegal)
4. You receive a loan from your parents to make the down payment on your first home, but when describing the source of the down payment on the mortgage application, you characterize it as a gift. (unethical, illegal)
5. Your manager asks you to book some sales revenue from the next quarter into this quarter's sales report to help reach target sales figures. You agree to do so. (unethical, illegal)

You probably labeled one or more of these five scenarios as unethical rather than illegal. The reality is that all of them are illegal. You may have chosen incorrectly because it is nearly impossible to know every detail of the highly complex laws relevant to these situations. Consider that there are ten thousand laws and regulations associated with the processing and selling of a single hamburger. Unless you are a lawyer who specializes in a particular area, it is difficult to know every law associated with your job. However, you can become more sensitized to what might be unethical or, in this case, illegal. One reason why ethics programs are required in one form or another is to help sensitize employees to the potential legal and ethical issues within their work environments.

As we have mentioned throughout this book, recent ethics scandals in U.S. business have destroyed trust in top management and significantly lowered the public's trust of business. As a result, the chairman of the Securities and Exchange Commission (SEC) issued a challenge for "American organizations to behave more ethically than the law requires to help restore investors' trust."[3] According to a survey by Golin/Harris International, there are five top recommendations to CEOs for rebuilding trust and confidence in American firms. These are making customers the top priority, assuming personal responsibility and accountability, communicating openly and frequently with customers, handling crises more honestly, and sticking to the code of business ethics no matter what.[4] This is a recurring theme among primary stakeholders. As shown in Figure 8–2, 80 percent of investors want more transparency in firms.

Understanding the factors that influence the ethical decision-making process, as discussed in Chapter 5, can help companies encourage ethical behavior and discourage undesirable conduct. Fostering ethical decision making within an organization requires terminating unethical persons and improving the firm's ethical standards. Consider the "bad apple–bad barrel" analogy. Some people are simply "bad apples" who will always do things in their own self-interest regardless of their organization's goals or accepted standards of conduct. Eliminating such bad apples through screening techniques and enforcement of the firm's ethical standards can help improve the firm's overall behavior.[5] For example, Countrywide Financial CEO Angelo Mozilo created a corporate culture focused on low-documentation and subprime mortgages. Until its demise, Mozilo made positive statements about the company, although he had sold $474 million of his company's stock prior to its sale to Bank of America.

FIGURE 8-2	Most Investors Want Transparency

Do you think that large corporations provide enough information about how they operate?

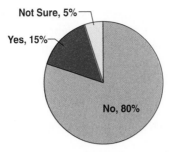

SOURCE: "TIAA-CREF Trust in America Survey of 1001 Respondents with Investments in Stocks, Bonds, or Other Investment Products," Snapshots, *USA Today,* January 5, 2006, B1.

Additionally, "liar loans," where borrowers' financial information is altered, were widespread in the company, putting the focus on the rewards of commissions for making loans with little concern for stakeholders.[6]

Organizations also can become "bad barrels," not because the individuals within them are bad, but because the pressures to succeed create opportunities that reward unethical decisions. In the case of such bad barrels, the firms must redesign their image and culture to conform to industry and social standards of acceptable behavior.[7] Most companies attempt to improve ethical decision making by establishing and implementing a strategic approach to improving their organization's ethics. Companies as diverse as Texas Instruments, Starbucks, Ford Motor Company, and Johnson & Johnson have adopted a strategic approach to organizational ethics and also continuously monitor their programs and make improvements when problems occur.

To promote legal and ethical conduct, an organization should develop an organizational ethics program by establishing, communicating, and monitoring the ethical values and legal requirements that characterize its history, culture, industry, and operating environment. Without such programs, uniform standards and policies of conduct, it is difficult for employees to determine what behaviors are acceptable within a company. As discussed in Chapters 6 and 7, in the absence of such programs and standards, employees generally will make decisions based on their observations of how their coworkers and superiors behave. A strong ethics program includes a written code of conduct, an ethics officer to oversee the program, careful delegation of authority, formal ethics training, rigorous auditing, monitoring, enforcement, and revision of program standards. Without a strong program, problems likely will occur. Such is the case in Latin America where a survey by a Latin American business magazine found that Argentine businesses have the greatest number of ethical problems. In Latin America, there is no method, rule, or corporate internal policy that controls in absolute terms what business managers plan, execute, or do, and only 26 percent of all executives follow the values of the founder or owner of the business in which they are employed.[8]

Although there are no universal standards that can be applied to organizational ethics programs, most companies develop codes, values, or policies to provide guidance on business conduct. However, it would be naïve to think that simply having a code of ethics will solve all the ethical dilemmas that a company might face.[9] Indeed, most of the companies that have experienced ethical and legal difficulties in recent years have had formal ethics codes and programs. The problem is that top managers have not integrated these codes, values, and standards into their firms' corporate culture where they can provide effective guidance for daily decision making. Tyco, for example, had an ethics program and was a member of the Ethics and Compliance Officer Association. However, it was never active in that organization, and its top managers were involved in misconduct that sacrificed public confidence in the company. CEO Dennis Kozlowski allegedly used millions of dollars of company funds for personal use and was indicted for criminal tax avoidance schemes.[10] If a company's leadership fails to provide the vision and support needed for ethical conduct, then an ethics program will not be effective. Ethics is not something to be delegated to lower-level employees while top managers break the rules.

To satisfy the public's escalating demands for ethical decision making, companies need to develop plans and structures for addressing ethical considerations. Some directions for improving ethics have been mandated through regulations, but companies must be willing to have in place a system for implementing values and ethics that exceeds the minimum requirements.

AN EFFECTIVE ETHICS PROGRAM

Throughout this book, we have emphasized that ethical issues are at the forefront of organizational concerns as managers and employees face increasingly complex decisions. These decisions are often made in a group environment composed of different value systems, competitive pressures, and political concerns that contribute to the opportunity for misconduct. In a national survey by KPMG International, 74 percent of the more than four thousand workers surveyed indicated that they had observed violations of the law or of company standards in the previous twelve months.[11] When opportunity to engage in unethical conduct abounds, companies are vulnerable to both ethical problems and legal violations if their employees do not know how to make the right decisions.

A company must have an effective ethics program to ensure that all employees understand its values and comply with the policies and codes of conduct that create its ethical culture. Because we come from diverse business, educational, and family backgrounds, it cannot be assumed that we know how to behave appropriately when we enter a new organization or job. At the pharmaceutical company Merck, for example, all employees are expected to uphold the organization's corporate code of conduct. Merck's sixty thousand employees participate in an interactive ethical business practices program that exposes them to real-life situations they might encounter. According to Merck's chief ethics officer, "We want employees to know how Merck's values apply to their day-to-day activities so that they can adhere to these standards and model these values whenever and wherever they conduct Merck business."[12]

According to a study by the Open Compliance Ethics Group (OCEG), among companies with an ethics program in place for ten years or more, none have experienced "reputation damage" in the last five years—"a testament to the important impact these programs can have over time." Companies that have experienced reputation damage in the past are much further along compared to their peers in establishing ethics and compliance programs. Companies in the study spent an average of $5.8 million in total compliance or ethics efforts for every $1 billion in revenues.[13]

An Ethics Program Can Help Avoid Legal Problems

As mentioned in Chapter 7, some corporate cultures provide opportunities for or reward unethical conduct because their management lacks concern or the company has failed to comply with the minimum requirements of the FSGO (Table 8–1). In such cases, the company may face penalties and the loss of public confidence if one of its employees breaks the law. The guidelines encourage companies to assess their key risk areas and to customize a compliance program that will address these risks and satisfy key effectiveness criteria. The guidelines also hold companies responsible for the misconduct of their employees. The KPMG organizational survey found that about half of those surveyed felt that their company would not discipline workers guilty of an ethical infraction, and 57 percent said that they felt pressure to do "whatever it takes" to meet business goals.[14]

At the heart of the FSGO is a "carrot-and-stick" philosophy. Companies that act to prevent misconduct by establishing and enforcing ethical and legal compliance programs may receive a "carrot" and avoid penalties should a violation occur. The ultimate "stick" is the possibility of being fined or put on probation if convicted of a crime. Organizational probation involves using consultants on site to observe and monitor a company's legal compliance efforts as well as to report the company's progress toward avoiding misconduct to the U.S. Sentencing Commission. Table 8–2 shows the fines that have been imposed on sentenced organizations for leading offenses, including

TABLE 8–1	Minimum Requirements for Ethics and Compliance Programs

1. Standards and procedures, such as codes of ethics, that are reasonably capable of detecting and preventing misconduct

2. High-level personnel who are responsible for an ethics and compliance program

3. No substantial discretionary authority given to individuals with a propensity for misconduct

4. Standards and procedures communicated effectively via ethics training programs

5. Establishment of systems to monitor, audit, and report misconduct

6. Consistent enforcement of standards, codes, and punishment

7. Continuous improvement of the ethics and compliance program

SOURCE: Adapted from U.S. Sentencing Commission, *Federal Sentencing Guidelines Manual*, effective November 1, 2004 (St. Paul: West, 2008).

TABLE 8-2	Mean and Median Fines Imposed on Sentenced Organizations in Four Offense Categories

	Cases with Fine Imposed							
	Cases with Fine Imposed (2007)				**Cases with Fine Imposed (2007)**			
Offense	**Total Number of Cases**	**Number**	**Mean Fine ($)**	**Median Fine ($)**	**Total Number of Cases**	**Number**	**Mean Fine ($)**	**Median Fine ($)**
Antitrust	12	12	164,167	175,000	15	11	115,691	50,000
Fraud	6,820	1,004	729,525	39,532	7,726	1,047	1,621,654	45,177
Environmental—wildlife	175	106	21,119	3,000	192	133	14,364	5,000

SOURCE: U.S. Sentencing Commission, *2003 Sourcebook of Federal Sentencing Statistics,* Table 15, www.ussc.gov/ANNRPT/2007/Table15.pdf (accessed January 14, 2009).

antitrust violations and fraud. The table compares two years of data; as can be seen from the table, fines for fraud, antitrust, and environmental wildlife offenses have all increased. Thus, moral issues are still a problem for the government.

The FSGO also requires federal judges to increase fines for organizations that continually tolerate misconduct and to reduce or eliminate fines for firms with extensive compliance programs that are making due diligence attempts to abide by legal and ethical standards. Until the guidelines were formulated, courts were inconsistent in holding corporations responsible for employee misconduct. There was no incentive to build effective programs to encourage employees to make ethical and legal decisions. Now companies earn credit for creating ethics programs that meet a rigorous standard. The effectiveness of a program is determined by its design and implementation: It must deal effectively with the risk associated with a particular business and has to become part of the corporate culture.

An ethics program can help a firm avoid civil liability, but the company still bears the burden of proving that it has an effective program. A program developed in the absence of misconduct will be much more effective than one imposed as a reaction to scandal or prosecution. A legal test of a company's ethics program is possible when an individual employee is charged with misconduct. The court system or the U.S. Sentencing Commission evaluates the organization's responsibility for the individual's behavior during the process of an investigation. If the courts find that the company contributed to the misconduct or failed to show due diligence in preventing misconduct, then the firm may be convicted and sentenced.

The Sarbanes–Oxley Act of 2002, as discussed in Chapter 3, established new requirements for corporate governance to prevent fraudulent behavior in business. The heart of this act is an accounting oversight board that establishes financial reporting requirements including instituting a code of conduct for senior financial officers. This legislation covers many issues related to corporate governance including the role of board members relative to the oversight of ethics programs. It also requires public corporations to file their code of ethics with the accounting oversight board or explain why they do not have a code of ethics.

Values versus Compliance Programs

No matter what their goals, ethics programs are developed as organizational control systems, the aim of which is to create predictability in employee behavior. Two types of control systems can be created. A **compliance orientation** creates order by requiring that employees identify with and commit to specific required conduct. It uses legal terms, statutes, and contracts that teach employees the rules and penalties for noncompliance. The other type of system is a **values orientation,** which strives to develop shared values. Although penalties are attached, the focus is more on an abstract core of ideals such as respect and responsibility. Instead of relying on coercion, the company's values are seen as something to which people willingly aspire.[15]

Research into compliance- and values-based approaches reveals that both types of programs can interact or work toward the same end but that a values orientation influences employees and creates ethical reasoning among employees. Values-based programs increase employees' awareness of ethics at work, their integrity, their willingness to deliver bad news to supervisors, and the perception that better decisions are made. Compliance-based programs are linked to employees' awareness of ethical issues at work, to their perception that decision making is better because of the program, and to their explicit knowledge of rules and expectations that makes decision making easier. In the final analysis, both orientations can be used to help employees and managers; however, it appears that a values-based program may be better for companies in the long run.

CODES OF CONDUCT

Most companies begin the process of establishing organizational ethics programs by developing **codes of conduct,** which are formal statements that describe what an organization expects of its employees. Such statements may take three different forms: a code of ethics, a code of conduct, and a statement of values.

A **code of ethics** is the most comprehensive and consists of general statements, sometimes altruistic or inspirational, that serve as principles and the basis for rules of conduct. A code of ethics generally specifies methods for reporting violations, disciplinary action for violations, and a structure of due process. A code of conduct is a written document that may contain some inspirational statements but usually specifies acceptable or unacceptable types of behavior. A code of conduct is more akin to a regulatory set of rules and, as such, tends to elicit less debate about specific actions. One problem with codes of conduct is that they tend to be developed without broad-based participation from stakeholders.[16] The final type of ethical statement is a **statement of values,** which serves the general public and also addresses distinct groups such as stakeholders. Values statements are conceived by management and are fully developed with input from all stakeholders. Despite our distinctions, it is important to recognize that these terms are often used interchangeably. Figure 8–3 indicates that most employees do not feel their company's code of conduct is comprehensive. While 38 percent appears low, this represents a 13 percent improvement over 2005. Because of legal regulations, 55 percent of publicly-held organizations have comprehensive codes, as opposed to a mere 27 percent in privately-held ones.[17]

Regardless of the degree of comprehensiveness, a code of ethics should reflect upper managers' desire for compliance with the values, rules, and policies that support

| FIGURE 8-3 | Percentage of Employees Who Identify Comprehensive Ethics and Compliance Programs in Their Own Companies |

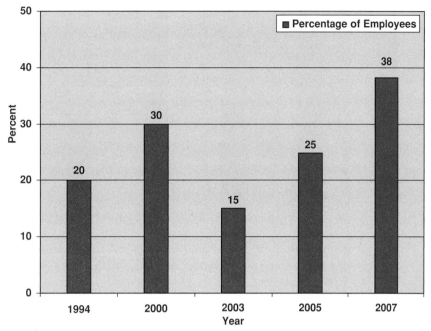

SOURCE: *National Business Ethics Survey, 2007,* Ethics Resource Center, 2007, p. 18.

an ethical culture. The development of a code of ethics should involve the president, board of directors, and chief executive officers who will be implementing the code. Legal staff should also be called on to ensure that the code has correctly assessed key areas of risk and that it provides buffers for potential legal problems. A code of ethics that does not address specific high-risk activities within the scope of daily operations is inadequate for maintaining standards that can prevent misconduct. Table 8–3 shows factors to consider when developing and implementing a code of ethics.

These codes may address a variety of situations, from internal operations to sales presentations and financial disclosure practices. Research has found that corporate codes of ethics often contain about six core values or principles in addition to more detailed descriptions and examples of appropriate conduct.[18] The six values that have been suggested as being desirable for codes of ethics include (1) trustworthiness, (2) respect, (3) responsibility, (4) fairness, (5) caring, and (6) citizenship.[19] These values will not be effective without distribution, training, and the support of top management in making these values a part of the corporate culture. Employees need specific examples of how these values can be implemented.

Codes of conduct will not resolve every ethical issue encountered in daily operations, but they help employees and managers deal with ethical dilemmas by prescribing or limiting specific activities. Many companies have a code of ethics, but it is not communicated effectively. A code that is placed on a website or in a training manual

TABLE 8-3	Developing and Implementing a Code of Ethics

1. Consider areas of risk and state the values as well as conduct necessary to comply with laws and regulations. Values are an important buffer in preventing serious misconduct.

2. Identify values that specifically address current ethical issues.

3. Consider values that link the organization to a stakeholder orientation. Attempt to find overlaps in organizational and stakeholder values.

4. Make the code understandable by providing examples that reflect values.

5. Communicate the code frequently and in language that employees can understand.

6. Revise the code every year with input from organizational members and stakeholders.

is useless if it is not reinforced every day. By communicating to employees both what is expected of them and what punishments they face if they violate the rules, codes of conduct curtail opportunities for unethical behavior and thereby improve ethical decision making. Fidelity Investment's code of ethics, for example, specifies that the sanctions for violating its code range from cautions and warnings to dismissal and criminal prosecution.[20] Codes of conduct do not have to be so detailed that they take into account every situation, but they should provide guidelines and principles that are capable of helping employees achieve organizational ethical objectives and addressing risks in an accepted way.

In the United States, Texas Instruments has gained recognition as having one of the nation's leading ethics programs. The company has won numerous ethics awards as well as being listed on the *Fortune* list of America's most admired companies where it ranked number one in the semiconductor industry for three years. It was also on the *Business Ethics* "100 Best Corporate Citizens" list in the last four years. Texas Instruments is extremely focused on ethics and social responsibility, it ensures that its employees are educated in ethics, and it does this through its "Code of Ethics" booklet and the ethics quick test that is an integral part of everything that Texas Instruments does. It is not only large companies that need to develop an ethics and compliance program; small companies need to and are doing it too. Next, let's look at Honda Engineering and how they developed an ethics program.

Honda Engineering

Honda Engineering North America, Inc. has four hundred associates and sales of $100 million to $200 million per year. It provides engineering services such as designing, building, and installing production tooling for Honda's plants in North America. There are many reasons why small companies should have an ethics program, especially to reduce the risk of compliance problems, because small companies usually have fewer internal controls and therefore have higher risks of compliance problems. It also gives small companies a competitive advantage; because their customers increasingly have an ethics program and want their suppliers to have one too. An ethics program can also improve hiring and reduce turnover because more and more employees become concerned about a corporation's ethical reputation when accepting a job offer. However, there are also problems that may not occur in a larger company;

for example, there may be a limited or nonexistent budget, a leaner staff, cultural differences, and difficulty getting management buy-in.

Honda Engineering was asked by its largest customer to establish an ethics program. The main concerns about implementing the program included concerns about the availability of workers and budget. Honda Engineering overcame these problems by using Honda of America (HAM) as a resource. They used HAM's code of conduct as a base and made minor changes to it using the same consultant as HAM. For code revisions, costs were kept low by not using a consultant. It has also been made available online, which reduces costs, and in a brochure format, which is only four pages. To address the worker-availability problem, Honda Engineering provided a toll-free number with a message, and they provided short, live training classes for all associates, which consisted of two hours for management and two hours for associates. All training was designed in-house with HAM support.

Honda Engineering runs an effective program by relying on the basic principles of building and maintaining trust. It does this through live training with frank discussions, asking the employees what they need, while maintaining independence and confidentiality. They use databases, surveys, and interviews with management to target the training and always follow up. Through effective communication, Honda Engineering ensures that employees are kept updated on changes to the code of conduct and any issues that arise. They send out an e-mail "Ethics@Work" a quarterly newsletter that is based on real situations and real concerns, Honda Engineering also addresses issues in the company newsletter. In this way, the company communicates the code to its employees while ensuring that employees know that it is everyone's responsibility to comply with the code at all times.[21]

ETHICS OFFICERS

Organizational ethics programs also must have oversight by high-ranking persons known to respect legal and ethical standards. These individuals—often referred to as **ethics officers**—are responsible for managing their organizations' ethics and legal compliance programs. They are usually responsible for (1) assessing the needs and risks that an organization-wide ethics program must address, (2) developing and distributing a code of conduct or ethics, (3) conducting training programs for employees, (4) establishing and maintaining a confidential service to answer employees' questions about ethical issues, (5) making sure that the company is in compliance with government regulation, (6) monitoring and auditing ethical conduct, (7) taking action on possible violations of the company's code, and (8) reviewing and updating the code. Ethics officers are also responsible for knowing thousands of pages of relevant regulations as well as communicating and reinforcing values that build an ethical corporate culture. According to the Ethics Resource Center survey, 65 percent of respondents reported that their firm has a designated office, person, or telephone line where they can get advice about ethics issues.[22] Corporate wrongdoings and scandal-grabbing headlines have a profound negative impact on public trust. To ensure compliance with state and federal regulations, many corporations are now appointing chief compliance officers and ethics and business conduct professionals to develop and oversee corporate compliance programs.[23]

The Ethics and Compliance Officer Association (ECOA) has over twelve hundred members, who are at the front lines of managing ethics programs.[24] The ECOA has members representing nearly every industry, they have members from more than 62 percent of the *Fortune* 100 companies, and they conduct business in more than 160 countries. In addition to U.S.–based organizations, members are based in Belgium, Canada, Germany, Great Britain, Greece, Hong Kong, India, Japan, the Netherlands, and Switzerland.[25] Ethics officers often move into their position from other jobs in their company rather than having formal ethics training. One-third of ECOA members have law degrees, one-fourth have financial backgrounds, and in some cases, they moved up through their companies' ranks and were selected because of their knowledge of the company and their ability to communicate and develop training programs. The financial reporting requirements of the Sarbanes–Oxley Act put more pressure on ethics officers to monitor financial reporting and the reporting of sales and inventory movements to prevent fraud in booking revenue and profits.[26]

In most firms, ethics officers do not report directly to the board of directors although that will likely change over the next few years. At Sun Microsystems, the ethics officer already reports to the board of directors, and employees can report concerns to someone outside the firm. If their concerns have merit, the outside help center can report directly to the appropriate board committee, which can request a full investigation. A Conference Board survey of one hundred senior ethics officers revealed that 60 percent indicated that their own board of directors is not sufficiently engaged in ethics issues. Fifty-seven percent said they have never engaged their board of directors in ethics training.[27]

ETHICS TRAINING AND COMMUNICATION

A major step in developing an effective ethics program is implementing a training program and communication system to educate employees about the firm's ethical standards. Figure 8–4 indicates that 69 percent of employees viewed that their organization provided ethics training by 2005. A significant number of employees report that they frequently find such training useful. Training can educate employees about the firm's policies and expectations, relevant laws and regulations, and general social standards. Training programs can make employees aware of available resources, support systems, and designated personnel who can assist them with ethical and legal advice. They can also empower employees to ask tough questions and make ethical decisions. Many companies are now incorporating ethics training into their employee and management development training efforts. At The Healthcare Company, for example, two hours of orientation training on the company's code of conduct is required for each employee within thirty days of employment, and a code of conduct refresher course is conducted for all employees annually.[28]

As we emphasized in Chapters 5 and 7, ethical decision making is influenced by corporate culture, by coworkers and supervisors, and by the opportunities available to engage in unethical behavior.[29] Ethics training can affect all three types of influence. Full awareness of the philosophy of management, rules, and procedures can strengthen both the corporate culture and the ethical stance of peers and supervisors. Such

| **FIGURE 8-4** | Presence of Ethics Training |

The response of employees when asked if their organization provides ethics training.

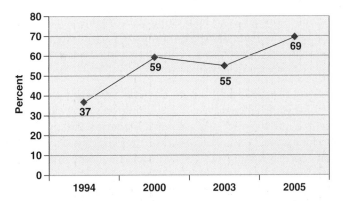

SOURCE: National Business Ethics Survey, *How Employees View Ethics in Their Organizations 1994–2005* (Washington, DC: Ethics Resource Center, 2005), 13.

awareness, too, arms employees against opportunities for unethical behavior and lessens the likelihood of misconduct. Thus, the existence and enforcement of company rules and procedures limit unethical practices in the organization. If adequately and thoughtfully designed, ethics training can ensure that everyone in the organization (1) recognizes situations that might require ethical decision making, (2) understands the values and culture of the organization, and (3) can evaluate the impact of ethical decisions on the company in the light of its value structure.[30]

If ethics training is to be effective, it must start with a foundation, a code of ethics, a procedure for airing ethical concerns, line and staff involvements, and executive priorities on ethics that are communicated to employees. Managers from every department must be involved in the development of an ethics-training program. Training and communication initiatives should reflect the unique characteristics of an organization: its size, culture, values, management style, and employee base. It is important for the ethics program to differentiate between personal and organizational ethics. Discussions in ethical-training programs sometimes break down into personal opinions about what should or should not be done in particular situations. To be successful, business ethics programs should educate employees about formal ethical frameworks and models for analyzing business ethics issues. Then employees can base ethical decisions on their knowledge of choices rather than on emotions.

Some of the goals of an ethics-training program might be to improve employees' understanding of ethical issues and their ability to identify them, to inform employees of related procedures and rules, and to identify the contact person who could help them resolve ethical problems. In keeping with these goals, the purpose of the Boeing Corporation's "Boeing Ethics and Business Conduct" program is as follows:

- ◆ Communicate Boeing's values and standards of ethical business conduct to employees.
- ◆ Inform employees of company policies and procedures regarding ethical business conduct.
- ◆ Establish processes to help employees obtain guidance and resolve questions regarding compliance with the company's standards of conduct and values.
- ◆ Establish criteria for ethics education and awareness programs and for coordinating compliance oversight activities.[31]

Boeing also asks employees to take ethics refresher training each year. On the company's "Ethics Challenge" webpage, employees (as well as the general public) can select from a variety of ethical dilemma scenarios, discuss them with their peers, and select from several potential answers. After clicking on the answer they think is most ethically correct, employees get feedback: the company's own opinion of the correct response and its rationale for it.

Indeed, most experts agree that one of the most effective methods of ethics training is exercise in resolving ethical dilemmas that relate to actual situations that employees may face in their jobs. Lockheed Martin, for example, developed a training game called "Gray Matters" that includes dilemmas that can be resolved in teams. Each team member can offer his or her perspective, thereby helping other team members understand the ramifications of a decision for coworkers and the organization.

A relatively new training device is behavioral simulation, which gives participants a short, hypothetical ethical-issue situation to review. Each participant is assigned a role within a hypothetical organization and is provided with varying levels of information about the scenario. Participants then must interact to develop recommended courses of action representing short-term, mid-term, and long-term considerations. Such simulations re-create the complexities of organizational relationships as well as the realities of having to address difficult situations with incomplete information. They help participants gain awareness of the ethical, legal, and social dimensions of business decision making; develop analytical skills for resolving ethical issues; and gain exposure to the complexity of ethical decision making in organizations. Research indicates that "the simulation not only instructs on the importance of ethics but on the processes for managing ethical concerns and conflict."[32]

Top executives must communicate with managers at the operations level (in production, sales, and finance, for instance) and enforce overall ethical standards within the organization. Table 8–4 lists the factors crucial to successful ethics training. It is most important to help employees identify ethical issues and give them the means to address and resolve such issues in ambiguous situations. In addition, employees should be offered direction in how to seek assistance from managers, the ethics officer, or other designated personnel when resolving ethical problems.

Although training and communication should reinforce values and provide employees with opportunities to learn about rules, they represent just one part of an effective ethics program. Moreover, ethics training will be ineffective if conducted solely because it is required or because it is something that competing firms are doing. The majority of ethics officers surveyed by the Conference Board said that even ethics training would not have prevented the collapse of Enron due to accounting improprieties.[33]

TABLE 8-4	Keys to Successful Ethics Training

1. Help employees identify the ethical dimensions of a business decision.

2. Give employees a means to address ethical issues.

3. Help employees understand the ambiguity inherent in ethics situations.

4. Make employees aware that their actions define the company's ethical posture both internally and externally.

5. Provide direction for employees to find managers or others who can help them resolve ethical conflicts.

6. Eliminate the belief that unethical behavior is *ever* justifiable by stressing that

   ◆ stretching the ethical boundaries results in unethical behavior.

   ◆ whether discovered or not, an unethical act is just that.

   ◆ an unethical act is *never* in the best interests of the company.

   ◆ the firm is held responsible for the misconduct of its members.

SOURCE: Adapted from Walter W. Manley II, *The Handbook of Good Business Practice,* 1992. Reprinted with permission of Thomson Publishing Services, Andover, Hampshire, England.

Enron executives knew they had the support of Arthur Andersen, the firm's auditing and accounting consulting partner, as well as that of law firms, investment analysts, and in some cases, government regulators. Enron's top managers therefore probably thought that their efforts to hide debt in off-balance-sheet partnerships would not be exposed.

In the Conference Board survey, 56 percent of ethics officers responded that they do not survey their employees to assess the effectiveness of their ethics programs, and 54 percent do not have ethics measurements as part of their performance appraisal systems.[34] Both of these activities could help determine the effectiveness of a firm's ethics training. If ethical performance is not a part of regular performance appraisals, this sends the message that ethics is not an important component of decision making. For ethics training to make a difference, employees must understand why it is conducted, how it fits into the organization, and what their own role in implementing it is.

SYSTEMS TO MONITOR AND ENFORCE ETHICAL STANDARDS

An effective ethics program employs a variety of resources to monitor ethical conduct and measure the program's effectiveness. Observing employees, internal audits, surveys, reporting systems, and investigations can assess compliance with the company's ethical code and standards. An external audit and review of company activities may sometimes be helpful in developing benchmarks of compliance. (We examine the process of ethical auditing in Chapter 9.)

To determine whether a person is performing his or her job adequately and ethically, observers might focus on how the employee handles an ethically charged situation. For example, many businesses employ role-playing exercises in training salespeople and managers. Ethical issues can be introduced into the discussion, and the results can be videotaped so that both participants and their superiors can evaluate the outcome of the ethics dilemma.

Questionnaires can serve as benchmarks in an ongoing assessment of ethical performance by surveying employees' ethical perceptions of their company, their superiors, their coworkers, and themselves, as well as gaining their ratings of ethical or unethical practices within the firm and industry. Then, if unethical conduct appears to be increasing, management will have a better understanding of what types of unethical practices may be occurring and why. A change in the company's ethics training may then be necessary.

The existence of an internal system by which employees can report misconduct is especially useful for monitoring and evaluating ethical performance. Many companies have set up ethics assistance lines—often called help lines—or help desks to offer support and give employees an opportunity to ask questions or report ethical concerns. A survey of *Fortune* 500 companies indicates that 90 percent offer toll-free help lines. It is interesting to note that Kenneth Lay, who was often a featured ethics speaker at conferences, did not offer employees at Enron a help line when he was Enron's CEO. Enron's auditor, Arthur Andersen, also had no help line.[35]

Although there is always some concern that employees may misreport a situation or abuse a help line to retaliate against a coworker, help lines have become widespread, and employees do use them. An easy-to-use help line or desk can serve as a safety net that increases the chance of detecting and responding to unethical conduct in a timely manner. Help lines serve as a central contact point where critical comments, dilemmas, and advice can be assigned to the person most appropriate for handling a specific case.[36] Figure 8–5 provides an overview of changes in employee propensity to report misconduct. Employees prefer to deal with ethical issues through their supervisor or

---

| **FIGURE 8–5** | Percentage of Employees Nationally Who Report Misconduct |

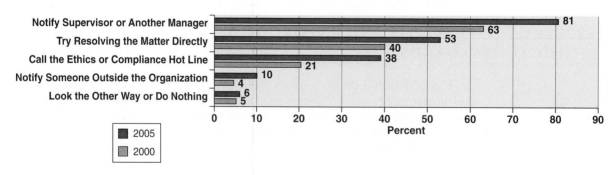

There were gains between 2000 and 2005 in the propensity of employees to report misconduct.

SOURCE: "KPMG Forensic Integrity Survey 2005–2006,"
http://www.kpmginsiders.com/display_analysis.asp?cs_id=148597 (accessed March 9, 2006).

manager or try to resolve the matter directly before using an anonymous reporting system such as a hot line.

Companies are increasingly using firms that provide professional case-management services and software. Software is becoming popular because it provides reports of employee concerns, complaints, or observations of misconduct, which can then be tracked and managed. It then allows the company to track investigations, analysis, resolutions, and documentation of misconduct reports. This helps prevent lawsuits, and the shared management and prevention can help a company analyze and learn about ethical lapses. However, it is important for companies to choose the right software for their company. They need to assess their current position and determine what they need going forward. Although only 10 to 15 percent of companies currently use some type of compliance management tool, many companies are moving toward the automated process that technology and software provide.

If a company is not making progress toward creating and maintaining an ethical culture, it needs to determine why and take corrective action, either by enforcing current standards more strictly or by setting higher standards. Corrective action may involve rewarding employees who comply with company policies and standards and punishing those who do not. When employees abide by organizational standards, their efforts should be acknowledged through public recognition, bonuses, raises, or some other means. On the other hand, when employees violate organizational standards, they must be reprimanded, transferred, docked, suspended, or even fired. If the firm fails to take corrective action against unethical or illegal behavior, the inappropriate behavior is likely to continue. In the Ethics Resource Center Survey, eight in ten employees who reported misconduct were dissatisfied with their organization's response because they did not believe that action taken by the organization was severe enough, suggesting that such corrective action is often not taken.[37]

Consistent enforcement and necessary disciplinary action are essential to a functional ethics or compliance program. The ethics officer is usually responsible for implementing all disciplinary actions for violations of the firm's ethical standards. Many companies are including ethical compliance in employee performance appraisals. During performance appraisals, employees may be asked to sign an acknowledgment that they have read the company's current ethics guidelines. The company must also promptly investigate any known or suspected misconduct. The appropriate company official, usually the ethics officer, needs to make a recommendation to senior management on how to deal with a particular ethical infraction. In some cases, a company may be required to report substantiated misconduct to a designated government or regulatory agency so as to receive credit. Under the FSGO, such credit for having an effective compliance program can reduce fines.[38]

Efforts to deter unethical behavior are important for companies' long-term relationships with their employees, customers, and community. If the code of ethics is aggressively enforced and becomes part of the corporate culture, it can effectively improve ethical behavior within the organization. If a code is not properly enforced, it becomes mere window dressing and will accomplish little toward improving ethical behavior and decisions.

Continuous Improvement of the Ethics Program

Improving the system that encourages employees to make more ethical decisions differs little from implementing any other type of business strategy. Implementation requires designing activities to achieve organizational objectives using available resources and given existing constraints. Implementation translates a plan for action into operational terms and establishes a means by which an organization's ethical performance will be monitored, controlled, and improved. Figure 8–6 indicates that organizations are more likely to have comprehensive ethics and compliance programs as they grow larger. This is in part due to increased resources, but also undoubtedly to increased stakeholder responsibilities and liabilities.

A firm's ability to plan and implement ethical business standards depends in part on how it structures resources and activities to achieve its ethical objectives. People's attitudes and behavior must be guided by a shared commitment to the business rather than mere obedience to traditional managerial authority. Encouraging diversity of perspectives, disagreement, and the empowerment of people helps align the company's leadership with its employees.

If a company determines that its ethical performance has been less than satisfactory, executives may want to reorganize how certain kinds of decisions are made. For example, a decentralized organization may need to centralize key decisions, at least for a time, so

FIGURE 8-6   Percentage of Employees Recognizing Own Companies as Having Comprehensive Ethics Programs Increases with Company Size

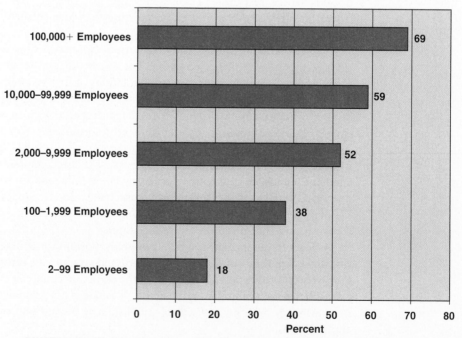

SOURCE: *National Business Ethics Survey,* 2007, Ethics Resource Center, 2007, p. 35.

that upper managers can ensure that the decisions are ethical. Centralization may reduce the opportunities that lower-level managers and employees have to make unethical decisions. Executives can then focus on initiatives for improving the corporate culture and infuse more ethical values throughout the firm by rewarding positive behavior and sanctioning negative behavior. In other companies, decentralizing important decisions may be a better way to attack ethical problems so that lower-level managers, familiar with the forces of the local business environment and local culture and values, can make more decisions. Whether the ethics function is centralized or decentralized, the key need is to delegate authority in such a way that the organization can achieve ethical performance.

Common Mistakes in Designing and Implementing an Ethics Program

Many business leaders recognize that they need to have an ethics program, but few take the time to answer fundamental questions about the goals of such programs. As mentioned previously, some of the most common program objectives are to deter and detect unethical behavior as well as violations of the law; to gain competitive advantages through improved relationships with customers, suppliers, and employees; and, especially for multinational corporations, to link employees through a unifying and shared corporate culture. Failure to understand and appreciate these goals is the first mistake that many firms make when designing ethics programs.

A second mistake is not setting realistic and measurable program objectives. Once a consensus on objectives is reached, companies should solicit input through interviews, focus groups, and survey instruments. Finding out what employees might do in a particular situation and what can help companies better understand how to correct unethical or illegal behavior either reactively or proactively. Research suggests that employees and senior managers often know that they are doing something unethical but rationalize their behavior as being "for the good of the company." As a result, ethics program objectives should contain some elements that are measurable.[39]

The third mistake is senior management's failure to take ownership of the ethics program. Maintaining an ethical culture may be impossible if CEOs do not support an ethical culture. In recent years, many firms, particularly in the telecommunications industry, have falsified revenue reports by recording sales that never took place, shipping products before customers agreed to delivery, or recording all revenue from long-term contracts up front instead of over the life of the contracts in order to keep earnings high and boost their stock prices. In a number of cases, top executives encouraged such fraud because they held stock options or other bonus packages tied to the company's performance. Thus, reporting higher revenues ensured that they earned larger payoffs. Of the most highly visible accounting fraud cases brought by the SEC, more than half involved falsifying revenue records. For example, the SEC, along with the Department of Justice and a congressional committee, investigated whether Qwest improperly recorded revenues from the sale of fiber-optic capacity as immediate gains even though most of the deals involved long-term leases.[40] If top managers behave unethically, creating and enforcing an ethical culture will be difficult, if not impossible.

The fourth mistake is developing program materials that do not address the needs of the average employee. Many compliance programs are designed by lawyers to ensure that the company is legally protected. These programs usually yield complex "legalese" that few within the organization can understand. To avoid this problem, ethics programs—including codes of conduct and training materials—should include feedback from employees from across the firm, not just the legal department. Including a question-and-answer section in the program, referencing additional resources for guidance on key ethical issues, and using checklists, illustrations, and even cartoons can help make program materials more user friendly.

The fifth common mistake made in implementing ethics programs is transferring an "American" program to a firm's international operations. In multinational firms, executives should involve overseas personnel as early as possible in the process. This can be done by developing an inventory of common global management practices and processes and examining the corporation's standards of conduct in this international context.

A final common mistake is designing an ethics program that is little more than a series of lectures. In such cases, participants typically recall less than 15 percent the day after the lecture. A more practical solution is to allow employees to practice the skills they learn through case studies or small-group exercises.

A firm cannot succeed solely by taking a legalistic approach to ethics and compliance with sentencing guidelines. Top managers must seek to develop high ethical standards that serve as a barrier to illegal conduct. Although an ethics program should help reduce the possibility of penalties and negative public reaction to misconduct, a company must want to be a good corporate citizen and recognize the importance of ethics to success in business.

SUMMARY

Ethics programs help sensitize employees to potential legal and ethical issues within their work environments. To promote ethical and legal conduct, organizations should develop ethics programs by establishing, communicating, and monitoring ethical values and legal requirements that characterize the firms' history, culture, industry, and operating environment. Without such programs and such uniform standards and policies of conduct, it is difficult for employees to determine what behaviors a company deems acceptable.

A company must have an effective ethics program to ensure that employees understand its values and comply with its policies and codes of conduct. An ethics program should help reduce the possibility of legally enforced penalties and negative public reaction to misconduct. The main objective of the Federal Sentencing Guidelines for Organizations is to encourage companies to assess risk and then self-monitor and aggressively work to deter unethical acts and punish unethical employees. Ethics programs are developed as organizational control systems to create predictability in employee behavior. These control systems may have a compliance orientation—which uses legal terms, statutes, and contracts that teach employees the rules and the penalties for noncompliance—or a values orientation—which consists of developing shared values.

Most companies begin the process of establishing organizational ethics programs by developing codes of conduct, which are formal statements that describe what an organization expects of its employees. Variations of codes of conduct include the code of ethics and the statement of values. A code of ethics must be developed as part of senior management's desire to ensure that the company complies with values, rules, and policies that support an ethical culture. Without uniform policies and standards, employees will have difficulty determining what is acceptable behavior in the company.

Having a high-level manager or committee who is responsible for an ethical compliance program can significantly enhance its administration and oversight. Such ethics officers are usually responsible for assessing the needs of and risks to be addressed in an organization-wide ethics program, developing and distributing a code of conduct or ethics, conducting training programs for employees, establishing and maintaining a confidential service to answer questions about ethical issues, making sure the company is complying with government regulation, monitoring and auditing ethical conduct, taking action on possible violations of the company's code, and reviewing and updating the code.

Successful ethics training is important in helping employees identify ethical issues and in providing them with the means to address and resolve such issues. Training can educate employees about the firm's policies and expectations, available resources, support systems, and designated ethics personnel, as well as about relevant laws and regulations and general social standards. Top executives must communicate with managers at the operations level and enforce overall ethical standards within the organization.

An effective ethics program employs a variety of resources to monitor ethical conduct and measure the program's effectiveness. Compliance with the company's ethical code and standards can be assessed through observing employees, performing internal audits and surveys, instituting reporting systems, and conducting investigations, as well as by external audits and review, as needed. Corrective action involves rewarding employees who comply with company policies and standards and punishing those who do not. Consistent enforcement and disciplinary action are necessary for a functioning ethical compliance program.

Ethical compliance can be ensured by designing activities that achieve organizational objectives, using available resources and given existing constraints. A firm's ability to plan and implement ethics business standards depends in part on its ability to structure resources and activities to achieve its ethics and objectives effectively and efficiently.

In implementing ethics and compliance programs, many firms make some common mistakes including failing to answer fundamental questions about the goals of such programs, not setting realistic and measurable program objectives, failing to have its senior management take ownership of the ethics program, developing program materials that do not address the needs of the average employee, transferring an "American" program to a firm's international operations, and designing an ethics program that is little more than a series of lectures. Although an ethics program should help reduce the possibility of penalties and negative public reaction to misconduct, a company must want to be a good corporate citizen and recognize the importance of ethics to successful business activities.

IMPORTANT TERMS FOR REVIEW		
compliance orientation	code of ethics	
values orientation	statement of values	
code of conduct	ethics officers	

RESOLVING ETHICAL BUSINESS CHALLENGES*

Jim, now in his fourth year with Cinco Corporation, was made a plant manager three months ago after completing the company's management-training program. Cinco owns pulp-processing plants that produce various grades of paper from fast-growing, genetically altered trees. Jim's plant, the smallest and oldest of Cinco's, is located in upstate New York, near a small town. It employs between 100 and 175 workers, mostly from the nearby town. In fact, the plant boasts about employees whose fathers and grandfathers have also worked there. Every year Cinco holds a Fourth of July picnic for the entire town.

Cinco's policy is to give each manager a free hand in dealing with employees, the community, and the plant itself. Its main measure of performance is the bottom line, and the employees are keenly aware of this fact.

Like all pulp-processing plants, Cinco is located near a river. Because of the plant's age, much of its equipment is outdated. Consequently, it takes more time and money to produce paper at Jim's plant than at Cinco's newer plants. Cinco has a long-standing policy of breaking in new managers at this plant to see if they can manage a work force and a mill efficiently and effectively. The tradition is that a manager who does well with the upstate New York plant will be transferred to a larger, more modern one. As a result, the plant's workers have had to deal with many managers and have become hardened and insensitive to change. In addition, most of the workers are older and more experienced than their managers, including Jim.

In his brief tenure as plant manager, Jim learned much from his workers about the business. Jim's secretary, Ramona, made sure that reports were prepared correctly, that bills were paid, and that Jim learned how to perform his tasks. Ramona had been with the plant for so long that she had become a permanent fixture. Jim's three foremen were all in their late 40s and kept things running smoothly. Jim's wife, Elaine, was having a difficult time adjusting to upstate New York. Speaking with other managers' wives, she learned that the "prison sentence," as she called it, typically lasted no longer than two years. She had a large calendar in the kitchen and crossed off each day they were there.

One morning as Jim came into the office, Ramona didn't seem her usual stoic self.

"What's up?" Jim asked her.

"You need to call the EPA," she replied. "It's not really important. Ralph Hoad said he wanted you to call him."

When Jim made the call, Ralph told him the mill's waste disposal into the river exceeded Environmental Protection Agency (EPA) guidelines, and he would stop by next week to discuss the situation. Jim hung up the phone and asked Ramona for the water sample results for the last six months from upstream, from downstream, and at the plant. After inspecting the data and comparing them with EPA standards, he found no violations of any kind. He then ordered more tests to verify the original data. The next day Jim compared the previous day's tests with the last six months' worth of data and still found no significant differences and no EPA violations. As he continued to look at the data, however, something stood out on the printouts that he hadn't noticed before. All the tests had been done on the first or second shifts. Jim called the foremen of the two shifts to his office and asked if they knew what was going on. Both men were extremely evasive in their answers and referred him to the third-shift foreman. When Jim phoned him, he, too, was evasive and said not to worry—that Ralph would explain it to him.

That night Jim decided to make a spot inspection of the mill and test the wastewater. When he arrived at the river, he knew by the smell that something was very wrong. Jim immediately went back to the mill and demanded to know what was happening. Chuck, the third-shift foreman, took Jim down to the lowest level of the plant. In one of the many rooms stood four large storage tanks. Chuck explained to Jim that when the pressure gauge reached a certain level, a third-shift worker opened the valve and allowed the waste to mix with everything else.

"You see," Chuck told Jim, "the mill was never modernized to meet EPA standards, so we have to divert the bad waste here; twice a week it goes into the river."

"Who knows about this?" asked Jim.

"Everyone who needs to," answered Chuck.

When Jim got home, he told Elaine about the situation. Elaine's reaction was, "Does this mean we're stuck here? Because if we are, I don't know what I'll do!" Jim knew that all the managers before him must have had the same problem. He also knew that there would be no budget for installing EPA-approved equipment for at least another two years. The next morning Jim checked the EPA reports and was puzzled to find that the mill had always been in compliance. There should have been warning notices and fines affixed, but he found nothing.

That afternoon Ralph Hoad stopped by. Ralph talked about the weather, hunting, fishing, and then he said, "Jim, I realize you're new. I apologize for not coming sooner, but I saw no reason to because your predecessor had taken care of me until this month."

"What do you mean?" Jim asked.

"Ramona will fill you in. There's nothing to worry about. I know no one in town wants to see the mill close down, and I don't want it to either. There are lots of memories in this old place. I'll stop by to see you in another couple of months." With that, Ralph left.

Jim asked Ramona about what Ralph had said. She showed him a miscellaneous expense of $100 a month in the ledgers. "We do this every month," she told him.

"How long has this been going on?" asked Jim.

"Since the new EPA rules," Ramona replied. She went on to clarify Jim's alternatives. Either he could continue paying Ralph, which didn't amount to much, or he could refuse to, which would mean paying EPA fines and a potential shutdown of the plant. As Ramona put it, "Headquarters only cares about the bottom line. Now, unless you want to live here the rest of your life, the first alternative is the best for your career. The last manager who bucked the system lost his job. The rule in this industry is that if you can't manage Cinco's upstate New York plant, you can't manage. That's the way it is."

QUESTIONS • EXERCISES

1. Identify the ethical and legal issues of which Jim needs to be aware.
2. Discuss the advantages and disadvantages of each decision that Jim could make.
3. Identify the pressures that have brought about the ethical and legal issues.
4. What is Jim's power structure and leadership position at the plant?

*This case is strictly hypothetical; any resemblance to real persons, companies, or situations is coincidental.

Check Your EQ

Check your EQ, or Ethics Quotient, by completing the following. Assess your performance to evaluate your overall understanding of the chapter material.

1.	A compliance program should be deemed effective if it addresses the seven minimum requirements for ethical compliance programs.	**Yes**	**No**
2.	The accountability and responsibility for appropriate business conduct rests with top management.	**Yes**	**No**
3.	Ethical compliance can be measured by observing employees as well as through investigating and reporting mechanisms.	**Yes**	**No**
4.	The key goal of ethics training is to help employees identify ethical issues.	**Yes**	**No**
5.	An ethical compliance audit is designed to determine the effectiveness of ethics initiatives.	**Yes**	**No**

ANSWERS: 1. No. An effective compliance program has the seven elements of a compliance program in place and goes beyond those minimum requirements to determine what will work in a particular organization. 2. Yes. Executives in the organization determine the culture and initiatives that support ethical behavior. 3. Yes. Sometimes external monitoring is necessary, but internal monitoring and evaluation are the norm. 4. No. It is much more than that—it involves not only recognition but also an understanding of the values, culture, and rules in the organization as well as the impact of ethical decisions on the company. 5. Yes. It helps in establishing the code and in making program improvements.

CHAPTER 9

Implementing and Auditing Ethics Programs

CHAPTER OBJECTIVES

- To define ethics auditing
- To identify the benefits and limitations of ethics auditing
- To examine the challenges of measuring nonfinancial performance
- To explore the stages of the ethics-auditing process
- To understand the strategic role that the ethics audit can play

CHAPTER OUTLINE

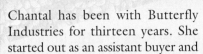

Chantal has been with Butterfly Industries for thirteen years. She started out as an assistant buyer and was later promoted to buyer. At one point, she married her boss, Juan, but they divorced several years later. After Juan left, Chantal threw herself into her work, and within a few years she had moved into the corporate offices, but with only Whiskers, a black-and-white cat, to cheer her progress up the corporate ladder.

During Chantal's tenure, Butterfly Industries grew from fewer than five hundred employees to more than thirty-five thousand. The company expanded all over the world and opened offices on every continent; it had nearly exclusive arrangements with suppliers from six different countries. Such rapid growth eroded the freedoms of a small firm in which one could do anything one wanted. So many employees—with different cultures, languages, time zones, varied clients—from so many countries, each with its own political realities, made corporate life much more complicated.

To Chantal, it seemed that the firm had grown at a whirlwind pace, and sometimes she thought that whirlwind had become an ugly black cloud. She had heard, for example, that some of Butterfly's suppliers in Puerto Rico mistreated their workers. In other foreign locations, Butterfly's products were bringing changes to the environment, as well as to local culture and gender roles. Because these workers tended to be women, children were being left to fend for themselves. In some Latin American countries, husbands were angry because their wives earned more than they did. And, then there were the rumors that retailers in some countries were selling Butterfly products without adequate service or, worse, diluting the products and selling them as "full strength."

After Butterfly went public, Chantal's sense of a foreboding whirlwind grew darker as headquarters' employees scrambled to satisfy shareholders' demands for specific information about products, projected earnings, employee benefit policies, and equal employment opportunity records. Chantal was also troubled that so many of the corporate people were

men; only she and one other woman were directly involved in the inner workings of the increasingly complex firm.

Six months ago, Chantal began hearing that some plant employees were suffering pay cuts while others weren't. In some cases, employees who had been working for Butterfly for fifteen years had been cut to thirty-six-hour workweeks, losing their full-time benefits. She began to notice political alliances being erected between marketing, finance, manufacturing, and corporate headquarters. Because each plant operated as an independent profit-making entity, each was guarded in its communication with other plants, knowing that if it could increase its profits it could also increase overall pay.

Chantal was not the only one to recognize that Butterfly needed guidance in a variety of areas, but no one had stepped forward. Then a month ago, Butterfly's president, Jermaine, asked Chantal to lunch. This was not unusual, but the conversation soon took a significant twist that Chantal was unprepared for.

"Chantal, you've been with the company for thirteen years now, right?" asked Jermaine.

"Yes, that's about right," Chantal answered.

"You know as well as anyone that I haven't kept pace with the growth," Jermaine continued with a mixture of sadness and determination. "When I founded this company, I could tell a few staffers to check out an idea, and several weeks later we'd talk about whether it would work. There was a time when I knew every employee, and even their families, but not anymore. Chantal, I think Butterfly has outgrown my style of management. What this company needs is a comprehensive set of rules and guidelines for every part of the company. I need to delegate more. That's why I wanted to talk to you."

Chantal, noticing her mouth was open, closed it and asked, "Jermaine, what are you saying to me?"

"Chantal, I've always been impressed with your work ethic and your sense of values. You know this company and its culture so well. I know you've heard some of the same rumors, so we both know that all is not well at Butterfly. What I'd like is for you to become the head of Butterfly's new ethics commit-tee. Of course, you know that we don't have an ethics committee, so that's where you come in."

"Me!?" Chantal asked with surprise.

"Yes, you. If you're willing, I want you to cre-ate this entity and run it so that we all can be proud of Butterfly again. So that people inside and outside the company know that we stand for what is right. You will be promoted to vice president, your salary will be doubled, and you can select your own team. Chantal, this is your chance to really make a huge difference. What's your answer?" asked Jermaine.

Chantal hesitated for a moment and then said, "Yes."

"Great! I knew I could count on you. The first thing I need is a proposed outline of the responsi-bilities of the new ethics committee, enforcement procedures—the works—and I want it in two weeks along with a list of people for the committee."

That night, as she stroked Whiskers, Chantal be-gan to plan.

QUESTIONS • EXERCISES

1. Prioritize the issues that Butterfly needs to ad-dress. How can an ethics program address these issues?
2. Develop an outline of who should be on the new ethics committee and describe what the committee's first steps should be toward im-plementing an effective ethics program.
3. Should the new ethics committee commission an ethics audit? If yes, when should this audit be conducted? If no, why not?

*This case is strictly hypothetical; any resemblance to real per-sons, companies, or situations is coincidental.

In Chapter 8, we introduced the idea of ethics programs as a way for organizations to improve ethical decision making and conduct in business. To properly imple-ment these programs and ensure their effectiveness, companies need to measure their impact. Increasingly, companies are applying the principles of auditing to ascer-tain whether their ethics codes, policies, and corporate values are having a positive im-pact on the firm's ethical conduct. These audits can help companies identify risks, noncompliance with laws and company policies, and areas that need improvement. An audit should provide a systematic and objective survey of the firm's ethical culture and values.

In this chapter, we examine the concept of an ethics audit as a way to implement an effective ethics program. We begin by defining the term *ethics audit* and exploring its relationship to a social audit. Next, we examine the benefits and limitations of this implementation tool, especially with regard to avoiding a management crisis. The chal-lenges of measuring nonfinancial ethical performance are examined and evolving stan-dards are reviewed from AA1000, the Integrity Institute, and the Open Compliance Ethics Group. We then detail our framework for the steps of an ethics audit, includ-ing securing the commitment of directors and top managers; establishing a commit-tee to oversee the audit; defining the scope of the audit process; reviewing the firm's mission, values, goals, and policies and defining ethical priorities; collecting and ana-lyzing relevant information; verifying the results; and reporting them. Finally, we con-sider the strategic importance of ethics auditing.

THE ETHICS AUDIT

An **ethics audit** is a systematic evaluation of an organization's ethics program and performance to determine whether it is effective. A major component of the ethics program described in Chapter 8, the ethics audit includes "regular, complete, and documented measurements of compliance with the company's published policies and procedures."[1] As such, the audit provides an opportunity to measure conformity to the firm's desired ethical standards. An audit can even be a precursor to setting up an ethics program in that it identifies the firm's current ethical standards and policies and risk areas so that an ethics program can effectively address problem areas. Although few companies have so far conducted ethics audits, recent legislation will encourage greater ethics auditing as companies attempt to demonstrate to various stakeholders that they are abiding by the law and have established programs to improve ethical decision making.

The concept of ethics auditing emerged from the movement to audit and report on companies' broader social responsibility initiatives, particularly with regard to the natural environment. An increasing number of companies are auditing their social responsibility programs and reporting the results so as to document their efforts to be more responsible to various interested stakeholder groups. A **social audit** is the process of assessing and reporting a business's performance in fulfilling the economic, legal, ethical, and philanthropic responsibilities expected of it by its stakeholders.[2] Social reports often discuss issues related to a firm's performance in the four dimensions of social responsibility as well as to specific social responsibility and ethical issues such as staff issues, community economic development, volunteerism, and environmental impact.[3] In contrast, ethics audits focus on more narrow issues related to assessing and reporting on a firm's performance in terms of ethical and legal conduct. However, an ethics audit can be a component of a social audit, and, indeed, many companies include ethical issues in their social audits. British Petroleum, for example, includes ethical performance in its "Environmental and Social Report."[4]

Regardless of the breadth of the audit, ethics auditing is a tool that companies can employ to identify and measure their ethical commitment to stakeholders. Employees, customers, investors, suppliers, community members, activists, the media, and regulators are increasingly demanding that companies be ethical and accountable for their conduct. In response, businesses are working to incorporate accountability into their actions, from long-term planning, everyday decision making, and rethinking processes for corporate governance and financial reporting to hiring, retaining, and promoting employees and building relationships with customers. The ethics audit provides an objective method for demonstrating a company's commitment to improving strategic planning, including its compliance with legal and ethical standards and social responsibility. The auditing process is important to business because it can improve a firm's performance and effectiveness, increase its attractiveness to investors, improve its relationships with stakeholders, identify potential risks, and decrease the risk of misconduct and adverse publicity that could harm its reputation.[5]

Ethics auditing is similar to financial auditing in that it employs similar procedures and processes to create a system of integrity that includes objective reporting. Like an accounting audit, an ethics audit may be conducted by someone with expertise from outside the organization. Although the standards used in financial auditing can be adapted to provide an objective foundation for ethics reporting, there are significant differences between the two audit types. Whereas financial auditing focuses on all systems related to money flow and on financial assessments of value for tax purposes and managerial accountability, ethics auditing deals with the internal and broad external impact of the organization's ethical performance. Another significant difference is that ethics auditing is not usually associated with regulatory requirements, whereas financial audits are required of public companies that issue securities. Because ethics and social audits are more voluntary, there are fewer standards that a company can apply with regard to reporting frequency, disclosure requirements, and remedial actions that it should take in response to results. This may change as more companies build ethics programs in the current environment—where regulatory agencies support giving boards of directors oversight of corporate ethics. For boards to track the effectiveness of ethics programs, audits will be required. In addition, nonfinancial auditing standards are developing with data available for benchmarking and comparing a firms nonfinancial ethical performance.

BENEFITS OF ETHICS AUDITING

There are many reasons why companies choose to understand, report on, and improve their ethical conduct. Recent accounting scandals and legal and ethical transgressions have encouraged companies to better account for their actions in a wide range of areas including corporate governance, ethics programs, customer relationships, employee relations, environmental policies, and community involvement. Cadence Design Systems, an electronics design company, restated its earnings in 2008 basically admitting that it had noted $24 million in revenue too early. A shareholder-filed lawsuit against the company alleges that Cadence inflated the stock price, violated federal securities laws, and took advantage of shareholders by causing the 25 percent stock price decline.[6]

At one extreme, a company may want to achieve the most ethical performance possible, whereas another firm may use an ethics audit merely to project a good image to hide its corrupt culture. Other firms may want to comply with the Federal Sentencing Guidelines for Organizations (FSGO) requirements that the board of directors oversee the discovery of ethical risk, design and implement an ethics program, and evaluate performance. Still other companies may see the auditing process as a key component of improving the financial performance of the organization. Thus, the real reasons why companies exceed the ethical-reporting standards prescribed by law actually lie along a vast spectrum.[7] For example, it is common for firms to conduct audits of business practices with legal ramifications such as employee safety, environmental impact, and financial reporting. Although these practices are important to a firm's ethics and social responsibility, they are also legally required and thus constitute the minimum level of commitment. However, because stakeholders are now demanding increased transparency and are taking a more active role through external organizations that represent their interests, government regulators are calling on companies to improve their ethical conduct and make more decisions based on principles rather than laws alone. The assessment of the ethical culture of an organization is necessary to improve ethical performance and to document in legal proceedings that a firm has an effective ethics program.

The auditing process can highlight trends, improve organizational learning, and facilitate communication and working relationships.[8] As such, auditing provides benefits for both organizations and their stakeholders. Auditing can help companies assess the effectiveness of their programs and policies, which often improves their operating efficiencies and reduces costs. Information from audits and reports can also help identify priorities among various activities so that the company can ensure that it is achieving the greatest possible impact with available resources.[9] The process of ethics auditing can also help an organization identify potential risks and liabilities and improve its compliance with the law. Furthermore, the audit report may help to document the firm's compliance with legal requirements as well as to demonstrate its progress in areas where it previously failed to comply such as by describing the systems it is implementing to reduce the likelihood of a recurrence of misconduct.[10]

For organizations, one of the greatest benefits of the auditing process is improved relationships with stakeholders who desire greater transparency. Many stakeholders have become wary of corporate public relations campaigns. Verbal assurances by corporate management are no longer sufficient to gain the trust of stakeholders. An ethics audit could have saved Enron if it identified and questioned millions of dollars in debt in off-balance-sheet partnerships. When companies and their employees, suppliers, and investors trust each other, the costs of monitoring and managing these relationships are lower. Companies experience less conflict with these stakeholders, which results in a heightened capacity for innovation and relationship building.

As a result, shareholders and investors have welcomed the increased disclosure that comes with corporate accountability. Figure 9–1 illustrates issues that are expected to have the most impact on shareholder value over the next five years. These issues can be considered major risk areas for ethics initiatives. Therefore, they represent subject-matter areas that could be important in an ethics audit. A growing number of investors are considering nonfinancial measures—such as the existence of ethics programs, legal compliance, board diversity and independence, and other corporate governance issues such as CEO compensation—when they analyze the quality of current and potential investments. Research suggests that investors may be willing to pay higher prices for the stock of companies that they deem to be accountable.[11] Consider that the "most admired companies" in the United States—General Electric, Berkshire Hathaway, Apple, FedEx, and Google—have generally avoided major ethical problems.[12] However, some companies have experienced some legal issues or had their ethics questioned. For example, Wal-Mart, who ranked twelfth in 2006, has been accused of treating its male and female employees differently and faces the largest private civil rights class-action discrimination suit from as many as 1.6 million female employees who say the giant retailer paid them lower wages and salaries than it did men in comparable positions. Pretrial proceedings uncovered discrepancies not only between the pay of men and women but also in the fact that men dominate higher-paying store manager

FIGURE 9-1	Top Issues over the Next Five Years

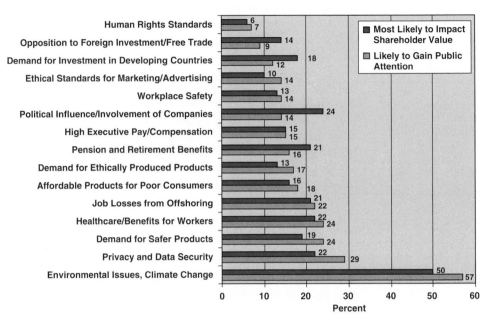

SOURCE: "From Risk to Opportunity—How Global Executives View Sociopolitical Issues: McKinsey Global Survey Results," *McKinsey Quarterly,* October 2008, http://www.mckinseyquarterly.com/Strategy/Strategic_Thinking/McKinsey_Global_Survey_Results_From_risk_to_opportunity_How_global_executives_view_sociopolitical_issues_2235 (accessed January 15, 2009).

positions while women occupy more than 90 percent of cashier jobs, most of which pay about $14,000 a year. Wal-Mart faces fines and penalties in the millions of dollars if found guilty of sexual discrimination.[13] Such problems could have been uncovered and addressed with a regular ethics audit. Even with its problems, Wal-Mart is the tenth most admired firm in the world, and Microsoft with a significant antitrust issue ranked sixth as the world's most admired company.[14]

Regular audits permit shareholders and investors to judge whether a firm is achieving the goals that it has established and whether it abides by the values that it has specified as important. Moreover, it permits stakeholders to influence the organization's behavior.[15] Increasingly, a broad range of stakeholder groups are seeking specific, often quantifiable, information from companies. These stakeholders expect companies to take a deeper look at the nature of their operations and to publicly disclose both their progress and problems in addressing these issues. Some investors are using their rights as stockholders to encourage companies to modify their plans and policies to address specific ethical issues. At Tyco, for example, shareholders voted to eliminate some executive benefits after a scandal involving unauthorized pay and fraudulent stock sales.[16]

Ethical Crisis Management and Recovery

A significant benefit of ethics auditing is that it may help prevent crises resulting from ethical or legal misconduct, crises that can potentially be more devastating than traditional natural disasters or technological disruptions. Just as companies develop *crisis management* plans to respond to and recover from natural disasters, they should also prepare for ethical disasters, which can not only result in substantial legal and financial costs but also disrupt routine operations, paralyze employees, reduce productivity, destroy organizational reputation, and erode stakeholder confidence. Ethical and legal crises have resulted in the demise of a number of well-known companies, including Enron and Arthur Andersen. Many other companies—HealthSouth, Firestone, Waste Management, Rite Aid, U.S. Foodservice, Qwest, Kmart, Mitsubishi Motors, Xerox, Daiwa Bank of Japan, Archer Daniels Midland, and Microsoft, to name but a few—survived ethical and legal crises. However, they paid a high price not only financially but also in terms of compromised reputation and declining stakeholder trust. Consider that Qwest spent $7 million a month on outside legal counsel to defend itself against allegations of accounting irregularities and fraud.[17] One study found that publicity about unethical corporate behavior lowers stock prices for at least six months.[18] A poll by Harris Interactive found many scandal-plagued firms at the bottom of its annual survey of perceived corporate reputation, including Enron, MCI (formerly WorldCom), Tyco International Ltd., and Adelphia. In the most recent survey, which ranks companies according to respondents' ratings of companies on twenty attributes, technology companies made an impressive showing, enjoying the strongest reputation of any industry. The technology business received positive ratings from 71 percent of the nearly twenty thousand Americans who took part in the survey. However, the overall reputation of American corporations, already weak, slipped further, despite corporate–governance reforms and a growing commitment to ethics and social responsibility. Seventy-one percent of respondents rated American businesses' reputation as "not good" or "terrible" up from the previous year when it was 68 percent.[19]

Despite the high costs of misconduct, a PricewaterhouseCoopers survey indicates that U.S. companies are failing to identify and manage ethical, social, economic, and environmental issues of concern. Although most companies recognize that these issues have the potential to harm their reputations and threaten their relationships with customers, suppliers, and other stakeholders, few are taking steps to identify, evaluate, and respond to them.[20] Figure 9–2 indicates that where employees are exposed to situations posing risk there is a high likelihood that they will also observe a violation taking place. For example, those who felt they were poorly prepared or felt pressure to deal with risk, 94 percent observed misconduct. Of those who encountered situations that they believed could result in misconduct, 74 percent observed at least one form of misconduct, and 64 percent of those in transitional organizations observed misconduct. Therefore, if employees feel pressured or aware of a risk factor in their work situation, they tend to observe misconduct. These findings mean that ethics audits could help more companies identify potential risks and liabilities so that they can implement plans to discover and eliminate or reduce risks before they reach crisis dimensions.

| **FIGURE 9-2** | Employee Observed Misconduct by Risk Factors |

Where employees are exposed to situations posing risk, there is high likelihood that they will also observe a violation taking place.

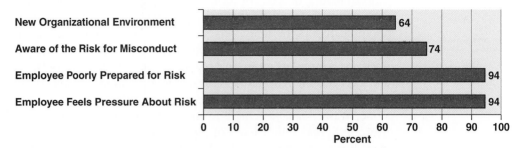

SOURCE: National Business Ethics Survey, *How Employees View Ethics in Their Organizations 1994–2005,* (Washington, DC: Ethics Resource Center, 2005), 36.

Organizational members who engage in questionable or even illegal conduct can cause ethical misconduct. These rogue employees can threaten the overall integrity of the organization. Top leaders in particular can magnify ethical misconduct to disastrous dimensions. Organizational disasters resulting from individuals' misconduct include Madoff family members at Madoff Investments, Andrew Fastow at Enron, Dennis Kozlowski at Tyco, and Bernie Ebbers at WorldCom.[21] An ethics audit can discover rogue employees who are violating the firm's ethical standards and policies or laws and regulations.

Ethical disasters follow recognizable phases of escalation, from ethical-issue recognition and the decision to act unethically to the organization's discovery of and response to the act. Appropriate anticipation of and intervention during these can stave off organizational disaster. Such contingency planning assesses risks, plans for these potential occurrences, and provides ready tools for responding to ethical crises. The process of ethical disaster–recovery planning involves assessing the organization's values, developing an ethics program, performing an ethics audit, and developing contingency plans for potential ethical disasters. The ethics audit itself provides the key link to preventing ethical disasters.

Challenges of Measuring Nonfinancial Performance

Although much of the regulatory focus of corporate ethics and compliance is driven by financial measures, the integrity of an organization also has to focus on nonfinancial areas of performance. The word *integrity* implies a balanced organization that not only makes ethical financial decisions but also is ethical in the more subjective aspects of its corporate culture. For example, the Sarbanes–Oxley Act has focused on questionable accounting and the metrics that destroy shareholder value. On the other hand, models have been developed—such as Six Sigma, the Balanced Scorecard, and the Triple Bottom Line—to capture structural and behavioral organizational ethical performance. *Six Sigma* is a methodology to manage process variations that cause defects, defined as unacceptable deviation from the mean or target, and to systematically work toward managing variation to eliminate those defects. The objective of Six Sigma is to deliver world-class performance, reliability, and value to the end customer.[22] The *Balanced Scorecard* is a method for measuring a company's activities in terms of its vision and strategies. A strategic management system that forces focus on the important performance metrics that drive success gives managers a comprehensive view of the performance of a business. It balances a financial perspective with customer, internal process, and learning and growth perspectives.[23] The *Triple Bottom Line* captures an expanded spectrum of values and criteria for measuring organizational (and societal) success—economic, environmental, and social. For some, a commitment to corporate social responsibility brings with it a need to institute Triple Bottom Line reporting.[24]

The purpose of nonfinancial measures is to determine the wholeness and soundness of the many aspects of a business that enhance ethics and profits without increasing risk. Companies that capitalize on ethical culture, communications, and other nonfinancial issues realize a financial "return on integrity."[25]

AccountAbility is an international membership organization committed to enhancing the performance of organizations and to developing the competencies of individuals in social and ethical accountability and sustainable development. Figure 9–3 illustrates the AccountAbility AA1000 framework for ethics and social responsibility. The AA1000 process standards link the definition and embedding of an organization's values to the development of performance targets and to the assessment and communication of organizational performance. By this process, focused around the organization's engagement with stakeholders, AA1000 ties social and ethical issues into the organization's strategic management and operations. AA1000 recognizes these different traditions. It combines the terms *social* and *ethical* to refer to the systems *and* individual behavior within an organization and to the *direct* and *indirect* impact of an organization's activities on stakeholders. *Social and ethical issues* (relating to systems, behavior and impacts) are defined by an organization's values and aims through the influence of the interests and expectations of its stakeholders and by societal norms and expectations. *Assessment* is measuring organizational responsiveness or the extent to which an organization takes action on the basis of stakeholder engagement. This is followed by *assurance* including control mechanisms and then reporting to document the process. *Embedding* of an organization's values to assure performance is a continuous process.

The Integrity Institute has developed ten validated models that create a diagnostic tool to help organizations recognize the structural weaknesses early on in order to avoid or address problems appropriately rather than to respond to and recover from a crisis, which often proves too late. Rather than focusing on *single-issue* assessments, a comprehensive model provides nonfinancial information that discovers and assesses the soundness, wholeness, and incorruptibility of a corporation, making it possible to pinpoint more accurately the weaknesses that may influence the health and welfare of a company and its sustainability. By measuring these components, it is possible to assess an organization's ability to withstand market forces (for example, ethical misconduct disasters) that may influence the company and destroy shareholder value.[26]

FIGURE 9-3 AA1000 Framework for Ethics and Social Accountability

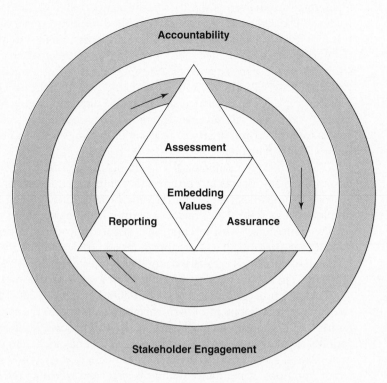

SOURCE: Adapted from AccountAbility AA1000 Series, http://www.accountability21.net/aa1000series (accessed March 12, 2009). Reprinted with permission of The Institute of Social and Ethical Accountability.

Table 9–1 illustrates the Integrity Institute's integrated model to standardize the measure of integrity. The model integrates ten drivers, or markers, that have the potential to weaken the overall structural soundness of the organization. These components include (1) communication, (2) compensation, (3) compliance and ethics, (4) corporate citizenship, (5) culture, (6) earnings, (7) governance, (8) leadership, (9) risk, and (10) stakeholder perceptions. While investors may already use many of these variables, the Integrity Institute Integria™ model establishes a standard that can predict the sustainability and success of the organization. This measurement to an established standard is used as a basis of certification of integrity by the Integrity Institute.

Figure 9–4 shows the Open Compliance Ethics Group framework overview. The Open Compliance Ethics Group (OCEG) (www.oceg.org) has worked with over one hundred companies to create a universal framework for compliance and ethics management. The OCEG focuses on nonfinancial compliance and the more qualitative elements of internal controls. The OCEG framework deals with complex issues of compliance and actual solutions to address the development of organizational ethics. The OCEG framework integrates some of the best thinking in several disciplines to

TABLE 9-1	The Integrity Institute Integrated Model to Standardize the Measure of Integrity
Communication integrity	Communicated information, messages, metamessages, and processes.
Compensation integrity	Excessive compensation, tactics used to motivate employees to take certain actions that can jeopardize the integrity of an organization.
Compliance and ethical integrity	Organizations that fail to comply with minimum legal requirements on a variety of fronts are being regularly dropped from investment and insurance portfolios.
Corporate citizenship integrity (environmental and social responsibility)	Integrity of the environmental policies and social responsibility practices of an organization. It measures the structure, not the morality, of corporate citizenship and identifies pressure being placed on companies to do the right thing.
Cultural integrity	Collective consciousness and values define the culture of the organization and whether it has integrity; whether the culture is sound, whole, and incorruptible and what predictive markers exist that may weaken the organization's ability to stand strong.
Earnings integrity	The extent to which corporate earnings are managed vs. manipulated has long been of interest to analysts, regulators, researchers, and other investment professionals.
Leadership integrity	Behavioral complexity in leadership and the strategy of leadership.
Risk integrity	Risks associated with intelligence and the sharing of data and related privacy issues. Risk integrity begins and ends with information and the transfer of that information.
Stakeholders perceptions of organizational integrity	After analyzing the nine nonfinancial performance indicators outlined above, measure them against the stakeholders' perceptions.

SOURCE: From *Managing Risks for Corporate Integrity: How to Survive An Ethical Misconduct Disaster* 1st edition by Brewer, Chandler, and Ferrell. Copyright © 2006. Reprinted with permission of South-Western, a division of Thomson Learning: www.thomsonrights.com. Fax 800 730-2215.

address compliance and ethics management. Using expertise from these disciplines, guidelines were developed. By establishing guidelines, rather than standards, OCEG provides a tool for each company to use as it sees fit, given its size, scope, structure, industry, and other factors that create individualized needs. The OCEG guidelines and benchmarking studies can be very valuable to a firm conducting an ethics audit. Most significant is the opportunity to benchmark an organization's current activities to those of other organizations. Table 4–10 provides the key findings from the 2005 OCEG benchmarking study.

Risks and Requirements in Ethics Auditing

Although ethics audits provide many benefits for individual companies and their stakeholders, they do have the potential to create risks. For example, a firm may uncover a serious ethical problem that it would prefer not to disclose until it can remedy the

---

| **FIGURE 9-4** | The Open Compliance Ethics Group Framework Overview |

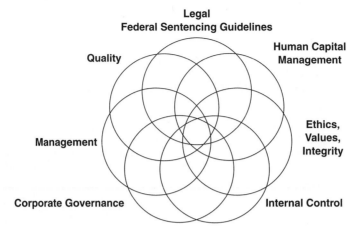

SOURCE: The Open Compliance Ethics Group Framework Overview, http://www.oceg.org/framework.asp (accessed April 4, 2006). Reprinted with permission.

situation. It may find that one or more of its stakeholders' criticisms cannot be dismissed or easily addressed. Occasionally, the process of conducting an ethics audit may foster stakeholder dissatisfaction rather than stifle it. Moreover, the auditing process imposes burdens (especially with regard to record keeping) and costs for firms that undertake it. Finally, the process of auditing and reporting a firm's ethics programs is no guarantee that it will avoid challenges related to its efforts.[27] In addition, because this type of auditing is relatively new, there are few common standards to judge disclosure and effectiveness or to make comparisons.[28]

Being viewed by the public as needing to be audited can motivate companies to conduct one so that they can signal their intention to respond to concerns.[29] Companies in the public eye because of questionable conduct or legal violations, such as Countrywide Financial, AIG, Fannie Mae, Freddie Mac, and Satyam, should conduct an ethics audit to demonstrate their visible commitment to improving decision making and business conduct.

Although ethics and social responsibility are defined and perceived differently by various stakeholders, a core of minimum standards for ethical performance is evolving. These standards represent a fundamental step toward the development of minimum ethics requirements that are specific, measurable, achievable, and meaningful to the business's impact on communities, employees, consumers, the environment, and economic systems. These standards help companies set measurable and achievable targets for improvement and form an objective foundation for reporting the firm's efforts to all direct stakeholders. There may still be disagreements on key issues and standards, but through these standards progress should be made.[30] Both the FSGO's seven steps for effective ethical compliance, as discussed in Chapters 3 and 8, and the Sarbanes–Oxley Act provide standards that organizations can use in ethics auditing.

THE AUDITING PROCESS[31]

Many questions should be addressed when conducting an audit, such as how broad the audit should be, what standards of performance should be applied, how often the audit should be conducted, whether and how the audit's results should be reported to stakeholders, and what actions should be taken in response to audit results. Thus, corporate approaches to ethics audits are as varied as organizations' approaches to ethics programs and responses to improve social responsibility.

It is our belief that an ethics audit should be unique to each company, reflecting its size, industry, corporate culture, and identified risks as well as the regulatory environment in which it operates. Thus, an ethics audit for a bank will differ from one for an automobile manufacturer or a food processor. Each has different regulatory concerns and unique risks stemming from the nature of its business. For this reason, we have mapped out a framework (see Table 9–2) that is somewhat generic and that most companies can therefore expand on when conducting their own ethics audit. The steps in our framework can also be applied to a broader social audit that includes specific ethical issues as well as other economic, legal, and philanthropic concerns of interest to various stakeholders. As with any new initiative, companies may choose to begin their effort with a smaller, less-formal audit and then work up to a more comprehensive social audit. For example, a firm may choose to focus on primary stakeholders in its initial audit year and then expand to secondary groups in subsequent audits.

Our framework encompasses a wide range of business responsibilities and relationships. The audit entails an individualized process and outcomes for a particular firm, as it requires the careful consideration of the unique issues that face a particular organization. For example, the auditing process at Kellogg Company includes the following:

> The Social Responsibility Committee of the Board of Directors shall identify, evaluate and monitor the social, political, environmental, occupational safety and health

---

TABLE 9–2   Framework for an Ethics Audit

◆ Secure commitment of top managers and board of directors.

◆ Establish a committee to oversee the ethics audit.

◆ Define the scope of the audit process, including subject-matter areas important to the ethics audit.

◆ Review the organization's mission, policies, goals, and objectives and define its ethical priorities.

◆ Collect and analyze relevant information in each designated subject-matter area.

◆ Have the results verified by an independent agent.

◆ Report the findings to the audit committee and, if approved, to managers and stakeholders.

SOURCES: These steps are compatible with the social-auditing methods prescribed by Warren Dow and Roy Crowe, *What Social Auditing Can Do for Voluntary Organizations* (Vancouver, Canada: Volunteer Vancouver, July 1999); Sandra Waddock and Neil Smith, "Corporate Responsibility Audits: Doing Well by Doing Good," *Sloan Management Review,* 41 (2000): 79.

trends, issues, and concerns, domestic and foreign, which affect or could affect the Company's business or performance.

The Committee shall make recommendations to assist in the formulation and adoption of policies, programs and practices concerning the matters set forth above including, but not limited to, environmental protection, employee and community health and safety, ethical business conduct, consumer affairs, alcohol and drug abuse, equal opportunity matters, and government relations, and shall monitor the Company's charitable contributions.[32]

Thus, although this chapter presents a structure and recommendations for both general social and ethics-specific audits, there is no generic approach that will satisfy every firm's circumstances. Nevertheless, the benefits and limitations that companies derive from auditing are relatively consistent.

Secure Commitment of Top Managers and Board of Directors

The first step in conducting any audit is securing the commitment of the firm's top management and, if it is a public corporation, its board of directors. Indeed, the push for an ethics audit may come directly from the board of directors in response to specific stakeholder concerns or in response to corporate governance reforms related to the Sarbanes–Oxley Act, which suggests that boards of directors should provide oversight for *all* auditing activities. In addition, court decisions related to the FSGO hold board members responsible for the ethical and legal compliance programs of the firms they oversee. New rules and regulations associated with the Sarbanes–Oxley Act require that boards include members who are knowledgeable and qualified to oversee accounting and other types of audits to ensure that these reports are accurate and include all material information. Although a board's financial audit committee will examine ethical standards throughout the organization as they relate to financial matters, it will also deal with the implementation of codes of ethics for top financial officers. Many of those issues relate to such corporate governance issues as compensation, stock options, and conflicts of interest. An ethics audit can demonstrate that a firm has taken steps to prevent misconduct, which can be useful in cases where civil lawsuits blame the firm and its directors for the actions of a rogue employee.

Pressure for an audit can also come from top managers who are looking for ways to track and improve ethical performance and perhaps give their firm an advantage over competitors that are facing questions about their ethical conduct. Additionally, under the Sarbanes–Oxley Act, CEOs and CFOs may be criminally prosecuted if they knowingly certify misleading financial statements. They may request an ethics audit as a tool to help improve their confidence in their firm's reporting processes. Some companies have established a high-level ethics office in conjunction with an ethics program, and the ethics officer may campaign for an ethics audit as a way to measure the effectiveness of the firm's ethics program. Regardless of where the impetus for an audit comes from, its success hinges on the full support of top management, particularly the CEO and the board of directors. Without this support, an ethics audit will not improve the ethics program and corporate culture.

Establish a Committee to Oversee the Ethics Audit

The next step in our framework is to establish a committee or team to oversee the audit process. Ideally, the board of directors' financial audit committee would oversee the ethics audit, but this is not the case in most companies. In most firms, managers or ethics officers, who do not always report to the board of directors, conduct social and ethics auditing. In any case, this team should include members who are knowledgeable about the nature and role of ethics audits and come from various departments within the firm. It may recruit individuals from within the firm or hire outside consultants to coordinate the audit and report the results directly to the board of directors. For example, the Chris Hani Baragwanath Hospital, the largest public hospital in the world, commissioned the Ethics Institute of South Africa to conduct an ethics audit.[33] As with the financial audit, an external auditor should not have other consulting or conflict-of-interest relationships with top managers or board members. Based on the best practices of corporate governance, audits should also be monitored by an independent board of directors' committee, as recommended by the Sarbanes–Oxley Act.

Define the Scope of the Audit Process

The ethics audit committee should establish the scope of the audit and monitor its progress to ensure that it stays on track. The scope of an audit depends on the type of business, the risks faced by the firm, and the opportunities available to manage ethics. This step includes defining the key subject matter or risk areas that are important to the ethics audit (for example, environment, discrimination, product liability, employee rights, privacy, fraud, financial reporting, legal compliance) as well as the bases on which they should be assessed. Assessments can be made on the basis of direct consultation, observation, surveys, or focus groups.[34] Table 9–3 lists some sample subject-matter areas and the audit items for each.

Review Organizational Mission, Values, Goals, and Policies and Define Ethical Priorities

Because ethics audits generally involve comparing an organization's ethical performance to its goals, values, and policies, the audit process should include a review of the current mission statement and strategic objectives. The company's overall mission may incorporate ethics objectives, but these may also be found in separate documents, including those that focus on social responsibility. For example, the firm's ethics statement or statement of values may offer guidance for managing transactions and human relationships that support the firm's reputation, thereby fostering confidence from the firm's external stakeholders.[35] Franklin Energy, for example, specifies five core values in managing its business which contribute to its success: ingenuity, results-orientation, frugality, integrity, and environmental stewardship.[36]

TABLE 9-3   The Ethics Audit

Organizational Issues*

Yes	No	1. Does the company have a code of ethics that is reasonably capable of preventing misconduct?
Yes	No	2. Does the board of directors participate in the development and evaluation of the ethics program?
Yes	No	3. Is there a person with high managerial authority responsible for the ethics program?
Yes	No	4. Are there mechanisms in place to avoid delegating authority to individuals with a propensity for misconduct?
Yes	No	5. Does the organization effectively communicate standards and procedures to its employees via ethics-training programs?
Yes	No	6. Does the organization communicate its ethical standards to suppliers, customers, and significant others that have a relationship with the organization?
Yes	No	7. Do the company's manuals and written documents guiding operations contain ethics messages about appropriate behavior?
Yes	No	8. Is there formal or informal communication within the organization about procedures and activities that are considered acceptable ethical behavior?
Yes	No	9. Does top management have a mechanism to detect ethical issues relating to employees, customers, the community, and society?
Yes	No	10. Is there a system for employees to report unethical behavior?
Yes	No	11. Is there consistent enforcement of standards and punishments in the organization?
Yes	No	12. Is there a committee, department, team, or group that deals with ethical issues in the organization?
Yes	No	13. Does the organization make a continuous effort to improve its ethical compliance program?
Yes	No	14. Does the firm perform an ethics audit?

Examples of Specific Issues That Could Be Monitored in an Ethics Audit†

Yes	No	1. Are there any systems and operational procedures to safeguard individual employees' ethical behavior?
Yes	No	2. Is it necessary for employees to break the company's ethical rules in order to get the job done?
Yes	No	3. Is there an environment of deception, repression, and cover-ups concerning events that would embarrass the company?
Yes	No	4. Are there any participatory management practices that allow ethical issues to be discussed?
Yes	No	5. Are compensation systems totally dependent on performance?
Yes	No	6. Is there sexual harassment?
Yes	No	7. Is there any form of discrimination—race, sex, or age—in hiring, promotion, or compensation?
Yes	No	8. Are the only standards about environmental impact those that are legally required?
Yes	No	9. Do the firm's activities show any concern for the ethical value systems of the community?
Yes	No	10. Are there deceptive and misleading messages in promotion?
Yes	No	11. Are products described in misleading or negative ways or without communicating their limitations to customers?
Yes	No	12. Are the documents and copyrighted materials of other companies used in unauthorized ways?
Yes	No	13. Are expense accounts inflated?
Yes	No	14. Are customers overcharged?
Yes	No	15. Is there unauthorized copying of computer software?

*A high number of yes answers indicates that ethical control mechanisms and procedures are in place within the organization.

†The number of yes answers indicates the number of possible ethical issues to address.

This review step should examine all formal documents that make explicit commitments to ethical, legal, or social responsibility as well as less-formal documents, including marketing materials, workplace policies, and ethics policies and standards for suppliers or vendors. This review may reveal a need to create additional statements to fill the identified gaps or to create a new comprehensive mission statement or ethical policy that addresses any deficiencies.[37]

It is also important to examine all of the firm's policies and practices with respect to the specific areas covered by the audit. For example, in an audit whose scope includes discrimination issues, this review step would consider the company's goals and objectives regarding discrimination, its policies on discrimination, the means available for communicating these policies, and the effectiveness of this communication. This assessment should also look at whether and how managers are rewarded for meeting their goals and the systems that employees have available to give and receive feedback. An effective ethics audit should review all these systems and assess their strengths and weaknesses.[38]

Concurrent with this step in the auditing process, the firm should define its ethical priorities. Determining these priorities is a balancing act because identifying the needs and assessing the priorities of each stakeholder can be difficult. Because there may be no legal requirements for ethical priorities, it is up to management's strategic planning processes to determine appropriate standards, principles, and duties as well as the action required to deal with ethics issues. It is very important in this stage to articulate these priorities and values as a set of parameters or performance indicators that can be objectively and quantitatively assessed. Because the ethics audit is a structured report that offers quantitative and descriptive assessments, actions should be measurable by quantitative indicators. However, it is sometimes not possible to go beyond description.[39]

At some point, the firm must demonstrate action-oriented responsiveness to those ethics issues it has given top priority. The Healthcare Company (HCA), for example, has developed a comprehensive corporate ethics and compliance program in response to its past ethical and legal problems. HCA's program requires not only that standards of compliance and ethical conduct be articulated but also that a system be implemented for auditing performance "in areas of compliance risk to ensure that established policies and procedures are being followed and are effective."[40]

Collect and Analyze Relevant Information

The next step in our ethical audit framework is to identify the tools or methods for measuring the firm's progress in improving employees' ethical decisions and conduct. In this step, the firm should collect relevant information for each designated subject-matter area. To understand employee issues, for example, the auditing committee will work with the firm's human resources department to gather employee survey information and other statistics and feedback. A thorough ethics audit will review all relevant reports, including external documents sent to government agencies and others. The information collected in this measurement step will help determine baseline levels of compliance as well as the internal and external expectations of the company. This step will also identify where the company has, or has not, met its commitments including those dictated by its mission statement and other policy documents. The documents reviewed in this process will vary from company to company, depending on the firm's size, the nature of its business, and the scope of the audit process.[41] For example, Ford Motor Company launched a formal inquiry to determine whether president and CEO Nick Scheele violated company purchasing policies when he ordered that all of Ford's advertising and marketing business be directed toward WPP Group PLC, a London-based advertising firm that already handles much of the advertising and for which Scheele's son works. Ford has a specific purchasing policy governing single-source contracts.[42] This inquiry would gather relevant information related to the subject of conflicts of interest and purchasing policies.

Some techniques for collecting evidence might involve examining both internal and external documents, observing the data-collection process (such as by consulting with stakeholders), and confirming information in the organization's accounting records. Auditors may also employ ratio analysis of relevant indicators to identify any inconsistencies or unexpected patterns. The importance of objective measurement is the key consideration of the ethics auditor.[43]

Figure 9–5 indicates the communication channels that employees feel comfortable using in providing feedback during data collection. Employees were asked to whom they would "feel comfortable" reporting misconduct if they suspected or became aware of it. Supervisors and local managers received the most favorable response, suggesting the need for organizations to ensure that front-line managers are equipped to respond

---

FIGURE 9–5   Employee-Preferred Channels for Reporting Misconduct

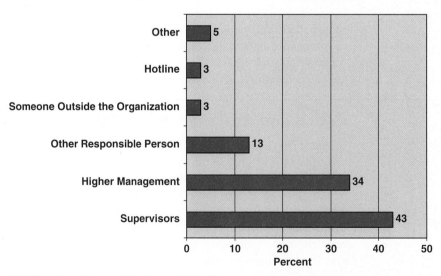

SOURCE: *National Business Ethics Survey, 2007,* Ethics Resource Center, 2007, p. 17.

appropriately to allegations. It is worth noting that those functions that are primarily charged with taking action in response to alleged misconduct (legal, internal audit, and board or audit committee functions) were cited among the less likely channels that employees would feel comfortable using to report allegations.

Because integrating stakeholder feedback in the ethics audit process is so crucial, these stakeholders must first be defined and then interviewed during the data-collection stage. For most companies, stakeholders include employees, customers, investors, suppliers, community groups, regulators, nongovernment organizations, and the media. Both social and ethics audits typically interview and conduct focus groups with these stakeholders to gain an understanding of how they perceive the company. For example, the Chris Hani Baragwanath Hospital (CHBH) in Johannesburg, South Africa, conducted an ethics audit that included focus groups with the hospital's management, doctors, nurses, related health professionals, support staff, and patients. Using the trends uncovered in these focus groups, CHBH then developed a questionnaire for an ethics survey, which it administered to a larger group of individual stakeholders.[44] The more stakeholders that auditors include in this measurement stage, the more time and resources the audit will consume. However, a larger sample of stakeholders may yield a more useful variety of opinions about the company. In multinational corporations, a decision must also be made whether to include in the audit only the main office or headquarters region or all facilities around the globe.[45]

Because employees carry out a business's operations, including its ethics initiatives, understanding employee issues is vital to a successful audit. Useful indicators for assessing employee issues include staff turnover and employee satisfaction. High turnover rates could indicate poor working conditions, an unethical culture, inadequate compensation, or general employee dissatisfaction. Companies can analyze these factors to determine key areas for improvement.[46] Questionnaires that survey employees' ethical perception of their company, their superiors, coworkers, and themselves, as well as ratings of ethical or unethical practices within the firm and industry, can serve as benchmarks in an ongoing assessment of ethical performance. Then, if unethical behavior is perceived to increase, management will better understand what types of unethical practices may be occurring and why. For example, the CHBH ethics survey asked employees about many issues including corporate culture and values, their physical workplace, human resources issues, misconduct, standards of patient care, and problems and sources of stress.[47] Most organizations recognize that employees will behave in ways that lead to recognition and rewards and avoid behavior that results in punishment. Thus, companies can design and implement human resources policies and procedures for recruiting, hiring, promoting, compensating, and rewarding employees that encourage ethical behavior.[48]

Customers are another primary stakeholder group because their patronage and loyalty determines the company's financial success. Providing meaningful feedback is critical to creating and maintaining customer satisfaction. Through surveys and customer-initiated communication systems such as response cards, e-mail, and toll-free telephone systems, an organization can monitor and respond to customer issues and its perceived social performance. Sears, for example, surveyed more than 2 million customers to investigate their attitudes toward products, advertising, and the social performance of the company.

A growing number of investors are seeking to include in their investment portfolios the stocks of companies that conduct ethics and social audits. They are becoming more aware of the financial benefits that can stem from socially responsible management systems—as well as the negative consequences of a lack of responsibility. For example, after the Securities and Exchange Commission (SEC) filed civil fraud charges against HealthSouth Corporation for overstating its earnings by $2.7 billion over a three-and-a-half-year period, the company's stock price plummeted 44 percent. The SEC suit sparked additional lawsuits against the company by its shareholders.[49] Thus, even the hint of wrongdoing can affect a company's relations with investors. Additionally, many investors simply do not want to invest in companies that engage in certain business practices, such as cigarette production, or that fail to provide adequate working conditions, such as sweatshops. It is therefore critical that companies understand the issues of this very important group of stakeholders and what they expect from corporations they have invested in, both financially and socially.

Organizations can obtain feedback from stakeholders through standardized surveys, interviews, and focus groups. Companies can also encourage stakeholder exchanges by inviting specific groups together for discussions. Such meetings also may include an office or facility tour or a field trip by company representatives to sites in the community. Regardless of how companies collect information about stakeholders' views, the primary objective is to generate a variety of opinions about how the company is perceived and whether it is fulfilling stakeholders' expectations.[50]

Once these data have been collected, the firm should then compare its internal perceptions to those discovered during the stakeholder assessment stage and summarize these findings. During this phase, the audit committee should draw some conclusions about the information it obtained in the previous stages. These conclusions may involve descriptive assessments of the findings, such as the costs and benefits of the company's ethics program, the strengths and weaknesses of the firm's policies and practices, feedback from stakeholders, and issues that should be addressed in future audits. In some cases, it may be appropriate to weigh the findings against standards identified earlier, both quantitatively and qualitatively.[51]

Data analysis should also include an examination of how other organizations in the industry are performing in the designated subject-matter areas. For example, the audit committee can investigate the successes of some other benchmark firm that is considered the best in a particular area and compare the auditing company's performance to it. Some common examples of the benchmark information available from most corporate ethics audits are employee or customer satisfaction, how community groups perceive the company, and the impact of the company's philanthropy. For example, the Ethics and Compliance Officer Association (ECOA) conducts research on legal and ethical issues in the workplace. These studies allow ECOA members to compare their responses to the aggregate results obtained through the study.[52] Such comparisons can help the audit committee identify best practices for a particular industry or establish a baseline for minimum requirements for ethics. It is important to note that a wide variety of standards are emerging that apply to ethics accountability. The aim of these standards is to create a tool for benchmarking and a framework for businesses to follow.[53]

Verify the Results

The next step is to have an independent party—such as a social/ethics audit consultant, a financial accounting firm that offers social auditing services (for example, KPMG), or a nonprofit special-interest group with auditing experience (for example, the New Economics Foundation)—verify the results of the data analysis. Business for Social Responsibility, a nonprofit organization supporting social responsibility initiatives and reporting, has defined *verification* as an independent assessment of the quality, accuracy, and completeness of a company's social report. Independent verification offers a measure of assurance that the company has reported its ethical performance fairly and honestly as well as providing an assessment of its social and environmental reporting systems.[54] As such, verification by an independent party gives stakeholders confidence in a company's ethics or social audit and lends the audit report credibility and objectivity.[55] British Petroleum, for example, had its "Environmental and Social Report," which includes ethical performance issues, verified by the accounting firm Ernst & Young.[56] However, a survey conducted by one of the Big Four accounting firms found that only a few social reports contained any form of external verification. This lack of third-party assurance may have contributed to the criticism that social and ethics auditing and reporting has more to do with public relations than genuine change. However, the number of outside verified reports is increasing.[57]

Although the independent validation of ethics audits is not required, an increasing number of companies are choosing to do so, much as they have their financial reports certified by a reputable auditing firm. Many public policy experts believe that an independent, objective audit can be provided only if the auditor has played no role in the reporting process—in other words, consulting and auditing should be distinctly separate roles. The Sarbanes–Oxley Act essentially legalized this belief.

The process of verifying the results of an audit should involve standard procedures that control the reliability and validity of the information. As with a financial audit, auditors can apply substantive tests to detect material misstatements in the audit data and analysis. The tests commonly used in financial audits—confirmation, observation, tracing, vouching, analytical procedures, inquiry, and recomputing—can be used in ethics and social audits as well. For example, positive confirmations can be requested from the participants of a stakeholder focus group to affirm that the reported results are consistent with what the focus group believes it found. Likewise, an ethics auditor can actually observe a company's procedures for handling ethical disputes to verify statements made in the report. And, just as a financial auditor traces from the supporting documents to the financial statements to test their completeness, an ethics auditor or verifier may examine employee complaints about an ethics issue to attest whether the reporting of such complaints was complete. An auditor can also employ analytical procedures by examining plausible relationships such as the prior year's employee turnover ratio or the related ratio commonly reported within the industry. With the reporting firm's permission, an auditor can contact the company's legal counsel to inquire about pending litigation that may shed light on ethical and legal issues currently facing the firm.[58]

Additionally, a financial auditor may be asked to provide a letter to the company's board of directors and senior managers to highlight inconsistencies in the reporting process. The auditor may request that management reply to particular points in the letter to indicate the actions it intends to take to address problems or weaknesses. The financial auditor is required to report to the board of directors' financial audit committee (or equivalent) any significant adjustments or difficulties encountered during the audit and any disagreements with management. Therefore, ethics auditors should be required to report to the company's audit committee the same issues that a financial auditor would report.[59]

Report the Findings

The final step in our framework is issuing the ethics audit report. This involves reporting the audit findings through a formal report to the relevant internal parties—namely, the board of directors and top executives—and, if approved, to external stakeholders. Although some companies prefer not to release the results of their auditing efforts to the public, more companies are choosing to make their reports available to a broad group of stakeholders. Some companies, including U.K.-based Co-operative Bank, integrate the results of the social audit with their annual report of financial documents and other important information. Many other companies, including The Body Shop, Johnson & Johnson, Shell, British Petroleum, and VanCity, also make their audit reports available on their corporate websites.[60]

Based on the guidelines established by the Global Reporting Initiative and Accountability, the report should spell out the purpose and scope of the audit, the methods used in the audit process (evidence gathering and evaluation), the role of the (preferably independent) auditor, any auditing guidelines followed by the auditor, and any reporting guidelines followed by the company.[61] The ethics audit of Johannesburg's Chris Hani Baragwanath Hospital follows these guidelines.[62] The report is more meaningful if integrated with other organizational information available such as financial reports, employee surveys, regulatory filings, and customer feedback. The use of information such as the OCEG Benchmarking Study, discussed earlier in the chapter, evaluates key elements of corporate and ethics programs that could help assess best practices across industry.[63]

As mentioned earlier, ethics audits may resemble financial audits, but they take quite different forms. In a financial audit, the Statement of Auditing Standards dictates literally every word found in a financial audit report in terms of content and placement. Based on the auditor's findings, the report issued can take one of the following four forms, among other variations. An *unqualified opinion* states that the financial statements are fairly stated, and a *qualified opinion* asserts that although the auditor believes the financial statements are fairly stated an unqualified opinion is not possible because of limitations placed on the auditor or minor issues involving disclosure or accounting principles. An *adverse opinion* states that the financial statements are not fairly stated, and, finally, a *disclaimer of opinion* qualifies that the auditor didn't have full access to records or discovered a conflict of interest. The technical difference between these various opinions has enormous consequences to the company.

THE STRATEGIC IMPORTANCE OF ETHICS AUDITING

Although the concept of auditing implies an official examination of ethical performance, many organizations audit their performance informally. Any attempt to verify outcomes and to compare them with standards can be considered an auditing activity. Many smaller firms probably would not use the word *audit*, but they do perform auditing activities. Organizations such as the Better Business Bureau (BBB) provide awards and assessment tools to help any organization evaluate their ethical performance. Companies with fewer resources may wish to use the judging criteria from the BBB's Torch Award Criteria for Ethical Companies (Table 9–4) as benchmarks for their informal self-audits. Past winners of this award include large companies such as IBM, Sony, and Niagara Mohawk. The award criteria even provides a category for companies with less than ten employees.

The ethics audit, like the financial audit, should be conducted regularly rather than in response to problems involving or questions about a firm's priorities and conduct. In other words, the ethics audit is not a control process to be used during a crisis although it can pinpoint potential problem areas and generate solutions in a crisis situation. As mentioned earlier, an audit may be comprehensive and encompass all the ethics and social responsibility areas of a business, or it can be specific and focus on one or two areas. One specialized audit could be an environmental-impact audit in which specific environmental issues, such as proper waste disposal, are analyzed. According to the KPMG International Survey of Corporate Responsibility Reporting, 79 percent of the top 250 companies in the Global *Fortune* 500 issued corporate responsibility reports and the same number issued sustainability reports.[64] Examples of other specialized audits include diversity, employee benefits, and conflicts of interest. Table 9–5 lists some issues related to quality and effectiveness in auditing.

Ethics audits can present several problems. They can be expensive and time consuming, and selecting the auditors may be difficult if objective, qualified personnel are not available. Employees sometimes fear comprehensive evaluations, especially by outsiders, and in such cases, ethics audits can be extremely disruptive.

Despite these problems, however, auditing ethical performance can generate many benefits as we have seen throughout this chapter. The ethics audit provides an assessment of a company's overall ethical performance as compared to its core values, ethics policy, internal operating practices, management systems, and, most important, key stakeholders' expectations.[65] As such, ethics and social audit reports are a useful management tool for helping companies identify and define their impact and facilitate important improvements.[66] This assessment can be used to reallocate resources and activities as well as focus on new opportunities. The audit process can also help companies fulfill their mission statements in ways that boost profits and reduce risks.[67] More specifically, a company may seek continual improvement in its employment practices, customer and community relations, and the ethical soundness of its general business practices.[68] Thus, the audit can pinpoint areas where improving operating practices can improve both bottom-line profits and stakeholder relationships.[69]

Most managers view profitability and ethics and social responsibility as a trade-off. This "either/or" mindset prevents them from taking a more proactive "both/and"

TABLE 9–4	Better Business Bureau's Torch Award Criteria for Ethical Companies

If you are the owner of the company, with no employees, explain how ethics are used in everyday business practices.

Management Practices

◆ Pertinent sections from an employee handbook, company manual, or training program (formal or informal) showing how ethics policies are communicated to and implemented by employees.

◆ Formal training and/or procedures used to address concerns an employee may have in dealing with an ethical dilemma.

◆ The existence of an ethics officer, compliance officer, or ombudsman should be noted, along with information concerning the responsibilities and authority of this position.

◆ Formal or informal management practices and policies that foster positive employee relations.

◆ Employee benefits and/or workplace practices that contribute to the quality of family life.

◆ Actions by the business to assess risks and take appropriate actions to prevent workplace injury.

◆ Examples of sound environmental practices.

Customer/Vendor/Supplier/Shareholder Relations

◆ Examples of how your business has prospered because of your belief in honesty, integrity, and doing the right thing.

◆ Complimentary feedback from customers, vendors, and/or suppliers.

◆ Company policies and practices that ensure excellence in quality products and/or services and demonstrate accountability to customers, vendors, and suppliers.

◆ Actions taken by your company showing that it went "beyond the call of duty."

◆ Examples of cases where your company had to make tough decisions that had negative short-term consequences but led to long-term benefits.

◆ If your company is publicly traded, discuss how the corporation demonstrates accountability to shareholders and adheres to good governance practices.

Marketing/Advertising/Communications/Sales Practices

◆ Descriptions of the methods that your company uses to ensure that all sales, promotional materials, and advertisements are truthful and accurate.

◆ Examples of efforts by your company to improve communications, advertising, marketing, and sales practices that benefit your industry as a whole.

◆ Sales-training policies and/or codes of ethics used by sales personnel that ensure all transactions are made in an upfront and ethical manner.

Reputation Within Industry and Community

◆ Articles in trade, industry publications, and news media that reflect your reputation in your industry and community as an ethical business.

◆ Awards, recognition, and/or complimentary letters from others within your industry or trade group.

◆ Recognition for charitable and/or community service projects.

SOURCE: Adapted from "International Torch Award Judging Criteria," Better Business Bureau, http://www.bbb.org/us/torch-awards/ (accessed January 15, 2009).

TABLE 9-5	Quality and Effectiveness in Ethics Auditing

◆ *Inclusivity* means that the audit process must include the views of all the principal stakeholders, not just the "noisy" stakeholders. Therefore, the assessment is based on many different views rather than just one.

◆ *Comparability* is the ability to compare the organization's performance from one audit period to another.

◆ *Completeness* means that no area of the company is excluded from the audit. This eliminates any "choice" selection of the best areas of the company, and it gives a more accurate and honest view.

◆ *Evolution* is what the company goes through when it fully commits to the audit.

◆ Management policies and systems are needed to ensure that the process of auditing is done in a controlled way.

◆ The information obtained from the audit must be disclosed if it is to be truly effective. The question of how many people to whom the information should be disclosed is continually debated.

◆ Continuous improvement ensures that the audit process is not only retrospective but also uncovers areas needing change and improvement.

SOURCE: "How to Do It," in *Business Corporate Accountability: The Emerging Practices in Social and Ethical Accounting, Auditing, and Reporting,* eds. Simon Zadek, Peter Pruzan, and Richard Evans (London: Earthscan, 1997), 35–49.

approach.[70] However, the auditing process can demonstrate the positive impact of ethical conduct and social responsibility initiatives on the firm's bottom line, convincing managers—and other primary stakeholders—of the value of adopting more ethical and socially responsible business practices.[71]

SUMMARY

An ethics audit is a systematic evaluation of an organization's ethics program and/or performance to determine its effectiveness. Such audits provide an opportunity to measure conformity to the firm's desired ethical standards. The concept of ethics auditing has emerged from the movement toward auditing and reporting on companies' broader social responsibility initiatives. Social auditing is the process of assessing and reporting a business's performance in fulfilling the economic, legal, ethical, and philanthropic social responsibilities expected of it by its stakeholders. An ethics audit may be conducted as a component of a social audit. Auditing is a tool that companies can employ to identify and measure their ethical commitment to stakeholders and to demonstrate their commitment to improving strategic planning, including their compliance with legal, ethical, and social responsibility standards.

The auditing process can highlight trends, improve organizational learning, and facilitate communication and working relationships. It can help companies assess the effectiveness of programs and policies, identify potential risks and liabilities, improve compliance with the law, and demonstrate progress in areas of previous noncompliance. One of the greatest benefits for businesses is improved relationships with stakeholders. A significant benefit of ethics auditing is that it may help prevent the public relations crises associated with ethical or legal misconduct. Although ethics audits provide many benefits for companies and their stakeholders, they do have the potential to create risks. In particular, the process of auditing cannot guarantee that the firm will not face challenges. Additionally, there are few common standards for judging disclosure and effectiveness or for making comparisons.

An ethics audit should be unique to each company based on its size, industry, corporate culture, identified risks, and the regulatory environment in which it operates. The chapter offered a framework for conducting an ethics audit that can also be used for a broader social audit.

The first step in conducting an audit is securing the commitment of the firm's top management and/or its board of directors. The push for an ethics audit may come directly from the board of directors in response to specific stakeholder concerns or corporate governance reforms or from top managers looking for ways to track and improve ethical performance. The audit's success hinges on the full support of top management.

The second step is establishing a committee or team to oversee the audit process. Ideally, the board of directors' financial audit committee would oversee the ethics audit, but in most firms, managers or ethics officers conduct auditing. This committee will recruit an individual from within the firm or hire an outside consultant to coordinate the audit and report the results.

The third step is establishing the scope of the audit, which depends on the type of business, the risks faced by the firm, and available opportunities to manage ethics. This step includes defining the key subject matter or risk areas that are important to the ethics audit.

The fourth step should include a review of the firm's mission, values, goals, and policies. This step should include an examination of both formal documents that make explicit commitments with regard to ethical, legal, or social responsibility and less-formal documents including marketing materials, workplace policies, and ethics policies and standards for suppliers or vendors. During this step, the firm should define its ethical priorities and articulate them as a set of parameters or performance indicators that can be objectively and quantitatively assessed.

The fifth step is identifying the tools or methods that can be employed to measure the firm's progress and then collecting and analyzing the relevant information. Some evidence-collection techniques might involve examining both internal and external documents, observing the data-collection process (such as stakeholder consultation), and confirming the information in the organization's accounting records. During this step, a company's stakeholders need to be defined and interviewed to understand how they perceive the company. This can be accomplished through standardized surveys, interviews, and focus groups. Once these data have been collected, they should be analyzed and summarized. Analysis should include an examination of how other organizations in the industry are performing in the designated subject-matter areas.

The sixth step is having an independent party—such as a social/ethics audit consultant, a financial accounting firm that offers social auditing services, or a nonprofit special-interest group with auditing experience—verify the results of the data analysis. Verification is an independent assessment of the quality, accuracy, and completeness of a company's audit process. Such verification gives stakeholders confidence in a company's ethics audit and lends the audit report credibility and objectivity. The process of verifying the results of an audit should employ standard procedures that control the reliability and validity of the information.

The final step in the audit process is reporting the audit findings to the board of directors and top executives and, if approved, to external stakeholders. The report should spell out the purpose and scope of the audit, the methods used in the audit process (evidence gathering and evaluation), the role of the (preferably independent) auditor, any auditing guidelines followed by the auditor, and any reporting guidelines followed by the company.

Although the concept of auditing implies an official examination of ethical performance, many organizations audit informally. The ethics audit should be conducted regularly. Although social auditing may present problems, it can generate many benefits. Through the auditing process, a firm can demonstrate the positive impact of ethical conduct and social responsibility initiatives on its bottom line, which may convince stakeholders of the value of adopting more ethical and socially responsible business practices.

IMPORTANT TERMS FOR REVIEW	ethics audit	social audit

RESOLVING ETHICAL BUSINESS CHALLENGES*

As Jerry looked around at the other members of the board, he wondered if it was too late to resign. How could he have been stupid enough to be dragged into this ethics audit quagmire! It had started innocently enough. With the passing of the Sarbanes–Oxley Act, everyone was aware of the consequences of accounting problems and their potential negative impact on a company, its board members, and its employees. So when Jerry's friend John, the president of Soumey Corporation, had asked him to be on the company's board of directors, Jerry had checked out the company. It wasn't that he didn't trust John; he just felt that he should never take unnecessary chances. But when Jerry's investigation of Soumey uncovered nothing unusual, he accepted the board position.

Soumey's board of directors included John Jacobs, Soumey's president; Alan Kerns, a retired Soumey executive; Alice Finkelstein, a retired executive from a similar company; Latisha Timme, a consultant within the industry; and Jerry. With Jerry on board, one of the board's first tasks was to conduct an ethics audit. The directors decided to contract the task to Teico, Inron, and Wurrel (TIW), an accounting firm highly recommended by Latisha. A few months later, TIW filed its final report of the audit with the board. The report indicated that, with a few exceptions, Soumey was doing a good job of monitoring ethical issues. Among the

recommendations that the report offered were that the company should appoint a person with high managerial authority to be responsible for its ethical compliance program, that it establish a confidential hot line for employees who had ethical or legal concerns, and that it create an ethics committee to address ethical issues in the organization.

At the next board meeting, John suggested that Alan be the ethics compliance officer because he lived close to the main offices and had time to do it. Alan quickly agreed, provided there was substantial remuneration for his time, which John affirmed. Jerry asked a few questions such as whether Alan had sufficient managerial authority.

Alice responded, "Jerry, this industry is rather small with only a few large players, Soumey being one of them. Trust me when I say that Alan, as a retired president of the company, will definitely have the respect of the employees."

Jerry had no more questions, and Alan became Soumey's new compliance officer. The confidential hot line was quickly installed, and announcements about its existence were widely distributed around the various offices and plant buildings to ensure it reached all of the firm's several thousand employees. The board also discussed TIW's final suggestion for an ethics committee, and all but Jerry agreed that the board could handle that task as well.

Jerry pointed out, "I don't think this is wise, John. This is a conflict of interest for you, isn't it?"

After a moment of hesitation, John replied, "You're right, Jerry, it is a conflict of interest that I be on the ethics committee." After another bit of silence, John suggested, "Wouldn't you agree that I should not be on the committee, Alan, Alice, and Latisha?" They all discussed the matter and agreed that Jerry's suggestion made perfect sense.

Time passed and the board held its quarterly meetings. Nothing unusual was brought up, just the same old issues that any publicly held company must deal with relative to shareholders, lawyers, regulators, and the public. Alan had suggested that the ethics compliance committee meet twice a year so that he could fill everyone in on what was happening. At these meetings, Alan would usually report the number of calls to the hot line, the status of complaints, and whether there were any serious allegations such as sexual harassment or any reported forms of race, sex, or age discrimination in hiring personnel.

After two years of quarterly board meetings and semiannual ethics meetings, Jerry suggested to Alan that they conduct another ethics audit.

"Why would we want to do that, Jerry? Things are going smoothly with the approach we're taking. Why have another outside audit? Do you think that we're doing a bad job!?"

Jerry hedged, "I'm not saying that, Alan. What I'm saying is that we may need to have an outside audit just to make sure everything looks good to the public. Why don't we discuss this with Latisha and Alice this week?"

Alan agreed but when the ethics committee met that week it was obvious to Jerry that Alan had spoken to Alice and Latisha about his and Alan's meeting. He wasn't surprised when the committee decided another audit would diminish the confidence in Alan's performance as ethics compliance officer. Several weeks later, John sent all the board members a letter announcing an increase in their pay as board directors as well as doubling their pay as ethics committee members. The letter stated, "Soumey Corporation has decided that your service to the company has been exemplary both as board members and as an ethics committee."

In Jerry's third year on the board of directors, he was finally able to attend Soumey's annual company picnic with his wife and children. They arrived late after all the introductions, and everyone was already in the generous buffet line. As a result, no one really knew who he was. The kids were having fun, and Jerry and his wife, Rosa, were too. However, after a while Jerry began to overhear some interesting comments. In one conversation, a production worker spoke about a toxic spill that had occurred because of the lack of safeguards. He told his companion, "Yeah, I know it was pretty messy, but only a few of my crew were hurt."

His friend asked, "Did they or you report it to management?"

He exclaimed, "Are you kidding? My guys don't want to lose their bonuses. Remember what happened to Bob's crew when the same thing happened and some of his guys complained. They had them filling out paperwork for a whole day, and the next week they were assigned a project with no incentives. They lost 40 percent of what they had been making with all the overtime and performance-based stuff. The guys and I agreed not to report it for those reasons."

Jerry couldn't help interrupting, "So why didn't the company fix the problem after it happened the first time?"

One of the men asked, "Are you new here?"

"Yeah, been here only a few weeks," Jerry lied.

The production worker answered, "You want to boost your pay, right? So you cut a few corners to get by."

Later that evening after Jerry and his family returned home, Rosa told him about a conversation she had overheard. "These women were talking about how unfair it is that most of the incentive-based pay seems to go to men with families. One woman said that she heard of a man over fifty-five who should have gotten a promotion but was turned down because his supervisor was told not to give it to him. Rumor was that this guy had bucked the last president of Soumey, and this was his payback. Jerry, you should have heard what they say about Alan, that he's like Santa Claus and the Grinch. You never see him, and if you do, it's not a pleasant experience. One woman told me that when she was working for him, he used to be a little too friendly. She said that's why no one really uses the ethics hot line for certain issues: They know that the fox is guarding the hen house."

A little later, one of Jerry's sons bounced into the room and asked him a question about the picnic. "Dad, how come all the Spanish workers are on the night shift? It really makes it hard for a couple of my friends to get their parents to drop them off for soccer."

The picnic had opened Jerry's eyes about an uglier side of Soumey. At the next board meeting, he indirectly addressed some of the problems he had noticed. But John responded, "We're going into a recession, and we have to cut a few corners to keep our dividends up to the market's expectations. Latisha has been watching and consulting me on the best way to keep ahead of the pack on this."

Latisha and Alice both commented, "Thank goodness we have a large Spanish workforce to offset some price increases. They're hard workers and don't complain."

"You're absolutely right," said Alan. "We don't have the EPA, OSHA, or other agencies on our backs because these people know how to work and keep quiet. If some federal agencies do start to poke around, I have some contingency plans to prevent any type of ethical disaster."

That evening Jerry and Rosa were talking about the situation. He told Rosa, "I think Soumey has some potentially ethical issues that need to be addressed, but what can I do?"

"Well," sighed Rosa, "We've lived in this town for a long time. We know the families that are on the board. They're good people. However, there's one thing you didn't hear at that picnic because of your lack of Spanish. I've told you that it's important to learn it, even if it's just for my family. A few of the people I overheard were talking about how the hot line isn't really anonymous. That's just not right, Jerry. You need to do something even if it does mean losing the extra income." Rosa's points struck a nerve because Jerry knew they were a little overextended financially.

"I'll see what I can do," he told her.

Still, she warned him, "That's good, honey, but remember I don't want you to make too many waves. We still have to live here, and you know we can't swing a dead cat and not hit one of the people at Soumey."

QUESTIONS • EXERCISES

1. What areas of its ethics audit should Soumey change?
2. Does Jerry have a legal duty to report any of the items that he has heard to an outside authority?
3. Discuss the makeup of Soumey's board of directors. Is it ethical?
4. Is Jerry liable for the problems associated with Soumey over the last three years? Explain why or why not.

*This case is strictly hypothetical; any resemblance to real persons, companies, or situations is coincidental.

Check Your EQ

Check your EQ, or Ethics Quotient, by completing the following. Assess your performance to evaluate your overall understanding of the chapter material.

1.	The ethics audit is required by the Sarbanes–Oxley Act of 2002.	Yes	No
2.	In public corporations, the ethics audit should be reported to the board of directors.	Yes	No
3.	The ethics audit helps identify risks and rogue employees.	Yes	No
4.	The scope of the ethics audit depends on the type of risks and the opportunities to manage them.	Yes	No
5.	Smaller companies can skip the step of verifying the results of the ethics audit.	Yes	No

ANSWERS: 1. No. Financial audits are required, and these may address some ethical issues. 2. Yes. This is consistent with good corporate governance but not required. 3. Yes. This is the main benefit of an ethics audit. 4. Yes. The scope determines the risks unique to the organization. 5. No. Verification is necessary to maintain integrity and accuracy.

CHAPTER 10

Business Ethics in a Global Economy

CHAPTER OBJECTIVES

- ◆ To understand the role of culture as a factor in business ethics
- ◆ To discuss cultural relativism and global business ethics
- ◆ To explore global values
- ◆ To assess the role of multinational corporations in business ethics
- ◆ To gain awareness of a number of ethical issues around the globe

CHAPTER OUTLINE

At the Dun and Ready (D&R) Company, Sid was responsible for monitoring the Japanese stock market to determine patterns and identify stocks that could become active. One of ten company representatives in Japan, Sid, who was of Japanese descent and fluent in the language, had been assigned to Tokyo. Being relatively new to the firm, he was told to gather information for his boss, Glenna. Glenna had been with D&R for ten years, but because of the cultural barriers, she was not enthusiastic about her Tokyo assignment. Glenna encouraged Sid to get to know the Japanese brokers, traders, and other key people in the business, and, thanks to his background, he found that he blended easily into the culture.

In Japan, ceremony and giving favors is a way of life. Sid learned that, by observing Japanese customs and perfecting his Japanese, he not only became an information resource on the Japanese stock market and its players for his company but also a resource for the Japanese who wanted to invest in the U.S. market. He found that the locals would talk to him about important investments rather than coming into the office to see Glenna.

Among Sid's duties was taking key customers to bars, restaurants, and vacation spots for entertainment. One day a government official in the group that Sid was entertaining hinted that he and the others would like to play golf on some famous U.S. courses. Sid understood what the government official wanted and relayed the request to Glenna, who told him that granting a favor of this kind would normally be against policy, but because such favors seemed to be the custom in Japan, they could do some "creative bookkeeping." "When in Rome, right, Sid?" was Glenna's response to the whole situation. By pulling some strings, Glenna managed to have these officials play at ten of the most exclusive U.S. golf courses. Later, several officials passed the word to people in Japan's elite financial circle about Sid's helpfulness.

Six months later, Glenna was transferred back to the States. Rumor had it that expenses were too high and revenue too low. Her replacement, Ron, didn't like being sent to Japan either. In his very first week on the job, he told the staff that he would shorten his tour in Tokyo by slashing expenses and increasing productivity. Ron was a "by-the-book" person. Unfortunately, company rules had not caught up with the realities of cultural differences. After two months with Ron, seven of the original ten company representatives had quit or been fired.

Sid was barely surviving. Then one of his contacts in the government repaid a favor by recommending several stocks to buy and sell. The information paid off, and Sid gained some breathing room from Ron. Around the same time, some of Sid's Japanese clients lost a considerable amount of money in the U.S. markets and wanted a "discount"—the term used for the practice in some large Japanese brokerage houses of informally paying off part of their best clients' losses. When Glenna was still in Tokyo, she had dipped into the company's assets several times to fund such discounts. Because everything required Ron's approval, Sid and his colleagues believed that this practice would not be tolerated. However, late one afternoon Sid and a few others provided the proper forms, and Ron signed them without realizing what he had done.

Several months passed and the three survivors had resorted to lowering their expenses by using their own funds. This in turn led to Sid churning some of his accounts; that is, he bought and sold stocks for the express purpose of increasing his own revenues. Churning was tolerated in Japan, along with other practices that would be deemed questionable in the United States. Ron was oblivious to what Sid was doing because his focus was on reducing expenses.

In the previous month, a group of important D&R clients had thrown a party for a few of their favorite brokers at one of their local haunts. After the customary toasts and small talk, it was suggested to Sid that a Japanese cartel might be interested in D&R. Sid was cautious and nothing else was mentioned. Several weeks later at another party, Sid and the two remaining D&R people were told that a takeover was imminent. But to make the takeover painless, the cartel needed certain sensitive information. Sid's reward for providing it would be a high position in the new, reorganized company and a "wink/nod" agreement that he could go anywhere in the world for his next assignment.

That week Ron had announced that headquarters was pleased with the productivity of the Tokyo group. "It's only a matter of time before I get transferred, and I want out of Tokyo," he told them. The office knew that if Ron were successful, his next position would be that of vice president. He also informed the group that corporate representatives would be coming to Tokyo the following week.

"It seems that they've heard rumors of a possible hostile takeover attempt on D&R from someone in Japan, and they want us to check it out," Ron said, adding with a tight smile. "There will be some changes next week."

Sid suspected that this meant there would be even fewer people working even harder. It might also mean, however, that someone knew that Sid and the two representatives had been talking to the wrong people. Or maybe one of the three had sold

out the other two. If Sid was to gather the information sought by the cartel, he would have to act quickly.

QUESTIONS • EXERCISES

1. What are the ethical issues here?
2. What moral philosophies were Sid, Glenna, and Ron using?
3. What are some control options that D&R could have introduced to create a more ethical culture?
4. Discuss the advantages and disadvantages of each decision that Sid could make.
5. Identify the pressures that have caused the ethical issues to develop.
6. Discuss Sid's power structure and leadership position at D&R and what it might be at the new D&R.

*This case is strictly hypothetical; any resemblance to real persons, companies, or situations is coincidental.

A dvances in communication, technology, and transportation have minimized the world's borders, creating a new global economy as more and more countries are attempting to industrialize and compete internationally. Because of these trends, more companies are doing business outside their home countries. These transactions across national boundaries define global business, a practice that brings together people from countries that have different cultures, values, laws, and ethical standards. Thus, the international businessperson must not only understand the values, culture, and ethical standards of his or her own country but also be sensitive to those of other countries. In addition, although about 90 percent of American companies have a written code of ethics, surveys indicate that ethical codes are found less frequently outside the United States. For example, 51 percent of German firms, 41 percent of British firms, and 30 percent of French firms surveyed had ethics codes in place.[1] Codes of ethics are also shifting within these various cultures. For example, ethical codes are increasingly concerned with conduct against the firm rather than with conduct on behalf of the firm; also becoming increasingly important are environmental affairs, a legal responsibility as the basis of codes, and enforcement/compliance procedures.[2]

In this chapter, we explore the ethical complexities and challenges facing businesses that operate internationally. We first consider the different perceptions worldwide of corporate ethics, cultural differences, and cultural relativism. We also discuss a global framework for ethical principles. Then we examine multinational corporations and the ethical problems they face. Finally, we highlight some of the major global ethical issues. As stated in earlier chapters, we do not attempt to offer absolute answers to the ethical issues. Our goal is to help you understand how international business activities can create ethical conflict and to help you improve your ethical decision-making ability.

ETHICAL PERCEPTIONS AND INTERNATIONAL BUSINESS

When businesspeople travel, they sometimes perceive that other business cultures have different modes of operation. There is at least the perception in the United States that American companies are different from those in other countries. This implied perspective of ethical superiority—"us" versus "them"—is also common in other countries. Table 10–1 indicates the countries that businesspeople, risk analysts, and the

TABLE 10–1	2008 Perceptions of Countries as Least/Most Corrupt	
Country Rank	**Least Corrupt Country**	**Most Corrupt Country**
1	Denmark	Somalia
1	New Zealand	Myanmar
1	Sweden	Iraq
4	Singapore	Haiti
5	Finland	Afghanistan
5	Switzerland	Sudan
7	Iceland	Guinea
7	Netherlands	Chad
9	Australia	Equatorial Guinea
9	Canada	Congo, Democratic Republic
11	Luxembourg	Zimbabwe
12	Austria	Uzbekistan
12	Hong Kong	Turkmenistan
14	Germany	Kyrgyzstan
14	Norway	Cambodia

SOURCE: Transparency International Corruptions Index, 2008, http://www.transparency.org/policy_research/surveys_indices/cpi (accessed January 13, 2009).

general public perceived as the most and least corrupt. In business, the idea that "we" differ from "them" is called the **self-reference criterion** (SRC).

The SRC is the unconscious reference to one's own cultural values, experiences, and knowledge. When confronted with a situation, we react on the basis of knowledge we have accumulated over a lifetime, which is usually grounded in our culture of origin. Our reactions are based on meanings, values, and symbols that relate to our culture but may not have the same relevance to people of other cultures. In the United States, for example, **dumping**—the practice of charging high prices for products sold in domestic markets while selling the same products in foreign markets at low prices, often below the costs of exporting them—is viewed negatively, and the United States has a number of antidumping laws. The U.S. Congress passed the Byrd amendment, which allows U.S. Customs to distribute money generated from foreign companies accused of dumping products to U.S. firms harmed by the dumping. However, the World Trade Organization (WTO) has ruled that this distribution of funds to U.S. firms violates its international trade rules and regulations. The WTO has recommended that the United States repeal the Byrd amendment, but the United States has officially rejected this recommendation. Although the United States is a member of the WTO, in this case, it has rejected its rules.[3] The WTO ruled that the amendment was inconsistent with the U.S. WTO obligations, and it authorized eight WTO members to retaliate against the United States.[4]

Culture as a Factor in Business

One of the most difficult concepts to understand and apply to the global business environment is culture. Because customs, values, and ethical standards vary from person to person, company to company, and even society to society, ethical issues that arise from international business activities often differ significantly from those that evolve from domestic business activities. Distinctively international issues are often related to differences in cultures. Thus, it is important to define and explore the concept of culture as it relates to the global setting.

Culture consists of everything in our surroundings that is made by people—both tangible items and intangible things like concepts and values. Language, religion, law, politics, technology, education, social organizations, general values, and ethical standards are all included within this definition. Each nation has a distinctive culture and, consequently, distinctive beliefs about what business activities are acceptable or unethical. Distinct subcultures can also be found within many nations. Thus, when transacting international business, individuals encounter values, beliefs, and ideas that may diverge from their own because of cultural differences. This chapter will allow you to test your own "cultural IQ."

One significant area of cultural differences is language. Problems of translation often make it difficult for businesspeople to express exactly what they mean. For example, when Bacardi created a fruity drink for the French market, it attempted to market the beverage in both France and Germany under the name Pavian. Unfortunately, "Pavian" translates as "baboon" in German. Even within the same language, words can mean different things in different countries. In Puerto Rico, for example, Tropicana brand orange juice was advertised as "Jugo de China," where "China" translates as "orange." But these same Spanish ads did not go over well with the Cuban population in Miami, Florida, for whom "Jugo de China" literally means "Chinese juice."[5]

Although blunders in communication may have their humorous side, they frequently offend or anger others, derail important business transactions, and even damage international business relations. When Touchstone Pictures, a subsidiary of Walt Disney, released the films *Father of the Bride, Part II; In the Army Now; Aladdin: The Return of Jafar; Kazaam;* and *GI Jane,* the International Arab League accused Disney of presenting a distorted image of Arabs. Although Disney generates a large portion of revenue from foreign distributions and activities, it failed to find success with these films in Islamic and Arab countries.[6] Furthermore, they alienated a culture that comprises a large percentage of the world's population. Worse than the Disney disaster was a 2006 Danish comic book that depicted a sacred Islamic entity. As a result of this international incident, hundreds of people died, embassies were closed, and the potential disaster of cultural sensitivity became a reality for Western countries.

Cultural differences in body language can also lead to misunderstandings. Body language consists of the nonverbal, usually unconscious way that we communicate through our gestures, posture, and facial expressions. Americans, for instance, nod their heads up and down to indicate "yes," but in Albania, an up-and-down nod means "no," whereas in Britain it indicates only that the person has heard, not that he or she agrees. Pointing an index finger, a commonplace gesture among Americans, is considered quite rude in Asia and Africa. Personal space—the distance at which one person feels comfortable when talking with another—also varies from culture to culture. American and British businesspeople prefer a larger space than do South American, Greek, and Japanese. This difference can make people from different countries ill at ease with each other in their negotiations.

Perceptions of time may likewise differ from country to country. Americans value promptness, but businesspeople from other lands approach punctuality in a more relaxed manner. An American firm lost a contract in Greece after it tried to impose its customs on the local negotiators by setting time limits for meetings. Greeks deem such limits insulting and lacking in finesse.[7] Americans, on the other hand, may view the failure to meet on time as a sign that future contractual obligations won't be met on a timely basis, thus increasing the potential cultural misperceptions.

Cultural differences can also become liabilities when firms transfer personnel. Consequently, large corporations spend thousands of dollars to ensure that the employees they send abroad are culturally prepared. Eastman Chemical Company, for example, has devised a preparation program so effective that 99 percent of participating employees successfully complete their term in a foreign country. Eastman's program provides cultural orientation for the entire family, not just the employee, and includes language training, a house-hunting trip, and counseling to prepare the family for life in a new culture.[8]

The seemingly innocuous customs of one country can be offensive or even dangerous in others. For example, employees of a California construction company presented green baseball caps to top Taiwanese company executives at a meeting. To traditional Taiwanese, however, green caps symbolize adultery. Unwittingly, the Americans had accused their associates of having unfaithful wives.[9] Table 10–2 lists acceptable standards of gift giving in selected areas of the world.

Divergent religious values can also create ethical issues in international business. For instance, before a British fast-food hamburger chain entered the Indian market, its market

TABLE 10–2	Gift-Giving Standards by Country and Culture

Locations in which a gift is expected

Europe: Czech Republic, Poland, Russia, Ukraine

Latin America: Bolivia, Colombia, Costa Rica

Pacific Rim: China, Hong Kong, Indonesia, Japan, Korea, Taiwan, Philippines, Thailand

Locations in which a gift is not expected on the first visit, but would be expected on a subsequent visit

Europe: Portugal, Spain

Latin America: Brazil, Chile, Guatemala, Nicaragua, Panama, Peru, Venezuela

Pacific Rim: Malaysia, Singapore

Scandinavia: Finland, Norway

Locations in which a gift is not expected, or gifts are less frequently exchanged

Africa, Australia

Europe: England, France, Hungary, Italy

Latin America: Uruguay

Scandinavia: Denmark

Middle East: Pakistan, Saudi Arabia

United States

Gift-Giving Procedures

Asia and the Middle East: Only use your right hand, or both hands, to offer or accept a gift.

Japan, Thailand, and Hong Kong: Use both hands to receive a gift.

Singapore: A recipient may "graciously refuse three times" before accepting your gift.

Chile: Gifts are accepted and opened immediately.

Indonesia: Small gifts are given on a frequent basis.

India: Don't offer a gift made from cowhide. Another prohibition for the Muslim faith is alcohol.

Greece, Spain, and Portugal: Don't give company logo gifts.

SOURCE: Developed by John Fraedrich, using the "Useful Links for International Trade," Federation of International Trade Associations, http://fita.org/webindex/browse.cgi/Entering_International_Markets/Cultural_Issues (accessed March 12, 2009).

research identified an issue. The members of the predominantly Hindu ruling class in India abstain from eating beef for religious reasons, and, although other Indian religions have no taboos regarding the consumption of beef, the British firm decided not to use beef for its burgers to avoid giving offense. Some companies are not always so considerate of other cultures' values and mores, however. When Walt Disney opened EuroDisney near Paris, there was a backlash of anti-Americanism. The French viewed the company as preaching American cultural values and responded with protests, rallies, and boycotts.

One of the critical ethical issues linked to cultural differences is the question of whose values and ethical standards take precedence during international negotiations and business transactions. When conducting business outside their own country, should businesspeople impose their own values, ethical standards, and even laws on members of other cultures? Or should they adapt to the values, ethical standards, and laws of the country in which they are doing business? As with many ethical issues, there are no easy answers to these questions.

Adapting Ethical Systems to a Global Framework

"When in Rome, do as the Romans do" or "You must adapt to the cultural practices of the country you are in" are rationalizations businesspeople sometimes offer for straying from their own ethical values when doing business abroad. By defending the payment of bribes or "greasing the wheels of business" and other questionable practices in this fashion, they are resorting to **cultural relativism,** the concept that morality varies from one culture to another and that business practices are therefore differentially defined as right or wrong by particular cultures. For example, Exxon Mobil Corporation and Royal Dutch/Shell Group have invested heavily in developing the oil reserves of Sakhalin Island, a Russian territory north of Japan. The companies have invested $22 billion in oil- and gas-drilling equipment not only because there may be as much as 13 billion barrels of oil in its waters but also because Russia's environmental rules are almost nonexistent and seldom enforced. However, the seismic blasting and toxic mud associated with developing the area's oil fields are hazardous to the endangered Western Pacific gray whale. If a spill or other accident were to occur, the nearest cleanup equipment is fifty miles away, making it impractical to save salmon and other animal species from harm.[10] Although the Russian government and people who live in the area are happy for the jobs, in this case the multinational investment group seems to be applying Russian cultural values toward the natural environment rather than the more stringent ones of their own countries.

Although companies in the United States are installing whistle-blower hot lines to meet Securities and Exchange (SEC) requirements under the Sarbanes–Oxley Act, recent rulings in France and Germany are challenging the legality of such hot lines. French authorities assert that the hot lines violate French privacy law because accusations can be anonymous; this creates concern that persons named by a whistle-blower aren't told of the complaint and don't have a chance to prove their innocence. Across Europe there are concerns about personal data and data protection. However, Xerox has an ethics help line in every country in which it operates, including Germany and France. The difference is that it is a *help* line, not a hot line, where people can ask general questions about policies. Xerox has had its code of conduct approved in every country where it applies.[11] It is not only the hot lines that are under pressure in other countries; in Germany a labor court ruled that parts of Wal-Mart Stores Inc.'s ethics code, including a ban on relationships between employees, violate German law. The same court also ruled against a proposed hot line for employees to report on colleagues' violations of the code of conduct. Labor representatives from the ninety-one German Wal-Mart stores sued the retail giant over the code after it was introduced without their prior approval. Under German law, employee–management councils must sign off on a wide range of workplace conditions.[12] Writing a code of conduct for a global workforce can be challenging. Table 10–3 provides a framework for writing an effective global code of conduct.

As with most philosophies, cultural relativists fall along a continuum. Some profess the belief that only one culture defines ethical behavior for the whole globe, without

| **TABLE 10–3** | Writing an Effective Global Code of Conduct |

1. *Form an international advisory group.* The group needs to provide content expertise and become local "champions" for the code. It should be a functionally diverse group that is geographically representative of the target markets as well as the company and management structure.

2. *Set clear objectives for the code.* It is important to establish some clear and realistic objectives for the document. Some of the most common objectives for codes of conduct are compliance, corporate social responsibility, suppliers, and partners or a values-based code. Companies need to make sure that they can follow through with enforcing a code once it is in place. If this does not occur, employees may become very cynical.

3. *Draft content.* This stage includes determining the issues, developing standards, and reviewing the preliminary draft of the code. There are four key components that should be included in each major standard: provide a rationale to explain the need for the standard, provide a clear definition of the issue, provide clear guidance (through examples, questions and answers, and the like), and discuss additional resources for information.

4. *Have knowledge about graphic design.* Cultural sensitivity plays a key role in graphic design and is required especially for the following areas: (1) the use of color—companies should be aware that color can have different meanings in different cultures; (2) use of symbols—the document should not rely on country-specific symbols such as the dollar symbol to represent currency; (3) use of photos—it is important to ensure that the photos represent the international character of the company and not one or two particular geographies.

5. *Hold focus groups and finalize content.* It is best to conduct focus groups in the native language and if possible with a translated code of conduct. Companies can use internal personnel or external personnel to conduct the focus group, but when using internal personnel, it is important to avoid using a member of management, which could stifle discussion and dissent.

6. *Translate the code.* It is important that companies understand when to translate the code and how to select translators. When there are fewer than twenty-five employees, it is best to provide a translation, but it is not necessary to reprint the code with graphics or in color. With more than one hundred employees, it is important to invest in translation and color reprinting of the code.

SOURCE: From Lori Tansey Martens, "Writing an Effective Code of Conduct," *International Business Ethics Review*, Vol. 8, No. 1, Spring/Summer 2005, pp. 1, 9–14. Reprinted with permission.

| **FIGURE 10–1** | Matrix for Global Relativists When Making Cross-Cultural Ethics Decisions |

Quadrants relate to the perceived ethicalness for global relativists doing business abroad.

Home Country Perceptions

		Ethical	**Unethical**
Foreign Country Perceptions	**Ethical**	Ethical	Ethical
	Unethical	Ethical	Unethical

exceptions. For the business relativist, for example, there may be no relevant ethical standards but the one of the culture in which his or her current transaction is taking place. Such individuals may adjust to the ethics of a particular foreign culture or use their own culture as a defense against something unethical as perceived in the foreign country. The disadvantage is that they may be in conflict with their own individual moral standards and perhaps with their own culture's values and legal system. Figure 10–1 shows a two-by-two matrix that relativists might use to make multicultural decisions. As business becomes more global and multinational corporations proliferate, the chances of ethical conflict increase.

GLOBAL VALUES

Many theorists have tried to establish a set of global or universal ethical standards. Table 10–4 lists six books and documents that suggest that there is a pattern of shared values—such as truthfulness, integrity, fairness, and equality—across the globe. When applied to global business, these values suggest a universal set of ethics. The Caux Round Table in Switzerland, in collaboration with business leaders in other European countries, Japan, and the United States, has created an international ethics code (www.cauxroundtable.org). The shared values assume that we all have basic rights and responsibilities that must be adhered to when doing business.

If there is a universal set of ethics, why then do businesspeople have trouble understanding what is ethical or unethical? Research suggests that there is variation between cultures and values, but there also appears to be consensus on sets of core values that many cultures may have, including integrity, altruism, collective motivation, and encouragement.[13] There are many more values that have been discussed in this context, and although the research still is not definitive, the important thing is how these basic rights, values, and responsibilities are operationalized or implemented. When someone from another culture mentions words such as *integrity* or *democracy,* most listeners feel reassured because these are familiar concepts. However, differences surface when someone from another culture explains what these concepts mean from the perspective of his or her culture.

Consider, for example, that honesty is valued in both Japan and the United States. Part of honesty is operationalized by trust. In Japan's banking industry, businesspeople demonstrated that trust by hiring retired Japanese bureaucrats to become auditors, directors, executives, and presidents—a practice known as *amakudari,* or "descent from heaven." Because these men were so trusted, bankers felt that nothing bad or unethical could happen to the banks. However, because the regulators implicitly trusted their former superiors, the relationship between regulated and regulator became fuzzy. In the United States, businesspeople may trust former superiors, but they also believe that there should be a separation between those who regulate and those who are regulated.[14]

Although honesty, charity, virtue, and beneficence may be universally desirable qualities, differences in implementing them can raise ethical issues. To address such problems, General Motors, Procter & Gamble, the Shell Group, and about thirty other companies agreed to abide by the Global Sullivan Principles (Table 10–5). These principles seek to encourage social responsibility around the world although some of these companies have

TABLE 10–4	Global Management Ethics

1993 Parliament of the World's Religions, The Declaration of a Global Ethic	State of California Handbook on . . . Moral and Civic Education . . .	Michael Josephson, Character Counts, Ethics: Easier Said Than Done
Nonviolence (love)	Morality	Trustworthiness
Respect for life	Truth	Honesty
Commitment	Justice	Integrity
Solidarity	Patriotism	Promise keeping
Truthfulness	Self-esteem	Loyalty
Tolerance	Integrity	Respect for others
Equal rights	Empathy	Responsibility
Sexual morality	Exemplary conduct	Fairness
	Reliability	Caring
	Respect for family, property, law	Citizenship

William J. Bennett, *The Book of Virtues*	Thomas Donaldson, *Fundamental International Rights*	Rushworth W. Kidder, *Shared Values for a Troubled World*
Self-discipline	Physical movement	Love
Compassion	Property, ownership	Truthfulness
Responsibility	No torture	Fairness
Friendship	Fair trial	Freedom
Work	Nondiscrimination	Unity
Courage	Physical security	Tolerance
Perseverance	Speech and association	Responsibility
Honesty	Minimal education	Respect for life
	Loyalty	Political participation
	Faith	Subsistence

SOURCE: Andrew Sikula, "Global Management Ethics," in *Applied Management Ethics* (1996), 127. Used by permission of the author, Andrew Sikula.

yet to implement these principles.[15] In addition, fifty of the world's largest corporations have signed the UN Global Compact, the purpose of which is to support free-trade unions, abolish child labor, and protect the natural environment. Signatory companies are required to post an annual update on their progress in these areas and are expected to cooperate with UN agencies on social projects in the developing countries in which they operate.[16] The International Organization for Standardization (ISO) recently met to begin the process of developing an international standard on social responsibility.[17]

A major challenge to businesses operating in global markets is how to accommodate inconsistencies in ethics and regulations and how to be proactive in developing responsible conduct. A review of regulatory efforts in some world regions shows that international consensus exists on approaches to encouraging ethical conduct in business organizations. The concern is to develop not only legal limitations for behavior but also incentives for self-regulation and ethical conduct that are acceptable in a global business environment. The challenge is enforcing ethical conduct and developing

TABLE 10-5	The Global Sullivan Principles

As a company which endorses the Global Sullivan Principles we will respect the law, and as a responsible member of society we will apply these Principles with integrity consistent with the legitimate role of business. We will develop and implement company policies, procedures, training and internal reporting structures to ensure commitment to these principles throughout our organization. We believe the application of these Principles will achieve greater tolerance and better understanding among peoples, and advance the culture of peace.

Accordingly, we will:

◆ Express our support for universal human rights and, particularly, those of our employees, the communities within which we operate, and parties with whom we do business.

◆ Promote equal opportunity for our employees at all levels of the company with respect to issues such as color, race, gender, age, ethnicity or religious beliefs, and operate without unacceptable worker treatment such as the exploitation of children, physical punishment, female abuse, involuntary servitude, or other forms of abuse.

◆ Respect our employees' voluntary freedom of association.

◆ Compensate our employees to enable them to meet at least their basic needs and provide the opportunity to improve their skill and capability in order to raise their social and economic opportunities.

◆ Provide a safe and healthy workplace; protect human health and the environment; and promote sustainable development.

◆ Promote fair competition including respect for intellectual and other property rights, and not offer, pay or accept bribes.

◆ Work with government and communities in which we do business to improve the quality of life in those communities—their educational, cultural, economic and social well-being—and seek to provide training and opportunities for workers from disadvantaged backgrounds.

◆ Promote the application of these principles by those with whom we do business.

We will be transparent in our implementation of these principles and provide information which demonstrates publicly our commitment to them.

SOURCE: Reprinted from *Ethikos: Examining Ethical and Compliance Issues in Business,* The Sullivan Foundation, http://www.thesullivanfoundation.org/gsp/principles/gsp/default.asp (accessed June 27, 2006).

organizational value systems that promote an ethical business environment. The best approaches for preventing violations and avoiding civil litigation are identifying ethical issues and implementing codes of conduct that incorporate both legal and ethical concerns. Companies and trade associations need to assess how to better develop the programs and determine the management practices that will result in excellent legal and ethical performance. Also key to improving global ethical and legal performance is determining the relationship between national differences in individuals' moral philosophies and the corporate core values in management systems.[18]

THE MULTINATIONAL CORPORATION

Multinational corporations (MNCs) are public companies that operate on a global scale without significant ties to any one nation or region. MNCs represent the highest level of international business commitment and are characterized by a global strategy of focusing on opportunities throughout the world. Examples of multinational corporations include Shell Oil, Nike, Monsanto, and Cisco Systems. Some of these firms have grown so large that they generate higher revenues than the gross domestic product (GDP)—the sum of all the goods and services produced in a country during one year—of some of the countries in which they do business, as shown in Table 10–6. Con-

| TABLE 10–6 | Comparison of World's Largest Corporations' Revenues to Countries' Gross Domestic Product |

Country/Company*	GDP/Revenues ($ billions)
North American Free Trade Agreement, China, Japan, and the European Union	36,535
India	2,660
Brazil	1,340
Russia	1,200
South Korea	865
Australia	466
Sweden	346
Turkey	302
Wal-Mart Stores U.S.	288
British Petroleum	285
Exxon Mobil	270
Royal Dutch/Shell	268
Indonesia	257
Saudi Arabia	250
South Africa	213
General Motors	193
Ireland	184
DaimlerChrysler	176
Toyota	172
Ford	172
Iran	161
General Electric	152
Argentina	152
Total	152
Chevron Texaco	148
Conoco Phillips	121
Axa	121
Alliance	118

TABLE 10-6	Comparison of World's Largest Corporations' Revenues to Countries' Gross Domestic Product (*continued*)

Country/Company*	GDP/Revenues ($ billions)
Malaysia	118
Israel	116
Volkswagen	110
Venezuela	108
Citigroup	108
Czech Republic	107
Singapore	106
ING Group	105
United Arab Emirates	104
Pakistan	103
Hungary	100
Nippon Telegraph & Telephone	100

*All other countries in the world are below $100 billion.

SOURCE: Adapted from "2006 IMF Country Rankings by GDP," Global Fortune 500, 2006, http://money.cnn.com/magazines/fortune/global500/ (accessed June 27, 2006).

sider Bill Gates, the CEO of Microsoft, whose total worth as of this writing is over $64 billion. To give this figure relevance, the world GDP is $40 trillion. Gates's income ranks fifty-second, just above the Ukraine's.

Because of their size and financial power, MNCs have been the subject of much ethical criticism, and their impact on the countries in which they do business has been hotly debated. Both American and European labor unions argue that it is unfair for MNCs to transfer jobs overseas, where wage rates are lower. Other critics have charged that multinationals use labor-saving devices that increase unemployment in the countries where they manufacture. MNCs have also been accused of increasing the gap between rich and poor nations and of misusing and misallocating scarce resources. Their size and financial clout enable MNCs to control money supplies, employment, and even the economic well-being of less-developed countries. In some instances, MNCs have controlled entire cultures and countries. For example, a Los Angeles judge recently ruled that Unocal may be liable for the conduct of the government of Myanmar (formerly known as Burma) because documents presented in court contended that forced labor was commonly used in Myanmar to build Unocal projects and that workers' refusal to work resulted in their imprisonment and/or execution at the hands of the Myanmar army. Unocal's financial size and determination to complete certain projects at any cost compelled the Myanmar government to sanction the use of forced labor.[19] In 2005, Unocal announced that it had reached a final settlement with the parties regarding several lawsuits related to the company's investment through subsidiaries in the Yadana natural gas pipeline project. The court documents have been sealed.

Critics believe that the size and power of MNCs create ethical issues involving the exploitation of both natural and human resources. One question is whether MNCs should be able to pay a low price for the right to remove minerals, timber, oil, and other natural resources and then sell products made from those resources for a much higher price. In many instances, only a small fraction of the ultimate sale price of such resources comes back to benefit the country of origin. This complaint led many oil-producing countries to form the Organization of Petroleum Exporting Countries (OPEC) in the 1960s to gain control over the revenues from oil produced in those lands.

Critics also accuse MNCs of exploiting the labor markets of host countries. Although some MNCs have been accused of paying inadequate wages, the ethical issue of fair wages is a complicated one. Sometimes MNCs pay higher wages than local employers can afford to match; then local businesses complain that the most productive and skilled workers go to work for multinationals. Measures have been taken to curtail such practices. For example, many MNCs are trying to help organize labor unions and establish minimum-wage laws. In addition, host governments have levied import taxes that increase the price that MNCs charge for their products and reduce their profits. Import taxes are meant to favor local industry as sources of supply for an MNC manufacturing in the host country. If such a tax raises the MNC's costs, it might lead the MNC to charge higher prices or accept lower profits, but such effects are not the fundamental goal of the law. Host governments have also imposed export taxes on MNCs to force them to share more of their profits.

The activities of MNCs may also raise issues of unfair competition. Because of their diversified nature, MNCs can borrow money from local capital resources in such volume that little is left for local firms. MNCs have also been accused of failing to carry an appropriate share of the cost of social development. They frequently apply advanced, high-productivity technologies that local companies cannot afford or cannot implement because they lack qualified workers. The MNCs thus become more productive and can afford to pay higher wages to workers. Because of their technology, however, they require fewer employees than the local firms would hire to produce the same product. And, given their economies of scale, MNCs can also negotiate lower tax rates. By manipulating transfer payments among their affiliates, they may pay little tax anywhere. All these special advantages explain why some claim that MNCs compete unfairly. For example, many heavy-equipment companies in the United States try to sell construction equipment to foreign companies that build major roads, dams, and utility complexes. They argue that this equipment will make it possible to complete these projects sooner, thus benefiting the country. Some less-developed countries counter that such equipment purchases actually remove hard currency from their economies and increase unemployment. Certain nations, such as India, therefore believe that it is better in the long run to hire laborers to do construction work than to buy a piece of heavy equipment. The country keeps its hard currency in its economy and creates new jobs, which increases the quality of life more than does having a project completed sooner.

Although it is unethical or illegal conduct by MNCs that grabs world headlines, some MNCs also strive to be good global citizens with strong ethical values. Texas Instruments (TI), for example, has adopted a three-level global approach to ethical integrity that asks (1) "Are we complying with all legal requirements on a local level?"

(2) "Are there business practices or requirements at the local level which impact how we interact with co-workers in other parts of the world?" and (3) "Do some of our practices need to be adapted based on the local laws and customers of a specific locale? On what basis do we define our universal standards that apply to TI employees everywhere?" Texas Instruments generally follows conservative rules regarding the giving and receiving of gifts. However, what may be considered an excessive gift in the United States may be viewed differently according to the local customs of other parts of the world. Texas Instruments used to define gift limits in terms of U.S. dollars, but now it just specifies that gift giving should not be used in a way that exerts undue pressure to win business or implies a quid pro quo.[20]

Many companies, including Coca-Cola, Du Pont, Hewlett-Packard, Levi Strauss & Co., Texaco, and Wal-Mart, endorse following responsible business practices abroad. These companies support a globally based resource system called Business for Social Responsibility (BSR). BSR tracks emerging issues and trends, provides information on corporate leadership and best practices, conducts educational workshops and training, and assists organizations in developing practical business ethics tools. It addresses such issues as community investment, corporate social responsibility, the environment, governance, and accountability. BSR has also established formal partnerships with other organizations that focus on corporate responsibility in Brazil, Israel, the United Kingdom, Chile, and Panama.[21]

Although MNCs are not inherently unethical, their size and power often seem threatening to less-developed countries. The ethical problems that MNCs face arise from the opposing viewpoints inherent in multicultural situations. Differences in cultural perspectives may be as important as differences in economic interests. Because of their size and power, MNCs must therefore take extra care to make ethical decisions that not only achieve their own objectives but also benefit the countries where they manufacture or market their products. Even premiere MNCs sometimes find themselves in ethical conflict and face liability as a result. After investigating the tires on Ford automobiles that were involved in sixty-two accidents and more than forty deaths in Venezuela, the Venezuelan attorney general determined that the incidents could lead to fines against or even criminal prosecution of the tires' manufacturer, Bridgestone/Firestone, Inc., and Ford. Ford reportedly had requested that Bridgestone/Firestone insert an extra nylon layer (referred to as a cap ply) between the tires' steel belt and tread to accommodate the hotter, more humid, and more demanding driving conditions in Venezuela. When Firestone's Venezuelan plant began producing the tires for Ford, however, the plant inadvertently began marketing tires without a cap ply causing many accidents and fatalities. The resulting international scandal forced Bridgestone's U.S. CEO to resign, as well as to dissolve a seventy-year-long agreement between Ford and Bridgestone. Ford has since switched to Michelin tires on all of its Explorers. Other tire suppliers, including Goodyear, are increasing the amount of testing that they do for all tires that go to Ford.[22]

Now let's turn our attention to some common global ethical issues that arise when companies transact business internationally. These include sexual and racial discrimination, human rights concerns, price discrimination, bribery, harmful products, pollution, telecommunications issues, and intellectual-property issues. Several organizations have been established to provide guidance on such international business issues. This list of issues is certainly not exhaustive but provides a sample of the complexity of ethical decision making in the global arena.

SEXUAL AND RACIAL DISCRIMINATION

Various U.S. and European laws prohibit businesses from discriminating on the basis of sex, race, religion, or disabilities in their hiring, firing, and promotion decisions. However, the problem of discrimination is still a reality in the world. In the United Kingdom, for example, East Indians have traditionally been relegated to the lowest-paying, least desired jobs. In Germany, the government will not grant citizenship to Turkish workers who have been living there for decades or even to second-generation Turkish German residents. Australian aborigines have long been the victims of social and economic discrimination. In many Southeast Asian and Far Eastern countries, employees from particular ethnic backgrounds may not be promoted. In Russia, job advertisements frequently specify the age and gender of prospective employees, and female entrepreneurs face endless bureaucracy, problems obtaining credit, and a tangled legal system. One female business owner was jailed for ten days with no charges filed, evidence brought, or, after she was released, apologies offered.[23]

Businesswomen remain a rarity in many Middle Eastern nations. In some Middle Eastern countries, for example, women are required to wear special clothing and cover their faces; in public, they may be physically separated from men. Because these countries prescribe only nonbusiness roles for women, companies negotiating with Middle Eastern firms have encountered problems when they use female sales representatives. Indeed, a Middle Eastern company may simply refuse to negotiate with saleswomen or may take an unfavorable view of the foreign organizations that employ them. The ethical issue in such cases is whether foreign businesses should respect Middle Eastern values and send only men to negotiate sales transactions, thus denying women employees the opportunity to further their careers and contribute to organizational objectives. The alternative would be for these firms to try to maintain their own ideas of social equality, knowing that female sales representatives will probably be unsuccessful because of the cultural norms in those societies.

Businesses around the world benefit by acknowledging and attempting to curb discrimination, including a decrease in employee turnover; people who believe they are hired, promoted, and treated according to their skills and abilities rather than their personal characteristics or beliefs are more likely to remain loyal. In turn, this can reduce the costs of hiring and training new employees because productivity naturally improves when jobs are filled with the most qualified persons. Additionally, when companies hire a diverse local workforce, they are more likely to enjoy the goodwill and support of the communities surrounding their facilities. Finally, companies that take steps to eliminate discrimination may receive favorable attention from such stakeholders as labor and women's rights groups, enhancing the reputation of the firm overall as well as its brands. Table 10–7 lists steps that BSR suggests companies take to be proactive on discrimination issues.

TABLE 10-7	Steps That Companies Can Take to Address Discrimination Issues

1. Establish a company policy on discrimination.

2. Communicate this policy both internally and externally.

3. Determine benchmarks for activities in which discrimination can arise.

4. Identify indicators of possible noncompliance.

5. Establish methods for identifying noncompliance.

6. Develop an action plan.

7. Take action.

SOURCE: *Discrimination*, by Business for Social Responsibility, Copyright © 2006. Reprinted with permission. http://www.bsr.org/CSRResources/IssueBriefDetail.cfm?DocumentID=50411 (accessed June 27, 2006).

HUMAN RIGHTS

Corporate concern for global human rights emerged in the 1990s as news stories depicting the opportunistic use of child labor, payment of low wages, and abuses in foreign factories helped reshape our attitudes about acceptable behavior for organizations. For example, eight clothing retailers, including Liz Claiborne and Tommy Hilfiger, settled a lawsuit alleging that they were responsible for abuses against foreign workers in textile factories on the Pacific Island of Saipan. As part of the settlement, the factory workers saw improved working conditions such as relaxed restrictions on bathroom breaks.[24]

Companies struggling with human rights issues sometimes make short-term decisions to boost profitability that have negative long-term implications. These issues include concerns about the treatment of minorities and women, as well as the issues of child labor and employee rights. Multinational corporations face even greater challenges in this area because of the nature of their relationships with manufacturers and subcontractors in other cultures. The International Labor Organization estimates that 250 million children between the ages of 5 and 14 years old work in developing countries (61 percent in Asia, 32 percent in Africa, and 7 percent in Latin America). Although only an estimated 5 percent of these child laborers work in export industries, this still represents an ethical issue for MNCs.[25]

Although concern about human rights issues is increasing, abuses still occur. Many believe that MNCs should view the law as constituting the "floor" of acceptable behavior and strive to improve workers' quality of life in every country. Understanding each country's culture can help MNCs make valuable improvements. At an annual Human Rights Survey meeting, the executive director of Human Rights Watch introduced three guidelines that managers should consider to advance human rights: (1) Companies need to establish an open dialogue between workers and management. (2) Businesses should be aware of the human rights issues and concerns in each country in which they do business, information which can be found through Amnesty International, an international nonprofit devoted to human rights issues. (3) Companies should adopt the prevailing legal standard but work to improve and embrace a "best practices" approach and standard. Internationally acceptable behavior in any country should be their goal.[26] Several organizations observe and report on corporate behavior:

◆ *Global Compact:* Developed by the UN Secretary-General, this organization asks businesses to adhere to human rights and labor standards as defined in international treaties.

◆ *Amnesty International:* The business unit of this London-based human rights group has established Human Rights Guidelines for Companies, a set of principles concerning the link between business and human rights.

◆ *Fair Labor Association:* A nonprofit organization whose members include manufacturers, universities, and groups promoting human, consumer, religious, shareholder, and labor rights. Participating firms agree to have their facilities and those of their contractors monitored by both internal and independent external organizations.

◆ *The Council on Economic Priorities Accreditation Agency:* This organization has established standards for assessing labor conditions in global manufacturing operations.

PRICE DISCRIMINATION

A major ethical issue in international business is how products sold in other countries are priced. When a firm charges different prices to different groups of customers, it may be accused of **price discrimination.** Differential pricing is legal if it does not substantially reduce competition or if it can be justified on the basis of costs—for example, the costs of taxes and import fees associated with bringing products into another country. However, price discrimination may become an ethical issue or even be illegal when (1) the practice violates either country's laws, (2) the market cannot be divided into segments, (3) the cost of segmenting the market exceeds the extra revenue from legal price discrimination, or (4) the practice results in extreme customer dissatisfaction.

When a market is artificially divided into segments and each segment is subject to different prices, inequalities may emerge that cannot be explained by added costs. Such pricing policies may be judged illegal if courts rule that they substantially decrease competition. In the United States, price discrimination that harms competition is prohibited under the Robinson–Patman Act. In other countries, judgments of illegality result from precedent or fairness rulings. The European Union (EU), for example, has fined numerous companies for price fixing, including European brewers ($201 million fine), the Swiss chemical firm Hoffman-La Roche ($63.5 million euros), and Archer Daniels Midland, a U.S. firm ($40 million euros).[27] But the largest EU price fixing fine to date has been 896 euros ($1.798 billion) against the four largest glass manufacturers in the world. Neelie Kroes, the EU's competition commissioner, said Guardian (Auburn Hills, Michigan), France's Compagnie de Saint-Gobain SA, British-based Pilkington Group Ltd., and Japan's Asahi Glass Co. colluded to fix prices within the European market. According to EU law, companies operating a cartel can be fined 10 percent of their annual sales in Europe. The largest fine ever imposed in Europe before this case was the $240 million (U.S.) levy in 1998 against Trans-Atlantic Shipping Alliance.[28]

When companies market their products outside their own countries, the costs of transportation, taxes, tariffs, and other expenses can raise their prices. But when prices increase beyond the level needed to meet the costs of these additional expenses, an ethical issue emerges. Increasing prices in this way is sometimes referred to as **gouging.** When the European Union converted to a single currency—the euro—many Europeans believed that individual shops as well as countries were gouging them.[29] Gouging also refers to charging exorbitant rates for a limited time to exploit situational shortages—for instance, when lumber suppliers charge premium prices to earthquake victims seeking to rebuild or when gas stations increased gasoline prices immediately after the terrorist attacks on September 11, 2001. But gouging can also be endemic. For example, Cemex SA, a cement manufacturer in Mexico, has five thousand cement distributors in poor neighborhoods in Mexico that charge monopoly prices and enjoy monopoly profits. Not surprisingly, cement costs more in Mexico than in any other country, which has a negative effect on poor homebuilders.[30] Most countries' laws forbid companies from charging exorbitant prices for lifesaving products, which include some pharmaceuticals. However, these laws do not apply to products that are not considered "lifesaving," even if they are in great demand and no substitutes are available.

As mentioned earlier in this chapter, dumping occurs when companies sell products in foreign markets at low prices that do not cover all the costs of exporting the products. The technique, which occurs for a variety of reasons, allows a company to enter a market quickly and capture a large market share. Sometimes dumping occurs when the domestic market for a firm's product is too small to support an efficient level of production. In other cases, technologically obsolete products that are no longer salable in the country of origin may be dumped overseas. Dumping is unethical if it interferes with competition or hurts firms and workers in other countries. Furthermore, if it substantially reduces competition, it is illegal under many international laws. Dumping is difficult to prove, however, but even the suspicion of dumping can lead to the imposition of import quotas, which can hurt innocent firms. After investigating complaints from U.S. steel producers and labor unions, the U.S. Department of Commerce determined that Russia has been dumping steel in the United States. It recommended assessing tariffs as high as 217 percent to reverse the effects of the dumping, which included the loss of ten thousand jobs in the U.S. steel industry. When the Department of Commerce announced that it would settle the case against Russia and suspend the tariffs, the announcement brought protests from attorneys general in four steel-producing states.[31] When the administration of President George W. Bush later attacked European steel imports with new tariffs, the European Union countered with its own tariffs against U.S. exports valued at $2.1 billion.[32]

Price differentials, gouging, and dumping create ethical issues because some groups of consumers have to pay more than a fair price for products. Pricing is certainly a complicated issue in international marketing because of the additional costs imposed by tariffs, taxes, customs fees, and paperwork, as well as the political desire to protect home markets. Nonetheless, businesses should take care to price their products so that they recover legitimate expenses and earn a reasonable profit while still competing fairly.

BRIBERY

In many cultures, giving bribes—also known as **facilitating payments**—is an acceptable business practice. In Mexico, a bribe is called *la mordida,* and South Africans call it *dash.* In the Middle East, India, and Pakistan, *baksheesh,* a tip or gratuity given by a superior, is widely used. The Germans call it *schmiergeld,* grease money, and the Italians call it *bustarella,* a little envelope. Companies that do business internationally should be aware that bribes are an ethical issue and that the practice is more prevalent in some countries than in others. Bribes and payoff requests are frequently associated with large construction projects, turnkey capital projects, and large commodity or equipment contracts.

But bribery is becoming more expensive around the world because of business transparency, leading more government agencies to crack down on the practice. For example, Gautam Sengupta, a foreign national who had worked as a task manager at the World Bank in Washington, pleaded guilty to a Justice Department charge that he had directed World Bank–financed projects to a Swedish consultant in exchange for kickbacks. J. Bryan Williams, a former senior executive with Mobil Oil, pleaded guilty to evading taxes on more than $7 million that he received for negotiating oil deals in Kazakhstan. Finally, the Titan Corporation, an intelligence and communications company in San Diego, pleaded guilty to violating the Corrupt-Practices Act and agreed to pay more than $28 million to settle charges that included making $2.1 million in payments to the election campaign of Mathieu Kerekou, president of the West African nation of Benin.[33]

Globally, consumers are becoming more aware of the costs of corruption. In a study completed by Transparency International, fifty-five thousand people in sixty-nine countries were polled to assess their views on corruption. When asked if corruption had increased or decreased over the past three years, citizens in forty-eight countries stated it had increased. In Colombia, Georgia, Indonesia, Hong Kong, Kenya, and Singapore, consumers believed it had declined, but, in Bolivia, Costa Rica, Dominican Republic, Ecuador, India, Israel, Nicaragua, Nigeria, Panama, Paraguay, Peru, Philippines, and Venezuela, over 50 percent of those responding felt that corruption had dramatically increased. Recently the Extractive Industries Transparency Initiative (EITI) agreed to adopt strict guidelines in order to eradicate bribery in the oil, gas, and mining business. The guidelines require signatory governments to publish all payments to them from oil and mining companies operating in their country, to subject all such revenues to an independent audit, and to consult with local nongovernment organizations about the monitoring of the industry.[34]

Table 10–8 demonstrates that other countries will not tolerate multinationals encroaching on their citizens' economic rights.

Because the world is shrinking technologically, people are becoming increasingly concerned with unethical activities and are making laws against them. Decades ago the United States began with the Foreign Corrupt Practices Act. The **Foreign Corrupt Practices Act** (FCPA) prohibits U.S. companies from offering or providing payments to officials of foreign governments for the purpose of obtaining or retaining business abroad. The FCPA was enacted after an SEC investigation in the mid-1970s revealed that four hundred U.S. firms admitted making questionable or illegal payments in excess of $300 million to foreign government officials, politicians, and political parties. Violators of the FCPA face corporate fines of up to $2 million, and company executives face a maximum of five years in prison or $10,000 in fines, or both. The FCPA does permit small "grease" payments to foreign ministerial or clerical government employees. Such payments are exempted because of their size and the assumption that they are used to persuade the recipients to perform their normal duties, not to do something critical to the distribution of new goods and services.

TABLE 10-8	European Union Price Fixing Cases and Fines		
		Euros	**USD**
1.	Compagnie de Saint-Gobain SA, car glass, 2008:	896 million	1,179,800 million
2.	ThyssenKrupp AG, elevators, under appeal, 2007:	479.7 million	631,642 million
3.	Hoffmann La Roche AG, vitamins, 2001:	462 million	608,290 million
4.	Siemens AG, power gear, under appeal, 2007:	396.56 million	522,129 million
5.	Pilkington PLC, car glass, 2008:	370 million	487,159 million
6.	Sasol Ltd., paraffin, 2008:	318.2 million	418,956 million
7.	Eni SpA, synthetic rubber, under appeal, 2006:	272.25 million	358,316 million
8.	Lafarge SA, plasterboard, under appeal, 2002:	249.6 million	328,506 million
9.	BASF AG, vitamins, 2001, reduced on court appeal:	236.8 million	311,659 million
10.	Otis Elevator Co., elevators, 2001, under appeal:	224.9 million	296,040 million

SOURCE: The Huffington Post, "Highest EU Price Fixing Fines," http://www.huffingtonpost.com/huff-wires/20081112/eu-eu-cartels-glance/ (accessed January 14, 2009).

Some critics of the FCPA contend that, although the law was designed to foster fair and equal treatment for all, it places U.S. firms at a disadvantage in the international business arena. The FCPA applies only to American businesses; other nations have not imposed such restraints on their companies doing business abroad. For example, if three companies—from the United States, France, and Korea—are bidding on a dam-building project in Egypt, the French and Korean firms could bribe Egyptian officials in their efforts to acquire the contract, but it would be illegal for the American firm to do so. Thus, the issue of bribery sets the values of one culture—the U.S. disapproval of bribery—against those of other cultures.

In 1988 the **Omnibus Trade and Competitiveness Act** (OTCA) reduced FCPA legislation in certain areas and repealed the Eckhardt amendment, which prevented senior managers from using agents or employees as scapegoats when bribes were given. The OTCA makes prosecution of bribery even more difficult, thus decreasing the power and applicability of the FCPA in global business settings. Subsequent support for the FCPA has come through a global treaty, the Convention on Combating Bribery of Foreign Public Officials in International Business Transactions, which has been signed by thirty-four nations. The Convention is dominated by some of the largest countries in the world, and the majority in support of the treaty are members of the Organisation of Economic Cooperation and Development (OECD). The treaty requires signatories to make it a criminal offense for any person to "offer, promise or give away undue pecuniary or other advantage . . . to a foreign public official" for the purpose of obtaining "business or other improper advantage in the conduct of international commerce." Punishment is to be swift and effective so as to deter future offenses and is to be determined by the country in which the company operates.[35] However, at the time of the Transparency International study, only eighteen of the thirty-four treaty-signing countries had deposited all the necessary ratification documents.[36]

HARMFUL PRODUCTS

Governments in advanced industrialized nations have banned the sale of certain products that are considered harmful. However, some companies in those nations continue to sell such products in other countries where they remain legal. For example, many recent news stories have focused on the safety of genetically engineered products, which have become very controversial in the United States and Europe. Investors have filed resolutions at American Home Products, Archer Daniels Midland, Dow Chemical, Du Pont, and Monsanto to prevent the marketing of genetically engineered products "until long-term safety testing has shown that they are not harmful to humans, animals, and the environment."[37] Similar proposals made to Coca-Cola and General Mills ask for labeling of genetically engineered ingredients until such ingredients are removed from the companies' products. Many countries, including Japan, Australia, and New Zealand, and those in the European Union, already require labeling of genetically engineered food products.[38]

Another ethical issue involves the export of tobacco products to less-developed countries. Cigarette sales in the United States are declining in the face of stricter tobacco regulations, increasing evidence that smoking causes illness and medical problems, and a decline in the social acceptability of smoking. However, as U.S. sales decline, tobacco companies have increased their efforts to market cigarettes and other tobacco products in other countries, particularly less-developed ones. As a result, U.S. cigarette exports now exceed $200 billion, which exceeds their domestic sales.[39] The ethical issue becomes whether tobacco marketers should knowingly sell a product in other countries that is considered harmful in their home country.

Many consumers in underdeveloped countries view tobacco as beneficial, both physically and economically. They argue that the tobacco industry provides jobs and stimulates economies and that cigarette consumers enjoy smoking. Many also cite the low longevity rates in these countries as a reason to discount the health hazards of tobacco. In the long run, however, as industrialization raises the standard of living in less-developed countries, in turn increasing longevity rates, those countries may change their views on tobacco. As people live longer and the health hazards of smoking begin to cost both the people and their governments more in time and money, ethical pressure in these countries will increase.

At times, products that are not harmful in some countries become harmful to consumers in others because of illiteracy, unsanitary conditions, or cultural values. For example, products marketed by the Nestlé Corporation in the 1970s included infant formulas, which are used in the supplemental feeding of infants and have been tested as safe when used correctly. When the company introduced its product into African countries as an alternative to breastfeeding, local mothers quickly adopted the product. As time passed, however, infant mortality rates rose dramatically. Investigators found that, because of high illiteracy rates, many mothers were not able to follow the instructions for using the formula correctly. In addition, the water they used to mix with the powdered formula was often unsafe, and poor mothers also diluted the formula to save money, which reduced the nutritional value of the feeding. Nestlé was criticized for its aggressive promotion of the infant formula. For example, the company had employed so-called milk nurses to discourage mothers from breastfeeding by portraying the practice as primitive and promoted Nestlé's infant formulas as a safer alternative. Under heated pressure from international agencies and boycotts by consumer groups, Nestlé agreed to stop promoting the infant formula. It also revised its product labeling and educational materials to point out the dangers of using the formula incorrectly and to assert that breastfeeding was actually preferable.[40] Eventually, however, the company reverted to its previous practices, and the World Health Organization has maintained its boycott. Thus, even traditionally safe and adequately tested products can create ethical issues when a marketer fails to evaluate foreign markets accurately or respond adequately to the health problems posed by its products in certain markets.

In the twenty-first century, the concern is growing over safe drinking water, genetically modified products, and tainted foodstuffs entering the food chain. For example, ConAgra Foods Inc. had to recall 19 million pounds of ground beef because sixteen people in the United States became ill with the *E. coli* bacteria.[41] In some cases, the consequences can be fatal. Among other products, Baxter International Inc. produces kidney-dialysis filters. Unfortunately, when some of the filters proved to be defective, at least ten people in Spain died as a result.[42]

Some companies are attempting to address the harmful product issue. For example, PepsiCo, long synonymous with fast food, is attempting to develop healthier snacks even knowing that fat, salt, and sugar are inherently tastier than broccoli, carrots, and tomatoes. The job of marketing healthier snacks with fewer calories and cholesterol is a challenge that PepsiCo is willing to meet to improve public health.[43]

POLLUTION AND THE NATURAL ENVIRONMENT

Whereas many legal and ethical violations have limited impacts, in the case of environmental issues, the effects of abuses can be far reaching and long term. For example, public concern over global warming has increased pressure on companies to dramatically increase energy efficiency. Pressure from environmentalists is also encouraging companies to scrutinize suppliers of wood and paper products to ensure that the trees are not endangered species and that companies are harvesting products using sustainable practices. Many companies are therefore working to create standards for environmental responsibility. For example, Delphi Automotive Systems Corporation is committed to protecting human health, natural resources, and the global environment. Delphi's Design for the Environment process requires teams to evaluate the environmental impacts of product designs, materials, and manufacturing processes before the manufacturing begins. A leading producer of products that reduce emissions and improve fuel efficiency, Delphi has gained certification in ISO14001, a global standard that recognizes facilities that proactively adopt systems that manage and reduce environmental impact.[44] Other companies have modified or halted the production and sale of products that have a negative impact on the environment. For example, after tests showed that Scotchguard does not decompose in the environment, 3M announced a voluntary end to production of the 40-year-old product, which had generated $300 million in sales.[45]

Seeking to defend their air and water quality, some countries are taking legal action against polluting firms. In Mexico, for example, firms that fail to cut back emissions or that deny access to inspectors during smog alerts face legal sanctions.[46] In other situations, outside organizations such as Greenpeace issue warnings on countries that engage in environmental abuses. Greenpeace has accused Israel, for example, of defying international convention by dumping toxic waste in the Mediterranean.[47]

In some countries, however, groups have lobbied governments to increase the level of pollution that they allow. For instance, Australia's per-capita emissions from energy consumption and industrial manufacturing will rise from 21 metric tons to 26 tons in 2010, making Australia the largest greenhouse-gas emitter in the world. One member of the Australia Institute stated that, "If they had been aware of the facts, other nations would not have agreed to Australia's demand for an increase in emission but would have required us to cut our emissions more than other countries."[48]

For organizations to thrive globally, their governments should form joint agreements, such as the North American Free Trade Agreement between the United States, Canada, and Mexico, that set reasonable standards for emissions for members. Many pollution-control efforts have relatively short payback periods and have a long-term positive effect on profitability. In contrast, violating environmental initiatives has both human and financial costs, with the human cost being the health hazards associated with pollution.

TELECOMMUNICATIONS ISSUES

With the advent of satellites, e-mail, and the Internet, information can be accessed in a matter of seconds instead of weeks; as a result businesses can become the victims as well as the perpetrators of unethical actions. The ease of information access poses ethical issues, particularly with regard to privacy, that can differ by country. Some Internet-based firms have responded to privacy issues responsibly, whereas others have not. Yahoo!, for example, revised its privacy policy to expand its ability to market its own products to Yahoo! users unless they expressly ask it not to. News of the policy change quickly circulated via the Web, and consumers exchanged ideas on how to change their personal preferences on Yahoo! to avoid getting Spam, junk mail, or telemarketing calls. The animosity was highlighted by a survey that reported that 75 percent of respondents described the new policy as "awful" while only 3 percent said it was good.[49]

Access to Internet users is becoming a huge business. For example, America Online (AOL) controls 138 million registered users, most with instant messaging, a popular form of Internet chat and a key Web technology. As a result, AOL has become the gatekeeper not only to its own subscribers but also to consumers tapping into the Internet from cell phones and TVs.[50] An even bigger gatekeeper has become Google, which in 1998 became an official company with paper assets of $1 million and real assets of just a fraction of that sum. In 2005 Google had become an incredibly powerful Internet force and cut a deal with AOL to invest $1 billion into a plan to control even more information and sell services.[51] AOL is now part of Time Warner and has been split up into many pieces.

The relevant ethical issues here relate to access, information mining, and monopolies. Information access gives Internet companies a revenue stream from charging companies to advertise on their server, and many websites collect various levels of personal information about their users that they subsequently sell to advertisers, a process that has exploded in the last ten years. One questionable technique that websites use is to link or connect one user to others, a tactic that involves sending a Web user an e-mail suggesting that if he or she gives them a friend's name, then the company will give him or her discounts on promoted products. The friend then receives the same e-mail and increasingly the amount of consumer information. Thus, companies are exploiting the human desire to obtain something for nothing.

The Internet seems to foster the something-for-nothing mentality. One of the largest problems associated with the Internet is fraud. From its most recent report, the Internet Fraud Complaint Center (IFCC) had received 103,959 complaints of fraud. The total dollar loss was $68.14 million with a median dollar loss of $219.56 per complaint. Internet auction fraud was the most reported offense (71.2 percent). Nondelivered merchandise and/or payment accounted for 15.8 percent of complaints, and credit/debit card fraud accounted for 5.4 percent of complaints. Check, investment, confidence fraud, and identity theft complete the top seven categories of complaints.

Information overload and Internet slowdowns are becoming more common, and sometimes they are intentionally caused. For example, the number of online attempts to criticize or disrupt corporate operations is increasing. Perpetrators have sent mass e-mail messages, used "distributed denial of service" tools to interrupt company website operations, and attempted to deflate stock prices by posting negative comments on online message boards.[52]

The speed of global communications has affected virtually all industries. The fashion industry is a good case in point. Imitations have always been a problem, as "knockoffs" usually enter the market a few months behind the originals by way of a few retailers. However, the practice has changed dramatically. A photograph can now be taken at a fashion show in Milan, scanned, and sent electronically to a factory in Hong Kong. The next day, a sample garment can be sent by overnight delivery to a New York showroom for retail buyers. Stores order these lower-priced "interpretations" for their own private-label collections and sometimes even show the costlier designer versions at the same time because competition in malls is fierce and fashion merchandise is highly perishable, the industry has become very competitive. Some designers are countering these imitations by suing and by bringing out affordable knock-off versions of their own clothes before anyone else can.

Questionable financial activities, such as money laundering, have also been made easier by global telecommunications. **Money laundering** consists of using or transferring illegally received funds in a financial transaction in order to conceal their source of ownership or to facilitate an illegal activity. Using telecommunications technology, drug traffickers and smugglers can move funds through wire transfers and checks sent to other countries. Allegations of money laundering have been lodged against officers of Mexican banks; as a result, many Mexicans have lost confidence in their banks due to concerns that banking controls are not enforced, despite statements by Mexico's then-president that his country would be a more law-abiding place.[53]

Russia has also experienced money-laundering issues at the banking and government level. For example, the Bank of New York was accused of helping Russians launder about $7 billion, while Barclays PLC of London was implicated in a $10 billion money-laundering scheme with Russian banks. Whether the money laundering is being done for illegal businesses or just as a tax haven, the global banking community is developing laws and regulations to plug the holes for unethical and illegal activities originating from or going through Russia.[54]

INTELLECTUAL-PROPERTY PROTECTION

Intellectual property refers to the ideas and creative materials that individuals develop to solve problems, to carry out applications, and to educate or entertain others. It is generally protected through patents, copyrights, and trademarks. A patent is a legal document issued to an inventor that grants him or her the right to exclude any other person from making, using, or selling the invention anywhere for a certain number of years (seventeen years in the United States). The patent document describes the invention in detail, including how to make or use it, and provides protection rights against infringers. India, for example, won a legal battle against Texas-based RiceTec Inc. over the name *basmati,* a particular rice that has been trademarked in India.[55]

Pharmaceuticals raise other patent issues, especially concerning the rights of multinational corporations to protect their patents on drugs so that they can recover their research costs and hinder the introduction of cheaper generic drugs. Future patent issues may relate to whether the human genome that identifies each gene in the human body should be patented. If this is permitted, people will no longer have the rights to their own genes.

A copyright is a protection that covers published and unpublished literary, scientific, and artistic works, in any form of expression, provided that the works are in a tangible or material form. Copyright laws were established to protect the originators of goods such as books and records. However, as use of the Internet and the World Wide Web has proliferated, it has become difficult for copyright owners to protect their works in various countries. The case of the popular song-swapping website, Napster, is illustrative. Napster enabled computer users worldwide to send and receive digital music files among themselves for free. The Recording Industry Association of America (RIAA) filed suit against Napster, alleging that its music-sharing service aided large-scale copyright infringement. Napster denied any wrongdoing, arguing that federal law permitting the copying of music for personal use protected its users. A federal judge disagreed and ruled that Napster had to halt the downloading of all copyrighted materials, a ruling later upheld on appeal. Napster's efforts to settle the suit were rebuffed by the RIAA, and its attempts to reinvent itself as a fee-based music-sharing site have thus far failed.[56] The RIAA continues to battle the proliferation of music-sharing sites.

Many manufacturing firms have been hurt by the fraudulent use of their trademarks, which occurs when other parties counterfeit a major name-brand company's product or ambiguously misrepresent their own products as a name brand. The problems involving name-brand fraud are as varied as the countries in which they occur. In Guatemala City, for example, downtown streets are filled with vendors selling copies of everything from Adidas sneakers to Ferrari jeans. Consumers can buy a fake pair of Lee's $40 rivet jeans for just $9. Business leaders and clothing manufacturers have urged Guatemala's president to veto a new law that would encourage contraband and counterfeiting. The problem with the law, however, according to an attorney for Lee

Apparel Company, Levi Strauss & Co., and Tommy Hilfiger Corporation, is that even if they confiscate counterfeit merchandise from a warehouse, they can do nothing to the people on the street selling it.[57] Consumer goods companies such as Unilever and Procter & Gamble say they lose millions of dollars annually in India and China to "look-alike" brands that use similar-sounding names and identical packaging. Procter & Gamble estimates its losses in India at more than $370 million annually and in China at about $6.5 million a year. The Houghton Mifflin Company found that counterfeit textbooks were being printed in India for world distribution. The counterfeiting problem has prompted some companies, including Coca-Cola Ltd. and Colgate-Palmolive Ltd., to form a brand-protection committee. The committee's website (http://www.fake-busters.com) was established to help consumers and officials verify packaging and identify the real brands.[58]

WORLD TRADE ORGANIZATION

The **World Trade Organization** (WTO) was established in 1995 at the Uruguay round of negotiations of the General Agreement on Tariffs and Trade (GATT). Today, the WTO has 133 member nations and an additional 33 nations that have applied for membership and hold observer status. On behalf of its membership, the WTO administers its own trade agreements, facilitates future trade negotiations, settles trade disputes, and monitors the trade policies of member nations. The WTO addresses economic and social issues involving agriculture, textiles and clothing, banking, telecommunications, government purchases, industrial standards, food sanitation regulations, services, and intellectual property. It also provides legally binding ground rules for international commerce and trade policy. The organization attempts to reduce barriers to trade between and within nations and settle trade disputes.

Although its goals are certainly lofty, the WTO has been criticized by a number of groups, especially environmental organizations. For example, after the U.S. Marine Mammal Act placed an embargo on tuna caught using methods that can also kill dolphins, Mexico denounced the act and sued the United States. In its Tuna–Dolphin Ruling, the WTO declared the U.S. law illegal under GATT rules, forcing the United States to rescind the law. A similar set of circumstances resulted in the WTO's Shrimp–Turtle Ruling. After the U.S. Environmental Protection Act required that all shrimp fishers use nets with turtle-excluder devices to protect endangered sea turtles, several Asian nations that refused to use the nets were excluded from selling shrimp in the United States. They filed suit, arguing that the United States cannot use import bans to influence fishing practices outside its own borders. The WTO agreed, and the United States eliminated this portion of the law.[59] Rulings such as these have led environmental organizations to question the effectiveness of the WTO.

SUMMARY

The global businessperson must not only understand the values, culture, and ethical standards of his or her own country but also be sensitive to those of other countries. Culture includes everything in our surroundings that is made by people—both tangible items and intangible concepts, including language, law, religion, politics, technology, education, social organizations, and general values and ethical standards. Each nation has a distinctive culture and different beliefs about what business activities are acceptable or unethical. Cultural differences that create ethical issues in international business include differences in language, body language, time perception, and religion. According to cultural relativism, morality varies from one culture to another, and business practices are defined as right or wrong by the particular culture in which they occur.

Numerous attempts have been made to establish a set of global or universal ethical standards. Although many cultures share certain values, differences surface when these values are explained from the perspective of a specific culture.

Multinational corporations operate on a global scale without significant ties to any one nation or region. Because of their size and financial power, MNCs can have a serious impact on the countries where they do business, which may create ethical issues.

Although U.S. laws prohibit American companies from discrimination in employment, discrimination in other countries is often justified on the basis of cultural norms and values. MNCs should strive to understand the human rights issues of each country in which they conduct business.

Price discrimination creates an ethical issue and may be illegal when the practice violates the laws of the countries in which it occurs, when the market cannot be segmented or the cost of segmenting exceeds the extra revenue gained from legal price discrimination, or when price discrimination results in customer dissatisfaction. When the foreign price of a product exceeds the full costs of exporting, the ethical issue of gouging arises. Dumping occurs when companies sell products in their home markets at high prices while selling the same products in foreign markets at low prices that do not cover the full costs of exporting. Price differentials, gouging, and dumping create ethical issues because some groups of consumers have to pay more than a fair price for products.

Bribery is an acceptable practice in many countries, but the U.S. Foreign Corrupt Practices Act (FCPA) prohibits American businesses from offering or providing payments to officials of foreign governments to obtain or retain business. The Omnibus Trade and Competitiveness Act reduced the force of the FCPA and has made the prosecution and applicability of the FCPA in global business settings nonthreatening.

Globally, companies have begun working together to minimize the negative effects of pollution and support environmental responsibility. Joint agreements and international cooperatives have successfully policed and prosecuted offenders of reasonable emission standards.

Advances in telecommunications have intensified such ethical issues as privacy protection, fraud, and patent, copyright, and trademark infringement. They have also made it easier to carry out questionable financial activities, notably money laundering, which involves transferring illegally received money or using it in financial transactions in order to conceal the source or ownership or to facilitate an illegal activity.

Intellectual property refers to the ideas and creative materials that individuals develop to solve problems, to carry out applications, and to educate or entertain others. It is generally protected through patents, copyrights, and trademarks.

World entities such as the World Trade Organization are in the process of redefining themselves in relation to the new global environment. Ethics in the twenty-first century has taken on a new importance and is seen as critical to the economic sustainability of corporations and countries, and international entities that do not recognize this new reality face global scrutiny.

IMPORTANT TERMS FOR REVIEW	self-reference criterion dumping culture cultural relativism multinational corporation price discrimination gouging	facilitating payment Foreign Corrupt Practices Act Omnibus Trade and Competitiveness Act money laundering intellectual property World Trade Organization

RESOLVING ETHICAL BUSINESS CHALLENGES*

George Wilson, the operations manager of the CornCo plant in Phoenix, Arizona, has a dilemma. He is in charge of buying corn and producing chips marketed by CornCo in the United States and elsewhere. Several months ago, George's supervisor, CornCo's vice president, Jake Lamont, called to tell him that corn futures were on the rise, which would ultimately increase the overall costs of production. In addition, a new company called Abco Snack Foods had begun marketing corn chips at competitive prices in CornCo's market area. Abco had already shown signs of eroding CornCo's market share. Jake was concerned that George's production costs would not be competitive with Abco's—hence, profitability would decline. Jake had already asked George to find ways to cut costs. If he couldn't, Jake said, then layoffs would begin.

George scoured the Midwest looking for cheap corn and finally found some. But when the railcars started coming in, one of the company's testers reported the presence of aflatoxin—a naturally occurring carcinogen that induces liver cancer in lab animals. Once corn has been ground into corn meal, however, the aflatoxin is virtually impossible to detect. George knew that by blending the contaminated corn with uncontaminated corn he could reduce the aflatoxin concentrations in the final product, which, he had heard, other managers sometimes did. According to U.S. law, corn contaminated with afla-

toxin cannot be used for edible products sold in the United States, and fines are to be imposed for such use. So far, no one has been convicted. No law, however, prohibits shipping the contaminated corn to other countries.

George knows that, because of his competitors' prices, if he doesn't sell the contaminated corn, his production costs will be too high. When he spoke to Jake, Jake's response was, "So how much of the corn coming in is contaminated?"

"It's about 10 percent," replied George. "They probably knew that the corn was contaminated. That's why we're getting such good deals on it."

Jake thought for a moment and said, "George, call the suspected grain elevators, complain to them, and demand a 50 percent discount. If they agree, buy all they have."

"But if we do, the blends will just increase in contamination!" said George.

"That's OK. When the blends start getting high, we'll stop shipping into the U.S. market and go foreign," Jake told him. "Remember, there are no fines for contaminated corn in Mexico."

George learned that one other person, Lee Garcia, an operations manager for the breakfast cereals division, had sold the contaminated corn once.

"Yeah, so what about it? I've got a family to support and house payments. For me there was no alternative. I had to do it or face getting laid off," Lee said.

As George thought about the problem, word spread about his alternatives. The following notes appeared in the plant suggestion box:

Use the corn or we all get laid off!

Process it and ship it off to Mexico!

It's just wrong to use this corn!

When George balked at Jake's proposed solution, Jake said, "George, I understand your situation. I was there once—just like you. But you've got to look at the bigger picture. Hundreds of workers would be out of a job. Sure, the FDA [Food and Drug Administration] says that aflatoxin is bad, but we're talking rats eating their weight in this stuff. What if it does get detected—so what? The company gets a fine, the FDA tester gets reprimanded for screwing up, and it's back to business as usual."

"Is that all that will happen?" asked George.

"Of course, don't worry," replied Jake.

But George's signature, not Jake's, was on the receipts for the contaminated railcars. "So if I do this, at what aflatoxin percentage do I stop, and will you sign off on this?" asked George.

"Look," said Jake, "that's up to you. Remember that the more corn chips that are produced for the U.S. market, the more profit the company gets and the higher your bonus. As for me signing off on this, I'm shocked that you would even suggest something like that. George, you're the operations manager. You're the one who's responsible for what happens at the plant. It just isn't done that way at CornCo. But whatever you do, you had better do it in the next several hours because, as I see it, the contaminated corn has to be blended with something, and the longer you wait, the higher the percentages will get."

QUESTIONS • EXERCISES

1. Discuss the corporate ethical issue of providing questionable products to other markets.
2. Discuss the suggestions submitted in the suggestion box in light of the decision that George must make. Should the suggestions have an influence?
3. Identify the pressures that have caused the ethical and legal issues in this scenario to arise.

*This case is strictly hypothetical; any resemblance to real persons, companies, or situations is coincidental.

Check Your EQ

Check your EQ, or Ethics Quotient, by completing the following. Assess your performance to evaluate your overall understanding of the chapter material.

1.	Most countries have a strong orientation toward ethical compliance or laws.	**Yes**	**No**
2.	The self-reference criterion is an unconscious reference to one's own cultural values, experience, and knowledge.	**Yes**	**No**
3.	Cultural differences also relate to differences in body language.	**Yes**	**No**
4.	Multinational corporations have identifiable home countries but operate globally.	**Yes**	**No**
5.	Certain facilitating payments are acceptable under the Foreign Corrupt Practices Act.	**Yes**	**No**

ANSWERS: 1. No. That's an ethnocentric perspective; in other countries laws may be viewed more situationally. 2. Yes. We react based on what we have experienced over our lifetimes. 3. Yes. Personal space, habits, and customs influence interaction among people of different cultures. 4. No. Multinational corporations have no significant ties to any nation or region. 5. Yes. A violation of the FCPA occurs when the payments are excessive or are used to persuade the recipients to perform other than normal duties.

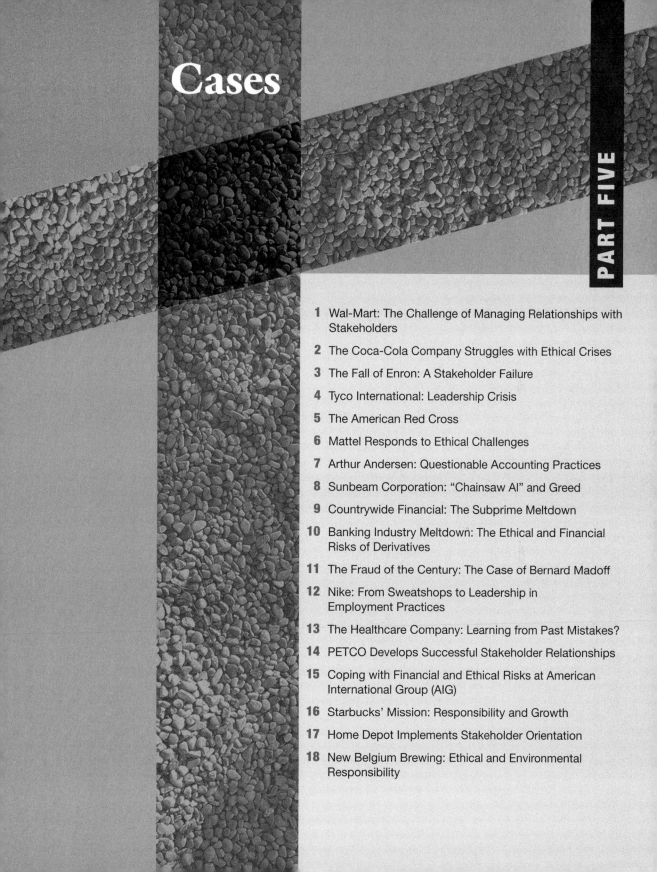

Cases

Wal-Mart: The Challenge of Managing Relationships with Stakeholders

Wal-Mart Stores Inc.—the world's largest retailer—is possibly the most controversial business in America. With sales over $312,000 billion in 2006 and approximately 1.7 million employees worldwide (of these, 1.3 million are U.S. employees), managing stakeholder relationships is a major challenge. The Wal-Mart that saves the average family an estimated $2329 per year has its critics. There are concerns about Wal-Mart's treatment of employees, suppliers, the environment, and the overall economic impact on communities. Feminists, human rights activists, anti-sprawl activists, and labor unions believe that Wal-Mart has engaged in misconduct to provide low prices to consumers. The company that banishes magazines with racy covers and CDs with edgy lyrics is seen as attempting to dictate its vision of American culture.

Wal-Mart claims that it is committed to improving the standard of living for their customers throughout the world. The key strategy is a broad assortment of quality merchandise and services at everyday low prices (EDLP) while fostering a culture that claims to reward and embrace mutual respect, integrity, and diversity. Wal-Mart has three basic beliefs: respect for the individual, service to their customers, and striving for excellence. How well the firm implements these beliefs is the focus of this case.

Wal-Mart, one of the most amazing success stories in the history of American business, has also shaped debate over the relationships between corporations and their stakeholders. Wal-Mart has excelled at market orientation, which is focusing on consumers, defeating competitors, and increasing shareholder value. Only recently has shareholder value lagged behind the major stock market–index performance. Other stakeholders such as employees, suppliers, and communities have been viewed as secondary to low prices for consumers. For example, the *Fortune* 100 best companies to work for does not include Wal-Mart. Number one in 2005 and number two in 2006 on the *Fortune* list was Wegmans Food Markets, with the very unusual motto of

This case was prepared by Melanie Drever, University of Wyoming, under the direction of O. C. Ferrell, for classroom discussion rather than to illustrate either effective or ineffective handling of an administrative, ethical, or legal decision by management. All sources used for this case were obtained through publicly available material and the Wal-Mart website.

employees first and customers second. Starbucks with its generous employee benefits, even for part timers, was number two in 2005 but dropped to twenty-ninth in 2006.

The story of Wal-Mart and its low prices shows both good and bad outcomes for society. The company has grown from a small chain to over five thousand stores in ten countries, making its early investors and some employees financially successful. It has been estimated that Wal-Mart saves consumers $100,000 billion a year. Wal-Mart's entrance into some markets lowers food prices 25 percent, including savings from competitors' price cuts. As competing supermarkets close, their union employees sometimes lose their jobs. One study found that total payroll wages per person declined by almost 5 percent where Wal-Mart stores are located due to Wal-Mart driving down wages. In 2005 an internal document made public by Wal-Mart Watch showed that 46 percent of Wal-Mart employees' children were on Medicaid or uninsured. Michael Hicks, an economist at the Air Force Institute of Technology found that Wal-Mart increased Medicaid costs an average of $1898 per worker. Armed with these alleged facts, the Maryland General Assembly passed the "Wal-Mart Bill" requiring employers with more than 10,000 workers to spend at least 8 percent of their payroll on employee health care or pay into a fund for the uninsured. Wal-Mart challenged the law; it appears that the law is not going to be implemented. Sarah Clark a Wal-Mart spokesperson was quoted in *USA Today:* "Wal-Mart does believe that everyone should have access to affordable healthcare, and this legislation adds nothing to accomplish this goal." The debate goes on with the question of the real costs to society for low prices.

HISTORY AND GROWTH OF WAL-MART

Wal-Mart's principal offices are in Bentonville, Arkansas. In 1945 in Newport, Arkansas, Sam Walton, the store's founder, opened a franchise Ben Franklin variety store. In 1946 his brother opened a similar store in Versailles, Missouri. Until 1962 the business was devoted entirely to the operation of variety stores. In 1962 the first Wal-Mart Discount City was opened, which was the first Wal-Mart discount store. In 1984 the first three Sam's Clubs were opened, and in 1988 the first supercenter opened. In 1999 the first neighborhood market was opened. Today the family of Wal-Mart founder Sam Walton has a combined fortune estimated at $90 billion.

The Wal-Mart business model includes two main segments: Wal-Mart Stores and Sam's Clubs. The Wal-Mart Stores come in three sizes: discount stores, which are about 100,000 square feet; supercenters, which are about 187,000 square feet; and the neighborhood markets, which are about 43,000 square feet in size. Sam's Clubs are membership warehouse clubs, which average 128,000 square feet and aim to provide exceptional value on brand-name merchandise at "members only" prices for both small businesses, nonprofit organizations, and personal use, especially large families.

Wal-Mart has continued to expand from its small roots in Arkansas, opening new stores at an accelerated rate. At present, Wal-Mart operates 2640 discount stores, 2396 supercenters, 670 Sam's Clubs, and 435 neighborhood markets in the United States. It has continued to open new stores every year, not only in the United States but also abroad. Much of the expansion overseas has been through acquisitions of existing operations in other countries.

Over 138 million people visit Wal-Mart every week, and 84 percent of Americans have shopped at Wal-Mart in the past year. People living in households with incomes of less than $30,000 a year give Wal-Mart its highest marks, proving that those who value Wal-Mart most need Wal-Mart's low prices the most.

Wal-Mart's first international initiative started in 1992 with a 50 percent joint venture in Mexico with Cifera discount stores. In 1998 they acquired control of Cifera and changed its name to Wal-Mart de Mexico. The first international venture was so successful that today Wal-Mart has 774 stores in Mexico. In addition, the company operates stores in Argentina (11), Brazil (295), Canada (278), Germany (88), South Korea (16), Puerto Rico (54), and the United Kingdom (315). Their joint ventures in China and Japan provide Wal-Mart with over 450 stores.

Wal-Mart became the largest grocery chain in 2002 with revenue larger than Safeway and Albertson's combined. It became the first retailer to be number one on the *Fortune* 500 list in 2005, with sales over $300 billion; in 2006 Wal-Mart was number two behind Exxon Mobil. Sales climbed 10 percent in 2005, and profits rose 13 percent to more than $10 billion. In addition to being number two on the *Fortune 500*, Wal-Mart was also named the "most admired company in America" in 2003 and 2004; in 2005, however, it slipped and ranked fourth on the list behind Dell, General Electric, and Starbucks; in 2006 it was ranked twelfth. Wal-Mart is the world's largest retailer as well as the largest employer.

RELATIONSHIPS WITH SUPPLIER STAKEHOLDERS

Wal-Mart is focused on keeping its costs low for its EDLP. It does this by streamlining its company and insisting its suppliers do the same. Wal-Mart is well known for its operational excellence in its ability to handle, move, and track merchandise, and it expects its suppliers to continually improve their systems too. It demands that its suppliers consistently lower prices of products from one year to the next by at least 5 percent; if a supplier is unwilling or unable to do so, Wal-Mart will no longer carry the product or will find another supplier for the product at the price they want.

Technology is a driving force in operational efficiency that lowers costs. The merchandise-tracking system—radio-frequency identification (RFID)—ensures that a product can be tracked from the time it leaves the supplier's warehouse to the time it enters and leaves a Wal-Mart store. In 2004 Wal-Mart insisted that its top one hundred suppliers ensure that all their pallets and products being shipped to Wal-Mart had RFID by January 2005. The cost to suppliers was much larger than the cost to Wal-Mart because suppliers needed to continually buy the RFID tags while all Wal-Mart needed was a system to read the tags. It has been estimated that the cost to one supplier could be $9 million to install and implement the RFID technology. Smaller Wal-Mart suppliers also have to install the tags, but they had until 2006 to comply.

RFID tags help Wal-Mart keep their shelves stocked and curbs the loss of retail products as they travel through the supply chain. RFID at Wal-Mart has directly resulted in a 16 percent reduction in stock-outs and a 67 percent drop in replenishment times. As customers go through checkout, the RFID system swiftly combines point-of-sale data on their purchases with RFID-generated data on what's available in the stockroom to produce pick lists that are automatically created in real time, based on sales. It also ensures that suppliers are notified when products are sold and can ensure that enough of a product is always at a particular store. This strategy also results in time and labor savings because associates (as employees are called at Wal-Mart) no longer need to scan store shelves to determine what is out of stock, nor do they have to scan cartons and cases arriving at the stockroom. The scanners tag incoming pallets and translate the data into supply chain–management database-forecasting models to address out-of-stock items and reduce stock–restocking mix-ups.

The power Wal-Mart has over its suppliers is more to do with its size and volume of products it needs than anything else. For example, Dial Corporation does 28 percent of its business with Wal-Mart. If it lost that one account, it would have to double its sales to its next nine customers just to stay even. Other companies that depend on Wal-Mart for sales are Clorox, which does 23 percent of its business with Wal-Mart; Revlon, 22 percent; Proctor & Gamble, 17 percent; Kraft Foods, 12 percent; General Mills, 12 percent; and Kellogg, 12 percent. This ensures that Wal-Mart dictates terms to its vendors rather than the other way around. However, there are benefits to suppliers because they become more efficient and streamlined, which helps their other customers too, as they improve their system for Wal-Mart.

Many companies believe that supplying Wal-Mart is the best thing for their business; there are the few, however, who believe that Wal-Mart is hurting their business and decide to no longer do business with them. An example of this is Snapper, a company with a 50-year heritage of making high-quality residential and commercial lawn equipment. CEO Jim Weir believed that Wal-Mart was incompatible with the company's strategy of high quality and, compared to Wal-Mart's typical lawn mowers, high prices. He felt that the long-term survival of the company meant that he should no longer sell to Wal-Mart. Wal-Mart tried to convince him that making a low-cost version of Snapper mowers specifically for Wal-Mart would be a good compromise, as Levi's did with their Levi's Signature brand made specifically for the Wal-Mart market. However, Weir would have none of it.

Weir said no to Wal-Mart and told his other customers about the decision. Wal-Mart accounted for 20 percent of his business, but he wanted to focus more on the other 80 percent of the independent dealers. The other dealers were happy with Weir's decision, and Snapper got much of the lost business back from the independent dealers by winning their hearts.

The constant drive by Wal-Mart for lower prices affects its suppliers in a more ominous way too. Many suppliers have had to move production from the United States to cheaper locations, such as China, to remain suppliers to Wal-Mart and maintain their business. Wal-Mart imports over $18 billion dollars worth of goods from China and encourages its suppliers to move their production operations to China to systematically lower cost. China and Wal-Mart have developed a unique partnership, and Wal-Mart accounts for 10 percent of the U.S. trade deficit with China. China's annual exports amount to $583 billion, and Wal-Mart ranks as China's eighth-largest trading partner, ahead of Australia, Canada, and Russia. Rubbermaid, once *Fortune*'s most admired company, has gone out of business, and much of its manufacturing equipment was sold to a Chinese company. Although the Rubbermaid brand name lives on, former Rubbermaid managers claim that the low prices that Wal-Mart demanded, including their reluctance to allow Rubbermaid to increase prices when the cost of raw materials increased, caused them to close and sell to a competitor. Companies such as Master Lock, Fruit of the Loom, and Levi's—as well as many other Wal-Mart suppliers—have all moved production overseas at the expense of U.S. jobs and all in the name of low prices for consumers.

ETHICAL ISSUES INVOLVING WAL-MART STAKEHOLDERS

Employee Stakeholders

DISCRIMINATION   The U.S. Equal Employment Opportunity Commission (EEOC) has filed fifteen lawsuits against Wal-Mart since 1994. Of these, ten are still pending, and five have been resolved.

FEMALE EMPLOYEES   Although women account for more than 67 percent of all Wal-Mart employees, women make up less than 10 percent of top-store managers. Wal-Mart insists that it adequately trains and promotes women, but in 2001 a Wal-Mart executive conducted an internal study that showed the company paid female store managers less than men in the same position.

In June 2004, a federal judge in San Francisco granted class-action status to a sex-discrimination lawsuit against Wal-Mart. It is the largest class-action lawsuit and involves 1.6 million current and former female employees at Wal-Mart. It claims that Wal-Mart discriminated against women in promotions, pay, training, and job assignments. Even Wal-Mart concludes in its annual report that if the company is not successful in its appeal of the class-action certification of the case, the resulting liability could be material to the company.

DISABLED EMPLOYEES   In January 2000, Wal-Mart agreed to pay two deaf applicants $132,500. The two applied to work at a Wal-Mart in Tucson, Arizona, but were denied employment because of their disabilities. Wal-Mart agreed to hire the two men as part of the settlement and to make corporate-wide changes in the hiring and training of new employees who are deaf or hearing impaired. However, in June 2001, for failure to comply with the original court order, Wal-Mart was fined $750,200, ordered to produce and air a TV ad stating that it had violated the Americans with Disabilities Act (ADA), reinstate William Darnell (one of the disabled workers), and create computer-based learning modules in American Sign Language and provide ADA training.

Another EEOC case took place in December 2001. The lawsuit alleged that Wal-Mart's preemployment questionnaire "Matrix of Essential Job Functions" violated the ADA, and the EEOC resolved the suit with a $6.8 million consent decree. In 2002 Wal-Mart agreed to pay $220,000 for rejecting a pregnant applicant. In February 2005, Wal-Mart paid a $7.5-million jury-verdict fine to a disabled former employee in a class-action lawsuit.

SWEATSHOP WORKERS   Another class-action lawsuit accuses Wal-Mart Stores Inc. of failing to monitor labor conditions at overseas factories that allegedly maintained sweatshop conditions. The plaintiffs are fifteen workers in Bangladesh, Swaziland, Indonesia, China, and Nicaragua who claim they were paid below minimum wage in their country, forced to work unpaid overtime, and in some cases even endured beatings by supervisors. It also includes four California workers who claim that Wal-Mart's entry into southern California forced their employers to reduce pay and benefits. The lawsuit could cover a class of anywhere from one hundred thousand to five hundred thousand workers.

ILLEGAL IMMIGRANTS   In October 2003, federal officials raided Wal-Mart stores across the United States and arrested 250 illegal immigrants working on cleaning crews at sixty-one stores in twenty-one states. The undocumented workers were from Mexico, eastern Europe, and other countries and were employed by several contractors used by Wal-Mart.

The investigation by the U.S. Immigration and Customs Enforcement evolved out of two earlier immigration probes in 1988 and 2001 and ended in March 2005 with a landmark $11 million civil settlement. Twelve corporations that provided janitorial services to Wal-Mart stores agreed to forfeit an additional $4 million and to enter corporate guilty pleas to criminal immigration charges.

However, according to a *Wall Street Journal* article in November 2005, three top Wal-Mart executives knew that its cleaning contractors used illegal immigrants who worked as many as seven days a week for less than the minimum wage. The executives allegedly encouraged the cleaning contractor to make "shells" of the company so that they could continue to hire the contractor if one of the companies was closed for hiring illegal workers. (Shell companies are created for either hiding something illegal or unethical. The company is called a shell because outsiders see it as a company, but in reality, many are just mail drops.)

Even after agreeing to make sure that no people working for Wal-Mart were illegal immigrants, another raid by federal, state, and local authorities in November 2005 netted 125 illegal immigrants. The illegal immigrants were arrested at a Wal-Mart construction site. The workers had been building a 1 million-square-foot distribution center in eastern Pennsylvania. In December 2005, another 14 illegal immigrants were arrested while installing shelves at one of Wal-Mart's distribution centers in Nebraska.

LOW BENEFITS   To work full time at Wal-Mart, an employee works a minimum of just 28 hours. Although wages tend to be higher than minimum wage, the few hours that employees are allowed to work ensures that associates can barely cover living expenses. This means that the taxpayer has to pay the difference. According to "The Case Against Wal-Mart," a typical Wal-Mart store with two hundred employees costs federal taxpayers $420,750 per year—about $2103 per employee. This pays for free and reduced lunches for Wal-Mart families, housing assistance, federal tax credits and deductions for low-income families, additional child tax credits, federal health-care costs of moving into state children's health insurance programs, and low-income energy assistance (electric and gas bills).

Wal-Mart fails to provide health insurance to more than 60 percent of its employees. Part-time employees are excluded from Wal-Mart's health program, and the company has an extra-long waiting period before employees become eligible for its health-care program. Even then, many are not eligible if they work part time, and those who are covered are underinsured. For employees who can get coverage, the deductibles can be prohibitively high for such low-income families, who then have to pay for most of the expenses themselves.

In a leaked Wal-Mart memo to the board of directors, Susan Chambers, Wal-Mart's executive vice president for benefits, described how 46 percent of Wal-Mart employees are uninsured or on Medicaid. The memo detailed how Wal-Mart's health plan requires such high out-of-pocket payments that the small number of employees hit by a very costly illness "almost certainly end up declaring personal bankruptcy." The memo also proposed that Wal-Mart rewrite job descriptions to involve more physical activity, in part to "dissuade unhealthy people from coming to work at Wal-Mart."

Another influence of Wal-Mart is the downward pressure on wages and benefits in towns when Wal-Mart enters the area. To compete against the retail giant, other stores in the area reduce their wages by about 3.5 percent. Overall payroll wages including Wal-Mart wages are reduced by 5 percent. But even with the decrease in wages, many stores still go out of business, causing many local residents to lose their jobs. According to the advocacy group Good Jobs First, Wal-Mart has received more than $1 billion in public subsidies just for building its stores (not counting the cost to state and local governments of picking up health-care costs of Wal-Mart employees).

WORKING CONDITIONS   In December 2005, Wal-Mart was ordered to pay $172 million to more than one hundred thousand California employees in a class-action lawsuit that claimed that Wal-Mart routinely denied workers meal breaks. California has a law that requires a thirty-minute meal break within the first five hours of a shift or an extra hour's pay. The employees also allege that they were denied rest breaks and that Wal-Mart managers deliberately altered timecards to keep people from earning overtime. Hours were regularly deleted from time records, and employees were reprimanded for claiming overtime. Another similar case in New Mexico and Colorado in 2000 ended with Wal-Mart reportedly paying $50 million to sixty-seven thousand employees.

According to www.WalMartFacts.com, forty pending wage-and-hour cases are currently seeking class certification. Wal-Mart states that any manager who requires or even tolerates "off-the-clock" work would be violating policy and labor laws.

UNIONS   Germany is the only place where Wal-Mart employees currently are unionized. Employees in German Wal-Mart stores have thirty-six days vacation a year and are paid overtime. Wal-Mart has, according to some sources, spent a considerable amount of money and resources on ensuring that Wal-Mart employees in the United States and the other fifteen countries in which it does business do not unionize. It has been alleged that when the word *union* surfaces in a Wal-Mart, the top dogs in Bentonville are called and action is taken immediately to thwart any union movements:

◆   In a Wal-Mart store in Loveland, Colorado, some employees in the Tire and Lube Express wanted to unionize. Wal-Mart found ways, according to some workers, to intimidate and brainwash its employees to pressure the few pro-union employees. Wal-Mart also hired more workers for the Tire and Lube Express to dilute the numbers who would vote for the union. The pressure ensured that once again Wal-Mart did not become unionized.

◆ In 2000 when seven of ten butchers in a store in Jacksonville, Texas, voted to join the United Food Workers Union, Wal-Mart responded by announcing that henceforth it would sell only precut meat in all of its supercenters, fired four of the union supporters, and transferred the rest into other divisions.

◆ In Canada, the United Food and Commercial Workers organized at Jonquiere, Quebec, Wal-Mart in 2004. In 2005 the retailer closed the store, claiming it was losing money and that union demands would prevent it from becoming profitable.

Wal-Mart is now facing a tough decision in China. If it wants to continue its growth into China, it might have to accept a union. According to some reports, employees in Chinese Wal-Marts were warned against speaking with trade-union officials during working hours. Poor working conditions in China and low wages are generating social unrest, and the government is trying to craft a new set of labor laws that give workers greater protection. These laws are likely to give greater power to the All-China Federation of Trade Unions. Whether Wal-Mart is forced to accept a union remains to be seen. As for Sam Walton, Wal-Mart's founder, he believed that unions were a divisive force and would make the company uncompetitive.

ETHICAL LEADERSHIP ISSUES: THOMAS COUGHLIN   In January 2005, Thomas Coughlin, vice chairman of Wal-Mart Stores Inc., resigned but remained on the Wal-Mart board of directors. At one time as vice chairman—the second-highest-ranking executive at Wal-Mart—he was a candidate to become CEO. Coughlin was a legend at Wal-Mart—a protégé and hunting buddy of Sam Walton. Coughlin would often spend a week on the road with Walton as they expanded Sam's Clubs. His compensation was over $6 million in 2004.

In March 2005, Coughlin was forced to resign from the board of directors for stealing as much as $500,000 from Wal-Mart in the form of bogus expenses and reimbursements, along with the unauthorized use of gift cards. Coughlin had worked at Wal-Mart for twenty-seven years, five of them as the second-most-powerful executive at the company. The case created new concerns about leadership, corporate governance, and the ethical culture of Wal-Mart.

In January 2006, Coughlin pled guilty to federal wire-fraud and tax-evasion charges. Although Coughlin took home millions of dollars in compensation, he secretly had Wal-Mart pay for some of his personal expenses, including hunting vacations, a $2590 dog enclosure at his home, and a $1359 pair of handmade alligator boots.

Coughlin's deceit was discovered when he asked a lieutenant to approve $2000 in expense payments without any receipts. Jared Bowen, a Wal-Mart vice president, says Coughlin mentioned that the money was for the union project. Coughlin claims that he told the Wal-Mart board of directors that he was using money for anti-union activities, including paying union staffers to identify pro-union workers in Wal-Mart stores. Wal-Mart issued statements that there were no anti-union activities and the funds were misappropriated for Coughlin's personal use. Paying union staffers to identify pro-union workers would be a criminal offense under the Taft–Hartley Act. The following day after Bowen reported the alleged misconduct, Wal-Mart fired him. As a whistle-blower on the expense-payment abuses, he could not understand why he was fired. He said that Wal-Mart officials indicated that "he wasn't forthcoming" and there was "a general lack of confidence." Bowen has asked federal prosecutors to investigate whether the company violated corporate whistle-blowing laws in his firing. In the meantime, Wal-Mart has rescinded Coughlin's retirement agreement, worth more than $10 million. Coughlin faced up to twenty-eight years in prison after pleading guilty to five counts of wire fraud and one count of filing a false tax return. He was sentenced to 27 months of home detention and five years probation. Wal-Mart spokesperson Mona Williams says the experience has been "embarrassing and painful. Someone we expected to operate with the highest integrity let us down in a very public way."

Environmental Stakeholders

The Environmental Protection Agency (EPA) and the states of Tennessee and Utah allege that Wal-Mart and some of its construction contractors violated the EPA's stormwater regulations at specified sites around the country. Wal-Mart settled the dispute without admitting any wrongdoing or violations of the regulations by paying a $3.1 million civil penalty and agreeing to implement a Supplemental Environmental Project valued at $250,000.

In 2001 the state of Connecticut filed suit against Wal-Mart for violations of state environmental laws and for failing to obtain the appropriate permits or to maintain the required records relating to stormwater-management practices at twelve stores. In 2003 the state also filed an amended complaint alleging that Wal-Mart also discharged wastewater associated with vehicle maintenance activities and photo-processing activities without proper permits. The company settled these suits without admitting any wrongdoing or violations of the regulations by paying $1.5 million and implementing new compliance procedures.

The EPA has alleged that Wal-Mart violated certain air-quality restrictions at various locations in Massachusetts and Connecticut, including state and local restrictions on the amount of time that truck engines are allowed to idle. Wal-Mart settled those allegations by agreeing to pay a $50,000 civil penalty, to implement new compliance procedures, and to implement a Supplemental Environmental Project valued at $100,000.

The district attorneys for Solano County and Orange County, California, allege that the Wal-Mart's store in Vacaville failed to comply with certain California statutes regulating hazardous waste– and hazardous materials–handling practices. Specifically, that Wal-Mart improperly disposed of a limited amount of damaged or returned product containing dry granular fertilizer and pesticides on or about April 3, 2002, and January 24, 2005. The cases have not yet been settled.

In another environmental case, the EPA alleges that Wal-Mart and one of its construction contractors violated EPA stormwater regulations at a site in Caguas, Puerto Rico. The administrative complaint filed by the agency proposes an administrative penalty in the amount of $157,500. The parties are currently negotiating toward a resolution of this matter.

In November 2005, Wal-Mart received a grand jury subpoena from the U.S. Attorney's Office in Los Angeles seeking documents and information relating to the company's receipt, transportation, handling, identification, recycling, treatment, storage, and disposal of certain merchandise that constitutes hazardous materials or hazardous waste. Wal-Mart also received administrative document requests from the California Department of Toxic Substances Control requesting similar documents and information with respect to two of the company's distribution facilities. California local government authorities and the state of Nevada have also initiated investigations into this matter. The company is cooperating fully with the respective authorities.

Many activists are concerned about urban sprawl created by Wal-Mart stores. The construction of a Wal-Mart supercenter can stress a city's infrastructure of roads, parking, and traffic flows. In addition, there are concerns about the number of acres of green space in a city that can be devoured by Wal-Mart constructing a new store. Another issue is the number of abandoned stores that Wal-Mart deserts after it outgrows the small discount stores and moves to a new supercenter location. There are over 26 million square feet of empty Wal-Marts, enough empty space to fill up 534 football fields. The annual figure of empty Wal-Marts is between 350 and 400 per year. It has been alleged that Wal-Mart goes out of its way to prevent other retail stores from buying its abandoned stores, especially competitors like Target.

WHAT IS WAL-MART DOING TO IMPROVE ITS REPUTATION?

Global Ethics Office

The Global Ethics Office was established on June 1, 2004. On June 4, 2004, Wal-Mart released a revised "Global Statement of Ethics" to communicate their ethical standards to all Wal-Mart facilities and stakeholders. The Global Ethics Office provides guidance in making ethical decisions based on the "Global Statement of Ethics" and a process for anonymous reporting of suspected ethics violation by calling the Ethics Helpline. The Ethics Helpline allows for an anonymous and confidential way for associates to contact the company regarding ethical issues. Wal-Mart's "Guiding Ethical Principles," added to the revised "Global Statement of Ethics," were designed to assist Wal-Mart associates and suppliers with making the right decision and doing the right thing:

1. Follow the law at all times.
2. Be honest and fair.
3. Never manipulate, misrepresent, abuse, or conceal information.
4. Avoid conflicts of interest between work and personal affairs.
5. Never discriminate against anyone.
6. Never act unethically—even if someone else instructs you to do so.
7. Never ask someone to act unethically.
8. Seek assistance if you have questions about the "Statement of Ethics" or if you face an ethical dilemma.
9. Cooperate with any investigation of a possible ethics violation.
10. Report ethics violations or suspected violations.

Environment

Although Wal-Mart has recycling locations at each of its stores, it has tied itself to other initiatives over the past couple of years to improve its environmental impact.

EXPERIMENTAL STORES   Wal-Mart opened two environmentally friendly stores—one in McKinney Texas, and the other in Aurora, Colorado. The two locations were chosen because they have different weather and climate considerations. The stores should provide examples of the way that building owners, scientists, engineers, architects, contractors, and landscape designers can work together to create stores that save energy, conserve natural resources, and reduce pollution. The stores are living laboratories, testing experimental technologies and products. Wal-Mart hopes to take what is learned at these two stores and use that at future stores.

The new stores include pervious pavement, experimental urban forest, water conservation, wildflower meadows, wind turbines, solar energy, recycling efforts, climate control, Xeriscape and bioswale (proenvironmental landscaping methods), and internal lighting and construction experiments.

WAL-MART ACRES FOR AMERICA   In 2005 Wal-Mart partnered with the National Fish and Wildlife Foundation to conserve critical wildlife habitats for future generations. It has committed $35 million for the next ten years to conserve at least one acre of priority wildlife habitat for every acre developed for company use. This puts the minimum total acres to be protected at 138,000.

ENERGY CONSERVATION MEASURES   There are three main ways that Wal-Mart is conserving energy:

◆ *Daylighting* (skylights/dimming): Most new stores include this feature, which enables the stores to dim or turn off lights as daylight increases and enters through the skylights, thereby reducing the demand for electricity during peak hours.
◆ *Heating* and *cooling:* The heating and cooling of Wal-Mart stores in the contiguous fory-eight states is centrally controlled in Bentonville, Arkansas, enabling Wal-Mart to actively control and manage energy consumption.

LIGHTING EFFICIENCY PROGRAM   All new Wal-Mart stores and supercenters use T-8 low-mercury fluorescent lamps and electronic ballasts, a very efficient lighting system. By retrofitting older stores with T-8 lighting rather than the T-12 systems, the amount of energy used by each store will be reduced by approximately 15 percent. Wal-Mart started retrofitting its older stores in 2000 and plans to have completed the process by 2007.

PLASTIC SANDWICH BALE   Wal-Mart partnered with Rocky Mountain Recycling in 2005 and introduced an innovation in the solid-waste and recycling industry. The Plastic Sandwich Bale is a new way to use existing equipment to reduce store waste. Plastic shopping bags, film from apparel bags, and shrink-wrap are "sandwiched" between layers of cardboard and then compacted for ease of plastic recovery within the store and transportation to end markets. From 2001 to 2006, Wal-Mart facilities in the United States have recycled 36,378 tons of plastic. In 2004 it launched a pilot program in 326 stores in Arizona, California, Colorado, Idaho, Montana, Nevada, New Mexico, Oregon, Utah, and Wyoming. It is proving to be a huge success and is keeping 5376 tons of plastic out of landfills per year.

KIDS RECYCLING CHALLENGE Wal-Mart introduced a recycling challenge for schools and children, which ran until May 2005. Over thirty-five schools participated, and for each sixty-gallon bag of plastic bags, schools received $5 from Wal-Mart. In the first six months of the program, over two thousand bags of bags were collected, and Wal-Mart gave over $28,000 to schools. The program was such a success that Wal-Mart has extended it, hoping to do it every school year.

2005 *WASTE NEWS* ENVIRONMENTAL AWARD Wal-Mart won the 2005 *Waste News* Environmental Award. *Waste News* editor stated that Wal-Mart had made the most significant environmental progress of any business in 2005.

IMPROVING ITS IMAGE AMONG CUSTOMERS

In 2005 Wal-Mart introduced a website (www.WalMartFacts.com) to counter claims made by its critics. The website has information about the litigation that Wal-Mart faces and what it thinks about the claims and lawsuits as well as information about the actions it is taking to help the environment. There are sections on community impact, an associate center, key topics, "Do You Know?" and "Talk with Us," as well as a list of all the awards and recognition that Wal-Mart has achieved. All of this is aimed at reducing misperceptions about Wal-Mart and ensuring that customers are better informed about all the "misleading" news that they hear about the retail giant.

In 2005 Wal-Mart also launched a full-page ad in more than one hundred newspapers across the country. The ad was a direct letter from Wal-Mart CEO H. Lee Scott, which said it was time for the public to hear the "unfiltered truth" about Wal-Mart and time for the company to stand up on behalf of a workforce that includes 1.2 million Americans. Scott called for Congress to increase the minimum wage and said that Wal-Mart has increased spending on health insurance for its workers. The firm says it insures six hundred thousand associates and more than three-fourths of Wal-Mart associates have health insurance.

Wal-Mart has also hired the public relations firm Hill and Knowlton and dozens of communications specialists to help it improve its overall image. This was combined with an aggressive advertising campaign publicizing the millions of dollars that Wal-Mart contributes to local community organizations, as well as focusing on other key concerns such as how Wal-Mart treats its employees and its employee diversity. Wal-mart has one of the most diverse work forces in the United States and is a leading employer of senior citizens in the United States, employing 164,000 workers aged 55 years or older. Of the fifteen board of director members, two Latinos sit alongside two women. It also employs 139,000 Hispanic associates, 208,000 African American associates, and 775,000 women. More than 76 percent of the management team at

Wal-Mart started as hourly associates, and as of 2006, the Wal-Mart website reports that more than 40 percent of Wal-Mart store management are women.

WAL-MART AND THE ECONOMY

Wal-Mart is a driving force in the U.S. economy. Wal-Mart saves working families $2329 a year, on average, according to a study analyzing the national and regional economic impact of Wal-Mart. The consumer savings continue to be especially meaningful to lower-income and retired consumers. Low prices are due to Wal-Mart's higher levels of capital investment in distribution and inventory-control assets, operational excellence, advanced information technology, low import prices from China, and greater efficiency in its whole supply chain.

The study by Global Insight, an independent economic analysis firm, concluded that the efficiencies that Wal-Mart has fostered in the retail sector have led to lower prices for the U.S. consumer. The expansion of Wal-Mart over the 1985–2004 period can be associated with a cumulative decline of 9.1 percent in food-at-home prices, a 4.2 percent decline in commodities prices, and a 3.1 percent decline in overall consumer prices as measured by the Consumer Price Index. The 3.1 percent decline in prices was partially offset by a 2.2 percent decline in nominal wages, but there was still a net increase in real disposable income of 0.9 percent. Wal-Mart also created 210,000 jobs nationwide.

In Dallas, Fort Worth, and Arlington, Texas, Wal-Mart's effect has been considerable. The cost savings have been 4 percent, and Wal-Mart has provided sixty-three hundred more jobs and a 2.6 percent increase in real disposable income in the Dallas–Fort Worth area.

For a new store with about 150 to 350 employees in an area, Wal-Mart typically increases employment in the area by 137 jobs in the short term, which levels off in the long term to an increase of 97 jobs. This is due to the net job decline in food, apparel, and accessory stores but an increase in building materials, garden supply, and general merchandise store jobs. Although Wal-Mart displaces other retail establishments in the short term, it stimulates the overall development of the retail sector, which leads to an overall positive impact (in terms of retail employment) for the countries in which Wal-Mart has expanded. Wal-Mart has contributed modestly to lower import prices because it has been able to purchase imported goods for 5 percent less than traditional retailers due to the high volume and distribution efficiencies.

HURRICANE KATRINA

Wal-Mart's response to Hurricane Katrina was fast, efficient, and significant. Wal-Mart contributed $17 million in cash to the hurricane relief effort, more than $3 million in merchandise, $15 million to the Bush–Clinton Katrina Fund, $1 million to the Salvation Army, and $1 million to the American Red Cross. Wal-Mart also provided more than $8.5 million in cash assistance to impacted associates through Wal-Mart's Associate Disaster Relief Fund. They gave $20,000 in cash donations to assist various animal shelters and organizations taking in lost animals in hurricane-impacted areas. In addition they also dispatched 2450 Wal-Mart truckloads, donated 70 pallets of clothes to help evacuees, set up donation centers in various shelters to help arriving evacuees needing personal health and beauty products, clothing, food, and water. For example, at the Houston Astrodome, Wal-Mart provided five trucks of relief supplies, forty-five associate volunteers, and a computer, fax machine, TV, VCR, and children's movies.

Wal-Mart donated one hundred truckloads of water and other supplies to the afflicted area. They also donated food for one hundred thousand meals and the promise of a job for every one of its displaced workers. Cliff Brumfield, executive vice president of the Brookhaven–Lincoln County Chamber of Commerce, said he was impressed with Wal-Mart's preparations: "They were ready before FEMA was." Scott, Wal-Mart's CEO from January 2000 to January 2009, appeared on *Larry King Live* to discuss the chain's response to the storm and was singled out and praised by former Presidents George H. W. Bush and Bill Clinton.

These measures have attempted to stem the tide of negative publicity that has focused on the company. Although it has tried to address all the major concerns of its various stakeholders, only time will tell whether these measures prove effective and whether Wal-Mart can overcome the negative publicity. Consumers always vote with their money.

THE FUTURE

Mike Duke became Wal-Mart's fourth CEO in January 2009. Perhaps changing the face of Wal-Mart executives will help to improve the corporation's image. Wal-Mart indicates it is willing to accept the challenge of improving stakeholder relationships. The firm claims that it is being singled out because of its large size. Moves by the company to enter into the banking industry were rejected due to the banking industry's fears that the retailer would quickly dominate the field.

Wal-Mart has also faced criticism for encouraging suppliers to join a group called Working Families for America, an organization that has more than one hundred thousand members and is helping Wal-Mart counter the wave of negative publicity. But because the group is funded in part by Wal-Mart, its suppliers are worried that if they don't join they will face repercussions. Wal-Mart has denied these claims and says that suppliers who do not join will not face any adverse consequences.

There is no doubt that Wal-Mart's size and rapid growth has put it at the center of a debate about its impact on workers, unions, suppliers, local communities, competition, and the environment. Wal-Mart's push to import most of its products from China and to force its suppliers to manufacture in China creates an issue that significantly affects the U.S. economy. However, Wal-Mart is continuing to move into new areas, increasing its focus on organic foods and even moving into more expensive products for upscale clientele.

Wal-Mart remains controversial and there are different points of view. Consider these quotes:

> Some well-meaning critics believe that Wal-Mart Stores today, because of our size, should, in fact, play the role that is believed that General Motors played after World War II. And that is to establish this post–World War middle class that the country is so proud of. . . . The facts are that retail does not perform that role in the economy.
> —Wal-Mart CEO H. Lee Scott

This is one of our nation's great companies. . . . The story of Wal-Mart exemplifies some of the very best qualities in our country—hard work, the spirit of enterprise, fair dealing and integrity.—Vice President Dick Cheney

It is extremely troubling when the vice president . . . praises a company that pays low wages and benefits, discriminates on the basis of gender, locks its own workers into stores at night, busts unions and violates child-labor laws.—Representative George Miller (D., Calif.)

It's time for Wal-Mart to understand that their company practices run counter to the very values that make this country great—fairness, opportunity and equality. —Senator Edward Kennedy (D., Mass.)

QUESTIONS

1. Evaluate how Wal-Mart has ranked and responded to various stakeholders.
2. Why do you think Wal-Mart has had a recent number of ethical issues that have been in the news almost constantly?
3. What do you think Wal-Mart could do to develop an improved ethical culture and respond more positively to its diverse stakeholders?

SOURCES: Stephanie Armour, "Maryland First to OK 'Wal-Mart Bill,'" *USA Today,* January 13, 2005, 1B; Associated Press, "Ex-Wal-Mart Vice Chairman Pleads Guilty in Fraud Case," *Wall Street Journal* online, January 31, 2006, www.online.wsj.com; James Bandler, "Former No. 2 at Wal-Mart Set to Plead Guilty," *Wall Street Journal,* January 7, 2006, A1; James Bandler and Ann Zimmerman, "A Wal-Mart Legend's Trail of Deceit," *Wall Street Journal,* April 8, 2005, A10; Michael Barbaro, "Image Effort by Wal-Mart Takes a Turn," *New York Times,* May 12, 2006, C1, C4; Michael Barbaro and Justin Gillis, "Wal-Mart at Forefront of Hurricane Relief," *Washington Post* online, September 6, 2005, www.WashingtonPost.com (accessed January 10, 2006); Matthew Boyle, "Wal-Mart Keeps the Change," *Fortune,* November 10, 2003, 46; "Buy Blue: Wal-Mart," Buy Blue, http://www.buyblue.org/node/ 2137/view/summary (accessed January 10, 2006); Lauren Coleman-Lochner, "Independent Look at Wal-Mart Shows Both Good and Bad. With Savings and Jobs Come Falling Wages and Rising Medicaid Costs," *[San Antonio] Express-News,* November 5, 2005, 4D; Cora Daniels, "Class Act: Women Scorned? He's on the Case," *Fortune,* September 20, 2004, 52; Kathleen Day, "Critics Fear a Wal-Mart Move into Banking Would Dominate the Industry," *Washington Post* in *The Branding Iron,* February 15, 2006, 6; "Dell Beats Wal-Mart as Most-Admired," *Fortune,* February 22, 2005, via http://money.cnn.com/ 2005/02/21/news/fortune500/most_admired/index.htm; "EEOC: Wal-Mart," Equal Employment Opportunity Commission, http://search.access.gpo.gov/eeoc/SearchRight.asp?ct=eeoc&q1=wal-mart (accessed January 2005); Lauren Etter, "China: Engagement or Containment," *Wall Street Journal,* November 19–20, 2005, A5; Lauren Etter, "Gauging the Wal-Mart Effect," *Wall Street Journal,* December 3–4, 2005, A9; "Event Highlights the Wal-Mart Health Care Crisis: New Study Declares Wal-Mart in Critical Condition," WalMartWatch, November 16, 2005, http://walmartwatch.com (accessed January 18, 2006); Jack Ewing, "Germany: Wal-Mart. Local Pipsqueek. The U.S. Giant Is Struggling in Germany Where Discounters Already Dominate," *BusinessWeek,* April 11, 2005, 54; Liza Featherstone, "Wal-Mart to the Rescue!" *The Nation* online, September 13, 2005, http://www.thenation.com/doc/ 20050926/featherstone (accessed January 2005); Teri Finneman, "When Wal-Mart Comes to Town; Supercenters Push into Western Minnesota, N.D.," *Forum,* August 7, 2005, via www.wakeupwalmart .com; Charles Fishman, "The Wal-Mart You Don't Know; Why Low Prices Have a High Cost," *Fast Company,* December 2003, 68–80; Charles Fishman, "The Man That Said No to Wal-Mart," *Fast Company,* January/February 2006, 66–71; Mei Fong and Ann Zimmerman, "China's Union Push Leaves Wal-Mart with Hard Choice," *Wall Street Journal,* May 13–14, 2006, A1, A6; "Global Insight

Releases New Study on the Impact of Wal-Mart on the U.S. Economy," Global Insight, http://www
.globalinsight.com/MultiClientStudy/MultiClientStudyDetail2438.htm (accessed January 23, 2005);
Russell Gold and Ann Zimmerman, "Papers Suggest Wal-Mart Knew of Illegal Workers." *Wall Street
Journal,* November 5, 2005, A3; Marcy Gordon, "Wal-Mart's Banking Bid Opposed, Critics Worried
About Safety of Local Banks," *USA Today,* April 11, 2006, B2; Lorrie Grant, "Wal-Mart Faces a New
Class Action," *USA Today,* September 14, 2005, 63; Lorrie Grant, "Wal-Mart Prepares for 2nd
Hurricane," *USA Today* online, September 23, 2005, http://www.usatoday.com/money/industries/
retail/2005-09-22-walmart-preparation_x.htm?csp=34; Robert Greenwald, *Wal-Mart—The High Cost of
Low Price,* a film by Robert Greenwald and Brave New Films, November 4, 2005, www.walmartmovie
.com; Thomas A. Hemphill, "Rejuvenating Wal-Mart's Business," Indiana University Kelley School of
Business, *Business Horizons* 48 (2005): 48, 11–21; Candace Hoke, www.walmartsurvivor.com; John
Johnson, "RFid Watch: Transmissions from the RFid Front Lines: How They Did It," DC Velocity,
January 2006, www.DCVelocity.com (accessed January 10, 2006); Del Jones, "Corporate Giving for
Katrina Reaches $547 million," *USA Today* online, September 13, 2005, http://www.usatoday.com/
money/companies/2005-09-12-katrina-corporate-giving_x.htm; Marcus Kabel, "Wal-Mart at War:
Retailer Faces Bruised Image, Makes Fizes," *Marketing News,* January 15, 2006, 25; David Koenig,
"Wal-Mart Wants to Be Where You Go for $500 Wine; New Texas Store Stocks Posh Products for
Upscale Clientele," *USA Today,* March 23, 2006, B2; Robert Levering and Milton Moskowitz, "The 100
Best Companies to Work For," *Fortune,* January 24, 2005, 61–88; Daniel McGinn, "Wal-Mart Hits the
Wall," *Newsweek,* November 14, 2005, 44–46; Ylan Q. Mui, "Wal-Mart List Racially Offensive,"
Washington Post/Denver Post, January 8, 2006, 14A; Harold Meyerson, "Open Doors, Closed Minds.
How One Wal-Mart True Believer Was Excommunicated for His Faith in Doing What He Thought the
Company Expected of Him: Crying Foul," Prospect, November 11, 2005, www.prospect.org (accessed
January 20, 2006); Al Norman, "The Case Against Wal-Mart." Raphel Marketing, 2004; Zena Olijnyk,
"The Wal-Mart Effect," *Canadian Business* 77, no. 8 (2004): 67–68; Karen Olsson, "Up Against Wal-
Mart," *Mother Jones* online, March/April 2003, http://www.motherjones.com/news/feature/
2003/03/ma_276_01.html (accessed January 10, 2006); Steve Quinn, "Wal-Mart Green with Energy,"
[Fort Collins] Coloradoan, July 24, 2005, E1–E2; "The Real Facts About Wal-Mart," Wakeupwalmart
.com, http://www.wakeupwalmart.com/facts/; Jim Renden "Wal-Mart Touts RFid Results,"
Search CIO, January 18, 2005, http://searchcio.techtarget.com/originalContent/0,289142,sid19
_gci1045698,00.html?bucket=NEWS (accessed January 10, 2006); Andy Serwer, "Bruised in
Bentonville," *Fortune,* April 18, 2005, 84–89; "Statement on Poll Showing Americans Believe Wal-Mart
Is a Good Place to Shop," WalMartfacts.com, http://www.walmartfacts.com/newsdesk/article
.aspx?id=1557 (accessed January 2005); "Statements Regarding Union-Funded 'Where would Jesus
Shop Campaign,'" WalMartfacts.com, http://www.walmartfacts.com/newsdesk/article.aspx?id=1539
(accessed January 2005); Laurie Sullivan, "Wal-Mart CEO: Hurricane Charlie Paved Way for Katrina
Response," *Information Week* online, September 19, 2005, www.informationweek.com; Jim Wagner,
"Wal-Mart RFID Tests Underway," *Wireless,* April 30, 2004, via www.internetnews.com (accessed
January 10, 2006); "Wal-Mart Annual Report 10-K"; "Wal-Mart Annual Report to Shareholders
2006";"Wal-Mart and the Environment," WalMartfacts.com, walmartfacts.com, http://www
.walmartfacts.com/eytopics/environment.aspx; "Wal-Mart Urged to 'Clean Up Act,'" BBC online, June
3, 2005, http://news.bbc.co.uk/2/hi/business/4605733.stm; www.WalMartfacts.com; Ann
Zimmerman, "Federal Officials Asked to Probe Wal-Mart Firing," *Wall Street Journal,* April 28, 2005,
via www.wakeupwalmart.com; Ann Zimmerman, "In Wal-Mart's Case, Its Enemies Aren't Terribly Good
Friends," *Wall Street Journal,* January 11, 2006, A1, A10; Ann Zimmerman and James Bandler, "How
Gift Cards Helped Trip Up Wal-Mart Aide," *Business News/Wall Street Journal,* July 15, 2005, via
http://www.post-gazette.com/pg/05196/538565.stm

The Coca-Cola Company Struggles with Ethical Crises

Coca-Cola has the most valuable brand name in the world and, as one of the most visible companies worldwide, has a tremendous opportunity to excel in all dimensions of business performance. However, over the last ten years, the firm has struggled to reach its financial objectives and has been associated with a number of ethical crises. Warren Buffet served as a member of the board of directors and was a strong supporter and investor in Coca-Cola but resigned from the board in 2006 after several years of frustration with Coca-Cola's failure to overcome many challenges.

Many issues were facing Doug Ivester when he took over the reins at Coca-Cola in 1997. Ivester was heralded for his ability to handle the financial flows and details of the soft-drink giant. Former-CEO Roberto Goizueta had carefully groomed Ivester for the top position that he assumed in October 1997 after Goizueta's untimely death. However, Ivester seemed to lack leadership in handling a series of ethical crises, causing some to doubt "Big Red's" reputation and its prospects for the future. For a company with a rich history of marketing prowess and financial performance, Ivester's departure in 1999 represented a high-profile glitch on a relatively clean record in one hundred years of business. In 2000 Doug Daft, the company's former president and chief operating officer, replaced Ivester as the new CEO. Daft's tenure was rocky, and the company continued to have a series of negative events in the early 2000s. For example, the company was allegedly involved in racial discrimination, misrepresenting market tests, manipulating earnings, and disrupting long-term contractual arrangements with distributors. By 2004 Daft was out and Neville Isdell had become president and worked to improve Coca-Cola's reputation.

We appreciate the work of Kevin Sample, who helped draft the previous edition of this case and Melanie Drever, who assisted in this edition. This case was prepared for classroom discussion rather than to illustrate either effective or ineffective handling of an administrative, ethical, or legal decision by management. All sources used for this case were obtained through publicly available material and the Coca-Cola website.

HISTORY OF THE COCA-COLA COMPANY

The Coca-Cola Company is the world's largest beverage company, and markets four of the world's top five leading soft drinks: Coke, Diet Coke, Fanta, and Sprite. It also sells other brands including Powerade, Minute Maid, and Dansani bottled water. The company operates the largest distribution system in the world, which enables it to serve customers and businesses in more than two hundred countries. Coca-Cola estimates that more than 1 billion servings of its products are consumed every day. For much of its early history, Coca-Cola focused on cultivating markets within the United States.

Coca-Cola and its archrival, PepsiCo, have long fought the "cola wars" in the United States, but Coca-Cola, recognizing additional market potential, pursued international opportunities in an effort to dominate the global soft-drink industry. By 1993 Coca-Cola controlled 45 percent of the global soft-drink market, while PepsiCo received just 15 percent of its profits from international sales. By the late 1990s, Coca-Cola had gained more than 50 percent of the global market in the soft-drink industry. Pepsi continued to target select international markets to gain a greater foothold in international markets. Since 1996 Coca-Cola has focused on traditional soft drinks, and PepsiCo has gained a strong foothold on new-age drinks, has signed a partnership with Starbucks, and has expanded rapidly into the snack-food business. PepsiCo's Frito-Lay division has 60 percent of the U.S. snack-food market. Coca-Cola, on the other hand, does much of its business outside of the United States, and 85 percent of its sales now come from outside the United States. As the late Roberto Goizueta once said, "Coca-Cola used to be an American company with a large international business. Now we are a large international company with a sizable American business."

Coca-Cola has been a successful company since its inception in the late 1800s. PepsiCo, although founded about the same time as Coca-Cola, did not become a strong competitor until after World War II when it began to gain market share. The rivalry intensified in the mid-1960s, and the "cola wars" began in earnest. Today, the duopoly wages war primarily on several international fronts. The companies are engaged in an extremely competitive—and sometimes personal—rivalry, with occasional accusations of false market-share reports, anticompetitive behavior, and other questionable business conduct, but without this fierce competition, neither would be as good a company as it is today.

By January 2006, PepsiCo had a market value greater than Coca-Cola for the first time ever. Its strategy of focusing on snack foods and innovative strategies in the non-cola beverage market helped the company gain market share and surpass Coca-Cola in overall performance.

COCA-COLA'S REPUTATION

Coca-Cola is the most-recognized trademark and brand name in the world today with a trademark value estimated to be about $25 billion. The company has always demonstrated a strong market orientation, making strategic decisions and taking actions to attract, satisfy, and retain customers. During World War II, for example, company president Robert Woodruff committed to selling Coke to members of the armed services for just a nickel a bottle. As one analyst said later, "Customer loyalty never came cheaper." This philosophy helped make Coke a truly global brand, with its trademark brands and colors recognizable on cans, bottles, and advertisements around the world. The advance of Coca-Cola products into almost every country in the world demonstrated the company's international market orientation and improved its ability to gain brand recognition. These efforts contributed to the company's strong reputation.

However, in 2000 Coca-Cola failed to make the top ten of *Fortune*'s annual "America's Most Admired Companies" list for the first time in a decade. Problems at the company were leadership issues, poor economic performance, and other upheavals. The company also dropped out of the top one hundred in *Business Ethics'* annual list of "100 Best Corporate Citizens" in 2001. For a company that spent years on both lists, this was disappointing, but perhaps not unexpected, given several ethical crises.

Coca-Cola's promise is that the company exists "to benefit and refresh everyone who is touched by our business." It has successfully done this by continually increasing market share and profits with Coca-Cola being the most-recognized brand in the world. Because the company is so well known, the industry so pervasive, and a strong history of market orientation, the company has developed a number of social responsibility initiatives to enhance its trademarks. These initiatives are guided by the company's core beliefs in the marketplace, workplace, community, and environment. For example, Coke wants to inspire moments of optimism through their brands and their actions, as well as creating value and making a difference everywhere they do business. Their vision for sustainable growth is fostered by being a great place to work where people are inspired to be the best they can be, by bringing the world a portfolio of beverage brands that anticipate and satisfy peoples' desires and needs, by being a responsible global citizen that makes a difference, and by maximizing return to shareowners while being mindful of their overall responsibilities.

SOCIAL RESPONSIBILITY FOCUS

Coca-Cola has made local education and community improvement programs a top priority for its philanthropic initiatives. Coca-Cola foundations "support the promise of a better life for people and their communities." For example, Coca-Cola is involved in a program called "Education on Wheels" in Singapore where history is brought to life in an interactive discovery adventure for children. In an interactive classroom bus, children are engaged in a three-hour drama specially written for the program. It challenges creativity and initiatives while enhancing communication skills as children discover new insights into life in the city.

Coca-Cola also offers grants to various colleges and universities in more than half of the United States, as well as numerous international grants. In addition to grants, Coca-Cola provides scholarships to more than 170 colleges, and this number is expected to grow to 287 over the next four years. It includes 30 tribal colleges belonging to the American Indian College Fund. Coca-Cola is also involved with the Hispanic Scholarship Fund. Such initiatives help enhance the Coca-Cola name and trademark and thus ultimately benefit shareholders. Each year 250 new Coca-Cola Scholars are designated and invited to Atlanta for personal interviews. Fifty students are then designated as National Scholars and receive awards of $20,000 for college; the remaining 200 are designated as Regional Scholars and receive $4,000 awards. Since the program's inception in 1986, a total of over twenty-five hundred Coca-Cola scholars have benefited from nearly $22 million for education. The program is open to all high school seniors in the United States.

The company recognizes its responsibilities on a global scale and continues to take action to uphold this responsibility, such as taking steps not to harm the environment while acquiring goods and setting up facilities. The company is proactive on local issues, such as HIV/AIDS in Africa, and has partnered with UNAIDS and other non-government organizations to put into place important initiatives and programs to help combat the threat of the HIV/AIDS epidemic.

Because consumers trust its products, and develop strong attachments through brand recognition and product loyalty, Coca-Cola's actions also foster relationship marketing. For these reasons, problems at a firm like Coca-Cola can stir the emotions of many stakeholders.

CRISIS SITUATIONS

The following documents a series of alleged misconduct and questionable behavior affecting Coca-Cola stakeholders. These ethical and legal problems appear to have had an impact on Coca-Cola's financial performance, with its stock trading today at the same price it did ten years ago. The various ethical crises have been associated with turnover in top management, departure of key investors, and the loss of reputation. There seems to be no end to these events as major crises continue to develop. It is important to try to understand why Coca-Cola has not been able to eliminate these events that have been so destructive to the company.

Contamination Scare

Perhaps the most damaging of Coca-Cola's crises—and the situation that every company dreads—began in June 1999, when about thirty Belgian children became ill after consuming Coca-Cola products. Although the company recalled the product, the problem soon escalated. The Belgian government eventually ordered the recall of all Coca-Cola products, leading officials in Luxembourg and the Netherlands to recall all Coca-Cola products as well. The company eventually determined that the illnesses were the result of a poorly processed batch of carbon dioxide. Coca-Cola took several days to comment formally on the problem, which the media quickly labeled a slow response. Coca-Cola initially judged the situation to be minor and not a health hazard, but by that time a public relations nightmare had begun. France soon reported more than one hundred people sick and banned all Coca-Cola products until the problem was resolved. Soon after, a shipment of Bonaqua, a new Coca-Cola water product, arrived in Poland, contaminated with mold. In each instance, the company's slow response and failure to acknowledge the severity of the situation harmed its reputation.

The contamination crisis was exacerbated in December 1999 when Belgium ordered Coca-Cola to halt its "Restore" marketing campaign in order to regain consumer trust and sales in Belgium. A rival firm claimed that the campaign strategy that included free cases of the product, discounts to wholesalers and retailers, and extra promotion personnel was intended to illegally strengthen Coca-Cola's market share. Under Belgium's strict antitrust laws, the claim was upheld, and Coca-Cola abandoned the campaign. This decision, along with the others, reduced Coca-Cola's market standing in Europe.

Competitive Issues

Questions about Coca-Cola's market dominance started government inquiries into its marketing tactics. Because most European countries have very strict antitrust laws, all firms must pay close attention to market share and position when considering joint ventures, mergers, and acquisitions. During the summer of 1999, Coca-Cola became very aggressive in the French market. As a result, the French government responded by refusing to approve Coca-Cola's bid to purchase Orangina, a French beverage company. French authorities also forced Coca-Cola to scale back its acquisition of Cadbury Schweppes, another beverage maker. Moreover, Italy successfully won a court case against Coca-Cola over anticompetitive prices in 1999, prompting the European Commission to launch a full-scale probe of the company's competitive practices. PepsiCo and Virgin accused Coca-Cola of using rebates and discounts to crowd their products off shelves, thereby gaining greater market share. Coca-Cola's strong-arm tactics proved to be in violation of European laws and once again demonstrated the company's lack of awareness of European culture and laws.

Despite these legal tangles, Coca-Cola products, along with many other U.S. products, dominate foreign markets throughout the world. According to some European officials, the pain that U.S. automakers felt in the 1970s because of Japanese imports is the same pain that U.S. firms are meting out in Europe. The growing omnipresence of U.S. products, especially in highly competitive markets, is why corporate reputation—both perceived and actual—is so important to relationships with business partners, government officials, and other stakeholders.

Racial Discrimination Allegations

In the spring of 1999, initially fifteen hundred African American employees sued Coca-Cola for racial discrimination but eventually grew to include two thousand current and former employees. Coca-Cola was accused of discriminating against them in pay, promotions, and performance evaluations. Plaintiffs charged that the company grouped African American workers at the bottom of the pay scale, where they typically earned $26,000 a year less than Caucasian employees in comparable jobs. The suit also alleged that top management had known of the discrimination since 1995 but had done nothing. Although in 1992 Coca-Cola had pledged to spend $1 billion on goods and services from minority vendors, it did not seem to apply to their workers.

Although Coca-Cola strongly denied the allegations, the lawsuit evoked strong reactions. To reduce collateral damage, Coca-Cola created a diversity council and paid $193 million to settle the racial discrimination lawsuit.

Problems with the Burger King Market Test

In 2002 Coca-Cola ran into more troubles when Matthew Whitley, a mid-level Coca-Cola executive, filed a whistle-blowing suit, alleging retaliation for revealing fraud in a market study performed on behalf of Burger King. To increase sales, Coca-Cola suggested that Burger King invest in and promote frozen Coke as a child's snack. The fast-food chain arranged to test market the product for three weeks in Richmond, Virginia, and evaluate the results before agreeing to roll out the new product nationally. The test market involved customers receiving a coupon for a free frozen Coke when they purchased a Value Meal (sandwich, fries, and drink). Burger King executives wanted to be cautious about the new product because of the enormous investment that each restaurant would require to distribute and promote the product. Restaurants would need to purchase equipment to make the frozen drink, buy extra syrup, and spend a percentage of their advertising funds to promote the new product.

When results of the test marketing began coming in to Coca-Cola, sales of frozen Coke were grim. Coca-Cola countered the bad statistics by giving at least one individual $10,000 to take hundreds of children to Burger King to purchase Value Meals including the frozen Coke. Coca-Cola's action netted seven hundred additional Value Meals out of nearly one hundred thousand sold during the entire promotion. But when the U.S. attorney general for the North District of Georgia discovered and investigated the fraud, the company had to pay $21 million to Burger King, $540,000 to the whistle-blower, and a $9 million pretax write-off had to be taken. Although Coca-Cola disputes the allegations, the cost of manipulating the frozen Coke research cost the company considerably in negative publicity, criminal investigations, a soured relationship with a major customer, and a loss of stakeholder trust.

Inflated Earnings Related to Channel Stuffing

Another problem that Coca-Cola faced during this period was accusations of channel stuffing. *Channel stuffing* is the practice of shipping extra inventory to wholesalers and retailers at an excessive rate, typically before the end of a quarter. Essentially, a company counts the shipments as sales although the products often remain in warehouses or are later returned to the manufacturer. Channel stuffing tends to create the appearance of strong demand (or conceals declining demand) for a product, which may result in inflated financial statement earnings thus misleading investors.

Coke was accused of sending extra concentrate to Japanese bottlers from 1997 through 1999 in an effort to inflate profits. In 2004 Coca-Cola reported finding statements of inflated earnings due to the company's shipping extra concentrate to Japan. Although the company settled the allegations, the Securities and Exchange Commission (SEC) did find that channel stuffing had occurred. Coca-Cola had pressured bottlers into buying additional concentrate in exchange for extended credit, which is technically considered legitimate.

To settle with the SEC, Coca-Cola agreed to avoid engaging in channel stuffing in the future. The company also created an ethics and compliance office and is required to verify each financial quarter that it has not altered the terms of payment or extended special credit. The company further agreed to work on reducing the amount of concentrate held by international bottlers. Although it settled with the SEC and the Justice Department, it still faces a shareholder lawsuit regarding channel stuffing in Japan, North America, Europe, and South Africa.

Trouble with Distributors

In early 2006, Coca-Cola faced problems with its bottlers, after fifty-four of them filed lawsuits seeking to block Coca-Cola from expanding delivery of Powerade sports drinks directly to Wal-Mart warehouses beyond the limited Texas test area. Bottlers alleged that the Powerade bottler contract did not permit warehouse delivery except for commissaries and that Coca-Cola had materially breached the agreement by committing to provide warehouse delivery of Powerade to Wal-Mart and by proposing to use a subsidiary, CCE, as its agent for warehouse delivery.

The problem was that Coca-Cola was trying to step away from the century-old tradition of direct-store delivery, known as DSD, wherein bottlers drop off product at individual stores, stock shelves, and build merchandising displays. Coca-Cola and CCE assert they were simply trying to accommodate a request from Wal-Mart for warehouse delivery, which is how PepsiCo distributes its Gatorade brand. CCE had also proposed making payments to some other bottlers in return for taking over Powerade distribution in their exclusive territories. But the bottlers had concerns that such an arrangement would violate antitrust laws and claimed that if Coca-Cola and CCE went forward with their warehouse delivery, it would greatly diminish the value of the bottlers' businesses.

The problems faced by Coca-Cola were reported negatively by the media and had a negative effect on Coca-Cola's reputation. When the reputation of one company within a channel structure suffers, all firms within the supply chain suffer in some way or another. This was especially true because Coca-Cola adopted an enterprise resource system that linked Coca-Cola's once almost classified information to a host of partners. Thus, the company's less-than-stellar handling of the ethical crises has introduced a lack of integrity in its partnerships. Although some of the crises had nothing to do with the information shared across the new system, the partners still assume greater risk because of their relationships with Coca-Cola. The interdependence between Coca-Cola and its partners requires a diplomatic and considerate view of the business and its effects on various stakeholders. Thus, these crises harmed Coco-Cola's partner companies, their stakeholders, and eventually, their bottom lines.

International Problems Related to Unions

Around the same time, Coca-Cola also faced intense criticism in Colombia where unions were making progress inside Coke's plants. Coincidently, at the same time, eight Coca-Cola workers died, forty-eight went into hiding, and sixty-five received death threats. The union alleges that Coca-Cola and its local bottler were complicit in these cases and is seeking reparations to the families of the slain and displaced workers. Coca-Cola denies the allegations, noting that only one of the eight workers was killed on the premises of the bottling plant. Also, the other deaths, all occurred off premises and could have been the result of Colombia's four-decade-long civil war.

Coke Employees Offer to Sell Trade Secrets

A Coca-Cola administrative secretary and two accomplices were arrested in 2006 and charged in a criminal complaint with wire fraud and unlawfully stealing and selling trade secrets from the Coca-Cola Company. The accused contacted PepsiCo executives and indicated that an individual identifying himself as "Dirk," who claimed to be employed at a high level with Coca-Cola, offered "very detailed and confidential information." When Coca-Cola received the letter from PepsiCo about the offer, the FBI was contacted, and an undercover FBI investigation began. The FBI determined that "Dirk" was Ibrahim Dimson of Bronx, New York. Dirk provided an FBI undercover agent with fourteen pages of Coca-Cola logo-marked "Classified—Confidential" and "CLASSIFIED—Highly Restricted." In addition, Dirk also provided samples of Coca-Cola top-secret products. The source of the information was Joya Williams, an executive administrative assistant for Coca-Cola's global brand director in Atlanta, who had access to some information and materials described by "Dirk." Employees should be held responsible for protecting intellectual property, and this breach of confidence by a Coca-Cola employee was a serious ethical issue.

ETHICAL RECOVERY?

Despite Coca-Cola's problems, consumers surveyed after the European contamination indicated they felt that Coca-Cola would still behave correctly during times of crises. The company also ranked third globally in a PricewaterhouseCoopers survey of most-respected companies. Coca-Cola managed to retain its strong ranking while other companies facing setbacks, including Colgate-Palmolive and Procter & Gamble, were dropped or fell substantially in the rankings.

Coca-Cola has taken the initiative to counter diversity protests. The racial discrimination lawsuit, along with the threat of a boycott by the NAACP, led to Daft's plan to counter racial discrimination. The plan was designed to help Coca-Cola improve employment of minorities.

When Coca-Cola settled the racial discrimination lawsuit, the agreement stipulated that the company (1) donate $50 million to a foundation to support programs in minority communities, (2) hire an ombudsman who would report directly to CEO Daft, (3) investigate complaints of discrimination and harassment, and (4) set aside $36 million for a seven-person task force and authorize it to oversee the company's employment practices. The task force includes business and civil rights experts and is to have unprecedented power to dictate company policy with regard to hiring, compensating, and promoting women and minorities. Despite the unusual provision to grant such power to an outside panel, Daft said, "We need to have outside people helping us. We would be foolish to cut ourselves off from the outside world."

Belgian officials closed their investigation of the health scare involving Coca-Cola and announced that no charges would be filed against the company. A Belgian health report indicated that no toxic contamination had been found in Coke bottles, even though the bottles were found to have contained tiny traces of carbonyl sulfide, which produces a rotten-egg smell; the amount of carbonyl sulfide would have to have been a thousand times higher to be toxic. Officials also reported that they found no structural problems with Coca-Cola's production plant and that the company had cooperated fully throughout the investigation.

CURRENT SITUATION AT COCA-COLA

While Coca-Cola's financial performance continues to lag, one issue that may have great impact on the success of the company is its relationship with distributors. Lawsuits that distributors have launched against Coca-Cola for its attempt to bypass them with Powerade have the potential of destroying trust and cooperation in the future. Other issues related to channel stuffing and falsifying market tests to customers indicate a willingness by management to bend the rules to increase the bottom line.

Although Coca-Cola seems to be trying to establish its reputation based on quality products and socially responsible activities, it has failed to manage ethical decision making in dealing with various stakeholders. An important question to consider is whether Coca-Cola's strong emphasis on social responsibility, especially philanthropic and environmental concerns, can help the company maintain its reputation in the face of highly public ethical conflict and crises.

CEO Isdell developed a two-year turnaround plan focused on new products, and the company created one thousand new products, including coffee-flavored Coca-Cola Blak to be marketed as an energy beverage and soft drink. The company is also adopting new-age drinks such as lower-calorie Powerade sports drink and flavored Dasani water. These moves are an attempt to catch up with PepsiCo who has become the noncarbonated-beverage leader. Coca-Cola continues developing products such as bottled coffee called Far Coast and black and green tea drinks called Gold Peak. Although PepsiCo has outexecuted Coca-Cola since 1996, Coca-Cola still has a 50 percent market share, but PepsiCo has become the larger company in 2006 and Coca-Cola's long-term earnings and sales have been lowered. If so many ethical issues had not distracted Coca-Cola, would its financial performance have been much better?

QUESTIONS

1. Why do you think Coca-Cola has had one ethical issue to resolve after another over the last decade or so?
2. A news analyst said that Coca-Cola could become the next Enron. Do you think this is possible and defend your answer?
3. What should Coca-Cola do to restore its reputation and eliminate future ethical dilemmas with stakeholders?

SOURCES: Elise Ackerman, "It's the Real Thing: A Crisis at Coca-Cola," *U.S. News & World Report,* October 4, 1999, 40–41; Ronald Alsop, "Corporate Reputations Are Earned with Trust, Reliability, Study Shows," *Wall Street Journal* online, September 23, 1999, http://interactive.wsj.com; "America's Most Admired Companies," *Fortune,* February 8, 2000, via www.pathfinder.com/fortune; "America's Most Admired Companies," *Fortune* online, www.fortune.com/fortune/mostadmired/(accessed

December 17, 2002); Paul Ames, "Case Closed on Coke Health Scare," Associated Press, April 22, 2000; Dan Beucke, "Coke Promises a Probe in Colombia," *BusinessWeek,* February 6, 2006, 11; James Bone, "Three Charged with Stealing Coca-Cola Trade Secrets," *Times Online,* July 6, 2006, http://www.timesonline.co.uk/printfriendly/0,,1-3-2259092-3,00.html (accessed July 7, 2006); Katrina Brooker, "The Pepsi Machine," *Fortune,* February 6, 2006, 68–72; Mary Jane Credeur, "Coke Poured Out 1000 New Products in 2005, Two-Year Turnaround Plan on Track, CEO Says," *USA Today,* December 8, 2005, B5; Coca-Cola Company, www2.coca-cola.com (accessed August 21, 2003); "Coca-Cola Introduces 'Real' Marketing Platform," *PR Newswire,* January 9, 2003, accessed via Lexis Nexis; "Coca-Cola Names E. Neville Isdell Chairman and Chief Executive Officer Elect," Coca-Cola press release, May 4, 2004, http://www2.coca-cola.com/presscenter/pc_include/nr_20040504 (accessed May 17, 2006); "Coke Rapped for Restore," *The Grocer,* December 4, 1999, 14; "Corporate Reputation in the Hands of Chief Executive," *Westchester County Business Journal,* May 18, 1998, 17; Patrick Crosby, "DOJ Statement, Evidence In Coke Trade-Secrets Case," *Wall Street Journal* online, July 5, 2006, http://online.wsj.com/article_print/SB115213927958898855.html (accessed July 7, 2006); T. C. Doyle, "Channel Stuffing Rears Its Ugly Head," *VARBusiness* online, May 6, 2003, www.varbusiness .com/showArticle.jhtml;jsessionid=PCVHTC511CHQ0QSNDBCSKHSCJUMEKJVN?article ID=18823602; James Faier, "The Name Is the Game," *Retail Traffic* online, http://retailtrafficmag .com/mag/retail_name_game/index.html (accessed May 15, 2006); Sharon Foley, "Cola Wars Continue: Coke vs. Pepsi in the 1990s," Harvard Business School Press, April 10, 1995, Case 9-794-055; Dean Foust and Geri Smith, "'Killer Coke' or Innocent Abroad? Controversy over Anti-Union Violence in Colombia Has Colleges Banning Coca-Cola," *BusinessWeek,* January 23, 2006, 46–48; "FYI," *Incentive* 176 (2002): 67; "Grand Jury to Investigate Coke on Channel Stuffing Allegations," *Atlanta Business Chronicle* online, May 3, 2004, http://atlanta.bizjournals.com/atlanta.stories/ 2004/05/03/daily2.html; Ann Harrington, "Prevention Is the Best Defense," *Fortune,* July 10, 2000, 188; Constance Hays, "Coca-Cola to Cut Fifth of Workers in a Big Pullback," *New York Times,* January 27, 2000, A1; Ernest Holsendolph, "Facing Suit, Coca-Cola Steps Up Diversity Efforts," *Atlanta Journal and Constitution,* May 27, 1999, F1; Anita Howarth, "Coca-Cola Struggles to Refurbish Image After Recent European Troubles," *Daily Mail,* January 16, 2000, accessed via Lexis Nexis Academic Universe; Tammy Joyner, "Generous Severance Packages," *Atlanta Journal and Constitution,* January 27, 2000, E1; Jeremy Kahn, "The World's Most Admired Companies," *Fortune,* October 11, 1999, 267–275; Marjorie Kelly, "100 Best Corporate Citizens," *Business Ethics* (Spring 2006): 23–24; Scott Leith, "Where Has Daft Been?" *Atlanta Journal and Constitution,* December 1, 2002, 1Q; Betty Lui, "Think of Us as a Local Company," *Financial Times,* January 20, 2003, 6; Betsy McKay and Chad Terhune, "Coca-Cola Settles Regulatory Probe; Deal Resolves Allegations by SEC That Firm Padded Profit by Channel Stuffing," *Wall Street Journal,* via http://proquest.umi.com/pqweb?did=823831501 &sid=1&Fmt=3&clientId=2945&RQT=309&Vname=PQD (accessed November 8, 2005); Betsy Morris and Patricia Sellers, "What Really Happened at Coke," *Fortune,* January 10, 2000, 114–116; Dan Morse and Ann Carrns, "Coke Rated 'Acceptable' on Diversity," *Wall Street Journal,* September 26, 2002, A9; Jon Pepper, "Europe Resents That Europeans Much Prefer to Buy American," *Detroit News* online, November 10, 1999, http://detnews.com/1999/business/9911/10/11100025.htm; Jordan T. Pine, "Coke Counters Protests with New Diversity Commitment," *Diversity Inc.* online, March 13, 2000, www.diversityinc.com; V. L. Ramsey, "$1 Billion Pledged to Vendors," *Black Enterprise,* July 1992, 22; Maria Saporta, "Transition at Coca-Cola: Ivester Paid a Price for Going It Alone," *Atlanta Journal and Constitution,* December 8, 1999, F1; "Second Annual List of '100 Best Corporate Citizens' Quantifies Stakeholder Service," *Business Ethics* online, www.business-ethics.com/newpage24.htm (accessed December 17, 2002); Patricia Sellers, "Coke's CEO Doug Daft Has to Clean Up the Big Spill," *Fortune,* March 6, 2000, 58–59; Christopher Seward, "Company Forewarned: Meaning of Goizueta's '96 Letter Echoes Today," *Atlanta Journal and Constitution,* January 27, 2000, E4; Chad Terhune, "Bottlers' Suit Challenge Coke Distribution Plan," *Wall Street Journal,* February 18–19, 2006, A5; Chad Terhune, "A Suit by Coke Bottlers Exposes Cracks in a Century-Old System," *Wall Street Journal,* March 13, 2006, A1; "Top 75: The Greatest Management Decisions Ever Made," *Management Review,* November 1998, 20–23; Henry Unger, "Revised Suit Cites Coca-Cola Execs," *Atlanta Journal and Constitution,* December 21, 1999, D1; Greg Winter, "Bias Suit Ends in Changes for Coke," *Austin American-Statesman* online, November 17, 2000, http://austin360.com/statesman.

The Fall of Enron: A Stakeholder Failure

Once upon a time, there was a gleaming headquarters office tower in Houston, with a giant tilted "E" in front, slowly revolving in the Texas sun. The Enron Corporation, which once ranked among the top *Fortune 500* companies, collapsed in 2001 under a mountain of debt that had been concealed through a complex scheme of off-balance-sheet partnerships and investor loss of confidence. Forced to declare bankruptcy, the energy firm laid off five thousand employees; thousands more lost their retirement savings, which had been invested in Enron stock. The company's shareholders lost tens of billions of dollars after the stock price plummeted. The scandal surrounding Enron's demise engendered a global loss of confidence in corporate integrity that continues to plague markets, and eventually it triggered tough new scrutiny of financial reporting practices such as the Sarbanes–Oxley Act in 2002. To understand what went wrong, let's examine the history, culture, and major players in the Enron scandal.

HISTORY

The Enron Corporation was created out of the merger of two major gas pipeline companies in 1985. Through its subsidiaries and numerous affiliates, the company provided products and services related to natural gas, electricity, and communications for its wholesale and retail customers. Enron transported natural gas through pipelines to customers all over the United States. It generated, transmitted, and distributed electricity to the northwestern United States and marketed natural gas, electricity, and other commodities globally. It was also involved in the development, construction, and operation of power plants, pipelines, and other energy-related projects all over the

We appreciate the work of Neil Herndon, who wrote the previous edition of this case under the direction of O. C. Ferrell, and Melanie Drever, who assisted in this edition. This case is for classroom discussion rather than to illustrate either effective or ineffective handling of an administrative, ethical, or legal decision by management. All sources used for this case were obtained through publicly available material and the Enron website.

world, including the delivery and management of energy to retail customers in both the industrial and commercial business sectors.

Throughout the 1990s, Chairman Kenneth Lay, chief executive officer (CEO) Jeffrey Skilling, and chief financial officer (CFO) Andrew Fastow transformed Enron from an old-style electricity and gas company into a $150 billion energy company and Wall Street favorite that traded power contracts in the investment markets. From 1998 to 2000 alone, Enron's revenues grew from about $31 billion to more than $100 billion, making it the seventh-largest company of the *Fortune* 500. Enron's wholesale energy income represented about 93 percent of 2000 revenues, with another 4 percent derived from natural gas and electricity. The remaining 3 percent came from broadband services and exploration. Enron-Online—the company's worldwide Internet trading platform—completed on average over five thousand transactions per day, buying and selling over eighteen hundred separate products online that generated over $2.5 billion in business every day.

There was every reason to believe that Enron was still financially sound in the third quarter of 2001, even though a bankruptcy examiner later reported a discrepancy in Enron's claimed net income and cash flow. This was done under certain accounting assumptions after the bankruptcy. For the third quarter of 2001, Enron's wholesale business generated a potential $754 million of earnings (before interest and taxes), an increase of 35 percent from the previous year. This represented over 80 percent of Enron's worldwide earnings. It was acknowledged by all parties that Enron's wholesale business was highly profitable and growing at a rapid rate. Even in the fourth quarter of 2001, Lay believed that Enron was still a growing viable company for the long run, based on physical volume moving through the pipelines.

A Timeline of the Enron Scandal

1985   Houston Natural Gas merges with Omaha-based InterNorth; the resulting company is eventually named Enron Corporation. Ken Lay, who had been CEO of Houston Natural Gas, becomes chairman and CEO the following year.

2000   Annual revenues reach $100 billion, and the Energy Financial Group ranks Enron as the sixth-largest energy company in the world, based on market capitalization.

February 2001   Jeff Skilling takes over as CEO. Lay remains chairman.

August 2001   Skilling unexpectedly resigns for "personal reasons," and Lay steps back into the CEO job. That same month, a letter from an Enron executive raises serious questions about the company's business and accounting practices.

October 2001   Enron releases third-quarter earnings, showing $1 billion in charges, including $35 million related to investment partnerships headed by Andrew Fastow, Enron's former CFO. Fastow is replaced as CFO.

October 22, 2001   Enron announces that the Securities and Exchange Commission (SEC) has launched a formal investigation into its "related party transactions."

November 8, 2001   Enron restates earnings for 1997 through 2000 and the first three quarters of 2001.

December 2, 2001   Enron files for protection from creditors in a New York bankruptcy court.

December 3, 2001   Enron announces that it is laying off four thousand employees.

January 9, 2002   The Justice Department announces that it is pursuing a criminal investigation of Enron.

(continued)

A Timeline of the Enron Scandal (continued)

January 14, 2002   U.S. House and Senate lawmakers return campaign contributions from Enron.

January 24, 2002   Lay resigns as chairman and CEO of Enron. The first of at least eight congressional hearings on Enron begins.

January 30, 2002   Enron names Stephen Cooper, a restructuring specialist, as acting CEO.

February 4, 2002   A report by a special committee of Enron's board investigating the energy trader's collapse portrays a company riddled with improper financial transactions and extensive self-dealing by company officials.

May 2, 2002   Enron announces plans to reorganize as a small company with a new name.

October 2, 2002   Fastow voluntarily surrenders to federal authorities after prosecutors indicate they will file charges for his role in the company's collapse.

October 31, 2002   Fastow is indicted on seventy-eight counts of masterminding a scheme to artificially inflate the energy company's profits.

February 3, 2003   Creditors of Enron sue Lay and his wife, Linda, to recover more than $70 million in transfers.

July 11, 2003   Enron finally announces a plan to restructure and pay off creditors after five deadline extensions.

July 2003   J. P. Morgan Chase and Citigroup pay nearly $300 million to settle allegations from the SEC, New York State and New York City, that they helped Enron manipulate its financial statements and mislead investors.

September 2003   Merrill Lynch avoids prosecution related to the Nigerian barge deal by acknowledging that some employees may have broken the law and by implementing reforms.

October 2003   Wesley Colwell, former chief accounting officer for Enron's trading unit, agrees to pay $500,000 to settle SEC allegations of manipulating earnings by using trading profits to offset massive losses in Enron's retail energy unit. He is still cooperating with the Justice Department but faces no criminal charges.

December 2003   Canadian Imperial Bank of Commerce avoids prosecution by accepting responsibility for crimes committed by employees who knowingly participated in complicated transactions that wrongly moved assets off of Enron's balance sheet so that the energy company could inflate earnings.

April 30, 2003   Fastow's wife, Lea, is charged with tax crimes and conspiracy for participating in husband's deals.

September 10, 2003   Former Enron treasurer Glisan pleads guilty to conspiracy and is sentenced to five years in prison.

January 14, 2004   Andrew Fastow pleads guilty to two counts of conspiracy and agrees to serve ten years in prison.

January 22, 2004   Causey pleads innocent to conspiracy and fraud charges.

February 19, 2004   Skilling, added to the Causey indictment, pleads innocent to more than thirty criminal counts including conspiracy, fraud, and inside trading.

May 6, 2004   Lea Fastow pleads guilty to filing a false tax form and is sentenced to the maximum sentence of one year in prison.

July 8, 2004   Lay surrenders after being indicted. He pleads innocent.

July 15, 2004   Bankruptcy judge confirms Enron's reorganization plan in which most creditors will receive about one-fifth of the about $63 billion they're owed in cash and stock.

October 19, 2004   Federal judge grants Lay a separate bank fraud trial but rules that Lay, Skilling, and Causey will be tried together on other charges.

February 2005   Raymond Bowen, Jr., finance chief at Enron from the aftermath of its failure through his resignation in October 2004, agrees to pay $500,000 to settle SEC allegations that he knew or should have known some assets were grossly overvalued to falsely inflate profits. Bowen did not admit or deny the allegations and faces no criminal charges.

(continued)

A Timeline of the Enron Scandal (continued)

May 31, 2005   The Supreme Court overturns the Arthur Andersen conviction.

December 28, 2005   Causey pleads guilty to securities fraud and agrees to serve seven years in prison in exchange for cooperating with the government.

January 30, 2006   The Lay and Skilling trial begins.

May 25, 2006   Lay and Skilling are convicted of conspiracy to commit securities and wire fraud. Lay is convicted in a separate bank fraud case.

July 5, 2006   Lay dies of a heart attack, erasing his conviction. A person who dies before an appeal is not considered convicted.

SOURCES: "A Chronology of Enron's Woes: The Accounting Debacle," *Wall Street Journal* online, March 20, 2003, http://online.wsj.com; "A Chronology of Enron's Woes: The Investigation," *Wall Street Journal* online, March 20, 2003, http://online.wsj.com; "Enron Timeline," *Houston Chronicle* online, January 17, 2002, http://www.chron.com/cs/CDA/story.hts/special/enron/1127125; Kristen Hays, "16 Cents on $1 for Enron Creditors," *Austin American-Statesman* online, July 12, 2003, http://www.statesman.com; "Key Dates Leading to Convictions of Lay, Skilling," *USA Today,* May 26, 2006, 3B; Associated Press; "Enron Who's Who," *USA Today* online, http://www.usatoday.com/money/industries/energy/2006-01-26-enron-whos-who_x.htm (accessed June 1, 2006).

ENRON'S CORPORATE CULTURE

When describing Enron's corporate culture, people like to use the words *arrogant* or *prideful,* perhaps justifiably. The firm employed competent, creative, and hard-working employees and recruited the best and brightest graduates from top universities. In 2001 *Fortune* magazine ranked Enron the twenty-second best company to work for in America. A large banner in the lobby at corporate headquarters proclaimed Enron "The World's Leading Company," and Enron executives blithely believed that competitors had no chance against it. Skilling even went so far as to tell utility executives at a conference that he was going to "eat their lunch." There was an overwhelming aura of pride, carrying with it the deep-seated belief that Enron's people could handle increasing risk without danger.

The culture also was about a focus on how much money could be made for many executives, at many levels, that shared in a stock option incentive program. For example, after the Enron collapse, it was alleged that Enron's compensation plans seemed less concerned with generating profits for shareholders than with enriching employee wealth. This may have been the result of the highly competent and aggressive employee culture that was motivated by the desire to improve their financial position. Enron's corporate culture reportedly encouraged risky behavior, if not breaking the rules.

Skilling appears to be the executive who created a system in which Enron's employees were rated every six months, with those ranked in the bottom 20 percent forced out. This "rank-and-yank" system helped create a fierce environment in which employees competed against rivals not only outside the company but also at the next desk. Delivering bad news could result in the "death" of the messenger, so problems in the trading operation, for example, were covered up rather than being communicated to management.

Lay once said that he felt that one of the great successes at Enron was the creation of a corporate culture in which people could reach their full potential. He said that he wanted it to be a highly moral and ethical culture and that he tried to ensure that people did in fact honor the values of respect, integrity, and excellence. On his desk was an Enron paperweight with the slogan "Vision and Values." Lay maintained that he was always concerned about ethics, and he continued to discuss the ethical and legal ramifications of the Enron disaster even after his conviction. The business ethics issue involved in his indictment was that he lied about the financial condition of Enron, but he continued to maintain that he had openly dealt with all issues that were brought to his attention. Some of the people inside Enron believed that nearly anything could be turned into a financial product and, with the aid of complex statistical modeling, traded for profit. Short on assets and heavily reliant on intellectual capital, Enron's corporate culture rewarded innovation and punished employees deemed weak. An important question is, How much does a CEO know about misconduct in a corporation?

Aggressive and highly intelligent Enron employees, in many divisions, were "pushing the limits" and bending the rules to achieve success. This highly competitive risk culture existed in a corporation that was trying to redefine how the energy industry did business. Lawyers, accountants, and the board of directors approved key decisions. As intelligent and creative as Enron's executives were, no one person, under Enron's organizational system of checks and balances, could orchestrate the schemes that created the demise of a company that large. The downfall took many layers of "pushing the envelope" and a great deal of complacency on the part of employees who, at many levels in the organization, saw wrongdoing and ignored it. To some extent, the Enron failure was the result of a free-enterprise system that rewarded risk taking and a corporate culture that pushed complex financial decisions to the edge. In addition, the right environmental conditions evolved in the financial markets, especially the dot-com bubble, contributing to Enron's stock collapse. Enron was the perfect corporate storm (or disaster) that required many failures by multiple stakeholders.

ENRON'S ACCOUNTING PROBLEMS

Enron's bankruptcy in December 2001 was the largest in U.S. corporate history at the time. The bankruptcy filing came after a series of revelations that the giant energy trader had been using partnerships, also called special-purpose entities (SPEs). These off-balance-sheet financing approaches are the heart of losses and write-offs that turned Enron into a disaster. In a meeting with Enron's lawyers in August 2001, the company's then CFO, Fastow, stated that Enron had established the SPEs to move assets and debt off its balance sheet and to increase cash flow by showing that funds were flowing through its books when it sold assets. Although these practices produced a very favorable financial picture, outside observers believed they might constitute fraudulent financial reporting because they did not accurately represent the company's true financial condition.

According to John C. Coffee, Columbia University law professor, once formed by Enron, the SPEs would then borrow debt from banks, and Enron would typically guarantee that debt. Although such guarantees are not unusual when SPEs are used, far less common (and indeed unique) was the fact that the principal asset of many Enron SPEs was Enron restricted stock. Thus, if Enron's stock price declined, the SPE's assets would be insufficient to cover the bank debt, and Enron would have to assume it.

In reality, these SPEs were legal entities, and many investment banks were involved as third-party investors becoming partners in these entities. Most companies engage in third-party transactions to move debt off the balance sheet. For example, a company builds its own plant or office building, sells it to a group of investors, and then leases back the property for its business purposes but still maintains some ownership. In other words, SPEs can be an asset that helps facilitate daily business operations.

Most of the SPEs at Enron were alleged to be entities in name only, and Enron funded them with its own stock and maintained control over them. This is not too different from leasing back property that can be used for storage, transportation, or other energy-related activities. After the crash of Enron's stock price, any assets associated with the SPE system had to be written off. Enron had to take a $1.2 billion reduction in equity in late 2001 because of the SPE write-off.

After Enron restated its financial statements for fiscal 2000 and the first nine months of 2001, its cash flow from operations dropped from a positive $127 million in 2000 to a negative $753 million in 2001. In 2001, with its stock price falling, Enron faced a critical cash shortage. Already shaken by questions about lack of disclosure in Enron's financial statements and by reports that executives had profited personally from the partnership deals, investor confidence collapsed, taking Enron's stock price with it.

For a time, it appeared that Dynegy might save the day by providing $1.5 billion in cash, secured by Enron's premier pipeline Northern Natural Gas, and then purchasing Enron for about $10 billion. But when Standard & Poor downgraded Enron's debt below investment grade on November 28, some $4 billion in off-balance-sheet debt came due, and Enron didn't have the resources to pay. Dynegy terminated the deal. On December 2, 2001, Enron filed for bankruptcy. Enron faced twenty-two thousand claims totaling about $400 billion.

Many complex accounting issues related to determining the value of Enron. For example, sometimes accounting rules changed, and different opinions emerged on which rules applied, such as the accounting rules governing goodwill. *Goodwill* is the difference between what a company pays for an entity and the book value of that company's net assets. For example, changes to the accounting rules governing goodwill required Enron to disclose impairments to certain of its assets including interests in Wessex Water, a business located in Bath, England. Companies such as Enron depend on accounting firms to determine what rules apply to valuing goodwill as well as other assets. The government alleged that Enron's claim of being committed to a water-growth strategy was flawed because it would require Enron to disclose impairments in certain of its assets related to goodwill. According to Lay, Enron's accounting firm, Arthur Andersen, communicated that the company was in compliance with the goodwill accounting rules and the government's claims of flawed disclosures were wrong.

THE WHISTLE-BLOWER

Assigned to work directly with Fastow in June 2001, Enron vice president Sherron Watkins, an eight-year Enron veteran, was given the task of finding some assets to sell off. With the high-tech bubble bursting and Enron's stock price slipping, Watkins was troubled to find unclear, off-the-books arrangements backed only by Enron's deflating stock. No one could explain to her what was going on. Knowing that she faced difficult consequences if she confronted then-CEO Skilling, she began looking for another job, planning to confront Skilling just as she left for a new position. Skilling, however, suddenly quit on August 14, saying he wanted to spend more time with his family. Chairman Lay stepped back in as CEO and began inviting employees to express their concerns and put them into a box for later collection. Watkins prepared an anonymous memo and placed it into the box. When Lay held a company-wide meeting shortly thereafter and did not mention her memo, however, she arranged a personal meeting with him.

On August 22, Watkins handed Lay a seven-page letter that she had prepared outlining her concerns. She told him that Enron would "implode in a wave of accounting scandals" if nothing was done. On the other hand, Watkins continued to perform her duties at Enron and participate in all business matters. Lay arranged to have Enron's law firm, Vinson & Elkins, look into the questionable deals. There is evidence that Lay followed up on Watkins's concerns with appropriate action. Watkins sold $30,000 worth of stock in August 2001 and some options in late September. She claimed that she was panicked by the 9/11 terrorist attacks and about the company. She sold another block and netted about $17,000. She had more information than most people, and it is possible the government could have charged her for insider trading if she truly believed Enron was going to become bankrupt.

Watkins alleges that her computer's hard drive was confiscated and she was moved from her plush executive office suite on the top floors of the Houston headquarters tower to a lower-level plain office with a metal desk. That desk was no longer filled with the high-level projects that had once taken her all over the world on Enron business. Instead, now a vice president in name only, she claimed she faced meaningless "make-work" projects. In February 2002, she testified before Congress about Enron's partnerships and resigned from Enron in November. Although Watkins claims to be a whistle-blower, most of her statements were made after Enron filed for bankruptcy and was a financial disaster. In addition, there is no factual evidence that her earlier claims and concerns had any merit.

THE CHIEF FINANCIAL OFFICER

CFO Fastow was indicted in October 2002 by the U.S. Department of Justice on ninety-eight federal counts for his alleged efforts to inflate Enron's profits. These charges included fraud, money laundering, conspiracy, and one count of obstruction of justice. Fastow pled guilty to two counts of conspiracy, admitting to orchestrating a myriad of schemes to hide Enron debt and inflate profits while enriching himself with millions. He surrendered nearly $30 million in cash and property and agreed to serve up to ten years in prison once prosecutors no longer needed his cooperation. He was a key government witness against Lay and Skilling. His wife, Lea Fastow, former assistant treasurer, quit Enron in 1997, first pled guilty to a felony tax crime, admitting to helping hide ill-gotten gains from her husband's schemes from the government. Withdrawing her plea, she then pled guilty to a newly filed misdemeanor tax crime. In July 2005, she was released from a yearlong prison sentence, followed by a year of supervised release.

Federal prosecutors argued that Enron's case is not about exotic accounting practices but fraud and theft. They contend that Fastow was the brain behind the partnerships used to conceal some $1 billion in Enron debt and that this led directly to Enron's bankruptcy. The federal complaints allege that Fastow defrauded Enron and its shareholders through the off-the-balance-sheet partnerships that made Enron appear to be more profitable than it actually was. They also allege that Fastow made about $30 million both by using these partnerships to get kickbacks that were disguised as gifts from family members who invested in them and by taking income himself that should have gone to other entities. Lay maintained that Enron found no visible flaws in Fastow's ethical background before hiring him as CFO and was taken by surprise when Fastow's personal gains from the off-balance-sheet partnerships were discovered. Lay believed that Fastow's manipulations of the off-balance-sheet partnerships were a key factor in the Enron disaster.

Fastow alleges that he was hired to arrange the off-balance-sheet financing and that Enron's board of directors, chairman, and CEO directed and praised his work. He also claims that both lawyers and accountants reviewed his work and approved what was being done and that "at no time did he do anything he believed was a crime." Skilling, chief operating officer (COO) from 1997 to 2000 before becoming CEO, reportedly championed Fastow's rise at Enron and supported his efforts to keep up Enron's stock prices.

The case against Fastow was largely based on information provided by the managing director, Michael Kopper, a key player in the establishment and operation of several of the off-the-balance-sheet partnerships. Kopper, a chief aide to Fastow, pled guilty to money laundering and wire fraud. He agreed to serve ten years in prison and to surrender some $12 million that he earned from his dealings with the partnerships. Others charged in the Enron affair were Timothy Belden, Enron's former top energy trader, who pled guilty to one count of conspiring to commit wire fraud and three British bankers—David Bermingham, Giles Darby, and Gary Mulgrew—who were indicted in Houston on wire-fraud charges related to a deal at Enron. They used secret investments to take $7.3 million in income that belonged to their employer, according to the Justice Department. The three, employed by the finance group Greenwich National Westminster Bank, were arrested in 2004, faced extradition, and pled innocent.

THE CHIEF EXECUTIVE OFFICER

Former CEO Skilling is widely seen as Enron's mastermind. He was so sure that he had committed no crime that he waived his right to self-incrimination and testified before Congress that "I was not aware of any inappropriate financial arrangements." However, Jeffrey McMahon, who took over as Enron's president and COO in February 2002, told a congressional subcommittee that he had informed Skilling about the company's off-the-balance-sheet partnerships in March 2000, when he was Enron's treasurer. McMahon said that Skilling had told him "he would remedy the situation."

Calling the Enron collapse a "run on the bank" and a "liquidity crisis," Skilling said that he did not understand how Enron went from where it was to bankruptcy so quickly. He also said that the off-the-balance-sheet partnerships were Fastow's creation. Skilling is also reported to have sold 39 percent of his Enron holdings before the company disclosed its financial troubles.

THE CHAIRMAN

Lay became chairman and CEO of the company that was to become Enron in February 1986. A decade later, Lay promoted Skilling to president and COO and then, as expected, stepped down as CEO in February 2001, to make way for Skilling. Lay remained as chairman of the board. When Skilling resigned in August 2001, Lay resumed the role of CEO.

Lay, who held a doctorate in economics from the University of Houston, contended that he knew little of what was going on even though he had participated in the board meetings that allowed the off-the-balance-sheet partnerships to be created. He said he believed the transactions were legal because attorneys and accountants approved them. In the late summer of 2001, he was reassuring employees and investors that all was well at Enron, based on strong wholesale sales and physical volume being delivered through the Enron marketing channel. Although cash flow does not always follow sales, there was every reason to believe that Enron was still a company with much potential. On February 12, 2002, on the advice of his attorney, Lay told the Senate Commerce Committee that he was invoking his Fifth Amendment rights not to answer questions that could be incriminating.

Prosecutors looked into why Lay began selling about $80 million of his own stock beginning in late 2000, even while he encouraged employees to buy more shares of the company. It appears that Lay drew down his $4 million Enron credit line repeatedly and then repaid the company with Enron shares. These transactions, unlike usual stock sales, do not have to be reported to investors. Lay said that he sold the stock because of margin calls on loans that he had secured with Enron stock and that he had no other source of liquidity.

VINSON & ELKINS

Enron was Houston law firm Vinson & Elkins' top client, accounting for about 7 percent of its $450 million revenue. Enron's general counsel and a number of members of Enron's legal department came from Vinson & Elkins. Vinson & Elkins seems to have dismissed Watkins's allegations of accounting fraud after making some inquiries, but this does not appear to leave it open to civil or criminal liability. Of greater concern are allegations that Vinson & Elkins helped structure some of Enron's special-purpose partnerships. Watkins, in her letter to CEO Lay, indicated that the law firm had written opinion letters supporting the legality of the deals. In fact, Enron could not have done many of the transactions without such opinion letters. Although the law firm denies that it has done anything wrong, legal experts say the key question is whether or not Vinson & Elkins approved deals that it knew were fraudulent.

Documents reviewed by *BusinessWeek* indicate that their experts felt that Vinson & Elkins had concerns about the legitimacy of Enron's business practices. So far, the law firm has yet to pay any damages nor have any of its lawyers faced professional misconduct charges by the Texas bar. Enron's bankruptcy trustee is attempting to settle with Vinson & Elkins for $30 million. The Securities and Exchange Commission (SEC) continues to investigate the advice provided to Enron by the firm. In addition, there is an attempt to hold Vinson & Elkins liable for the $40 billion in investor losses resulting from the Enron collapse.

MERRILL LYNCH

The prestigious brokerage and investment banking firm of Merrill Lynch faced scrutiny by federal prosecutors and the SEC for its role in Enron's 1999 sale of Nigerian barges. Merrill Lynch allegedly bought the barges for $28 million, of which Enron financed $21 million through Fastow's oral assurance that Enron would buy Merrill Lynch's investment out in six months with a 15 percent guaranteed rate of return. Merrill Lynch went ahead with the deal despite an internal Merrill Lynch document that suggested that the transaction might not be appropriate. Merrill Lynch denies that the transaction was a sham and said that it never knowingly helped Enron to falsify its financial reports.

The barge deal was not among the financial blunders that pushed Enron into bankruptcy in 2001. However, prosecutors claimed that it showed Enron was willing to employ suspect financial practices to meet lofty earnings targets. Four former Merrill Lynch executives and two former mid-level Enron executives were charged with conspiracy and fraud related to the transaction. The defense attorneys disputed the government's claims. Enforcement Director Stephen Cutler said,

> Even if you don't have direct responsibility for a company's financial statements, you cannot turn a blind eye when you have reason to know what you are doing will help make those statements false and misleading. At the end of 1999, Merrill Lynch and the executives we are suing today did exactly that: They helped Enron defraud its investors through two deals that were created with one purpose in mind—to make Enron's financial statements look better than they actually were.

ARTHUR ANDERSEN LLP

In its role as Enron's auditor, Arthur Andersen was responsible for ensuring the accuracy of Enron's financial statements and internal bookkeeping. Andersen's reports were used by potential investors to judge Enron's financial soundness and future potential before they decided whether to invest and by current investors to decide if their funds should remain invested there. These investors would expect that Andersen's certifications of accuracy and application of proper accounting procedures were independent and without any conflict of interest. If Andersen's reports were in error, investors could be seriously misled. However, Andersen's independence has been called into question. The accounting firm was a major business partner of Enron, with more than one hundred employees dedicated to its account, and it sold about $50 million a year in consulting services to Enron. Some Andersen executives even accepted jobs with the energy trader.

Andersen was found guilty of obstruction of justice in March 2002 for destroying Enron-related auditing documents during an SEC investigation of Enron. As a result, Andersen has gone out of business. The U.S. Supreme Court overturned the obstruction-of-justice decision, but Andersen had closed its doors.

It is still not clear why Andersen auditors failed to ask Enron to better explain its complex partnerships before certifying Enron's financial statements. Some observers believe that the large consulting fees received from Enron unduly influenced Andersen. However, an Andersen spokesperson said that the firm had looked hard at all available information from Enron at the time. But shortly after she spoke to Enron CEO Lay, Watkins had taken her concerns to an Andersen audit partner, who reportedly conveyed her questions to senior Andersen management responsible for the Enron account. It is not clear what action, if any, Andersen took.

THE BREAKUP OF ENRON'S ASSETS

Enron's demise caused tens of billions of dollars of investor losses, triggered a collapse of electricity-trading markets, and ushered in an era of accounting scandals that precipitated a global loss of confidence in corporate integrity. Now companies must defend legitimate but complicated financing arrangements, even legitimate financing tools tainted by association with Enron. On a more personal level, thousands of former Enron employees struggle to find jobs, while many retirees have been forced to return to work in a bleak job market because their Enron-heavy retirement portfolios were wiped out. One senior Enron executive committed suicide.

In July 2003, Enron announced its intention to restructure and a plan to pay off its creditors. Pending creditor and court approval of the plan, most creditors would receive between 14.4 cents and 18.3 cents for each dollar they were owed—more than most expected. Under the plan, creditors would receive about two-thirds of the amount in cash and the rest in equity in three new companies, none of which would carry the tainted Enron name. The three companies were CrossCountry Energy Corporation, Prisma Energy International Inc., and Portland General Electric.

CrossCountry Energy would retain Enron's interests in three North American natural gas pipelines. CrossCountry Energy, formed from Enron's domestic gas pipeline assets, was immediately placed on the market for creditor compensation. On September 1, 2004, Enron announced an agreement to sell CrossCountry Energy to CCE Holdings LLC (a joint venture between Southern Union Company and a unit of General Electric) for $2.45 billion. The money would be used for debt repayment and represented a substantial increase over the previous offer made by NuCoastal LLC earlier in 2004.

Prisma Energy International would take over Enron's nineteen international power and pipeline holdings. Prisma Energy International, formed out of Enron's remaining overseas assets, emerged from bankruptcy as a main-line descendant of Enron through a stock offering to Enron creditors. Currently, many of Prisma's assets remain under direct Enron ownership with Prisma operating in a management capacity.

The third company, Portland General Electric (PGE), was founded in 1889 and ranks as Oregon's largest utility. PGE was acquired by Enron during the 1990s and emerged from bankruptcy as an independent company through a private stock offering to Enron creditors.

All remaining assets not related to CrossCountry, Prisma, or PGE were liquidated. As of 2006, CrossCountry was under CCE Holdings ownership, while the PGE and Prisma deals remained to be consummated. Enron emerged from Chapter 11 bankruptcy protection in November 2004 but will likely be wound down once the recovery plan is carried out. Enron's remaining assets are grouped under two main subsidiary companies: Prisma Energy International and PGE, both of which will likely be spun off.

On November 14, 2004, all of Enron's outstanding common stock and preferred stock was canceled. Each person who was the record holder of Enron Corporation stock on that day was allocated an uncertificated, nontransferable interest in one of two trusts that held new shares of Enron Corporation. In the very unlikely event that the value of Enron's assets exceeds the amount of its allowed claims, distributions would be made to the holders of these trust interests in the same order of priority of the stock that they previously held.

According to the Enron website in 2006, it was in the midst of liquidating its remaining operations and distributing its assets to its creditors. Even with the conviction of Enron executives, the justice system will not reform the way that corporate America runs businesses. Many businesspeople see this as an event outside their lives and businesses, very much like passing the traffic accident and thinking it can never happen to them. To prevent future Enron-type failures, the corporate culture, corporate governance, and reward systems will have to change in many organizations. In most cases, a CEO acting alone cannot "sink the ship," and many of the structural, cultural, and corporate governance conditions that caused the collapse of Enron haven't been removed from corporate America.

THE LAY AND SKILLING TRIAL

On May 25, 2006, a Houston jury found Kenneth Lay and Jeffrey Skilling guilty on all counts of conspiring to hide the company's financial condition in 2000 and 2001. During the case, the judge dealt a blow to the two defendants when he told the jury that they could find the defendants guilty of consciously avoiding knowing about wrongdoing at the company. Many former Enron employees refused to testify because they were not guaranteed that their testimony would not be used against them at future trials convicting them. Many questions about the accounting fraud remained after the trial. The verdict was a total victory for federal prosecutors who had spent four years building a criminal case against the two men who had played a key role in building

Enron as a role model for the energy industry. Sean M. Berkowitz, director of the Justice Department's Enron Task Force, said "You can't lie to shareholders, you can't put yourself in front of your employees' interests, and no matter how rich and powerful you are you have to play by the rules." The verdict was a blow to Lay and Skilling who testified that "Enron was a fundamentally sound company brought low in a market panic spurred by short sellers and negative media reports." On the other hand, the government maintained that Enron used deceptive accounting and bogus claims of the growth potential of new business units.

The jury found Lay, 64 years old, guilty of six counts of conspiracy and fraud. Skilling, 52 years old, was convicted on eighteen counts of conspiracy and securities fraud but acquitted on nine out of ten counts of illegal insider trading. On the way out of the courtroom, Lay said he was "shocked" by the verdict. "I firmly believe I am innocent of the charges against me as I've said from day one." Then juror Wendy Vaughan said, "I felt it was their duty to know what was going on." Outside the courthouse, prosecutors said the trial should send a message to executives who manipulate their companies' earnings.

Many people don't feel much sympathy for Skilling and Lay because so many people lost a lot of money, but there is an alternative viewpoint. A number of law professors and lawyers have concerns about the Enron Task Force's prosecution of Lay and Skilling, accusing the government of "criminalizing corporate agency costs." In other words, the government is accused of misusing criminal laws to punish questionable business transactions and bad management decisions. In a civilized society, do we imprison people for the rest of their lives because they may have made some bad business decisions?

No doubt, this was a very complex case, and even the most hard-core antibusiness types are queasy with the conclusion of this tragedy. There was not conclusive evidence that there was intent to defraud investors, although investor losses were massive. The important question is, Was there complacency at all managerial levels about rule bending among some employees or was there massive corruption at all levels? One of the key prosecution elements was complacent negligence, that Skilling and Lay just turned a blind eye.

The truth is that the jury would have had to understand the entire corporate culture as well as many systemic embedded business decisions at Enron to know for sure that Lay and Skilling were guilty of their charges. Bad business decisions were made, but there is uncertainty as to the true involvement and intent of many of the CEO's decisions. Society and the courts tend to simplify events and blame all that goes wrong on just a few individuals. At this stage of understanding, there are few people who understand how an organizational culture can evolve with complacency and constant reinforcement from coworkers driving bad decisions. In our society, we are taught that the opinion of trusted professionals such as accountants and lawyers can be followed in business decisions. In this case, the accounting firm Arthur Andersen, internal and external attorneys, as well as the board of directors approved the key decisions at Enron.

Lay said he never intended to harm anyone; in fact, he came back as CEO after Skilling stepped down and at the insistence of the Enron board of directors to provide leadership and attempt to save the company. A decision that he and his wife both regretted. As CEO, Lay was responsible for thirty thousand employees operating in thirty countries. He managed an exceptional group of employees, as eluded to in the film *Enron: The Smartest Men in the Room*. Great leaders are often given accolades for their accomplishments, and Lay was no exception in the "heyday" of Enron. But most will acknowledge that the heart of their success, or in this case, ultimate failure, is the people with whom they surround themselves and place in positions of authority. The people who Lay trusted, such as Fastow (convicted former CFO), were key operatives in the day-to-day decision making at Enron. It was a complex maze of events that caused the failure of Enron.

On July 5, 2006, Ken Lay died of a heart attack in Aspen, Colorado. He was awaiting sentencing and still maintaining his innocence. Lay had endured a five-month trial but was working hard to develop an appeal of his conviction. He did not feel that it was possible to get a fair trial in Houston and indicated that the jury had not even read his indictment. He thought he was convicted because as CEO he was charged with responsibility for what happened at Enron, even if he was unaware of wrongdoing. The heart of the case against Lay was that he allegedly lied about the financial condition at Enron. Federal courts, including the Fifth Court of Appeals, hold that a defendant's death erases a conviction. Lay stated that he wanted to be of use to society and would continue to do that in any way possible. In the five weeks before his death, he read several drafts of this case and tried to provide insights about what happened at Enron. He wanted to share his knowledge and perspective about Enron with future business leaders.

QUESTIONS

1. How did the corporate culture of Enron contribute to its bankruptcy?
2. Did Enron's bankers, auditors, and attorneys contribute to Enron's demise? If so, what was their contribution?
3. What role did the CFO play in creating the problems that led to Enron's financial problems?

SOURCES: Personal conversations with Ken Lay between May 27, 2006, and June 20, 2006, by O. C. Ferrell and Linda Ferrell; Associated Press, "Enron Who's Who," *USA Today* online, http://www .usatoday.com/money/industries/energy/2006-01-26-enron-whos-who_x.htm (accessed June 1, 2006); Mark Banineck and Mary Flood, "Enron's Top Execs Are Guilty, Guilty," *San Antonio Express News,* May 26, 2006, 1A; Alexei Barrionuevo, Jonathan Weil, and John R. Wilke, "Enron's Fastow Charged with Fraud," *Wall Street Journal,* October 3, 2002, A3–A4; Eric Berger, "Report Details Enron's Deception," *Houston Chronicle,* March 6, 2003, 1B, 11B; Maria Bartiromo, "The Ones Who Got Away," *BusinessWeek* online, June 12, 2006, http://www.businessweek.com/magazine/content/06_24/b3988122 .htm?campaign_id=search (accessed June 7, 2006); Christine Y. Chen, "When Good Firms Get Bad Chi," *Fortune,* November 11, 2002, 56; Andrew Dunn and Laurel Brubaker Calkins, "Death to Hinder Feds," *Denver Post,* July 6, 2006, C1; Peter Elkind and Bethany McLean, "Feds Move Up Enron Food Chain," *Fortune,* December 30, 2002, 43–44; John R. Emshwiller, "Enron's Kenneth Lay is Dead at 64," *Wall Street Journal* online, July 6, 2006, A1, http://www.online.wsj.com/article_print/ SB115210822917098397.html (accessed July 6, 2006); "Enron's Last Mystery," *BusinessWeek* online, June 12 2006, http://www.businessweek.com/magazine/content/06_24/b3988056.htm?campaign _id=search (accessed June 7, 2006); Enron Website, for facts about Enron, www.enron.com (accessed

May 18, 2006); "Enron Whistle-Blower Resigns," MSNBC News, www.msnbc.com/news/835432.asp (accessed December 2, 2002); Greg Farrell, "Lay, Skilling found guilty," *USA Today,* May 26, 2006, A1, B1; Greg Farrell, "Former Enron CFO Charged," *USA Today,* October 3, 2002, B1; Greg Farrell, Edward Iwata, and Thor Valdmanis, "Prosecutors Are Far from Finished," *USA Today,* October 3, 2002, 1B–2B; "Fastow Indicted on 78 Counts," MSNBC News, www.msnbc.com/news/828217.asp (accessed November 6, 2002); O. C. Ferrell, "Ethics," *BizEd,* May/June 2002, 43–45; Jeffrey A. Fick, "Report: Merrill Replaced Enron Analyst," *USA Today,* July 30, 2002, B1; "Finger-Pointing Starts as Congress Examines Enron's Fast Collapse," *Investor's Business Daily,* February 8, 2002, A1; Daren Fonda, "Enron: Picking over the Carcass," *Fortune,* December 30, 2002, 56; Mike France, "One Big Client, One Big Hassle," *BusinessWeek,* January 28, 2002, 38–39; Bryan Gruley and Rebecca Smith, "Keys to Success Left Kenneth Lay Open to Disaster," *Wall Street Journal,* April 26, 2002, A1, A5; Tom Hamburger, "Enron CEO Declines to Testify at Hearing," *Wall Street Journal,* December 12, 2001, B2; Kristen Hays, "16 Cents on $1 for Enron Creditors," *Austin American-Statesman* online, July 12, 2003, http://statesman .com; Kristen Hays, "Conspiracy with Merrill Lynch Charged in Enron Trial," *Washington Post* online, http://www.washingtonpost.com/wp-dyn/articles/A39044-2004Sep21.html (accessed June 7, 2006); Edward Iwata, "Merrill Lynch Will Pay $80M to Settle Enron Case," *USA Today* online, February 20, 2003, www.usatoday.com; Jeremy Kahn, "The Chief Freaked Out Officer," *Fortune,* December 9, 2002, 197–198, 202; Kenneth Lay Speech, Houston Forum, December 13, 2005, www.kenlayinfo.com/public /pag142.aspx (accessed June 7, 2006); Kathryn Kranhold and Rebecca Smith, "Two Other Firms in Enron Scheme, Documents Say," *Wall Street Journal,* May 9, 2002, C1, C12; Peter Lattman, "Enron: Two Very Different Views from the Peanut Gallery," *Wall Street Journal* online, May 26, 2006, http://blogs.wsj.com/law/2006/05/26/enron-two-very-different-views-from-the-peanut-gallery (accessed May 31, 2006); Bethany McLean, "Why Enron Went Bust," *Fortune,* December 24, 2001, 58, 60–62, 66, 68; Jodie Morse and Amanda Bower, "The Party Crasher," *Fortune,* December 30, 2002, 53–56; Belverd E. Needles, Jr., and Marian Powers, "Accounting for Enron," in *Houghton Mifflin's Guide to the Enron Crisis* (Boston: Houghton Mifflin, 2003), 3–6; *New York Times* coverage of the Enron trial, http://www.nytimes.com/business/businessspecial3/index.html?adxnnl=1&adxnnlx=114798623 z56Vd16RUkp6eHnHTTXBHw (accessed May 18, 2006); Michael Orey, "Lawyers: Enron's Last Mystery?" *BusinessWeek* online, June 1, 2006, www.businessweek.com/investor/content/may2006/ pi20060531_972686.htm; Mitchell Pacelle, "Enron's Creditors to Get Peanuts," *Wall Street Journal* online, July 11, 2003, http://online.wsj.com; "Primer: Accounting Industry and Andersen," *Washington Post* online, www.washingtonpost.com (accessed October 2, 2002); Miriam Schulman, "Enron: What Ever Happened to Going Down with the Ship?" Markkula Center for Applied Ethics, www.scu.edu/ethics/publications/ethicalperspectives/schulman0302.html (accessed September 11, 2002); Chris H. Sieroty, "3 Ex-Bankers Charged in Enron Scandal," *Washington Times* online, www.washtimes.com (accessed October 2, 2002); William Sigismond, "The Enron Case from a Legal Perspective," in *Houghton Mifflin's Guide to the Enron Crisis* (Boston: Houghton Mifflin, 2003), 11–13; Elliot Blair Smith, "Panel Blasts Enron Tax Deals," *USA Today* online, February 13, 2003, www.usatoday.com; Rebecca Smith and Kathryn Kranhold, "Enron Knew Portfolio's Value," *Wall Street Journal,* May 6, 2002, C1, C20; Rebecca Smith and Mitchell Pacelle, "Enron Plans Return to Its Roots," *Wall Street Journal,* May 2, 2002, A1; Jake Ulick, "Enron: A Year Later," CNN/Money, www.money.cnn.com/2002/11/26/news/companies/enron_anniversary/index.htm (accessed December 2, 2002); U.S. Securities and Exchange Commission, "SEC Charges Merrill Lynch, Four Merrill Lynch Executives with Aiding and Abetting Enron Accounting Fraud," 2003, http://www.sec.gov/news/press/2003-32.htm (accessed June 7, 2006); Joseph Weber, "Can Andersen Survive?" *BusinessWeek,* January 28, 2002, 39–40; Wikipedia, http://en.wikipedia.org/wiki/Enron (accessed May 18, 2006); Winthrop Corporation, "Epigraph," in *Houghton Mifflin's Guide to the Enron Crisis* (Boston: Houghton Mifflin, 2003), 1; Wendy Zellner, "A Hero—and a Smoking-Gun Letter," *BusinessWeek,* January 28, 2002, 34–35.

Tyco International: Leadership Crisis

On September 12, 2002, Tyco International's former chief executive officer, L. Dennis Kozlowski, and former chief financial officer, Mark H. Swartz, were seen in handcuffs on national television after they were arrested and charged with misappropriating more than $170 million from the company. They were also accused of stealing more than $430 million through fraudulent sales of Tyco stock and concealing the information from shareholders. The two executives were charged in a Manhattan federal court with numerous counts of grand larceny, enterprise corruption, and falsifying business records. Another executive, former general counsel Mark A. Belnick, was also charged with concealing $14 million in personal loans. Months after the initial arrests, charges and lawsuits were still being filed in a growing scandal that threatened to eclipse the notoriety of other companies facing accounting fraud charges in the early 2000s.

TYCO'S HISTORY

Tyco Inc., was founded by Arthur J. Rosenberg in 1960, in Waltham, Massachusetts, as an investment and holding company focusing on solid-state science and energy conversion. It developed the first laser with a sustained beam for medical procedures. With a shifting of focus to the commercial sector, Tyco became a publicly traded company in 1964. It also began a pattern of acquisitions—sixteen different companies by 1968—that would continue through 1982 as the company sought to fill gaps in its development and distribution network. The rapidly growing and diversifying firm grew from $34 million in sales in 1973 to $500 million in 1982.

In 1982, Tyco reorganized into three business segments (fire protection, electronics, and packaging) to strengthen itself from within. By 1986 Tyco had returned

---

We appreciate the work of Linda G. Mullen in helping draft the previous edition of this case. This case was prepared for classroom discussion rather than to illustrate either effective or ineffective handling of an administrative, ethical, or legal decision by management. All sources used for this case were obtained through publicly available material and the Tyco website.

to a growth-through-acquisitions mode. In the 1990s Tyco maintained four core segments: electrical and electronic components, health-care and specialty products, fire and security services, and flow control. The company changed its name to Tyco International in 1993 to signal its global presence to the financial community. By 2000 the firm had acquired more than thirty major companies, including well-known firms such as ADT, Raychem, and the CIT Group.

THE RISE OF DENNIS KOZLOWSKI

Leo Dennis Kozlowski was born in Newark, New Jersey, in 1946. His parents, Leo Kelly and Agnes Kozlowski, were second-generation Polish Americans. His father worked for Public Service Transport (later the New Jersey Transport), and his mother was a school crossing guard in Newark's predominantly Polish neighborhood. Kozlowski attended public school and graduated from West Side High in 1964. He lived at home while he studied accounting at Seton Hall University in South Orange, New Jersey.

After brief stints at SCM Corp. and Nashua Corporation, Kozlowski went to work for Tyco in 1976. He soon found a friend and mentor in CEO Joseph Gaziano, whose lavish style—including company jets, extravagant vacations, company cars, and country club memberships—impressed Kozlowski. However, the luxurious lifestyle came to an end when Gaziano died of cancer in 1982. Fellow MIT graduate John F. Fort III, who differed sharply in management style, replaced Gaziano. Where Gaziano had been extravagant, Fort was analytical and thrifty, and Wall Street responded approvingly to his new course and direction for Tyco. Fort's goal was to increase profits for the shareholders of Tyco and cut out extravagant spending that had characterized Gaziano's tenure.

Kozlowski, who had thrived under Gaziano, had to shift gears to adapt to the abrupt change in leadership. However, Kozlowski's accounting background helped push him up the ranks at Tyco. He was very adept at crunching numbers and helping achieve Fort's vision of taking care of shareholders first. Fort soon noticed Kozlowski's talents.

Kozlowski's first major promotion within Tyco was to president of Grinnell Fire Protection Systems Co., Tyco's largest division. At Grinnell, Kozlowski cut out extras and reduced overhead, eliminated 98 percent of the paperwork, and reworked compensation programs. Although he slashed managers' salaries, he also set up a bonus compensation package that gave them greater control over the money they could earn. He gave public recognition to high achievers at a yearly banquet, but he also recognized the underachievers, giving out an award for the worst-producing unit as well as the best. Perhaps most important, Kozlowski systematically began to buy out and acquire each of the fire protection division's competitors. As described in a *BusinessWeek* article, he gained a reputation as a "corporate tough guy, respected and feared in roughly equal measure."

Over the next few years, Kozlowski continued his rise up Tyco's corporate ladder, becoming the company's president in 1987, before rising to CFO and eventually CEO in 1992. However, his aggressive approach to acquisitions and mergers during this period became a concern for then-CEO Fort, who wanted to slow the rate of activity in Kozlowski's division. His largest acquisition was Wormald International, a $360 million global fire-protection concern. However, integrating Wormald proved problematic and Fort was reportedly not happy with so large a purchase. Fort and Kozlowski also disagreed over the rapid changes that Kozlowski made in the fire-protection division. Kozlowski responded by lobbying to convince Tyco's board of directors that the problems with Wormald were a "bump in the road" and the firm should continue its strategy of acquiring profitable companies that met its guidelines. The board sided with Kozlowski, and Fort resigned as CEO and later as chairman of the board, although he remained a member of Tyco's board of directors until 2003.

KOZLOWSKI'S TYCO EMPIRE

At the age of 46, Kozlowski found himself at the helm of Tyco International in 1992. He eventually moved out of his North Hampton home, leaving his wife and two daughters for a waitress, Karen Lee Mayo Locke, whom he eventually married in 2000. Before 2000 Kozlowski's lifestyle was comparatively ordinary for a person of such rank; however, some subtle changes in lifestyle did occur after the North Hampton move but before his second marriage. His new lifestyle—which included parties that were regular gossip-column fodder and homes in Boca Raton, Nantucket, Beaver Creek, and New York City—appeared to emulate that of Kozlowski's mentor, former CEO Joseph Gaziano. Indeed, Kozlowski's aggressive strategy of mergers and acquisitions made Tyco look more like the company it had been under Gaziano.

Kozlowski had learned Tyco and its businesses from the bottom up, giving him an advantage in his determination to make Tyco the greatest company of the new century. Among other things, he recognized that one of the conglomerate's major shortcomings was its reliance on cyclical industries. Thus, he decided to diversify into more non-cyclical industries. His first major acquisition toward that objective was the Kendall Company, a manufacturer of medical supplies, which had emerged from bankruptcy just two years before. Kozlowski quickly revived the business, which became very profitable and doubled Tyco's earnings. Although Tyco's board of directors had initially balked at the Kendall acquisition, the directors were pleased with the subsidiary's turnaround and contribution to profits. Kozlowski made Kendall the core of his new Tyco Healthcare Group, which quickly grew to become the second-largest producer of medical devices behind Johnson & Johnson. The board rewarded Kozlowski's performance by increasing his salary to $2.1 million and giving him shares of the company's stock.

Kozlowski's next strategic move was the acquisition of ADT Security Services, a British-owned company located in Bermuda, in 1997. By structuring the deal as a "reverse takeover," Tyco acquired a global presence as well as ADT's Bermuda registration, which allowed the firm to create a network of offshore subsidiaries to shelter its foreign earnings from U.S. taxes.

While Kozlowski continued to acquire new companies to build his vision of Tyco, he handpicked a few trusted people and placed them in key positions. One of these individuals was Mark Swartz, who was promoted from director of Mergers and Acquisitions to CFO. Swartz, who had developed a strong financial background as an auditor for Deloitte & Touche and a reputation for being more approachable than Kozlowski, was aware of Kozlowski's business practices. Kozlowski also recruited Mark Belnick to become Tyco's general counsel.

By this time, Tyco's corporate governance system was composed of Kozlowski as CEO and the firm's board of directors, which had eleven members, including Joshua Berman, a vice president of Tyco and former outside counsel; Mark Swartz, CFO; Lord Michael Ashcroft, a British dignitary who came with the ADT merger; James S. Pasman, Jr., also from ADT; W. Peter Slusser, also from ADT; Richard S. Bodman, a venture capitalist; Stephen W. Foss, CEO of a textile concern; Joseph F. Welch, CEO of snack-food maker Bachman Co.; Wendy Lane, a private equity investor; John F. Fort III, former CEO and chairman of Tyco; and Frank E. Walsh, Jr., director of the board. Kozlowski particularly liked the prestige of Lord Ashcroft being associated with his company. The majority of the directors had been on the board for ten to twenty years, and they were very familiar with Tyco's strategies and Kozlowski's management style. As directors, they were responsible for protecting Tyco's shareholders by disclosing any questionable situations or issues that might seem unethical or inappropriate, such as conflicts of interest. However, after the arrests of Kozlowski and Swartz, investigations subsequently uncovered the following troubling relationships among the board's members:

◆ Swartz participated in loan-forgiveness programs.
◆ Bodman invested $5 million for Kozlowski in a private stock fund managed by Bodman.
◆ Walsh received $20 million for helping arrange the acquisition of CIT Group without the knowledge of the rest of the board of directors.
◆ Walsh also held controlling interest in two firms that received more than $3.5 million for leasing an aircraft and providing pilot services to Tyco between 1996 and 2002.
◆ Foss received $751,101 for supplying a Cessna Citation aircraft and pilot services.
◆ Ashcroft used $2.5 million in Tyco funds to purchase a home.

With his handpicked board in place, Kozlowski decided to open a Manhattan office overlooking Central Park. However, the firm maintained its humble Exeter, New Hampshire, office, where Kozlowski preferred to be interviewed. According to *BusinessWeek,* he bragged to a guest that, "We don't believe in perks, not even executive parking spots." The unpublicized Manhattan office essentially became the firm's unofficial headquarters, and Kozlowski lavished it with every imaginable perk. He used Tyco funds to purchase and furnish apartments for key executives and employees in New York's pricey Upper East Side as well.

Meanwhile, Jeanne Terrile, an analyst for Tyco at Merrill Lynch, was not so impressed with Kozlowski's activities and Tyco's performance. Stock analysts like those at Merrill Lynch make recommendations to investors whether to buy, hold, or sell a particular stock. After Terrile wrote a less than favorable review of Tyco's rapid acquisitions and mergers and refused to upgrade Merrill's position on Tyco's stock, Kozlowski met with David Komansky, the CEO of Merrill Lynch. Although the subject of the meeting was never confirmed, shortly thereafter, Terrile was replaced by Phua Young, who immediately upgraded Merrill's recommendation for Tyco to "buy" from "accumulate." Merrill Lynch continued to be one of Tyco's top underwriters as well as one of its primary advisers for mergers and acquisitions.

Between 1997 and 2001, Tyco's revenues climbed 48.7 percent a year, and its pretax operating margins increased to 22.1 percent. The pace of mergers and acquisitions escalated with the assistance of Swartz, Tyco's CFO. In February 2002, Tyco announced that it had spent more than $8 billion on more than seven hundred acquisitions in the last three years. Among these were AMP Inc., an electronics maker for $11.3 billion in stock, and CIT Group, a commercial finance company. However, some of the merged companies were less than satisfied with the arrangement. Kozlowski forced acquired companies to scale back sharply and eliminate anything—and anyone—that did not produce revenue. The toll on human capital was enormous. Tyco shareholders and directors, however, were very happy with Kozlowski's performance, as demonstrated by his rapid salary increases from $8 million in 1997, to $67 million in 1998, to $170 million in 1999, which made him the second-highest paid CEO in the United States. A transaction that would be considered somewhat pivotal in Kozlowski's personal life was his 1997 purchase of a four-acre, three-bedroom, 7000-square-foot house in Nantucket, Massachusetts for $5 million.

During 1997–2002, Kozlowski's charismatic leadership style together with the firm's decentralized corporate structure meant that few people, including members of the board of directors, had a true picture of the firm's activities and finances. The company was organized into four distinct divisions—fire protection (53 percent); valves, pipes, and other "flow-control" devices (23 percent); electrical and electronic components (13 percent); and packaging materials (11 percent)—and there was little interaction among them. Each division's president reported directly to Kozlowski, who in turn reported to the board.

Those who saw red flags at Tyco International were shot down, including Jeanne Terrile at Merrill Lynch and David W. Tice, a short seller who questioned whether Tyco's use of large reserves in connection with its acquisitions was obscuring its results. A nonpublic investigation by the Securities and Exchange Commission (SEC) resulted only in Tyco amending its earnings per share for 1999.

THE FALL OF DENNIS KOZLOWSKI

At the beginning of 2002, Kozlowski announced that Tyco would split into four independent, publicly traded companies: security and electronics, health care, fire protection and flow control, and financial services. Tyco believed these actions would increase shareholder value. Kozlowski stated that

> I am extremely proud of Tyco's performance. We have built a great portfolio of businesses and over the five years ended September 30, 2001, we have delivered earnings per share growth at a compounded annual rate of over 40% and industry-leading operating profit margins in each of our businesses. During this same period, we have increased annual free cash flow from $240 million in 1996 to $4.8 billion in fiscal 2001. Nonetheless, even with this performance, Tyco is trading at a 2002 P/E multiple of 12.0x, a discount of almost 50% to the S&P 500.

But then everything began to fall apart, especially when the board of directors learned that one of its members, Walsh, had received a $20 million bonus for his part in securing and aiding in the CIT merger. Walsh promptly resigned from the board. Troubled by the idea that Kozlowski had made such a major payment without their knowledge, the remaining board members launched an investigation to determine whether other board members had earned such "commissions." The probe uncovered numerous expense abuses. Finally, after learning that he was about to be indicted for tax evasion, Kozlowski agreed to resign as CEO of Tyco on June 2, 2002.

Months earlier, the New York State Bank Department had observed large sums of money going into and out of Tyco's accounts. This would not have been unusual except that the funds were being transferred into Kozlowski's personal accounts. Eventually, authorities discovered that Kozlowski had allegedly avoided $3.1 million in New York state taxes by appearing to ship rare artwork to New Hampshire when in fact it was sent to New York. On June 3, Kozlowski was arrested for tax evasion, but the scandal was only just beginning.

On September 12, 2002, Kozlowski and Swartz, who had also resigned from Tyco, were indicted on thirty-eight felony counts for allegedly stealing $170 million from Tyco and fraudulently selling an additional $430 million in stock options. Among other allegations, Kozlowski was accused of taking $242 million from a program intended to help Tyco employees buy company stock so that he could buy yachts, fine art, and luxury homes. Together with former legal counsel Mark Belnick, the three face criminal charges and a civil complaint from the SEC. Kozlowski was also accused of granting $106 million to various employees through "loan forgiveness" and relocation programs. Swartz was also charged with falsifying documents in this loan program in the amount of $14 million. Belnick was charged with larceny and trying to steer a federal investigation, as well as taking more than $26 million from Tyco.

In addition, several former board members were cited for conflict-of-interest issues. Walsh, a former board member who received a $20 million bonus for the CIT merger, pleaded guilty and agreed to repay the $20 million plus an additional $2 million in court costs. Moreover, Jerry Boggess, the president of Tyco Fire and Security Division was fired and accused of creating a number of "bookkeeping issues" that had a negative impact on earnings to shareholders. Richard Scalzo, the Pricewaterhouse-Coopers auditor who signed off on Tyco's 2002 audit, was removed. Tyco's stock plunged from $60 per share in January 2002 to $18 per share by December, and investors lost millions of dollars. Many of the firm's 260,000 employees were also shareholders and watched their savings dwindle. Tyco's retirees found that their savings and retirement plans, which were tied up in company shares, plummeted with the company's stock price.

REBUILDING AN EMPIRE

After Kozlowski's resignation, he was replaced as CEO by Edward Breen (see Table C4-1). The company filed suit against Kozlowski and Swartz for more than $100 million. The SEC allows companies to sue for profits made by "insiders" who are profiting by buying and selling company stock within a six-month period. The company

| **TABLE C4-1** | Tyco Timeline and Statements from Tyco Press Releases |

June 3, 2002 Dennis Kozlowski resigns as chairman of the board and CEO for personal reasons. Kozlowski also steps down from the board of directors. At the request of Tyco's board, John Fort agrees to assume primary executive responsibilities during an interim period while a search for a permanent replacement is completed.

June 10, 2002 Tyco replaces its general counsel, Mark Belnick, with Irving Gutin. Gutin previously served as general counsel of Tyco.

June 17, 2002 Tyco files suit against Belnick for a broad pattern of misconduct, including using company funds for personal gain.

June 17, 2002 Tyco files suit against Frank Walsh, former member of the board of directors, for breaching his fiduciary obligations in the company's CIT Group acquisition.

July 25, 2002 The board of directors appoints Edward Breen, former president and COO of Motorola, Inc., as chairman of the board and CEO.

August 6, 2002 Tyco appoints Eric Pillmore as senior vice president of corporate governance. Breen, chairman and CEO, said, "I have made an absolute commitment to establishing the highest standards of corporate governance in every aspect of this company's financial reporting, operations and management."

September 11, 2002 David FitzPatrick is appointed executive vice president and CFO and succeeds Mark Swartz, who has resigned from the company.

September 12, 2002 Tyco board of directors nominates five business leaders to fill expected vacancies:

◆ Jerome York is chairman, president, and CEO of Micro Warehouse, Inc. Before joining Micro Warehouse, York was the vice chairman of Tracinda Corporation from 1995 to 1999, was CFO of IBM Corporation from 1993 to 1995, and held various positions at Chrysler Corporations from 1979 to 1993. York graduated from the U.S. Military Academy and received an MS from the Massachusetts Institute of Technology and an MBA from the University of Michigan.

◆ Mackey McDonald served as the chairman, president, and CEO of VF Corporation. McDonald began his tenure at VF Corporation in 1982 and was named chairman, president, and CEO in 1998. He also was a director of operations at Hanes Corporation. McDonald graduated from Davidson College and received an MBA in marketing from Georgia State University.

◆ George Buckley is the chairman and CEO of Brunswick Corporation. Formerly serving as the chief technology officer and president of two divisions throughout his career at Emerson Electric Company from 1993 to 1997, Buckley joined Brunswick in 1997 and has held the role of chairman and CEO for over two years. Buckley combined postgraduate work at Huddersfield and Southampton Universities and received a doctorate at the University of Huddersfield in 1977.

◆ Bruce Gordon is the president of retail markets at Verizon Communications, Inc. Gordon fulfilled a variety of positions at Bell Atlantic Corporation, including group president, vice president of marketing and sales, and vice president of sales. Gordon graduated from Gettysburg College and received an MS from Massachusetts Institute of Technology.

◆ Sandra Wijnberg is a senior vice president and CFO at Marsh & McLennan Companies, Inc. Before joining Marsh & McLennan in January 2000, Wijnberg served as a senior vice president and treasurer of Tricon Global Restaurants, Inc., and held various positions at PepsiCo, Inc.; Morgan Stanley Group, Inc.; and American Express Company. Wijnberg is a graduate of the University of California, Los Angeles, and received an MBA from the University of Southern California.

November 8, 2002 The board of directors nominates Admiral Dennis C. Blair (U.S. Navy, Ret.) to be on the board. Blair retired as commander in chief of the U.S. Pacific Fleet in 1999 after more than thirty years of service in the armed forces. Previously, Blair served as vice admiral and director of the Joint Staff and member of the Reserve Forces Policy Board for the Department of Defense. During his career, he had also worked closely with the White House, the National Security Council, and the Central Intelligence Agency and served as rear admiral and commander of the *Kitty Hawk* Battle Group. Blair graduated from the U.S. Naval Academy and holds a master's degree from Oxford University.

November 18, 2002 Jerome York, chairman, president, and CEO of Micro Warehouse, Inc., and Mackey McDonald, chairman, president, and CEO of VF Corporation, are appointed to the board of directors. York fills the seat vacated by Ashcroft, and McDonald serves in place of Pasman. Ashcroft and Pasman, who submitted letters of resignation to Tyco chairman and CEO Breen, were the first Tyco directors to resign following the board's unanimous decision not to nominate or support for reelection at the company's 2003 annual meeting any of the nine current directors who were members of the board prior to July 2002. Ashcroft said, "After 18 years of service on the Board, it was time for me to move on and allow the company's new management team to do its job. I am pleased that the Board agreed with my suggestion of appointing as advisors to the Board two current directors. I have, however, told the Board that I do not wish to serve in this capacity because there are others more suitable than I for this role. Looking ahead, I wish the company well in successfully meeting the challenges of rebuilding Tyco." Pasman said, "I believe that a new Board will help propel Tyco to the levels of operating performance, shareholder value and investor confidence that the company deserves. Even though I am leaving my position as director, I will always remain a staunch supporter of this business and the people of Tyco."

(continued)

TABLE C4-1	Tyco Timeline and Statements from Tyco Press Releases (continued)

January 30, 2003 H. Carl McCall, former comptroller of the state of New York, is nominated to join the board of directors. He began his term as New York state comptroller in May 1993, was reelected to his second term as comptroller in November 1998, and served until November 2002 when he became the Democratic nominee for governor of the state of New York. Previous to his position as comptroller, McCall was a vice president of Citicorp for eight years. He has also served as the president of the New York City Board of Education, ambassador to the United Nations, commissioner of the Port Authority of New York and New Jersey, and commissioner of the New York State Division of Human Rights, and he was elected to three terms as New York state senator. He received a bachelor's degree from Dartmouth College and a master's degree of divinity degree from Andover-Newton Theological School in Andover, Massachusetts, and is an ordained minister of the United Church of Christ. He is a member of the New York Stock Exchange board of directors where he serves as chairman of the board's Audit and Finance Committee. He also cochaired the board's Committee on Corporate Accountability.

March 29, 2004 The board of directors approves stock option and restricted-stock awards for the company's chairman and CEO Breen. The awards consist of two hundred thousand restricted shares, which vest on the third anniversary of the grant date, and six hundred thousand premium-priced stock options with strike prices ranging from $33 to $40, which vest in equal annual installments over a three-year period beginning immediately after the grant date.

January 18, 2005 Tyco nominates Raj Gupta, chairman and CEO of Rohm and Haas Company, for election to Tyco's board of directors. Gupta, age 59, would become Tyco's twelfth director and its eleventh independent director. Gupta also serves on the board of trustees for Drexel University and is a board member of The Vanguard Group.

March 14, 2005 The board of directors approves stock option and restricted-stock awards for the company's chairman and CEO Breen. The awards consist of 160,000 restricted shares, which vest on the third anniversary of the grant date, and 600,000 premium-priced stock options with strike prices ranging from $37 to $45, which vest in three equal annual installments beginning on the first anniversary of the grant date. The board feels that premium-priced stock options provide an effective vehicle to align Breen's incentives with shareholder interests.

stated that "to hold him accountable for his misconduct, we seek not only full payment for the funds he misappropriated but also punitive damages for the serious harm he did to Tyco and its shareholders." Additionally, Tyco is suing for monies paid by Kozlowski to keep some of those closest to him from testifying against him.

Breen launched a review of the company's accounting and corporate governance practices to determine whether any other fraud had occurred. Although the probe uncovered no fraud, the firm announced in late 2002 that it would restate its 2002 financial results by $382.2 million. Tyco's new management declared in a regulatory filing that the firm's previous management had "engaged in a pattern of aggressive accounting which, even when in accordance with Generally Accepted Accounting Principles, was intended to increase reported earnings above what they would have been if more conservative accounting had been employed." Although Tyco's investigations found no further fraud, the company repeatedly restated its financial results or took accounting charges totaling more than $2 billion over the next six months.

In 2004 Kozlowski and Swartz went before a jury that ended in a mistrial. However, in 2005 both were found guilty on twenty-two of twenty-three counts of grand larceny and conspiracy, falsifying business records, and violating business law. The judge also ordered both to pay $134 million to Tyco. Kozlowski also must pay a $70 million fine and Swartz a $35 million fine. Kozlowski's total bill came to $167 million in fines and restitution. The prison time for both appears to be a little less than seven years in a state facility. Both are appealing their sentences while incarcerated. Kozlowski has so far raised over $105.8 million by selling off a Monet, a Renoir, his three-bedroom condominium in Beaver Creek, Colorado, and his Nantucket home.

To restore investors' faith in the company, Tyco's new management team worked hard to reorganize the company and recover some of the funds taken by Kozlowski. At its annual meeting, shareholders elected a completely new board of directors and voted to make future executive severance agreements subject to shareholder approval and to require the board chairman to be an independent person, rather than a Tyco CEO. However, the shareholders elected to keep the company incorporated in Bermuda. In 2006 Breen announced that Tyco would be splitting into three entities: Tyco Healthcare ($10 billion, 40,000 employees), one of the world's leading diversified health-care companies; Tyco Electronics ($12 billion, 88,000 employees), the world's largest passive electronic components manufacturer; and the combination of Tyco Fire & Security and Engineered Products & Services (TFS/TEPS) ($18 billion, 118,000 employees), a global business with leading positions in residential and commercial security, fire protection, and industrial products and services. Tyco has survived the doomsday predictions with over $40 billion in revenue, and their employees have sighed a breath of relief for their jobs and pensions.

QUESTIONS

1. What are the ethical and legal issues in this case?
2. What role did Tyco's corporate culture play in the scandal?
3. What roles did the board of directors, CEO, CFO, and legal counsel play?
4. Have Tyco's recent actions been sufficient to restore confidence in the company?
5. What other actions should the company take to demonstrate that it intends to play by the rules?
6. How will the implementation of the Sarbanes–Oxley Act of 2002 prevent future dilemmas in Tyco?
7. Can the SEC trust Tyco's new board?

SOURCES: Bud Angst, "The Continuing Tyco Saga: December 2002," *[Valley View, PA] Citizen Standard*, January 1, 2003, via http://budangst.com/news/News763.htm; James Bandler and Jerry Guidera, "Tyco Ex-CEO's Party for Wife Cost $2.1 Million, but Had Elvis," *Wall Street Journal*, September 17, 2002, A1; Anthony Bianco, William Symonds, and Nanette Byrnes, "The Rise and Fall of Dennis Kozlowski," *BusinessWeek*, December 23, 2002, 64–77; Laurie P. Cohen, "Tyco Ex-Counsel Claims Auditors Knew of Loans," *Wall Street Journal* online, October 22, 2002, http://online.wsj.com/article_print0,,SB103524176089398951,00.html; Laurie P. Cohen and John Hechinger, "Tyco Suits Say Clandestine Pacts Led to Payments," *Wall Street Journal*, June 18, 2002, A3, A10; Laurie P. Cohen and Mark Maremont, "Tyco Ex-Director Faces Possible Criminal Charges," *Wall Street Journal*, September 9, 2002, A3, A11; Laurie P. Cohen and Mark Maremont, "Tyco Relocations to Florida Are Probed," *Wall Street Journal*, June 10, 2002, A3, A6; "Corporate Scandals: Tyco, International," MSNBC, www.msnbc.com/news/corpscandal_front.asp?odm=C2ORB (accessed April 4, 2003); "Former Tyco Execs Face Fraud Charges," Canadian Broadcasting Corporation online, September 12, 2002, www.cbc.ca/stories/2002/09/12/tyco020912; Charles Gasparino, "Merrill Replaced Its Tyco Analyst After Meeting," *Wall Street Journal*, September 17, 2002, C1, C13; Jerry Guidera, "Veteran Tyco Director Steps Down," *Wall Street Journal*, November 12, 2002, A8; "History," Tyco International, www.tyco.com/tyco/history.asp (accessed April 25, 2003); Arianna Huffington, "Pigs at the Trough Sidebars," Arianna Online, www.ariannaonline.com/books/pigs_updown.html (accessed April 25, 2003); Louis Lavelle, "Rebuilding Trust in Tyco," *BusinessWeek*, November 25, 2002, 94–96; Robin

Londner, "Tyco to Consider Reincorporation, Auditor Removed," *[South Florida] Business Journal* online, March 10, 2003, http://southflorida.bizjournal.com/southflorida/stories/2003/03/10/daily2.html; Loann Lublin and Jerry Guidera, "Tyco Board Criticized on Kozlowski," *Wall Street Journal,* June 7, 2002, A5; Mark Maremont, "Tyco May Report $1.2 Billion in Fresh Accounting Problems" *Wall Street Journal* online, April 30, 2003, http://online.wsj.com/article/0,,SB105166908562976400,00.html?mod=home_whats_news_us; Mark Maremont, "Tyco Seeks Hefty Repayments from Former Financial Officer," *Wall Street Journal,* October 7, 2002, A6; Mark Maremont and Laurie P. Cohen, "Ex-Tyco CEO Is Likely to Face Charges over Unauthorized Pay," *Wall Street Journal,* September 12, 2002, A1, A8; Mark Maremont and John Hechinger, "Tyco's Ex-CEO Invested in Fund Run by Director," *Wall Street Journal* online, October 23, 2002, http://online.wsj.com/article_print0,,SB1035329530787240111,00.html; Mark Maremont and Jerry Markon, "Former Tyco Chief, Two Others Face New Charges and Lawsuits," *Wall Street Journal,* September 13, 2002, A3, A6; Mark Maremont and Jerry Markon, "Former Tyco Executives Are Charged," *Wall Street Journal* online, September 13, 2002, http://online.wsj.com/article_print0,SB1031836600798528755,00.html; Mark Maremont and Jerry Markon, "Tyco's Kozlowski Is Indicted on Charges of Tax Evasion," *Wall Street Journal,* June 5, 2002, A1, A7; Samuel Maull, "Kozlowski Claims Tyco Owes Him Millions," *Real Cities* online, March 14, 2003, www.realcities.com/mld/realcities/business/financial_markets/5395148.htm; Kevin McCoy, "Tyco Acknowledges More Accounting Tricks," *USA Today,* December 31, 2002, 3B; Kevin McCoy, "Investigators Scrutinize $20M Tyco Fee," *USA Today,* September 16, 2002, 1B; Kevin McCoy, "Directors' Firms on Payroll at Tyco," *USA Today,* September 18, 2002, 1B; Gary Panter, "The Big Kozlowski," *Fortune,* November 18, 2002, 123–126; Stephen Taub, "Tyco on Tyco: Errors Made, but No Fraud," CFO.com, December 31, 2002, www.cfo.com/article/1,5309,8596,00.html?f=related; "Tyco's History Under Kozlowski," *Washington Post* online, June 3, 2002, www.washingtonpost.com; "Tyco's Shareholders Defeat Proposal to Leave Bermuda," *USA Today* online, March 6, 2003, www.usatoday.com/money/industries/retail/2003-03-06-tyco_x.htm; "Tyco Smells Smoke at Fire Unit," TheStreet.com, March 12, 2003, www.thestreet.com/_yahoo/tech/earnings.10073763.html; 2006, http://www.tyco.com/livesite.

The American Red Cross

BRIEF HISTORY

The American Red Cross (ARC) is an independent organization supported by public financial donations and volunteerism. Its mission is to "provide relief to victims of disasters and help people prevent, prepare for and respond to emergencies." The ARC was initially founded in 1881 by Clara Barton, who had been inspired by the work of the International Red Cross while on a trip to Europe during the Franco-Prussian War of 1870–1871. Barton was determined to bring the model back to the United States, and subsequently led the organization through its first domestic and international relief missions, including assisting the U.S. military during the Spanish-American War in 1898. The ARC is one of a handful of organizations chartered by the United States government, receiving its first federal charter in 1900.

As a member of the International Federation of Red Cross and Red Crescent Societies, the ARC joins more than 175 other national societies in bringing aid to victims of disasters throughout the world. The ARC follows the seven fundamental bylaws to which all Red Cross societies must conform: humanity, impartiality, neutrality, independence, voluntary service, unity, and universality.

ORGANIZATIONAL STRUCTURE

Today the American Red Cross consists of roughly half a million volunteers and 35,000 employees. For many years the ARC has been a fifty-member, all-volunteer Board of Governors. The President of the United States is the honorary chairman of the Red Cross and appoints eight governors, including the chairman of the board. The

We appreciate the work of Michelle Watkins and John Paul Schilling, under the direction of O. C. Ferrell and Jennifer Jackson, in the writing of this case. This case was developed for classroom discussion rather than to illustrate either effective or ineffective handling of an administrative, ethical, or legal discussion by management. All sources used for this case were obtained through publicly available material.

chairman nominates and the board elects the president, who is responsible for carrying into effect the policies and programs of the board. This arrangement is undergoing changes that will be discussed later in the case.

The ARC is made up of over 700 local chapters across the country. These chapters receive funding from the national Red Cross. Directors of local chapters are authorized to run day-to-day operations. Representatives of the local chapters dominate the board of governors. In recent history, the board has clashed with top national leadership.

TROUBLE AT THE TOP: EXECUTIVE TURNOVER

The past decade has seen a high rate of turnover in the boardroom at the Red Cross. Since Elizabeth Dole's resignation as Chair in 1999, the ARC has had seven different permanent or acting heads. President Bernadine Healy (1999–2001) was forced to resign following mismanagement of the response to the September 11 attacks. Similarly, president and chief executive officer Marsha J. Evans (2002–2005) was ousted after the Hurricane Katrina debacle, though the official reason for her departure was communication problems with the board. More recently, Mark W. Everson was President and CEO for the brief period between May 29, 2007, and November 27, 2007. Everson was forced to resign after an inappropriate sexual relationship with a subordinate came to light.

This constant executive turnover has significantly weakened the venerable organization's ability to carry out its federal mandate. Some blame the oversized board of directors. "The board seems to think it is a hiring and firing agency, and does not see its role as building a strong Red Cross," said Paul C. Light, a professor of public service at New York University. "The constant change in leadership is debilitating and does nothing to address the real problem, which is years and years of underinvestment in telecommunications, technology and other infrastructure to help the organization with its mission." In the cases of both Ms. Healy and Mr. Everson, the board spent a considerable amount of time and money conducting a search for the "right person," nearly two years and eighteen months, respectively.

Further tarnishing the reputation of the agency, the ARC has a history of awarding large severance packages for ousted executives, no matter how short the term served. Bernadine Healy received $1.9 million in salary and severance pay upon her departure in late 2001. Marsha Evans received a total of $780,000 in December 2005; this comprised eighteen months' severance pay and a $36,495 unpaid bonus. Speaking of the damage to the organization, Diana Aviv, president and chief executive of the Independent Sector, a nonprofit trade association, said, "The tragedy of this is that the American Red Cross is probably the best-known nonprofit organization in this country. When the stories about it are more about governance and management and less about how it saves lives, it's sad and not just for the Red Cross."

Leadership troubles have extended into the local chapters as well, indicating systemic problems. In a story on the ARC, CBS News cited a laundry list of misconduct: "the fundraiser in Louisiana caught padding her own bank account with donations; the manager in Pennsylvania who embezzled to support her crack cocaine habit; and the executive in Maryland who forged signatures on purchase orders meant for disaster victims." One of the biggest charity frauds in history occurred at the ARC's Hudson County chapter in New Jersey. Chief executive Joseph Lecowitch and bookkeeper

Catalina Escoto stole well over $1 million in Red Cross funds, squandering it on gambling and gifts to themselves. Escoto also gave herself at least $75,000 in bonuses. Even after Congress mandated changes meant to do away with such problems, in May 2007 an executive in Orange County pleaded guilty to federal charges that she embezzled at least $110,000 of the organization's money.

The systemic problems at the American Red Cross have continued through 2008, with the nonprofit running about a $200 million deficit and eliminating 1000 jobs that year. Management turmoil and a slow economy combined to dampen fund-raising, and the new CEO, Gail McGovern, split the organization's number-two executive position into three separate president-level positions. McGovern filled two of these positions with former AT&T executives with whom she had worked. The ARC was forced to respond by asking for a $150 million appropriation, along with funding to help victims of wildfires, tornadoes, and floods.

Organizational Changes at the Top

It was in late 2006 that Congress took action to try to right the organization after the scandals of September 11, Hurricane Katrina, and the myriad problems at local chapters. Senator Charles E. Grassley filed legislation to overhaul the American Red Cross. This marked the first time in almost sixty years that Congress has moved to amend the organization's charter. The legislation sought to assuage the difficulties in the board by cutting its numbers by more than half, to twenty members by the year 2012. It also restructured the role of the President of the United States in making board appointments. In the past, the President has appointed the chairperson and eight board members, typically cabinet secretaries who rarely attended meetings. Under the proposed legislation, the board would nominate a chairperson for approval and appointment by the president. All other presidential appointments to the board were abolished. An independent ombudsman position was created to take charge of annually reporting to Congress as well as assisting whistle-blowers should agency misconduct be reported.

The American Red Cross Code of Business Ethics and Conduct was updated in January 2007. All employees and volunteers are required to read and sign the two-page document. The ARC offers a "24-hour, confidential and anonymous, 'Concern Connection Line' that provides American Red Cross staff, volunteers and members of the public a way to report concerns or questions regarding potentially illegal, unsafe or unethical conduct." The ARC also published an eight-page "Ethics Rules and Policies," which outlines how business funds, property, and time may be allocated, as well as addressing conflicts of interest, record keeping, and addressing media inquiries. By far the longest section of this document is the page addressing writings by employees and volunteers about September 11, 2001, which details a policy for "creating, marketing and selling books and other literary works relating to the events of September 11, 2001."

The word "ethics" does not appear a single time in the main promotional document the ARC provides governmental agencies. "Compliance" appears only in reference to the ARC's requirements related to the collection of blood donations. No mention is made of employee or volunteer ethics training in any official ARC documents available at its website. While such a program may in fact exist, it is clear from the lack of mentions that this is not a high priority for the organization. In the light of such scandals as have plagued the ARC, stakeholders must be assured repeatedly of the genuine efforts the organization is making to institutionalize ethical best practices. It may be possible that the ARC believes that because its mission is to respond to assist people in need that organizational ethics will automatically occur. Perhaps the assumption is that all employees will be ethical without direction or training.

SEPTEMBER 11, 2001

Slow Response

After the September 11 attacks on New York City's World Trade Center, the ARC was widely criticized for its response. The criticisms began the very day of the incident, as the Pentagon called the office of Red Cross President Bernadine Healy at noon to ask, "Where the hell are you guys? Where is the Red Cross?" The Virginia-based command center known as the Disaster Operations Center (DOC) had, for more than a day afterwards, failed to activate the specialized teams normally sent out after a plane crash or similar disaster. The trouble did not stop there. In the days and weeks following the attacks, the ARC was continually criticized for its management of the donations from thousands of Americans, both financial donations and blood donations.

Monetary Donation Mismanagement

After September 11 monetary donations poured in at an unprecedented rate. Healy set up a separate fund, the "Liberty Fund," for donations earmarked for victims. By the end of October, the fund had received $543 million in pledges. It had, however, distributed less than one-third of those funds to 9/11 relief efforts. The ARC announced that over half would be spent to increase the organization's ability to prepare for and respond to future catastrophes instead. Angry outcries prompted a U.S. Congressional hearing in November 2001. Healy attempted to defend the use of the money, saying it was clear to donors that not all gifts would go directly to immediate relief efforts. To this, Representative Billy Tauzin replied, "it was specially funded for this event, for September 11, and we're also being told parenthetically, 'by the way, we're going to give two thirds of it away to other important Red Cross needs.'" The ethical issue of asking for funds for 9/11 relief efforts, and then appropriating those funds for other purposes, created an explosive debate. At the time of the hearing, Healy had already been forced to resign as ARC president and was on her way out. The ARC subsequently announced that all Liberty Funds monies would go to September 11 victims and their families.

HURRICANE KATRINA

ARC and FEMA Miscommunication

During August and September of 2005, the American Red Cross responded to the disastrous effects of Hurricanes Katrina and Rita, the largest national emergency in the history of the organization. Katrina hit New Orleans on August 23 as a category 3 storm, making it the sixth strongest hurricane ever recorded in the Atlantic. It was also the costliest hurricane in history. Hurricane Rita hit the coast of Louisiana and Texas only a month later and was an even larger category 3 storm. The ARC was able to raise over $2 billion in private donations to fund massive relief efforts for both these disasters.

Yet again, following this outpouring of charitable giving, the American public was left largely unsatisfied by the inadequate and untimely relief efforts depicted in the media. These subpar emergency responses were the outcome of a host of fraudulent, questionable, and inefficient decisions made by the ARC, as well as its federal, state, and local disaster relief counterparts. As a result of these faulty responses, and at the request of various congressional committees, the Government Accountability Office (GAO) wrote a report detailing the inadequacies of the ARC and the Federal Emergency Management Agency (FEMA).

The GAO found that the National Response Plan written by the Department of Homeland Security (DHS) in December 2004 was not properly followed and that coordination between the ARC and FEMA was not satisfactory. The DHS plan depicted the ARC as the primary agency responsible for coordinating federal mass care assistance in support of state and local governments and other voluntary organizations, in charge of meeting needs such as shelter, food, and emergency first aid. During their disaster relief efforts, FEMA and ARC officials disagreed about their roles and responsibilities and failed to communicate appropriate point of contacts for each agency. Additionally, ARC staff was criticized for rotating support positions every two to three weeks. This made it difficult for ARC staff to maintain working relationships with counterparts or to gain expertise in their job functions. Lastly, FEMA failed to implement a comprehensive system to track requests for assistance received from the ARC. One of the ARC's main objectives is properly categorizing and responding to requests for specific goods or necessary services by state and local governments as well as other voluntary organizations.

Donation Mismanagement

FRAUDULENT USE OF FUNDS Along with the failures in communication between FEMA and the ARC, there have been numerous accusations as to the improper management of donated funds. A *New York Times* article summarizes these actions as follows: "The accusations include the improper diversion of relief supplies, failure to follow Red Cross procedures in tracking and distributing supplies, and use of felons as volunteers in the disaster area in violation of Red Cross rules." Numerous Katrina volunteers reported the disappearance of rented cars, electricity generators, and even some 3000 air mattresses. During the relief efforts the ARC had over 235,000 volunteers working in the hurricane disaster areas, more than five times the previous peak of 40,000 volunteers for other relief efforts. It has been reported that several of these volunteers had arrest warrants or other felony charges in their backgrounds. The ARC has a screening process that normally would detect potential volunteers with criminal backgrounds, but during Katrina, the organization was so overwhelmed with people seeking to volunteer that it dropped its usual standards.

Other volunteers complained of unauthorized possession and use of Red Cross computer equipment by staff and volunteers. This equipment was equipped with software to add donated money to debit cards for immediate use by hurricane victims and could easily be misused by unscrupulous volunteers. Other incidents included an ARC call center employee writing money orders in the names of various relief victims and fraudulently cashing them herself.

In response, the ARC has launched an investigation into claims that as an organization, it had virtually no cost controls, little oversight of inventory, and no mechanism for basic background checks on volunteers that were given substantial responsibilities. These examples of mismanagement of charitable funds pose questions regarding the ARC's ability to prevent fraud and protect resources amid the chaos of major national disasters.

Encouragement of Corporate Partnerships

Another storyline that emerged from relief efforts for Hurricane Katrina victims regards the ARC's acceptance and choice of corporate partnerships. During the national emergency situation, many corporations were eager to help. Corporate donations not only help victims, but it casts companies in a good light as it shows their compassion and concern for stakeholders. As a nonprofit organization, and the lead agency in charge of various aspects of the disaster relief, the ARC had a duty to scrutinize the corporate donations.

There are various examples of corporate partnerships during Katrina disaster relief efforts, including Coca-Cola donating water, Anheuser Busch canning and delivering water in Anheuser Busch cans, Master Card and J.P. Morgan issuing ATM cards with access to ARC donated funds for relief victims, and lastly the ARC accepting funds raised by the Southwest Drycleaners Association (SDA) intended to help the SDA portray themselves as a compassionate and community-involved industry.

In a national emergency, these corporate partnerships help to provide access to resources that otherwise may not be available. The ARC deserves praise for incorporating the generosity of private corporations effectively into its overall disaster relief strategy. However, it should be noted that in the future a more active approach to monitoring private firms' donations would benefit the transparency and overall goals of keeping the ARC apolitical and independent from large businesses. This would allow the ARC to assure regular citizens that their charitable donations will not be affected or misused, regardless of corporate involvement. The ARC must be especially careful with whom it is willing to partner during times of national disaster.

An article published in the *Harvard Business Review* states that entities such as the ARC would benefit from greater cooperation and partnerships with private businesses. "It's a good thing when companies pitch in after natural disasters or other calamities. It would be a far better thing if they partnered with aid agencies to make plans before disaster struck." As an example, the authors use the agreement for a partnership between Abbott Laboratories and the ARC to supply blood screening equipment to prove their point that preplanned private partnerships with aid agencies could expedite relief efforts to disaster victims. Through this agreement, Abbott Laboratories will donate a variety of pharmaceutical products ranging from antibiotics to baby food.

Donation Acceptance and Insufficient Capacity

The last point worth mentioning in this analysis of the ARC's donation management involves the actual capacity to electronically accept these donations. The ARC's website has become the main source for receiving individual charitable donations. After September 11, 2001, the organization had to expand its Web-based infrastructure to accommodate additional Web traffic. After the tsunami in Southeast Asia, the ARC found itself once again overwhelmed with Internet traffic to donate money. Internet technology staff was forced to offload some of the expansion capabilities work to contractors in the technology processing industry.

The magnitude of donations for Hurricane Katrina victims was unprecedented in the ARC's history. Internet donors immediately overwhelmed the ARC website's capacity. Over fifty Internet technology staff members worked around the clock to expand capacity six-fold. The ARC once again outsourced some of the workload to Akamai Technologies, Inc.

There is a lesson to be learned from these continued action-and-reaction scenarios regarding online donation acceptance capacity. The lesson is that the ARC would benefit greatly from a plan outlining how to deal with the next crisis of insufficient capacity. Dave Clark, the chief technology officer at the ARC, believes that it would be a good idea to install a collaboration system. This would consist of a plan to effectively partner with various Internet technology firms to alleviate long-term problems regarding online capacity needs, as well as to deter the ARC from dealing with each disaster on a case by case basis, thus better serving the increasingly large online donor community.

MARKETING CHALLENGES AT THE RED CROSS

After much bad press, the ARC faces the many challenges of marketing itself as a prominent, ethical, and transparent nonprofit organization. The ARC must effectively reduce perceived risk associated with giving to it. The ARC must carefully choose partnerships with private corporations that will continue to encourage blood donations. The ARC must also be able to overcome any frivolous lawsuits that might damage its reputation. Lastly, the ARC must focus on marketing the positive impacts the organization has on society, including the vital role it plays in disaster relief. These marketing efforts would ideally translate into increased positive exposure and enhanced support for the organization.

Perceived Risks of Charitable Giving

Unfortunately for the ARC, many donors have been irritated by the numerous reports of fraudulent use of donations. Donors now associate a degree of uncertainty with giving to the ARC, as they question whether the funds will be used properly. Additionally, the number of nonprofit organizations searching for donor funds has increased dramatically over the past twenty years. In 1987 there were 422,000 nonprofits in the United States, and by 2005 the number nearly doubled to 800,000 nonprofit organizations. This growth obviously increases competition for charitable donations, especially in tough economic times. In order to maintain a strong donor base and continue to increase the monetary amount of donations, the ARC must increase transparency to assure donors that their money is being used responsibly.

Partnerships and the Red Cross Symbol

In the fall of 2004, the ARC joined in a unique marketing partnership with the independent film studio Lionsgate to co-market the release of a horror film entitled *Saw IV* while promoting blood collection services. The *Saw* "Give Till It Hurts" blood drive was a key element of the marketing campaign for the fourth installment of the most successful horror franchise of all time. Due in large part to promotions like the *Saw* blood drive in 2004, filmgoers' donations increased from 4200 pints to 41,000 pints of blood in 2007. In October 2008, the *Saw* franchise again held a nationwide blood drive to draw attention to the release of *Saw V.* Marketing efforts such as this benefit both the film producers and the ARC by adding to its main goal, increasing blood supplies, while promoting the film. Many marketers believe that this sort of age-specific marketing strategy, accompanied by word-of-mouth advertising, is recommended to reach a new pool of potential volunteers.

Lastly, the ARC benefits from brand recognition in the form of its internationally recognized Red Cross symbol. This same symbol has also generated controversy in the form of a lawsuit filed by Johnson & Johnson Co. regarding licensing the Red Cross icon for use on commercial products. In 1887, Johnson & Johnson Co. began using the symbol on its surgical packages and registered the trademark for commercial use with the U.S. Patent Office in 1906. The ARC, on the other hand, cites its Federal charter from the year 1900 as the adoption date for its emblem. The ARC further points out that the image was developed in Switzerland in 1863 by the International Committee of the Red Cross where the group decided that "volunteer nurses braving battlefields shall wear in all countries, as a uniform distinctive sign, a white armlet with a red cross." In total, the ARC has sold first aid kits, preparedness kits, and related products that have generated over $2 million in revenue. Johnson & Johnson believed that the ARC was benefiting from consumers confusing the ARC packages for those of Johnson & Johnson, which has very similar packaging. However, the lawsuit was resolved in 2008, with both parties dismissing their suits and countersuits.

Focusing on Positive International Effects

From a marketing perspective, the largest benefit the ARC possesses is its ability to focus on the positive doings of its sister international organizations. The International Federation of Red Cross and Red Crescent Societies have written a report discussing discrimination against women, the elderly, and the disabled in disasters. The IFRC concluded in this report that these situations, as well as sexual violence, can be prevented with an improvement in disaster-preparedness programs. This conclusion effectively states that with stronger support by charitable organizations, such harsh discriminations can be reduced or eliminated in the future.

Even in incidents where the International Committee of the Red Cross (ICRC) is forced to evacuate a country, such as in the case of Myanmar in 2006, the ARC gains publicity from write-ups on its International association. An article in the *Economist* summarizes Myanmar's decision regarding removal of the ICRC. "Last year the organization paid individual visits to more than 3,000 prisoners in 55 places. It has also been providing aid—foods, medicines, help with sanitation, and so on—to villages on the border." The *Economist* goes on to state that "the ICRC announced that the ruling junta last month ordered it to close its five field offices in the country." Thus, even in negative circumstances, the positive coverage on the ICRC benefits the overall marketability of the ARC.

ETHICAL RISKS AND CHALLENGES

The American Red Cross faces many ethical risks and challenges. Some are common challenges for any organization of its size, such as executive compensation, preventing and handling employee misconduct, and considering all stakeholders in its operating model. Other risks are unique to the Red Cross, such as transparent and accurate representation of the organization's need for, and use of, monetary donations, volunteer time, and blood donations. Also unique ethical challenges are maintaining effective and efficient operations to respond to disasters and transparently reporting the organization's accomplishments, failures and opportunities for improvement in disaster response activities.

The executive turnover experienced by the ARC in recent years has also brought to light the compensation awarded top executives. On leaving the company in 2001, Bernadine Healy was given $19 million in salary and severance. Marsha Evans was given $780,000 when she left in 2005. Much time and money was also spent in the search and training for top executives. Employee misconduct has also been an issue, from the discrimination in disbursing relief after disasters to employee embezzlement. Such misconduct has occurred from New Orleans to Maryland and New Jersey, indicating a systemic problem. Addressing stakeholder needs, particularly those of the ARC's thousands of donors, is an ongoing challenge. Donors have a multitude of choices among nonprofits to support with their money and their time. They need open, honest, and transparent communication as to how their resources are allocated and why such decisions are made. Issues like misrepresenting the use of the "Liberty Fund" collected after September 11 must be prevented if the ARC wishes to continue to be relevant.

The ARC must also address the specific ethical risks with its disaster response duties. Clear and efficient communications with Federal and local government agencies is a challenge, as seen in the aftermath of Hurricane Katrina. The ARC must develop strategic plans to better accomplish disaster response goals. These plans must also include how to respond to organizational missteps and failures. Transparent, honest reporting of the ARC's goals, accomplishments, opportunities for improvement, and mistakes would go a long way to restoring the country's trust in the organization.

SUMMARY

In short, the American Red Cross has a stakeholder obligation to fulfill its charter's expectations and deliver these promises effectively and efficiently. Charitable donations fund the nonprofit's operations and volunteers comprise 95 percent of its workers. The ARC staff and volunteers need to be well managed by capable directors and executives within ARC. Improvements to the ARC as an organization must begin with executive leadership and flow downwards to every level of the group. Congressional oversight and interaction with federal, state, and local organizations must also continue to be reviewed and modified to suit current needs.

Disaster relief cooperation in the form of partnering with private corporations to provide efficient and effective responses to victims of disasters should be continued. Joint-marketing practices between the ARC and private businesses should also continue, as long as the mission of the ARC is not compromised by unethical interactions or associations. Close monitoring must also continue to be carried out by the many stakeholders of the ARC, including donors, staff, volunteers, and society in general.

QUESTIONS

1. Explain the possible problems in the ethical culture of the Red Cross that created the issues discussed in this case.
2. Name some of the problems the ARC has encountered with handling donation money.
3. What are some of the reasons for the ARC's ethical dilemmas and how do you suggest it guarantees these problems do not recur in the future?
4. What effect does organizational structure and compensation have on ethical behavior among chief executives at ARC?

SOURCES: "Overview of Red Cross Services," *The American Red Cross,* 2008, 3; "About Us," *ARC,* http://www.redcross.org/aboutus (accessed November 27, 2008); The American Red Cross, "Ethics Rules and Policies," 7–8; Stephanie Strom, "Firing Stirs New Debate Over Red Cross," *New York Times,* November 29, 2007, http://www.nytimes.com/2007/11/29/us/29cross.html?ref=us (accessed April 14, 2008); Stephanie Strom, "President of Red Cross Resigns; Board Woes, Not Katrina, Cited," *New York Times,* December 14, 2005, http://www.nytimes.com/2005/12/14/politics/14redcross.html (accessed December 22, 2008); Jacqueline L. Salmon, "Red Cross Gave Ousted Executive $780,000 Deal," *Washington Post,* March 4, 2006, A9; Sharyl Attkisson, "Disaster Strikes in Red Cross Backyard," *CBS Evening News,* July 29, 2002, http://www.cbsnews.com/stories/2002/07/29/eveningnews/main516700.shtml (accessed April 21, 2008); Randal C. Archibold, "California: Ex-Executive at Red Cross Pleads Guilty," *New York Times,* May 26, 2007, http://www.nytimes.com/2007/05/26/us/26brfs-EXEXECUTIVEA_BRF.html?_r=l (accessed December 22, 2008); Mike Spector, "Red Cross CEO Shuffles Executive Ranks," *Wall Street Journal,* September 23, 2008, http://online.wsj.com/article/SB122220688507068655.html (accessed October 21, 2008); Stephanie Strom, "Bill Would Restructure Red Cross," *New York Times,* December 5, 2006, http://www.nytimes.com/2006/12/05/washington/05cross.html (accessed April 17, 2008); Deborah Sontag, "What Brought Bernadine Healy Down?" *New York Times,* December 21, 2001, http://query.nytimes.com/gst/fullpage.html?res=9C02EEDC173EF930A15751ClA9679C8B63 (accessed December 22, 2008); Ray Suarez, "Red Cross Woes," *The NewsHour with Jim Lehrer,* December 19, 2001; United States Government Accountability Office, "Coordination Between FEMA and the Red Cross Should Be Improved for the 2006 Hurricane Season," *Report to Congressional Committees: Hurricanes Katrina and Rita,* June 2006, 2; Stephanie Strom, "Red Cross Sifting Internal Charges Over Katrina Aid," *New York Times,* March 24, 2006, A2; Yochi Dreazen, "More Katrina Woes: Incidents of Fraud at Red Cross Centers," *Wall Street Journal,* October 14, 2005, B1; Jeremy Mullman, "Shoe on the Other Foot for Marin Institute," *Advertising Age* 77, no. 20 (2006): 8; David Breitkopf, "Stored-Value Cards for Katrina Victims," *American Banker* 170, no. 173 (2005): 20; Anisya Thomas and Lynn Fritz, "Disaster Relief, Inc.," *Harvard Business Review* 84, no. 11 (2006): 121; Carmen Nobel, "Donations Test Red

Cross Staff," *Eweek* 22, no. 37 (2005): 23; "Caveat, Donor," *Searcher* 15, no. 2 (2007): 14; "Red Crossing the Line," *Brandweek,* September 3, 2007, 38; Franz Hackl and Gerald Josef Pruckner, "Demand and Supply of Emergency Help: An Economic Analysis of Red Cross Services," *Health Policy* 77, no. 3 (2006): 338; "The Battle Stations of the Cross," *Modern Healthcare,* August 20, 2007, 36; "Johnson & Johnson and American Red Cross Announce Resolution to Lawsuit," *Fox Business Online,* June 17, 2008, http://www.foxbusiness.com/story/markets/industries/health-care/johnson—johnson-american-red-cross-announce-resolution-lawsuit (accessed December 22, 2008); "Discrimination in Disasters," *Time,* December 31, 2007, 31; "Red Cross Does Not Mark the Spot," *Economist,* December 2, 2006, 47.

Mattel Responds to Ethical Challenges

Mattel, Inc. is a world leader in the design, manufacture, and marketing of family products. Well-known for toy brands such as Barbie, Fisher-Price, Disney, Hot Wheels, Matchbox, Tyco, Cabbage Patch Kids, and board games such as Scrabble, the company boasts nearly $6 billion in annual revenue. Headquartered in El Segundo, California, with offices in thirty-six countries, Mattel markets its products in over one hundred and fifty nations.

It all started in a California garage workshop when Ruth and Elliot Handler and Matt Matson founded Mattel in 1945. Mattel started out making picture frames, but the founders soon recognized the profitability of the toy industry and switched their emphasis to toys. Mattel became a publicly-owned company in 1960, with sales exceeding $100 million by 1965. Over the next forty years, Mattel went on to become the world's largest toy company in terms of revenue.

Mattel has had its share of losses over its history. During the mid- to late-1990s, Mattel lost millions in declining sales and bad business acquisitions. In January 1997, Jill Barad took over as Mattel's CEO. Barad's management style was characterized as strict and her tenure at the helm proved challenging for many employees. While Barad had been successful in building the Barbie brand to $2 billion by the end of the twentieth century, growth slowed in the early twenty-first century. Declining sales at outlets such as Toys "Я" Us marked the start of some difficulties for the retailer, responsibilities for which Barad accepted and resigned in 2000.

Robert Eckert replaced Barad as CEO. Aiming to turn things around, Eckert sold unprofitable units and cut hundreds of jobs. In 2000, under Eckert, Mattel was granted the highly sought-after licensing agreement for products related to the *Harry Potter* series of books and movies. The company continued to flourish and build its reputation, even earning the Corporate Responsibility Award from UNICEF in 2003. Mattel released its first Annual Corporate Responsibility Report the following year. By 2008 Mattel had fully

This case was written by Debbie Thorne, John Fraedrich, O. C. Ferrell, and Jennifer Jackson, with the editorial assistance of Jennifer Sawayda. This case was developed for classroom discussion rather than to illustrate either effective or ineffective handling of an administrative, ethical, or legal discussion by management. All sources used for this case were obtained through publicly available material.

realized a turnaround and was recognized as one of *Fortune* magazine's "100 Best Companies to Work For" and *Forbes* magazine's "100 Most Trustworthy U.S. Companies."

MATTEL'S CORE PRODUCTS

Barbie and American Girl

Among its many lines of popular toy products, Mattel is famous for owning top girls' brands. In 1959, Mattel introduced a product that would change its future forever: the Barbie doll. One of the founders, Ruth Handler, had noticed how her daughter loved playing with paper cutout dolls. She decided to create a doll based on a young adult rather than on a baby. Barbie took off to become one of Mattel's critical product lines and the number-one girls' brand in the world. Since her introduction, Mattel has sold more than 1 billion Barbie dolls in over one hundred and fifty countries. The Barbie line today includes dolls, accessories, Barbie software, and a broad assortment of licensed products such as books, apparel, food, home furnishings, home electronics, and movies.

To supplement the Barbie line, in 1998 Mattel acquired a popular younger type of doll. Mattel announced it would pay $700 million to Pleasant Co. for its high-end American Girl collection. American Girl dolls are sold with books about their lives, which take place during important periods of U.S. history. The American Girl brand includes several book series, accessories, clothing for dolls and girls, and a magazine that ranks in the top ten American children's magazines.

Hot Wheels

Hot Wheels roared into the toy world in 1968. More than thirty years later, the brand is hotter than ever and includes high-end collectibles, NASCAR (National Association for Stock Car Auto Racing) and Formula One models for adults, high-performance cars, track sets, and play sets for children of all ages. The brand is connected with racing circuits worldwide. More than 15 million boys aged 5 to 15 are avid collectors, each owning forty-one cars on average. Two Hot Wheels cars are sold every second of every day. The brand began with cars designed to run on a track and has evolved into a "lifestyle" brand with licensed Hot Wheels shirts, caps, lunch boxes, backpacks, and more. Together, Hot Wheels and Barbie generate 45 percent of Mattel's revenue and 65 percent of its profits.

Cabbage Patch Kids

Since the introduction of mass-produced Cabbage Patch Kids in 1982, more than 90 million dolls have been sold worldwide. In 1994, Mattel took over selling these beloved dolls after purchasing production rights from Hasbro. In 1996, Mattel created a new line of Cabbage Patch doll, called Snacktime Kids, which was expected to meet with immense success. The Snacktime Kids had moving mouths that enabled children to "feed" them plastic snacks. However, the product backfired. The toy had no on/off switch and reports of children getting their fingers or hair caught in the dolls' mouths surfaced during the 1996 holiday season. Mattel voluntarily pulled the dolls from store shelves by January

1997, and offered consumers a cash refund of $40 on returned dolls. The U.S. Consumer Product Safety Commission applauded Mattel's handling of the Snacktime Kids situation. Mattel effectively managed a situation that could easily have created bad publicity or a crisis situation. Mattel stopped producing Cabbage Patch Kids in 2000.

MATTEL'S COMMITMENT TO ETHICS AND SOCIAL RESPONSIBILITY

Mattel's core products and business environment create many ethical issues. Because the company's products are designed primarily for children, it must be sensitive to social concerns about children's rights. It must also be aware that the international environment often complicates business transactions. Different legal systems and cultural expectations about business can create ethical conflict. Finally, the use of technology may present ethical dilemmas, especially regarding consumer privacy. Mattel has recognized these potential issues and taken steps to strengthen its commitment to business ethics. The company also purports to take a stand on social responsibility, encouraging its employees and consumers to do the same.

Privacy and Marketing Technology

One issue Mattel has tried to address repeatedly is that of privacy and online technology. Advances in technology have created special marketing issues for Mattel. The company recognizes that because it markets to children, it must communicate with parents regarding its corporate marketing strategy. Mattel has taken steps to inform both children and adults about its philosophy regarding Internet-based marketing tools, such as the Hot Wheels website. This website contains a lengthy online privacy policy, part of which is excerpted below:

> Mattel, Inc. and its family of companies ("Mattel") are committed to protecting your online privacy when visiting a website operated by us. We do not collect and keep any personal information online from you unless you volunteer it and you are 13 or older. We also do not collect and keep personal information online from children under the age of 13 without consent of a parent or legal guardian, except in limited circumstances authorized by law and described in this policy. . . .[1]

By assuring parents that their children's privacy will be respected, Mattel demonstrates that it takes its responsibility of marketing to children seriously.

Expectations of Mattel's Business Partners

Mattel, Inc. is also making a serious commitment to business ethics in their dealings with other industries. In late 1997, the company completed its first full ethics audit of each of its manufacturing sites as well as the facilities of its primary contractors. The audit revealed that the company was not using any child labor or forced labor, a problem plaguing other overseas manufacturers. However, several contractors were found

---

[1] Mattel, Inc., Online Privacy Policy, http://www.hotwheels.com/policy.asp (accessed December 3, 2008).

to be in violation of Mattel's safety and human rights standards and were asked to change their operations or risk losing Mattel's business. The company now conducts an independent monitoring council audit in manufacturing facilities every three years.

In an effort to continue its strong record on human rights and related ethical standards, Mattel instituted a code of conduct entitled Global Manufacturing Principles in 1997. One of these principles requires all Mattel-owned and contracted manufacturing facilities to favor business partners committed to ethical standards comparable with those of Mattel. Other principles relate to safety, wages, and adherence to local laws. Mattel's audits and subsequent code of conduct were designed as preventative, not punitive measures. The company is dedicated to creating and encouraging responsible business practices throughout the world.

Mattel also claims to be committed to its workforce. As one company consultant noted, "Mattel is committed to improving the skill level of workers . . . [so that they] will experience increased opportunities and productivity." This statement reflects Mattel's concern for relationships between and with employees and business partners. The company's code is a signal to potential partners, customers, and other stakeholders that Mattel has made a commitment to fostering and upholding ethical values.

Legal and Ethical Business Practices

Mattel favors to partner with businesses similarly committed to high ethical standards. At a minimum, partners must comply with the local and national laws of the countries in which they operate. In addition, all partners must respect the intellectual property of the company, and support Mattel in the protection of assets such as patents, trademarks, or copyrights. They are also responsible for product safety and quality, protecting the environment, customs, evaluation and monitoring, and compliance.

Mattel's business partners must have high standards for product safety and quality, adhering to practices that meet Mattel's safety and quality standards. In recent years, however, safety standards have been seriously violated, which will be discussed in more detail later. Also, because of the global nature of Mattel's business and its history of leadership in this area, the company insists that business partners strictly adhere to local and international customs laws. Partners must also comply with all import and export regulations. To assist in compliance with standards, Mattel insists that all manufacturing facilities provide the following:

- ◆ Full access for on-site inspections by Mattel or parties designated by Mattel
- ◆ Full access to those records that will enable Mattel to determine compliance with its principles
- ◆ An annual statement of compliance with Mattel's Global Manufacturing Principles, signed by an officer of the manufacturer or manufacturing facility[2]

With the creation of the Mattel Independent Monitoring Council (MIMCO), Mattel became the first global consumer products company to apply such a system to facilities and core contractors worldwide. The company seeks to maintain an independent monitoring system that provides checks and balances to help ensure that standards are met.

---

[2] "Mattel's Commitment to Ethics," *eBusiness Ethics*, http://www.e-businessethics.com/mattel9.htm.

If certain aspects of Mattel's manufacturing Principles are not being met, Mattel will try to work with its partners to help them fix their problems. New partners will not be hired unless they meet Mattel's standards. If corrective action is advised but not taken, Mattel will terminate its relationship with the partner in question. Overall, Mattel is committed to both business success and ethical standards, and it recognizes that it is part of a continuous improvement process.

Mattel Children's Foundation

Mattel takes its social responsibilities very seriously. Through the Mattel Children's Foundation, established in 1978, the company promotes philanthropy and community involvement among its employees and makes charitable investments to better the lives of children in need. Funding priorities have included building a new Mattel Children's Hospital at the University of California, Los Angeles (UCLA), sustaining the Mattel Family Learning Program, and promoting giving among Mattel employees.

In November 1998, Mattel donated a multiyear, $25 million gift to the UCLA Children's Hospital. The gift was meant to support the existing hospital and provide for a new state-of-the-art facility. In honor of Mattel's donation, the hospital was re-named Mattel Children's Hospital at UCLA.

The Mattel Family Learning Program utilizes computer learning labs as a way to advance children's basic skills. Now numbering more than eighty throughout the United States, Hong Kong, Canada, and Mexico, the labs offer software and technology designed to help children with special needs or limited English proficiency.

Mattel employees are also encouraged to participate in a wide range of volunteer activities as part of "Mattel Volunteers: Happy to Help." Employees serving on boards of local nonprofit organizations or helping with ongoing nonprofit programs are eligible to apply for volunteer grants supporting their organizations. Mattel employees contributing to higher education or to nonprofit organizations serving children in need are eligible to have their personal donations matched dollar for dollar up to $5,000 annually.

International Manufacturing Principles

As a U.S.-based multinational company owning and operating facilities and contracting worldwide, Mattel's Global Manufacturing Principles reflect not only Mattel's need to conduct manufacturing responsibly, but to respect the cultural, ethical, and philosophical differences of the countries in which it operates. These Principles set uniform standards across Mattel manufacturers and attempt to benefit both employees and consumers.

Mattel's Principles cover issues such as wages, work hours, child labor, forced labor, discrimination, freedom of association, and working conditions. Workers must be paid at least minimum wage or a wage that meets local industry standards (whichever is greater). No one under the age of 16 or the local age limit (whichever is higher) may be allowed to work for Mattel facilities. Mattel refuses to work with facilities that use forced or prison labor, or to use these types of labor itself. Additionally, Mattel does not tolerate discrimination. The company states that an individual should be hired and employed based on his or her ability—not on individual characteristics or beliefs. Mattel recognizes all employees' rights to choose to affiliate with organizations or associations without interference. Regarding working conditions, all Mattel facilities and its business partners must provide safe working environments for their employees.

OVERSEAS MANUFACTURING

Despite Mattel's best efforts, not all overseas manufacturers have faithfully adhered to its high standards. Mattel has recently come under scrutiny over their sale of unsafe products. In September 2007, Mattel announced recalls of toys containing lead paint. The problem surfaced when a European retailer discovered lead paint on a toy. An estimated 10 million individual toys produced in China were affected. Mattel quickly stopped production at Lee Der, the company officially producing the recalled toys, after it was discovered that Lee Der had purchased lead-tainted paint to be used on the toys. Mattel blamed the fiasco on the manufacturers' desire to save money in the face of increasing prices. "In the last three or five years, you've seen labor prices more than double, raw material prices double or triple," CEO Eckert said in an interview, "and I think that there's a lot of pressure on guys that are working at the margin to try to save money."

The situation began when Early Light Industrial Co., a subcontractor for Mattel owned by Hong Kong toy tycoon Choi Chee Ming, subcontracted the painting of parts of *Cars* toys to another China-based vendor. The vendor, named Hong Li Da, decided to source paint from a nonauthorized third-party supplier—a violation of Mattel's requirement to use paint supplied directly by Early Light. The products were found to contain "impermissible levels of lead."

On August 2, 2007, it was announced that another of Early Light's subcontractors, Lee Der Industrial Co., used the same lead paint found on *Cars* products. China immediately suspended the company's export license. Afterward, Mattel pinpointed three paint suppliers working for Lee Der—Dongxin, Zhongxin, and Mingdai. This paint was used by Lee Der to produce Mattel's line of Fisher-Price products. It is said that Lee Der purchased the paint from Mingdai due to an intimate friendship between the two companies' owners. On August 11, 2007, Zhang Shuhong, operator of Lee Der, hung himself after paying his 5,000 staff members.

Later that month, Mattel was forced to recall several more toys because of powerful magnets in the toys that could come loose and pose a choking hazard for young children. If more than one magnet is swallowed, the magnets could attract each other inside the child's stomach, causing potentially fatal complications. Over 21 million Mattel toys were recalled in all, and several lawsuits were filed by parents claiming their children had been harmed by these Mattel products.

At first, Mattel blamed Chinese subcontractors for the huge toy recalls; but the company later accepted a portion of the blame for its troubles, while maintaining that Chinese manufacturers were largely at fault. The Chinese view the situation quite differently. As reported by the state-run Xinhua news agency, the spokesman for China's General Administration of Quality Supervision and Inspection and Quarantine said, "Mattel should improve its product design and supervision over product quality. Chinese original equipment manufacturers were doing the job just as importers requested, and the toys conformed to the U.S. regulations and standards at the time of the production." Mattel also faced criticism from many of its consumers, who believed Mattel was denying culpability by placing much of the blame on China. Mattel was later awarded the 2007 "Bad Product" Award by Consumers International.

How did this crisis occur under the watch of a company praised for its ethics and high safety standards? Although Mattel had investigated its contractors, it did not audit the entire supply chain, including subcontractors. This left room for these violations to occur. Mattel has also moved to enforce a rule that subcontractors cannot hire suppliers two or three tiers down. In a statement, Mattel says it has spent more than 50,000 hours investigating its vendors and testing its toys. Mattel also announced a three-point plan. This plan aims to tighten Mattel's control of production, discover and prevent the unauthorized use of subcontractors, and test the products itself rather than depending on contractors.

THE CHINESE GOVERNMENT'S REACTION

Chinese officials eventually did admit the government's failure to properly protect the public. The Chinese government is now promising to tighten supervision of exported products, but effective supervision is challenging in such a large country that is so burdened with corruption. In January 2008, the Chinese government launched a four-month-long nationwide product quality campaign, offering intensive training courses to domestic toy manufacturers to help them brush up on their knowledge of international product standards and safety awareness. As a result of the crackdown, the State Administration for Quality Supervision and Inspection and Quarantine (AQSIQ) announced that it had revoked the licenses of more than 600 Chinese toy makers. As of 2008, the State Administration for Commerce and Industry (SACI) released a report claiming that 87.5 percent of China's newly-manufactured toys met quality requirements. While this represents an improvement, the temptation to cut corners remains strong in a country that uses price, not quality, as its main competitive advantage. Where there is demand, there will be people trying to turn a quick profit.

MATTEL VERSUS FORMER EMPLOYEE AND MGA

Since 2004, Mattel has been embroiled in a bitter intellectual property rights battle with former employee Carter Bryant and MGA Entertainment Inc. over rights to MGA's popular Bratz dolls. Carter Bryant, an on-again/off-again Mattel employee, designed the Bratz dolls and pitched them to MGA. A few months after the pitch Bryant left Mattel to work at MGA, which began producing Bratz in 2001. In 2002, Mattel launched an investigation into whether Bryant had designed the Bratz dolls while employed with Mattel. After two years of investigation, Mattel sued Bryant. A year later MGA fired off a suit of its own, claiming that Mattel was creating Barbies with looks similar to those of Bratz in an effort to eliminate the competition. Mattel answered by expanding its own suit to include MGA and its CEO, Isaac Larian.

For decades, Barbie has reigned supreme on the doll market. However, Bratz dolls have recently given Barbie a run for her money. In 2005, four years after the brand's debut, Bratz sales were at $2 billion. At the same time, Barbie was suffering from declining sales. Between June and April 2008, Barbie's gross sales fell by 6 percent. The past year has shown that Bratz is not immune to sluggish sales either, however, as consumers cut back their spending across the board.

Much evidence appears to point toward Bryant having conceived of Bratz dolls while at Mattel. Four years after the initial suit was filed, Bryant settled with Mattel under an undisclosed set of terms. And, although some decisions have been made, the battle between Mattel and MGA continues. In July 2008, a jury deemed MGA and its CEO liable for what it termed "intentional interference" regarding Bryant's contract with Mattel. In August 2008, Mattel received damages in the range of $100 million. Although Mattel first requested damages of $1.8 billion, the company is pleased with the principle behind the victory.

In December 2008, Mattel appeared to win another victory when a California judge banned MGA from issuing or selling any more Bratz dolls. However, the company was allowed to keep Bratz on the shelves until after Christmas. In the worst-case scenario, MGA will have to discontinue its line of Bratz dolls completely or hand Bratz over to Mattel. Some analysts, however, think this outcome is unlikely. Instead, they expect Mattel to work out a deal with MGA in which MGA can continue to sell Bratz dolls as long as Mattel shares in some of the profits. MGA plans to appeal the court ruling. Whatever the outcome, Mattel has managed to gain some control over Barbie's stiffest competition.

MATTEL LOOKS TOWARD THE FUTURE

Like all major companies, Mattel has weathered its share of storms. In recent years, the company has faced a series of difficult and potentially crippling challenges. During the wave of toy recalls, some analysts suggested that the company's reputation was battered beyond repair. Mattel, however, has refused to go quietly. Although the company admits to poorly handling recent affairs, it is attempting to rectify its mistakes and to prevent future mistakes as well. The company appears dedicated to shoring up its ethical defenses to protect both itself and its customers. With the economic future of the United States uncertain, Mattel may be in for slow growth for some time to come. What is certain is Mattel's commitment to rebuilding its reputation as an ethical company. Mattel is hard at work restoring goodwill and faith in its brands, even as it continues to be plagued with residual distrust over the lead paint scandal. Reputations are hard won and easily lost, but Mattel appears to be steadfast in its commitment to corporate ethics and delivering quality products.

QUESTIONS

1. Do manufacturers of products for children have special obligations to consumers and society? If so, what are these responsibilities?
2. How effective has Mattel been at encouraging ethical and legal conduct by its manufacturers? What changes and additions would you make to the company's Global Manufacturing Principles?
3. To what extent is Mattel responsible for issues related to its production of toys in China? How might Mattel have avoided these issues?
4. Do you feel that Mattel should receive control of MGA's Bratz dolls? If so, what actions should Mattel take regarding Bratz?

SOURCES: "About Mattel—Company History," "Responsibility—Executive Summary," "Cabbage Patch Kids Overview," "Barbie Overview," "Hot Wheels Overview," "Mattel Press Releases: 9/29/00," "Responsibility—Independent Monitoring," and "Mattel Children's Foundation" Mattel, www.mattel.com (all accessed January 17, 2001); Lisa Bannon and Carlta Vitzhum, "One-Toy-Fits-All: How Industry Learned to Love the Global

Kid," *Wall Street Journal,* April 30, 2003, http://online.wsj.com; Adam Bryant, "Mattel CEO Jill Barad and a Toyshop That Doesn't Forget to Play," *New York Times,* October 11, 1998; Bill Duryea, "Barbie-holics: They're Devoted to the Doll," *St. Petersburg Times,* August 7, 1998; Rachel Engers, "Mattel Board Members Buy $30 Million in Stock: Insider Focus," Bloomberg.com, December 22, 2000; "Global Manufacturing Principles," Mattel, 1998, p. 1; James Heckman, "Legislation," *Marketing News,* December 7, 1998, 1, 16; Mattel, Inc., Hot Wheels website, www.hotwheels.com/; "Independent Monitoring Council Completes Audits of Mattel Manufacturing Facilities in Indonesia, Malaysia and Thailand," Mattel, press release, November 15, 2002, www.shareholder.com/mattel/news/20021115-95295.cfm; "Investors and Media," "Mattel Children's Foundation," and "Mattel Independent Monitoring Council," Mattel, www.mattel.com/about_us/ (all accessed April 30, 2003); "Mattel and U.S. Consumer Product Safety Commission Announce Voluntary Refund Program for Cabbage Patch Kids Snacktime Kids Dolls," U.S. Consumer Product Safety Commission, Office of Information and Public Affairs, Release No. 97-055, January 6, 1997; "Mattel, Inc., Launches Global Code of Conduct Intended to Improve Workplace, Workers' Standard of Living," *Canada NewsWire,* November 21, 1997 (for more information on Mattel's code, the company can be contacted at 310-252-3524); "Mattel, Inc., Online Privacy Policy," Mattel, www.hotwheels.com/policy.asp (accessed April 30, 2003); Marla Matzer, "Deals on Hot Wheels," *Los Angeles Times,* July 22, 1998; Patricia Sellers, "The 50 Most Powerful Women in American Business," *Fortune,* October 12, 1998; "Toymaker Mattel Bans Child Labor," *Denver Post,* November 21, 1998; Michael White, "Barbie Will Lose Some Curves When Mattel Modernizes Icon," *Detroit News,* November 18, 1997; Laura S. Spark, "Chinese Product Scares Prompt US Fears," *BBC News,* July 10, 2007, http://news.bbc.co.uk/2/hi/americas/6275758.stm (accessed April 5, 2008); Benjamin B. Olshin, "China, Culture, and Product Recalls," S2R, August 20, 2007, http://www.s2r.biz/s2rpapers/papers-Chinese_Product.pdf (accessed April 5, 2008); "Mattel Recalls Batman™ and One Piece™ Magnetic Action Figure Sets," Consumer Product Safety Commission, August 14, 2007, http://service.mattel.com/us/recall/J1944CPSC.pdf (accessed April 2, 2008); Parker, "Magnetic Toy Sets," YourLawyer.com, April 2, 2008, http://www.yourlawyer.com/topics/overview/magnetic_toy_sets; "Product Recall," Mattel Consumer Service, April 1, 2008, http://service.mattel.com/us/recall.asp; David Barboza and Louise Story, "Toymaking in China, Mattel's Way," *New York Times,* July 26, 2007, http://www.nytimes.com/2007/07/26/business/26toy.html? pagewanted=1&_ r=3&hp (accessed April 6, 2008); Shu-Ching Chen, "A Blow to Hong Kong's Toy King," Forbes.com, August 15, 2007, http://www.forbes.com/2007/08/15/mattel-china-choi-face-markets-cx_jc_0815autofacescan01. html (accessed April 7, 2008); David Barboza, "Scandal and Suicide in China: A Dark Side of Toys," Iht.com, August 23, 2007, http://www.iht.com/articles/2007/08/23/business/23suicide.php?page=1 (accessed April 6, 2008); "The United States Has Not Restricted Imports Under the China Safeguard," United States Government Accountability Office, September 2005, http://www.gao.gov/new.items/d051056.pdf (accessed April 4, 2008); Jack A. Raisner, "Using the 'Ethical Environment' Paradigm to Teach Business Ethics: The Case of the Maquiladoras," *Journal of Business Ethics,* 1997, http://www.springerlink.com/content/nv62636101163v07/fulltext.pdf (accessed April 10, 2008); "87.5% Toys Meet Requirements on Domestic Market," China Toy Association, Xinhua, April 10, 2008, http://www.toy-cta.org/en/news_open.asp?id= 3118&columnid=143&columnlayer=0143; "Mattel Awarded $100M in Doll Lawsuit," *USA Today,* August 27, 2008, B-1; Nicholas Casey, "Mattel Prevails Over MGA in Bratz-Doll Trial," *Wall Street Journal,* July 18, 2008, B-18–B-19; Nicholas Casey, "Mattel to Get Up to $100 Million in Bratz Case," *Wall Street Journal,* August 27, 2008, http://online.wsj.com/article_print/SB121978263398273857.html (accessed August 28, 2008); American Girl, www.americangirl.com (accessed September 14, 2008); "Barbie," www.mattel.com, http://www.mattel.com/our_toys/ot_barb.asp (accessed September 14, 2008); Mattel Annual Report 2007, http://www.shareholder.com/mattel/downloads/2007AR.pdf (accessed September 14, 2008); "Mattel History," http://www.mattel.com/about_us/history/default.asp?f=true (accessed December 3, 2008); "Learning from Mattel," Tuck School of Business at Dartmouth, http://mba.tuck.dartmouth.edu/pdf/2002-1-0072.pdf (accessed December 3, 2008); "Mattel to Sell Learning Company," *Direct,* October 2, 2000, http://directmag.com/news/marketing_mattel_sell_learning/ (accessed December 3, 2008); Miranda Hitti, "9 Million Mattel Toys Recalled," WebMD, August 14, 2007, http://children.webmd.com/news/20070814/9_million_mattel_toys_recalled (accessed December 3, 2008); "Third Toy Recall by Mattel in Five Weeks," *Business Standard,* September 6, 2006, http://www.business-standard.com/india/storypage.php? autono=297057 (accessed December 3, 2008); "International Bad Product Awards 2007," Consumers International, http://www.consumersinternational.org/Shared_ASP_Files/UploadedFiles/527739D3-1D7B-47AF-B85C-6FD25779149B_InternationalBad ProductsAwardspressbriefing.pdf (accessed December 3, 2008); Gina Keating, "MGA 'Still Assessing' Impact of Bratz Ruling: CEO," Yahoo! News, December 4, 2008, http://news.yahoo.com/s/nm/20081205/bs_nm/us_mattel_larian_1 (accessed December 5, 2008); "Bratz Loses Battle of the Dolls," *BBC News,* December 5, 2008, http://news.bbc.co.uk/2/hi/business/7767270.stm (accessed December 5, 2008).

Arthur Andersen: Questionable Accounting Practices

Arthur Andersen and partner Clarence DeLany founded Arthur Andersen LLP in Chicago in 1913. Over a span of nearly ninety years, the Chicago accounting firm would become known as one of the "Big Five" largest accounting firms in the United States, together with Deloitte & Touche, PricewaterhouseCoopers, Ernst & Young, and KPMG. For most of those years, the firm's name was nearly synonymous with trust, integrity, and ethics. Such values are crucial for a firm charged with independently auditing and confirming the financial statements of public corporations, whose accuracy investors depend on for investment decisions.

In its earlier days, Andersen set standards for the accounting profession and advanced new initiatives on the strength of its then undeniable integrity. One example of Andersen's leadership in the profession occurred in the late 1970s when companies began acquiring IBM's new 360 mainframe computer system, the most expensive new computer technology available at the time. Many companies had been depreciating computer hardware on the basis of an assumed ten-year useful life. Andersen, under the leadership of Leonard Spacek, determined that a more realistic life span for the machines was five years. Andersen therefore advised its accounting clients to use the shorter time period for depreciation purposes, although this resulted in higher expenses charged against income and a smaller bottom line. Public corporations that failed to adopt the more conservative measure would receive an "adverse" opinion from Andersen's auditors, something they could ill afford.

Arthur Andersen once exemplified the rock-solid character and integrity that was synonymous with the accounting profession. But high-profile bankruptcies of clients such as Enron and WorldCom capped a string of accounting scandals that eventually cost investors nearly $300 billion and hundreds of thousands of people their jobs. As a result, the Chicago-based accounting firm was forced to close its doors after ninety years of business.

We appreciate the work of Heather Stein, Colorado State University, in helping draft the previous edition of this case. This case was prepared for classroom discussion rather than to illustrate either effective or ineffective handling of an administrative, ethical, or legal decision by management. All sources used for this case were obtained through publicly available material.

THE ADVENT OF CONSULTING

Leonard Spacek joined the company in 1947 following the death of founder Arthur Andersen. He was perhaps best known for his uncompromising insistence on auditor independence, which was in stark contrast to the philosophy of combining auditing and consulting services that many firms, including Andersen itself, later adopted. Andersen began providing consulting services to large clients such as General Electric and Schlitz Brewing in the 1950s. Over the next thirty years, Andersen's consulting business became more profitable per partner than its core accounting and tax services businesses.

According to the American Institute of Certified Public Accountants (AICPA), the objective of an independent audit of a client's financial statements is "the expression of an opinion on the fairness with which [the financial statements] present, in all material respects, financial position, results of operations, and its cash flows in conformity with generally accepted accounting principles." The primary responsibility of an auditor is to express an opinion on a client firm's financial statements after conducting an audit to obtain reasonable assurance that the client's financial statements are free of material misstatement. It is important to note that financial statements are the responsibility of a company's management and not the outside auditor.

At Andersen, growth became the priority, and its emphasis on recruiting and retaining big clients perhaps came at the expense of quality and independent audits. The company linked its consulting business in a joint cooperative relationship with its audit arm, which compromised its auditors' independence, a quality crucial to the execution of a credible audit. The firm's focus on growth also generated a fundamental change in its corporate culture, one in which obtaining high-profit consulting business seems to have been regarded more highly than providing objective auditing services. Those individuals who could deliver the big accounts were often promoted ahead of the practitioners of quality audits.

Andersen's consulting business became recognized as one of the fastest-growing and most profitable consulting networks in the world. Revenues from consulting began catching up with the auditing unit in the early 1980s and surpassed it for the first time in 1984. Although Andersen's consulting business was growing at a rapid pace, its audit practice remained the company's bread and butter. Ten years later, Arthur Andersen merged its operational and business systems consulting units and set up a separate business consulting practice in order to offer clients a broader range of integrated services. Throughout the 1990s, Andersen reaped huge profits by selling consulting services to many clients whose financial statements it also audited. This lucrative full-service strategy would later pose an ethical dilemma for some Andersen partners, who had to decide how to treat questionable accounting practices discovered at some of Andersen's largest clients.

Thanks to the growth of Andersen's consulting services, many viewed it as a successful model that other large accounting firms should emulate. However, this same model eventually raised alarm bells at the Securities and Exchange Commission (SEC), concerned over its potential for compromising the independence of audits. In 1998, then SEC chairman Arthur Levitt publicly voiced these concerns and recommended new rules that would restrict the nonaudit services that accounting firms could provide to their audit clients—a suggestion that Andersen vehemently opposed.

Nonetheless, in 1999 Andersen chose to split its accounting and consulting function into two separate—and often competing—units. Reportedly, under this arrangement, competition between the two units for accounts tended to discourage a team spirit and instead fostered secrecy and selfishness. Communication suffered, hampering the firm's ability to respond quickly and effectively to crises. As revenues grew, the consulting unit demanded greater compensation and recognition. Infighting between the consulting and auditing units grew until the company was essentially split into two opposing factions.

In August 2000, following an arbitration hearing, a judge ruled that Andersen's consulting arm could effectively divorce the accounting firm and operate independently. By that time, Andersen's consulting business consisted of about eleven thousand consultants and brought in global revenues of nearly $2 billion. Arthur Andersen as a whole employed more than eighty-five thousand people worldwide. The new consulting company promptly changed its name to Accenture the following January. The court later ordered Arthur Andersen to change its name to Andersen Worldwide in order to better represent its new global brand of accounting services.

Meanwhile, in January 2001, Andersen named Joseph Berardino as the new CEO of the U.S. auditing practice. His first task was to navigate the smaller company through a number of lawsuits that had developed in prior years. The company paid $110 million in May 2001 to settle claims brought by Sunbeam shareholders for accounting irregularities and $100 million to settle with Waste Management shareholders over similar charges a month later. In the meantime, news that Enron had overstated earnings became public, sending shock waves through the financial markets. Over the following year, many companies, a number of them Andersen clients, were forced to restate earnings. The following sections describe a few of the cases that helped lead to Andersen's collapse.

THE COLLAPSE OF ANDERSEN

Baptist Foundation of Arizona

In what would become the largest bankruptcy of a nonprofit charity in U.S history, the Baptist Foundation of Arizona (BFA), which Andersen served as auditor, bilked investors out of about $570 million. BFA, an agency of the Arizona Southern Baptist Convention, was founded in 1948 to raise and manage endowments for church work in Arizona. It operated like a bank, paying interest on deposits that were used mostly to invest in Arizona real estate. The foundation also offered estate and financial planning services to the state's more than four hundred Southern Baptist churches and was one of the few foundations to offer investments to individuals.

BFA invested heavily in real estate, a more speculative investment strategy than other Baptist foundations in the state traditionally used. Profits from investments were supposed to be used to fund the churches' ministries and numerous charitable causes.

Problems began when the real estate market in Arizona suffered a downturn, and BFA's management came under pressure to show a profit. To do so, foundation officials allegedly concealed losses from investors beginning in 1986 by selling some properties at inflated prices to entities that had borrowed money from the foundation and were unlikely to pay for the properties unless the real estate market turned around. In what court documents would later label a "Ponzi scheme" after a famous swindling case, foundation officials allegedly took money from new investors to pay off existing investors in order to keep cash flowing. In the meantime, the foundation's top officers received six-figure salaries. With obligations to investors mounting, the scheme eventually unraveled, leading to criminal investigations and investor lawsuits against BFA and Andersen; more than half of the foundation's 133 employees were laid off. Finally, the foundation petitioned for Chapter 11 bankruptcy protection in 1999, listing debts of about $640 million against assets of about $240 million.

The investor lawsuit against Andersen accused the auditing firm of issuing false and misleading approvals of BFA's financial statements, which allowed the foundation to perpetuate the fraud. Andersen, in a February 2000 statement, responded that it sympathized with BFA investors but stood by the accuracy of its audit opinions. The firm blamed BFA management for the collapse, arguing that it was given misleading information on which to conduct the audits. However, during nearly two years of investigation, reports surfaced that Andersen had been warned of possible fraudulent activity by some BFA employees, and the firm eventually agreed to pay $217 million to settle the shareholder lawsuit in May 2002.

Sunbeam

Andersen's troubles over Sunbeam Corporation began when its audits failed to address serious accounting errors that eventually led to a class-action lawsuit by Sunbeam investors and the ouster of CEO Albert Dunlap in 1998. Boca Raton–based Sunbeam is the maker of such notable home appliance brands as Mr. Coffee, Mixmaster, Oster, Powermate, and others. Both the lawsuit and a civil injunction filed by the SEC accused Sunbeam of inflating earnings through fraudulent accounting strategies such as "cookie jar" revenues, recording revenue on contingent sales, and accelerating sales from later periods into the present quarter. The company was also accused of using improper "bill-and-hold" transactions, which involves booking sales months ahead of actual shipment or billing, temporarily inflating revenue through accounts receivable, and artificially boosting quarterly net income. As a result, Sunbeam was forced to restate six quarters of financial statements. The SEC's injunction also accused Phillip Harlow, then a partner at Arthur Andersen, of authorizing clean or "unqualified" opinions on Sunbeam's 1996 and 1997 financial statements despite his awareness of many of Sunbeam's accounting and disclosure improprieties. On February 6, 2001, Sunbeam Corporation filed a voluntary petition with the U.S. Bankruptcy Court for the Southern District of New York under Chapter 11 of Title 11 of the Bankruptcy Code. In August 2002, a federal judge approved a $141 million settlement in the case. In it, Andersen agreed to pay $110 million to resolve the claims without admitting fault or liability. Sunbeam's losses to shareholders amounted to over $4.4 billion and seventeen hundred lost jobs. In 2002 Sunbeam Corporation successfully emerged from bankruptcy protection as a private company and new identity—American Household, Inc. (AHI). Its former household products division became the subsidiary Sunbeam Products, Inc. In 2005 AHI was sold to Jarden Consumer Solutions, a wholly owned subsidiary of Jarden Corporation.

Waste Management

Andersen also found itself in court over questionable accounting practices with regard to $1.4 billion of overstated earnings at Waste Management. A complaint filed by the SEC charged Waste Management with perpetrating a "massive" financial fraud over a period of more than five years. According to the complaint, the company's senior management itself violated and aided and abetted others' violations of antifraud, reporting, and record-keeping provisions of federal securities laws, resulting in a loss to investors of more than $6 billion. Andersen was named in the case as having aided the fraud by repeatedly issuing unqualified audit opinions on Waste Management's materially misleading financial statements.

According to SEC documents, Waste Management capped the amount of fees it would pay for Andersen's auditing services, but it advised Andersen that it could earn additional fees through "special work." At first, Andersen identified improper accounting practices and presented them to Waste Management officials in a report called "Proposed Adjusting Journal Entries," which outlined entries that needed to be corrected to avoid understating Waste Management's expenses and overstating its earnings. However, Waste officials refused to make the corrections and instead allegedly entered into a closed-door agreement with Andersen to write off the accumulated errors over a ten-year period and change its underlying accounting practices, but only in future periods. The SEC viewed this agreement as an attempt to cover up past frauds and to commit future frauds.

The result of these cases was that Andersen paid some $220 million to Waste Management shareholders and $7 million to the SEC. Four Andersen partners were sanctioned, and an injunction was obtained against the firm. Andersen, as part of its consent decree, was forced to promise not to sign off on spurious financial statements in the future or it would face disbarment from practicing before the SEC—a promise that it would later break with Enron. After the dust settled, Waste Management shareholders lost about $20.5 billion, and about eleven thousand employees were laid off. In 2001 Waste Management agreed to pay out $457 million for a class-action lawsuit related to Andersen.

Enron

In October 2001, the SEC announced that it was launching an investigation into the accounting of Enron, one of Andersen's biggest clients. Indeed, Andersen's new CEO, Joseph Berardino, had perhaps viewed the $1 million a week in audit fees Enron paid to Andersen, along with the consulting fees it paid to Andersen's spin-off firm, Accenture, as a significant opportunity to expand revenues at Andersen. And, with Enron as a client, Andersen had been able to make 80 percent of the companies in the oil and gas industry its clients. However, on November 8, 2001, Enron was forced to restate five years' worth of financial statements that Andersen had signed off on, accounting for $586 million in losses. Within a month, Enron filed for bankruptcy. The U.S. Justice Department began a criminal investigation into Andersen in January 2002, prompting both Andersen's clients and its employees to jump ship. The auditing firm eventually admitted to destroying a number of documents concerning its auditing of Enron, which led to an indictment for obstruction of justice on March 14, 2002. CEO Berardino stepped down by the end of the month.

As Andersen's obstruction-of-justice trial progressed, Nancy Temple, Andersen's Chicago-based lawyer, demanded Fifth Amendment protection and thus did not have to testify. Many others named her as the "corrupt persuader" who led others astray. She allegedly instructed David Duncan, Andersen's supervisor of the Enron account, to remove her name from memos that could have incriminated her. On June 15, 2002, the jury found Andersen guilty of obstruction of justice, the first accounting firm ever to be convicted of a felony. The company agreed to stop auditing public companies by August 31, 2002, essentially shutting down the business.

Telecommunication Firms

Unfortunately for Andersen, the accusations of accounting fraud did not end with Enron. News soon surfaced that WorldCom, Andersen's largest client, had improperly accounted for nearly $3.9 billion of expenses and had overstated earnings in 2001 and the first part of 2002. After WorldCom restated its earnings, its stock price plummeted, and investors launched a barrage of lawsuits that sent WorldCom into bankruptcy court. WorldCom's bankruptcy filing eclipsed Enron's as the largest in U.S. history. Andersen blamed WorldCom for the scandal, insisting that the expense irregularities had not been disclosed to its auditors and that it had complied with SEC standards in its auditing of WorldCom. WorldCom, however, pointed the finger of blame not only at its former managers but also at Andersen for failing to find the accounting irregularities. The SEC filed fraud charges against WorldCom, which fired its CFO.

While the Enron and WorldCom scandals continued, more telecommunications firms, including Global Crossing and Qwest Communications, came under investigation for alleged accounting improprieties. Both firms had been issued unqualified or clean opinions on audits by Andersen. At the heart of both cases is the issue of fake asset swaps, in which the accused telecommunication companies allegedly exchanged fiber-optic broadband capacity at inflated prices in order to show huge gains. An investor lawsuit was filed against Global Crossing and Andersen alleging that Global Crossing had artificially inflated earnings and that Andersen had violated federal securities laws by issuing unqualified (positive) audit opinions on Global Crossing's financial statements, though it knew or failed to discover they contained material misstatements. Global Crossing filed for Chapter 11 bankruptcy protection and fired Andersen as its auditor. Qwest, which thus far has avoided bankruptcy court, admitted to using improper accounting methods and will likely be forced to restate profits for 1999 through 2001, including $950 million in relation to the swaps and up to $531 million in cash sales of optical capacity.

CORPORATE CULTURE AND ETHICAL RAMIFICATIONS

As the details of these investigations into accounting irregularities and fraud came to light, it became apparent that Andersen was more concerned about its own revenue growth than where the revenue came from or whether its independence as an auditor had been compromised. One of the reasons for this confusion in its corporate culture may have been that numerous inexperienced business consultants and untrained auditors were sent to client sites that were largely ignorant of company policies. Another factor may have been its partners' limited involvement in the process of issuing opinions. As the company grew, the number of partners stagnated. There is also evidence that Andersen had limited oversight over its audit teams and that such visibility was impaired by a relative lack of checks and balances that could have identified when audit teams had strayed from accepted policies. Audit teams had great discretion in terms of issuing financial statements and restatements.

In February 2002, Andersen hired former Federal Reserve Board chairman Paul Volcker to institute reform and help restore its reputation. Soon after Volcker came on board, however, Andersen was indicted for obstruction of justice in connection with the shredding of Enron documents. During the investigations, Andersen had been trying to negotiate merger deals for its international partnerships and salvage what was left of its U.S operations. But amid a mass exodus of clients and partners and Berardino's resignation, the company was forced to begin selling off various business units and ultimately laid off more than seven thousand employees in the United States.

During this time, Alaska Air Group, an Andersen client, restated its 2001 results, which resulted in an *increase* in shareholder equity of $31 million. Alaska Air made the restatement on the recommendation of its new auditor, Deloitte & Touche, which had replaced Andersen in May 2002.

After Andersen was convicted of obstruction of justice, it was fined $500,000, among other penalties. Andersen agreed to cease auditing public corporations by the end of August, essentially marking the end of the ninety-year-old accounting institution. Accenture, its spin-off consulting unit, is free and clear of all charges although the consulting firm seems reluctant to mention its origins and association with Andersen: Nowhere on Accenture's website is the word *Andersen* to be found.

In 2005 the U.S. Supreme Court threw out Arthur Andersen's obstruction-of-justice conviction. A federal jury found Andersen guilty of obstructing justice by "corruptly persuading" workers to shred documents related to alleged improprieties by Enron. But the Supreme Court said the jury instructions diluted the meaning of "corruptly" to the point that it could have covered the type of innocent shredding that companies do each day. The Court did not rule on whether Andersen's shredding was wrong; rather, the case revolved entirely around the adequacy of the jury instructions at the company's trial.

Although some experts believe that the Court's ruling was strictly based on technical issues rather than whether or not Andersen was guilty of obstruction of justice, the fact remains that Andersen may not have gone out of business if this ruling had been made available during the trial. Looking back at this event, accounting consultants and many business executives believe that the quick rush to destroy Arthur Andersen's accounting and auditing business may have had a negative effect on competition and the cost of auditing for all public corporations. On the other hand, Arthur Andersen's involvement with so many accounting fraud cases caused what could have been an overreaction by regulatory entities. Unfortunately for many thousands of Arthur Andersen employees who were not involved in accounting fraud, their lives were affected by all of the events associated with this case.

IMPLICATIONS FOR REGULATION AND ACCOUNTING ETHICS

The accounting scandals of the early twenty-first century sent many Andersen clients into bankruptcy court and subjected even more to greater scrutiny. They also helped spur a new focus on business ethics, driven largely by public demands for greater corporate transparency and accountability. In response, Congress passed the Sarbanes–Oxley Act of 2002, which established new guidelines and direction for

TABLE C7-1 Intentions of the Sarbanes–Oxley Act

Sarbanes–Oxley Act	What It Will Do	What It Could Prevent
Section 104: Inspection of Registered Public Accounting Firms	Verify that financial statements are accurate	Using questionable/illegal accounting practices
Section 201: Services Outside the Scope of Auditors; Prohibited Activities	Restrict auditors to audit activities only	Fostering improper relationships; reducing the likelihood of compromising a good audit for more revenue
Section 203: Audit Partner Rotation	Rotate partners assigned to client so that "fresh eyes" see paperwork	Fostering "partner-in-crime" relationship
Section 204: Auditor Reports to Audit Committees	Auditors must report to committee, who work for the board, not the company	Powerlessness of auditors by giving the board power to investigate and rectify
Section 302: Corporate Responsibility for Financial Reports	Making CEOs personally liable for ensuring that statements are reported accurately	Publishing misleading statements
Section 303: Improper Influence on Conduct of Audits	Removes power from company personnel	Withholding information from auditors by making this illegal
Section 404: Management Assessment of Internal Controls	Gives auditor a voice outside of the audit to attest to policies demonstrated by the company	Information slipping by the SEC and stakeholders by giving more visibility to the firm
Title VIII: Corporate and Criminal Fraud Accountability Act of 2002	Makes it a felony to impede federal investigation; provides whistle-blower protection; allows investigators to review work of auditors	Destruction of documents
Section 1102: Tampering with a Record or Otherwise Impeding an Official Proceeding	Persons acting to corrupt or destroy evidence liable for extended prison term	Others from attempting to interfere in an official investigation

SOURCE: Table adapted from Mandy Storeim, *Andersen LLP: An Assessment of the Company's Dilemmas in Corporate Crisis*, BG660 Final Project, Colorado State University, November 13, 2002.

corporate and accounting responsibility. The act was enacted to combat securities and accounting fraud and includes, among other things, provisions for a new accounting oversight board, stiffer penalties for violators, and higher standards of corporate governance. Table C7–1 discusses some of the components of the act and how it could prevent these types of situations from occurring again.

For the accounting profession, the Sarbanes–Oxley Act emphasizes auditor independence and quality, restricts accounting firms' ability to provide both audit and nonaudit services for the same clients, and requires periodic reviews of audit firms. All are provisions that the Arthur Andersen of the past would likely have supported wholeheartedly. Some are concerned, however, that such sweeping legislative and regulatory reform may be occurring too quickly in response to intense public and political pressure. The worry is that these reforms may not have been given enough forethought and cost–benefit consideration for those public corporations that operate within the law, which comprise the vast majority of corporate America.

QUESTIONS

1. Describe the legal and ethical issues surrounding Andersen's auditing of companies accused of accounting improprieties.
2. What evidence is there that Andersen's corporate culture contributed to its downfall?
3. How can the provisions of the Sarbanes–Oxley Act help minimize the likelihood of auditors failing to identify accounting irregularities?

SOURCES: "$141M Sunbeam Fraud Case Settled; Andersen to Pay Bulk," New York State Society of Certified Public Accountants, August 9, 2002, http://nysscpa.org/home/2002/802/1week/article58.htm; "Alaska Air Restatement Adds Shareholder Value," *Seattle Times,* January 11, 2003, C1; "Andersen's Fall from Grace," BBC News online, June 17, 2002, www.news.bbc.co.uk/1/hi/business/2049237.stm; Joan Biskupic, "Ruling: Instructions to Jury Were Flawed," *USA Today* online, June, 1, 2005, http://www.keepmedia.com/pubs/USATODAY/2005/06/01/875172; John A. Byrne, "Fall from Grace," *BusinessWeek,* August 12, 2002, 50–56; Nanette Byrnes, Mike McNamee, Diane Brady, Louis Lavelle, Christopher Palmeri, et al., "Accounting in Crisis," *BusinessWeek,* January 28, 2002, 44–48; Dave Carpenter, "Andersen's WorldCom Story Familiar to Enron Excuse," *Houston Chronicle* online, June 27, 2002, www.chron.com/cs/CDA/printstory.hts/special/andersen/1474232; "The Fall of Andersen," *Chicago Tribune* online, September 1, 2002, www.chicagotribune.com/business/showcase/chi-0209010315sep01.story; Greg Farrell, "Jury Will Hear of Andersen's Past Scandals," *USA Today* online, May 8, 2003, www.usatoday.com/money/energy/enron/2002-05-07-andersen-trial.htm; "First Trial of Arizona Baptist Foundation Case Starts This Week," *Baptist Standard* online, March 4, 2002, http://baptiststandard.com/2002/3_4/print/arizona.html; Jonathan D. Glater, "Auditor to Pay $217 Million to Settle Suits," Yahoo! News, March 2, 2002, http://premium.news.yahoo.com/news?tmpl=story&u=/nytp/20020302/880914; "Global Crossing Drops Andersen; Being Investigated by FBI, SEC," New York State Society of Certified Public Accountants, February 2, 2002, www.nysscpa.org/home/2002/202/1week/article45.htm; Floyd Norris, "$217 Million New Settlement by Andersen in Baptist Case," Yahoo! News, May 7, 2002, http://premium.news.yahoo.com/news?tmpl=story&u=/nytp/20020507/918059; Bruce Nussbaum, "Can You Trust Anybody Anymore?" *BusinessWeek,* January 28, 2002, 31–32; Barbara Powell, "Bankrupt WorldCom Says Financial Woes Persisting," Yahoo! News, October 22, 2002, http://story.news.yahoo.com/news?tmpl=story&u=/ap/20021022/ap_wo_en_po/

us_worldcom_110/27/02; "Q&A: What Now for Andersen?" BBC News online, June 16, 2002, http://news.bbc.co.uk/1/hi/business/2048325.stm; "Qwest Admits Improper Accounts," BBC News online, July 29, 2002, http://news.bbc.co.uk/2/hi/business/2158135.stm; David Schepp, "Analysis: Verdict Signals Andersen's End," BBC News online, June 15, 2002, http://news.bbc.co.uk/1/hi/business/2047381.stm; "SEC Sues Former CEO, CFO, Other Top Officers of Sunbeam Corporation in Massive Financial Fraud," U.S. Securities and Exchange Commission, May 15, 2001, www.sec.gov/news/headlines/sunbeamfraud.htm; Stephen Taub, "Andersen Pays $110 Million in Sunbeam Settlement," CFO.com, May 2, 2001, www.cfo.com/printarticle/0,53172947/A,00.html; "Telecoms Bosses Deny 'Fake' Swap Deals," BBC News online, October 1, 2002, http://news.bbc.co.uk/2/hi/business/2290679.stm; Kathy Booth Thomas, "Called to Account," *Time,* June 18, 2002, 43–45; "Waste Management Founder, Five Other Former Top Officers Sued for Massive Fraud," U.S. Securities and Exchange Commission, March 26, 2002, www.sec.gov/news/headlines/wastemgmt6.htm; "WorldCom, Andersen Play Blame Game," *USA Today* online, July 8, 2002, www.usatoday.com/money/telecom/2002-07-08-worldcom-hearings-ap.htm; "WorldCom R evelations Another Mark Against Andersen," *Atlanta Journal-Constitution* online, June 27, 2002, www.accessatlanta.com/ajc/business/0602/worldcom/27andersen.html; Wendy Zellner, Stephanie Forest Anderson, and Laura Cohn, "A Hero—and a Smoking-Gun Letter," *BusinessWeek,* January 28, 2002, 34–35.

Sunbeam Corporation: "Chainsaw Al" and Greed

When John Stewart and Thomas Clark founded the Chicago Flexible Shaft Company in Dundee, Illinois, in 1897, they probably never expected that their fledgling company would grow into a huge conglomerate and face ethical and financial dilemmas more than a hundred years later. Like many corporations, the firm has changed and faced many crises. It has changed its name several times, acquired rival companies, added totally new product lines, gone through bankruptcy, rebounded, restructured, relocated, and hired and fired many CEOs, including "Chainsaw Al" Dunlap. Today, Sunbeam has grown into a well-known designer, manufacturer, and marketer of consumer products used for cooking, health care, and personal care. A few of the most recognized brand names owned by Sunbeam include Coleman, First Alert, Grillmaster, Healthometer, Mixmaster, Mr. Coffee, Oster, Osterizer, Powermate, and Campingaz.

MORE THAN ONE HUNDRED YEARS OF CHANGE

The first products that Sunbeam manufactured and sold were agricultural tools. In 1910 the company began manufacturing electrical appliances, one of the first being a clothes iron. At that time, Stewart and Clark began using the name Sunbeam in advertising campaigns although the company would not officially change its name to the Sunbeam Corporation until 1946. Sunbeam's electric products sold well even during the Great Depression of the 1930s when homemakers throughout the country quickly accepted the Sunbeam Mixmaster, automatic coffee maker, and pop-up toaster. The years following the Great Depression were times of growth and innovation for Sunbeam. The next major development came in 1960 when Sunbeam acquired rival

We appreciate the work of Carol Rustad and Linda E. Rustad in helping draft the previous edition of this case, and Melanie Drever, University of Wyoming, who assisted in this edition. This case was prepared for classroom discussion rather than to illustrate either effective or ineffective handling of an administrative, ethical, or legal decision by management. All sources used for this case were obtained through publicly available material and the Sunbeam website.

appliance maker John Oster Manufacturing Company, which helped make Sunbeam the leading manufacturer of electric appliances.

During the 1980s, a period of relatively high inflation and interest rates, corporations were going through acquisitions, mergers, restructurings, and closings—doing whatever they could to continue operating profitably. In 1981 Allegheny International, an industrial conglomerate, acquired Sunbeam. Allegheny retained the Sunbeam name and added John Zink (air pollution–control devices) and Hanson Scale (bathroom scales) to the Sunbeam product line. After sales of other divisions of Allegheny International declined, the company was forced into bankruptcy in 1988.

In 1990 investors Michael Price, Michael Steinhardt, and Paul Kazarian bought the Sunbeam division from Allegheny International's creditors. They renamed the division the Sunbeam-Oster Company and took it public two years later. The following year, Kazarian was forced out of his chairman position and out of the company. Sunbeam-Oster also relocated to Florida and purchased the consumer products unit of DeVilbiss Health Care. In 1994 Sunbeam-Oster acquired Rubbermaid's outdoor-furniture business. The company changed its name back to Sunbeam Corporation in 1995.

By the time Albert Dunlap took over the company in 1996, Sunbeam had more than twelve thousand stock-keeping units (SKUs), or individual variations of its product lines. The company also had twelve thousand employees, as well as twenty-six factories worldwide, sixty-one warehouses, and six headquarters. Its earnings had been declining since December 1994; by 1996 the stock was down 52 percent, and its earnings had declined by 83 percent. The company needed help.

ALBERT DUNLAP, AKA "CHAINSAW AL"

Before taking the reins at Sunbeam, Dunlap had acquired a reputation as one of the country's toughest executives—as well as nicknames like "Chainsaw Al," "Rambo in Pinstripes," and "The Shredder"—because he eliminated thousands of jobs while restructuring and turning around financially troubled companies. His reputation and business philosophy were recognized throughout the world. His operating philosophy was to make extreme cuts in all areas of operations, including extensive layoffs, so as to streamline a business and return it to profitability. He even authored a book, entitled *Mean Business*, in which he stressed that the most important goal of any business is making money for shareholders. To achieve this goal, Dunlap developed four simple rules of business: (1) Get the right management team, (2) cut back to the lowest costs, (3) focus on the core business, and (4) get a real strategy. By following those four rules, Dunlap helped turn around companies in seventeen states and across three continents, including—according to Dunlap—Sterling Pulp & Paper, American Can, Lily-Tulip, Diamond International, Canenham Forest Industries (formerly Crown-Zellerback), Australian National Industries, Consolidated Press Holdings, and Scott Paper Company.

Michael Price and Michael Steinhardt hired Dunlap as the CEO and chairman of the board for Sunbeam Corporation in July 1996. Price and Steinhardt, two of the original investors who had bought Sunbeam from bankrupt Allegheny International and together owned 42 percent of the stock, had originally tried to sell Sunbeam. Unsuccessful in that effort, they decided to see if "Chainsaw Al" could save their company, although they well knew Dunlap's reputation for extensive layoffs and huge operating cuts. They believed, however, that such drastic efforts were necessary to turn Sunbeam around and increase stock prices and profits. In fact, Sunbeam's stock price did increase, almost instantly, vaulting 49 percent on July 19, 1996, the day Dunlap was named chairman and CEO. The rise from $12\frac{1}{2}$ to $18\frac{5}{8}$ added $500 million to Sunbeam's market value. The stock continued to increase, reaching a record high of $52 per share in March 1998. Although Dunlap's acceptance of the helm at Sunbeam helped boost the company's stock, he realized that his reputation alone would not hold the stock price up and that he needed to start the process of turning Sunbeam around.

DUNLAP'S FIRST STEP AT SUNBEAM

In accordance with his management rules, Dunlap's first move at Sunbeam was to get the right management team. His very first hire was Russ Kersh, a former employee of Dunlap, as executive vice president of finance and administration. The new management team also included twenty-five people who had previously worked for Dunlap at various companies. Dunlap saw logic in hiring these people because they had all worked with him and had been successful in past turnarounds. He retained only one senior executive from Sunbeam's old management team. Once this first step had been accomplished, Dunlap and his "Dream Team for Sunbeam" quickly went into action implementing his second rule: Cut back to the lowest costs.

SECOND STEP: CUT BACK

In his book *Mean Business,* Dunlap had written, "Sunbeam's employees wanted a leader and knew things had to change. Employees want stability. Restructuring actually brings stability, because the future is more clear." Sunbeam's employees certainly knew of Dunlap's reputation for slashing jobs. Some would argue, however, that what people want and need is job security, and knowing Dunlap's reputation did not make Sunbeam's employees feel secure. The need for security relates to psychologist Abraham Maslow's hierarchy of needs, which can be applied to employee motivation. According to Maslow, people strive to satisfy five basic needs—physiological, security, social, esteem, and self-actualization—in a hierarchical order. Security needs—second in the hierarchy of needs—relate to protecting oneself from physical and economic harm. At Sunbeam, Dunlap's reputation for layoffs left many employees feeling threatened and insecure.

As expected, after less than four months as chairman and CEO of Sunbeam, Dunlap announced plans to eliminate half of Sunbeam's twelve thousand employees worldwide. The layoffs affected all levels at Sunbeam. Management and clerical staff positions were cut from 1529 to 697, and headquarters staff was cut by 60 percent, from 308 to 123 employees. On hearing of Dunlap's layoff plans, U.S. Labor Secretary Robert Reich reportedly remarked, "There is no excuse for treating employees as if they are disposable pieces of equipment." Around the same time, the company's share prices rose to the mid-$20 range, and one of the original investors, Michael Steinhardt, sold his shares and divested himself of his Sunbeam connection altogether.

Another method used by Dunlap to cut back to the lowest costs was to reduce the number of SKUs from twelve thousand to fifteen hundred. When Dunlap took over, Sunbeam had thirty-six variations of styles and colors for one clothes iron. Such variation allows for product differentiation, a common business strategy, but some argued that thirty-six variations of a consumer product such as an iron were unnecessary and costly to maintain. Instead of many product variations, Dunlap pursued service as the area to differentiate Sunbeam from competitors in the appliance business.

Eliminating 10,500 SKUs also enabled Dunlap to close a number of factories and warehouses—another cost-saving method. He disposed of eighteen factories worldwide, reducing their number from twenty-six to eight, and reduced the number of warehouses from sixty-one to eighteen. The layoff of thousands of employees, coupled with the reduction of SKUs, factories, and warehouses meant that fewer headquarter locations would be needed. Thus, Dunlap consolidated Sunbeam's six headquarters into one facility in Delray Beach, Florida—Dunlap's primary residence.

STEPS THREE AND FOUR

Once the cost-cutting strategies had been implemented, Dunlap began to practice his third rule—that is, to focus on Sunbeam's core business, which first needed to be defined. Dunlap and his Dream Team defined Sunbeam's core business as electric appliances and appliance-related businesses. They identified five categories surrounding the core business as vital to Sunbeam's success: kitchen appliances, health and home, outdoor cooking, personal care and comfort, and professional products. Any product that did not fit into one of the five categories was sold. Dunlap applied a simple criterion to decide whether to keep or divest a product line. Because he believed firmly that consumers recalled the Sunbeam brand name fondly, he retained any product that related to the Sunbeam brand name. Identifying Sunbeam's core business and paring down to it was the goal in implementing the third rule.

The final of Dunlap's four rules of business called for developing and implementing a real strategy. Dunlap and his team defined Sunbeam's strategy as driving the growth of the company through core business expansions by further differentiating Sunbeam's products from competitors', moving into new geographic areas around the globe, and introducing new products that were linked directly to emerging customer trends as lifestyles evolved around the world. As the first step in implementing this strategy, the company reengineered electrical appliances to 220 volts so they could be marketed and used internationally. Another step was reclaiming the differentiation between the Oster and Sunbeam lines. Each was designed, packaged, and advertised to target different markets. Oster products were positioned as upscale, higher-end brands and sold at completely different retailers than the Sunbeam lines. The Sunbeam line of products was positioned as an affordable, middle-class brand. Early in 1997, Sunbeam opened ten factory-outlet stores to increase brand awareness, sales, and ultimately shareholder wealth. Dunlap made all these changes within seven months of taking up the challenge to turn around Sunbeam. The stock rose to more than $48 per share, a 284 percent increase since July 1996.

THE TURNAROUND OF SUNBEAM

Just fifteen months after accepting the position as chairman and CEO, Dunlap issued a press release in October 1997 announcing that the turnaround of Sunbeam was complete and that Morgan Stanley of Stanley Dean Witter & Co. had been hired to find a buyer for Sunbeam. However, according to John A. Byrne in his book *Chainsaw,* "No one was the least bit interested." Byrne also reported that Dunlap misled a journalist into reporting that Philips, a Dutch electronics giant, was interested in purchasing Sunbeam for $50+ per share but that Dunlap wanted $70.

On March 2, 1998, Dunlap announced plans to buy three consumer products companies. Sunbeam acquired 82 percent of Coleman (camping gear) from Ronald Perelman for $2.2 billion. Perelman received a combination of cash and stock, which gave him 14 percent ownership of Sunbeam. Sunbeam also acquired 98.5 percent of Signature Brands (Mr. Coffee) and 95.7 percent of First Alert (smoke and gas alarms) from Thomas Lee for $425 million in cash. Two days after announcing the purchase of the three companies, Sunbeam's stock closed at a record high of $52 a share. With the stock price at an all-time high and 1997 net income reported at $109.4 million, Sunbeam truly seemed to have been turned around—at least on paper.

Dunlap publicly praised himself and his "Dream Team for Sunbeam" for turning around the failing corporation within seven months of taking over. He was so confident in the success of their mission at Sunbeam that he added a complete chapter to his book *Mean Business* titled, "Now There's a Bright Idea. Lesson: Everything You've Read So Far About Restructuring Works. This Chapter Proves It—Again." Dunlap stated that Kersh and a dozen other people tried to dissuade him from taking the Sunbeam job because they were convinced that even he could not save the troubled company. Dunlap had disagreed with them, pointing out that he saw opportunity where others saw the impossible. He mentioned that he did not need to take the position at Sunbeam or with any other company because of his wealth. Dunlap also wrote that the tremendous media attention given to the first edition of his book made it an unofficial handbook for Sunbeam employees and also provided free publicity for the company. A whole section of the chapter recalled how the media arrived in full force to cover the promotional tour and signing of his book. Dunlap also mentioned how strangers, including a Greek Orthodox cleric, praised him and his book, and pointed out that he was at the top of the most admired CEOs list in a survey of business students at U.S. colleges and universities. In the concluding paragraph of the chapter, Dunlap suggested that all CEOs and boards of directors should read his book and use him as a role model in running their companies.

At the time, Dunlap's management philosophy seemed to underlie his success at Sunbeam. He streamlined the company and attained what he considered the most important goal of any business: to make money for shareholders. In February 1998, Sunbeam's board of directors expressed satisfaction with Dunlap's leadership and signed a three-year employment contract with him that included 3.75 million shares of stock.

SUNBEAM'S ACCOUNTING PRACTICES RAISE QUESTIONS

Although Dunlap accomplished what he had set out to do at Sunbeam, the share-holder wealth did not last. Nor did the board's satisfaction. Sunbeam again faced tough times—and not because of excessive costs or lack of a strategy. The three purchases that more than doubled Sunbeam's size and helped push the company's stock price to $52 also helped cause a second upheaval and restructuring of Sunbeam. Rumors began surfacing that these purchases had been made to disguise losses through write-offs.

Paine Webber, Inc. analyst Andrew Shore had been following Sunbeam since the day Dunlap was hired. As an analyst, Shore's job was to make educated guesses about investing clients' money in stocks. Thus, he had been scrutinizing Sunbeam's financial statements every quarter and considered Sunbeam's reported levels of inventory for certain items to be unusual for the time of year. For example, he noted massive increases in the sales of electric blankets in the third quarter although they usually sell well in the fourth quarter. He also observed that sales of grills were high in the fourth quarter, which is an unusual time of year for grills to be sold, and noted that accounts receivable were high. On April 3, 1998, just hours before Sunbeam announced a first-quarter loss of $44.6 million, Shore downgraded his assessment of the stock. By the end of the day Sunbeam's stock prices had fallen 25 percent.

Shore's observations were indeed cause for concern. In fact, Dunlap had been using a bill-and-hold strategy with retailers, which boosted Sunbeam's revenue, at least on the balance sheet. A *bill-and-hold strategy* entails selling products at large discounts to retailers and holding them in third-party warehouses to be delivered at a later date. By booking sales months ahead of the actual shipment or billing, Sunbeam was able to report higher revenues in the form of accounts receivable, which inflated its quarterly earnings. The strategy essentially shifted sales from future quarters to the current one, and in 1997 the strategy helped Dunlap boost Sunbeam's revenues by 18 percent.

The bill-and-hold strategy is not illegal and follows the generally accepted accounting principles (GAAP) of financial reporting. Nevertheless, Sunbeam's share-holders filed lawsuits, alleging that the company had made misleading statements about its finances and deceived them so they would buy Sunbeam's artificially inflated stock. A class-action lawsuit was filed on April 23, 1998, naming both Sunbeam Corporation and CEO Albert Dunlap as defendants. The lawsuit alleged that Sunbeam and Dunlap had violated the Securities and Exchange Act of 1934 by misrepresenting and/or omitting material information concerning the business operations, sales, and sales trends of the company. The lawsuit also alleged that the motivation for artificially inflating the price of the common stock was to enable Sunbeam to complete millions of dollars of debt financing in order to acquire Coleman, First Alert, and Signature Brands. Sunbeam's subsequent reporting of earnings significantly below the original estimate caused a huge drop in its stock.

Dunlap continued to run Sunbeam and the newly purchased companies as if nothing had happened. On May 11, 1998, he tried to reassure two hundred major investors and Wall Street analysts that the first-quarter loss would not be repeated and that Sunbeam would post increased earnings in the second quarter. That same day he announced another fifty-one hundred layoffs at Sunbeam and the acquired companies, possibly to gain back investor confidence and divert attention away from the losses and lawsuits. The tactic failed. The press continued to report on Sunbeam's bill-and-hold strategy and the accounting practices that Dunlap had allegedly used to artificially inflate revenues and profits.

DUNLAP'S REPUTATION BACKFIRES

Dunlap called an impromptu board meeting on June 9, 1998, to address and rebut the reported charges. A partner from Sunbeam's outside auditors, Arthur Andersen LLP, assured the board that the company's 1997 numbers were in compliance with accounting standards and firmly stood by Arthur Andersen's audit of Sunbeam's financial statements. Robert J. Gluck, the controller at Sunbeam, who was also present at the board meeting, did not counter the auditor's statement. The meeting seemed to be going well until Dunlap was asked if the company would make its projected second-quarter earnings. His response that sales were soft was not what the board expected to hear. Nor was his statement that he had a document in his briefcase outlining a settlement of his contract for his departure from Sunbeam. The document was never reviewed. However, Dunlap's behavior made board members suspicious, which led to an in-depth review of Dunlap's practices.

The review took place during the next four days in the form of personal phone calls and interviews between board members and select employees—without Dunlap's knowledge. A personal conversation with Sunbeam's executive vice president, David Fannin, reportedly revealed that the 1998 second-quarter sales were considerably below Dunlap's forecast and that the company was in crisis. Dunlap had forecast a small increase, but the numbers provided by Fannin indicated that Sunbeam could lose as much as $60 million that quarter. Outside the boardroom and away from Dunlap, Gluck (the controller) revealed that the company had tried to do things in accordance with GAAP, but allegedly everything had been pushed to the limit.

These revelations led the board of directors to call an emergency meeting. On Saturday, June 13, 1998, the board of directors, along with Fannin, and a pair of lawyers, discussed the informal findings. They agreed that they had lost confidence in Dunlap and his ability to turn Sunbeam around. The board of directors unanimously agreed that Dunlap had to go and drafted a letter calling for his immediate departure. "Chainsaw Al" was told that same day, in a one-minute conference call, that he was the next person to be cut at Sunbeam.

SUNBEAM LOOKS FORWARD

Once again, Sunbeam faced the need to revitalize itself. It was again looking for a new CEO; its stock price had dropped to as low as $10 per share; shareholder lawsuits had been filed; legal action regarding Dunlap's firing was under way; the Securities and Exchange Commission (SEC) was scrutinizing Sunbeam's accounting practices; the audit committee of the board of directors was requiring Sunbeam to restate its au-dited financial statements of 1997, possibly for 1996, as well as for the first quarter of 1998; and creditors were demanding payment in full. Additionally, on August 24, 1998, Sunbeam announced that it would discontinue a quarterly dividend of 1 cent per share. Shareholder confidence was at an all-time low.

Less than two years after Dunlap was hired, Sunbeam again reorganized and brought in a new senior management team. Jerry W. Levin accepted the position of pres-ident and CEO. He outlined a new strategy for Sunbeam, focusing on growth through increased product quality and customer service. The plan was to decentralize opera-tions while maintaining centralized support and organizing into three operating groups. Four of the eight plants that were scheduled to be closed under Dunlap's management remained open to ensure consistency of supply. In a press release, Levin outlined his strat-egy for revitalizing Sunbeam: "Our goal is to increase accountability at the business unit level, and to give our employees the tools they need to build their businesses. We are shifting Sunbeam's focus to increasing quality in products and customer service."

On October 21, 1998, Sunbeam announced that it had signed a memorandum of understanding to settle, subject to court approval, the class-action lawsuit brought by public shareholders of Coleman Company, Inc. The court approved, and on January 6, 2000, Sunbeam completed the acquisition of the publicly held shares of Coleman. The terms of the merger allowed all public stockholders of Coleman to receive $6.44 in cash, 0.5677 of a share of Sunbeam common stock, and 0.381 of a warrant to pur-chase one share of Sunbeam common stock for each of their shares of Coleman stock.

There were legal ramifications from Dunlap's firing. In an interview on July 9, 1998, Dunlap stated that he intended to challenge Sunbeam's efforts to deny him sev-erance under his contract, although both Dunlap and Sunbeam agreed not to take le-gal action against each other for a period of six months. Dunlap claimed that his mission was aborted prematurely and that three days after receiving the board of director's support he was fired without being given a reason. On March 15, 1999, Dunlap filed an arbitration claim against Sunbeam to recover $5.5 million in unpaid salary, $58,000 worth of accrued vacation, and $150,000 in benefits as well as to have his stock op-tions repriced at $7 a share. Additionally, he sued the company for dragging its feet in reimbursing him for more than $1.4 million in legal and accounting fees he had racked up defending himself in lawsuits that alleged securities fraud. Although the board made it clear that they had no intention of paying Dunlap any more money, a judge ruled in his favor in June 1999.

In a letter to the shareholders at the beginning of 1999, Levin stated that Sunbeam had gone back to basics and intensified its focus on its powerful family of brands. He also wrote that the lending banks had extended covenant relief and waivers of past de-faults until April 10, 2000. The $1.7 billion credit agreement was extended until April 14, 2000, at which time Sunbeam hoped to have a definitive agreement extending the covenant relief and waivers for an additional year. Sunbeam was required to restate its audited accounting reports. It took auditors four months to unravel the accounting statements from Dunlap's tenure, which were confirmed to be legal—just inaccurate. The 1997 net income was restated from $109.4 million to $38.3 million.

In the meantime, Sunbeam moved forward, creating a new company—Thalia Products, Inc. (thinking and linking intelligent appliances)—to produce smart appliances and services and to license home-linking technology to other manufacturers. At the International Housewares show in January 2000, Sunbeam and Thalia introduced nine new products that automatically network when plugged in and "talk" to each other to coordinate tasks. Such tasks include an alarm clock turning on the coffee pot ten minutes before the alarm goes off—no matter what time it is set for—and an alarm that will ring if water has not been added to the coffee pot. Sunbeam announced on March 23, 2000, that its Thalia Products division had an agreement with Microsoft Corporation to join the Universal Plug and Play (UPnP) Forum, which would further the companies' shared objective of establishing industry-leading standards for home appliance networking.

At this point, CEO Levin still had confidence in Sunbeam's ability to recover. A press release on May 10, 2000, stated that the first-quarter results showed that net sales had increased 3 percent to $539 million and that operating results had narrowed to a loss of $3 million. Levin stated,

> These results, though improved, are not indicative of the value we have created, and will continue to create for Sunbeam's shareholders. Looking forward, we expect operating results to further improve as we execute our long-range strategy that focuses on consumer-oriented new products.

However, on January 25, 2001, Sunbeam announced that it had been notified by the New York Stock Exchange (NYSE) that the company was not in compliance with minimum listing criteria. As a result, the NYSE "delisted" the company's common stock. This meant that the stock ceased to be traded. The bad news continued when Sunbeam announced on February 6, 2001, that it planned to reorganize under Chapter 11 of the U.S. Bankruptcy Code due to its $3.2 billion in debt, some of which accrued from Dunlap's acquisitions. The company expected no interruption in production or distribution. Senior management committed themselves to remaining in place and leading Sunbeam throughout the bankruptcy process and beyond.

In September 2002, Dunlap agreed to pay $500,000 to settle the SEC's charges that he defrauded investors by inflating sales at Sunbeam so as to make the company more attractive to a prospective buyer. According to the SEC, Sunbeam's accounting practices inflated the company's income by $60 million in 1997, "contributing to the false picture of a rapid turnaround in Sunbeam's financial performance." In settling the charges, Dunlap did not admit or deny any wrongdoing and agreed never to work as an executive or director of a public corporation again. Dunlap's chief financial officer, Russell Kersh, agreed to the same ban and paid $200,000 to settle the SEC's suit. The month before, Dunlap paid $15 million to settle a class-action lawsuit brought by shareholders with similar allegations.

Sunbeam emerged from Chapter 11 bankruptcy proceedings in December 2002 and changed its name to American Household, Inc. Its former household products division became the subsidiary Sunbeam Products, Inc. In September 2004, the Jarden Corporation purchased American Household, Inc., of which it is now a subsidiary.

Jarden Consumer Solutions is a wholly owned subsidiary of Jarden Corporation. They have many brands including Bionaire®, BRK®, Crock-Pot®, First Alert®, Food-Saver®, Healthometer®, Holmes®, Mr. Coffee®, Oster®, Patton®, Rival®, Seal-a-Meal®, Sunbeam®, and VillaWare®. They are a company whose employees—nearly thirteen thousand strong in ten countries—are committed to a set of core values that empha-size integrity, community service, and entrepreneurship. They are always looking for solutions to help make consumers' lives easier, safer, and fun. Jarden Consumer Solutions operates in approximately twenty-five offices and manufacturing facilities in ten countries. Although Sunbeam-Oster no longer exists as a company, the brands can still be found in many major stores.

QUESTIONS

1. How did pressures for financial performance contribute to Sunbeam's culture where quarterly sales were manipulated to influence investors?
2. What were Dunlap's contributions to the financial and public relations embar-rassments at Sunbeam that caused investors and the public to question Sunbeam's integrity?
3. Identify ethical issues that Dunlap's management team may have created by adopt-ing a short-run focus on financial performance. What lessons could be learned from the outcome?

SOURCES: Alexander Law Firm, via http://defrauded.com/sunbeam.shtml (accessed September 13, 1998); "American Household, Inc.," *Hoover's* online, www.hoovers.com/co/capsule/4/0,2163,11414,00.html (accessed April 16, 2003); Douglas Bell, "Take Me to Your Leader," *ROB Magazine* online, June 10, 2000, www.robmagazine.com/archive/2000ROBfebruary/html/idea_log.html; Martha Brannigan and Ellen Joan Pollock, "Dunlap Offers Tears and a Defense," *Wall Street Journal*, July 9, 1998, B1; John A. Byrne, "How Al Dunlap Self-Destructed," *BusinessWeek*, July 6, 1998, 58–65; John A. Byrne, "The Notorious Career of Al Dunlap in the Era of Profit-at-Any-Price," in *Chainsaw* (New York: HarperCollins, 1999); John A. Byrne, "Chainsaw Al Dunlap Cuts His Last Deal," *BusinessWeek* online, September 5, 2002, www.businessweek.com/bwdaily/dnflash/sep2002/nf2002095_2847.htm; Albert J. Dunlap and Bob Aldeman, "How I Save Bad Companies and Make Good Companies Great," *Mean Business*, rev. ed. (New York: Simon & Schuster, 1997); "Dunlap and Kersh Resign from Sunbeam Board of Directors," *Company News On-Call*, via www.prnewswire.com (accessed September 13, 1998); Daniel Kadlec, "Chainsaw Al Gets the Chop," *Time*, June 29, 1998, via http://cgi.pathfinder.com/time/ham...29/business.chainsaw-al-get15.html; "Letter from CEO Jerry W. Levin," Sunbeam, June 10, 2000, www.sunbeam.com; Steve Matthews, "Sunbeam's Ex-CEO Seeks $5.25 Million in Arbitration Claim," *Bloomberg News*, March 15, 1999; Andy Ostmeyer, "'Chainsaw Al' Agrees to Settle Suit," *Joplin [Missouri] Globe* online, January 16, 2002, www.joplinglobe.com/archives/2002/020116/regional/story5.html; Andy Ostmeyer, "Sunbeam's Bankruptcy Protection Plan OK'd," *Joplin [Missouri] Globe* online, November 27, 2002, www.joplinglobe.com/archives/2002/021127/regional/story2.html; Neil Roland and Judy Mathewson, with Robert Schmidt, "Sunbeam Ex-CEO 'Chainsaw Al' Dunlap Settles SEC Case," *Bloomberg News*, September 4, 2002; Matthew Schifrin, "Chainsaw Al to the Rescue," *Forbes* online, August 26, 1996, www.forbes.com/forbes/082696/5805042a.htm; Matthew Schifrin, "The Unkindest Cuts," *Forbes* online, May 4, 1998, www.forbes.com/forbes/98/0504/6109044a.htm; Matthew Schifrin, "The Sunbeam Soap Opera: Chapter 6," *Forbes*, July 6, 1998, 44–45; Patricia Sellers, "First: Sunbeam's Investors Draw Their Knives—Exit for Chainsaw?" *Fortune*, June 8, 1998, 30–31; "Sunbeam Announces Eastpak Sale Complete," *PR Newswire*, May 30, 2000, www.prnewswire.com; "Sunbeam Balks at Dunlap's Demand for $5.5 Million," *Naples [Florida] Daily News*, March 17, 1999; "Sunbeam Completes Acquisition of Coleman Publicly Held Shares," Sunbeam press release, January 6, 2000, www.sunbeam.com; "Sunbeam Corporation," *Hoover's* online, www.hoovers.com/premium/profiles/11414.html (accessed September 19, 1998); "Sunbeam Corporation Announces Plan to Reorganize under Chapter 11," Sunbeam press release, February 6, 2001, www.sunbeam.com/

media_room/soc_reorg.htm; "Sunbeam Credit Waivers Extended to April 14, 2000," *PR Newswire,* April 11, 2000, www.prnewswire.com; "Sunbeam Joins Microsoft in the Universal Plug and Play Forum to Establish a 'Universal' Smart Appliance Technology Standard," Sunbeam press release, March 23, 2000, www.sunbeam.com; "Sunbeam Outlines New Strategy, Organizational Structure, Senior Management Team," *Company News On-Call,* via www.prnewswire.com (accessed September 13, 1998); "Sunbeam Reports First Quarter 2000 Results," Sunbeam press release, May 10, 2000, www.sunbeam.com; "Sunbeam to Restate Financial Results," *Company News On-Call,* via www.prnewswire.com (accessed September 13, 1998); "Sunbeam Signs Memorandum of Understanding to Settle Coleman Shareholder Litigation," *PR Newswire,* October 21, 1998, www.prnewswire.com; "Time for Smart Talk Is Over," Sunbeam press release, January 14, 2000, www.sunbeam.com; "VF to Acquire Eastpak Brand," Sunbeam press release, March 20, 2000, www.sunbeam.com.

Countrywide Financial: The Subprime Meltdown

Not too long ago, Countrywide Financial seemed to have everything going for it. Co-founded in part by Angelo Mozilo in 1969, it had become the largest provider of home loans in the United States within a few decades. By the 2000s, one in six U.S. loans originated with Countrywide. In 1993, loan transactions reached the $1 trillion mark. Additionally, it was the number-one provider of home loans to minorities in the United States and had lowered the barriers of homeownership for lower-income individuals. Countrywide offered services such as loan closing, capital market, insurance, and banking. In the 1970s, Countrywide had diversified into the securities market as well.

In 1992, Countrywide created a program called "House America" that enabled more consumers to qualify for home loans, as well as to make smaller down payments. In 2003, they proposed the "We House America" program with a goal to provide $1 trillion in home loans to low-income and minority borrowers by 2010. The strategies of both programs were similar and included:

- Expanded approval/timely payment rewards
- Multiunit loan programs
- FHA and VA loan programs
- New immigrants initiatives
- Location-efficient mortgages
- Down-payment and closing-cost assistance programs
- Rural housing loans
- Mortgage revenue bond programs
- Rehabilitation loan programs

At the time, Countrywide's reputation in the industry was stellar. *Fortune* magazine called it the "23,000% stock" because between 1982 and 2003, Countrywide delivered

This case was written by John Fraedrich, O. C. Ferrell, and Jennifer Jackson, with the editorial assistance of Jennifer Sawayda. This case was developed for classroom discussion rather than to illustrate either effective or ineffective handling of an administrative, ethical, or legal discussion by management. All sources used for this case were obtained through publicly available material.

investors a 23,000 percent return, exceeding the returns of Washington Mutual, Wal-Mart, and Warren Buffett's Berkshire Hathaway. In 1999, the company serviced $216.5 billion in loans. In 2000, the increase in revenues was attributed, in part, to home equity and subprime loans. The Annual Report for that year states: "Fiscal 2000 shows a higher margin for home equity and subprime loans" (which, due in part to their higher cost structure charge a higher price per dollar loaned). Subprime loans were a factor to Countrywide's immense success. However, the company's reliance on what was originally intended to aid low-income individuals ended up contributing to its downfall.

UNDERSTANDING SUBPRIME LOANS

To understand Countrywide's failure, one must first understand the concept of subprime lending. Simply put, subprime lending means lending to borrowers, generally people who would not qualify for traditional loans, at a rate higher than the prime rate, although how far above depends on factors like credit score, down payment, debt-to-income ratio, and recent payment delinquencies. Subprime lending is risky because clients are less likely to be able to pay back their loans.

Although subprime loans can be made for a variety of purposes, mortgages have gained the most news coverage. Subprime mortgages fall into three categories. First is the interest-only mortgage, through which borrowers pay only the loan's interest for a set period of time. The second type allows borrowers to pay monthly, but this often means that borrowers opt to pay an amount smaller than that needed to reduce the amount owed on the loan. Third, borrowers can find themselves with mortgages featuring a fixed interest rate for a period, converting to variable rates after a while.

Typically, subprime loans are offered to high-risk clients who do not qualify for conventional loans. The average borrower has a credit score of below 620 and is generally low-income. However, a 2007 *Wall Street Journal* study revealed that from 2004–2006 the rate of middle- and upper-income subprime loan borrowers rose dramatically. During the early- to mid-2000s, when real estate prices were booming and confidence levels were high, even clients who could have qualified for regular loans chose to take out subprime loans to finance their real estate speculations. As real estate prices peaked, more well-to-do investors turned to subprime mortgages to finance their expensive homes.

In relation to the loan market as a whole, subprime loans comprise a relatively small part. In 2008, over 6 million U.S. homeowners had subprime loans with a combined value of over $600 billion. In comparison, all other U.S. loans amounted to over $10 trillion. Although they only make up a small chunk of the loan market, many consider subprime loans to be a key contributor to the 2008 financial crisis.

One of the tools of the subprime loan was the adjustable rate mortgage (ARM) that allowed borrowers to pay low introductory payments for three to five years that would then be adjusted annually as the prime interest rate increased or decreased. Another type of ARM was to pay interest for a set number of years with balloon payments, meaning that people would only make interest payments for the life of the loan, and then would be expected to pay the entire principal at once upon maturity of the loan. These tools worked as long as the housing market remained on an upward trajectory, but when housing prices fell or interest rates increased people found themselves unable to pay. Many financial experts contributed to the problem by telling clients that in the future they would certainly have more income because of the increases in their property's value. They assured home buyers that even if payments increased, they would be able to afford them because the value of their home would have increased so much. Even consumers with good credit looking to refinance were attracted to the low interest rates without fully recognizing the possible consequences.

THE SUBPRIME CRISIS

When introduced, the new financial tool of subprime loans was praised for lowering barriers to homeownership. The U.S. Department of Housing and Urban Development stated that subprimes were helping many minorities afford homes, and were therefore a good tool.

Although subprime lending has only become a major news topic recently, the subprime concept began in the 1970s in Orange County, California. At this time, rural farmland was being converted into the suburbs, and subprime loans were a way for people to afford to buy homes, even if their credit was poor. The typical subprime recipient would not have met normal lending standards. Yet in the 1970s, the subprime loans made sense as a means to fuel southern California's growth. Homes were appreciating rapidly, so if a family decided to buy a house and live there for three to five years, they could reasonably expect that home to sell for over 50 percent more than what they had originally paid. In addition, Congress passed the Equal Credit Opportunity Act in 1974 to help ensure that all consumers had an equal chance to receive a loan. Potential homeowners, in theory, would no longer be rejected based on sex, race, national origin, or any other factor considered discriminatory.

Contractors also wanted a part of the action. They began to build houses and "flip" them. Flipping is when the contractor builds homes, (without buyers) on credit, and takes the sale of some of the homes to the lending institution as collateral to obtain more credit to build more homes. Speculators also flipped existing homes by buying them on credit with no intention of keeping them, waiting until the value had increased, and selling them at a profit. Industries that supplied home builders were profiting as well, and costs of materials increased with the high demand. Real estate agents were motivated to push sales through because of commissions they could earn (on average 6 percent of the sales price). Many mortgage officers were also compensated by commissions. Even real estate appraisers began to inflate the value of homes to ensure loans would go through. This was to become one of the chief accusations against Countrywide during the financial crisis.

But then something happened that no one had considered. The U.S. economy began to slow. People started working more and earning less money. Jobs started moving abroad, health insurance became more expensive, gas prices increased, and the baby boomers began to sell their homes to fund their retirement. In spite of this, builders kept on building, and the financial industry continued to lend to increasingly risky buyers. Homeowners found that they had less disposable income to make housing payments.

The result was a surplus of housing that homeowners could no longer afford. Banks began to foreclose on houses when the homeowners could not pay. As the demand for housing decreased, banks lost significant amounts of money. Many other industries, like the automobile industry and insurance companies, were also negatively affected as struggling citizens tried to cope with the economic downturn. With plummeting stock prices, the United States began experiencing a financial crisis that had a rippling effect across the world. Economist Alan Greenspan said the crisis could be "the most wrenching since the end of the Second World War."

Starting late in 2007 and continuing into 2008 marked the tipping-point for the burgeoning mortgage crisis. Foreclosure rates skyrocketed and borrowers and investors began to feel the full ramifications of taking the subprime risk. Mortgage defaults played a part in triggering a string of serious bank and financial institution failures as well. In 2007, investors began to abandon their mortgage-backed securities, causing huge institutions such as Morgan Stanley, Merrill Lynch, and Citigroup to lose large sums of money. Morgan Stanley, for example, lost over $265 billion internationally. Bear Stearns required government intervention to stay afloat. Analysts have attributed the banks' failings to poor intra-bank communication and a lack of effective risk management.

Although the Chief Financial Officer (CFO) is supposed to be in charge of risk management, it appears that many institutions viewed the role as merely advisory. It was highly risky for these firms to downplay the importance of the CFO. Not only did many of these banks fail at risk management, they were in violation of the Sarbanes–Oxley Act—which requires that a company verify its ability to internally control its financial reporting. A CFO not directly in charge of a company's finances is signing off on something that he or she actually knows little about. The extent of the 2008–2009 financial crisis has made it clear to many that a massive overhaul of the financial industry's regulatory system is needed.

COUNTRYWIDE'S INVOLVEMENT IN THE SUBPRIME CRISIS

During the early 2000s, Countrywide reaped the benefits of subprime loans. In 2001, mortgages contributed to 28 percent of Countrywide's earnings with subprime loans up to $280 million (the year before, subprime loans represented $86.9 million). In 2002, Countrywide's loan portfolio to minorities, low- to moderate-income borrowers, and low- to moderate-income tracts had dramatically increased from years past. Countrywide had also increased its commissioned sales force by nearly 60 percent, to 3484 in 2003, with the goal of increasing overall market share. Some critics have argued that salespeople were given incentives to undertake riskier transactions in order to continue to grow the company at a rapid rate. One allegation against Countrywide is that in order to increase its profit, it would even offer subprime loans to people who qualified for regular loans. Leading the day-to-day operations of the Consumer Markets Division was David Sambol, who would later be implicated in the scandal.

After years of fast growth and upbeat projections, Countrywide's 2007 Annual Report had a somber tone. The financial crisis had begun and the company was feeling its negative effects. A significant amount of the report focused on the details of accounting for its mortgage portfolio and default rates. In one year, Countrywide depreciated over $20 billion and absorbed over $1 billion in losses. By 2008, the company had accrued over $8 billion in subprime loans with 7 percent delinquent. The industry average was 4.67 percent delinquency. That year foreclosures doubled, and the firm planned to lay off 10 to 20 percent of its employees, or 10,000 to 20,000 people.

The company attempted to ease loan terms on more than 81,000 homeowners with a program called the Countrywide Comprehensive Home Preservation Program. The program allowed consumers to refinance or modify loans with an adjustable rate mortgage for a lower interest rate or switch to a fixed rate mortgage. President and Chief Operating Officer David Sambol stated, "Countrywide believes that none of our subprime borrowers that have demonstrated the ability to make payments should lose their home to foreclosure solely as a result of a rate [increase]. This is yet another step in our continuing effort to identify and improve existing programs that assist our customers." Countrywide also created special divisions to work to help borrowers and actively informed their customers about their options. The company offered phone counseling teams, personalized resource mailings, and counselors within communities who could meet face-to-face. Countrywide appeared to be genuine in its attempts to help homeowners, but it was too little too late. By then questions and accusations had begun to develop against company leaders.

In 2008, Alphonso Jackson, Secretary of Housing and Urban Development (HUD), reported that over 500,000 Countrywide consumers were in danger of facing foreclosure. The blame for this was focused primarily on subprime lending and adjustable rate mortgages. Countrywide Financial countered that there were other reasons for delinquencies and foreclosures. It maintained the main causes of delinquencies and foreclosures were unrelated to the company's investment decisions—issues like medical problems, divorce, and unemployment—not adjustable rate mortgages. It further claimed less than 1 percent of its consumers had defaulted on account of adjustable rate mortgages. Still, consumers began to question whether Countrywide's risky lending played a role in the larger financial crisis.

ISSUES RELATED TO THE BANK OF AMERICA ACQUISITION

In 2008, Bank of America, one of the United States' top financial institutions with $683 billion in assets, offered to buy Countrywide Financial for $4 billion. The price tag was a substantial discount on what the company was actually worth. Bank of America paid approximately $8/share while shares were valued at $20/share earlier in the year. Kenneth D. Lewis, Chairman, President, and Chief Executive Officer said at the time, "We are aware of the issues within the housing and mortgage industries. The transaction reflects those challenges. Mortgages will continue to be an important relationship product, and we now will have an opportunity to better serve our customers and to enhance future profitability." At the time, Bank of America held $1.5 trillion in assets, which better equipped them to deal with the crisis. "Their balance sheet can take a shock much better than Countrywide," said CreditSights senior analyst David Hendler. "When you take the shocks at Countrywide, they have a big, busting consequence that's negative." Bart Narter, senior analyst at Celent, a Boston-based financial research and consulting firm, said, "There's still plenty of risk involved. He's brave to do it. But I think that it's very likely down the road to be profitable, maybe not immediately, but long-term."

However, there could be more reasons why Countrywide allowed Bank of America to acquire it. It may be better able to handle the ethical investigations concerning Countrywide currently underway by the government. Among other issues, Countrywide is coming under increased scrutiny for giving out so-called *liar loans.* Liar loans are mortgages that required no proof of the borrowers' income or assets. These loans allowed consumers to purchase homes with few or no assets. With the additional burden of the financial crisis, many homeowners with liar loans cannot pay their mortgages, nor are they able to refinance their homes because housing prices have plummeted. Some are being forced to foreclose, generating substantial losses for mortgage companies and the economy. One economic site estimated that the true cost of liar loans could total over $100 billion in losses.

Countrywide Financial was one of the top providers of liar loans. These loans allowed the industry to profit, at least for a little while, because people with liar loans were riskier clients, and therefore had to pay higher fees and interest rates to the mortgage company. Many accuse Countrywide of negligence, of giving out highly risky loans to people who could not afford them for the sake of quick profits. Others accuse the company of even more unethical dealings. Some homeowners who are now struggling under liar loans are accusing Countrywide of *predatory lending,* saying the company misled them. Although some homeowners may have been truly misled into liar loans, more than 90 percent of liar loan applicants overstated their income, with three out of five overstating it by at least 50 percent. This rampant dishonesty, critics charge, could not have occurred without the mortgage company's awareness. It has sparked new investigations into whether Countrywide *aided* borrowers in falsifying information. Hence, some attest that Countrywide's buyout by Bank of America may have been more than just an economic choice. Instead, it could have been a way to prepare for the onslaught of criticism that would arise against Countrywide.

In March 2008, Bank of America decided to retain David Sambol, Executive Managing Director of Business Segment Operations at Countrywide, as well as to pay him a hefty compensation package. Indeed, his credentials show he is qualified. He received a Bachelor's degree in Business Administration and Accounting from California State University, Northridge in 1982. Prior to joining Countrywide in 1985, Sambol served as a Certified Public Accountant with the accounting firm of Ernst & Whinney. After getting hired at Countrywide, his unit led all revenue generating functions of the company. He was instrumental in Countrywide's mortgage division expanding to become the most comprehensive in the industry. In 2007, David Sambol's compensation package was $4,025,000. In March 2008, Bank of America agreed to set up a $20 million retention account, payable in equal installments on the first and second anniversaries of the merger, for Sambol, plus $8 million in restricted stock. Sambol's retention package also included the use of a company car or car allowance, country club dues, and financial consulting services through the end of 2009. He was also to continue to have access to a company airplane for business and personal travel.

Much of the public was outraged that Sambol would receive such high compensation after taking part in Countrywide's bad business dealings. At the end of May, Senator Charles E. Schumer, D-N.Y., Chairman of Congress' Joint Economic Committee, asked Bank of America to reconsider the decision to put Sambol in charge of home lending. "There seem to be two economic realities operating in our country today," Representative Henry A. Waxman, Democrat of California, the committee chairman, said. "Most Americans live in a world where economic security is precarious and there are real economic consequences for failure. But our nation's top executives seem to live by a different set of rules. The question before the committee was: when companies fail to perform, should they still give millions of dollars to their senior executives?" After the hearings Bank of America announced that Sambol was being replaced by Barbara Desoer, Bank of America's chief technology and operations officer. Sambol would continue to receive some, though not all, of his perks.

THE ROLE OF COUNTRYWIDE'S
CEO ANGELO MOZILO

Angelo Mozilo is being investigated by the Securities and Exchange Commission due to the sale of company stock options that earned him over $400 million between 2002 and 2008. In a 2007 interview Maria Bartiromo of *BusinessWeek* asked Mozilo about allegations that he profited from over $100 million on stock sales in the previous year. Mozilo asserted, "I have not sold any stock—to my recollection—in 10 years. Everything I've sold was options. The selling is because [when the options] expire, I no longer have the benefit of what I have built and what this team has built for the last 40 years. Up until this debacle, I created $25 billion in value for shareholders. There have been very few—only about 11 stocks—that have performed better over the last 25 years than Countrywide. I could have sold all of those shares at 40 bucks a share and didn't because I want to be aligned with the shareholders."

The public did not seem to believe Mozilo's defense, especially after he received a $100 million severance package when Countrywide was sold to Bank of America. In 2007–2008, Mr. Mozilo was named as a defendant in many lawsuits. The plaintiffs include:

◆ International Brotherhood of Electrical Workers Local 98 Pension Fund
◆ Norfolk County Retirement System
◆ Arkansas Teacher Retirement System, Fire & Police Pension Association of Colorado
◆ Public Employees' Retirement System of Mississippi
◆ Argent Classic Convertible Arbitrage Fund
◆ New Jersey Carpenters' Pension Fund
◆ New York City Employees' Retirement System

One lawsuit alleged misconduct and disregard of fiduciary duties, including a lack of good faith and lack of oversight of Countrywide's lending practices. The lawsuit also accused Countrywide of improper financial reporting and lack of internal controls, alleging that Mozilo was paid $10 million more than was disclosed. Additionally, the company claimed that Countrywide's officers and directors unlawfully sold over $848 million of stock between 2004 and 2008 at inflated prices while in possession of insider information.

Mr. Mozilo's pay also drew heavy scrutiny from members of Congress. Federal securities regulators and congressional investigators found that the use of a flawed peer group and easy bonus targets helped inflate his pay. In the hearings about executive pay, Congressman Elijah E. Cummings of Maryland said, "We've got golden parachutes drifting off to the golf course and have people I see every day who are losing their homes and wondering where their kids will do their homework." He then asked Mr. Mozilo about an e-mail message he sent demanding that the taxes due on his wife's travel on the corporate jet be covered by the company. "It sounds out of whack today because it is out of whack, but in 2006 the company was going great," said Mozilo. "In today's world I would never write that memo." He also apologized for another e-mail message in which he complained about his compensation. "It was an emotional time," he said. But in the same hearings, Mr. Mozilo also reminded the audience that Countrywide's stock price had appreciated over 23,000 percent from 1982 to 2007. His performance-based bonuses were approved by shareholders and he exercised the options as he prepared for retirement. "In short, as our company did well, I did well," he said.

BANK OF AMERICA PLANS A RECOVERY

In July 2008, Bank of America bought Countrywide without Sambol and Mozilo. Since 2001, Bank of America has been focused on profit, not growth. However, it might be a while before Bank of America profits from the acquisition of Countrywide. According to the Securities and Exchange Commission, Bank of America has taken on $16.6 billion in Countrywide's debts. Exiting the subprime lending markets is part of Bank of America's long-term plan. The company planned to liquidate its $26.3 billion subprime real estate portfolio in 2008–2009 and said it would manage its existing $9.7 billion portfolio over its remaining term. Bank of America clearly understood that by buying Countrywide it inherited a volatile earning stream that had become unattractive from a risk-reward standpoint. Kenneth Lewis, CEO of Bank of America, said at the time, "We are committed to achieving consistent, above-average shareholder returns and these actions are aimed at achieving that mission." Bank of America plans to replace Countrywide's brand with its own.

In addition to managing Countrywide's debt, Bank of America must also handle the stream of lawsuits being filed against the company. Many of these lawsuits claim that the company duped homeowners with predatory loan practices. Countrywide recently agreed to provide $8 billion in loan and foreclosure relief to over 397,000 homeowners. It also agreed to adjust the terms of ARMs according to income. Bank of

America's Barbara Desoer, who replaced David Sambol, said the company is committed to helping homeowners and is cutting interest rates to as low as 2.5 percent.

Countrywide is facing additional investigations for other alleged misconduct. In March 2008, the FBI started an investigation to find out whether Countrywide misrepresented its financial information. Additionally, the FBI is investigating Countrywide's VIP program which, according to an insider, provided special mortgage deals to certain high-up officials, known as "Friends of Angelo's." These deals included discount rates and fees not offered to ordinary Countrywide customers. Those implicated in these dealings include Democratic Senators Chris Dodd and Kent Conrad, two former cabinet members, and two CEOs from Fannie Mae. These officials denied that they knew they were getting special discounts. Prosecutors are looking into whether these discounts constituted as improper gifts and whether they qualified as illegal on Countrywide's part.

Despite these proceedings, Bank of America's Barbara Desoer remains optimistic about the future. Like so many others, Bank of America suffered horrendous losses as 2008 came to a close, with a drop in net income of 95 percent in the fourth quarter. Yet Desoer has cited some improvements. She said, "But last quarter, the first quarter that Countrywide and Bank of America operated as one company, we made 250,000 first mortgages, worth $51 billion of principal, plus $6 billion of home-equity loans." The company is predicting that home prices will stabilize by late 2009.

CONCLUSION

Countrywide was not the only cause of the financial crisis. Numerous Wall Street companies are being investigated for unethical practices related to this scandal. (This list includes the Bank of America, which has been investigated for potential breaches of fiduciary duty concerning employee retirement funds.) However, Countrywide's unethical behavior was a key contributor to the problems of the economy in 2008–2009. Many consider it to be one of the central villains in this crisis. They allege that Countrywide knowingly engaged in risky loans, offering subprime loans even to those who qualified for regular loans, in order to profit from the higher rates. In the process, it may have helped to falsify lender information, allowing those with no assets to obtain loans. The consequence was a surplus of housing, plummeting housing prices, and a slew of foreclosures, all of which placed the economy in a precarious state. The result is that the United States has lost global credibility as an economic superpower of the free world.

The Countrywide scandal has brought up other issues, including that of executive compensation. Should executives receive hefty compensation packages and severance pay when their companies flounder? Should they be called into account for not exercising due care? Many people think so, as evidenced by the enormous public outrage facing those like David Sambol and Angelo Mozilo. It is clear that Countrywide has failed the majority of its stakeholders. Ethical misconduct and high-risk business practices helped to create the disaster at Countrywide. It remains to be seen whether its acquisition by the Bank of America will be enough to salvage its reputation and to save the business that was once Countrywide Financial.

QUESTIONS

1. Are subprime loans an unethical financial instrument, or are they ethical but misused in a way that created ethical issues?
2. Discuss the ethical issues that caused the downfall of Countrywide Financial.
3. What was the role of founder and CEO Angelo Mozilo in Countrywide's demise?
4. How should Bank of America deal with potential ethical and legal misconduct discovered at Countrywide?

SOURCES: Scott Reckard, "Countrywide Head Ousted by Bank of America," *Los Angeles Times,* May 29, 2008, http://www2.tbo.com/content/2008/may/29/bz-countrywide-head-ousted-by-bank-of-america/?news-money (accessed June 2008); "A Bad Week for Countrywide's David Sambol," May 30, 2008, Fox, united-states-district-court-central-district-of-califo « WordPress.com Tag Feed; "Judge Rules Mozilo and Countrywide Execs Must Face Multi-Million Dollar Federal Lawsuit," May 22, 2008, Fox; Senate Hearings accessed at http://www.nytimes.com/2008/03/07/business/07cnd-pay.html?_r=1&oref=slogin; Patrick McGeehan and Riva D. Atals, "How Bank of America Stumbled," September 28, 2008, http://query.nytimes.com/gst/fullpage.html?res=9405E4DF133DF93BA1575AC0A9659C8B63; Bartiromo Maria, "Countrywide Feels the Heat," *BusinessWeek,* August 29, 2007, http://www.businessweek.com/bwdaily/dnflash/content/aug2007/db20070829_117563.htm?chan=search (accessed March 16, 2008); "Countrywide Financial," Countrywide Financial Corporation, http://about.countrywide.com (accessed March 16, 2008); "Countrywide Moves to Ease Mortgage Misery," *BusinessWeek,* October 23, 2007, http://www.businessweek.com/investor/content/oct2007/pi20071023_454573.htm (accessed March 16, 2008); "Equal Credit Opportunity Act," Federal Trade Commission, http://www.ftc.gov/bcp/conline/pubs/credit/ecoa.shtm (accessed March 16, 2008); Roben Farzad, "In Search of a Subprime Villain," *BusinessWeek,* January 24, 2008, http://www.businessweek.com/magazine/content/08_05/b4069077193810.htm?chan=search (accessed March 16, 2008); Carl Gutierrez, "Countrywide's New Bad News," *Forbes,* March 10, 2008, http://www.forbes.com/markets/2008/03/10/countrywide-fbi-mortgage-markets-equity-cx_cg_0310markets26.html (accessed March 16, 2008); Liz Moyer, "A Subprime Solution," *Forbes,* December 6, 2007, http://www.forbes.com/wallstreet/2007/12/05/subprime-paulson-bush-biz-wall-cx_lm_1206subprime.html (accessed March 25, 2008); "Mortgage Industry Statistics," LenderRATEMATCH, freeratesearch.com/en/newsroom/mortgage_statistics/ (accessed April 1, 2008); "Subprime Lending," United States Department of Housing and Urban Development, http://www.hud.gov/offices/fheo/lending/subprime.cfm (accessed March 16, 2008); Rick Wartzman, "The Countrywide Conundrum," *BusinessWeek,* November 9, 2007, http://www.businessweek.com/managing/content/nov2007/ca2007119_693870.htm?chan=search (accessed March 16, 2008); Lisa Myers and Amna Nawaz, October 30, 2008, "Feds Probe Countrywide's 'VIP' Program," NBC News, http://deepbackground.msnbc.msn.com/archive/2008/10/30/1613877.aspx (accessed November 14, 2008); "Bank of America Assumes $16.6B in Countrywide Debt," *Dayton Business Journal,* November 10, 2008, http://www.bizjournals.com/dayton/stories/2008/11/10/daily7.html (accessed November 14, 2008); "Countrywide Agrees to Help Kansas Homeowners," November 13, 2008, http://www.kansascw.com/Global/story.asp?S=9344671 (accessed November 14, 2008); Geoff Colvin, "Signs of Life from the Mortgage Frontline," *Forbes,* November 13, 2008, http://money.cnn.com/2008/11/12/magazines/fortune/colvin_desoer.fortune/?postversion=2008111311 (accessed November 14, 2008); Angela Caputo, "Countrywide Accord Paves Way for More Loan Remodifications," Progress Illinois, November 12, 2008, http://progressillinois.com/2008/11/12/loan-modification-plan; Meg Marco, "Subprime Meltdown: Inside the Countrywide Subprime Lending Frenzy," *The Consumerist,* August 27, 2009, http://consumerist.com/consumer/subprime-meltdown/inside-the-countrywide-subprime-lending-frenzy-293902.php (accessed November 13, 2008); Carl Gutierrez,

"Countrywide's New Bad News," *Forbes,* March 10, 2008, http://www.forbes.com/ markets/2008/03/10/countrywide-fbi-mortgage-markets-equity-cx_cg_0310markets26.html (accessed November 13, 2008); "'Liar Loans' Threaten to Prolong Mortgage Mess," MSNBC, August 18, 2008, http://www.msnbc.msn.com/id/26270434/ (accessed November 14, 2008); Mark Gimein, "Inside the Liar's Loan: How the Mortgage Industry Nurtured Deceit," Slate, April 24, 2008, http://www.slate.com/id/2189576/ (accessed November 14, 2008); Alan Greenspan, "We Will Never Have a Perfect Model of Risk," Financial Times.com, March 16, 2008, http://www.ft.com/cms/s/ 0/edbdbcf6-f360-11dc-b6bc-0000779fd2ac.html?nclick_check=1 (accessed November 15, 2008).

Banking Industry Meltdown: The Ethical and Financial Risks of Derivatives

OVERVIEW

The 2008–2009 global recession was caused in part by a failure of the financial industry to take appropriate responsibility for its decision to utilize risky and complex financial instruments. Corporate cultures were built on rewards for taking risks rather than rewards for creating value for stakeholders. Unfortunately, most stakeholders, including the public, regulators, and the mass media, do not always understand the nature of the financial risks taken on by banks and other institutions to generate profits. Problems in the subprime mortgage markets sounded the alarm in the most recent economic downturn. Very simply, the subprime market was created by making loans to people who normally would not qualify based on their credit rating. The debt from these loans was often repackaged and sold to other financial institutions in order to take it off lenders' books and reduce their exposure. When the real estate market became overheated, many people were no longer able to make the payments on their variable rate mortgages. When consumers began to default on payments, prices in the housing market dropped and the values of credit default swaps (CDSs—the repackaged mortgage debt) lost significant value. The opposite was supposed to happen. CDSs were sold as a method of insuring against loss. These derivatives, investors were told, would act as an insurance policy to reduce the risk of loss. Unfortunately, losses in the financial industry were so widespread that even the derivatives contracts that had been written to cover losses from unpaid subprime mortgages could not be covered by the financial institutions that had written these derivatives contracts. The financial industry and managers at all levels have become focused on the rewards for the transaction without concerns about how their actions could potentially damage others.

This case was written by John Fraedrich, O. C. Ferrell, and Jennifer Jackson, with the editorial assistance of Jennifer Sawayda. This case was developed for classroom discussion rather than to illustrate either effective or ineffective handling of an administrative, ethical, or legal discussion by management. All sources used for this case were obtained through publicly available material.

In addition to providing a simplified definition of what derivatives are, this case allows for a review of questionable, often unethical or illegal, conduct associated with a number of respected banks in the recent financial crisis. First, we review the financial terminology associated with derivatives, as they were an integral part of the downfall of these financial institutions. Derivatives were, and still are, considered a legal and ethical financial instrument when used properly, but they inherently hold a lot of potential for mishandling. When misused, they provide a ripe opportunity for misconduct. To illustrate the types of misconduct that can result, this case employs a number of examples. First we examine Barings Bank, which ceased to exist because of a rogue trader using derivatives. Next, we look at United Bank of Switzerland (UBS) and its huge losses from bad mortgages and derivatives. Bear Stearns, an investment bank that suffered its demise through derivatives abuse, is the third example. Finally, Lehman Brothers is an investment bank that was involved with high-risk derivatives that also led to its bankruptcy. At the conclusion of this case we examine the risk of derivatives and potential ethical risks associated with the use of these instruments in the financial industry.

DERIVATIVES DEFINED

Derivatives are financial instruments with values that change relative to underlying variables, such as assets, events, or prices. In other words, the value of derivatives is based on the change in value of something else, called the *underlying* trade or exchange. The main types of derivatives are futures, forwards, options, and swaps. A futures contract is an agreement to buy or sell a set quantity of something at a set rate at a predetermined point in the future. The date on which this exchange is scheduled to take place is called the delivery, or settlement, date. *Futures* contracts are often associated with buyers and sellers of commodities who are concerned about supply, demand, and changes in prices. They can only be traded on exchanges. Almost any commodity, such as oil, gold, corn, or soybeans can have a futures contract defined for a specific trade. *Forwards* are similar to futures, except they can be traded between two individuals. A forward contract is a commitment to trade a specified item at a specific price in the future. The forward contract takes whatever form the parties agree to. An *option* is a less binding form of derivative. It conveys the right, but not the obligation, to buy or sell a particular asset in the future. A *call option* gives the investor the right to buy at a set price on delivery day. A *put option* gives the investor the option to sell a good or financial instrument at a set price on the settlement date. It is a financial contract with what is called a *long position*, giving the owner the right, but not the obligation, to sell an amount at a preset price and maturity date. Finally, *swaps* live up to their name. A swap can occur when two parties agree to exchange one stream of cash flows against another one. Swaps can be used to hedge risks such as changes in interest rates, or to speculate on the changing prices of commodities or currencies. Swaps can be difficult to understand, so here is an example. JP Morgan developed CDSs that bundled together as many as three hundred different assets, including subprime loans. Credit default swaps were meant as a form of insurance. In other words, securities were bundled into one financial package and companies such as JP Morgan were essentially paying insurance premiums to the investors who purchased them, who were now on the hook if payments of any of the securities included in the CDS did not come through.

As mentioned before, the value of derivatives is based on different types of underlying values, including assets such as commodities, equities (stocks), bonds, interest rates, exchange rates, or indexes such as a stock market index, consumer price index (CPI), or even an index of weather conditions. For example, a farmer and a grain storage business enter into a futures contract to exchange cash for grain at some future point. Both parties have reduced a future risk. For the farmer it's the uncertainty of the future grain price and for the grain storage business it's the availability of the grain at a predetermined price.

Some believe derivatives lead to market volatility because enormous amounts of money are controlled by relatively small amounts of margin or option premiums. The job of a derivatives trader is something like a bookie taking bets on how people will bet. *Arbitrage* is defined as attempting to profit by exploiting price differences of identical or similar financial instruments, on different markets or in different forms. As a result, derivatives can suffer large losses or returns from small movements in the underlying asset's price. Investors are like gamblers in that they can bet for or against the price (going up or down) and can consequently lose or win large amounts.

BARINGS BANK

Barings Bank, which had been in operation in the United Kingdom for 233 years, ceased to exist on February 26, 1995, when a futures trader named Nick Leeson lost approximately $1.4 billion in company assets. The extinction was, in part, due to a large holding position in the Japanese futures market. Leeson, chief trader for Barings Futures in Singapore, accumulated a large number of opening positions on the Nikkei Index. He then generated losses in the first two months of 1995 when the Nikkei dropped more than 15 percent. To try and recover these losses, Leeson placed what is called a short "straddle" on the Singapore and Tokyo stock markets. He was betting that the stock market would not move significantly in the short term. This strategy is risky but can be profitable in stable markets. Yet when the Kobe earthquake hit and sent the Japanese stock market plummeting, Leeson lost a lot of money. He did not, however, change his approach. In fact, Leeson tried to cover his losses through a series of other risky investments. They, instead, only increased the losses. When he finally quit his job, Leeson sent a fax to his manager stating "sincere apologies for the predicament that I have left you in." Barings was purchased by ING, a Dutch bank, for £1 (approximately $1 U.S. dollar), which then sold it under the name Baring Asset Management (BAM) to MassMutual and Northern Trust in March 2005.

Nick Leeson's life is a rags-to-riches tale. Son of a plasterer, he started his career in 1984 as a clerk with royal bank Coutts and later worked briefly for Morgan Stanley. He then got a position in operations at Barings, and later was transferred to Jakarta. Leeson worked in a back office solving clients' problems of wrongly denominated certificates and difficulties of delivery. Before long, Leeson was appointed manager of a new operation in the futures markets on the Singapore Monetary Exchange (SIMEX). Leeson had the authority to hire traders and staff and to sell six financial products, but his main business was doing inter-exchange arbitrage or "switching." Switching is betting on small differences between contracts by buying and selling futures simultaneously on two different stock exchanges. For example, if a contract was worth the equivalent of $3 in London and $2.75 in Singapore, Leeson would buy in Singapore and sell in London, making a 25 cent profit.

The key to Leeson's strategy in the 1980s was the knowledge that one stock market was slower in processing trades than the other. To hide any bad bets, Leeson created an error account (named 8888 for its auspiciousness in Chinese numerology) for his losses. Because no one could see the losses hidden by this account, Leeson was widely regarded as a brilliant trader. He had assured Barings that he was not trading with company money and all the positions were perfectly hedged and virtually risk-free. Barings managers had little knowledge in trading and did not suspect Leeson of deception. Based on their trust, Barings put a billion dollars into Leeson's account and made no attempt to check his statements. All it took to bring down this house of cards was one earthquake.

When the Kobe earthquake hit in January 1995 Leeson's luck finally ran out. He fled to Malaysia, Thailand, and Germany; and was finally arrested for fraud in Frankfurt on February 23, 1995. He was extradited back to Singapore and sentenced to six-and-a-half years in Singapore's Changi prison where he was diagnosed with colon cancer and was divorced by his wife. During that time, Leeson wrote *Rogue Trader: How I Brought Down Barings Bank and Shook the Financial World,* which was later made into a movie. He was released from prison in July 1999. Since then he has become CEO of the Galway United Football Club. Although he has tried to atone for his actions, to many he is still considered to be the rogue trader who, through his misuse of derivatives, destroyed the United Kingdom's oldest bank.

UBS

United Bank of Switzerland (UBS) is a diversified global financial services company, headquartered in Switzerland. It is the world's largest manager of private wealth assets and the second-largest bank in Europe with overall invested assets of approximately $3.167 trillion U.S. dollars. In 2000, UBS acquired PaineWebber Group Inc. to become the world's largest wealth management firm for private clients. On June 9, 2003, all UBS business groups rebranded under the UBS name as the company began operating as one large firm. As a result of the rebranding, UBS took a $1 billion writedown for the loss of goodwill associated with the retirement of the PaineWebber brand. UBS is no longer an acronym but is the company's brand name. Its logo of three keys stands for confidence, security, and discretion. UBS had offices in the world's financial centers in fifty countries, and employs approximately eighty-two thousand people.

Recently, UBS has come under scrutiny for questionable practices. In 2008, Internal Revenue Service investigators asked for some 20,000 American client names suspected of hiding as much as $20 billion in assets to avoid at least $300 million in federal taxes on funds in offshore accounts. The issue is complicated because using offshore accounts is not illegal in the United States, but hiding income in undeclared accounts is. However, Switzerland does not consider tax evasion a crime and using undeclared accounts is legal. In May 2008, former UBS bankers Mario Staggl and Bradley Birkenfeld were indicted in Florida for helping an American property developer evade taxes by creating bogus trusts and corporations to hide the ownership and control of offshore assets. They are also accused of advising clients to destroy bank records and of helping them to file false tax returns. UBS asked bankers to sign papers saying that they, not the bank, would be responsible if they broke non-Swiss tax laws. Indian authorities are probing suspected violations of foreign exchange controls involving accounts held at UBS by two companies controlled by India's richest man. The accusations involve transactions that were allegedly arranged by unspecified parties by taking overdrafts on accounts held with UBS London.

However, tax evasion is not the only problem UBS faces. It too has suffered from the subprime crisis due to its heavy dependence on derivatives and mortgage-related securities. In fact, UBS suffered more losses than any other lender in Europe. By November 2008, the bank had been forced to write-down over $46 billion in losses on bad mortgages and derivatives (write-downs represent a reduction in an asset's book value). The bank blamed weak risk controls and risky investment dealings for its loss.

In 2008, UBS appealed to the Swiss government, which doled out an aid package of approximately $59.2 billion to the ailing bank. In exchange, UBS agreed to forgo nearly $27.7 million in pay to the company's top three executives. From now on, the bank promises, bonuses will depend more on the bank's performance, a decision that comes as a relief to those who have criticized what they see as the bank's excessive pay for CEOs. Additionally, some CEOs who resigned promised to return some of the compensation they received. Time will tell whether these combined decisions will be able to resolve the bank's burgeoning problems.

BEAR STEARNS

Unlike many companies that existed before the Great Depression of 1929, Bear Stearns thrived through much of the twentieth century. Unfortunately, nearly eighty years later, Bear Stearns would encounter another severe economic crisis that it would not survive. JP Morgan acquired the company in March 2008 after it lost billions in the subprime crisis.

Bear Stearns was a global investment bank and a securities and brokerage firm. Located in New York, NY, it began as an equity trading-house in 1923 founded by Joseph Bear, Robert Stearns, and Harold Mayer. With an initial $500,000 in capital, the company thrived in the 1920s and 1930s, even after the stock market crash. In fact, the company did so well that while other banks were failing by the dozens, Bear Stearns was able to pay out bonuses. By 1933, the company employed seventy-five people and opened its first regional office in Chicago.

About twenty years later, the company began operating international offices. Bear Stearns continued to grow and prosper, and in 1985 it formed a holding company known as Bear Stearns Companies, Inc. In 2002, while other firms were struggling, Bear Stearns was the only securities firm to report a first-quarter profit increase. It also began focusing more on the housing industry, which would spell out its doom a mere five years later.

In 2005, Bear Stearns was listed as *Fortune* magazine's "America's Most Admired Securities Firm" for the second time in three years. At the end of November 2006, the company's total capital was $66.7 billion and its assets totaled $350.4 billion. The subprime crisis first hit Bear Stearns early in 2007. Previously, the bank had seen a fifty-two-week high of $133.20 per share. By September 2007, two of Bear Stearns' hedge funds had collapsed and the company's third-quarter profit had decreased by 61 percent. By November it had written off $1.2 billion in mortgage securities. In March 2008, the Federal Reserve attempted to bail out the company, but it could not save Bear Stearns. JP Morgan agreed to buy Bear Stearns for a mere $2 per share, which was a decrease of $131 per share in about a year. After lawsuits and intense negotiations, JP Morgan raised the buying price to $10 per share.

What caused a long-standing institution like Bear Stearns to fall? Its investment in subprime loans was a significant factor, but derivatives could also be a major reason. Since its failure, information has come out that Bear Stearns widely misrepresented client information on loan applications in order to make them appear more desirable mortgage recipients. Once these risky subprime loans were given out, the company packaged and sold the debt as securities to other institutions. The securities were backed by cash flow from the loans, which only works when loan payments come in when they are supposed to. In this way, Bear Stearns managed to keep the risky subprime lending debt off of its books and moved the onus to investors. Bear Stearns had derivatives amounting to $13.4 trillion at the end of November 2007.

Since its failure, the Bear Stearns scheme has since been exposed as a risky "house of cards." Executives have been charged with misleading investors by concealing that hedge funds were failing as the mortgage market crumbled. Investors lost $1.6 billion in assets. Executives Ralph R. Cioffi and Matthew M. Tannin were arrested and face criminal charges. Yet this does little to console investors or Bear Stearns employees as they have watched the company's fall and acquisition by JP Morgan.

LEHMAN BROTHERS

Even though the firm had been around for over 150 years, Lehman Brothers found that it too could not survive the subprime mortgage crisis. On September 14, 2008, Lehman Brothers, the fourth-largest investment bank in the United States, filed for Chapter 11 bankruptcy.

Lehman Brothers was founded by Henry, Emanuel, and Mayer Lehman, German immigrants who migrated to America in the mid-nineteenth century. It opened its first store in Montgomery, Alabama, in 1850. As cotton was the cash crop of the South, the brothers often accepted payment in cotton and began acting as brokers for those who were buying and selling the crop. The brothers' business expanded quickly, and they opened an office in New York in 1858. Soon they had transformed from brokerage to merchant banking and Lehman Brothers became a member of the New York Stock Exchange in 1887.

The company continued to thrive even through the stock market crash of 1929. It began advising and financing several businesses, including Halliburton, Digital Equipment, and Campbell Soup. The firm opened its first international office in Paris in 1960. After going public in 1994, Lehman Brothers joined the S&P 100 Index in 1998 and watched its stock rise to $100 per share by the early 2000s. In 2007, the same year as the beginning of the subprime crisis, Lehman Brothers was ranked number one on the *Fortune* "Most Admired Firms" list. CEO Richard Fuld was placed on the list of the world's thirty best CEOs. For its third-quarter, Lehman Brothers possessed assets worth $275 billion.

Then the subprime mortgage crisis hit. By August 2008 the company's shares had lost 73 percent of their value. Even as the company asked for government aid, its executives continued to pocket millions of dollars in bonuses, an action that caused public outrage. In September, the company filed for bankruptcy with $613 billion in debt. Company shares rapidly fell 90 percent to 21 cents per share. The bank received some relief after Barclay PLC agreed to purchase much of Lehman Brothers for $1.75 billion. The purchase of Lehman Brothers was welcome news for some workers, as many of them thought they were going to lose their jobs. Yet this does little to help many shareholders, who had already seen their stocks reduced to nothing. Even CEO Fuld had lost $600 million since December 2007.

What caused such a well-established company like Lehman Brothers to go belly-up? Its dependence on subprime mortgages was the central factor. Additionally, some are accusing the firm of unethical behavior in its dealings with First Alliance Mortgage, a company accused of "predatory lending." Lehman Brothers helped bundle millions of dollars in mortgages into derivatives instruments for First Alliance and helped make them seem like appealing investment vehicles for Wall Street. Of course, when the loans defaulted, it contributed to the massive financial crisis of today.

Lehman Brothers had also acquired several credit default swaps (CDSs). The company had acquired large amounts of subprime mortgage debt and other lower rated assets when securitizing the underlying mortgages. Even though Lehman had closed its subprime mortgage division in 2007, it maintained much of its subprime mortgage liability through 2008, resulting in large losses from the collapse of the subprime market. Creditors of Lehman Brothers, AIG among them, had taken out credit default swaps to hedge against the case of a Lehman bankruptcy. The estimated amount of settling these swaps stands at $100 to $400 billion. Additionally, many major money market funds had significant exposure to Lehman Brothers, the bankruptcy of which caused the investors in these money market accounts to lose millions. Undoubtedly, the fall of Lehman Brothers will have severe effects on businesses across the world for a long time, a negative legacy of this once great company.

ETHICAL ISSUES WITH DERIVATIVES

Derivatives (especially swaps) expose investors to counterparty risk. For example, if a business wants a fixed interest loan but banks only offer variable rates, the business swaps payments with another business that wants a variable rate, creating a fixed rate for the first business. However, if the second business goes bankrupt, the first business loses its fixed rate and has to pay the variable rate. If interest rates increase to the point where the first business cannot pay back the loan, it causes a chain reaction of failures. Derivatives may also pose high amounts of risk for the small or inexperienced investors.

Because derivatives offer the possibility of large rewards, they offer an attraction to individual investors. But the basic premise of derivatives is to transfer risk among parties based on their willingness to assume additional risk, or hedge against it. Many smaller investors do not comprehend this until they lose. As a result, a chain reaction leading to a domestic or global economic crisis can occur. Warren Buffett, a well-known investor, has stated that he regards derivatives as "financial weapons of mass destruction." Derivatives have been used to leverage the debt in an economy, sometimes to a massive degree. When something unexpected happens, an economy will find it very difficult to pay its debts, thus causing a recession or even depression. Marriner S. Eccles, U.S. Federal Reserve Chairman from 1934 to 1948, stated that an excessively high level of debt was one of the primary causes of the Great Depression.

Some experts believe derivatives have significant benefits as well. Although it is always the case with derivatives that someone loses while someone else gains, under normal circumstances, derivatives should not adversely affect the economic system because it is not a zero-sum game—derivatives theoretically allow for absolute economic growth; meaning while one party gains in relation to the other, both gain relative to their previous positions. Former Federal Reserve Board Chairman Alan Greenspan commented in 2003 that he believed that derivatives softened the impact of the economic downturn at the beginning of the twenty-first century and UBS, for example, believed derivatives were part of its future.

However, derivatives have a checkered history. In the 1900s, derivatives trading and bucket shops were rampant. Bucket shops are small operators in options and securities that lure clients into transactions and then flee with the money, setting up shop elsewhere. In 1922, the federal government attempted to stop this practice with the Grain Futures Act, and in 1936 options on grain futures were temporarily banned in the United States as well as in other countries. In 1972, the Chicago Mercantile Exchange (the Merc) created the International Monetary Market, allowing trading in currency futures representing the first futures contracts associated with nonphysical commodities. In 1975, the Merc responded with the Treasury bill futures contract that was based purely on interest rate futures. In 1977 and 1982, T-bond (Treasury) futures contracts, Eurodollar contracts, and stock index futures were created. The 1980s marked the beginning of swaps and other over-the-counter derivatives. Soon large, and even some not so large, corporations were using derivatives to hedge a wide variety of investment risks. Derivatives soon became too complex for the average person to understand, and Wall Street turned to mathematicians and physicists to create models and computer programs that could analyze these exotic instruments.

Finally, the ethical issues in using derivatives rest with managers and traders who use this highly complex and risky financial instrument. Derivatives are used in sales transactions where there is an opportunity of great financial rewards that does not take into account the level of risk for investors or other stakeholders. If the risk associated with a derivative is not communicated to the investor, this could result in deception or even fraud. It has become apparent that the use of derivatives such as credit default swaps became so profitable that traders and managers lost sight of anything but their incentives for selling these instruments. In other words, financial institutions were selling what could be called defective products because a true risk of these financial instruments was not understood or disclosed to the customer. In some cases these defective products were given to traders to sell without any due diligence from the company as to the level of risk.

CONCLUSION

While derivatives, including *credit default swaps,* were not the only cause of the failure of the banks discussed in this case, the use of these instruments by decision makers resulted in taking enormous risks. In hindsight these actions seem to be unwise and unfair to stakeholders. An ethical issue relates to the level of transparency that exists in using complex financial instruments to create profits for customers. If purchasers do not understand the potential risks and the possibility of loss of their money, then a chance for deception exists. In the banks examined in this case, there is no doubt that a number of key decision makers not only pushed the limits of legitimate risk-taking, but also engaged in manipulation, and in some cases fraud, to deceive stakeholders.

At this point, it is doubtful whether banks have learned enough about the 2008–2009 financial crisis to avoid future failures. Investors and shareholders need to start looking beyond short-term results and need to start understanding the value of long-term thinking. The CEO and Board of Directors need to develop a transparent business model that balances risk with market opportunity. The ethical risks of lower-level managers using deception and manipulation to create profits, often through loopholes and unregulated areas of decision making, are high. Through ethical leadership and compliance programs these risks can be minimized.

QUESTIONS

1. What are the ethical risks associated with derivatives?
2. What is the difference between making a bad business decision associated with derivatives and engaging in unethical conduct using derivatives?
3. What kinds of investment decisions drove Barings Bank, UBS, Bear Stearns, and Lehman Brothers to financial disasters?
4. How can an ethical corporate culture with adequate internal controls, including ethics and compliance policies, prevent future disasters in financial companies?

SOURCES: Lynn T. Drennan, "Ethics, Governance, and Risk Management," Caledonian Business School, Scotland, UK: Centre for Risk and Governance; David Koenig, "Case Study: Nick Leeson and Barings Bank." 2008, Ductilibility, http://www.ductilibility.com/uploads/Case_Study_-_Barings_Bank_and_Nick_Leeson.pdf (accessed March 4, 2009); Sam Bhugaloo, "Commodities Trading: Nick Leeson, Internal Controls and the Collapse of Barings Bank," Trade Futures, Ltd., http://www.tradefutures .co.uk/Nick_Leeson_Barings_Bank.pdf (accessed March 4, 2009); S.C. Gwynne, Book Review: "Total Risk: Nick Leeson and the Fall of Barings Bank," *Washington Monthly,* 11 Apr. 2008, http://findarticles .com/p/articles/mi_m1316/is_/ai_17761531 (accessed March 4, 2009); Staff writer, "Nick Leeson Blames the Banks." Sox First, 11 Apr. 2008, http://www.soxfirst.com/50226711/nick_leeson_blames_ the_banks.php (accessed March 4, 2009); Howard Chua-Eoan, "The Top 25 Crimes of the Century: #18 The Collapse of Barings Bank, 1995," *TIME,* November 18, 2007, http://www.time.com/time/2007/ crimes/18.html (accessed March 4, 2009); Staff writer, "Down the Matterhorn: UBS Falls From Grace,"

The Economist, July 12, 2007, http://www.economist.com/finance/displaystory.cfm?story_id=E1_ JQRPGNT (accessed March 4, 2009); John Downey, "BofA Asks $20M in Dispute vs. Ex-employees," *Charlotte Business Journal,* July 22, 2002, http://www.bizjournals.com/charlotte/stories/2002/07/ 22/story7.html (accessed March 4, 2009); Lynnley Browning, "Wealthy Americans Under Scrutiny in UBS Case," *New York Times,* June 6, 2008, http://www.nytimes.com/2008/06/06/business/ worldbusiness/06tax.html?scp=1&sq=Wealthy%20Americans%20Under%20Scrutiny%20in%20UBS% 20Case&st=cse (accessed March 4, 2009); Lynnley Browning, "Federal Prosecutors Declare European Banker a Fugitive," *New York Times,* May 23, 2008, http://www.nytimes.com/2008/05/23/ business/worldbusiness/23bank.html?scp=1&sq=Federal+Prosecutors+Declare+European+Banker +a+Fugitive&st=nyt (accessed March 4, 2009); Philip Aldrick, "UBS Sub-Prime Warning Fails to Rattle Markets," *Telegraph.co.uk,* October 3, 2007, http://www.telegraph.co.uk/finance/markets/2816866/ UBS-sub-prime-warning-fails-to-rattle-markets.html (accessed March 4, 2004); Jeffrey Cane, "A Pilot for UBS Foundering Ship," *Conde Nast Portfolio,* February 13, 2008, http://www.portfolio.com/ news-markets/top-5/2008/02/13/A-Pilot-for-UBS-Foundering-Ship (accessed March 4, 2009); Katharina Bart, "UBS Joins the 'Bonus Chop' for Executives, *Wall Street Journal,* November 17, 2008, http://online.wsj.com/article/SB122693338045733273.html (accessed March 4, 2009); Michael Grynbaum, "Bear Stearns Profit Plunges 61% on Subprime Woes," *New York Times,* http://www.nytimes.com/ 2007/09/21/business/20cnd-wall.html?scp=1&sq=Bear%20Stearns%20Plunges%2061%%20on% 20Subprime%20Woes&st=cse (accessed March 4, 2009); Landon Thomas Jr. and Eric Dash, "Seeking Fast Deal, JPMorgan Quintuples Bear Stearns Bid," *New York Times,* March 25, 2008, http://www.nytimes.com/2008/03/25/business/25bear.html?scp=1&sq=Seeking+Fast+Deal%2C+ JPMorgan+Quintuples+Bear+Stearns+Bid&st=nyt (accessed March 4, 2009); Landon Thomas Jr., "Prosecutors Build Bear Stearns Case on E-Mails," *New York Times,* June 20, 2008, http://www.nytimes.com/2008/06/20/business/20bear.html?_r=1&hp&oref=slogin (accessed March 4, 2009); Dealbook Blog, "Could Bear Stearns Do Better?" *New York Times,* http://www.nytimes.com/2008/03/17/business/17dealbook-could-be21779.html?_r=1 (accessed November 20, 2008); Jesse Eisinger, "The $58 Trillion Elephant in the Room," November 20, 2008, http://www.portfolio.com/views/columns/wall-street/2008/10/15/Credit-Derivatives-Role-in-Crash#page1, (October 13, 2008), Staff writer, "Lehman's CDS Mess: Who's on the Hook?" Seeking Alpha, October 13, 2008, http://seekingalpha.com/article/99619-lehman-s-cds-mess-who-s-on-the-hook (accessed on November 21); Kim Lengle, "A Warning Sign from Lehman," CBS News, October 20, 2008, http://www.cbsnews.com/stories/2008/10/20/cbsnews_investigates/main4535072.shtml (accessed March 4, 2009); Brian Ross, "Lehman Had Long Relationship with Suspect Mortgage Brokers," ABC News, September 15, 2008, http://abcnews.go.com/Blotter/story?id=5807408&page = (accessed March 4, 2009); Randall Smith, Diya Gullapalli, and Jeffery McCracken, "Lehman, Workers Score Reprieve," *Wall Street Journal,* September 17, 2008, http://online.wsj.com/article/ SB122156586985742907.html (accessed March 4, 2009); Alice Gomstyn, "Bleeding Green: The Fall of Fuld," ABC News, October 6, 2008, http://abcnews.go.com/Business/Economy/Story?id =5951669&page=1 (accessed March 4, 2009); Sam Mamudi, "Lehman Folds with Record $613 Billion Debt," Market Watch, September 15, 2008, http://www.marketwatch.com/news/story/ lehman-folds-613-billion-debt/story.aspx?guid={2FE5AC05-597A-4E71-A2D5-9B9FCC290520} (accessed March 4, 2009); Simon Kennedy, Greg Morcroft, and Robert Schroeder, "Lehman Failure, AIG Struggle Drive Financials Lower," Market Watch, September 15, 2008, http:// www.marketwatch.com/news/story/lehman-falls-80-firm-readies/story.aspx?guid={8E886D48 -E3C7-4CE2-95F4-7099CE1A49DB}&dist=msr_2 (accessed March 4, 2009).

The Fraud of the Century: The Case of Bernard Madoff

The fraud perpetrated by Bernard Madoff, which was discovered in December 2008, is based upon a Ponzi scheme. Madoff took money from new investors to pay earnings for existing customers. The greater the payout to retiring and withdrawing customers, the more revenue or clients he would need to start an "investment relationship" with. The Ponzi scheme was named after Charles Ponzi, who in the early twentieth century, saw a way to profit from international reply coupons. International reply coupons were a guarantee of return postage in response to an international letter. Charles Ponzi determined that he could make money, legally, by swapping out these coupons for more expensive postage stamps in countries where the stamps were of higher value. While making a significant profit with this system, Ponzi got the idea of enticing investors to provide him more capital to trade coupons for higher priced postage stamps. His promise to investors was a 50 percent profit in a few days.

Touted as a financial wizard and the "Warren Buffett" of his day, Ponzi lived outside Boston; he had a fairly opulent life, bringing in as much as $250,000/day. Part of Ponzi's success came from his personal charisma and ability to con even savvy investors. The promised payout was supported by the new investors anxious to take advantage of these robust returns because he appeared to create an image of power, trust, and responsibility. In July of 1920, the *Boston Post* ran an article exposing the scheme and soon after, regulators raided his offices and charged him with mail fraud, knowing that his fabricated investment reports were mailed to his clients. The foundational operating principle of a Ponzi scheme is that you must constantly attract new investors to pay the old investors the "gains" they were promised. Most Ponzi schemes self-destruct fairly quickly as the ability to keep attracting new investors dwindles. In the case of Bernard Madoff, he may have perpetrated the fraud for many years.

BERNARD L. MADOFF INVESTMENT SECURITIES LLC: "ALL IN THE FAMILY"

Bernie Madoff started in the investment business by legally buying and selling stocks not listed on the New York Stock Exchange (NYSE). Starting in 1960 as a sole proprietorship, he served as a "wholesaler" between institutional investors. In the early days, working with investment firms such as A.G. Edwards, Charles Schwab, and others, he made his money based on the variance between the offer price and sales price of stocks. In the 1990s, Madoff Securities was trading up to 10 percent of the Nasdaq shares on certain days. Early success and competitive advantage came from Bernie working with his brother Peter (the first of several family members to join his firm), who after graduating from law school joined Madoff's company and developed superior technology for trading, buying, and selling at the best prices. Madoff did not operate a hedge fund, which charges a fee for services and holds the money at a custodial bank. Madoff controlled the funds in-house and made his money, in this division, from commissions on sales and profits and as far as has been revealed, the profits were not based on fraud.

As Madoff became more successful, he moved the company's headquarters from Wall Street to Third Avenue to the red granite "Lipstick Building" built by famed architect Philip Johnson. Not unlike Ken Lay and his lobbying efforts to deregulate the energy and gas industry, Bernie became more involved in lobbying for regulatory changes which would make it easier to trade electronically. Peter took on more oversight of the firm's securities business. Bernie served as Chairman of the Nasdaq in 1990, 1991, and 1993. Through his successful networking, visibility at the Nasdaq, and promise of consistent returns (10–12 percent) Bernie was drawing billions of dollars from hundreds of investors. In addition, he held a seat on the government advisory board on stock market regulation, served on charitable boards, and started his own foundation, which added to his credibility. He developed respectability and trust as a highly knowledgeable investment specialist. His inaccessibility and "invitation only" approach to new investors created an air of exclusivity and desire to be involved. It could be equated to the most exclusive of country clubs—the greatest enjoyment is the status of membership. Ruth Madoff, Bernie's wife, also worked at the firm for a time, indicating a family network of relationships in the firm.

Peter's niece, Shana Madoff, was a rules and compliance officer at Madoff's firm and worked under her father who was head of compliance in the market making arm (not the firm's money management business). Shana, although not charged with any crimes, is married to Eric Swanson, a former SEC compliance lawyer. Shana Madoff has a respected career and was honored by the Girl Scouts of America as a "woman of distinction."

Although under investigation, neither of Madoff's sons, Mark or Andrew, has been charged with any wrongdoing. They were responsible for turning their father in when he confessed to the fraudulent nature of his investment firm. Andrew did have money invested in his father's firm whereas Mark took his money out of the firm eight years earlier. The two deny any knowledge of the fraud. The family emphasizes the separation of the stock trading business (run on the 19th floor) and the investment management business (run on the 17th floor) by Bernie Madoff.

In March, 2009 when Bernard Madoff stated his guilt, he never indicated the involvement of any other company employees or family members. He stated in the Allocution that, "I want to emphasize today that while my investment advisory business—the vehicle of my wrongdoing—was part of Bernard L. Madoff Securities, the other businesses that my firm engaged in, proprietary trading and market making, were legitimate, profitable, and successful in all respects. Those businesses were managed by my brother and my two sons" (Madoff Plea Allocution, p. 2). Further investigation will determine the extent and level of external support which Madoff had in defrauding thousands. His hiring philosophy for the investment business was to hire inexperienced individuals with no background in finance. They may have been unknowing participants.

EXPLAINING THE GROWTH NUMBERS

Madoff claimed he could consistently generate 10 to 12 percent returns for investors. Many of his clients were already wealthy and looking for a stable and constant rate of return. His stated investment strategy was to buy stocks while also trading options on those stocks as a way to limit the potential losses on those stocks. His market timing strategy was called the "split strike conversion." With the large financial portfolio Madoff managed, many indicate at least one "red flag" would have been the fact that he would have overtaken the market had he traded the options in the volumes necessary to meet his financial goals. In his "Plea Allocution" statement in March of 2009, he indicated that he never invested any of his client's funds. Madoff simply moved money between Chase Manhattan Bank in New York and Madoff Securities International Ltd., a United Kingdom Corporation. Madoff stated that his fraud began in the early 1990s.

Madoff had relationships with intermediaries also known as "feeders" to his investment fund. These "feeders" trusted Madoff and at this point do not appear to be integrally involved in the fraud. One such middleman, Rene-Thierry Magon de la Villehuchet committed suicide on December 23, 2008, after losing his life savings to Madoff. The middlemen profited by receiving fees, and Madoff had a stream of money flowing into his operation. Robert Jaffe operated as a middleman for Madoff starting in 1989 when he became the manager of Boston-based Cohmad Securities, a firm co-owned by Madoff to attract investors. Jaffe was the son-in-law of one of Madoff's earliest investors and was a member of the Palm Beach Country Club, where he solicited new investors. He earned a small profit when Madoff took on an investor Jaffe introduced to him.

Stanley Chais was a private investor from Beverly Hills who consistently brought in returns of 10 to 15 percent. Chais was funneling all his clients' money to Madoff. Investors with Chais claim they thought he was personally managing their money and were not aware of the Madoff connection. In June, Chais sent a letter to clients informing them that he was moving to Jerusalem for six months for medical reasons and his son would take over in his absence. Chais's fortune is claimed to be devastated as is that of his clients. In addition, Chais lost significant money in his own charitable fund.

Jeffrey Tucker was an attorney for eight years at the SEC. Tucker also facilitated the meeting between Fairfield Greenwich Group and Madoff resulting in the loss of $7.3 billion (the biggest known single loss). Andres Piedrahita wed one of the daughters of Fairfield Greenwich's co-founder Walter Noel. Piedrahita joined Greenwich and attracted significant revenue from Europe's wealthiest families, operating out of a London office. Wealthy Spanish clients invested just under $50 million with the Group and Madoff.

Robert Schulman operated Tremont Group Holdings after gaining experience working with Smith Barney and Shearson Lehman Brothers. Investors with Tremont, who ended up with Madoff, lost an estimated $3.3 billion. Tremont is part of Massachusetts Life Insurance Company that oversees billions of dollars in Oppenheimer Funds mutual fund assets. Tremont helped Mass Mutual enter the hedge fund business. Schulman, at the age of 62, retired from Tremont in the summer of 2008 (nearly six months before Madoff's fraud was exposed). Schulman claims to have lost money in the Madoff funds and now operates a charity helping women and children who are poor or abused. None of his charities' funds were invested with Madoff at the time the scandal broke.

Swiss Bank Union Bancaire Privee (UBP) placed $700 million of wealthy clients' money in Madoff's Ponzi scheme. Top management received warnings from the bank's research department that Madoff's fund should be eliminated from a list of approved funds. The bank's senior executives were aware of the concerns and continued to leave hundreds of millions of investor funds with Madoff. UBP told its clients it was the victim of "massive fraud" and that it had conducted due diligence in managing client funds.

FINANCIAL SUPPORT NEAR THE END AND THE ARREST

The week and a half before Madoff admitted to his sons that he was operating a Ponzi scheme, 95-year-old Palm Beach philanthropist and entrepreneur Carl Shapiro gave Madoff $250 million. Shapiro lost the $250 million that he provided to Madoff as well as the loss of $100 million in a charitable organization he had invested with the firm. Madoff had made requests of many others for funds to save his business and Martin Rosenman provided $10 million. Rosenman is the President of a fuel company in New York. Rosenman is suing Madoff for the money, alleging that Madoff proposed the solicitation was for a new fund and he was sent a nineteen-page promotional piece in advance of the investment.

Madoff was arrested on December 11, 2008, accused of operating a $50 billion Ponzi scheme after confessing his failure to his sons Andrew and Mark, who worked with their father in the firm. The official charge is criminal securities fraud. Madoff declared to his sons that he had roughly $200 to $300 million left in the business and that he wanted to provide the money to employees before turning himself over to authorities. The sons thought the investment arm of the business held between $8 billion and $15 billion in assets. SEC records showed that the firm had $17 billion in assets at the beginning of 2008.

THE INVESTIGATION AND CHARGES

Investigators in this case include the Securities and Exchange Commission (SEC), FBI, federal prosecutors from the U.S. attorney's office for the Southern District of New York, and the Financial Industry Regulatory Authority. Forensic accountants will try to pull together the trail of investments and spending to determine where the money went. There is a belief that multiple offshore funds have been created by Madoff to shelter assets prior to the collapse of the firm. Madoff's business was not registered with the SEC until 2006 after a SEC investigation.

Bernard Madoff is charged with fraud. Investigators are evaluating documents dating back to January 1, 2000. The charges were not new when exposed to the SEC. Beginning in 1992, federal regulators investigated allegations of wrongdoing by Madoff. Table C11-1 is a summary of the nature of these investigations.

INVESTORS IMPACTED

The list of Madoff clients is a who's who of organizations, nonprofits, successful entrepreneurs, and businesspeople as well as entertainers. The Fairfield Greenwich Group had around $7.5 billion or more than half of its assets invested in the firm. Tremont Group Holdings, owned by Oppenheimer, had $3.3 billion invested. Ezra Merkin, head of GMAC, operated a hedge fund which lost $1.8 billion to Madoff. For a list of selected victims of the fraud see Table C11-1.

TABLE C11-1	Government and Regulatory Investigations of Bernard Madoff

Year	Nature of the Investigation
1992	SEC—Madoff's name came up in Florida accounting investigation
1999	SEC—reviews Madoff's trading practices
2001	SEC—Harry Markopolos, securities industry executive, raises question regarding Madoff's returns
2004	SEC—review into allegations of improper trading practices
2005	SEC—interviews Madoff and family finding no improper trading activities
2005	Industry-based regulatory group finds no improper trading activities
2005	SEC—meets with Harry Markopolos who claims Madoff operates world's largest Ponzi scheme
2006	SEC—enforcement investigation finds misleading behavior and Madoff registers as an investment advisor
2007	Financial Industry Regulatory Authority investigates and no regulatory action was taken

SOURCE: Associated Press, "The Many Fruitless Probes into Bernie Madoff," *APNewswire,* January 5, 2009,
http://news.moneycentral.msn.com/provider/providerarticle.aspx?feed=AP&date=20090105&id=9486677 (accessed January 5, 2009).

Several victims have shared their "stories" and relationship with Bernie Madoff. Richard Sonking met with Madoff in the mid-1990s after his father, who had an account with Madoff, recommended the investment for the steady 8 to 14 percent returns. Sonking pulled together the minimum $100,000 required for investment at that time and was reminded how selective Madoff was in developing relationships. After selling his business, importing porcelain collectibles from France, he placed additional funds in Madoff's hands. He was pleased with the returns and pleased with the monthly, detailed seven- to eight-page statements provided (including detail on equity trades). Upon retiring in 2005, Sonking requested quarterly distributions from his account and the amount could be increased with a faxed request. Until the news stories in December 2008 there was no warning of any fraudulent activities.

Loretta Weinberg, a New Jersey state senator and conservative investor, embraced her late husband's philosophy that you live on half of what you make and save the rest. She was invested with Stanley Chais, a Los Angeles money manager who provided quarterly investment reports and a 10 to 14 percent annual return. Until the Madoff scandal hit the press, Weinberg had not heard of Madoff. As a 73-year-old state senator making $49,000/year she will have to cope with the loss of her $1.3 million in life savings. In addition, she is concerned for her family who were all invested with Chais and, unknowingly, Madoff.

Joseph Gurwin is 88 years old and lives in Palm Beach. He came to know Madoff and became his friend through the Palm Beach social and philanthropic community. Gurwin noted Madoff's reputation for secure and conservative financial management. Gurwin's Foundation (The J. Gurwin Foundation, Inc.) operating with around $28 million in assets donated $1.2 million in one year. The Foundation was invested heavily with Madoff. He indicated no warning signs and when he requested withdrawals, the money came quickly. Gurwin's Foundation supports health care, as well as services and programs for frail, elderly, or disabled younger adults.

Law firms in Florida are representing clients who believed they were investing with Westport National Bank (a regulated banking institution in Connecticut) not Madoff Investments. On December 12 the investors received a letter from Westport National indicating that they had a custodial agreement with Westport, giving full discretionary authority to Bernard L. Madoff Investment Securities.

RESTITUTION FOR INVESTORS

Some investors are suing the SEC for negligence in its regulatory responsibility and not being able to identify the fraud. Such attempts represent the first time investors have sought restitution from a regulatory agency. Christopher Cox, SEC Chairman at the start of the fraud investigation, indicated that the SEC examiners had missed "red flags" in reviewing the Madoff firm. Allegations of wrongdoing started nearly ten years ago. Repeated investigations and examinations by the SEC showed no investment fraud. Because many SEC employees end up working in the investment business on Wall Street, there was speculation that an overall lack of objectivity clouded these investigations.

Most investors are looking for minor compensation from the Securities Investor Protection Group (SIPC), which is a security-industry group started by Congress to provide up to $500,000 per customer for theft in a relationship between a broker and direct investor. The trustee has mailed claim forms to more than eight thousand Madoff customers. Many experts believe that third-party investors (those who invested indirectly in the Madoff accounts) will not be eligible for SIPC funds.

Some investors are engaging in "clawback suits." This litigation would attempt to secure funds from "investors" who had been able to successfully withdraw funds and reallocate that money among the defrauded clients. To protect their assets, many who have received payout funds from Madoff are transferring the money to irrevocable trusts, homes, annuities, or life insurance policies to protect them from seizure (Kim, 2009).

A search of Madoff's office by federal prosecutors and investigators found about 100 signed checks for nearly $173 million. The court-appointed trustee has obtained $29 million in assets and identified another $830 million in liquid assets, which could be recovered and returned to investors.

Perhaps the greatest restitution for some investors came as Bernard Madoff was handcuffed on March 12, 2009 and taken to prison after his 12-minute confession of guilt in a Lower Manhattan court house. Some victims asked the judge for a trial to uncover more about this extensive fraud and to determine why the governments' regulatory system failed many investors. Judge Chin indicated there would be no trial as there was a plea of guilt and ongoing investigation at hand (Lucchetti, 2009).

THE FUTURE OF CHARITABLE GIVING

Due to the widespread impact of the Madoff-related losses upon charities, nonprofits, and educational institutions, donor skepticism and withdrawal are not unexpected consequences. As mentioned earlier, some of the organizations affected include the Elie Wiesel Foundation for Humanity, Yeshiva University, and Wunderkinder Foundation (Steven Spielberg's Fund). This wariness comes at a time when the global recession has resulted in losses of around 30 percent for many foundation endowments. The vast majority of nonprofits indicate that the economy was having a negative/very negative impact on fund-raising, before the Madoff scandal was exposed. There is an increased care and sensitivity that will accompany charitable giving and shape the questions and stipulations placed upon donations. Some guidelines provided for evaluating responsible charities include the following:

1. See what materials are readily available to potential investors/donors from the organization (annual reports, audited financial statements, payroll, and overhead)?
2. Who is the charity invested with and how much of their funds are invested?
3. Who is managing the fund/charity and is there an independent investment committee (who's on this committee)?
4. Is the investment portfolio appropriately diversified?
5. Who is auditing the fund/charity?
6. Is there objectivity among board members through written "conflict of interest" statements that prevent direct business dealings while serving on the board?

CONCLUSION

Bernard Madoff is accused of creating a Ponzi scheme that destroyed $50 billion in investments. Many people are trying to understand how so many experienced investors, including banks, insurance companies, and nonprofit foundations lost billions of dollars to an individual who was able to deceive them as well as regulators. Investigators are trying to determine who helped Madoff carry off what some say could be a thirty-year scheme that caused the $65 billion in losses and may have impacted over 4,800 people. Accountants, auditors, and regulators are supposed to be gatekeepers who protect the public interest. Investigators believe that Madoff had a trading strategy that failed, then after a while, he made few trades for many years and his operation consisted of taking money from new clients and paying it out to existing clients, a classic Ponzi scheme.

From an ethical perspective, this would be an example of white-collar crime. White-collar crime creates victims by establishing trust and respectability. As in this case, victims of white-collar crime are trusting clients who believed there were many checks and balances that certified the Madoff investment operation as legitimate. Madoff appears to be the classic white-collar criminal. He was an educated and experienced individual in a position of power, trust, respectability, and responsibility who abused his trust for personal gains. From the inception of his investment business, he knew that he was operating a Ponzi scheme and defrauding his clients. In the end, he said he "knew this day would come."

An important question is how one individual could deceive so many people who certified his operation as legitimate. Madoff's accountants, family, and other employees will have to answer to authorities about their knowledge of the operations. For example, investigators have issued a subpoena for David Friehling, a New York accountant, who audited Madoff's financial statements. Frank DiPascili, who dealt with client accountants and worked at Madoff's firm for twenty-two years, "responded evasively" and many of his answers to investigators were "incomprehensible." While only Madoff has been charged with misconduct at this time, if there were other participants, they will face responsibility for their actions.

White-collar crime is unique in that it is often done knowingly by a rogue individual to steal, cheat, or manipulate in order to damage others. Often, the only way to prevent white-collar crime is to have internal controls and compliance standards that detect misconduct. Perhaps the most difficult white-collar crime and fraud to expose is that perpetrated by the top executive. We count on leadership within an organization to create, manage, and motivate an ethical organizational culture with all the checks and balances in place. In the Madoff case there was the opportunity to deceive others without effective audits or transparency and an understanding of the true nature of his operations. As a result of this case, individual investors, institutions, and hopefully regulators will exert more diligence in demanding transparency and honesty from those who manage investments.

QUESTIONS

1. What are the ethical issues involved in the Madoff case?
2. Do you believe that Bernard Madoff worked alone, or do you think he had help in creating and sustaining his Ponzi scheme? Would this represent a conflict of interest?
3. What should be done to help ensure that Ponzi schemes like this one do not happen in the future?

SOURCES: "Madoff's Victims," *Wall Street Journal*, http://s.wsj.net/public/resources/documents/st_madoff_victims_20081215.html (accessed January 9, 2009); "Plea Allocution of Bernard L. Madoff," http://online.wsj.com/public/resources/documents/20090315madoffall.pdf, March 12, 2009, accessed March 12, 2009; "Victims of Scandal Reflect on Shocking Turnabout," *Wall Street Journal*, online.wsj.com/article/SB122972955226822819.html (accessed December 23, 2008); Elizabeth Bernstein, "After Madoff, Donors Grow Wary of Giving," *Wall Street Journal*, online.wsj.com/article/SB122999068109728409.html (accessed December 23, 2008); Cassel Bryan Law, "Inside a Swiss Bank, Madoff Warnings," *Wall Street Journal*, January 14, 2009, 1A; Thomas Catan, Christopher Bjork, and Jose De Cordoba, "Giant Bank Probe Over Ties to Madoff," *Wall Street Journal*, online.wsj.com/article/SB123179728255974859.html (accessed January 13, 2009); Amir Efrati, "Q&A on the Madoff Case," *Wall Street Journal*, online.wsj.com/articles/SB123005811322430633.html (accessed January 9, 2009); Amir Efrati, "Scope of Alleged Fraud Is Still Being Assessed," *Wall Street Journal*, online.wsj.com/article/SB122953110854314501.html (accessed December 23, 2008); Amir Efrati and Chad Bray, "U.S.: Madoff Had $173 Million in Checks," *Wall Street Journal*, online.wsj.com/article/SB123143634250464871.html (accessed January 9, 2009); Amir Efrati, Aaron Lucchetti, and Tom Lauricella, "Probe Eyes Audit Files, Role of Aide to Madoff," *Wall Street Journal*, online.wsj.com/article/SB122999256957528605.html (accessed December 23, 2008); Robert Frank and Amir Efrati, "Madoff Tried to Stave Off Firm's Crash Before Arrest," *Wall Street Journal*, online.wsj.com/article/SB123129835145559987.html (accessed January 7, 2009); Robert Frank and Tom Lauricella, "Madoff Created Air of Mystery," *Wall Street Journal*, online.wsj.com/article/SB122973208705022949.html (accessed December 23, 2008); Kara Scannell, "Investor Who Lost Money in Alleged Scheme Seeks Relief from SEC," *Wall Street Journal*, online.wsj.com/article/SB122999646876429063.html (accessed December 22, 2008); Jane J. Kim (2009) "As 'Clawback' Suits Loom, Some Investors Seek Cover," *Wall Street Journal*, March 12, p. C3; Aaron Lucchetti, (2009) "Victims Welcome Madoff Imprisonment," *Wall Street Journal*, March 12, http://online.wsj.com/article/SB123687992688609801.html, accessed March 12, 2009; Jenny Strasburg, "Madoff 'Feeders' Under Focus," *Wall Street Journal*, December 27–28, 2008, A1, A8; Jenny Strasburg, "Mass Mutual Burned by Madoff," *Wall Street Journal*, December 22, 2008, C1; Ethan Trex, "Who Was Ponzi—What the Heck Was His Scheme?" CNN.com, http://www.cnn.com/2008/LIVING/wayoflife/12/23/mf.ponzi.scheme/index.html (accessed December 23, 2008); Elizabeth Williamson, "Shana Madoff's Ties to Uncle Probed," *Wall Street Journal*, online.wsj.com/article/SB122991035662025577.html (accessed December 23, 2008).

Nike: From Sweatshops to Leadership in Employment Practices

> The Nike product has become synonymous with slave wages, forced overtime and arbitrary abuse.—Nike chairman Phil Knight at a speech to the National Press Club, May 12, 1998

The biography of Phil Knight, the driving force behind Nike, has been recounted repeatedly as an example depicting a "self-made billionaire." Philip H. Knight, seventieth on the *Forbes* ranking of the world's richest people in 2006, is now worth $7.3 billion, has come a long way from selling shoes out of his car trunk in 1964. In contrast to its meteoric rise in the 1980s after going public, the late 1990s for Nike was a period composed of combating allegations about subcontractor labor and human rights violations in third-world countries. Nike's response was considered by its critics to be more of a public relations, damage-control stunt rather than a sincere attempt at labor reform.

Knight founded Nike in 1964 under the name "Blue Ribbon Sports." The idea, born as a result of a paper written by Knight during his MBA program at Stanford, was to import athletic shoes from Japan into the U.S. market otherwise dominated by German competitors. The Nike brand was created in 1972 ("Nike" after the Greek goddess of victory), the company went public in 1980, and today Nike is one of the largest manufacturers of athletic goods in the world.

THE SCANDAL

Sweatshops and product origin permeated the public consciousness, when Kathy Lee Gifford discovered that her endorsed clothing line was actually made in Honduran sweatshops. Nike is known as a footwear company, but approximately one-third of its

We appreciate the work of Deepa Pillai, Alexi Sherrill, and Melanie Drever who assisted in this edition of the case. This case was prepared for classroom discussion rather than to illustrate either effective or ineffective handling of an administrative, ethical, or legal decision by management. All sources used for this case were obtained through publicly available material and the Nike website.

revenue comes from apparel, and that manufacturing takes place mostly in factories located in Asia. Contracts with suppliers from Korea and Taiwan replaced Nike's original contracts with Japanese producers. The company's increasing scope and size of operations, along with increasing costs, have meant that these suppliers have had subcontracts with cheaper labor markets in other third-world countries such as Indonesia, China, and Vietnam.

Nike employees were assigned to the new manufacturing facilities in these countries in order to monitor operations. According to Nike's Corporate Responsibility Report (2001), the pool of suppliers came from over seven hundred factories in fifty countries. The lower costs of production coupled with innovative advertising and marketing were the main reasons for Nike's growth.

Since the mid-1990s, Nike has faced a barrage of criticism from labor rights activists, the media, and others for human rights violations in their factories in third-world countries. The accusations include deficiencies in health and safety conditions, extremely low wages, and indiscriminate hiring and firing practices. The attention given to this issue by the national media is evident in the number of reports and editorials in leading newspapers as well as programs on television—all lending support to the cause of labor activists campaigning against Nike's unfair labor practices.

In Indonesia, where Korean suppliers owned a majority of Nike factories, several cases of human rights abuses were revealed by nongovernment organizations—for example, Roberta Baskin's CBS report on the conditions in Nike's manufacturing facilities in Indonesia in 1993 and Bob Herbert's op-ed article in the *New York Times* in 1996.

Another of Nike's problems was factory conditions in Vietnam, which became public knowledge. Ernst and Young, commissioned by Nike to audit one of the factories, reported extreme, unacceptable standards of chemicals in the factory and cases of employee health problems caused as a result of this and other infringements of the established code of conduct. Unfortunately for Nike, it was leaked to the press, resulting in the *New York Times* running it as a front-page article.

THE FALLOUT AND RESPONSE

Public protests against Nike took the forms of boycotts and picketing of Nike stores, and universities began canceling their deals with Nike to produce branded athletic goods. In 1998 Nike revenues and stock prices decreased by approximately 50 percent, leading to the laying off of sixteen hundred workers.

Nike had already established its code of conduct in 1992 in the wake of increasing public interest in the operations of multinational corporations in developing countries; Nike was following suit with other companies operating in these areas. In theory, suppliers were required to sign the code of conduct and display it in their factories, but this was not enforced. More recent efforts to enforce standards have been made in the form of monitoring, both through Nike's own production department and by independent consultants; the objective is the dual goal of retaining cost effectiveness while honoring the cost of labor and human rights issues.

The initial reactions of Nike officials to specific criticisms was to ignore them, the rationale being that they did not own the factories and were therefore not responsible for labor and human rights violations. They claimed to be marketers and designers lacking knowledge about manufacturing. However, in 1996 Knight claimed full responsibility for working conditions wherever its products were produced. But in his speech on May 12, 1998, Knight denied that Nike had a sweatshop problem and claimed the problems had to do with public relations rather than actual factory conditions.

During this time, Nike sought to counter the allegations about labor and human rights violations through an extensive public relations campaign. A workplace code of conduct was established to regulate working conditions in foreign factories. In the mid-1990s, Nike finally intervened in the wage policy of its factories in Indonesia and announced wage raises above the legal minimum wage in 1999. In 1998 a statement of corporate responsibility addressing the various allegations against Nike was issued and included several specific steps that Nike intended to implement in its factories.

Nike used a number of other tactics in attempting to repair its tarnished image. Michael Jordan was recruited as a Nike spokesperson. Because universities formed a core segment of Nike's market and repercussions had already been felt in this area with several deals being canceled, letters detailing the acceptable conditions in the factories and stressing Nike's commitment to corporate responsibility were sent to U.S. universities. Representatives from Nike also visited campuses and spoke to students, assuring them of Nike's intention toward responsible corporate citizenship. A key visit in this context was Knight's to the University of North Carolina at Chapel Hill; numerous press conferences were also held with college newspapers across the United States.

MORE PROBLEMS: *NIKE VS. KASKY*

Nike hired Andrew Young, a former UN ambassador, to visit and report on conditions in its third-world factories. The 1997 report stated that a survey of twenty factories in several Asian countries had revealed that (1) there were no infringements of health and labor codes of conduct and (2) the pay in Nike-controlled factories was substantially higher than the required minimum wage. The report claimed that Nike typically subsidized meals and medical treatment of factory employees. As part of its intensive public relations campaign, Nike used press releases in newspapers and ran full-page advertisements based on parts of Young's report, mentioning that Nike was doing a good job but could do better.

In 1998 Marc Kasky, a self-styled corporate critic, responded to the conflict between Nike's claims and the content of the report by Ernst and Young filing a lawsuit against Nike. The case was to be a landmark one not only from Nike's perspective but also from the perspective of commercial speech laws. Among other allegations, it was claimed that Nike was consciously misleading the public when it claimed that workers in its factories were being paid in accordance with minimum wage laws, that they were being paid substantially more than the minimum wage, and that they received free/subsidized meals and health services. The decision of the California Supreme Court in

2002 went against Nike, and the company was held accountable for its deceptive public statements regarding its labor practices. Nike appealed to the U.S. Supreme Court, but the case was sent back to the San Francisco District Court of Appeals. Faced with the prospect of extended litigation, Nike agreed to settle with Kasky. The settlement included $1.5 million to be paid over three years to the Fair Labor Association—a worker rights–monitoring group in Washington, DC—and $500,000 a year to subsidize entrepreneurial ventures of foreign employees and forums in Nike's factories. Nike officials stated that settling was the correct choice because the focus was on benefits to workers and to Nike's commitment of corporate responsibility.

Nike Recovers and Excels in Managing Social Responsibility

The company has been making numerous changes, learning that an open-minded approach to the issues facing its industry is better than denial. As part of this evolution, Nike has moved away from focusing on its own code of conduct and toward creating a standard code of conduct throughout the industry.

As part of the new Nike, they have moved beyond its old monitoring systems and employ three different types in its factories. First, it uses the SHAPE inspection to determine basic compliance to regulations regarding environment, safety, and health. Nike's field-based production staff generally performs this inspection. The second method is the Management Audit (M-Audit). Nike hired twenty-one staff members and trained them in labor-auditing practices. The M-Audit, an in-depth inspection, is designed to uncover problems that may not be readily obvious. Finally, Nike encourages independent monitoring by the Fair Labor Association. Nike now has a compliance team composed of over ninety people in twenty-one countries.

Nike has also opened the doors of a number of its contract factories to research groups from the Sloan School of Management at the Massachusetts Institute of Technology who are studying the business drivers and outcomes. The company hopes that through this research it can learn more about the business process and how to better manage production flow and work hours in its factories. Nike has also implemented the balanced scorecard, a lettered grading system, to better assess factory compliance with the code of conduct. This system gives the company a reliable method for rewarding high-performance, compliant factories. The balanced scorecard is also used to help Nike avoid pushing factories in one direction to the detriment of others; for example, the card measures cost, delivery, and quality, and all need to be addressed equally for production to flow smoothly.

In addition to building up its monitoring processes, Nike is now disclosing its contract factory base. Doing so is part of the corporate movement toward transparency. By disclosing its supply chain, Nike believes it can be more successful at monitoring and at making changes, not only in its own factories but also industry-wide, once issues have been uncovered. Nike hopes that by disclosing its own supply chain it can encourage other companies to do the same. It hopes to standardize a code of conduct followed by all companies and factories in the industry. Nike also feels that transparency should work as a motivator for contract factories. Those with high compliance rankings can be confident that business will come their way.

Another part of Nike's evolution is finding new production methods to avoid the toxic chemicals typically used to make their products. It is also coming up with innovative ways to recycle old shoes and to create products made of recycled polyester or organic cotton. Nike has become more aware of its impact on the environment and is taking steps to make this impact a better one.

Although challenging, putting corporate responsibility at the forefront of Nike's business is a positive move. The company is learning to deliver equal value to its five different stakeholder groups: consumers, shareholders, business partners, employees, and the community. With a focus on corporate responsibility, Nike hopes to build and improve its relationships with consumers, achieve a high-quality supply chain, and create top quality, innovative products. Although this evolution is a difficult one filled with lessons learned along the way, employees worldwide and the company itself are reaping the benefits.

As part of a movement toward corporate responsibility, Knight stepped down as CEO in 2004 although he still is chairman of the board. His reason was to put someone in who was an expert in corporate responsibility. Bill Perez was hired as the new CEO, based on his track record in this area and a belief that companies must invest in and improve the communities in which they coexist. In 2006 Nike veteran Mark Parker, formerly copresident, took over as CEO and director. Parker, who has been with Nike for twenty-seven years, has been part of most of Nike's top innovative plans and is recognized as a product visionary.

As a result of the changes, Nike appeared in *Business Ethics* magazine's "100 Best Corporate Citizens" list for 2005 and 2006. It entered the list in 2005 at number thirty-one and climbed to number thirteen in 2006. *Business Ethics* cites its reasons for listing Nike as the strength of Nike's commitment to community and environment. Nike was actually ranked number one in the magazine's environmental category due to its efforts to eliminate waste and toxic substances from production processes. Nike also made *Fortune* magazine's "100 Best Companies to Work For" list for the first time in 2006, coming in at number 100 and has received a perfect score on the Human Rights Campaign Foundation's Corporate Equality Index two years in a row. Although Nike admits that it has a long way to go, it is being rewarded for its efforts along the way, both by positive results and industry response.

QUESTIONS

1. What were Nike's mistakes in handling the negative publicity?
2. Discuss the intent of their public relations tactics.
3. Do you think Nike is doing enough to improve conditions in its contract factories? What might they do differently or better?
4. How would you rank Nike's improvements?

SOURCES: Academics Studying the Athletic and Campus Apparel Industry, "Academics Studying Nike," maintained by David M. Boje, PhD, updated January 2006, http://business.nmsu.edu/~dboje/nike/nikemain1.html (accessed May 17, 2006); "Business Ethics Magazine Lists "100 Best Corporate Citizens for 2006," Nike, http://www.nike.com/nikebiz/nikebiz.jhtml?page=59&item=tppr&year=2006&release=05a

(accessed May 16, 2006); James Ciment, ed. "The Promise and Perils of Globalization: The Case of Nike," in *Social Issues in America: An Encyclopedia* (Armonk, NY: Sharpe, 2006); Ronald K. L. Collins and David M. Skover, "Symposium: *Nike v. Kasky* and the Modern Commercial Speech," June 2004, via http://www.law.seattleu.edu/fachome/skover/articles/nike/ (accessed May 17, 2006); Tim Connor, "Still Waiting for Nike to Do It; Nike's Labor Practices in the Three Years Since CEO Phil Knight's Speech to the National Press Club," Global Exchange, 2001, via http://www.cleanclothes.org/ ftp/ 01-05NikeReport.pdf (accessed July 14, 2006); John H. Cushman, Jr., "Nike Pledges to End Child Labor and Apply U.S. Rules Abroad," *New York Times,* May 13, 1998, via http://www.corpwatch.org/ article.php?id=12965 (accessed July 14, 2006); Tony Emerson, "Swoosh Wars: In an Operation Modeled on the Clinton Campaign Machine, Nike Takes on Its Enemies," *Newsweek International,* March 12, 2001, http://www.msu.edu/~jdowell/pdf/SwooshWars.pdf (accessed July 14, 2006); "Evolution: Shifting Our Approach to Labor Compliance," Nike website, updated April 2005, http://www.nike .com/nikebiz/nikebiz.jhtml?page=25&cat=approach (accessed May 16, 2006); Bob Herbert, "In America: Nike's Pyramid Scheme," *New York Times,* June 10, 1996, via http://www.geocities .com/Athens/Acropolis/5232/NYT061096.htm (accessed July 14, 2006); Holman W. Jenkins, Jr., "The Rise and Stumble of Nike," *Wall Street Journal,* June 3, 1998, A6; Jackie Krentzman, "The Force Behind the Nike Empire," *Stanford Magazine* online, http://www.stanfordalumni.org/ news/magazine/1997/janfeb/articles/knight.html (accessed May 17, 2006); "Labors' Pains," PBS online, April 14, 1997, http://www.pbs.org/newshour/bb/business/jan-june97/sweatshops_4-14 .html (accessed May 17, 2006); "A Letter from Nike Brand's Presidents: Three Areas of Focus for the Future," Nike website, updated April 2005, http://www.nike.com/nikebiz/nikebiz.jhtml?page=54&item= direction (accessed May 16, 2006); "A Message from Phil Knight," Nike website, updated April 2005, http://www.nike.com/nikebiz/nikebiz.jhtml?page=54&item=letter (accessed May 16, 2006); "Nike-Funded Study Claims Workers at Nike's Indonesian Factories Are Subject to Abuse and Harassment," Institute for Global Ethics, *Ethics Newsline,* February 26, 2001, http://www.globalethics .org/newsline/members/issue.tmpl?articleid=02260116252837 (accessed May 17, 2006); "Nike, Inc. Names Mark Parker CEO, William D. Perez Resigns," Nike press release, January 23, 2006, http://www.nike.com/nikebiz/news/pressrelease.jhtml?year=2006&month=01&letter=d (accessed May 17, 2006); "Niketimeline" and "Highlights," Nike website, http://www.nike.com/nikebiz/ media/nike_timeline/nike_timeline.pdf (accessed May 17, 2006); "Workers in Contract Factories," Corporate Responsibility Report 2004, Nike website, http://www.nike.com/nikebiz/gc/r/fy04/ docs/workers_factories.pdf (accessed May 16, 2006); "The World's Billionaires, 2006: #70 Philip Knight," *Forbes* online, March 9, 2006, http://www.forbes.com/lists/2006/10/2KZ5.html (accessed May 17, 2006); Matt Zwolinski, "In the News: International (Global) Business Ethics," *BizEd* online, April 15, 2005, http://www.bized.ac.uk/dataserv/chron/news/2331.htm (accessed May 17, 2006).

The Healthcare Company: Learning from Past Mistakes?

In 1968 Dr. Thomas Frist, Sr., Jack C. Massey, and Dr. Thomas Frist, Jr., founded the Hospital Corporation of America (HCA) to manage Park View Hospital in Nashville, Tennessee. The firm grew rapidly over the next two decades by acquiring and building new hospitals and contracting to manage additional facilities for their owners. The firm merged with Columbia Hospital Corporation to become Columbia/HCA Healthcare Corporation in 1994, and Columbia founder Richard Scott became chairman and CEO of the combined companies. By 1997 Columbia/HCA Healthcare Corporation had grown to become one of the largest health-care services companies in the United States, operating 343 hospitals, 136 outpatient surgery centers, and approximately 550 home-health locations. It also provided extensive outpatient and ancillary services in thirty-seven states, as well as in the United Kingdom and Switzerland. The firm's comprehensive network included more than 285,000 employees and used economies of scale to increase profits.

Columbia/HCA's stated mission was "to work with our employees, affiliated physicians and volunteers to provide a continuum of quality healthcare, cost-effectively for the people in the communities we serve." Its vision was "to work with employees and physicians, to build a company that is focused on the well-being of people, that is patient-oriented, that offers the most advanced technology and information systems, that is financially sound, and that is synonymous with quality, cost-effective health-care." Columbia/HCA's goals included measuring and improving clinical outcome and patient satisfaction as well as reducing costs and providing services with compassion. With these goals, the company built the nation's largest chain of hospitals based on cost effectiveness and financial performance. It competed by capitalizing on its size and creating economies of scale in the internal control of its costs and sales activities. The focus was bottom-line performance and new business acquisitions.

We appreciate the work of Mike Thomas, who helped draft this edition of the case. This case is for classroom discussion rather than to illustrate either effective or ineffective handling of an administrative, ethical, or legal decision by management. All sources used for this case were obtained through publicly available material and the HCA website.

However, a number of critics charged that health-care services and staffing at Columbia/HCA often took a back seat to the focus on profits. For example, the company employed shorter training periods than competing hospitals provided. One former administrator reported that training that typically should take six months was sometimes accomplished in as little as two weeks at a Columbia/HCA hospital. In addition, the company was accused of "patient dumping"—discharging emergency-room patients or transferring them to other hospitals when they are not yet in stable condition. In 1997 officials at the Department of Health and Human Services Inspector General's Office indicated that they were considering imposing fines on Columbia/HCA for an unspecified number of patient-dumping cases. Additionally, the corporate watchdog INFACT publicly challenged the company's practices, inducting Columbia/HCA into its "Hall of Shame" for corporations that manipulate public policy to the detriment of public health.

ETHICAL AND LEGAL PROBLEMS BEGIN

In late July 1997, Fawcett Memorial Hospital in Port Charlotte, Florida, a Columbia/HCA hospital, became the focal point of the biggest case of health-care fraud in the industry. A government investigation resulted in the indictment of three mid-level Columbia/HCA Healthcare Corporation executives for filing false cost reports for Fawcett, which resulted in losses of more than $4.4 million from government programs. The government alleged that Columbia/HCA had gained at least part of its profit by overcharging for Medicare and other federal health programs; that is, executives had billed the government for nonreimbursable interest expenses. Other concerns were alleged illegal incentives to physicians and the possible overuse of home-health services. Federal investigators accused Columbia/HCA of engaging in a "systematic effort to defraud government health care programs." In a seventy-four-page document, federal investigators quoted confidential witnesses who stated that Columbia/HCA's former CEO, Richard Scott, and former president, David Vandewater, were briefed routinely on issues relating to Medicare reimbursement claims that the government charged were fraudulent. Samuel Greco, Columbia/HCA's former chief of operations, was also implicated in the scandal.

One of the issues was whether Columbia/HCA had fraudulently overstated home-health care laboratory-test expenses and knowingly miscategorized other expenditures so as to inflate the amounts for which it sought reimbursement. For example, Columbia/HCA's Southwest Florida Regional Medical Center in Fort Myers reportedly claimed $68,000 more in property taxes than it paid. Moreover, documents showed that the hospital had set aside money to return to the government in case auditors caught the inflated figure. Technically, expenses claimed on cost reports must be related to patient care and fall within the realm of allowable Medicare reimbursements. However, medical billing can be confusing, chaotic, imprecise, and subject to interpretation. Hence, it is not unusual for hospitals to keep two sets of accounting books. One set is provided to Medicare, and the other set, which includes records for set-aside money, is held in case auditors interpret the Medicare cost report differently than the hospital does. Some believe it is appropriate for a hospital to set aside money to return to the government if the hospital in good faith believes the Medicare cost claims are legitimate. However, if administrators believe strongly or know that certain claims are not allowable yet still file the claims and note them in the second set of books, charges of fraud may result.

Confidential witnesses said that Columbia/HCA had made an effort to hide from federal regulators internal documents that could have disclosed the alleged fraud. In addition, Columbia/HCA's top executive in charge of internal audits had instructed employees to soften the language used in internal financial audits that were critical of Columbia/HCA's practices. According to FBI agent Joseph Ford, "investigation by the [Federal Bureau of Investigation] and the [Defense Criminal Investigative Service] has uncovered a systematic corporate scheme perpetrated by corporate officers and managers of Columbia/HCA's hospitals, home health agencies, and other facilities in the states of Tennessee, Florida, Georgia, Texas, and elsewhere to defraud Medicare, Medicaid, and the [Civilian Health and Medical Program of the Uniformed Services]." Indicted Columbia/HCA officials pleaded not guilty, and defense lawyers for Columbia/HCA tried to diminish the importance of the allegations contained in the government's affidavits.

DEVELOPING A NEW ETHICAL CLIMATE AT COLUMBIA/HCA

Soon after the investigation was launched, Dr. Thomas Frist, Jr., was hired as chairman and CEO of Columbia/HCA. Frist, who had been president of HCA before it merged with Columbia, vowed to cooperate fully with the government and to develop a one-hundred-day plan to change the troubled firm's corporate culture. Under the Federal Sentencing Guidelines for Organizations (FSGO), companies that have effective due diligence compliance programs can reduce their fines if they are convicted of fraud. For penalties to be reduced, however, an effective compliance program must be in place before misconduct occurs. Although the FSGO requires that a senior executive be in charge of the due diligence compliance program, Columbia/HCA's general counsel had been designated to take charge of the program.

After a hundred days as chairman and CEO of Columbia/HCA, Frist outlined changes that would reshape the company. His reforms included a new mission statement as well as plans to create a new senior executive position to oversee ethical compliance and quality issues. Columbia/ HCA's new mission statement emphasized a commitment to quality medical care and honesty in business practices. It did not, however, mention financial performance. "We have to take the company in a new direction," Frist said. "The days when Columbia/HCA was seen as an adversarial or in your face, a behind-closed-doors kind of place, is a thing of the past." (It has been claimed that some managers viewed Columbia/HCA's corporate culture as so unethical that they resigned before the fraud investigation had even started.)

Columbia/HCA hired Alan Yuspeh as the senior executive to oversee ethical compliance and quality issues. Yuspeh, senior vice president of ethics, compliance, and corporate responsibility, was given a staff of twelve at the corporate headquarters and assigned to work with group, division, and facility presidents to create a "corporate culture where Columbia workers feel compelled to do what is right." Yuspeh's first initiatives were to refine monitoring techniques, boost workers' ethics and compliance training, develop a code of conduct for employees, and create an internal mechanism for workers to report any wrongdoing.

Because of the investigation, consumers, doctors, and the general public lost confidence in Columbia/HCA, and its stock price dropped more than 50 percent from its all-time high. The new management seemed more concerned about developing the corporation's ethical compliance program than about its growth and profits. For instance, at a conference in Phoenix, Arizona, twenty Columbia managers were asked to indicate by a show of hands how many of them had escaped taunts from friends that they were crooks. Not a single hand went up. The discussion that followed that question did not focus on surgery profit margins. It focused on resolving the investigation and on the importance of the corporation's intangible image and values.

COLUMBIA/HCA LAUNCHES AN ETHICS, COMPLIANCE, AND CORPORATE RESPONSIBILITY PROGRAM

Columbia/HCA released a press statement indicating that it was taking a critical step in developing a company-wide ethics, compliance, and corporate responsibility program. To initiate the program, the company designated more than five hundred employees as facility ethics and compliance officers (ECOs). The new ECOs began their roles with a two-day training session in Nashville. The local leadership provided by these facility ECOs was thought to be the key link in ensuring that the company continued to develop a culture of ethical conduct and corporate responsibility.

As part of the program, Yuspeh made a fifteen-minute videotape that was sent to managers throughout the Columbia/HCA system. The tape announced the launching of the compliance-training program and the unveiling of a code of ethics that was designed to effectively communicate Columbia/HCA's new emphasis on compliance, integrity, and social responsibility. Frist stated that "we are making a substantial investment in our ethics and compliance program in order to ensure its success" and that "instituting a values-based culture throughout this company is something our employees have told us is critical to forming our future. The ethics and compliance initiative is a key part of that effort."

Training seminars for all employees, conducted by each facility's ECO, included introductions to the training program, the Columbia/HCA code of conduct, and the company's overall ethics and compliance program. The training seminars also included presentations by members of senior management and small-group discussions in which participants discussed how to apply the new Columbia/HCA code of conduct in ethics-related scenarios.

Although the company wanted individuals to bring their highest sense of personal values to work each day, the purpose of the program was to help employees understand the company's strict definition of ethical behavior rather than to change their personal values. Columbia/HCA's ethical guidelines tackled basic issues such as whether nurses can accept $100 tips—they cannot—as well as complicated topics such as what constitutes Medicare fraud. In addition, the company developed certification tests for the employees who determine billing codes. In 1998 a forty-minute training video was shown to all the firm's employees; it featured three ethical scenarios for employees to examine. Columbia/HCA apparently recognized the importance of ethical conduct and quality service to all of its constituents.

RESOLVING THE CHARGES

In 1997–1998, Columbia/HCA Healthcare settled with the Internal Revenue Service (IRS) for $71 million over allegations that it had made excessive compensation and "golden parachute" payments to some one hundred executives. As a result of the settlement, the IRS, which had sought $276 million in taxes and interest, agreed to drop its charges that Columbia/HCA had awarded excessive compensation by allowing the executives to exercise stock options after a new public offering of Columbia/HCA stock. Frist had reportedly earned about $125 million by exercising stock options after that public offering, and seventeen other top executives each made millions on the deals.

In August 2000, Columbia/HCA became the first corporation ever to be removed from INFACT's Hall of Shame. The executive director of INFACT announced that Columbia/HCA had drastically reduced its political activity and influence. For example, the corporation has no active federal lobbyists and has a registered lobbying presence in only twelve states. According to INFACT's executive director, "This response to grassroots pressure constitutes a landmark development in business ethics overall and challenges prevailing practices among for-profit health care corporations."

In December 2000, Columbia/HCA announced that it would pay the federal government more than $840 million in criminal fines and civil penalties. The company agreed in June 2003 to pay $631 million to settle the last of the government's charges that it had filed false Medicare claims, paid kickbacks to doctors, and overcharged at wound-care centers. No senior executives of the company have ever been charged with a crime. However, the company has paid out a total of $1.7 billion in fines, refunds, and lawsuit settlements after admitting that it had, through two subsidiaries, offered financial incentives to doctors in violation of antikickback laws, falsified records to generate higher payments for minor treatments or treatments that never occurred, charged for laboratory tests that were never ordered, charged for home-health care for patients who did not qualify for it, and falsely labeled ads as "community education." KPMG, the firm's auditor, denied any wrongdoing on its part but agreed to pay $9 million to settle a whistle-blower lawsuit related to the charges. Columbia/HCA also signed a "Corporate Integrity Agreement" in 2000 that subjected the firm to intense scrutiny until 2009. In the same year, the company was officially renamed HCA—The Healthcare Company.

In January 2001, Frist relinquished the title of CEO to focus on other interests but remained involved in corporate strategy as chairman of HCA's board of directors. Jack Bovender, Jr. (formerly CFO) replaced him. Of the fraud investigation, Bovender said, "We think the major issues have been settled," although the company still has some "physician relations issues and cost report issues" to resolve in civil actions involving individual hospitals. Since 1997 the company has closed or consolidated more than one hundred hospitals. It is currently composed of locally managed facilities that include 175 hospitals and 80 outpatient surgery centers in twenty-four states, England, and Switzerland.

HCA'S COMPLIANCE PROGRAM AT WORK

Today, HCA spends $4 million a year on its ethics program, which includes an ethics and compliance committee of independent board directors, two separate corporate committees that draft ethics policy and monitor its use, and a twenty-member department that implements the program. In all, twenty-six executives oversee ethics and compliance for a variety of issues, ranging from taxes to pollution to the Americans with Disabilities Act.

The ethics compliance program set up by Yuspeh includes seven components: (1) articulating ethics through a code of conduct and a series of company policies and procedures; (2) creating awareness of these standards of compliance and promoting ethical conduct among everyone in the company through ethics training, compliance training, and other ongoing communication efforts; (3) providing a twenty-four-hour, toll-free telephone hot line to report possible misconduct; (4) monitoring and auditing employees' performance in areas of compliance risk to ensure that established policies and procedures are being followed and are effective; (5) establishing organizational supports for the ethics compliance effort; (6) overseeing the company's implementation of and adherence to the Corporate Integrity Agreement; and (7) undertaking other efforts such as clinical ethics and pastoral services.

Training continues to play a major role in helping employees understand HCA's new focus on ethics and legal compliance. Every new employee is required to undergo two hours of "orientation" on the firm's code of conduct within thirty days of employment. At that time, new employees receive a copy of the code of conduct, participate in training using videotapes and games, and sign an acknowledgment card. All employees complete one hour of refresher training on the firm's code of conduct every year.

HCA's new ethics hot line helps the firm identify misconduct and take corrective action where necessary. For example, in the spring of 2002, an anonymous caller to the toll-free line accused a hospital supply clerk of stealing medical gear and reselling it online through eBay. After investigators verified the complaint, the clerk was fired. Since its inception, the ethics program has fielded hundreds of such ethics-related complaints.

The effort to change HCA's corporate culture quickly and become the model corporate citizen in the health-care industry was a real challenge. This health-care provider learned the hard way that maintaining an organizational ethical climate is the responsibility of top management. As Bovender says, "Internal controls can always be corrupted. We've tried to come up with a system that would require a lot of people to conspire. It would be very hard for Tyco-type things to happen here." HCA seems to have recovered well from all of its problems, and at the time of writing this case, a number of companies were trying to acquire it, an indication that they view it as a great business opportunity. ◆

QUESTIONS

1. What were the organizational ethical leadership problems that resulted in Columbia/HCA's misconduct?
2. Discuss the strengths and weaknesses of HCA's current ethics program. Does this program appear to satisfy the provisions of the Federal Sentencing Guidelines for Organizations and the Sarbanes–Oxley Act?
3. What other suggestions could Columbia/ HCA have implemented to sensitize its employees to ethical issues?

SOURCES: Columbia/HCA Healthcare Corporation, *1996 Annual Report to Stockholders;* "Columbia/HCA Launches Ethics and Compliance Training Program," AOL News, February 12, 1998, http://cbs.aol.com; "Columbia/HCA to Sell Part of Business," *Commercial Appeal,* June 3, 1998, B8; "Corporate Influence Curtailed," *PR Newswire,* August 2, 2000; Kurt Eichenwald, "Reshaping the Culture at Columbia/HCA," *New York Times,* November 4, 1997, C2; Kurt Eichenwald and N. R. Kleinfield, "At Columbia/HCA, Scandal Hurts," *Commercial Appeal,* December 21, 1997, C1, C3; "Ethics, Compliance, and Corporate Responsibility: Introduction," HCA, http://ec.hcahealthcare.com/ (accessed April 24, 2003); "HCA Tentatively Agrees to Multimillion Fraud Settlement," American Medical News, January 27, 2003, www.ama-assn.org/sci-pubs/amnews/pick_03/gvbf0127.htm; "History," HCA, http://hca.hcahealthcare.com/CustomPage.asp?guidCustomContentID=C2E6928A-D8B1-42AF-BA44-6C2B591282D5 (accessed April 24, 2003); "INFACT Urges Columbia/HCA to Remove Itself from the Hall of Shame," *PR Newswire,* www.prnewswire.com (accessed May 27, 1999); Lucette Lagnado, "Columbia Taps Lawyer for Ethics Post: Yuspeh Led Defense Initiative of 1980s," *Wall Street Journal,* October 14, 1997, B6; Tom Lowry, "Columbia/HCA Hires Ethics Expert," *USA Today,* October 14, 1997, 4B; Tom Lowry, "Loss Warning Hits Columbia/HCA Stock," *USA Today,* February 9, 1998, 2B; Duncan Mansfield, "HCA Names Bovender Chief Executive," January 8, 2001, Yahoo! News, http://biz.yahoo.com/apf/010108/hca_change_ 2.html (accessed January 16, 2001); Charles Ornstein, "Columbia/HCA Prescribes Employee Ethics Program," *Tampa Tribune,* February 20, 1998, 4; Eva M. Rodriguez, "Columbia/HCA Probe Turns to Marketing Billing," *Wall Street Journal,* August 21, 1997, A2; Neil Weinberg, "Healing Thyself," *Forbes* online, March 17, 2003, www.forbes.com/forbes/2003/0317/064.html; Chris Woodyard, "FBI Alleges Systemic Fraud at Columbia," *USA Today,* October 7, 1997, 1B.

PETCO Develops Successful Stakeholder Relationships

BACKGROUND AND HISTORY

PETCO Animal Supplies Inc. is the nation's number-two pet supply specialty retailer of premium pet food, supplies, and services with over 750 stores in forty-eight states and the District of Columbia. Their pet-related products include pet food, pet supplies, grooming products, toys, novelty items, vitamins, veterinary supplies, and small pets such as fish, birds, other small animals (excluding cats and dogs). PETCO's strategy is to offer their customers a complete assortment of pet-related products and services at competitive prices, with superior levels of customer service at convenient locations and through their e-commerce site www.petco.com.

PETCO stores offer the broad merchandise selection, convenient location, and knowledgeable customer service of a neighborhood pet-supply store. PETCO believes that this combination differentiates their stores and provides them with a competitive advantage. Their principal format is a 12,000- to 15,000-square-foot store, conveniently located near local neighborhood shopping destinations, including supermarkets, bookstores, coffee shops, dry cleaners, and video stores, where their target "pet parent" customer makes regular weekly shopping trips. PETCO believes that their stores are well positioned, both in terms of product offerings and location, to benefit from favorable long-term demographic trends: a growing pet population and an increasing willingness of pet owners to spend on their pets.

Since mid-2001, all new stores have been opened in their new formats, which incorporate a more dramatic presentation of their companion animals and emphasize higher-margin supplies categories. Each store has approximately ten thousand pet-related items, including premium cat and dog foods, collars, leashes, grooming products, toys, and animal habitats. The stores also offer grooming, obedience training, and

This case was prepared by Melanie Drever, University of Wyoming, under the direction of O. C. Ferrell, for classroom discussion rather than to illustrate either effective or ineffective handling of an administrative, ethical, or legal decision by management. All sources used for this case were obtained through publicly available material and the PETCO website.

veterinary services, and they sponsor pet adoption for cats and dogs with local animal-welfare organizations. PETCO has 16,900 employees, 9,000 of which are full time.

Walter Evan founded PETCO in 1965 as a mail-order veterinary-supplies store. The original name was UPCO, United Pharmacal Company. In 1976 they opened their first retail store in La Mesa, California, buying quality pet and veterinary supplies and selling them directly to animal professionals and the public at discount prices. In 1979 UPCO became PETCO. PETCO's vision is to promote the highest level of well-being for companion animals and to support the human–animal bond. Their aim is to provide a broad array of premium products, companion animals, and services and a fun and exciting shopping experience. Their value proposition to the pet parent/ customer is provided through friendly, knowledgeable associates (employees) in convenient, community-based locations.

The pet food, supplies, and services industry is benefiting from a number of favorable demographic trends that are continuing to support a steadily growing pet population. The U.S. pet population has now reached 378 million companion animals, including 143 million cats and dogs, with an estimated 62 percent of all U.S. households owning at least one pet, and three-quarters of those households owning two or more pets. It is widely believed that the trend for more pets and for more pet-owning households will continue, driven by an increasing number of children under 18 years of age and a growing number of empty nesters whose pets have become their new "children." Estimates have suggested that U.S. retail sales of pet food, supplies, small animals (excluding cats and dogs), and services increased to approximately $34 billion in 2004. PETCO believes they are well positioned to benefit from several key growth trends within the industry.

THE PET INDUSTRY

The pet industry is growing and getting stronger. Harley Davidson has a line of leather dog jackets, and Paul Mitchell has a line of pet shampoos. Hotels are offering pet-friendly rooms, and Japanese pet-toy company Takara has introduced Bow-Lingual, a device that translates dog barks. Pet owners continue to treat their pet as part of their families. They often lavish as much care and attention on the pet as they do on other family members; this means that many pet owners are prepared to spend considerable sums of money on pet products. However, not all the trends affect the industry in a positive way; for example, pet owners are moving away from dogs toward cats, which means that volumes of pet food will decrease.

PETCO does business in a highly competitive industry and competes against such names as diverse as PetSmart and Wal-Mart. This competition can be categorized into three different segments: (1) supermarkets, warehouse clubs, and mass merchants; (2) specialty pet store chains; and (3) traditional pet stores and independent service providers. The principal competitive factors influencing PETCO are product selection and quality, convenient store locations, customer service, and price. PETCO believes that they compete effectively within their various geographic areas. However, some of their competitors are much larger in terms of sales volume and have access to greater capital and management resources than PETCO does.

THE RISKS ASSOCIATED WITH THE PET INDUSTRY

Most organizations' greatest fear is not discovering risk associated with operating their business. Regardless of the industry, there is concern that the public or a special-interest group can uncover some activity that can immediately be used by critics and the mass media, competitors, or simply skeptical stakeholders to undermine a firm's reputation. Therefore, an ethical risk assessment is an important activity that is included in most companies' ethics initiatives. A single negative incident can influence perceptions of a corporation's image and reputation instantly and possibly continue for years afterwards.

Not all ethical concerns are of a company's making, and there are certainly those disgruntled antagonists who will distort the truth for their own self-interest. Because pets are such a strong emotional attachment for many, assessing risk of accusations in this industry is especially important. For all companies who sell pets, the question is not if there will be accusations, but when the accusations are made, can there be a rapid enough response to explain or correct activities that are in question to mitigate possible negative perceptions. The important focus should be on a commitment to make the right decisions and to constantly assess and deal with the risk of operating a business.

PETCO is committed to pets and animals in general. However, as with other companies, selling animals has inherent risks. Between 2000 and 2005, People for the Ethical Treatment of Animals (PETA) alleged questionable conditions at PETCO. PETA, a special-interest group that makes strong demands not always supported by the general public, is highly critical of most organizations that sell or use animals for commercial purposes.

PETA made complaints regarding cruelty and neglect to animals in PETCO's care, and they filed a complaint against PETCO with the Securities and Exchange Commission (SEC). PETA had concerns about the handling of their animals for sale. PETCO responded and made changes. In particular, PETA was concerned about the sale of large birds; specifically, such birds need plenty of space to move around and exercise. Also, when kept as "companions," large birds need a great deal of socialization and attention—at least eight hours a day. Most parrots die from diseases caused by the same conditions that adversely affect humans—for example, obesity, high-stress environments, and too-little exercise. Many large birds also have multiple guardians in their lifetimes because they tend to outlive one human family after another; their lifespan is typically between forty and seventy years. Adding further to the problem is that about 70 percent of parrots suffer from "miner's lung" disease (pneumoconiosis) because of living in dry, stuffy, indoor environments.

On April 12, 2005, PETA and PETCO announced an agreement that would advance animal welfare across the country. PETA agreed to end its campaign against the national pet food and supply retailer, to take down all references to "PETNO," and dismantle its "PETCOCruelty" website. PETCO agreed to end the sale of large birds in its stores upon completion of the sale of the limited number they had in stock. It also would continue to work with its shelter partners to help those groups adopt not only dogs and cats but also homeless birds of all sizes, as part of PETCO's established "Think Adoption First" program. PETCO also agreed to make some changes to benefit rats and mice; these changes included separating the animals by gender to prevent breeding. Although not required to answer to PETA, PETCO decided to respond to indicate its desire to cooperate, resolve issues and misunderstandings, and improve operations.

Another incident occurred in May 2004 when PETCO paid nearly $1 million in precedent-setting settlements of two California lawsuits involving the mistreatment of animals in PETCO stores in five California counties. After PETA released undercover footage of extreme neglect at North American Pet Distributor, Inc. (NAPD), which supplied at least fifty-five PETCO stores, PETCO halted its business with NAPD because it had established a response system to deal quickly with any knowledge about supplier abuse of animals. Resolving any activity that is not in compliance with an organization's standards of conduct is easy once they have been developed.

Other problems have also plagued PETCO. In 2002 inspectors and customers found sick finches, a moldy dead turtle, dead birds, and a toad "cooked to death" at two San Francisco PETCO stores that were also overcharging customers on sale items. PETCO settled this case in 2004, agreeing to pay more than $900,000—most of which would be spent on new scanners in its stores. PETCO also agreed it would increase training for its managers and employees in regard to caring and looking after animals. Again, this demonstrated the desire to do the right thing and respond to mistakes made by employees. With over sixteen thousand employees, individuals will step outside the bounds of PETCO's desired conduct, but the ability to expose and correct these situations illustrates an effective ethics program.

In 2004 PETCO agreed to settle a Federal Trade Commission charge that it did not take reasonable or appropriate measures to prevent commonly known attacks by hackers to obtain customer information. The settlement required PETCO to implement a comprehensive information security program for its website.

Another worry that PETCO has addressed is pet owners' concerns over pet food-portion control; this concern has been addressed by selling the Electronic Portion Control Le Bistro by Petmate. This product dispenses food at certain times throughout the day. PETCO has also started a PetHotel, a form of kenneling called Best Friends Pet Care, Inc., which includes TV sets tuned to animal shows and special ventilation systems. PETCO is trying hard to find the issues that concern their customers and address them. One issue that might affect PETCO in the future could include concerns about avian flu; this particularly concerns people who buy their bird feed from PETCO.

Managing risk is an important aspect of any business but especially for companies that sell animals. PETCO has tried to limit its risk by selling only a few types of animals and not selling large animals such as dogs or cats. This has limited the extent to which it is at risk and avoided the negative effect of the risk. Animal sales make up only 5 percent of PETCO's revenues; pet supplies and services make up the rest. By avoiding this risk, PETCO ensures that it keeps not only its customers and investors happy but also the animals in its care protected from abuse.

THE PETCO ETHICS PROGRAM

PETCO has a comprehensive code of ethics. Its main emphasis is that animals always come first, and PETCO wants to ensure that all the employees adhere to this code. One of their most important missions is to promote the health, well-being, and humane treatment of animals. They do this through their vendor selection programs, pet adoption programs, and their partnerships with animal-welfare organizations. PETCO was founded on the principle of "connecting with the community."

In 1999 PETCO established the PETCO Foundation to help them promote charitable, educational, and other philanthropic activities for the betterment of animals everywhere. The PETCO Foundation is dedicated to serving the "Four Rs": Reduce, Rescue, Rehabilitate, Rejoice. The PETCO Foundation promotes the welfare of companion animals and the importance of the person–animal bond. The foundation raises funds for animal-welfare groups and promotes pet adoption to all their customers. The PETCO Foundation, a nonprofit organization, has raised more than $28 million since its inception. Through a combination of programs and fundraisers—"Round Up," "Think Adoption First," "Spring a Pet," "Tree of Hope," "National Pet Adoption Days," and "Kind News"—more than thirty-three hundred nonprofit grassroots animal-welfare organizations have received support. They are also responsible for the donation of in-kind goods and services to worthwhile organizations with the same mission of strengthening the bond between people and pets. With an exclusive long-term agreement with Petfinder.com, they also support over seven thousand additional animal welfare agencies.

The code of ethics also has a section relating to dealing with customers and others. It emphasizes that employees should treat customers with the utmost care and that their privacy should be respected at all times. PETCO also ensures that its selling practices, advertising policies, and pricing and buying practices are mentioned in its code. It is against the code to promote one brand over any other brand; associates are expected to interact honestly with each customer and to clearly explain the purpose and benefits of the products and services. PETCO makes efforts to ensure that their advertising is not misleading and that pricing decisions are made without influence from vendors, contractors, or competitors.

The matter of courtesy, dignity, and respect among associates is taken very seriously. The code of ethics addresses concerns about sexual and other types of harassment that could occur in the workplace. If any employee makes a complaint about harassment, it will be treated with confidentiality and appropriate corrective action. Discipline will be directed at offending parties, which may include dismissal. Drug abuse, asset protection, and violence in the workplace are also concerns for PETCO and are addressed in the code. PETCO has implemented measures that aim to increase associate, vendor, and customer protection with the goal of providing a safe working environment.

PETCO associates are to avoid conflicts of interest or what appear to be conflicts of interest. This means that PETCO associates must not place themselves in situations that might force them to choose between their own personal or financial interests and the interests of PETCO. Associates are encouraged to communicate any conflicts of interest to management to determine whether a conflict actually exists.

The code of ethics addresses the acceptance of gifts and entertainment. PETCO associates are prohibited from accepting gifts or gratuities from vendors or potential vendors, whether it is money, merchandise, services, lavish entertainment, travel, or any other form. Associates who receive such gifts are asked to contact their supervisor or the PETCO hot line for guidance and ask vendors to refrain from giving gifts in the future. Acceptance of reasonable entertainment in accordance with customary practice is acceptable, as long as it is kept within reasonable limits.

Employment with suppliers, vendors, or others doing business with PETCO is expected to be done at the discretion of associates, and their supervisors are expected to be contacted. Investments in vendors made by associates or their immediate families are not permitted without prior approval from the Ethics Committee. PETCO discourages workplace romances when there is a direct or indirect reporting relationship because undue pressure may occur. Outside interests are allowed; however, they should not be endorsed, funded, or sponsored by PETCO. It is considered inappropriate for associates to publicly make negative remarks about PETCO. If associates have a grievance or concern, they are asked to work with the company to obtain a mutually satisfactory resolution.

Associates must also agree to not interfere with PETCO's business by directly or indirectly soliciting the business of any persons or entities who were the customers of PETCO, or soliciting an associate of PETCO to terminate his or her position for a period of six months immediately after the termination of her or his employment. Trade secrets and other proprietary information must also be kept in strict confidence both during employment and forever following separation.

After the scandals of Enron and other publicly traded companies, PETCO strived for and explicitly called for accurate accounting records of all its assets, liabilities, expenses, and other transactions. No unrecorded or undisclosed fund or asset of PETCO or its subsidiaries may be established or maintained for any purpose. Furthermore, PETCO insists that no confidential or proprietary information relating to PETCO, its suppliers, vendors, or customers can be disclosed at any time. All PETCO property and information systems can only be used for conducting company business. Occasional personal use is permitted as long as it does not interfere with or impedes PETCO's business. Knowingly duplicating copyrighted computer software is also prohibited.

All associates are encouraged to comply with accounting laws including the Sarbanes–Oxley Act and the generally accepted accounting principles. Internal controls and procedures are designed to ensure that PETCO's financial records are accurately and completely maintained. It is also against PETCO policy to buy or sell PETCO stock while in possession of important information not publicly available.

The code of ethics also addresses other concerns such as workplace safety, wage and hour laws, and reporting time worked. Political contributions from PETCO funds are not allowed, as are payments to government personnel. PETCO also respects the environment and strives to conserve natural resources as much as possible.

A section concerning managers and supervisors encourages them to be role models when dealing with employment decisions. When dealing with the media, managers and supervisors are asked to discuss any situations with all parties to determine an appropriate media response if necessary. An associate may also at no time submit or knowingly accept false or misleading information, documents, or proposals. When in doubt, associates are encouraged to phone the code of ethics hot line or ask a supervisor on the appropriate course of action to take.

The code of ethics also presents a chain of command to follow in case an employee is faced with an ethical dilemma. There is also an anonymous 24-hour hot line for associates to call if they do not feel that their immediate supervisor is being responsive or if it involves their immediate supervisor. The code of ethics is reviewed on an annual basis. The company also has an internal Ethics Committee, which oversees compliance with the code and continually monitors related best practices.

PETCO FOUNDATION FUNDRAISERS

The "Round Up" Program

Every year between 5 and 10 million pets are euthanized in the United States. PETCO launched an annual "Spay Today" initiative in 2000 to address the significant and growing problem of pet overpopulation. Overpopulation due to unwanted litters sends millions of animals to animal shelters each year. The "Spay Today" funds come from customer donations at PETCO stores where customers are encouraged to round up their purchases to the nearest dollar or more. Each PETCO store selects one or more spay/neuter–focused charitable partners to which the funds are donated. In addition, 10 percent of all funds raised are donated to the Petfinder.com Foundation to assist their spay/neuter efforts. In 2000 PETCO allowed pet owners to purchase a voucher at PETCO stores to have a cat spayed or neutered for $10 and a dog spayed or neutered for $20 (compared to the regular price of more than $100). In 2004 this program raised $817,000 for local animal-welfare organizations across the country.

The "Think Adoption First" Program

"Think Adoption First," launched in 2005, supports and promotes the person–animal bond. It is a program that sets the standard for responsibility and community involvement for the industry. Each year, 8 to 12 million pets are relinquished to shelters and rescue groups. PETCO, the PETCO Foundation, and Petfinder.com offer a second chance for those orphaned companion animals. "Think Adoption First" recommends the adoption of companion animals beyond dogs and cats as an alternative first choice to consider. They provide access to rescued animals through their partnership network of rescue groups and then work with their partners to make companion animals available for in-store adoption. They have strengthened their relationship with Petfinder.com, and together they have found homes for over 2 million animals. This program reinforces PETCO's commitment to both social responsibility and financial success.

The "Spring a Pet" Program

The "Spring a Pet" fundraiser encourages pet lovers to donate $1, $5, $10, or $20 to animal-welfare causes. Donors receive a personalized cutout bunny to display in their neighborhood store or take home as a reminder of their generosity. Each PETCO store selects an animal-welfare organization to be the recipient of the money raised at its location. In the past, the money has provided veterinary care for homeless and abused animals and outreach programs to help handicapped and disadvantaged individuals adequately care for their companion animals. In 2005 this program raised $1.51 million.

The "Tree of Hope" Program

Customers visiting one of PETCO's 760 stores during the Christmas season can purchase card ornaments for $1, $5, $10, or $20. They can also choose from red or blue "Making a Difference" wristbands or a 2006 PETCO Foundation calendar loaded with coupons. All funds go toward the "Tree of Hope." Anyone donating $20 or more receives a PETCO Foundation hand-painted globe ornament. In 2005, this program raised $2.1 million.

The "National Pet Adoption Days" Program

More than fourteen thousand animals were adopted during "National Pet Adoption Days" on April 2–3, 2005. Not only did dogs and cats find new homes but also hundreds of birds, reptiles, and small mammals.

The "Kind News" Program

"Kind News" is a Humane Education Program that educates children about the humane treatment of companion animals and fellow human beings. It features stories about responsible pet environmental concerns and issues as well as information on all types of animals. It contains many learning tools to reinforce the concept of compassion and concern for all living things.

PETCO'S CHALLENGES AND ACCOMPLISHMENTS

Most companies focus on customers to help establish their reputation and success, but PETCO has adopted a stakeholder orientation and is concerned about its impact on society. Although PETCO wants quality products for its customers, with information and advice for caring for pets, it is also concerned about important issues related to the existence and role of animals in our society. For example, the "Think Adoption First" and the "Round Up" program to encourage spaying/neutering of pets illustrates important contributions to society. Especially important is the PETCO Foundation support of "Kind News" to educate children about proper humane treatment of animals and fellow human beings. PETCO, like any organization, experiences risk associated with doing business and has developed a comprehensive ethics program to manage relationships with stakeholders. For example PETCO addressed the concerns of PETA and has taken a proactive approach to addressing any accusations or concerns about its operations.

All organizations in the retail area are subject to criticisms and have to work hard to maintain internal controls that provide assurance that employees follow ethical codes. PETCO accomplishes this through an ethics office and by developing an ethical corporate culture. PETCO's code of ethics addresses all organizational risk related to human resources, conflicts of interests, and appropriate behavior in the workplace. All large organizations know that misconduct will occur somewhere in the organization, so discovering, exposing, and addressing any event before it can cause reputation damage are important. For PETCO, the desire to do the right thing and to train all organizational members to make ethical decisions ensures success in the marketplace and a significant contribution to society.

1. What are the ethical risks associated with selling pets and pet products in a retail environment?
2. How has PETCO managed the various ethical concerns that have been expressed by stakeholders?
3. Assess the ethical culture of PETCO.

SOURCES: All websites were accessed between January 23 and July 5, 2006. "Animal Abuse Case Details. PETCO Lawsuit—Mistreating Animals San Diego, CA," May 28, 2004, Pet-Abuse, http://www.pet -abuse.com/cases/2373/CA/US; Catherine Colbert, "PETCO Animal Supplies, Inc.," *Hoovers* online, http://www.hoovers.com/petco-(holding)/ID__17256—/free-co-factsheet.xhtml; "*Fortune* 500 2006: Our Annual Ranking of America's Largest Corporations," CNN/Money, http://money.cnn.com/ magazines/fortune/fortune500/snapshots/2154.html; Michelle Higgins, "When the Dog's Hotel Is Better Than Yours," *Wall Street Journal,* June 30, 2004, D1; "Just Say No! Petco—The Place Where Pets Die," Kind Planet, http://www.kindplanet.org/petno.html (accessed July 5, 2006); Melissa Kaplan, "PETCO Settles Suit Alleging Abuse, Overcharging," May 27, 2004, CBS News online, http://www .anapsid.org/pettrade/petocit2.html; Ilene Lelchuk, "San Francisco Alleges Cruelty at 2 PETCOs," *San Francisco Chronicle,* via June 19, 2002, http://www.anapsid.org/pettrade/petcocit2.html; "Lifestyle Trends Affect Pet Markets," *Pet Age* online, January 2006, http://www.petage.com/News010607.asp; Robert McMillan, "PETCO Settles Charge It Left Customer Data Exposed," IDG News Service, November 17, 2004, http://www.networkworld.com/news/2004/1117petcosettl.html; Chris Penttila, "Magic Markets" *Entrepreneur's StartUps* online, September 2004, http://www.entrepreneur.com/ article/0,4621,316866-2,00.html; "PETA and PETCO Announce Agreement," PETA, April 2005, http://www.peta.org/feat/PETCOAgreement/default.asp; "Petco Animal Supplies Inc. (PETC)," Yahoo! Finance, http://finance.yahoo.com/q?s=PETC; "PETCO Annual Report to Shareholders" and "PETCO 10-K Annual Report," www.petco.com; "PETCO's Bad Business Is Bad for Animals," PETA, Spring 2003, http://www.peta.org/living/at-spring2003/comp2.html; "PETCO Code of Ethics," http://ir.petco.com/phoenix.zhtml?c=93935&p=irol-govConduct; "PETCO Foundation to 'Round-Up' Support for Spay/Neuter Programs," *Forbes,* online, July 13, 2005 http://www.forbes.com/ prnewswire/feeds/prnewswire/2005/07/13/prnewswire200507131335PR_NEWS_B_WES_LA_LAW 067.html; "PETCO Looks to the Web to Enhance Multi-Channel Marketing," *Internet Retailer,* January 16, 2006; "PETCO Pays Fine to Settle Lawsuit," PETA, Annual Review 2004, http://www.peta.org/feat/annual_review04/notToAbuse.asp; "PETCO Settles FTC Charges," Federal Trade Commission, November 17, 2004, http://www.ftc.gov/opa/2004/11/petco.htm; "PETCO 'Spring a Pet' Campaign Blossoms for Animals Nationwide," Corporate Social Responsibility press release, Citizenship at Boston College, May 11, 2005, http://www.csrwire.com/ccc/article.cgi/ 3910.html; "The Pet Market—Market Assessment 2005," Research and Markets, http://www.researchandmarkets.com/reports/c26485/; "Pet Portion Control," *Prevention,* February 2006, 201; "Pet Store Secrets: PETA Uncovers Shocking Back-Room Secrets," PETA, Summer 2000, http://www.peta.org/living/at-summer2000/petco.html; "Say No to PETCO," PETA, Spring 2002, http://www.peta.org/living/at-spring2002/specialrep/; Julie Schmidt, "Pet Bird Buyers Asking Sellers About Avian Flu," *USA Today,* November 28, 2005, via http://www .citizen-times.com/apps/pbcs.dll/article?AID=/20051129/HEALTH/511290304/1008/ HEALTH (accessed July 5, 2006); Jessica Stannard-Freil, "Corporate Philanthropy: PR or Legitimate News?" *On Philanthropy* online, May 5, 2005 http://www.onphilanthropy.com/tren_comm/ tc2005-05-20.html.

Coping with Financial and Ethical Risks at American International Group (AIG)

When American International Group (AIG) collapsed in September 2008 and was subsequently saved by a government bailout, it became one of the most controversial players in the 2008–2009 financial crisis. The corporate culture at AIG had been involved in a high-stakes risk-taking scheme supported by managers and employees that appeared entirely focused on short-term financial rewards. One unit, AIG Financial Products, was chiefly to blame. The Financial Products unit specialized in derivatives and other complex financial contracts that were tied to subprime mortgages or commodities. While its dealings were risky, the unit generated billions of dollars of profits for AIG. Nevertheless, during his long tenure as CEO of AIG, Maurice "Hank" Greenberg had been open about his suspicions of AIG's Financial Products unit. However, after Greenberg resigned as chief executive of AIG in 2005, the Financial Products unit became even more speculative in its activities. The perfect storm formed with the subprime mortgage crisis and a sudden sharp downturn in the value of residential real estate. Since much of the speculation in the Financial Products unit was tied to derivatives, even small movements in the value of financial measurements could result in catastrophic losses.

In this case, we trace the history of AIG as it evolved into one of the largest and most respected insurance companies in the world, and the more recent events that led to its demise. AIG had a market value of $180 billion in 2007, and by 2009 this amount had fallen to a mere $5 billion. Only a government rescue of $152 billion prevented AIG from facing total bankruptcy in late 2008. Saving AIG was not meant as a reward, however. The government rescued the company not to keep it from bankruptcy, but to prevent the bankruptcies of many other global financial institutions that depended on AIG as counterparty on collateralized debt obligations. If AIG had been allowed to fail, it is possible that the financial meltdown that occurred in 2008–2009 would have been worse. The following case examines the events leading up to the 2008 meltdown, including the philosophy of top management and the corporate

This case was written by John Fraedrich, O. C. Ferrell, and Jennifer Jackson, with the editorial assistance of Jennifer Sawayda. This case was developed for classroom discussion rather than to illustrate either effective or ineffective handling of an administrative, ethical, or legal discussion by management. All sources used for this case were obtained through publicly available material.

culture that set the stage for AIG's demise. We will review the events that occurred in 2008, including ethical issues related to transparency and failed internal controls. Finally, we will look at the role of the government and its decision to bail out AIG, taking a 79.9 percent ownership in a company that grossly mishandled its responsibility to its stakeholders.

AIG'S HISTORY

The saga of American International Group (AIG) began in 1919 with the U.S.-born Cornelius Vander Starr, who founded a company in Shanghai representing American insurance companies selling fire and marine coverage in Asia. Starr's success in Shanghai quickly led to expansion across Asia, and to the United States in 1926. While AIG began as a representative of American insurance companies abroad, in the United States it provided insurance risk coverage to insurance companies as a way to disperse liabilities. Reinsurers such as AIG were created to remove some of the risk associated with large disasters. Because of AIG and others, insurance companies could grow faster than ever before.

Insurance companies are educated risk takers. When insurance companies feel they have too much risk, they go to their reinsurance companies, such as AIG, to take out insurance so that if something catastrophic happens, they can still pay their clients. AIG utilizes models to determine how much insurance it can sell to insurers and still pay out. To put it simply, AIG charges insurance companies a premium in order to allow them to spread their risk so that they can sell insurance policies and grow more rapidly.

In 1968, Maurice "Hank" Greenberg, a native New Yorker and experienced insurance executive who had been with AIG for many years, took over as CEO. AIG grew exponentially during his tenure. By the end of the 1980s, the company had become the largest underwriter of commercial and industrial coverage in the United States and the leading international insurance organization. AIG continued to expand throughout the 1990s, led by its return to China as the first foreign insurance organization granted a license by the Chinese authorities to operate a wholly-owned insurance business in Shanghai. AIG later expanded to Guangzhou, Shenzhen, Beijing, and Vietnam. In 2001, AIG established two joint ventures in general insurance and life insurance in India with the Tata Group, the leading Indian industrial conglomerate. New AIG subsidiary companies followed the fall of the Soviet Union into Eastern Europe, with general and life insurance companies formed in Russia, Poland, Hungary, and the Czech Republic, among other emerging markets.

In 2001, AIG purchased American General Corporation, a top U.S. life insurer. This acquisition made AIG a leader in the U.S. life insurance industry and consumer lending. Today, the four principal business areas of AIG are General Insurance, Life Insurance and Retirement Services, Financial Services, and Asset Management. For the individual consumer, business, financial professional, or insurance professional, AIG provides Accident and Health Insurance; Auto Insurance; Life Insurance; Banking and Loans; Retirement Services; Travel Insurance; Additional Services; and Annuities. Before its 2008 collapse, AIG had revenues exceeding $110 billion, with total assets of over $1 trillion, and 116,000 employees around the world.

AIG'S CULTURE

Maurice "Hank" Greenberg was the CEO of AIG for thirty-eight years, and was therefore a key player in shaping the modern face and corporate culture of the company. Many considered Greenberg a genius in the insurance business, and arguably he was one of the most successful and influential executives in the business for over forty years. But critics called him autocratic in his drive to expand the company into an international powerhouse. During his career, Greenberg championed innovative products that insured almost any type of risk, including Internet identity theft and hijacking. At least four U.S. presidents sought Greenberg's advice on international affairs and financial markets. And Greenberg was always known for utilizing his contacts and influence to help advance the company. Over the years, Greenberg aggressively lobbied for laws and rulings favorable to AIG. He was very involved with international politics and helped the U.S. government to secure information and develop backdoor channels for classified dealings. In return, AIG was given the benefit of the doubt when regulation agencies came questioning the company's doings. When billions or trillions of dollars are involved, global corporations have powers equal to or greater than those of governments or regulatory agencies.

In spite of Greenberg's active networking, the early 2000s found AIG under investigation by the Securities and Exchange Commission for its "finite insurance" deals—contracts that covered specific amounts of losses rather than unexpected losses of indeterminate size—and what appeared to be loans (since premiums were structured to match policy payouts and eliminate risk) rather than genuine risk allocation vehicles. A federal inquiry later found information that Greenberg might have been personally involved in creating a bogus reinsurance transaction with General Re to fraudulently boost AIG's reserves. New York Attorney General Spitzer subpoenaed Greenberg, who treated the summons far more lightly than he should have. As rumors swirled, AIG's stock began to plummet, and the AIG board started to become concerned. On March 15, 2005, Greenberg was forced out as CEO. Martin Sullivan succeeded him and held the CEO position for three years, followed by Robert Willumstad for three months. Willumstad was forced to step down in 2008 in the wake of the corporation's meltdown. The current CEO is Edward Liddy, the former CEO of The Allstate Corporation.

WHAT HAPPENED AT AIG TO CAUSE ITS DEMISE?

AIG's troubles were, at the heart, caused by a kind of derivative called credit default swaps (CDSs). As a reinsurer, AIG used CDSs as a kind of insurance policy on complex collateralized debt obligations (CDOs). The company issued the swaps and promised to pay these institutions, AIG's counterparties, if the debt securities defaulted. However, AIG did not have a large enough safety net to weather the subprime mortgage collapse. These insurance contracts became essentially worthless because many people could not pay back their subprime mortgages and AIG did not have the creditworthiness for the big collateral call.

The government took the drastic step to bail out the company, providing the funds to purchase the CDOs that were being held by banks, hedge funds, and other financial institutions, and in the process ended up with 79.9 percent ownership of AIG. The U.S. government is now the senior partner in a special-purpose entity that will receive interest and share the liability in the ownership of these tainted investment instruments. If AIG had been allowed to go bankrupt, the fear was that many banks would have also gone bankrupt throughout the world.

While overall AIG had a diversified insurance business, one unit, AIG Financial Products, was the source of many of the company's woes. Formed more than two decades ago to trade over-the-counter derivatives, its creation was timed perfectly to ride the derivatives market boom. By and large, Financial Products was run like a hedge fund out of London and Wilton, Connecticut. Hedge funds are a special type of fund available to a select range of investors. They seek to utilize a wide variety of investment tools to mitigate, or *hedge,* risk—oftentimes the term refers to funds that use short selling as a means of increasing investment returns. Short selling is betting that the stock price of a company will change during a specified period of time. When the stocks move the expected direction, the investor makes money.

AIG Financial Products specialized in derivatives that generated billions of dollars in profits over the years. Derivatives are financial contracts or instruments whose value is derived from something else such as commodities (corn, wheat, soybeans, etc.), stocks, bonds, and even home mortgages. Gains or losses from derivatives come from betting correctly on the movement of these values. The unit also dealt with the mortgage securities, a sector that turned rancid with the collapse of the housing bubble. Former New York Attorney General Eliot Spitzer, a champion of financial sector reform, claimed that AIG Financial Products was "the black hole of AIG." While AIG can be described as a conservative global conglomerate selling insurance policies to businesses and individuals, the Financial Products unit was staffed by quantitative specialists with doctorate-degreed individuals in finance and math whom, it seems, were very willing to take risks. This unit thought it was above the insurance operations and its employees conducted themselves like investment bankers. The AIG Financial Products unit was founded in 1987 by Howard Sosin. When Sosin joined AIG he was given an unusual deal: a 20 percent stake in the unit and 20 percent of its profits.

In the late 1990s under the leadership of Joseph Cassano, AIG Financial Products ramped up its business of selling credit default swaps, which are the heart of the most recent financial meltdown. Credit default swaps are financial products that transfer the credit exposure (risk) of fixed income products (bonds) between parties. The buyer of a credit swap receives credit protection, whereas the seller of the swap guarantees the credit worthiness of the product. By doing this, the risk of default is transferred from the holder of the fixed income security to the seller of the swap. One credit default swap can be valued at hundreds of millions of dollars. AIG Financial Products expanded into writing swaps to cover debt that was backed by mortgages. The unit sold swaps to large institutional investors. These collateralized debt obligations were backed by mortgages, and the swaps issued by AIG backed some $440 billion worth of obligations. These types of products were known as collateralized debt obligations (CDOs). AIG made millions selling CDOs and was able to post modest margin requirements, which is the amount the company keeps as a deposit to protect against the risk of loan defaults or non-payments. For example, to buy stock on margin, you must have at least 50 percent of the purchase price in your account. AIG was able to make these CDO deals with a very small fraction of actual money on hand. Unfortunately, some of these CDOs were attached to home mortgages. In spite of the risk, the company involved itself in bad mortgage lending by financial institutions that did not have sufficient capital to cover the loans, which in turn had bought this type of insurance from AIG that created an unstable financial environment. The loans and the CDOs were often sold to people who could not repay their debt. CEO Greenberg became concerned about this unit's derivative dealings and asked a group to shadow its trades. Greenberg was uncomfortable with the results and thought the unit was taking too many risks. However, Greenberg left the company in 2005 because of regulators investigating AIG over its accounting practices.

AIG sold credit protection on CDOs by simply writing pieces of paper that stated that AIG would cover the losses in case these obligations went bad. AIG agreed to either take over the obligations or cover the losses on CDOs. While AIG made billions of dollars in profits and managers received millions of dollars in compensation for selling these so-called insurance policies, it turned out to be a high-risk house of cards. The tools, CDOs and CDSs, were used recklessly and failed to assess systemic risk of counterparties not measuring their own exposures and not paying their obligations. The Financial Products unit has been under ongoing investigations around the world, including by the United Kingdom's Serious Fraud Office.

While they have gained notoriety by now, before 2008 derivatives were not widely understood by the public, mass media, regulators, and many of the executives that were providing the oversight for their use. AIG could have taken another approach by buying mortgages or CDOs and then having some other party package them into a credit default swap as insurance, but since AIG was an insurer it simply wrote policies on CDOs, thus increasing revenues with the hope that only a few would default. Of course, AIG guessed wrong and became the epicenter of a financial nightmare that has caused many bank failures and a worldwide financial depression.

AIG LACKED TRANSPARENCY

There is evidence that AIG knew of potential problems in valuing derivative contracts before the 2008–2009 financial meltdown occurred. Outside auditors raised concerns about being excluded from conversations on the evaluation of derivatives. But during this time period, AIG executives Cassano and Sullivan continued to reassure investors and auditors that AIG had accurately identified all areas of exposure to the U.S. residential housing market and stated their confidence in their evaluation methods.

PricewaterhouseCoopers (PwC), AIG's auditor, had a right to know about the models and about market indications that indicated that the value of AIG swaps should be lowered. If prosecutors find evidence that investors and PwC were misled, it could be considered a criminal fraud. The market indicators in question came in the form of demands for collateral by AIG trading partners. At a congressional hearing, Sullivan stated that he believed the evaluations to be accurate, based on the information he possessed at the time. This situation is similar to executives at Enron who claimed that they did not know that Enron utilized derivatives and off-the-books balance sheet partnerships that caused its demise. Many Enron executives ended up being found guilty of crimes. Some are in prison while others are still awaiting their fates and prison time.

AIG PROVIDED INCENTIVES TO TAKE RISKS

What were the factors within the corporate culture of AIG that promoted speculative risk-taking? Part of the problem may have been AIG's incentives. The AIG culture was focused on a reward system that placed little responsibility on executives who made very poor decisions. Although they produced nearly $40 billion in losses in 2008, a number of managers were selected to receive large bonuses. AIG offered cash awards and other perks to thirty-eight executives and a retention program with payments from $92,500 to $4 million for employees earning salaries between $160,000 and $1 million. After receiving more than $152 billion in federal rescue funds, AIG publicly claimed that it would eliminate some of these bonuses for senior executives while all the time planning to hand out cash awards that doubled or tripled the salaries of some. AIG asserted that these types of payments were necessary to keep top employees at AIG, even as control of the company was being handed over to the government. The ethical ramifications of the rewards doled out in the face of excessive risk-taking and possible misconduct have been highly criticized by most stakeholders. The central reason AIG was bailed out at all was that the government was seeking to prevent the failure of some of the world's largest banks, thereby potentially causing a global financial catastrophe. AIG's actions reflect an ethical culture that neglects the most important stakeholders who support a business.

The demise of AIG's Financial Products unit, in part, resulted from excessive risk-taking by academic economists and financial scholars using computer models that failed to take into account real-world market risks. For example, Gary Gorton, a finance professor at the Yale School of Management, was an academic scholar whose work was cited in speeches by Federal Reserve Chairman Ben Bernanke. AIG paid him large consulting fees for developing computer models to gauge risk for more than $400 billion complicated credit default swaps. Remember that these swaps can be for hundreds of millions of dollars each. AIG relied on his models to determine which swap deals were low risk. Unfortunately, Gorton's models did not anticipate how market forces and contract terms could turn swaps into huge financial liabilities. It was not Gorton's failing however, as AIG did not assign him to assess those threats and his models therefore did not consider them. However, the failure to assess the risk of credit default swaps correctly caused the demise of AIG and pushed the federal government to rescue it and the U.S. banking system.

AIG entered a very lucrative but perilous new market without understanding the sheer complexity of the financial products that it was selling. AIG is not alone in placing faith in people like Gorton and exotic computer models to determine trades and risk. However, computers and academic experts cannot determine all of the variables, forces, and weights that cause a high- or low-risk investment to go bad. The true blame lays in business placing too much trust in models with faulty assumptions. Models cannot predict with absolute certainty what humans will do because humans are not always rational. Warren Buffett, chief executive of Berkshire Hathaway and billionaire many times over, said, "all I can say is, beware of geeks. . . bearing formulas."

AIG ultimately owed Wall Street's biggest firms about $100 billion for speculative trades turned bad. This $100 billion debt is particularly challenging because the $150 billion rescue package for AIG does not include provisions for these debts. Questions remain about how the insurer will cover these debts. The company allegedly placed billions of dollars at risk through speculation on the movements of various mortgage pools and the bottom line is there are no actual securities backing these speculative positions on which AIG is losing money. The losses stem from market wagers that were essentially bets on the performance of bundles of derivatives linked to subprime residential mortgages. The government rescue of AIG protected many of its policyholders and counterparties from immediate losses on traditional insurance contracts, but these speculative trades by AIG were not a part of the government risk rescue. AIG's activities indicate managers and traders were focused on financial rewards for assembling high-risk contracts, and the Financial Products division was conducting itself like a gambler in a casino who irrationally expected all bets to pay off. AIG had lost its underlying mission, the importance of strong moral principles, and good compliance programs that respect stakeholders.

The controversies regarding AIG did not end with government ownership. In fact, the problems critics identified regarding the company's culture and reckless spending were put on full display a mere two months after receiving its bailout money. Top AIG executives were spotted holding a lavish conference at a posh Point Hilton Squaw Peak Resort in Phoenix for one hundred fifty financial planners and top AIG executives. The three-day event reportedly cost over $343,000. Representatives of the corporation defend the conference, stating that most of the costs were underwritten by sponsors—however, such an episode mere weeks after receiving its government bailout did not sit well with stakeholders. Many believe that it demonstrates how little remorse AIG has for the decisions leading up to the failure, and how little has changed since receiving government money.

AIG'S CRISIS AND BAILOUT

It was September 16, 2008, when the other shoe dropped and AIG's problems came to a boil. Due to the many issues outlined above, AIG's stock was downgraded by the rating companies, which caused the stock to drop, causing a run on the reinsurer's liquid assets (cash on hand) that revealed its lack of liquidity. Simply put, AIG did not have the capital to repay investors asking for their money back.

The federal government came to the rescue, not out of concern for AIG, but to prevent the string of bank failures that would surely follow an AIG bankruptcy. Over the course of a month, the government doled out $152.5 billion of taxpayer money, creating a line of credit for the company and buying up AIG stock. This was a highly controversial decision, particularly since the government did not do the same thing for the other financial giant Lehman Brothers. On March 2, 2009, the government made the controversial decision to dole out another $30 billion in capital to the failing institution. The decision was made even more contentious when it was revealed that $165 million of the bailout money went to bonuses of employees of the failed Financial Products unit. While the government concluded that it could not get the money back, it did resolve to increase the oversight of new bailout funds. When questioned about the decision to repeatedly bail out AIG, Federal Reserve Chairman Ben Bernanke told U.S. lawmakers that "AIG exploited a huge gap in the regulatory system. . . . There was no oversight of the financial products division. This was a hedge fund, basically, that was attached to a large and stable insurance company." He stated that AIG is the single case out of the entire 2008–2009 financial crisis that made him the angriest. However, Bernanke went on to say that "We had no choice but to try to stabilize the system because of the implications that the failure would have had for the broad economic system.

Although the bailouts were massive, it did not cover all that AIG owed and the company had to sell off numerous assets. Two-thirds of the company needed to be sold in a tough market for sellers, resulting in auctions of dozens of the company's units around the world. Many of these sales have resulted in disappointing prices for AIG. For example, Munich Re, the world's biggest reinsurer, agreed to buy American International Group Inc.'s Hartford unit for $742 million, about a third less than AIG paid for it eight years before. The company also has given more than two thousand employees cash incentives to stop them from quitting, saying that the payments are necessary. "Anybody who wants to start an insurance company or beef up their position, they will come to our organization and pick people off," Edward Liddy, the current CEO, said in the interview. "If that happens, we can't maintain the businesses we want to keep and we won't be able to sell them for the kinds of values that we need."

Greenberg maintains his innocence, and insists that the company's upper management was the root cause of the collapse after he left. "AIG had a unique culture when I was its CEO, particularly in comparison with the way many large public companies operate today," he said. "Neither I nor other members of my senior management team had employment contracts. I received no severance package in connection with my retirement, and I never sold a single share of AIG stock during the more than 35 years that I served as CEO." Greenberg continues to hold substantial stock in the company. At the end of 2008, he and his firm, Starr International, owned more than 268 million shares, or nearly 10 percent.

In a 2008 interview, Greenberg explained what he sees as the real cause of the financial collapse. He blames low interest rates and excessively easy credit for the reckless risk-taking and poor decisions made within the financial industry. He also cites excessive leveraging and mark-to-market accounting practices as contributing to the meltdown. Mark-to-market is assigning a value to a position held in a financial instrument based on the current market price for the instrument. For example, the final value of a financial contract (grain futures) that expires in nine months will not be known until it expires. If it is marked to market, for accounting purposes, it is assigned the value that it would have at the end of each day. Greenberg believes that the above factors all grew out of control to the point where the entire system had nowhere to go but toward failure.

CONCLUSION

The question remains: Was a bailout really necessary? Some say yes, like Greenberg himself. "You have to have a bailout. But I would call it something else rather than a bailout. That implies the wrong thing. It is really also helping Main Street, not just Wall Street, because if the economy doesn't grow, jobs are going to be lost and we're going to go into a depression rather than a recession. . . . The taxpayer is not going to take a hit long term because the money involved will be repaid over a period of time." Others are not so certain. Critics of AIG's and the auto industry bailout, for example, cite lack of accountability in how the funds are used. Many also oppose this level of government intervention in corporations because it seems to be rewarding companies that blatantly ignored the needs and desires of their stakeholders in favor of enriching themselves in the short term. Without a doubt, the failure of AIG was massive, and bailout or not, its effects have rippled across the globe.

QUESTIONS

1. Discuss AIG's corporate culture as to what role it played, if any, in its downfall.
2. Discuss the variables that may have caused AIG to need a bailout by the U.S. government and would it have been better to give, as Greenberg suggested, a bridge loan.
3. Discuss ethical decision making at AIG in relation to risks.
4. Discuss AIG's executives' ethical conduct and how a strengthened ethics program might help the company to strengthen the ethics of its corporate culture.

SOURCES: Jenny Anderson, "A.I.G. Profit Is Reduced by $4 Billion," *New York Times,* June 1, 2005, http://query.nytimes.com/gst/fullpage.html?res=9C01E1D81F39F932A35755C0A9639C8B63 (accessed December 10, 2008); Jenny Anderson, "Greenberg Fires Back At Directors," *New York Times,* August 5, 2005, http://query.nytimes.com/gst/fullpage.html?res=9A02E7DE163EF 936A3575BC0A9639C8B63&sec=&spon=&pagewanted=2 (accessed December 10, 2008); Beverly Behan, "Memo to the Board of AIG," *BusinessWeek,* November 16, 2008, http://www.businessweek.com/managing/content/nov2008/ca20081118_408443.htm (accessed December 22, 2008); Lynnley Browning, "A.I.G.'s House of Cards," *Portfolio,* September 29, 2008, http://www.portfolio.com/news-markets/top-5/2008/09/29/AIGs-Derivatives-Run-Amok? (accessed December 22, 2008); Nanette Byrnes, "The Unraveling of AIG," *BusinessWeek,* September 16, 2008, http://www.businessweek.com/bwdaily/dnflash/content/sep2008/db20080915_552271.htm (accessed December 22, 2008); Jesse Drucker, "AIG's Tax Dispute With U.S. Has Twist of Irony," *Wall Street Journal,* November 14, 2008, C2; *The Economist,* "The Great Untangling," November 8, 2008, 85–86; Kurt Eichenwald and Jenny Anderson, "How a Titan of Insurance Ran Afoul of the Government," *New York Times,* April 4, 2005, http://www.nytimes.com/2005/04/04/business/04aig.html?scp=1&sq=%22how+a+titan+of+insurance %22&st=nyt (accessed January 7, 2009); Mauma Desmond, "AIG. CDOs. CDS. It's a Mess," Forbes.com, November 15, 2008, http://www.forbes.com/markets/2008/11/15/aig-credit-default -markets-equity-cx_md_1110markets24.html (accessed November 19, 2008); David Henry, Matthew Goldstein, and Carol Matlack, "How AIG's Credit Loophole Squeezed Europe's Banks," *BusinessWeek,* October 16, 2008, http://www.businessweek.com/magazine/content/08_43/b4105032835044.htm (accessed December 22, 2008); Carol J. Loomis, "AIG: The Company That Came to Dinner," *Fortune,*

January 19, 2009, 70–78; Carrick Mollenkamp, Serena Ng, Liam Pleven, and Randall Smith, "Behind AIG's Fall, Risk Models Failed to Pass Real-World Test," *Wall Street Journal,* November 3, 2008, A1, A16; Gretchen Morgenson, "A.I.G.: Whiter Shade of Enron," *New York Times,* April 3, 2005, http://www.nytimes.com/2005/04/03/business/yourmoney/03gret.html?_r=1&scp=1&sq= %22whiter%20shade%20of%20enron%22&st=cse (accessed January 7, 2009); Serena Ng and Liam Pleven, "Revised AIG Rescue Is Bank Boon," *Wall Street Journal,* November 12, 2008, C1, C5; Serena Ng, Carrick Mollenkamp, and Michael Siconolfi, "AIG Faces $10 Billion in Losses on Trades," *Wall Street Journal,* December 10, 2008, A1, A2; Timothy L. O'Brian, "Guilty Plea Is Expected in A.I.G.-Related Case," *New York Times,* June 10, 2005, http://query.nytimes.com/gst/fullpage.html?res =9801E3DC1138F933A25755C0A9639C8B63&sec=&spon=&pagewanted=2 (accessed December 10, 2008); Liam Pleven and Amir Efrati, "Documents Show AIG Knew of Problems with Valuations," *Wall Street Journal,* October 11–12, 2008, B1, B2; Justine A. Rosenthal, "Maurice Greenberg on What's Next for Wall Street," *National Interest Online,* October 2, 2008, http://www.nationalinterest.org/ Article.aspx?id=19970 (accessed December 22, 2008); Ron Scherer, "A Top Insurance Company as the New Enron? An Accounting Probe at AIG Worries Wall Street, and Involves Some of America's Richest Men," *Christian Science Monitor,* April 1, 2005, http://www.csmonitor.com/2005/0401/p03s01 -usju.html (accessed January 7, 2009); Hugh Son, "AIG Says More Managers Get Retention Payouts Topping $4 Million," Bloomberg.com, December 9, 2008, http://www.bloomberg.com/apps/ news?pid=newsarchive& sid=aKIvmgvNl6zA (accessed December 10, 2008); Hugh Son, "AIG Plans to Repay U.S. in 2009, Liddy Tells CNBC," Bloomberg.com, December 22, 2008, http://www.bloomberg.com/ apps/ news?pid=20601087&sid=aDXR6Ayuezx4&refer=home (accessed December 22, 2008); Mary Williams Walsh, "Bigger Holes to Fill," *Wall Street Journal,* November 11, 2008, B1, B5, Ken Sweet, "Bernanke Tells Congress He's 'Angry' About AIG," Fox Business, March 03, 2009, http://www .foxbusiness.com/story/markets/economy/bernanke-recovery-hinges-financial-turnaround/ (accessed March 5, 2009); Jonathan Weisman, Sudeep Reddy, and Liam Pleven, "Political Heat Sears AIG," *The Wall Street Journal,* March 17, 2009, http://online.wsj.com/article/SB123721970101743003.html (accessed March 17, 2009).

Starbucks' Mission: Responsibility and Growth

Three partners founded Starbucks in 1971, with the first store opening in Seattle's open-air Pike Place Market. The company is named after the first mate in Herman Melville's *Moby Dick*. In 1982 Howard Schultz joined Starbucks as director of retail operations and marketing. After visiting Milan, Italy, with its fifteen hundred coffee bars, Schultz saw the opportunity to develop a similar retail coffee-bar culture in Seattle. In 1985 the first downtown Seattle coffeehouse was tested, and the first Starbucks café latte was served. Since then Starbucks has been expanding across the United States where it operates eight thousand stores and over thirty-two hundred stores in thirty-seven countries. It opens about five new stores a day and serves over 30 million customers a week. Of its customers, 24 percent visit sixteen times per month. No other fast-food chain can post numbers even close to this. Its goal is to have thirty thousand stores globally, which compares to thirty-one thousand operated by McDonald's.

Starbucks purchases and roasts high-quality whole-bean coffees and sells them, along with fresh-brewed coffees, Italian-style espresso beverages, cold blended beverages, a variety of complementary food items, coffee-related accessories and equipment, a selection of premium teas, and a line of compact discs. Starbucks also sells coffee and tea products and licenses its trademark through other channels; through certain of its equity investors, Starbucks produces and sells bottled Frappuccino® coffee drinks and Starbucks DoubleShot® espresso drink and a line of superpremium ice creams.

The company's objective is to establish Starbucks as the most recognized and respected brand in the world. To achieve this goal, Starbucks plans to continue rapid expansion of its retail operations, to grow its specialty operations, and to selectively pursue other opportunities to leverage the Starbucks brand through the introduction of new products and the development of new channels of distribution. Starbucks

---

This case was prepared by Ben Siltman, University of Wyoming, and Melanie Drever, University of Wyoming, under the direction of Linda Ferrell for classroom discussion rather than to illustrate either effective or ineffective handling of an administrative, ethical, or legal decision by management. All sources used for this case were obtained through publicly available material and the Starbucks website.

manages successful growth through careful consideration of stakeholder interests and its corporate social responsibility.

STARBUCKS CULTURE

In 1990 Starbucks' senior executive team created a mission statement that laid out the guiding principles behind the company. They hoped that the principles included in the mission statement would help their partners (employees) determine the appropriateness of later decisions and actions. As Orin Smith explained, "Those guidelines are part of our culture and we try to live by them every day." After drafting the mission statement, the executive team asked all Starbucks partners to review and comment on the document. Based on their feedback, the final statement put "people first and profits last." In fact, the number-one guiding principle in Starbucks' mission statement was to "provide a great work environment and treat each other with respect and dignity."

Starbucks does three things to keep the mission and guiding principles alive. First, it distributes a copy of the mission statement and comment cards for feedback during orientation to all new partners. Second, when presentations are made, Starbucks continually relates decisions back to the guiding principle(s) that they support. Third, the company formed a "Mission Review" system so that any partner could comment on a decision or action relative to its consistency with one of the six principles. The partner with the most knowledge pertaining to the comment had to respond directly within two weeks, or if it was anonymous, the response would appear in the monthly report. This continual emphasis on the guiding principles and the underlying values has become the cornerstone of Starbucks.

The efforts have fostered a strong organizational culture that employs a predominately young educated workforce who are proud to work for Starbucks. According to Smith, "It's extremely valuable to have people proud to work for [the company] and we make decisions that are consistent with what our partners expect of us."

In 2006 Starbucks ranked seventeenth on the *Business Ethics* "100 Best Corporate Citizens" list (2005: forty-fifth; 2004: forty-fifth; 2003: twenty-first; 2002: twenty-first) and on the *Fortune* "100 Best Companies to Work For" list for eight years (2006: twenty-ninth). However, being a great employer comes at a high cost. In 2005 Starbucks spent more on health insurance for its employees than on raw materials to brew its coffee. Starbucks provides health-care coverage to employees who work at least twenty hours a week and has faced double-digit increases in insurance costs each of the last four years. In 2005 Starbucks spent $200 million on health care for its eighty thousand U.S. employees. But the benefits policy is the key reason for low employee turnover and high productivity.

QUESTIONING STARBUCKS' MISSION AND IMPACT

Starbucks has flourished in thirty-eight countries, but this success has also attracted harsh criticism on issues such as fair-trade coffee, bovine growth hormone (BGH) milk, Schultz's alleged financial links to the Israeli government, and the accusations that

Starbucks' growth is forcing locally run coffee shops out of business. A survey by Global Marketing Institute found that even Starbucks customers view the company as "arrogant, intrusive, and self-centered." As a result Starbucks has invested significantly in corporate social responsibility (CSR) activities. They offer grants to charities and produce an annual CSR report. Starbucks was one of the first major coffeehouse brands to introduce "ethical" coffee in 2002 when it began offering a "fair-trade coffee of the week" and shortly after permanently added it to the main menu. Although a fine gesture, many competitors followed suit and switched to 100 percent fair-trade coffee, leaving Starbucks as an ethical trailer instead of a pioneer.

Criticism extends far beyond fair-trade policies in that accusations have centered on Starbucks' clustering strategy that saturates areas with branches, forcing many local coffee shops out of business. *Ethical Consumer* magazine researcher Ruth Rosselson says, "Starbucks has a number of useful policies in how it sources coffee, and its dialogue with Oxfam is progress. However, we would recommend consumers choose non-chain shops that offer fair-trade coffee. Starbucks operates like the supermarkets: it puts local companies out of business and with this policy can never be 100 percent ethical." Corporate Watch researcher Chris Grimshaw feels that Starbucks' CSR program is being used as a "smokescreen to create the illusion of ethics," adding that the company is committed solely to making money for shareholders.

CORPORATE SOCIAL MISSION

Just as treating partners well is one of the pillars of Starbucks, so is contributing to the communities it serves and to the environment. As a result of their pillars, Starbucks supports causes in both the communities where stores are located and the countries where Starbucks coffee is grown.

In 1991 Starbucks began contributing to CARE, a worldwide relief and development foundation, as a way to give back to coffee-origin countries. By 1995 Starbucks was CARE's largest corporate donor, pledging more than $100,000 a year and specifying that its support go to coffee-producing countries. The company's donations helped with such projects as clean-water systems, health and sanitation training, and literacy. In that year, Starbucks contributed more than $1.8 million to CARE.

In 1998 Starbucks partnered with Conservation International, a nonprofit organization that helps promote biodiversity in coffee-growing regions and supports producers of shade-grown coffee. Conservation International coffee came from cooperatives in Chiapas, Mexico, and was introduced as a limited edition in 1999. The cooperatives' land bordered the El Triunfo Biosphere Reserve, an area designated by Conservation International as one of twenty-five "hot spots" that is home to over half of the world's known plants and animals. Since 1999 Starbucks has funded seasonal promotions of this coffee every year, with the hope of adding it to its lineup of year-round offerings. The results of the partnership have proven positive for both the environment and Mexican farmers. Shade acreage has increased by 220 percent while farmers receive a price premium of 65 percent above market price and have increased their exports by 50 percent. Finally, through this partnership, Starbucks made loan guarantees that helped provide over $750,000 to farmers. This financial support enabled farmers to nearly double their income.

Although Starbucks has supported responsible business practices virtually since its inception, as the company has grown, so has the importance of defending its image. At the end of 1999, Starbucks created a CSR department, and Dave Olsen was named the department's first senior vice president. According to Sue Mecklenburg, "Dave really is the heart and soul of the company and is acknowledged by others as a leader. By having Dave as the first Corporate Responsibility SVP, the department had instant credibility within the company," Between 1994 and 2001, Starbucks' CSR department had grown from only one person to fourteen. Starbucks is concerned about the environment and its employees, suppliers, customers, and communities.

The Environment

In 1992 Starbucks developed an environmental mission statement to articulate more clearly how the company interacted with the environment, eventually creating an Environmental Starbucks Coffee Company Affairs team tasked with developing environmentally responsible policies and minimizing the company's "footprint." Additionally, Starbucks was active in using environmental purchasing guidelines, reducing waste through recycling and energy conservation, and continually educating partners through the company's "Green Team" initiatives.

Employees

Schultz proved that businesses can still make money while maintaining fair labor practices and a social conscience. The son of a blue-collar worker, Schultz grew up in Brooklyn, New York, and lost faith in the American dream after his father suffered a tragic injury that left him unemployed with no benefits. "I watched what would happen to the plight of working class families when society and companies turned their back on the worker," Schultz said. "I wanted to build the kind of company my father never got to work for." The result of this is all Starbucks employees, including part-time workers, are entitled to receive health benefits (including health, medical, dental, and vision benefits) and individuals who work more than twenty hours a week can receive stock options, known as Bean Stock. Schultz's key to maintaining a strong business is by "creating an environment where everyone believes they're part of something larger than themselves but believes they also have a voice." Understanding how vital employees are, Schultz is first to admit that his company focuses on personal interactions. "We are not in the coffee business serving people, but in the people business serving coffee."

Starbucks embraces diversity as an essential component in the way they do business. The company has 91,056 employees with 11,444 outside the United States. Of these, 28 percent are minorities, and 64 percent are women. This has proved successful: Starbucks has a partner turnover rate of 60 percent compared to the restaurant industry average of 200 percent. Furthermore, 82 percent of the partners rated being "very satisfied" and 15 percent as "satisfied" with their jobs when asked by outside audit agencies. Most satisfaction rates this high can only be found in small companies and is practically unheard of for large, publicly traded corporations.

Suppliers

While striving to meet its goal to establish Starbucks as the most recognized and re-spected brand of coffee in the world, it maintains an excellent reputation for social re-sponsibility and business ethics throughout the coffee community. It builds relationships with the farmers who supply the coffee while working with governments in the vari-ous countries in which it operates. Starbucks also practices conservation by using Star-bucks Coffee and Farmer Equity Practices, a set of socially responsible coffee-buying guidelines, and by offering preferential buying status for participants who score the highest on verified reports. Starbucks pays coffee farmers premium prices that help support their families instead of other illegal crops. The company also invests in social development programs that help build schools, health clinics, and other projects that benefit coffee-growing communities.

Starbucks collaborates with farmers through the Farmer Support Center, located in Costa Rica, to provide technical support and training that promotes high-quality coffee for the future. They are also involved in purchasing conservation and certified coffees—including Fair Trade Certified, shade-grown, and certified organic coffee—to promote responsible environmental and economic efforts.

Social responsibility, fair trade, and support for the environment are a part of the total product for consumers that are concerned about these social issues.

Customers

Starbucks continually works to grow their business by diversifying. The Hear Music platform includes media bars in stores where customers can download music; as of 2006, forty-one music media bars were in service. Starbucks also has more than three hundred drive-through stores. They also provide wireless Internet access with T1 speeds in more than forty-three hundred U.S. and European stores. At Starbucks.com, one can find the closest "Wireless Hotspot Available" by simply using a store locator.

Communities

Starbucks firmly believes that opening a store adds immediate value to the community because the store becomes a gathering spot, drawing people together. Additionally, store managers are granted discretion to donate to local causes and provide coffee for local fundraisers. One Seattle store donated more than $500,000 to Zion Preparatory Academy, an African American school for inner-city youth. In 1998 Starbucks and Earvin "Magic" Johnson's company, Johnson Development Corporation, formed a joint partnership and created Urban Coffee Opportunities. Subsequently, twenty-eight stores opened in urban communities, providing new employment and revitalization to several U.S. cities.

Schultz personally believes that literacy has the power to change lives and foster hope for young children who live in underserved neighborhoods. Accordingly, Schultz used the advance and ongoing royalties from his book, *Pour Your Heart Into It,* to create the Starbucks Foundation that provides "opportunity grants" to nonprofit literacy groups, sponsors young writers' programs, and partners with Jumpstart, an organization helping Headstart children.

SUCCESS AND CHALLENGE

Starbucks is trying to change pop culture: what we eat and drink, when we work and play, and how we spend our time and money. Some people call it the "Starbuckization" of society. Starbucks is not only the kingpin of expensive coffee but also among the top trendsetters of our time. Starbucks thinks that "if you love the taste of our coffee, you will love our taste in pop culture."

There are some negative aspects of this new pop culture. Starbucks is changing what we eat (but it is not always healthy). Portions are too big, and the drinks are full of calories and fat. It is possible that healthier food is in their future, but success has made them a target for people who are concerned about a healthy lifestyle.

On the positive side, Starbucks has added more than a teaspoon of social responsibility into its coffee, and there is a cost for social responsibility. Employee benefits and socially responsible actions come with a cost. Starbucks has made the $4 coffee drink acceptable and opened the door for other competitors to charge similar prices.

Psychologist Joyce Brothers says Starbucks has a positive effect in that "there is a sense of security when you go there." On the other hand, Starbucks is changing urban streetscapes; it is impossible in many cities to go more than a few blocks without seeing the familiar Starbucks logo. Even advertisements for apartments for rent point out that they are near a Starbucks. All of this is helping Starbucks become a cultural curator.

Starbucks has achieved amazing growth, creating financial success for shareholders while positioning itself as socially responsible. Its reputation has been built on product quality, stakeholder concerns, and a balanced approach to its business activities. Starbucks receives criticism for its ability to beat the competition, putting other coffee shops out of business, and creating a uniform retail culture in many cities, but it excels in its relationship with its employees and is a role model for the fast-food industry in employee benefits. In addition, in an age of shifts in supply chain power, Starbucks is as concerned about their suppliers and meeting their needs as any other primary stakeholder. One of the areas where the company faces challenges is catching up with some of its competition in providing fair-trade coffee. The future looks bright for Starbucks, but the company must continue to focus on a balanced stakeholder orientation that has been so key to its success.

QUESTIONS

1. Why do you think Starbucks has been so concerned with social responsibility in its overall corporate strategy?
2. Is Starbucks unique in being able to provide a high level of benefits to its employees?

3. Do you think that Starbucks has grown rapidly because of its ethical and socially responsible activities or because it provides products and an environment that customers want?

SOURCES: "Brewing Up a Strong Starbucks Alternative," MSNBC, February 5, 2006, http://www.msnbc .msn.com/id/4163701/; "Coca-Cola May Take on Starbucks," MSNBC, January 30, 2006, http://www .msnbc.msn.com/id/11101825/; Anne Fifield, "Starbucks and Global Exchange," *Tuck Today,* Summer 2003, online, via http://mba.tuck.dartmouth.edu/pdf/2002-1-0023.pdf (accessed May 18, 2006); "'*Fortune*' Magazine's 100 Best Companies to Work For List 2006," Money/CNN, http://money.cnn .com/magazines/fortune/bestcompanies/full_list/ (accessed July 24, 2006); "Health Care Takes Its Toll on Starbucks," MSNBC, September 14, 2005, http://www.msnbc.msn.com/id/9344634; Adam Horowitz, David Jacobson, Mark Lasswell, and Owen Thomas, "101 Dumbest Moments in Business," *Business 2.0,* February 1, 2006, via http://money.cnn.com/magazines/business2/101dumbest/full_list/ page6.html; Bruce Horovitz, "Starbucks Aims Beyond Lattes to Extend Brand to Films, Music and Books," *USA Today,* May 19, 2006, A1, A2; "In Rare Flop, Starbucks Scraps Chocolate Drink," MSNBC, February 10, 2006, http://www.msnbc.msn.com/id/11274445/; "100 Best Corporate Citizens 2006," *Business Ethics* online, Spring 2006, http://www.business-ethics.com/media/Chart%20of %20100%20Best %20Corp%20Citizens%20for%202006.pdf (accessed July 24, 2006); Starbucks, http://www.starbucks.com/ retail/thewayiseeit_default.asp (accessed July 24, 2006); Starbucks, http://www.starbuckseverywhere.net/ (accessed July 24, 2006); "Starbucks Annual Report 10-K," Starbucks, www.starbucks.com (July 24, 2006); "Starbucks Company Fact Sheet," Starbucks, http://www.starbucks.com/aboutus/ Company_Fact_Sheet_Feb06.pdf (accessed July 24, 2006); "Starbucks: Selling the American Bean," *BusinessWeek* online, December 1, 2005, http://www.businessweek.com/print/innovate/content/ dec2005/id20051201_506349.htm (accessed July 24, 2006); Mariam Subjally, "Starbucks Creator Recounts Company's Rise, Emphasizes Importance of Ethical Approach," Emory Wheel, http://www .emorywheel.com (accessed February 8, 2005).

Home Depot Implements Stakeholder Orientation

When Bernie Marcus and Arthur Blank opened the first Home Depot store in Atlanta in 1979, they forever changed the hardware and home-improvement retailing industry. Marcus and Blank envisioned huge warehouse-style stores stocked with an extensive selection of products offered at the lowest prices. Today, do-it-yourselfers and building contractors can browse from among 40,000 different products for the home and yard, from kitchen and bathroom fixtures to carpeting, lumber, paint, tools, and plants and landscaping items. If there is a product not provided in one of the stores, Home Depot offers 250,000 other products that can be special ordered. Some Home Depot stores are open twenty-four hours a day, but customers can also order products online and pick them up from their local Home Depot stores or have them delivered. The company also offers free home-improvement clinics to teach customers how to tackle everyday projects like tiling a bathroom. For those customers who prefer not to "do it yourself," most stores offer installation services. Trained employees, recognizable by their orange aprons, are on hand to help customers find the right item or demonstrate the proper use of a particular tool.

Today, Home Depot employs 345,000 people and operates approximately 2042 Home Depot stores, EXPO Design Centers, and Villager's Hardware stores in the United States, Canada, and Mexico. It also operates four wholly owned subsidiaries: Apex Supply Company, Georgia Lighting, Maintenance Warehouse, and National Blinds and Wallpaper Company sales are over $81 billion annually, making it the largest home-improvement retailer in the United States. Home Depot continues to do things on a grand scale, including putting its corporate muscle behind a tightly focused social responsibility agenda. Every week 22 million customers visit Home Depot, and that means some conflict associated with providing services in a retail environment will occur.

We appreciate the work of Gwyneth Walters, who helped draft the previous edition of this case, and Melanie Drever, who assisted in this edition. This case was prepared for classroom discussion rather than to illustrate either effective or ineffective handling of an administrative, ethical, or legal decision by management. All sources used for this case were obtained through publicly available material and the Home Depot website.

MANAGING CUSTOMER RELATIONSHIPS

In 2006 John Costello was the chief marketing officer or, as he states, chief customer officer. Costello consolidated marketing and merchandising functions to help consumers achieve their goals in home improvement projects more effectively and efficiently.

According to Costello, "Above all else, a brand is a promise. It says here's what you can expect if you do business with us. Our mission is to empower our customers to achieve the home or condo of their dreams." When he arrived in 2002, Home Depot's reputation was faltering. His plan called for overhauling the Home Depot website as well as integrating mass marketing and direct marketing with the in-store experience. It was all integrated with the new Home Depot mantra: "You can do it. We can help." Teams of people from merchandising, marketing, visual merchandising, and operations attempted to provide the very best shopping experience at Home Depot. The philosophy was simple; Home Depot believed that customers should be able to read why one ceiling fan is better than another, while associates (employees) should be able to offer installation and design advice.

Unfortunately, Home Depot has to deal with negative publicity associated with customer-satisfaction measures provided by outside sources. The University of Michigan's annual American Customer Satisfaction Index in 2006 showed Home Depot slipping to last among major U.S. retailers. With a score of 67, down from 73 in 2004, Home Depot scored 11 points behind Lowe's and 3 points lower than Kmart. "This is not competitive and too low to be sustainable. It's very serious," wrote Claes Fornell, professor of business at the University of Michigan. Fornell believes that the drop in satisfaction is one reason why Home Depot's stock was stagnant.

On the other hand, CEO Robert Nardelli said that the survey was a "sham." Nardelli points out that Fornell created his own ethical concerns when he shorted (purchased options that would profit from Home Depot's stock price decreasing) his personal portfolio before the survey came out in 2003. Fornell says the trades were part of his research into a correlation between companies' customer-satisfaction scores and stock price performance, but the University of Michigan banned the practice indicating there were concerns about the practice.

Some former managers at Home Depot blame service issues on a culture that focused on military principles for execution. Some employees felt paranoid about being terminated unless they followed directions in a required manner. But Harris Interactive's 2005 Reputation Quotient survey ranked Home Depot number twelve among major companies and said that customers appreciated Home Depot's quality services. In 2006 Home Depot ranked thirteenth in *Fortune*'s "America's Most Admired Companies."

A good example of a socially responsible activity to connect with customers is Home Depot's program, called the Kids Workshop, to teach children the skills related to home improvements. The workshops are free, with how-to-clinics designed for ages 5 to 12 years old. Children, accompanied by an adult, use their skills to create objects that can be used in and around their homes or communities. Useful projects have included the creation of toolboxes, fire trucks, and mail organizers, as well as more educational projects such as window birdhouses and Declaration of Independence frame kits. Since 1997 more than 12 million projects have been built at Kids Workshops with more than 650,000 children building their first toolbox at Home Depot. Home Depot also provides workshops specially designed for women or people who have recently bought a new home. These workshops are free of charge, and anyone can attend.

ENVIRONMENTAL INITIATIVES

Cofounders Marcus and Blank nurtured a corporate culture that emphasizes social responsibility, especially with regard to the company's impact on the environment. Home Depot began its environmental program in 1990 on the twentieth anniversary of Earth Day by adopting a set of environmental principles (Table C17–1). These principles have since been adopted by the National Retail Hardware Association and Home Center Institute, that represent more than forty-six thousand retail hardware stores and home centers.

Guided by these environmental principles, Home Depot has initiated a number of programs to minimize the firm's—and its customers'—impact on the environment. In 1991 the retailer began using recycled content materials for store and office supplies, advertising, signs, and shopping bags. It also established a process for evaluating the environmental claims made by suppliers. The following year, the firm launched a program to recycle wallboard-shipping packaging, which became the industry's first reverse-distribution program. It also opened the first drive-through recycling center,

---

TABLE C17–1   Home Depot's Environmental Principles

Home Depot acknowledges the importance of conservation. The following principles are Home Depot's response:

♦ We are committed to improving the environment by selling products that are manufactured, packaged and labeled in a responsible manner, that take the environment into consideration and that provide greater value to our customers.

♦ We will support efforts to provide accurate, informative product labeling of environmental marketing claims.

♦ We will strive to eliminate unnecessary packaging.

♦ We will recycle and encourage the use of materials and products with recycled content.

♦ We will conserve natural resources by using energy and water wisely and seek further opportunities to improve the resource efficiency of our stores.

♦ We will comply with environmental laws and will maintain programs and procedures to ensure compliance.

♦ We are committed to minimizing the environmental health and safety risk for our associates and our customers.

♦ We will train our employees to enhance understanding of environmental issues and policies and to promote excellence in job performance and all environmental matters.

♦ We will encourage our customers to become environmentally conscious shoppers.

SOURCE: "The Home Depot Environmental Principles," Home Depot, www.homedepot.com/HDUS/EN_US/corporate/ corp_respon/environ_principles.shtml (accessed May 16, 2006). Reprinted by permission from the Home Depot Headquarters, Homer TLC.

in Duluth, Georgia. Home Depot became the first home-improvement retailer to offer wood products from tropical and temperate forests certified as well managed by the Scientific Certification System's Forest Conservation Program. The company also began to replace wooden shipping pallets with reusable slip sheets to minimize waste and energy use and to reduce pressure on hardwood resources used to make wood pallets.

In 1999 Home Depot announced that it would endorse independent, third-party forest certification and wood from certified forests. The company joined the Certified Forests Products Council, a nonprofit organization that promotes responsible forest product–buying practices and the sale of wood from Certified Well-Managed Forests. But environmentalists believed that the company was only being politically correct and had no real intent, so they picketed company stores in protest of Home Depot's practice of selling wood products from old-growth forests. Led by the Rainforest Action Network, environmentalists have picketed Home Depot and other home center stores for years to stop the destruction of the world's old-growth forests. On our planet, only 20 percent of the old-growth forests survive. Later that year, during Home Depot's twentieth anniversary celebration, Arthur Blank announced,

> Our pledge to our customers, associates, and stockholders is that Home Depot will stop selling wood products from environmentally sensitive areas. . . . Home Depot embraces its responsibility as a global leader to help protect endangered forests. In 2002, Home Depot eliminated . . . wood from endangered areas—including lauan, redwood, and cedar products—and gave preference to "certified" wood.

To be certified by the Forest Stewardship Council, a supplier's wood products must be tracked from the forest, through manufacturing and distribution, to the customer, and harvesting, manufacturing, and distribution practices must ensure a balance of social, economic, and environmental factors. Blank also challenged competitors to follow Home Depot's lead, and within two years, Lowe's (the number-two home-improvement retailer), Wickes (a lumber company), and Andersen Corporation (a window manufacturer) had met that challenge. By 2003 Home Depot reported that it had reduced its purchases of Indonesian lauan, a tropical rain-forest hardwood used in door components, by 70 percent, and continues to increase its purchases of certified sustainable wood products.

Home Depot has also donated $25 million in 2005 to nonprofit groups like Keep America Beautiful, the Tampa Audubon Society, the World Wildlife Fund Canada, and the Nature Conservancy. In 2002 the company founded the Home Depot Foundation, which provides resources to assist nonprofit organizations throughout the United States and Canada. The foundation awards grants to eligible nonprofits three times per year and partners with successful, innovative nonprofits across the country that are working to increase awareness and successfully demonstrate the connection between housing, the urban forest, and the overall health and economic success of their communities. The company has established a carpooling program for more than three thousand employees in the Atlanta area and remains the only North American home-improvement retailer with a full-time staff dedicated to environmental issues. These efforts have yielded many rewards such as improved relations with environmental stakeholders. Home Depot's environmental programs earned the company an A on the

Council on Economic Priorities Corporate Report Card, a Vision of America Award from Keep America Beautiful, and, along with Scientific Certification Systems and Collin Pine, a President's Council for Sustainable Development Award. The company was also voted *Fortune* magazine's "America's Most Admired Specialty Retailer" in 2005 and 2006. It was also recognized by the U.S. Environmental Protection Agency with its Energy Star Retail Commitment Award.

CORPORATE PHILANTHROPY

In addition to its environmental initiatives, Home Depot focuses corporate social responsibility efforts on disaster relief, affordable housing, and at-risk youth. In 2005 the company supported thousands of nonprofit organizations with nearly $40.6 million in material and financial contributions. The company also posts a Social Responsibility Report on its website, detailing its annual charitable contributions and the community programs in which it has become involved over the years.

Home Depot works with more than 350 affiliates of Habitat for Humanity, a nonprofit organization that constructs and repairs homes for qualified low-income families. In 2005 it helped build 21 Habitat for Humanity homes with over 160 homes built since its partnership began. The company also works with Christmas in April, a nonprofit organization that rehabilitates housing for the elderly and disabled. Home Depot has renovated more than 20,000 homes for the elderly and disabled in more than 230 communities as part of Rebuilding Together with Christmas in April. Through such programs, thousands of Home Depot associates volunteer, using products supplied by the company, to help build or refurbish affordable housing for their communities, thereby reinforcing their own skills and familiarity with the company's products. Home Depot also provides support to dozens of local housing groups around the country, as well as specific community events, like Hands on San Francisco Day.

Home Depot also supports YouthBuildUSA, a nonprofit organization that provides training and skill development for young people. YouthBuildUSA gives students the opportunity to help rehabilitate housing for homeless and low-income families. Home Depot contributes to many at-risk youth programs, including Big Brothers/Big Sisters, KaBOOM!, and the National Center for Missing and Exploited Children. Home Depot believes that every child should have a safe and fun place to play. In 2005 Home Depot partnered with KaBOOM! on 248 projects in the United States, Canada, and Mexico and also pledged $25 million to build one thousand playgrounds in one thousand days. It has been a partner with KaBOOM! for over ten years and has helped build and refurbish more than four hundred playgrounds.

Home Depot has also addressed the growing need for relief from disasters such as hurricanes, tornadoes, and earthquakes. When Hurricane Floyd devastated parts of North Carolina, the company donated nearly $100,000 in cleanup and rebuilding supplies to relief agencies, sent more than fifty thousand gallons of water to storm victims, extended credit to more than fifty communities, and sponsored clinics on how to repair damage resulting from the storm. After the 911 terrorist attacks, the company set up three command centers with more than two hundred associates to help coordinate relief supplies such as dust masks, gloves, batteries, and tools to victims and rescue workers. When a deadly tornado struck Oklahoma City, Home Depot helped by rebuilding roofs, planting trees, and clearing roads. After Hurricanes Katrina, Rita, and Wilma, Home Depot, the Home Depot Foundation, their suppliers, and The Homer Fund contributed $9.3 million in cash and materials to support recovery. Their rebuilding Hope & Homes program will provide more than $1.25 million to rebuild lives and communities on the U.S. Gulf Coast. Home Depot also donated $500,000 to support the American Red Cross's tsunami relief efforts in Southeast Asia. They also hosted more than twenty hurricane-preparation events in eight states, educating the public on necessary steps and precautions. The National Hurricane Conference awarded them the 2004 award for hurricane-awareness efforts. The company has contributed emergency relief funds, supplies, and labor to American Red Cross relief efforts. Home Depot also partners with the Weather Channel in Project SafeSide, a national severe weather public awareness program.

EMPLOYEE RELATIONS

Home Depot encourages employees to become involved in their communities through volunteer and civic activities. In 2005 employees volunteered 795,558 hours to community causes. The Home Depot devoted a week to community service in 2004 with Associates throughout the United States, Canada, Mexico, and China donating more than 260,000 volunteer-hours and an additional 17,000 family members helping. These hours led to the completion of more than sixteen hundred projects in a week. In 2005 Home Depot took part in the Corporate Month of Service, which with the nonprofit Hands On Network allowed more than 40,000 volunteers from the Home Depot to help their own communities logging more than 320,000 hours on thirteen hundred neighborhood projects.

Home Depot also strives to apply social responsibility to its employment practices, with the goal of assembling a diverse work force; however, the company settled a class-action lawsuit brought by female employees who claimed they were paid less than male employees, awarded fewer pay raises, and promoted less often. The $87.5 million settlement represented one of the largest settlements of a gender discrimination lawsuit in U.S. history at the time. In announcing the settlement, the company emphasized that it was not admitting to wrongdoing and defended its record, saying it "provides opportunities for all of its associates to develop successful professional careers and is proud of its strong track record of having successful women involved in all areas of the company."

The settlement required Home Depot to establish a formal system to ensure that employees can notify managers of their interest in advancing to a management or sales position. The company's Job Preference Program (JPP), an automated hiring and promotion computer program, opens all jobs and applicants to the company-wide network, eliminates unqualified applications, and helps managers to learn employee aspirations and skills in a more effective manner. The JPP brought changes for many women and minority managers working at Home Depot. Despite these efforts, the company faced a new sexual discrimination lawsuit brought by the U.S. Equal Employment Opportunity Commission in 2002 on behalf of a woman who claimed that she had been rejected for several positions at a Los Angeles–area store in favor of less-qualified men. Denying the accusations, a spokesperson for Home Depot declared, "The company has a zero tolerance for discrimination of any kind." The company is still in litigation.

A STRATEGIC COMMITMENT
TO SOCIAL RESPONSIBILITY

Knowing that stakeholders, especially customers, feel good about a company that actively commits resources to environmental and social issues, company executives believe that social responsibility can and should be a strategic component of Home Depot's business operations. The company remains committed to its focused strategy of philanthropy and volunteerism. This commitment extends throughout the company, fueled by top-level support from the cofounders and reinforced by a corporate culture that places great value on playing a responsible role within the communities it serves.

QUESTIONS

1. Rank the relative power of Home Depot's various stakeholders. Defend why you have ranked the first three as most important.
2. Evaluate Home Depot's philanthropic activities as a link to its overall corporate strategy.
3. How do you think Home Depot has handled ethical issues such as gender discrimination and other human resource issues over the last ten years?

SOURCES: *1999 Annual Report,* Home Depot, 2000 http://www.buck.com/10k?tenkyear=99&idx= h&co=HD&nam=DEMO&pw=DEMO (accessed July 25, 2006); *2005 Annual Report,* Home Depot 2005, http://ir.homedepot.com/reports.cfm (accessed July 25, 2006); Jim Carlton, "How Home Depot and Activists Joined to Cut Logging Abuse," *Wall Street Journal,* September 26, 2000, A1ff.; John Caulfield, "Social Responsibility: Retailer's Community Affairs Agenda Includes Disaster Relief, Housing, Youth and the Environment," *National Home Center News,* December 17, 2001, via www.findarticles.com; Cora Daniels, "To Hire a Lumber Expert, Click Here," *Fortune,* April 3, 2000, 267–270; John Galvin, "Chief Customer Officer," *Point,* April 2005, 21–25; Kirstin Downey Grimsley, "Home Depot Settles Gender Bias Lawsuit," *Washington Post,* September 20, 1997, D1; Brian Grow, "Renovating Home Depot," *BusinessWeek* online, March 6, 2006, http://www.businessweek.com/ magazine/content/06_10/b3974001.htm (accessed July 25, 2006); "Hands on San Francisco Announces Fifth Annual Citywide Day of Volunteerism on May Tenth," *Business Wire,* April 30, 2003, www.businesswire.com; "Home Depot Faces Federal Sex Discrimination Suit," *USA Today* online, September 6, 2002, www.usatoday.com/money/industries/retail/2002–09–06-home-depot-sued_x.htm; "Home Depot Lambasted for Attempt to Go Green," Environmental News Network, March 15, 1999, www.enn.com/; "The Home Depot Launches Environmental Wood Purchasing Policy," Rainforest Action Network, August 26, 1999, www.ran.org/ran_campaigns/old_growth/ news/hd_pr.html; "Home Depot Retools Timber Policy," *Memphis Business Journal* online, January 2, 2003, www.bizjournals.com/memphis/stories/2002/12/30/daily12.html; Home Depot website, www.homedepot.com (accessed May 5, 2003); Susan Jackson and Tim Smart, "Mom and Pop Fight Back," *BusinessWeek,* April 14, 1997, 46; Janice Revell, "Can Home Depot Get Its Groove Back?" *Fortune* online, February 3, 2003, www.fortune.com/fortune/investing/articles/0,15114,409691,00.html.

New Belgium Brewing: Ethical and Environmental Responsibility

Most of the companies frequently cited as examples of ethical and socially responsible firms are large corporations, but it is the social responsibility initiatives of small businesses that often have the greatest impact on local communities and neighborhoods. These businesses create jobs and provide goods and services for customers in smaller markets that larger corporations often are not interested in serving. Moreover, they also contribute money, resources, and volunteer time to local causes. Their owners often serve as community and neighborhood leaders, and many choose to apply their skills and some of the fruits of their success to tackling local problems and issues that benefit everyone in the community. Managers and employees become role models for ethical and socially responsible actions. One such small business is the New Belgium Brewing Company, Inc., based in Fort Collins, Colorado.

HISTORY OF THE NEW BELGIUM BREWING COMPANY

The idea for the New Belgium Brewing Company began with a bicycling trip through Belgium. Belgium is arguably the home of some of the world's finest ales, some of which have been brewed for centuries in that country's monasteries. As Jeff Lebesch, an American electrical engineer, cruised around that country on his fat-tired mountain bike, he wondered if he could produce such high-quality beers back home in Colorado. After acquiring the special strain of yeast used to brew Belgian-style ales, Lebesch returned home and began to experiment in his Colorado basement. When his beers earned thumbs up from friends, Lebesch decided to market them.

We appreciate the work of Nikole Haiar, who helped draft the previous edition of this case, and Melanie Drever, who assisted in this edition. This case was prepared for classroom discussion rather than to illustrate either effective or ineffective handling of an administrative, ethical, or legal decision by management. All sources used for this case were obtained through publicly available material and the New Belgium Brewing website.

The New Belgium Brewing Company (NBB) opened for business in 1991 as a tiny basement operation in Lebesch's home in Fort Collins. Lebesch's wife, Kim Jordan, became the firm's marketing director. They named their first brew Fat Tire Amber Ale in honor of Lebesch's bike ride through Belgium. New Belgium beers quickly developed a small but devoted customer base, first in Fort Collins and then throughout Colorado. The brewery soon outgrew the couple's basement and moved into an old railroad depot before settling into its present custom-built facility in 1995. The brewery includes an automated brewhouse, two quality-assurance labs, and numerous technological innovations for which NBB has become nationally recognized as a "paradigm of environmental efficiencies."

The craft brewing market is the only major segment of the beer market that is growing. Figure C18–1 shows craft brewing's share of the U.S. market. Many of the craft brewers engage in reserve bottling and special seasonal brands. Craft brew sales grew 9 percent to 7.1 million barrels in 2005, following a 7 percent increase in 2004. This makes craft beers the fastest-growing segment of the U.S. alcoholic-beverage market. As a part of this fast-growing craft market, NBB competes with companies such as Wyoming-based Grand Teton brewing company, Chicago's Goose Island brewing company, and San Diego–based Stone brewing company. Coors is attempting to enter this market with Bluemoon wheat-beer brand, and Anheuser Busch has acquired Red Hook brewing company. NBB has positioned itself based on the quality of its products and its concern for stakeholders.

Today, NBB offers a variety of permanent and seasonal ales and pilsners. The company's standard line includes Sunshine Wheat, Blue Paddle Pilsner, Abbey Ale, Trippel Ale, 1554 Black Ale, and the original Fat Tire Amber Ale, still the firm's best seller. Some customers even refer to the company as the Fat Tire Brewery. The brewery also markets two types of specialty beers on a seasonal basis. Seasonal ales include Frambozen and Abbey Grand Cru, which are released at Thanksgiving and Christmas, and Farmhouse Ale, which is sold during the early fall months. The firm occasionally offers one-time-only brews, such as LaFolie, a wood-aged beer, which are sold only until the batch runs out.

FIGURE C18–1   Craft Brewing's Share of the U.S. Beer Market

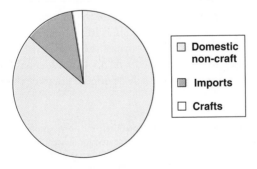

SOURCE: Craft Brewers Association 2005.

Until 2005 NBB's most effective form of advertising has been its customers' word of mouth. Indeed, before New Belgium beers were widely distributed throughout Colorado, one liquor store owner in Telluride is purported to have offered people gas money if they would stop by and pick up New Belgium beer on their way through Fort Collins. Although New Belgium beers are distributed in just one-third of the United States, the brewery receives numerous e-mails and phone calls every day inquiring when its beers will be available elsewhere.

With expanding distribution, however, the brewery recognized a need to increase its opportunities for reaching its far-flung customers. It consulted with David Holt, an Oxford professor and branding expert. After studying the young company, Holt, together with Marketing Director Greg Owsley, drafted a seventy-page "manifesto" describing the brand's attributes, character, cultural relevancy, and promise. In particular, Holt identified in New Belgium an ethos of pursuing creative activities simply for the joy of doing them well and in harmony with the natural environment. With the brand thus defined, New Belgium went in search of an advertising agency to help communicate that brand identity; it soon found Amalgamated, an equally young, independent New York advertising agency. Amalgamated created a $10 million advertising campaign for New Belgium that targets high-end beer drinkers, men ages 25 to 44, and highlights the brewery's image as being down to earth. The grainy ads focus on a man rebuilding a cruiser bike out of used parts and then riding it along pastoral country roads. The product appears in just five seconds of each ad between the tag lines, "Follow Your Folly . . . Ours Is Beer." The ads helped position the growing brand as whimsical, thoughtful, and reflective. In addition to the ad campaign, the company maintained its strategy of promotion through event sponsorships.

NEW BELGIUM ETHICAL CULTURE

According to Owsley, beyond a desire for advertising and promotion ethics, there is a fundamental focus on the ethical culture of the brand. Although consumer suspicion of business is on fully raised eyebrow, those in good standing—as opposed to those trading on hype—are eyed with iconic-like adoration. From this off polarization comes a new paradigm in which businesses that fully embrace citizenship in the community they serve can forge enduring bonds with customers. Meanwhile, these are precarious times for businesses that choose to ignore consumer's looking at brands from an ethical perspective. More than ever before, what the brand says and what the company does must be synchronized. NBB believes the mandate for corporate social responsibility gains momentum beyond the courtroom to the far more powerful marketplace. Any current and future manager of business must realize that business ethics are not so much about the installation of compliance codes and standards as they are about the spirit in which they are integrated. Thus, the modern-day brand steward—usually the most externally focused member of the business management team—must prepare to be the internal champion of the bottom-line necessity for ethical, values-driven company behavior.

At NBB a synergy of brand and values occurred naturally as the firm's ethical culture, in the form of core values and beliefs, and was in place long before NBB had a marketing department. Back in early 1991, NBB was just a home-brewed business plan of Jeff Lebesch, an electrical engineer, and his social worker wife, Kim Jordan. Before they signed any business paperwork, the two took a hike into Rocky Mountain National Park. Armed with a pen and a notebook, they took their first stab at what the fledgling company's core purpose would be. If they were going forward with this venture, what were their aspirations beyond profitability? What was the real root cause of their dream? What they wrote down that spring day, give or take a little wordsmithing, was the core values and beliefs that you can read on the NBB website today. More important, ask just about any New Belgium worker, and she or he can list for you many, if not all, of these shared values and can inform you which are the most personally poignant. For NBB, branding strategies are as rooted in their company values as in other business practices.

NEW BELGIUM'S PURPOSE AND CORE BELIEFS

NBB's dedication to quality, the environment, and its employees and customers is expressed in its mission statement: "To operate a profitable brewery which makes our love and talent manifest." The company's stated core values and beliefs about its role as an environmentally concerned and socially responsible brewer include

- ◆ Producing world-class beers
- ◆ Promoting beer culture and the responsible enjoyment of beer
- ◆ Continuous, innovative quality and efficiency improvements
- ◆ Transcending customers' expectations
- ◆ Environmental stewardship: minimizing resource consumption, maximizing energy efficiency, and recycling
- ◆ Kindling social, environmental, and cultural change as a business role model
- ◆ Cultivating potential through learning, participative management, and the pursuit of opportunities
- ◆ Balancing the myriad needs of the company, staff, and their families
- ◆ Committing ourselves to authentic relationships, communications, and promises
- ◆ Having fun

Employees believe that these statements help communicate to customers and other stakeholders what NBB, as a company, is about. These simple values developed over fifteen years ago are still meaningful to the company and its customers today, even though there has been much growth.

EMPLOYEE CONCERNS

Recognizing the employees' role in the company's success, NBB provides many generous benefits. In addition to the usual paid health and dental insurance and retirement plans, employees get a free lunch every other week and a free massage once a year; they can bring their children and dogs to work. Employees who stay with the company for five years earn an all-expenses paid trip to Belgium to "study beer culture." Perhaps most important, employees can also earn stock in the privately held corporation, which grants them a vote in company decisions. NBB's employees now own one-third of the growing brewery. Open-book management lets employees see the financial costs and performance.

ENVIRONMENTAL CONCERNS

NBB's marketing strategy involves linking the quality of its products, as well as their brand, with the company's philosophy toward affecting the planet. From leading-edge environmental gadgets and high-tech industry advancements to employee-ownership programs and a strong belief in giving back to the community, NBB demonstrates its desire to create a living, learning community.

NBB strives for cost-efficient energy-saving alternatives to conducting its business and reducing its impact on the environment. In staying true to the company's core values and beliefs, the brewery's employee-owners unanimously agreed to invest in a wind turbine, making NBB the first fully wind-powered brewery in the United States. Since the switch from coal power, NBB has been able to reduce its carbon dioxide emissions by 1800 metric tons per year. The company further reduces its energy use by employing a steam condenser that captures and reuses the hot water that boils the barley and hops in the production process to start the next brew. The steam is redirected to heat the floor tiles and de-ice the loading docks in cold weather. Another way that NBB conserves energy is by using "sun tubes," which provide natural daytime lighting throughout the brewhouse all year long.

NBB also takes pride in reducing waste through recycling and creative reuse strategies. The company strives to recycle as many supplies as possible, including cardboard boxes, keg caps, office materials, and the amber glass used in bottling. The brewery also stores spent barley and hop grains in an on-premise silo and invites local farmers to pick up the grains, free of charge, to feed their pigs. NBB even encourages its employees to reduce air pollution by using alternative transportation. As an incentive, NBB gives its employees "cruiser bikes"—like the one pictured on its Fat Tire Amber Ale label—after one year of employment and encourages them to ride to work.

NBB has been a long-time participant in green building techniques. With each expansion of the facility, they have incorporated new technologies and learned a few lessons along the way. In 2002 NBB agreed to participate in the U.S. Green Building Council's Leadership in Energy and Environment Design for Existing Buildings pilot program. From sun tubes and day lighting throughout the facility to reusing heat in the brewhouse, they continue to search for new ways to close loops and conserve resources.

Reduce, Reuse, Recycle are the three Rs of being an environmental steward. The reuse program includes heat for the brewing process, cleaning chemicals, water, and much more. Recycling at NBB takes on many forms, from turning waste products into something new and useful (like spent grain to pig feed) to supporting the recycling market in creative ways (like turning their keg caps into table surfaces). They also buy recycled whenever they can, from paper to office furniture. Reduction surrounds them—from motion sensors on the lights throughout the building to induction fans that pull in cool winter air to chill their beer—because offsetting their energy needs is the cornerstone to being environmentally efficient.

SOCIAL CONCERNS

Beyond its use of environment-friendly technologies and innovations, NBB strives to improve communities and enhance people's lives through corporate giving, event sponsorship, and philanthropic involvement.

Since its inception, NBB has donated more than $1.6 million to organizations in the communities in which they do business. For every barrel of beer sold the prior year, NBB donates $1 to philanthropic causes within their distribution territory. The donations are divided between states in proportion to their percentage of overall sales. This is their way of staying local and giving back to the communities who support and purchase NBB products. In 2006 Arkansas, Arizona, California, Colorado, Idaho, Kansas, Missouri, Montana, Nebraska, Nevada, New Mexico, Oregon, Texas, Washington, and Wyoming received funding.

Funding decisions are made by the NBB Philanthropy Committee, which is composed of employees throughout the brewery, including owners, employee-owners, area leaders, and production workers. NBB looks for nonprofit organizations that demonstrate creativity, diversity, and an innovative approach to their mission and objectives. The committee also looks for groups that involve the community to reach their goals.

NBB maintains a community bulletin board in its facility where it posts an array of community involvement activities and proposals. This community board allows tourists and employees to see the different ways they can help out the community, and it gives nonprofit organizations a chance to make their needs known. Organizations can apply for grants through the NBB website, which has a link designated for this purpose.

NBB sponsors a number of events, with a special focus on those that involve "human-powered" sports that cause minimal damage to the natural environment. Through event sponsorships, such as the Tour de Fat, NBB supports various environmental, social, and cycling nonprofit organizations. New Belgium sponsored the MS 150 "Best Damn Bike Tour," a two-day, fully catered bike tour, from which all proceeds went to benefit more than five thousand local people with multiple sclerosis. NBB also sponsored the Ride the Rockies bike tour, which donated the proceeds from beer sales to local nonprofit groups. The money raised from this annual event funds local projects such as improving parks and bike trails. In the course of one year, NBB can be found at anywhere from 150 to 200 festivals and events, across all fifteen western states.

ORGANIZATIONAL SUCCESS

NBB's efforts to live up to its own high standards have paid off with numerous awards and a very loyal following. It was one of three winners of *Business Ethics* magazine's Business Ethics Awards for its "dedication to environmental excellence in every part of its innovative brewing process." It also won an honorable mention in the Better Business Bureau's 2002 Torch Award for Outstanding Marketplace Ethics competition. Jordan and Lebesch were named the recipients of the Rocky Mountain Region Entrepreneur of the Year Award for manufacturing. The company also captured the award for best mid-sized brewing company of the year and best mid-sized brewmaster at the

Great American Beer Festival. In addition, New Belgium took home medals for three different brews, Abbey Belgian Style Ale, Blue Paddle Pilsner, and LaFolie specialty ale.

According to David Edgar, director of the Institute for Brewing Studies, "They've created a very positive image for their company in the beer-consuming public with smart decision-making." Although some members of society do not believe that a company whose major product is alcohol can be socially responsible, NBB has set out to prove that, for those who make a choice to drink responsibly, the company can do everything possible to contribute to society. Its efforts to promote beer culture and the connoisseurship of beer has even led it to design a special "Worthy Glass," the shape of which is intended to retain foam, show off color, enhance the visual presentation, and release aroma. NBB also promotes the responsible appreciation of beer through its participation in and support of the culinary arts. For instance, it frequently hosts New Belgium Beer Dinners, in which every course of the meal is served with a complementary culinary treat.

According to Owsley, although the Fat Tire brand has a bloodline straight from the enterprise's ethical beliefs and practices, the firm's work is not done. They must continually reexamine ethical, social, and environmental responsibilities. In 2004 NBB received the Environmental Protection Agency's regional Environmental Achievement Award.

There are still many ways for NBB to improve as a corporate citizen. They still don't produce an organic beer. The manufacturing process is a fair distance from being zero waste or emission free. There will always be a need for more public dialogue on avoiding alcohol abuse. Practically speaking, they have a never-ending to-do list. NBB also must acknowledge that as their annual sales increase, the challenges for the brand to remain on a human scale and culturally authentic will increase too. How to boldly grow the brand while maintaining its humble feel has always been a challenge.

Every six-pack of New Belgium Beer displays the phrase, "In this box is our labor of love, we feel incredibly lucky to be creating something fine that enhances people's lives." Although Lebesch has semiretired from the company to focus on other interests, the founders of NBB hope that this statement captures the spirit of the company. According to employee Dave Kemp, NBB's environmental concern and social responsibility give it a competitive advantage because consumers want to believe in and feel good about the products they purchase. NBB's most important asset is its image—a corporate brand that stands for quality, responsibility, and concern for society. Defining itself as more than just a beer company, NBB also sees itself as a caring organization that is concerned with all stakeholders, including the community, the environment, and employees.

QUESTIONS

1. What environmental issues does the New Belgium Brewing Company work to address? How has NBB taken a strategic approach to addressing these issues? Why do you think the company has chosen to focus on environmental issues?
2. Are NBB's social initiatives indicative of strategic philanthropy? Why or why not?

3. Some segments of society vigorously contend that companies that sell alcoholic beverages and tobacco products cannot be socially responsible organizations because of the nature of their primary products. Do you believe that NBB's actions and initiatives are indicative of an ethical and socially responsible corporation? Why or why not?

4. What else could NBB do to foster ethical and responsible conduct?

SOURCES: Peter Asmus, "Goodbye Coal, Hello Wind," *Business Ethics* 13 (1999): 10–11; Robert Baun, "What's in a Name? Ask the Makers of Fat Tire," *[Fort Collins] Coloradoan*, October 8, 2000, E1, E3; Rachel Brand, "Colorado Breweries Bring Home 12 Medals in Festival," *Rocky Mountain News,* via www.insidedenver.com/news/1008beer6.shtml (accessed November 6, 2000); Stevi Deter, "Fat Tire Amber Ale," The Net Net, www.thenetnet.com/reviews/fat.html (accessed April 29, 2003); DirtWorld, www.dirtworld.com/races/Colorado_race745.htm (accessed November 6, 2000); Robert F. Dwyer and John F. Tanner, Jr., *Business Marketing* (Columbus, OH: Irwin/McGraw-Hill, 1999), 104; "Fat Tire Amber Ale," *Achwiegut* (The Guide to Austrian Beer), www.austrianbeer.com/beer/b000688.shtml (accessed January 19, 2001); "Four Businesses Honored with Prestigious International Award for Outstanding Marketplace Ethics," Better Business Bureau press release, September 23, 2002, www.bbb.org/alerts/2002torchwinners.asp; Julie Gordon, "Lebesch Balances Interests in Business, Community," *[Fort Collins] Coloradoan*, February 26, 2003; Del I. Hawkins, Roger J. Best, and Kenneth A. Coney, *Consumer Behavior: Building Marketing Strategy,* 8th ed. (Columbus, OH: Irwin/McGraw-Hill, 2001); David Kemp, Tour Connoisseur, New Belgium Brewing Company, personal interview by Nikole Haiar, November 21, 2000, 1:00 P.M.; New Belgium Brewing Company, Fort Collins, CO, www.newbelgium.com (accessed April 29, 2003); New Belgium Brewing Company Tour by Nikole Haiar, November 20, 2000, 2:00 P.M.; "New Belgium Brewing Wins Ethics Award," *Denver Business Journal* online, January 2, 2003, http://denver.bizjournals.com/denver/stories/2002/12/30/daily21.html; New Belgium Brewing Company, http://www.newbelgium.com/sustainability.php and http://www.newbelgium.com/philanthropy.php (accessed May 17, 2006); Greg Owsley, "The Necessity for Aligning Brand with Corporate Ethics," in *Fulfilling Our Obligation, Perspectives on Teaching Business Ethics,* ed. Sheb L. True, Linda Ferrell, and O. C. Ferrell (Kennesaw, GA: Kennesaw State University Press, 2005), 128–132; Dan Rabin, "New Belgium Pours It on for Bike Riders," *Celebrator Beer News* online, August/September 1998, www.celebrator.com/9808/rabin.html.

Foundational Concepts in Understanding the Ethical Dimensions of the Financial Meltdown

At the beginning of 2009, the U.S. economy found itself mired in red ink. Over a six-month period, the largest banks and brokerage houses around the globe became victims of what many called an "unforeseeable" set of events. In truth, what happened had been far from unforeseeable. As early as 2004 many signs were present that the United States and world financial systems were in failing health. Regardless of whether the 2008 meltdown could have been accurately predicted, governments, analysts, executives, and stakeholders have been left to sort through the mess. Economists, financial analysts, and governmental officials are attempting to find the root cause that forced the U.S. government to inject the economy with over $750 billion in 2008 and another $789 billion stimulus in February 2009 to attempt to stabilize the system.

A major part of the problem was in the financial industry's culture of focusing on rewards and the bottom line. Wall Street is a highly interconnected system rife with opaque decision making, lack of accountability, and unreliable accounting methods. CEOs received sometimes hundreds of millions of dollars, even for poor performance or when misconduct occurred during their watch. Even lower-level traders received huge commissions for transactions, regardless of the economic outcome for the firm. Ethical concerns were simply isolated in a silo and the codes of conduct became little more than window dressing. Combine this with rampant leveraging and the widespread use of complex computer models that few understood, and one is left with a volatile house of cards. It did not take much to bring the entire system to its knees. Many who should have been in-the-know were ignorant of the risks because of risk compartmentalization, wherein strategic business units within corporations were unaware of the big picture in terms of the consequences of their actions. As a result, no one person, company, or agency should be blamed—the problems were systemic. While most companies endeavored to comply with the legal system, they often looked for loopholes and unregulated means of maximizing profits and financial rewards. The regulatory system needed remaking to better govern over safety, conduct, and systematic risk. Derivatives, capital requirements, and hedge funds were underregulated, which increased risks to investors. Many companies were trying to do what was ethical; however, because of the complex nature of the global economy everyone was looking at their trees, their own self-interest, and did not see the forest, the collapse of the system, until it was too late.

The ripple effect was felt in late October 2008 when institutions around the world came together to engineer a financial strategy to stabilize the financial markets of all the developed countries. The meltdown had caused many to question governmental institutions' oversight, as well as the responsibility of those who managed the money of individuals, corporations, and nonprofits. A lack of trust has caused major investors to question the once-perceived competency, fairness, and truthfulness of regulatory institutions. This situation has caused further instability and mistrust in the entire financial system. As a result, many now are starting to question the foundations of capitalism and the policies needed to make it function. Today some of the fundamental tenants or assumptions of capitalism are under debate, and may be modified. The changes in the system will need to address issues such as the law, ethics, and the required level of compliance to minimize risk.

As governments, public policy makers, and business begin the debate, it behooves them to understand the major players in what we define as *modified capitalism*. Modified capitalism is different from pure capitalism in that the government intervenes and regulates business to some extent. Modified capitalism is based on the assumption that government regulatory agencies such as the Securities and Exchange Commission (SEC) protect investors and the public. Many nations exist as mixed economies that borrow elements from more than one type of economic system. One of the many exports from the United States is the capitalistic ideology, the invisible hand, less regulation, and maximizing shareholder wealth. Barney Frank, Chairman of the House Financial Services Committee, has provided leadership on the future of the regulatory structure of Wall Street. Not since the 1930s has Washington assumed so much power over private industry so rapidly.

In the discussion that follows we help you understand the factors that caused the global financial crisis and about the legal, regulatory, and ethical dimensions that will change our world. For example, this section explains what collateral debt obligations, specifically derivatives, are and why they are legal and yet may become illegal. We review the nature and purpose of the securities markets, and the role of speculation in them. We will define and explain key concepts related to the recent financial crisis. Additionally, we will discuss how collateralized debt obligations and subprime loans opened the door to opportunities for extreme risk-taking and misconduct. The explanation of the financial meltdown will help you to understand why corporate social responsibility, corporate governance, executive pay, governmental regulation, and business ethics will increase in importance in the next decade and why you should be aware of the possible coming changes.

BACKGROUND OF THE FINANCIAL CRISIS

Let us start with some very basic concepts. We all have heard about the stock market, yet many do not understand its main function, which is to provide *capital* (money) to companies that want to expand but do not have sufficient funds to do so. Companies create *stocks* (shares) that give partial ownership of the company to others for an expected rate of return. The *dividend* was originally the greatest source of value to investors. If the company keeps the number of stocks in circulation constant, stock prices rise or fall depending upon what others believe will happen to the company. This belief is called *speculation*. Speculation has many factors that can affect a stock's value. The factors that drive speculation can be company news, macroeconomic, political, technological, environmental, and even gossip. Performance factors such as cash flow, sales, or earnings are used as well as historical ratios and statistics. In the long run, speculation is the precursor to the stock's actual value. The stock market provides the opportunity to trade not only stocks, but also currency, bonds, real estate, commodities, derivatives, and other financial instruments.

A critical concept within the financial meltdown is *collateralized debt*. Collateralized debt is a financial instrument similar to a bond in that it has a value and interest and the debts are repaid by the borrower. Collateralized debt obligations (CDOs) are sophisticated financial tools that repackage individual loans into a product that can be sold on the secondary market for banks and other financial institutions. These packages consist of auto loans, credit card debt, or corporate debt. They are called collateralized because they have some type of real asset (car, house, etc.) behind them. CDOs are called asset-backed commercial paper if they consist of corporate debt and mortgage-backed securities if the loans are mortgages. If the mortgages are made to those with a less than prime (best) credit history, they are called subprime mortgages. CDOs were created to provide more liquidity or invisible money into the economy. It allows banks and corporations to sell off debt, which frees up more capital to invest or loan. The creation of CDOs is one reason why the U.S. economy has grown so fast.

However, the downside of CDOs is that it allows the originators of the loans to avoid having to collect on them when they become due, since the loans are now owned by other investors. Before investors buy the CDOs they usually always look to rating companies (e.g., Standard & Poor's) to determine their risk. CDOs have also led many to be less disciplined in adhering to strict lending and accounting standards. Another downside is that they are complex to the extent that often the buyers really cannot be sure what they are buying. Often, investors rely on the banks and rating companies selling the CDOs without doing enough research to be sure the package is really worth the price. If something happens to make sellers lose their trust in the product, the CDOs become difficult to resell. To insure against losses from owning a CDO, the owner can purchase credit default swaps (CDSs). CDSs are insurance products that businesses buy and sell, and are considered a counterparty risk reduction instrument. Usually, large insurance companies such as AIG sell CDSs like insurance policies for businesses so that if anything catastrophic happens, they assume the risk by paying out the money lost. They gamble that they will have enough money to handle isolated catastrophes and still make a profit.

CDSs are derivatives, which are financial contracts or instruments whose value is derived from something else such as commodities (corn, wheat, soybeans, etc.), stocks, bonds, and even home mortgages. Gains or losses from derivatives come from betting correctly on the movement of these values and are part of what are called futures, forwards, options, and swaps. A *futures* contract is an agreement to buy or sell a set quantity of something at a set rate at a predetermined point in the future. Futures contracts are often associated with buyers and sellers of commodities who are concerned about supply, demand, and changes in prices. *Forwards* are similar to futures, except they can be traded between two individuals. A forward contract is a commitment to trade a specified item at a specific price in the future. The forward contract takes whatever form the parties agree to. An *option* is a less binding form of derivative. It conveys the right, but not the obligation, to buy or sell a particular asset in the future. A *call option* gives the investor the right to buy at a set price on delivery day. A *put option* gives the investor the option to sell a good or financial instrument at a set price on the settlement date. It is a financial contract with what is called a *long position*, giving the owner the right, but not the obligation, to sell an amount at a preset price and maturity date. Finally, *swaps* occur when two parties agree to exchange one stream of cash flows against another one. Swaps can be used to hedge risks such as changes in interest rates, or to speculate on the changing prices of commodities or currencies.

Derivatives have been linked to the financial meltdown. For example, in 1998 multi-billionaire investor Warren Buffett purchased a reinsurance company called General Re. At the same time there was a collapse of a company called Long Term Capital Management. This company experienced a relatively small $5 billion trading loss that nevertheless almost destroyed the global monetary system. From this event, the financial markets were warned that excessive leveraging and the complexity of the trades could lead to such events again. It took Warren Buffett four years to finally untangle himself from General Re because of this problem. By 2007 derivatives had globally grown to a $516 trillion industry. Paul B. Farrell of MarketWatch.com, a website published by Dow Jones & Company, concluded that derivatives have grown to such a large part of the investment world because of the following: Sarbanes–Oxley increased corporate disclosures and government oversight; Federal Reserve's cheap money policies created the subprime-housing boom; war budgets burdened the U.S. Treasury and future entitlements programs; trade deficits with China and others destroyed the value of the U.S. dollar; and oil- and commodity-rich nations demanded equity payments rather than debt.

To put the $516 trillion into perspective, Farrell provides the following figures: U.S. annual gross domestic product (GDP) is about $15 trillion; U.S. money supply is also about $15 trillion; U.S. government's maximum legal debt is $9 trillion; world's GDP for all nations is approximately $50 trillion; unfunded Social Security and Medicare benefits $50 trillion to $65 trillion; total value of the world's real estate is estimated at about $75 trillion; total value of world's stock and bond markets is more than $100 trillion.

The reality of how deep of a hole the global economy was in came to a head when the federal government bailed out AIG with $152.5 billion of taxpayer money. Many companies made credit decisions based on bad ratings that were poorly thought out. For the last ten years, credit has become so easy to get and leverage became so high that companies were leveraging twenty or thirty times their capital. Toxic products or investments like subprime mortgages that were rated as prime exacerbated the situation.

BREAKDOWN OF TRUST AND THE GATEKEEPERS

As mentioned, trust is the glue that holds businesses and transactions together. Ethics helps create the foundational trust between two parties in a transaction. Trust gives way to confidence and allows businesses to depend upon one another as they make transactions or exchange value. There are many people who must trust and be trusted to make business work properly. Columbia University corporate governance expert Dr. John Coffee has defined gatekeepers as "reputational intermediaries who provide verification and certification of services to investors." Gatekeepers not only include accountants, who are essential to certifying the accuracy of financial information, but also lawyers, financial rating agencies, and even financial reporting services. All of these groups are critical in providing information that allows stakeholders to gain an understanding of the financial position of an organization. Most of these gatekeepers operate with professional codes of ethics and face legal consequences, or even disbarment, if they fail to operate within agreed-upon principles of conduct. Therefore, there is a strong need for gatekeepers to retain ethical standards and independence using standard methods and procedures that can be audited by other gatekeepers, the regulatory system, and investors.

ACCOUNTANTS

One major gatekeeper group that controls access to important information is accountants. Accountants measure and disclose financial information, with an assurance of accuracy, to the public. Managers, investors, tax authorities, and other stakeholders who make resource allocation decisions are all groups who use the information provided by accountants. Accountants assume certain basic principles about their clients. One assumption is that the corporation is an entity that is separate and distinct from its owners, and that it will continue to operate as such in the future. Another assumption is that a sort of stable monetary system (dollar) is in place and that all necessary information concerning the business is available and presented in an understandable manner. Accountants have their own set of rules, one of which is that, if there is a choice between equally acceptable accounting methods, they should use the one that is least likely to overstate or misdirect.

Recently many accountants have not been adhering to this rule. For example, Arthur Andersen was once a standard-bearer for integrity. But at Andersen, growth became the priority, and its emphasis on recruiting and retaining big clients came at the expense of quality and independent audits. The company linked its consulting business in a joint cooperative relationship with its audit arm, which compromised its auditors' independence, a quality crucial to the execution of a credible audit. The firm's focus on growth generated a fundamental change in its corporate culture, one in which obtaining a high profit consulting business was regarded as more important than providing objective auditing services. The lucrative full-service strategy would later pose an ethical dilemma for some Andersen partners when they had to decide how to treat questionable accounting practices discovered at some of Andersen's largest clients. Ultimately, Arthur Andersen was dissolved because of its ties to the Enron scandal. Gatekeepers such as lawyers, financial rating agencies, and even financial reporting services must have high ethical standards. These groups must be trusted by all stakeholders, and most operate with professional codes of ethics.

RISK ASSESSMENT

Another critical gatekeeper group in the financial meltdown was risk assessors of financial products. The top three companies in the world that independently assess financial risks are Standard & Poor's, Moody's, and Fitch. They assess risk and express it through letters ranging from "AAA," which is the highest grade, to "C," which is junk. Different rating services use the same letter grades, but use various combinations of upper- and lower-case letters to differentiate themselves.

As early as 2003, financial analysts and the three global rating firms suspected that there were some major problems with the way their models were assessing risk. In 2005, Standard & Poor's realized that their algorithm for estimating the risks associated with debt packages was flawed. As a result, they asked for comments on improving their equations. In 2006–2007 many governmental regulators and others started to realize what the rating agencies had known for years: Their ratings were not very accurate. One report stated that the high ratings given to debt were based on inadequate historical data and companies were ratings shopping between companies so as to obtain the best rating possible. It was found that investment banks were among some of the worst offenders, paying for ratings and therefore causing conflicts of interest. The amount of revenue these three companies annually receive is approximately $5 billion.

Further investigations uncovered many disturbing problems. First, Moody's, S&P's, and Fitch had all violated a code of conduct that required analysts to consider only credit factors, not "the potential impact on Moody's, or an issuer, an investor or other market participant." Also, these companies had become overwhelmed by an increase in the volume and sophistication of the securities they were asked to review. Finally, analysts, faced with less time to perform the due diligence expected of them, began to cut corners. Evidence provided to Congress in the form of instant messages and e-mails demonstrate the unethical behavior prevalent in the ratings business, and the high level of awareness among participants: (IM exchange from April 2007, between two S&P analysts):

> Rahul [Dilip Shah] btw – that deal is ridiculous, [Shannon Mooney] I know right . . . model def does not capture half of the risk, [Shah] we should not be rating it., [Mooney] it could be structured by cows and we would rate it.; [S&P analyst]; Rating agencies continue to create an ever-bigger monster, the CDO market. Let us hope we are all wealthy and retired by the time this house of cards falters.

GOVERNMENT INSURANCE AGAINST INVESTOR LOSS

Some experts contend that the government and its regulators were the cause of the mortgage problem. Governmental agencies that were supposed to provide insurance and oversights against investor and bank losses were the Federal Deposit Insurance Corporation (FDIC) and the Securities Investor Protection Corporation (SIPC). These organizations may have failed in their contract of trust to the American people.

The Federal Deposit Insurance Corporation

The FDIC is supposed to guarantee the safety of checking and savings deposits in banks for the public. It is the agency that investigates banks, their directors, and their accounting practices; yet the agency did not warn Congress of impending problems. Some say the agency was too slow and did too little to steer banks away from risky mortgage loans. Because of the losses of trust in banks, the FDIC increased insurance on bank accounts to $250,000, from $100,000, per account in late 2008. This is because savers feared their banks would fail and they would lose their funds valued over $100,000.

The Securities Investor Protection Corporation

The Securities Investor Protection Corporation (SIPC) also lost the trust of many investors. SIPC has the role of returning funds and securities to investors if financial companies go bankrupt. SIPC does not protect against market risk, but it does protect the value of the securities held by its members up to $500,000 per customer, including up to $100,000 for cash. Not all investments are protected by SIPC, such as unregistered investment contracts, unregistered limited partnerships, fixed annuity contracts, or commodity futures contracts and commodity options. The SIPC is supposed to keep alert for financial misconduct and to promote trust. However, the organization may not have been doing an adequate job in keeping that trust contract. For example, when the SIPC examined Bernard Madoff, who ran the largest Ponzi scheme ever discovered and bilked investors of approximately $65 billion over the course of decades, the organization did not see anything wrong. In the case of the Madoff fraud, some investors have the potential to recover up to a maximum of $500,000 of their investments because of losses stemming from the fraud, not market risk losses. Investors can only recover money directly invested through Madoff, and not other investors or hedge funds. SIPC's president, Stephen Harbeck, said the firm's financial records were "utterly unreliable." Yet a year ago those same records were considered reliable. Many, including Congress, have been left wondering how trained professionals could have been keeping a watch over Madoff's bogus books for years without seeing anything wrong with them. SIPC personnel have cited a lack of resources as the organization's principal reason for the oversight.

The Securities and Exchange Commission

The Securities and Exchange Commission (SEC) is also meant to play a crucial role in protecting investors, overseeing markets, and facilitating capital formation. Its primary responsibilities are to enforce federal securities laws, and to regulate the securities industry, the nation's stock and options exchanges, and other electronic securities markets. The SEC exists to be an advocate for investors; but many have criticized the organization for not fulfilling its mission. Some say that Wall Street and SEC employees have enjoyed a far-too-cozy relationship for decades. This has created a situation where, in some cases, those who make and enforce the rules are the same who profit from rule changes. Without a level of objective distance between SEC officials and the financial sector, enforcement can become quite difficult. In the case of the 2008–2009 financial crisis, many of the officials who should have seen trouble brewing in the financial industry did not realize the scope of the subprime mortgage and derivatives problems, or at least made no public announcement, until it was too late.

For example, in the case of Madoff and the missing $65 billion, credible allegations of financial wrongdoing going back to at least 1999 were repeatedly brought to the attention of SEC staff, yet nothing was done. Some suggest that poor training of junior and inspector-level staff was the problem. In some cases, it is alleged that those checking for fraud had not received enough training to enable them to do their job. "The people doing the examinations have no clue what the right questions are to ask," said Bill Brodsky, the chief executive of the Chicago Board Options Exchange in an interview. "Going in and asking questions out of a manual doesn't help you understand how a business works."

The Sarbanes–Oxley Act

The Enron and WorldCom scandals did much to create regulations and laws with which to comply. As a result of these corporate scandals, the Sarbanes–Oxley Act (SOX) of 2002 was created. Governed by the SEC, the goal of SOX is to improve financial reporting. It has also generated considerable controversy. SOX implementation is expensive, and many in the financial community are starting to question whether it is worth the cost. For example, *CFO Magazine* reported that 48 percent of public companies will spend at least $500,000 in the first year of compliance with SOX.

Supporters contend that SOX is necessary and plays a useful role in restoring public confidence in the nation's capital markets by, among other things, strengthening corporate accounting controls. Opponents claim that it has reduced America's international competitive edge against foreign financial service providers, claiming it has introduced an overly complex and regulatory environment into U.S. financial markets. SOX provides independent oversight of public accounting firms, mandates that senior executives take individual responsibility for the accuracy and completeness of corporate financial reports, and requires reporting of corporate reports to the SEC or its agents. SOX also defines codes of conduct for securities analysts and requires disclosure of conflicts of interest. Included within SOX is the Corporate and Criminal Fraud Act, which describes specific criminal penalties for fraud by manipulation, destruction, or alteration of financial records or other interference with investigations, while providing certain protections for whistle-blowers. The White Collar Crime Penalty Enhancement Act is another subject included within SOX that increases the criminal penalties associated with white-collar crimes and recommends sentencing guidelines. Finally, SOX includes the Corporate Fraud Accountability Act that makes it illegal to tamper or change company records and provides for jail time instead of simply fines.

Federal Sentencing Guidelines for Organizations

The Federal Sentencing Guidelines for Organizations (FSGO) came into effect on November 1, 1991, and was to create uniformity and certainty in sentencing, and in particular to increase the punishment of those committing "white-collar" crimes. Much has been said about FSGO being, in effect, a "carrot and stick" to encourage business ethics. A stick because the guidelines impose stiff fines on organizations that commit illegal acts. A carrot because if firms convince the legal entities they had an effective compliance program, fines are reduced. According to FSGO standards, an effective compliance program must have the following:

- Compliance standards and assessment of ethical and legal risk
- Development of a Code of Conduct
- Oversight by high-level personnel, who had not been involved in unethical or illegal activity
- Due care in delegating substantial discretionary authority
- Effective Communication to all levels of employees
- Reasonable steps to achieve compliance, which include systems for monitoring, auditing, and reporting suspected wrongdoing without fear of reprisal
- Consistent enforcement of compliance standards including disciplinary mechanisms
- Reasonable steps to respond to and prevent further similar offenses upon detection of a violation that provides corrective action

Upper management implementing an ethics program should take care to ensure that the care and diligence should flow downward throughout the organization. Although the guidelines were meant to help with sentencing, the concept of the "stick" as an effective driver to ethical behavior is problematic according to critics. Some people and companies calculate the odds of getting caught and never take into account the rights of others.

A 2004 amendment expands the FSGO to require that a business's management and board of directors be well-informed about its ethics program regarding content, implementation, and effectiveness. The board must assure that there is a high-ranking manager accountable for the operational oversight of the ethics program; that mechanisms are in place that assure employees means of reporting misconduct without recrimination; and the board must oversee the discovery of risks in order to better deal with them.

Ethics programs should be built upon the philosophy of risk avoidance or at the least, risk management. It becomes a cost of doing business. Creating programs creates a more ethical culture only to the extent that it will create a more legal culture, but will not create a values-driven culture. The motivation for compliance is to cover exposure the company might have, not to assure that decisions are made due to values shared by the organization and the employee. The motivation and the culture of upper management who will be implementing the ethics program should flow downward throughout the organization. Implementing the sentencing guidelines was to create uniformity and certainness in sentencing and to exact a fair and just punishment. But the concept of the "stick" as an effective driver to values-driven management is problematic. As a society, when we reach a certain level of frustration with a certain type of already prohibited behavior we often conclude that the unwanted behavior continues because the consequences are not severe enough to stop the particular behavior. Sometimes this tenet holds true, while other times it does not.

For example, you may be tempted to speed on your way to a destination. In making the decision, you may conduct a mental cost-benefit analysis. A rational person will balance the cost of a ticket multiplied by the risk and the cost of getting caught (i.e., the cost of the ticket, inconvenience, and effect on driver's license). If you knew the chance was 100 percent that you would be pulled over, you would not likely speed unless the economic rewards for arriving quicker outweighed any negative consequences. You probably did not factor in safety, because people generally do not plan on getting in an accident.

Would a greater fine change the evaluation? It would depend on how much of an increase it was. If the fine were raised to $10,000, then you probably would not spend much time debating whether the benefits of speeding outweigh the costs. However, there are some drivers who will miscalculate the chances of being caught, or not even think about the consequences. To those there is no "stick" effect, even on behavior.

Higher fines or increased penalties have not resulted in more ethical businesspeople, nor has it forced people to use more ethical decision-making processes. It has simply forced people into behaviors that hew more closely to the law. When it comes to values-driven or ethical leadership the important issue is how a person's decisions or behaviors will affect others. Threatening punishment for doing the wrong thing, or limiting the punishment of a wrongdoer because of some good, may not be the most effective way of creating an environment of ethical decision making. The principles of human rights, the greatest good, or enlightened self-interest are not the factors encouraged by the Sentencing Guidelines or any type of penal system.

EXAMINING THE CAUSES
OF THE FINANCIAL CRISIS

The financial meltdown was not caused by one event or one agency not doing its job, nor can it be blamed on a group of "bad" people. These events represent a systemic failure that did not take into account the basic nature of people, profit making companies, and the agencies and laws that were supposed to be enforced so that all could trust the financial system. Many good ideas on how to improve the profits of stockholders and stakeholders combined to form the toxic environment that resulted in the financial disaster. To understand the complexity and in order to propose a partial remedy, we summarize the findings from above.

The first is our fundamental understanding of how economies work and the concepts taught to students in business. The fields of economics and finance have a perceived need to explain economics, finance, and business decision making in mathematical terms. By reducing people's attitudes, perceptions, and behaviors to equations one assumes that man is rational: this is not always the case. Because economics is based in the behavior of man that creates systems to bring increased value to exchanges in the form of currency, all equations must have an uncertainty or error term. In business this error term is called risk and we quantify it, but many forget that it is always there. Second, businesses must make a profit whether one calls it profit, revenue, earnings per share, or accrued value. As people attempt to obtain this goal, their own personal values that are not usually based in profit can come into conflict with the firm's and society. In our society money is the value we place on our work that feeds, clothes, and supports.

Third, in order to create value or do business, one must have trust. To establish trust we have created rules, regulations, accounting procedures, and independent agencies in and outside of government. To ensure trust and conformity within our society we have established laws. These laws have created companies that have rules and procedures that may or may not always coincide. A faulty assumption is that laws are static, they do not change. What was once ethical can become unethical, and if it is unethical to many stakeholders it can become illegal. Finally, competition will always exist, thus increasing risk to other firms and people's way of life.

After the Cold War, modified capitalism was seen as the best alternative to create wealth. In the 1990s, the world of business became more complex. Academics in economics, finance, and business were creating strategies to become more efficient, effective, and competitive. The pressure to cut corners has always existed, but with the advent of the global economy, financial products were created that masked economic risk on a worldwide scale. Because of the interdependency among financial systems products such as collateralized debt obligations (CDOs), derivatives, and the packaging, selling, and reselling of them created a world financial analysts and managers of financial institutions thought they understood. Add competition to the mix, and managers were pushing gatekeepers such as accountants and lawyers to stretch rules and even create new ones for the firms' benefit. While this was happening, the governments that should have understood how to preserve the trust of the system were not doing their job. This was partly because the markets and products were so complex and partly because the economic models suggested that no intervention was needed. This is one reason why agencies such as the SEC hired investment bankers to work for them. In turn they wrote regulations that may or may not have been for the benefit of the people, but rather just for the benefit of financial institutions. Next came the independent agencies that were supposed to be impartial, but they were primarily being paid by the institutions that were selling the products they were to be grading. To be competitive, agencies such as Standard & Poor's may have started to cut corners. Also, the financial models used were not factoring risk correctly.

Simultaneously, agencies within the government were establishing more rules; however, the probability of getting caught was known to be low and if caught, monetary fines were the solution. Eventually the numbers started to become larger and larger. We went from millions to billions to trillions and the financial industry did not flinch or question because they assumed they knew all the risks and had them covered: but they did not. As a result they gambled by leveraging or using the same money to back more and more debt. When people tried to actually pay back their debts they discovered they couldn't. With people not being able to pay, banks could no longer pay their debts, so they went to the business of debt insurers. Unfortunately these companies had backed so many deals with the same money they couldn't pay up. When they couldn't pay, the banks couldn't because the people in their homes couldn't pay. This became the spiral of financial death that has taken hold of the world. Now that we are in it, how do we get out? The answer is simple. We begin by building trust in the financial sector as well as within governmental and nongovernmental agencies that are affiliated with the financial world.

BUILDING FINANCIAL TRUST IN THE FUTURE

To build back financial trust, businesses must first assess their accounting procedures to determine if they truly represent financial reality. Second, transparency must emerge as a top priority. Third, a solution to the reality that corporate decisions can threaten the existence of sovereign countries and their financial integrity must be discussed. Fourth, there needs to be a reappraisal of people's real worth. Executive pay as it relates to their employees' pay will be debated, and the concept of maximizing shareholder wealth will be debated as it relates to other stakeholders. Corporate governance procedure will change. A world standard of living will emerge. Environmental issues that were considered ethical will become unethical and illegal. So will certain financial products, accounting practices, and business opportunities. For example, entities such as venture capital groups may be questioned by governments as to their actual contribution or worth to society.

New laws in the United States and abroad will make certain practices within the financial markets illegal and money will be spent on simplifying, enforcing, and punishing, with jail time, white-collar actions. Over the next few years, CEOs and other top managers in leading financial firms will be prosecuted by the Justice Department and the SEC. They will face hordes of civil plaintiff lawyers who will claim damage to their clients. Since today's financial collapse has vaporized about $9 trillion in investment capital, prosecutors will try to determine what went wrong during specific transactions. These lawyers will not seek to be historians and analyze what happened to the economy. Prosecutors and lawyers will focus on very familiar concepts: lying, cheating, and stealing. Decision makers at firms such as Bear Stearns, AIG, Lehman Brothers, Fannie Mae, and Freddie Mac will be targets for investigations or possible misconduct.

The new Federal Sentencing Guidelines for Organizations as well as more law enforcement will increase the probability of being caught and the chances of going to jail. If these actions are taken and seriously implemented, trust will be created in our global financial institutions and people will begin to crawl out of the economic death spiral. Students who are not aware of the new financial world order and its changing rules, laws, corporate governance, and stakeholders will find themselves possibly not being hired, or maybe fired or in jail, not because they intentionally acted unethically or illegally but rather they weren't sensitized to the ethical decision-making process. The new financial world may be less tolerant of blissful ignorance.

CONCLUSION

While the legal and regulatory system has attempted to make it more difficult to engage in misconduct, it seems that the regulatory system and government incentives for ethical conduct failed us in the 2008–2009 financial meltdown. Although the executives during this time were at a far greater risk of criminal and civil liability than at any other time before, they continued to push the edge of ethical risk-taking in order to reap the financial rewards of salaries, bonuses, and executive stock option programs. There is much evidence that there is a significant correlation between long-term business performance and companies that exhibit good corporate governance and effective ethics and compliance programs. These companies often get better insurance coverage and rates, higher bond ratings, and improve stock performance.

Most public corporations treated Sarbanes–Oxley as an expensive compliance program and failed to embrace the ethical dimensions of financial transparency and responsibility to stakeholders. Lawmakers and regulatory agencies believed they had fixed the problems that resulted in the 2001–2002 financial scandals associated with Enron and WorldCom. Now we have a graveyard of new companies that failed including Lehman Brothers, Wachovia Bank, Washington Mutual Bank, and organizations such as Fannie Mae, Freddie Mac, AIG, and many others on life-support provided by the government.

In reality, the regulatory system was better at being reactive rather than proactive in looking forward to potential problems. If financial companies had taken the 2004 amendments to the Federal Sentencing Guidelines seriously they would have focused on not only legal compliance requirements but also on how to maximize the effectiveness of ethics programs. Ethics and compliance programs provide a business a better way to look at the enterprise, improving processes and creating a culture to enhance reputation and achieve overall objectives. These programs are becoming more proactive and value training to provide knowledge and skills to employees with strategic or operational responsibilities. The Open Compliance Ethics Group has found that one of the key benefits of an ethics and compliance program is creating integration amongst all aspects of enterprise, and when the program has a good working relationship with all business functions and processes, a culture evolves to prevent misconduct.

In the latest financial meltdown there was no enterprise-wide assessment of risk-taking linked to environmental threats. Avoiding future ethical and financial disasters will require the linking of financial risk-taking to responsibilities to stakeholders. We will continue to have systemic breakdowns in our financial system if we only approach the system with a bottom-line mentality and individuals, business units, and organizations look at short-term profits and rewards. Every part of our financial system including companies and the regulatory system needs to embrace business ethics linking responsibilities to stakeholders.

SOURCES: Jenny Anderson and Vikas Bajaj, "Rating Firms Seem Near Legal Deal on Reforms," *New York Times,* June 4, 2008, http://www.nytimes.com/2008/06/04/business/04cuomo.html?_r =1&scp=1&sq=June%204%202008%20Rating%20Frims&st=cse (accessed January 7, 2009); Mark J. Astarita, "SIPC Disappointment Down the Road for Madoff Investors," The Securities Law Home Page, December 29, 2008, http://seclaw.blogspot.com/2008/12/sipc-disappointment-down-road-for .html (accessed January 7, 2009); Vikas Bajaj, "At Moody's, Some Debt Was Rated Incorrectly," *New York Times,* July 2, 2008, http://query.nytimes.com/gst/fullpage.html?res= 9505E3DB173DF931A35754C0A96E9C8B63&scp=1&sq=At+Moody%27s%2C+some+debt+was +rated+incorrectly%2C+july+2%2C+2008&st=nyt (accessed January 7, 2009); John C. Coffee, "What Caused Enron?: A Capsule Social and Economic History of the 1990's," Columbia Law School, The Center for Law and Economic Studies, http://www.law.columbia.edu/law~economicstudies, January 20, 2003, 1–49; Paul B. Farrell, "Derivatives the New 'Ticking Bomb,' Buffett and Gross Warn: $516 Trillion Bubble Is a Disaster Waiting to Happen," MarketWatch, March 10, 2008, http://www .marketwatch.com/news/story/ derivatives-new-ticking-time-bomb/story.aspx?guid= %7BB9E54A5D-4796-4D0D-AC9E-D9124B59 D436%7D (accessed January 7, 2009); Finra Investors, "Your Rights Under SIPC Protection," http://www.finra.org/Investors/ProtectYourself/ AfterYouInvest/YourRightsUnderSIPCProtection/index.htm (accessed January 7, 2009); Michael M. Grynbaum, "Study Finds Flawed Practices at Ratings Firms," *New York Times,* July 9, 2008, http://www .nytimes.com/2008/07/09/business/09credit. html?scp=1&sq=Study%20Finds%20Flawed,%20July% 209,2008&st=cse (accessed January 7, 2009); Alix Nyberg, "Sticker Shock: The True Cost of Sarbanes–Oxley Compliance," *CFO Magazine,* September 1, 2003, 51–62; Roger Parloff, "Wall Street: It's Payback Time," *Fortune,* January 19, 2009, 57–69; Andrew Rice, "Barney Frank Has Got Your Number," *Conde Nast Portfolio,* February 2009, 100–105, 110–12; Andrew Ross Sorkin, "S.I.P.C. Chief

Calls Madoff's Records 'Utterly Unreliable'," *Dealbook, New York Times,* December 16, 2008, http://dealbook.blogs.nytimes.com/2008/12/16/sipc-chief-calls-madoffs-records-utterly-unrealiable (accessed January 7, 2009); Zachary Roth, "It Could Be Structured By Cows and We Would Rate It: How The Ratings Agencies Helped Cause The Financial Crisis," Talking Points Memo Muckraker, November 19, 2008, http://tpmmuckraker.talkingpointsmemo.com/2008/11/ it_could_be_structured_by_cows.php (accessed January 7, 2009); Pete Yost and Marcy Gordon, "AG Takes Himself Out of Madoff Fraud Probe," Yahoo News, December 17, 2008, http://news .yahoo.com/s/ap/20081217/ap_on_bi_ge/madoff_scandal (accessed January 7, 2009).

Notes

Chapter 1

1. "Full Survey: Trust in Governments, Corporations and Global Institutions Continues to Decline," World Economic Forum, December 15, 2005, Geneva, Switzerland.

2. "New National Poll: Nearly 40% of 'Ethically Prepared' Teens Believe Lying, Cheating, or Violence Necessary to Succeed," Junior Achievement/ Deloitte Teen Ethics Survey, http://www.ja.org/ about/releases/about/newsitem435.asp (accessed January 13, 2009).

3. "Teens Respect Good Business Ethics," *USA Today,* December 12, 2005, B1.

4. Marianne Jennings, "An Ethical Breach by Any Other Name," *Financial Engineering News,* January/February 2006.

5. Paul W. Taylor, *Principles of Ethics: An Introduction to Ethics,* 2nd ed. (Encino, CA: Dickenson, 1975), 1.

6. Adapted and reproduced from *The American Heritage Dictionary of the English Language,* 4th ed. Copyright © 2002 by Houghton Mifflin Company.

7. Wroe Alderson, *Dynamic Marketing Behavior* (Homewood, IL: Irwin, 1965), 320.

8. Ethics Resource Center, *2005 National Business Ethics Survey: How Employees Perceive Ethics at Work* (Washington, DC: Ethics Resource Center, 2005), 4, 28, 29.

9. Heather Timmons and Bettina Wassener, "Satyam Chief Admits Huge Fraud," www.nytimes.com/ 2009/01/01/business/worldbusiness/ 08satyam.html (accessed January 13, 2009).

10. Ronald Alsop, "Scandal-Filled Year Takes Toll on Firms' Good Names," *Wall Street Journal* online, February 12, 2003, http://online.wsj.com.

11. "Ex-Goldman Associate Is Sentenced to Insider Trading," *New York Times,* January 13, 2009, http://dealbook.blogs.nytimes.com/2008/01/03/ ex-goldman-associate-is-sentenced-in-insider- trading-case/ (accessed January 13, 2009).

12. "PWC Accounting Firm Reaches $97 Million Settlement with Ohio in AIG Case," *Insurance Journal,* http://www.insurancejournal.com/news/ national/2008/10/06/94335.htm (accessed January 14, 2009).

13. Jeffrey M. Jones, "Effects of Year's Scandals Evident in Honesty and Ethics Ratings," Gallup Organization press release, December 4, 2002, www.gallup.com/poll/releases/pr021204.asp.

14. John Lyman, "Who Is Scooter Libby? The Guy Behind the Guy," *Center for American Progress* (October 28, 2005).

15. Charles Piller, "Bell Labs Says Its Physicist Faked Groundbreaking Data," *Austin American-Statesman* online, September 26, 2002, www.austin360.com/ statesman/.

16. Hwang Woo-Suk, http://en.wikipedia.org/wiki/ Hwang_Woo-Suk (accessed June 27, 2006).

17. Jay Glazer, "Giants' Burress Accidentally Shoots Self in Leg," *Fox Sports* on MSN, http://msn.foxsports. com/nfl/story/8866348/Giants'-Burress- accidentally-shoots-self-in-leg (accessed January 14, 2009).

18. Keith H. Hammonds, "Harry Kraemer's Moment of Truth," *Fast Company* online, November 2002, www.fastcompany.com/online/64/kraemer.html.

19. Archie B. Carroll and Ann K. Buchholtz, *Business and Society: Ethics and Stakeholder Management* (Cincinnati: South-Western, 2006), 452–455.

20. Alan R. Yuspeh, "Development of Corporate Compliance Programs: Lessons Learned from the DII Experience," in *Corporate Crime in America: Strengthening the "Good Citizenship" Corporation* (Washington, DC: U.S. Sentencing Commission, 1995), 71–79.

21. Eleanor Hill, "Coordinating Enforcement Under the Department of Defense Voluntary Disclosure Program," in *Corporate Crime in America: Strengthening the "Good Citizenship" Corporation* (Washington, DC: U.S. Sentencing Commission, 1995), 287–294.

22. "Huffing and Puffing in Washington: Can Clinton's Plan Curb Teen Smoking?" *Consumer Reports* 60 (1995): 637.

23. Arthur Levitt, with Paula Dwyer, *Take on the Street* (New York: Pantheon Books, 2002).

24. Hill, "Coordinating Enforcement."

25. Richard P. Conaboy, "Corporate Crime in America: Strengthening the Good Citizen Corporation," in *Corporate Crime in America: Strengthening the "Good Citizenship" Corporation* (Washington, DC: U.S. Sentencing Commission, 1995), 1–2.

26. *United States Code Service* (Lawyers' Edition), 18 U.S.C.S. Appendix, Sentencing Guidelines for the United States Courts (Rochester, NY: Lawyers Co-operative Publishing, 1995), sec. 8A.1.

27. Anthony Bianco, William Symonds, and Nanette Byrnes, "The Rise and Fall of Dennis Kozlowski," *BusinessWeek,* December 17, 2002, 65–77.

28. "WorldCom CEO Slaps Arthur Andersen," CNN, July 8, 2002, www.cnn.com.

29. "Fraud Inc.," CNN/Money, http://money.cnn .com/news/specials/corruption/ (accessed February 5, 2002); "SEC Formalizes Investigation into Halliburton Accounting," *Wall Street Journal* online, December 20, 2002, http://online.wsj.com.

30. "Full Survey: Trust in Governments, Corporations and Global Institutions."

31. "Corporate Reform Bill Passed," CNN, July 25, 2002, www.cnn.com.

32. "Keeping an Eye on Corporate America," *Fortune,* November 25, 2002, 44–46.

33. Ethics and Compliance Officer Association homepage, "Membership," http://www.theecoa.org/ AboutMemb.asp (accessed March 6, 2006).

34. Chip Cummins. "Shell Trader, Unit Are Fined over Bogus Oil Trades," *Wall Street Journal,* January 5, 2006, C3.

35. Avi Shafran, "Aaron Feuerstein: Bankrupt and Wealthy," aish.com, June 30, 2002, www.aish.com/ societyWork/work/Aaron_Feuerstein_Bankrupt_ and__Wealthy.asp.

36. Thomas L. Friedman, "A Green Dream in Texas," *New York Times* online, January 18, 2006, http://topi<<friedman.new.184.jpg>>cs.nytimes .com/top/opinion/editorialsandoped/oped/ columnists/thomaslfriedman/index.html?inline= nyt-per (accessed January 19, 2006).

37. Bernard J. Jaworski and Ajay K. Kohli, "Market Orientation: Antecedents and Consequences," *Journal of Marketing* 57 (1993): 53–70.

38. Ethics Resource Center, *2000 National Business Ethics Survey: How Employees Perceive Ethics as Work* (Washington, DC: Ethics Resource Center, 2000), 67.

39. "Wal-Mart Commits Additional $15 million to Katrina Relief," September 1, 2005, http:// walmartstores.com/GlobalWMStoresWeb/ navigate.do?catg=26&contId=4856 (accessed March 6, 2006).

40. Terry W. Loe, "The Role of Ethical Culture in Developing Trust, Market Orientation and Commitment to Quality" (PhD diss., University of Memphis, 1996).

41. Ethics Resource Center, *2000 National Business Ethics Survey,* 5.

42. John Galvin, "The New Business Ethics," SmartBusinessMag.com, June 2000, 99.

43. Ibid.

44. "Investors Prefer Ethics over High Return," *USA Today,* January 16, 2006, B1.

45. David Rynecki, "Here Are 8 Easy Ways to Lose Your Shirt in Stocks," *USA Today,* June 26, 1998, B3.

46. Zogby International Survey, reported in *Marketing News,* February 15, 2006, 3.

47. "Trend Watch," *Business Ethics,* March/April 2000, 8.

48. Marjorie Kelly, "Holy Grail Found. Absolute, Definitive Proof That Responsible Companies Perform Better Financially," *Business Ethics,* Winter 2004.

49. Kris Hudson, "Wal-Mart to Offer Improved Health-Care Benefits." *Wall Street Journal,* February 24, 2006, A2.

50. "Today's Briefing," *Commercial Appeal,* October 12, 2000, C1.

51. Nikebiz.com, "The Inside Story," http://www.nike .com/nikebiz/nikebiz.jhtml?page=24 (accessed March 6, 2006).

52. Loe, "The Role of Ethical Culture."

53. O. C. Ferrell, Isabelle Maignan, and Terry W. Loe, "The Relationship Between Corporate Citizenship and Competitive Advantage," in *Rights, Relationships, and Responsibilities,* ed. O. C. Ferrell, Lou Pelton, and Sheb L. True (Kennesaw, GA: Kennesaw State University, 2003).

54. S. B. Graves and S. A. Waddock, "Institutional Owners and Corporate Social Performance: Maybe Not So Myopic After All," *Proceedings of the International Association for Business and Society,* San Diego, 1993; S. Waddock and S. Graves, "The Corporate Social Performance–Financial Performance Link," *Strategic Management Journal* 18 (1997): 303–319.

55. Melissa A. Baucus and David A. Baucus, "Paying the Payer: An Empirical Examination of Longer Term Financial Consequences of Illegal Corporate Behavior," *Academy of Management Journal* (1997): 129–151.

56. Healthsouth Statement Regarding Scrushy Press Conference, http://www.healthsouth.com/medinfo/home/app/frame?2=article.jsp,0,091505_Scrushy_Press (accessed March 7, 2006).

57. Kurt Eichenwald and N. R. Kleinfeld, "At Columbia/HCA, Scandal Hurts," *Commercial Appeal,* December 21, 1997, C1, C3.

58. Galvin, "The New Business Ethics."

59. Curtis C. Verschoor, "A Study of the Link Between a Corporation's Financial Performance and Its Commitment to Ethics," *Journal of Business Ethics* 17 (1998): 1509.

Chapter 2

1. Vikas Anand, Blake E. Ashforth, and Mahendra Joshi, "Business as Usual: The Acceptance and Perpetuation of Corruption in Organizations" *Academy of Management Executive* 18, no. 2 (2004): 39–53.

2. Debbie Thorne, O. C. Ferrell, and Linda Ferrell, *Business and Society* (Boston: Houghton Mifflin, 2003), 64–65.

3. "Enron 101," *BizEd* (May/June 2002): 40–46.

4. Lynn Brewer, Robert Chandler, and O. C. Ferrell, "Managing Risks for Corporate Integrity: How to Survive an Ethical Misconduct Disaster," (Mason OH: Texere/Thomson, 2006), 11.

5. Roger Parloff, "Wall Street: It's Payback Time," *Fortune,* January 19, 2009, 61.

6. Press Release, "JP Morgan Chase Completes Bear Stearns Acquisition," http://www.bearstearns.com/includes/pdfs/PressRelease_BSC_31May08.pdf.

7. Ji Lee, "The End," *Conde Nast Portfolio,* December 9, 2008, 116–117.

8. Worth Civils, "Radio Shack Cleans House," *Wall Street Journal,* March 1, 2006, B1.

9. Brewer, Chandler, and Ferrell, "Managing Risks for Corporate Integrity," 11.

10. Adapted from Isabelle Maignan, O. C. Ferrell, and Linda Ferrell, "A Stakeholder Model for Implementing Social Responsibility in Marketing," *European Journal of Marketing* 39 (2005): 956–977.

11. Ibid.

12. Ibid.

13. Thorne, Ferrell, and Ferrell, *Business and Society.*

14. Isabelle Maignan and O. C. Ferrell, "Corporate Social Responsibility: Toward a Marketing Conceptualization," *Journal of the Academy of Marketing Science* 32 (2004), 3–19.

15. Ibid.

16. Ibid.

17. Amy Merrick, "Gap Report Says Factory Inspections Are Getting Better," *Wall Street Journal,* July 13, 2005, B10.

18. Maignan and Ferrell, "Corporate Social Responsibility."

19. G. A. Steiner and J. F. Steiner, *Business, Government, and Society* (New York: Random House, 1988).

20. Milton Friedman, "Social Responsibility of Business Is to Increase Its Profits," *New York Times Magazine,* September 13, 1970, 122–126.

21. "Business Leaders, Politicians and Academics Dub Corporate Irresponsibility 'An Attack on America from Within,'" *Business Wire,* November 7, 2002, via America Online.

22. Adam Smith, *The Theory of Moral Sentiments,* Vol. 2. (New York: Prometheus, 2000).

23. Theodore Levitt, *The Marketing Imagination* (New York: Free Press, 1983).

24. Norman Bowie, "Empowering People as an End for Business," in *People in Corporations: Ethical Responsibilities and Corporate Effectiveness,* ed. Georges Enderle, Brenda Almond, and Antonio Argandona (Dordrecht, Netherlands: Kluwer Academic Press, 1990), 105–112.

25. "1997 Cone/Roper Cause-Related Marketing Trends in 'Does It Pay to Be Ethical?'" *Business Ethics* (March–April 1997): 15.

26. Isabelle Maignan, "Antecedents and Benefits of Corporate Citizenship: A Comparison of U.S. and French Businesses," (PhD diss., University of Memphis, 1997).

27. "Leading the Way: Profiles of Some of the '100 Best Corporate Citizens' for 2002," *Business Ethics* online, May 16, 2002, www.business-ethics.com/newpage.htm.

28. Bruce Horovitz, "Whole Foods Setting Clean Energy Example," *USA Today,* January 16, 2006, www.Coloradoan.com (accessed January 16, 2006).

29. Ibid.

30. Steve Quinn, "Wal-Mart Green with Energy," *[Fort Collins] Coloradoan,* July 24, 2005, E1–E2.

31. Tobias Webb, James Rose, and Peter Davis, "ISO 26000 Indicates Immaturity: If Corporate Responsibility Is to Be Effective, Prominence Has to Be Given to Both Quantitative and Qualitative Analyses," *Ethical Corporation* (December 2005): 9.

32. Alex Frangos, "Timber Business Backs A New 'Green' Standard," *Wall Street Journal,* March 29, 2006, B6.

33. Ibid.

34. Archie B. Carroll, "The Pyramid of Corporate Social Responsibility: Toward the Moral Management of Organizational Stakeholders," *Business Horizons* 34 (1991): 42.

35. Isabelle Maignan, O. C. Ferrell, and G. Tomas M. Hult, "Corporate Citizenship: Cultural Antecedents and Business Benefits," *Journal of the Academy of Marketing Science* 27 (1999): 457.

36. Better Business Bureau/Gallup Trust in Business Index, April 2008, http://us.bbb/org/WWWRoot/storage/0/Shared%20Documents/Survey%20II%20-%20BBB%20Gallup%20-%20Executive%20Summary%20-%2025%20Aug%2008.pdf (accessed January 13, 2009).

37. *Dodge v. Ford Motor Co.,* 204 Mich.459, 179 N.W. 668, 3 A.L.R. 413 (1919).

38. Alfred Marcus and Sheryl Kaiser, "Managing Beyond Compliance: The Ethical and Legal Dimensions of Corporate Responsibility," *North Coast Publishers,* 2006, 79.

39. Ben W. Heineman, Jr., "Are You a Good Corporate Citizen?" *Wall Street Journal,* June 28, 2005, B2.

40. Jerry Markon, "Former Executive of Adelphia Plans to Plead Guilty," *Wall Street Journal,* November 14, 2002, A5.

41. Darryl Reed, "Corporate Governance Reforms in Developing Countries," *Journal of Business Ethics* 37 (2002): 223–247.

42. Bryan W. Husted and Carlos Serrano, "Corporate Governance in Mexico," *Journal of Business Ethics* 37 (2002): 337–348.

43. Maria Maher and Thomas Anderson, *Corporate Governance: Effects on Firm Performance and Economic Growth* (Paris: Organisation for Economic Co-operation and Development, 1999).

44. A. Demb and F. F. Neubauer, *The Corporate Board: Confronting the Paradoxes* (Oxford, Eng.: Oxford University Press, 1992).

45. Sandy Shore, "Ex-Qwest Exec Settlement Said Collapsed," *Associated Press,* January 20, 2006, http://accounting.smartpros.com/x51431.xml (accessed March 15, 2006).

46. Maher and Anderson, *Corporate Governance.*

47. Organisation for Economic Co-operation and Development, *The OECD Principles of Corporate Governance* (Paris: Organisation for Economic Co-operation and Development, 1999).

48. Louis Lavelle, "The Best and Worst Boards," *BusinessWeek,* October 7, 2002, 104–114.

49. Andrew Backover, "Overseer Confident WorldCom Will Come Back," *USA Today,* December 31, 2002, 8A.

50. Melvin A. Eisenberg, "Corporate Governance: The Board of Directors and Internal Control," *Cordoza Law Review* 19 (1997): 237.

51. Geoffrey Colvin, "CEO Knockdown," *Fortune,* April 4, 2005.

52. "Billionaire Warren Buffett Leaving Coca-Cola Board," *Atlanta Business Chronicle,* February 14, 2006, http://atlanta.bizjournals.com/atlanta/stories/2006/02/13/daily10.html.

53. James Covert, "Wal-Mart Urged to Review Controls," *Wall Street Journal,* June 2, 2005.

54. Amy Borrus, "Should Directors Be Nervous," *BusinessWeek* online, March 6, 2006 (accessed March 8, 2006).

55. John A. Byrne, with Louis Lavelle, Nanette Byrnes, Marcia Vickers, and Amy Borrus, "How to Fix Corporate Governance," *BusinessWeek,* May 6, 2002, 69–78.

56. "How Business Rates: By the Numbers," *BusinessWeek,* September 11, 2000, 148–149.

57. Kaja Whitehouse, "Investors Sue H-P over Size of Fiorina Severance Package," *Wall Street Journal,* March 8, 2006.

58. Sarah Anderson, John Cavanagh, Scott Klinger, and Liz Stanton, "Executive Excess 2005. Defense Contractors Get More Bucks for the Bang. 12th Annual CEO Compensation Survey," *Institute for Policy Studies, United for a Fair Economy,* August 30, 2005, http://www.faireconomy.org/

press/2005/EE2005_pr.html (accessed March 15, 2006).

59. Sarah Anderson, John Cavanagh, Ralph Estes, Chuck Collins, and Chris Hartman, *A Decade of Executive Excess: The 1990s Sixth Annual Executive.* Boston: United for a Fair Economy, 1999, online, June 30, 2006, http://www.faireconomy.org/.

60. Louis Lavelle, "CEO Pay, The More Things Change . . . ," *BusinessWeek,* October 16, 2000, 106–108.

61. "2007 Trends in CEO Pay," The American Federation of Labor and Congress of Industrial Organizations, http://www.aflcio.org/corporatewatch/paywatch/pay/index.cfm (accessed January 14, 2009).

62. Joann S. Lublin, "Boards Tie CEO Pay More Tightly to Performance," *Wall Street Journal,* February 21, 2006, A1.

63. Gary Strauss, "America's Corporate Meltdown," *USA Today,* June 27, 2002, 1A, 2A.

64. Phyllis Plitch, "Firms with Governance Disclosure See Higher Returns—Study," *Wall Street Journal* online, March 31, 2003, http://online.wsj.com/.

65. Adapted from Isabelle Maignan, O. C. Ferrell, & Linda Ferrell, "A Stakeholder Model for Implementing Social Responsibility in Marketing," *European Journal of Marketing,* Sept./Oct. 2005, pp. 956–977. Reprinted with permission.

66. Marjorie Kelly, "Business Ethics 100 Best Corporate Citizens 2005," *Business Ethics* (Spring 2005): 20–25.

67. "Obesity Becomes Political Issue as Well as Cultural Obsession," Washington Wire, *Wall Street Journal* online, March 3, 2006, www.wsj.com (accessed March 21, 2006).

68. "Readers on Health Care," *Wall Street Journal* online, January 9, 2006, www.wsj.com (accessed March 21, 2006).

69. "Corporate Social Responsibility at Starbucks," http://www.starbucks.com/aboutus/csr.asp (accessed March 21, 2006).

70. Stephanie Armour, "Maryland First to OK 'Wal-Mart Bill' Law Requires More Health Care Spending," *USA Today,* January 13, 2006, B1.

71. Kris Hudson, "Wal-Mart to Offer Improved Health-Care Benefits," *Wall Street Journal,* February 24, 2006, A2.

Chapter 3

1. Joseph B. White and Lee Hawkins, Jr., "GM Will Restate Results for 2001 in Latest Stumble," *Wall Street Journal,* November 10, 2005, A1, A13.

2. John J. Fialka, "Top Oil Executives Defend Gas Prices Amid Scrutiny," *Wall Street Journal,* November 10, 2005, A4.

3. Eric H. Beversluis, "Is There No Such Thing as Business Ethics?," *Journal of Business Ethics* 6 (1987): 81–88. Reprinted by permission of Kluwer Academic Publishers, Dordrecht, Holland.

4. Carolyn Said, "Ellison Hones His 'Art of War' Tactics," *San Francisco Chronicle,* June 10, 2003, A1.

5. Michael Liedtke, "Oracle CEO to Pay $122M to Settle Lawsuit," Associated Press, *Washington Post* online, November 22, 2005, washingtonpost.com.

6. Beversluis, "Is There No Such Thing as Business Ethics?," 82.

7. Vernon R. Loucks, Jr., "A CEO Looks at Ethics," *Business Horizons* 30 (1987): 4.

8. The Workplace Bullying Institute, *U.S. Workplace Bullying Survey,* September 2007, bullyinginstitute.org (accessed January 15, 2009).

9. David Whelan, "Only the Paranoid Resurge," *Forbes,* April 10, 2006, 42–44.

10. Sarah Lueck and Anna Wilde Mathews, "Former FDA Head Held Shares in Regulated Firms as Late as '04," *Wall Street Journal,* October 26, 2005, A2.

11. "The Company We Keep: Why Physicians Should Refuse to See Pharmaceutical Representatives," *Annals of Family Medicine* 3, no. 1, (2005): 82–85.

12. "GAO Document B-295402," Lockheed Martin Corporation, February 18, 2005; "Decision; Matter of: Lockheed Martin Corporation," February 18, 2005, http://www.gao.gov/decisions/bidpro/295402.htm.

13. John Byrne, "Fall from Grace," *BusinessWeek,* August 12, 2002, 50–56.

14. Press release: "A World Built on Bribes?" March 2005, http://www.transparency.org/pressreleases_archive/2005/2005.03.16.gcr_relaunch.html.

15. Ira Winkler, *Corporate Espionage: What It Is, Why It's Happening in Your Company, What You Must Do About It* (New York: Prima, 1997); Ira Winkler, *Spies Among Us: How to Stop the Spies, Terrorists, Hackers, and Criminals You Don't Even Know You Encounter Every Day* (Indianapolis: Wiley, 2005); Kevin D. Mitnick and William L. Simon, *The Art of Intrusion: The Real Stories Behind the Exploits of*

Hackers, Intruders and Deceivers (Indianapolis: Wiley, 2005).

16. "U.S. Equal Employment Opportunity Commission: An Overview," U.S. Equal Employment Opportunity Commission, www.eeoc.gov/overview.html (accessed February 4, 2003).

17. Bureau of the Census, *Statistical Abstract of the United States, 2001* (Washington, DC: Government Printing Office, 2002), 17.

18. Randall Smith, "African-American Broker Sues Alleging Bias at Merrill Lynch," *Wall Street Journal,* December 1, 2005, C3.

19. John C. Hendrickson, "EEOC Charges Sidley & Austin with Age Discrimination," Equal Employment Opportunity Commission, January 13, 2005, http://www.eeoc.gov/press/1-13-05.html.

20. Sue Shellenberger, "Work and Family," *Wall Street Journal,* May 23, 2001, B1.

21. "What Is Affirmative Action?" HR Content Library, October 12, 2001, www.hrnext.com/content/view.cfm?articles_id=2007&subs_id=32.

22. "What Affirmative Action Is (and What It Is Not)," National Partnership for Women & Families, www.nationalpartnership.org/content.cfm?L1=202&DBT=Documents&NewsItemID=289&HeaderTitle=Affirmative%20Action (accessed February 4, 2003).

23. "What Is Affirmative Action?"

24. "What Affirmative Action Is (and What It Is Not)."

25. Debbie Thorne McAlister, O. C. Ferrell, and Linda Ferrell, *Business and Society: A Strategic Approach to Social Responsibility,* 2nd ed. (Boston: Houghton Mifflin, 2005), 255–259.

26. Joe Millman, "Delayed Recognition; Arab-Americans Haven't Put Much Effort into Advancing Their Rights as a Minority. Until Relatively Recently, That Is." *Wall Street Journal,* November 14, 2005, R8.

27. See http://www.eeoc.gov/stats/harass.html for EEOC statistics.

28. Paula N. Rubin, "Civil Rights and Criminal Justice: Primer on Sexual Harassment Series: NIJ Research in Action," October 1995, http://www.ncjrs.org/txtfiles/harass.txt.

29. *Zabkowicz v. West Bend Co.,* 589 F. Supp. 780, 784, 35 EPD Par. 34, 766 (E.D. Wis. 1984).

30. Iddo Landau, "The Law and Sexual Harassment," *Business Ethics Quarterly* 15, no. 2 (2005): 531–536.

31. "Enhancements and Justice: Problems in Determining the Requirements of Justice in a Genetically Transformed Society," *Kennedy Institute Ethics Journal* 15, no. 1 (2005): 3–38.

32. "EEOC Settles Sexual Harassment and Retaliation Case for $1 Million," June 29, 2004, http://www.epexperts.com/print.php?sid=1515.

33. William T. Neese, O. C. Ferrell, and Linda Ferrell, "An Analysis of Mail and Wire Fraud Cases Related to Marketing Communication: Implications for Corporate Citizenship," working paper, 2003.

34. "Snapshot," *USA Today,* October 3, 2002.

35. Paul Davies, "Former Refco Officers Are Sued," *Wall Street Journal,* November 15, 2005, C3.

36. Matt Kranz, "More Earnings Restatements on Way," *USA Today,* October 25, 2002, 3B.

37. Nicole Bullock, "Qwest's Credit Ratings Reflect Risks Despite Recent Debt Swap," *Wall Street Journal,* December 30, 2002, B4.

38. Cassell Bryan-Low, "Accounting Firms Face Backlash over the Tax Shelters They Sold," *Wall Street Journal* online, February 7, 2003, http://online.wsj.com.

39. "WorldCom Finds Another $3.3B in Errors," CNN, August 8, 2002, www.cnn.com/2002/BUSINESS/asia/08/08/US.worldcom.biz/index.html.

40. *Gillette Co. v. Wilkinson Sword, Inc.,* 89-CV-3586, 1991 U.S. Dist. Lexis 21006, *6 (S.D.N.Y. January 9, 1991).

41. *Am. Council of Certified Podiatric Physicians & Surgeons v. Am. Bd. of Podiatric Surgery, Inc.,* 185 F.3d 606, 616 (6th Cir. 1999); *Johnson & Johnson-Merck Consumer Pharms. Co. v. Rhone-Poulenc Rorer Pharms., Inc.,* 19 F.3d 125, 129–30 (3d Cir. 1994); *Coca-Cola Co. v. Tropicana Prods., Inc.,* 690 F.2d 312, 317 (2d Cir. 1982).

42. Jeff Bater, "FTC Says Companies Falsely Claim Cellphone Patches Provide Protection," *Wall Street Journal* online, February 21, 2002, http://online.wsj.com.

43. Archie B. Carroll, *Business and Society: Ethics and Stakeholder Management* (Cincinnati: South-Western, 1989), 228–230.

44. "Netgear Settles Suit over Speed Claims," *Wall Street Journal,* November 28, 2005, C5.

45. "AT&T Settles Lawsuit Against Reseller Accused of Slamming," *Business Wire,* via America Online, May 26, 1998.

46. "Newsletter; Federal Trade Commission Report: ID Theft #1 Complaint," February 2005, http://www.machine-solution.com/_Article+FTC+ID+Theft.html.

47. "Retail Theft and Inventory Shrinkage," *What You Need to Know about . . . Retail Industry,* http://retailindustry.about.com/library/weekly/02/aa021126a.htm (accessed February 6, 2003).

48. Daryl Koehn, "Consumer Fraud: The Hidden Threat," University of St. Thomas, www.stthom.edu/cbes/commentary/HBJCONFRAUD.html (accessed February 6, 2003).

49. Robert Tomsho, "Two Plead Guilty to Fraud Charges Related to Charter One Acquisition," *Wall Street Journal,* November 4, 2005.

50. Anna Wilde Mathews, "Copyrights on Web Content Are Backed," *Wall Street Journal,* October 27, 2000, B10.

51. "Today's Briefing," *Commercial Appeal,* November 15, 2000, C1.

52. Electronic Protection Information Center, http://www.epic.org/crypto/ (accessed June 10, 2006).

53. Nora J. Rifon, Robert LaRose, and Sejung Marina Choi, "Your Privacy Is Sealed: Effects of Web Privacy Seals on Trust and Personal Disclosures," *Journal of Consumer Affairs* 39, no. 2 (2002): 339–362.

54. Steven Ward, Kate Bridges, and Bill Chitty, "Do Incentives Matter? An Examination of On-line Privacy Concerns and Willingness to Provide Personal and Financial Information," *Journal of Marketing Communications* 11, no. 1 (2005): 21–40.

55. "Electronic Monitoring and Surveillance Survey: Many Companies Monitoring, Recording, Videotaping—and Firing—Employees," *New York Times,* May 18, 2005, via http://www.amanet.org/press/amanews/ems05.htm.

56. "Sonera Executive Is Arrested in a Widening Privacy Probe," *Wall Street Journal* online, November 22, 2002, http://online.wsj.com.

57. "Privacy (Employee)," Business for Social Responsibility, www.bsr.org/ (accessed February 6, 2003).

58. John Galvin, "The New Business Ethics," SmartBusinessMag.com (June 2000): 97.

59. "Ethical Issues in the Employer–Employee Relationship," *Society of Financial Service Professionals,* www.financialpro.org/press/Ethics/es2000/Ethics_Survey_2000_Report_FINAL.cfm (accessed February 6, 2003).

60. Mitch Wagner, "Google's Pixie Dust," *InformationWeek,* issue 1061 (2005): 98.

61. Stephenie Steitzer, "Commercial Web Sites Cut Back on Collections of Personal Data," *Wall Street Journal,* March 28, 2002, http://online.wsj.com.

62. Christopher Conkey, "FTC Goes After Firm That Installs Spyware Secretly," *Wall Street Journal,* October 6, 2005, D4.

63. Eve M. Caudill and Patrick E. Murphy, "Consumer Online Privacy: Legal and Ethical Issues," *Journal of Public Policy & Marketing* 19 (2000): 7.

64. Galvin, "The New Business Ethics," 98.

65. Steitzer, "Commercial Web Sites Cut Back on Collections of Personal Data."

66. Christopher Conkey, "Credit-Card Use Is Up Despite Concern About Fraud," *Wall Street Journal,* October 6, 2005, D2.

67. Sarah Ellison, "Why Kraft Decided to Ban Some Food Ads to Children," *Wall Street Journal,* October 31, 2005, A1.

Chapter 4

1. "Targeting Illegal Tax Shelters," Democratic Leadership Council, http://www.dlc.org/ndol_ci.cfm?kaid=139&subid=900082&contentid=252601 (accessed January 14, 2009).

2. Kate Kaye, "Failed Deals and Ad Targeting Controversy Drew Attention in '08," *ClickZ News,* December 31, 2008, http://www.clickz.com/3632230 (accessed January 14, 2009).

3. "Drug Firms Agree to Settle Lawsuit over Cardizem," *Wall Street Journal,* January 28, 2003, A1.

4. Stephen Scheibal, "Civic Group Takes Issue with Chain Bookstore," *Austin American-Statesman* online, December 11, 2002, www.austin360.com/statesman/.

5. Gary Martin, "Clear Channel Accused of Stifling Competition, Bullying Musicians," *Austin American-Statesman* online, January 31, 2003, www.austin360.com/statesman/; Yochi J. Dreazen and Joe Flint, "FCC Eases Media-Ownership Caps, Clearing the Way for New Mergers," *Wall Street Journal* online, June 3, 2003, http://online.wsj.com.

6. Gregory T. Gundlach, "Price Predation: Legal Limits and Antitrust Considerations," *Journal of Public Policy & Marketing* 14 (1995): 278.

7. Quoted in "Software Publishers Association Applauds Department of Justice Antitrust Competition Action; Department Acts in Support of Software Industry Competition Principles," PRNewswire.com, May 18, 1998.

8. "Store Files Antitrust Lawsuit Against Microsoft," PRNewswire.com, May 18, 1998.

9. Don Clark, Mark Wigfield, Nick Wingfield, and Rebecca Buckman, "Judge Approves Most of Pact, in Legal Victory for Microsoft," *Wall Street Journal* online, November 1, 2002, http://online.wsj.com; Kim Peterson, Brier Dudley, and Bradley Meacham, "Microsoft Settles with California for $1 Billion," *Seattle Times,* January 11, 2003, A1, A10.

10. "10 Ways to Combat Corporate Espionage," *About .com,* http://bizsecurity.about.com/od/ physicalsecurity/a/Espionage.htm (accessed January 14, 2009).

11. "A Child Shall Lead the Way: Marketing to Youths," *Credit Union Executive,* May–June 1993, 6–8.

12. Rich Stim, "Dad, What's a Cookie? Complying with COPPA," Nolos Patent, Copyright and Trademark Blog, February 22, 2008, http://www .patentcopyrighttrademarkblog.com/2008/02/ dad-whats-a-cookie-complying-w.html (accessed January 14, 2009).

13. Otto Krusius, "From Out of the Mouses of Babes," *Kiplinger's,* November 2000, 32.

14. "Women's Earnings as a Percentage of Men's 1951–2007," U.S. Women's Bureau and the National Committee on Pay Equity, http://www.pay-equity.org (accessed January 14, 2009).

15. Steve Alexander, "Wal-Mart to Pay $54 Million to Settle Suit Over Unpaid Work," *Minneapolis Star Tribune,* December 9, 2008, http://www.startribune.com/ business/35819094.html (accessed January 14, 2009).

16. Steve Alexander, "Wal-Mart to Pay $54 Million to Settle Suit Over Unpaid Work," *Minneapolis Star Tribune,* December 9, 2008, http://www.startribune.com/ business/35819094.html (accessed January 14, 2009).

17. Michael Arndt, Wendy Zellner, and Peter Coy, "Too Much Corporate Power," *BusinessWeek,* September 11, 2000, 149.

18. Dave Bryan, "Royal Caribbean Guards Against Pollution," *USA Today* online, www.usatoday.com/ life/travel/lt092.htm (accessed October 13, 2000).

19. John Yaukey, "Discarded Computers Create Waste Problem," *USA Today* online, www.usatoday.com/ news/ndsmonl4.htm (accessed October 13, 2000).

20. Andrew Park, "Stemming the Tide of Tech Trash," *BusinessWeek,* October 7, 2002, 36A–36F.

21. "Corporate Reform Bill Passed," CNN, July 25, 2002, www.cnn.com.

22. Penelope Patsuris, "The Corporate Scandal Sheet," *Forbes* online, August 26, 2002, www.forbes.com/ home/2002/07/25/accountingtracker.html.

23. Nelson D. Schwartz, "The Looting of Kmart, Part 2," *Fortune,* February 17, 2003, 30; Elliot Blair Smith, "Probe: Former Kmart CEO 'Grossly Derelict,'" *USA Today,* January 27, 2003, B1.

24. David McHugh, "Business Wants to Restore Public Trust," America Online, January 28, 2003.

25. Amy Borrus, "Learning to Love Sarbanes–Oxley," *BusinessWeek,* November 21, 2005, 126–128.

26. Stephen Taub, "SEC:1300 'Whistles' Blown Each Day: Most Tips Concerning Accounting Problems at Public Companies; 'A Tremendous Source of Leads,'" CFO.com, August 3, 2004, http://www.cfo.com/ article.cfm/3015607 (accessed March 15, 2006).

27. Julie Homer, "Overblown: In the Wake of Sarbanes–Oxley, Some Serious Misconceptions Have Arisen About What Blowing the Whistle Actually Means," CFO.com, October 1, 2003.

28. David Katz, "A Tough Act to Follow: What CFOs Really Think About Sarbox—and How They Would Fix the *!#& Thing," CFO.com, March 15, 2006, http://www.cfo.com/article.cfm/5598373 (accessed March 16, 2006).

29. Tim Reason, "Feeling the Pain: Are the Benefits of Sarbanes–Oxley Worth the Cost?" CFO.com, May 2005, http://www.cfo.com/article.cfm/3909558 (accessed March 15, 2006).

30. "Sarbanes–Oxley Act Improves Investor Confidence, but at a Cost," *CPA Journal,* October 2005, http:// www.nysscpa.org/ cpajournal/2005/ 1005/perspectives/p19.htm (accessed March 16, 2006).

31. Tricia Bisoux, "The Sarbanes–Oxley Effect," *BizEd,* July/August 2005, 24–29.

32. Ibid.

33. James C. Hyatt, "Birth of the Ethics Industry," *Business Ethics* (Summer 2005): 20–27.

34. Amy Borrus, "Learning to Love Sarbanes–Oxley," *BusinessWeek,* November 21, 2005, 126–128.

35. Win Swenson, "The Organizational Guidelines' 'Carrot and Stick' Philosophy, and Their Focus on 'Effective' Compliance," in *Corporate Crime in America: Strengthening the "Good Citizenship" Corporation* (Washington, DC: U.S. Sentencing Commission, 1995), 17–26.

36. *United States Code Service* (Lawyers' Edition), 18 U.S.C.S. Appendix, Sentencing Guidelines for the United States Courts (Rochester, NY: Lawyers Cooperative Publishing, 1995), sec. 8A.1.

37. O. C Ferrell and Linda Ferrell, "Current Developments in Managing Organizational Ethics and

Compliance Initiatives," University of Wyoming, white paper, Bill Daniels Business Ethics Initiative 2006.

38. Ibid.

39. Lynn Brewer, "Capitalizing on the Value of Integrity: An Integrated Model to Standardize the Measure of Non-financial Performance as an Assessment of Corporate Integrity," in *Managing Risks for Corporate Integrity. How to Survive an Ethical Misconduct Disaster,* ed. Lynn Brewer, Robert Chandler, and O. C. Ferrell (Mason, OH: Thomson/Texere, 2006), 233–277.

40. Poulomi Saha, "Enabling Customers: McDonald's New Packaging Initiative Has Been Welcomed by Anti-obesity Campaigners," *Ethical Corporation,* December 2005, 13–14.

41. Ingrid Murro Botero, "Charitable Giving Has 4 Big Benefits," *Business Journal of Phoenix* online, January 1, 1999, www.bizjournals.com/phoenix/stories/1999/01/04/smallb3.html.

42. "2004 Contributions: $248.52 Billion by Source of Contributions," Giving USA Foundation–American Association of Fundraising Counsel (AAFRC) Trust for Philanthropy/Giving USA 2005, http://www.aafrc.org/gusa/chartbysource.html (accessed June 27, 2006).

43. Marjorie Kelly, "100 Best Corporate Citizens 2005," *Business Ethics* (Spring 2005): 25.

44. "Wal-Mart Giving," Walmartfacts.com http://www.walmartfacts.com/community/walmart-foundation.aspx (accessed March 17, 2006).

45. Steve Hilton, "Bisto: Altogether now, 'Aah . . . ,' " *Ethical Corporation,* December 2005, 50.

46. "McDonald's Employees Honor Ray Kroc's Birthday by Giving Back to Communities Nation-wide," PRNewswire.com (accessed October 13, 2000).

47. "CSR Case Study: The Home Depot: Giving Back to Communities," Interdepartmental Working Group on Corporate Social Responsibility (CSR), http://www.fivewinds.com/uploadedfiles_shared/CSRHomeDepot.pdf (accessed March 17, 2006).

48. "About Home Depot, Community Relations Quick Facts, Declaration of Independence Road Trip," http://www.independenceroadtrip.org/Media/faqsheets_homedepot.html (accessed March 17, 2006).

49. Swenson, "The Organizational Guidelines' 'Carrot and Stick' Philosophy."

Chapter 5

1. Thomas M. Jones, "Ethical Decision Making by Individuals in Organizations: An Issue-Contingent Model," *Academy of Management Review* 16 (February 1991): 366–395; O. C. Ferrell and Larry G. Gresham, "A Contingency Framework for Understanding Ethical Decision Making in Marketing," *Journal of Marketing* 49 (Summer 1985): 87–96; O. C. Ferrell, Larry G. Gresham, and John Fraedrich, "A Synthesis of Ethical Decision Models for Marketing," *Journal of Macromarketing* 9 (Fall 1989): 55–64; Shelby D. Hunt and Scott Vitell, "A General Theory of Marketing Ethics," *Journal of Macromarketing* 6 (Spring 1986): 5–16; William A. Kahn, "Toward an Agenda for Business Ethics Research," *Academy of Management Review* 15 (April 1990): 311–328; Linda K. Trevino, "Ethical Decision Making in Organizations: A Person-Situation Interactionist Model," *Academy of Management Review* 11 (March 1986): 601–617.

2. Jones, "Ethical Decision Making," 367, 372.

3. Donald P. Robin, R. Eric Reidenbach, and P. J. Forrest, "The Perceived Importance of an Ethical Issue as an Influence on the Ethical Decision-Making of Ad Managers," *Journal of Business Research* 35 (January 1996): 17.

4. "Lead Attorneys in Enron Shareholder Litigation: Wall St. Banks Operated Giant Ponzi Scheme," Corporate Governance Fund Report, August 14, 2002, www.cgfreport.com/NewsFlashMilberg.htm.

5. Roselie McDevitt and Joan Van Hise, "Influences in Ethical Dilemmas of Increasing Intensity," *Journal of Business Ethics* 40 (October 2002): 261–274.

6. Anusorn Singhapakdi, Scott J. Vitell, and George R. Franke, "Antecedents, Consequences, and Mediating Effects of Perceived Moral Intensity and Personal Moral Philosophies," *Journal of the Academy of Marketing Science* 27 (Winter 1999): 19.

7. Ibid.

8. Ibid.

9. Ibid., 17.

10. "2005 Draft Remarks of Attorney General Alberto Gonzales," Adelphia Victims Press Conference, http://www.usdoj.gov/ag/speeches/2005/draft_remarks_ag042505.htm (accessed February 11, 2006).

11. T. W. Loe, L. Ferrell, and P. Mansfield, "A Review of Empirical Studies Assessing Ethical

Decision-Making in Business," *Journal of Business Ethics* 25 (2000): 185–204.

12. Michael J. O'Fallon, and Kenneth D. Butterfield, "A Review of the Empirical Ethical Decision-Making Literature: 1996–2003," *Journal of Business Ethics* 59 (July 2005): 375–413; P. M. J. Christie, J. I. G. Kwon, P. A. Stoeberl, and R. Baumhart, "A Cross-Cultural Comparison of Ethical Attitudes of Business Managers: India, Korea and the United States," *Journal of Business Ethics* 46 (September 2003): 263–287; G. Fleischman and S. Valentine, "Professionals' Tax Liability and Ethical Evaluations in an Equitable Relief Innocent Spouse Case," *Journal of Business Ethics* 42 (January 2003): 27–44; A. Singhapakdi, K. Karande, C. P. Rao, and S. J. Vitell, "How Important Are Ethics and Social Responsibility? A Multinational Study of Marketing Professionals," *European Journal of Marketing* 35 (2001): 133–152.

13. R. W. Armstrong, "The Relationship Between Culture and Perception of Ethical Problems in International Marketing," *Journal of Business Ethics* 15 (November 1996): 1199–1208; J. Cherry, M. Lee, and C. S. Chien, "A Cross-Cultural Application of a Theoretical Model of Business Ethics: Bridging the Gap Between Theory and Data," *Journal of Business Ethics* 44 (June 2003): 359–376; B. Kracher, A. Chatterjee, and A. R. Lundquist, "Factors Related to the Cognitive Moral Development of Business Students and Business Professionals in India and the United States: Nationality, Education, Sex and Gender," *Journal of Business Ethics* 35 (February 2002): 255–268.

14. J. M. Larkin, "The Ability of Internal Auditors to Identify Ethical Dilemmas," *Journal of Business Ethics* 23 (February 2000): 401–409; D. Peterson, A. Rhoads, and B. C. Vaught, "Ethical Beliefs of Business Professionals: A Study of Gender, Age and External Factors," *Journal of Business Ethics* 31 (June 2001): 225–232; M. A. Razzaque and T. P. Hwee, "Ethics and Purchasing Dilemma: A Singaporean View," *Journal of Business Ethics* 35 (February 2002): 307–326.

15. J. Cherry and J. Fraedrich, "An Empirical Investigation of Locus of Control and the Structure of Moral Reasoning: Examining the Ethical Decision-Making Processes of Sales Managers," *Journal of Personal Selling and Sales Management* 20 (Summer 2000): 173–188; M. C. Reiss and K. Mitra, "The Effects of Individual Difference Factors on the Acceptability of Ethical and Unethical Workplace Behaviors," *Journal of Business Ethics* 17 (October 1998): 1581–1593.

16. O. C. Ferrell and Linda Ferrell, "Role of Ethical Leadership in Organizational Performance," *Journal of Management Systems* 13 (2001): 64–78.

17. James Weber and Julie E. Seger, "Influences upon Organizational Ethical Subclimates: A Replication Study of a Single Firm at Two Points in Time," *Journal of Business Ethics* 41 (November 2002): 69–84.

18. Sean Valentine, Lynn Godkin, and Margaret Lucero, "Ethical Context, Organizational Commitment, and Person-Organization Fit," *Journal of Business Ethics* 41 (December 2002): 349–360.

19. Bruce H. Drake, Mark Meckler, and Debra Stephens, "Transitional Ethics: Responsibilities of Supervisors for Supporting Employee Development," *Journal of Business Ethics* 38 (June 2002): 141–155.

20. Ferrell and Gresham, "A Contingency Framework," 87–96.

21. R. C. Ford and W. D. Richardson, "Ethical Decision-making: A Review of the Empirical Literature," *Journal of Business Ethics* 13 (March 1994): 205–221; Loe, Ferrell, and Mansfield, "A Review of Empirical Studies."

22. National Business Ethics Survey, *How Employees Perceive Ethics at Work* (Washington, DC: Ethics Resource Center, 2000), 30.

23. "Employee Theft Solutions," *The Shulman Center*, http://www.employeetheftsolutions.com/ (accessed January 14, 2009).

24. Niraj Sheth, Jackie Range, and Geeta Anand, "Corporate Scandal Shakes India," *Wall Street Journal*, January 8, 2009, http://online.wsj.com/article/SB123131072970260401.html (accessed January 9, 2009).

25. National Business Ethics Survey, 30.

26. R. Eric Reidenbach and Donald P. Robin, *Ethics and Profits* (Englewood Cliffs, NJ: Prentice-Hall, 1989), 92.

27. "Small Virtues: Entrepreneurs Are More Ethical," *BusinessWeek* online, March 8, 2000, www.businessweek.com/smallbiz/0003/ib3670029.htm?scriptFramed.

28. Constance E. Bagley, "The Ethical Leader's Decision Tree," *Harvard Business Review*, January–February 2003, 18.

29. John Byrne, "How Al Dunlap Self-Destructed," *BusinessWeek*, July 6, 1998, 44–45.

30. "Sunbeam Ex-CEO 'Chainsaw Al' Dunlap Settles SEC Case," Securities Class Action Clearinghouse, Stanford Law School press release, September 4, 2002, http://securities.stanford.edu/news-archive/2002/20020904_Settlement03_Roland.htm.

31. Daniel J. Brass, Kenneth D. Butterfield, and Bruce C. Skaggs, "Relationship and Unethical Behavior: A Social Science Perspective," *Academy of Management Review* 23 (January 1998): 14–31.

32. Andrew Kupfor, "Mike Armstrong's AT&T: Will the Pieces Come Together?" *Fortune,* April 26, 1999, 89.

33. From *Managing Risks for Corporate Integrity: How to Survive an Ethical Misconduct Disaster* 1st edition by Brewer, Chandler, and Ferrell. Copyright © 2006. Reprinted with permission of South-Western, a division of Thomson Learning: www.thomsonrights.com. Fax 800 730-2215.

34. J. M. Burns, *Leadership* (New York: Harper & Row, 1985).

35. Royston Greenwood, Roy Suddaby, and C. R. Hinings, "Theorizing Change: The Role of Professional Associations in the Transformation of Institutionalized Fields," *Academy of Management Journal* 45 (January 2002): 58–80.

36. "WorldCom Chief Outlines Initial Turnaround Strategy," *Wall Street Journal* online, January 14, 2003, http://online.wsj.com.

37. Stephen R. Covey, *The 7 Habits of Highly Effective People* (New York: Simon & Schuster, 1989).

38. Archie B. Carroll, "Ethical Leadership: From Moral Managers to Moral Leaders," in *Rights, Relationships and Responsibilities,* Vol. 1, ed. O. C. Ferrell, Sheb True, and Lou Pelton (Kennesaw, GA: Kennesaw State University, 2003), 7–17.

39. Andy Serwer, "Wal-Mart: Bruised in Bentonville," *Fortune* online, April 4, 2005, www.fortune.com/fortune/subs/print/0,15935,1044608,00.html.

40. Thomas I. White, "Character Development and Business Ethics Education," in *Rights, Relationships and Responsibilities,* Vol. 1, ed. O. C. Ferrell, Sheb True, and Lou Pelton (Kennesaw, GA: Kennesaw State University, 2003), 137–166.

41. Carroll, "Ethical Leadership," 11.

42. Keith H. Hammonds, "Harry Kraemer's Moment of Truth," *Fast Company* online, November 2002, www.fastcompany.com/online/64/kraemer.html.

43. Carroll, "Ethical Leadership," 11.

44. Chad Terhune, "Pepsi, Vowing Diversity, Isn't Just Image Polish, Seeks Inclusive Culture," *Wall Street Journal,* April 19, 2005, B1.

45. Carroll, "Ethical Leadership," 12.

46. Steve Quinn, "Wal-Mart Green with Energy," *[Fort Collins] Coloradoan,* July 24, 2005, E1.

47. Brent Smith, Michael W. Grojean, Christian Resick, and Marcus Dickson, "Leaders, Values and Organizational Climate: Examining Leadership Strategies for Establishing an Organizational Climate Regarding Ethics," *Journal of Business Ethics,* as reported at "Research @ Rice: Lessons from Enron—Ethical Conduct Begins at the Top," Rice University, June 15, 2005, www.explore.rice.edu/explore/NewsBot.asp?MODE=VIEW&ID=7478&SnID=878108660.

48. "New Belgium Brewing: Environmental and Social Responsibilities," New Belgium Brewing Company, www.newbelgium.com (accessed August 25, 2005); Greg Owsley, "The Necessity for Aligning Brand with Corporate Ethics," in *Fulfilling Our Obligation: Perspectives on Teaching Business Ethics,* ed. Sheb L. True, Linda Ferrell, and O. C. Ferrell (Kennesaw, GA: Kennesaw University Press, 2005), 127–139.

49. Herb Baum and Tammy Kling, "The Transparent Leader," in LeaderPoints, Centerpoints for Leaders, December 2004, www.centerpointforleaders.org/newsletters/dec04.html.

50. Monica Langley, "Course Correction: Behind Citigroup Departures: A Culture Shift by CEO Prince," *Wall Street Journal,* August 24, 2005, A1.

Chapter 6

1. James R. Rest, *Moral Development Advances in Research and Theory* (New York: Praeger, 1986), 1.

2. "Business Leaders, Politicians and Academics Dub Corporate Irresponsibility 'An Attack on America from Within,'" *Business Wire,* November 7, 2002, via America Online.

3. Abhijit Biswas, Jane W. Licata, Daryl McKee, Chris Pullig, and Christopher Daughtridge, "The Recycling Cycle: An Empirical Examination of Consumer Waste Recycling and Recycling Shopping Behaviors," *Journal of Public Policy & Marketing* 19 (2000): 93.

4. "Court Says Businesses Liable for Harassing on the Job," *Commercial Appeal,* June 27, 1998, A1.

5. Richard Brandt, *Ethical Theory* (Englewood Cliffs, NJ: Prentice-Hall, 1959), 253–254.

6. J. J. C. Smart and B. Williams, *Utilitarianism: For and Against* (Cambridge, UK: Cambridge University Press, 1973), 4.

7. C. E. Harris, Jr., *Applying Moral Theories* (Belmont, CA: Wadsworth, 1986), 127–128.

8. Gordon Fairclough, "Tainting of Milk Is Open Secret in China," *Wall Street Journal,* November 3, 2008, http://online.wsj.com/article/SB122567367498791713.html (accessed January 13, 2009).

9. Immanuel Kant, "Fundamental Principles of the Metaphysics of Morals," in *Problems of Moral Philosophy: An Introduction,* 2nd ed., ed. Paul W. Taylor (Encino, CA: Dickenson, 1972), 229.

10. Example adapted from Harris, *Applying Moral Theories,* 128–129.

11. Gerald F. Cavanaugh, Dennis J. Moberg, and Manuel Velasquez, "The Ethics of Organizational Politics," *Academy of Management Review* 6 (1981): 363–374; U.S. Bill of Rights, www.law.cornell.edu/constitution/constitution.billofrights.html (accessed February 17, 2003).

12. Marie Brenner, "The Man Who Knew Too Much," *Vanity Fair,* May 1996, available at www.jeffreywigand.com/*insider/*vanityfair.html (accessed February 17, 2003).

13. Norman E. Bowie and Thomas W. Dunfee, "Confronting Morality in Markets," *Journal of Business Ethics* 38 (2002): 381–393.

14. Kant, "Fundamental Principles," 229.

15. Thomas E. Weber, "To Opt In or Opt Out: That Is the Question When Mulling Privacy," *Wall Street Journal,* October 23, 2000, B1.

16. C. R. Bateman, J. P Fraedrich, and R. Iyer, "The Integration and Testing of the Janus-Headed Model Within Marketing," *Journal of Business Research* 56 (2003): 587–596; J. B. DeConinck and W. F. Lewis, "The Influence of Deontological and Teleological Considerations and Ethical Culture on Sales Managers' Intentions to Reward or Punish Sales Force Behavior," *Journal of Business Ethics* 16 (1997): 497–506; J. Kujala, "A Multidimensional Approach to Finnish Managers' Moral Decision-Making," *Journal of Business Ethics* 34 (2001): 231–254; K. C. Rallapalli, S. J. Vitell, and J. H. Barnes, "The Influence of Norms on Ethical Judgments and Intentions: An Empirical Study of Marketing Professionals," *Journal of Business*

Research 43 (1998): 157–168; M. Shapeero, H. C. Koh, and L. N. Killough, "Underreporting and Premature Sign-Off in Public Accounting," *Managerial Auditing Journal* 18 (2003): 478–489.

17. William K. Frankena, *Ethics* (Englewood Cliffs: Prentice-Hall, 1963).

18. R. E. Reidenbach and D. P. Robin, "Toward the Development of a Multidimensional Scale for Improving Evaluations of Business Ethics," *Journal of Business Ethics* 9, no. 8 (1980): 639–653.

19. Patrick E. Murphy and Gene R. Laczniak, "Emerging Ethical Issues Facing Marketing Researchers," *Marketing Research* 4, no. 2 (1992): 6–11.

20. T. K. Bass and Barnett G. Brown, "Religiosity, Ethical Ideology, and Intentions to Report a Peer's Wrongdoing," *Journal of Business Ethics* 15, no. 11 (1996): 1161–1174; R. Z. Elias, "Determinants of Earnings Management Ethics Among Accountants," *Journal of Business Ethics* 40, no. 1 (2002): 33–45; Y. Kim, "Ethical Standards and Ideology Among Korean Public Relations Practitioners," *Journal of Business Ethics* 42, no. 3 (2003): 209–223; E. Sivadas, S. B. Kleiser, J. Kellaris, and R. Dahlstrom, "Moral Philosophy, Ethical Evaluations, and Sales Manager Hiring Intentions," *Journal of Personal Selling & Sales Management* 23, no. 1 (2003): 7–21.

21. Manuel G. Velasquez, *Business Ethics Concepts and Cases,* 4th ed. (Upper Saddle River, NJ: Prentice-Hall, 1998), 132–133.

22. Ibid.

23. Adapted from Robert C. Solomon, "Victims of Circumstances? A Defense of Virtue Ethics in Business," *Business Ethics Quarterly* 13, no. 1 (2003): 43–62.

24. Ian Maitland, "Virtuous Markets: The Market as School of the Virtues," *Business Ethics Quarterly* (January 1997): 97.

25. Ibid.

26. Stefanie E. Naumann and Nathan Bennett, "A Case for Procedural Justice Climate: Development and Test of a Multilevel Model," *Academy of Management Journal* 43 (2000): 881–889.

27. Joel Brockner, "Making Sense of Procedural Fairness: How High Procedural Fairness Can Reduce or Heighten the Influence of Outcome Favorability," *Academy of Management Review* 27 (2002): 58–76.

28. "Wainwright Bank and Trust Company Award for Social Justice Inside and Out," *Business Ethics,* November/December 1998, 11.

29. John Fraedrich and O. C. Ferrell, "Cognitive Consistency of Marketing Managers in Ethical

Situations," *Journal of the Academy of Marketing Science* 20 (1992): 245–252.

30. Manuel Velasquez, Claire Andre, Thomas Shanks, S. J., and Michael J. Meyer, "Thinking Ethically: A Framework for Moral Decision Making," *Issues in Ethics* (Winter 1996): 2–5.

31. Lawrence Kohlberg, "Stage and Sequence: The Cognitive Developmental Approach to Socialization," in *Handbook of Socialization Theory and Research,* ed. D. A. Goslin (Chicago: Rand McNally, 1969), 347–480.

32. Adapted from Kohlberg, "Stage and Sequence."

33. Clare M. Pennino, "Is Decision Style Related to Moral Development Among Managers in the U.S.?" *Journal of Business Ethics* 41 (2002): 337–347.

34. A. K. M. Au and D. S. N. Wong, "The Impact of Guanxi on the Ethical Decision-Making Process of Auditors—An Exploratory Study on Chinese CPA's in Hong Kong," *Journal of Business Ethics* 28, no. 1 (2000): 87–93; D. P Robin, G. Gordon, C. Jordan, and E. Reidenback, "The Empirical Performance of Cognitive Moral Development in Predicating Behavioral Intent," *Business Ethics Quarterly* 6, no. 4 (1996): 493–515; M. Shapeero, H. C. Koh, and L. N. Killough, "Underreporting and Premature Sign-Off in Public Accounting," *Managerial Auditing Journal* 18, no. 6 (1996): 478–489; N. Uddin and P. R. Gillett, "The Effects of Moral Reasoning and Self-Monitoring on CFO Intentions to Report Fraudulently on Financial Statements," *Journal of Business Ethics* 40, no. 1 (2002): 15–32.

35. David O. Friedrichs, *Trusted Criminals, White Collar Crime in Contemporary Society* (Belmont, CA: Wadsworth, 1996).

36. Kari & Associates, White Collar Crime website, http://www.karisable.com/crwc.htm (accessed March 9, 2006).

37. Diana B. Henriques and Jack Healy, "Madoff's Bail Revoked After Guilty Pleas to All Charges," *The New York Times,* March 12, 2009, http://www.nytimes.com/2009/03/13/business/13madoff.html?hp (accessed March 12, 2009).

38. H. J. Eysenck, "Personality and Crime: Where Do We Stand?" *Psychology, Crime & Law* 2, no. 3 (1996): 143–152; S. J. Listwan, *Personality and Criminal Behavior: Reconsidering the Individual,* UMI Digital Dissertations Abstracts, 2000, http://www.lib.umi.com/dissertations/.

39. J. M. Rayburn and L. G. Rayburn, "Relationship Between Machiavellianism and Type A Personality and Ethical-Orientation," *Journal of Business Ethics* 15, no. 11 (1996): 1209–1219.

40. Quoted in Marjorie Kelly, "The Ethics Revolution," *Business Ethics,* Summer 2005, 6.

41. O. C. Ferrell and Larry G. Gresham, "A Contingency Framework for Understanding Ethical Decision Making in Marketing," *Journal of Marketing* 49 (2002): 261–274.

42. Thomas I. White, "Character Development and Business Ethics Education," in *Fulfilling Our Obligation: Perspectives on Teaching Business Ethics,* ed. Sheb L. True, Linda Ferrell, and O. C. Ferrell (Kennesaw, GA: Kennesaw State University Press, 2005), 165.

43. Ibid., 165–166.

Chapter 7

1. Richard Gibson, "McDonald's Faces the Costly Issue of Employee Rudeness," Dow Jones News Service, http://www.s-t.com/daily/07-01/07-15-01/b03bu066.htm (accessed March 30, 2006).

2. Richard L. Daft, *Organizational Theory and Design* (Cincinnati: South-Western, 2007).

3. Stanley M. Davis, quoted in Alyse Lynn Booth, "Who Are We?" *Public Relations Journal* (July 1985): 13–18.

4. T. E. Deal and A. A. Kennedy, *Corporate Culture: Rites and Rituals of Corporate Life* (Reading, MA: Addison-Wesley, 1982), 4.

5. G. Hofstede, "Culture's Consequences: International Differences," in *Work-Related Values* (Beverly Hills, CA: Sage, 1980), 25.

6. N. M. Tichy, "Managing Change Strategically: The Technical, Political and Cultural Keys," *Organizational Dynamics* (Autumn 1982): 59–80.

7. J. W. Lorsch, "Managing Culture: The Invisible Barrier to Strategic Change," *California Management Review* 28 (1986): 95–109.

8. "Transforming Our Culture: The Values for Success," Mutual of Omaha, www.careerlink.org/emp/mut/corp.htm (accessed February 19, 2003).

9. William Clay Ford, Jr., "A Message from the Chairman," Ford Motor Company, www.ford.com/en/ourCompany/corporateCitizenship/ourLearningJourney/message (accessed February 19, 2003); "GM and Ford: Roadmaps for Recovery,"

BusinessWeek online, March 14, 2006, http://www
.businessweek.com/print/investor/content/
mar2006/pi20060314_416862.htm (accessed
March 30, 2006).

10. "Southwest Airlines Adopt-a-Pilot Educational Program Encourages School-to-Career Path," PR
Newswire, February 6, 2006, www.southwest.com/
about_swa/press/prindex.html (accessed March 30,
2006).

11. N. K. Sethia and M. A. Von Glinow, "Arriving at
Four Cultures by Managing the Reward System," in
Gaining Control of the Corporate Culture (San Fran-
cisco: Jossey-Bass, 1985), 409.

12. Gigi Stone, "Are Pension Cuts Snuffing Out Workers' Dreams?" February 19, 2006, http://abcnews
.go.com/WNT/PersonalFinance/story?id=1636508
(accessed March 30, 2006).

13. Roger Yu, "Airlines' Performance Near 20-year
Low," *USA Today*, April 7, 2008, http://www
.usatoday.com/travel/flights/2008-04-06-airline
complaintsN.htm (accessed January 13, 2009).

14. "UPS Deploys 167 'Green' Trucks,"
http://www.pressroom.ups.com/pressreleases/
archives/archive/0,1363,4991,00.html (accessed
January 13, 2009).

15. "US: U.S. Foodservice Auditors Committed Misconduct—SEC," Reuters, February 16, 2006, www
.corpwatch.org/article.php?id=13287; www.hoovers
.com/u.s.-foodservice (accessed March 31, 2006).

16. Peter Lattman, "Boeing's Top Lawyer Spotlights
Company's Ethical Lapses," January 31, 2006,
http://blogs.wsj.com/law/2006/01/31/
boeings-top-lawyer-rips-into-his-company/
(accessed March 31, 2006).

17. Business Ethics: The Magazine of Corporate
Responsibility, http://www.business-ethics.com/
node/75 (accessed January 13, 2009); Green
Mountain Home Website, http://www.gmcr.com/
csr/AboutOurCompany.aspx (accessed January 13,
2009).

18. United Nations Millennium Development Website,
http://www.un.org/millenniumgoals/ (accessed
January 13, 2009).

19. Christopher Lawton, "Judge Sanctions Gateway
for Destroying Evidence," *Wall Street Journal*,
March 31, 2006, A3.

20. Isabelle Maignan, O. C. Ferrell, and Thomas Hult,
"Corporate Citizenship, Cultural Antecedents and
Business Benefit," *Journal of the Academy of Mar-
keting Science* 27 (1999): 455–469.

21. R. Eric Reidenbach and Donald P. Robin, *Ethics
and Profits* (Englewood Cliffs, NJ: Prentice-Hall,
1989), 92.

22. E. Sutherland and D. R. Cressey, *Principles of Criminology*, 8th ed. (Chicago: Lippincott, 1970), 114.

23. O. C. Ferrell and Larry G. Gresham, "A Contingency Framework for Understanding Ethical Decision Making in Marketing," *Journal of Marketing*
49 (1985): 90–91.

24. Edward Wong, "Shuttle Insulator Admits to Short-
cuts," *Austin American-Statesman* online, February
18, 2003, http://austin360.com/statesman.

25. James S. Bowman, "Managerial Ethics in Business
and Government," *Business Horizons* 19 (1976):
48–54; William C. Frederick and James Weber,
"The Value of Corporate Managers and Their Crit-
ics: An Empirical Description and Normative
Implications," in *Research in Corporate Social
Performance and Social Responsibility*, ed. William C.
Frederick and Lee E. Preston (Greenwich, CT: JAI
Press, 1987), 149–150; Linda K. Trevino and Stuart
Youngblood, "Bad Apples in Bad Barrels: A Causal
Analysis of Ethical Decision Making Behavior,"
Journal of Applied Psychology 75 (1990): 38.

26. Richard Lacavo and Amanda Ripley, "Persons of the
Year 2002—Cynthia Cooper, Coleen Rowley, and
Sherron Watkins," *Time* online, December 22,
2002, www.time.com/personoftheyear/2002;
Thomas S. Mulligan, "Whistle Blower Recounts Enron Tale," *Los Angeles Times* online, March 16,
2006, http://www.latimes.com/business/
la-fi-enron16mar16,1,5771701.story?ctrack=
1&cset=true (accessed April 3, 2006).

27. Mulligan, "Whistle Blower Recounts Enron Tale."

28. John W. Schoen, "Split CEO–Chairman Job, Says
Panel," MSNBC.com, January 9, 2003, www.msnbc
.com/news/857171.asp (accessed June 27, 2006).

29. "Former Wal-Mart Exec Files Complaints,"
CNN/Money, May 24, 2005, www.money.cnn.com.

30. "Making Your Whistleblower Case Succeed: Basic
Workings of Whistleblower Complaints,"
www.jameshoyer.com/practice_qui_tam.html?se=
Overture (accessed April 5, 2006).

31. Paula Dwyer and Dan Carney, with Amy Borrus,
Lorraine Woellert, and Christopher Palmeri, "Year
of the Whistleblower," *BusinessWeek*, December 16,
2002, 106–110.

32. Darren Dahl, "Learning to Love Whistleblowers,"
Inc., March 2006, 21–23.

33. John R. P. French and Bertram Ravin, "The Bases of Social Power," in *Group Dynamics: Research and Theory,* ed. Dorwin Cartwright (Evanston, IL: Row, Peterson, 1962), 607–623.

34. Lynn Brewer, Robert Chandler, and O. C. Ferrell, *Managing Risks for Corporate Integrity* (Mason, OH: Thomson/Texere, 2006), 35.

35. "Ex-Worldcom Comptroller Gets Prison Time," "Ex-Worldcom CFO Gets Five Years," CNN/ Money, August 11, 2005, www.money.cnn.com (accessed August 11, 2005).

36. Lyman W. Porter, "Job Attitudes in Management: II. Perceived Importance of Needs as a Foundation of Job Level," *Journal of Applied Psychology* 47 (1963): 141–148.

37. Clayton Alderfer, *Existence, Relatedness, and Growth* (New York: Free Press, 1972), 42–44.

38. Louis P. White and Long W. Lam, "A Proposed Infrastructural Model for the Establishment of Organizational Ethical Systems," *Journal of Business Ethics* 28 (2000): 35–42.

39. Gary Edmondson, Kate Carlisle, Inka Resch, Karen Anhalt, and Heidi Dawley, "Human Bondage," *BusinessWeek,* November 27, 2000, 147–160.

40. Stanley Holmes, "Cleaning Up Boeing," *Business-Week* online, March 13, 2006, http://www .businessweek.com/print/magazine/content/ 06_11/ b3975088.htm?chan=gl (accessed April 6, 2006).

41. Spencer Ante, "They're Hiring in Techland," *BusinessWeek* online, January 23, 2006, http://www .businessweek.com/print/technology/content/jan 2006/tc20060123_960426.htm (accessed April 6, 2006).

42. Joseph A. Belizzi and Ronald W. Hasty, "Supervising Unethical Sales Force Behavior: How Strong Is the Tendency to Treat Top Sales Performers Leniently?" *Journal of Business Ethics* 43 (2003): 337–351.

43. John Fraedrich and O. C. Ferrell, "Cognitive Consistency of Marketing Managers in Ethical Situations," *Journal of the Academy of Marketing Science* 20 (1992): 243–252.

44. Michael Connor, "Philip Morris: More Spent on Health Ads," Yahoo! News, May 23, 2000, http:// dailynews.yahoo.com/h/nm/2000523/bs/ tobacco_engle_1.html; "Philip Morris U.S.A. Expresses Confidence in Its Youth Smoking Prevention Advertising Based on Extensive Research Findings," Business Wire, May 29, 2002, via www .findarticles.com, "About Youth Smoking Prevention," Phillip Morris, http://www.philipmorrisusa .com/en/policies_practices/ysp/about_ysp.asp (accessed April 6, 2006).

Chapter 8

1. Bob Lewis, "Survival Guide: The Moral Compass— Corporations Aren't Moral Agents, Creating Interesting Dilemmas for Business Leaders," *InfoWorld,* March 11, 2002, via www.findarticles.com.

2. Marjorie Kelly, "Business Ethics 100 Best Corporate Citizens 2006," *Business Ethics* (Spring 2006), 22.

3. "SEC Chief Donaldson Pushes Ethics," MSNBC News, February 28, 2003, www.msnbc.com/news/ 878994.asp.

4. "62% of Americans Tell CEOs 'You're Not Doing Enough to Restore Trust and Confidence in American Business,'" Golin/Harris International press release, June 20, 2002, www.golinharris.com/news/ releases.asp?ID=3788.

5. Linda K. Trevino and Stuart Youngblood, "Bad Apples in Bad Barrels: Causal Analysis of Ethical Decision Making Behavior," *Journal of Applied Psychology* 75 (1990): 378–385.

6. Roger Parloff, "Wall Street: It's Payback Time," *Fortune,* January 19, 2009, 69.

7. Trevino and Youngblood, "Bad Apples in Bad Barrels."

8. "AmericaEconomia Annual Survey Reveals Ethical Behavior of Businesses and Executives in Latin America," AmericaEconomia, December 19, 2002, via www.prnewswire.com.

9. Constance E. Bagley, "The Ethical Leader's Decision Tree," *Harvard Business Review* (February 2003): 18–19.

10. "Ex-Tyco CFO Indicted for Tax Evasion," CNN/ Money, February 19, 2003, http://money.cnn .com/; "A Guide to Corporate Scandals," MSNBC .com, www.msnbc.com/news/wld/business/brill/ Corporate Scandal_DW.asp (accessed February 26, 2003).

11. "Fast Fact," *Fast Company,* September 2000, 96.

12. Merck & Co., Inc., 1999 Annual Report, 29.

13. "How Am I Doing?" *Business Ethics* (Fall 2005): 11.

14. "KPMG Integrity Survey 2005–2006," http://www .us.kpmg.com/RutUS_prod/Documents/9/ ForIntegritySurv_WEB.pdf (accessed March 24, 2006).

15. Gary R. Weaver and Linda K. Trevino, "Compliance and Values Oriented Ethics Programs: Influences on

Employees' Attitudes and Behavior," *Business Ethics Quarterly* 9 (1999): 315–335.

16. Peter R. Kendicki, "The Options Available in Ethics Programs," *National Underwriter*, November 12, 2001, 57–58.

17. *National Business Ethics Survey, 2007*, Ethics Resource Center, 2007, 18.

18. Mark S. Schwartz, "A Code of Ethics for Corporate Code of Ethics," *Journal of Business Ethics* 41 (2002): 37.

19. Ibid.

20. "2002 Fidelity Investments Code of Ethics Summary," Fidelity Investments, http://personal .fidelity.com/myfidelity/InsideFidelity/index.html (accessed March 3, 2003).

21. Cate Whitfield, Staff Administrator, Honda Engineering N.A. Inc. "A Small Company Case Study," Annual Business Ethics and Compliance Conference, 2005.

22. National Business Ethics Survey, *How Employees View*, 56.

23. "USSC Commissioner John Steer Joins with Compliance and Ethics Executives from Leading U.S. Companies to Address Key Compliance, Business Conduct and Governance Issues," *Society for Corporate Compliance and Ethics*, PR Newswire, October 31, 2005.

24. Allynda Wheat, "Keeping an Eye on Corporate America," *Fortune*, November 25, 2002, 44–45.

25. "About the ECOA," At A Glance, http://www .theecoa.org/AboutEOA.asp (accessed June 27, 2006).

26. Wheat, "Keeping an Eye on Corporate America."

27. "Top Corporate Ethics Officers Tell Conference Board That More Business Ethics Scandals Are Ahead; Survey Conducted at Conference Board Business Ethics Conference," PR Newswire, June 17, 2002, via www.findarticles.com.

28. "Ethics, Compliance, and Corporate Responsibility," HCA Healthcare, http://ec.hcahealthcare.com (accessed March 3, 2003).

29. O. C. Ferrell and Larry Gresham, "A Contingency Framework for Understanding Ethical Decision Making in Marketing," *Journal of Marketing* 49 (1985): 87–96.

30. Diane E. Kirrane, "Managing Values: A Systematic Approach to Business Ethics," *Training and Development Journal* 1 (1990): 53–60.

31. "Ethics and Business Conduct," www.boeing.com/ companyoffices/aboutus/ethics/index.htm

(accessed February 25, 2003), courtesy of Boeing Business Services Company.

32. Debbie Thorne LeClair and Linda Ferrell, "Innovation in Experiential Business Ethics Training," *Journal of Business Ethics* 23 (2000): 313–322.

33. "Top Corporate Ethics Officers Tell Conference Board."

34. Ibid.

35. Janet Wiscombe, "Don't Fear Whistle-Blowers: With HR's Help, Principled Whistle-Blowers Can Be a Company's Salvation," *Workforce*, July 2002, via www.findarticles.com.

36. Mael Kaptein, "Guidelines for the Development of an Ethics Safety Net," *Journal of Business Ethics* 41 (2002): 217.

37. National Business Ethics Survey, *How Employees View*, 32.

38. Curt S. Jordan, "Lessons in Organizational Compliance: A Survey of Government-Imposed Compliance Programs," *Preventive Law Reporter* (Winter 1994): 7.

39. Lori T. Martens and Kristen Day, "Five Common Mistakes in Designing and Implementing a Business Ethics Program," *Business and Society Review* 104 (1999): 163–170.

40. Anne C. Mulkern, "Auditors Smelled Trouble," *Denver Post*, October 2, 2002, A1.

Chapter 9

1. John Rosthorn, "Business Ethics Auditing—More Than a Stakeholder's Toy," *Journal of Business Ethics* 27 (2000): 9–19.

2. Debbie Thorne, O. C. Ferrell, and Linda Ferrell, *Business and Society: A Strategic Approach to Corporate Citizenship*, 2nd ed. (Boston: Houghton Mifflin, 2005).

3. Rosthorn, "Business Ethics Auditing."

4. "Environmental and Social Report," British Petroleum, www.bp.com/environ_social/guide_environ _social/ (accessed March 17, 2003).

5. "Accountability," Business for Social Responsibility, www.bsr.org/BSRResources/WhitePaperDetail .cfm?DocumentID=259 (accessed February 13, 2003).

6. Frank Reynolds, "Earnings Announcement Caused 25 Percent Stock Drop, Suit Says," November 26, 2008, http://news.findlaw.com/andrews/bf/ cod/20081126/20081126_cadence.html (accessed January 14, 2009).

7. "Why Count Social Performance," in *Building Corporate Accountability: The Emerging Practices in*

Social and Ethical Accounting, Auditing and Reporting, ed. Simon Zadek, Peter Pruzan, and Richard Evans (London: Earthscan, 1997), 12–34.

8. Kevin J. Sobnosky, "The Value-Added Benefits of Environmental Auditing," *Environmental Quality Management* 9 (1999): 25–32.

9. "Accountability," Business for Social Responsibility.

10. Trey Buchholz, "Auditing Social Responsibility Reports: The Application of Financial Auditing Standards," Colorado State University, professional paper, November 28, 2000, 3.

11. "Accountability," Business for Social Responsibility.

12. "America's Most Admired Companies," *Fortune,* March 17, 2008, http://money.cnn.com/magazines/fortune/mostadmired/2008/index.html (accessed January 14, 2009).

13. Wendy Zellner, "No Way to Treat a Lady?" *BusinessWeek,* March 3, 2003, 63–66.

14. Fisher, "America's Most Admired Companies," 72.

15. John Pearce, *Measuring Social Wealth* (London: New Economics Foundation, 1996) as reported in Warren Dow and Roy Crowe, *What Social Auditing Can Do for Voluntary Organizations* (Vancouver, Canada: Volunteer Vancouver, July 1999), 8.

16. Mark Maremont, "Tyco Holders Reject Proposal to Reincorporate in the U.S.," *Wall Street Journal* online, March 7, 2003, http://online.wsj.com.

17. Dennis K. Berman, "Qwest Spends Top Dollar to Defend Its Accounting," *Wall Street Journal* online, March 10, 2003, http://online.wsj.com.

18. "The Effect of Published Reports of Unethical Conduct on Stock Prices," reported in "Business Ethics," Business for Social Responsibility, www.bsr.org/BSRResources/WhitePaperDetail.cfm?DocumentID=270 (accessed March 5, 2003).

19. Ronald Alsop, "Ranking Corporate Reputations—Tech Companies Score High in Yearly Survey as Google Makes Its Debut in Third Place; Autos, Airlines, Pharmaceuticals Lose Ground," *Wall Street Journal,* December 6, 2005, B1.

20. "U.S. Companies Risk Reputations and Finances Due to Broadening Public Concern with All Forms of Corporate Behavior," PRNewswire, August 19, 2002, via www.findarticles.com.

21. Penelope Patsuris, "The Corporate Accounting Scandal Sheet," *Forbes* online, August 26, 2002, www.forbes.com/2002/07/25/accountingtracker.html.

22. "Six Sigma," http://en.wikipedia.org/wiki/Six_Sigma (accessed April 4, 2006).

23. "The Balanced Scorecard," http://en.wikipedia.org/wiki/Balanced_scorecard (accessed April 4, 2006).

24. "The Triple Bottom Line," http://en.wikipedia.org/wiki/Triple_bottom_line (accessed April 4, 2006).

25. Lynn Brewer, "Capitalizing on the Value of Integrity: An Integrated Model to Standardize the Measure of Non-Financial Performance as an Assessment of Corporate Integrity," in Lynn Brewer, Robert Chandler, and O. C. Ferrell, *Managing Risks for Corporate Integrity: How to Survive an Ethical Misconduct Disaster* (Mason, OH: Thomson/Texere, 2006), 233–277.

26. Brewer, Chandler, and Ferrell, *Managing Risks for Corporate Integrity,* 49–50.

27. Dow and Crowe, *What Social Auditing Can Do for Voluntary Organizations,* 15–18.

28. Peter Raynard, "Coming Together: A Review of Contemporary Approaches to Social Accounting, Auditing and Reporting in Non-Profit Organizations," *Journal of Business Ethics* 17 (1998): 1471–1479.

29. Tracy Swift and Nicole Dando, "From Methods to Ideologies: Closing the Assurance Expectations Gap in Social and Ethical Accounting," *Journal of Corporate Citizenship* (Winter 2002): 81–90.

30. "What Is Corporate Social Responsibility?" Vasin, Heyn & Company, www.vhcoaudit.com/SRAarticles/WhatIsCSR.htm (accessed February 13, 2003).

31. The methodology in this section was adapted from Thorne, Ferrell, and Ferrell, *Business and Society.*

32. "Accountability," Business for Social Responsibility.

33. Johann Mouton, "Chris Hani Baragwanath Hospital Ethics Audit," Ethics Institute of South Africa, 2001, available at www.ethicsa.org/report_CHB.html.

34. "Verification," Business for Social Responsibility, www.bsr.org/BSRResources/White PaperDetail.cfm?DocumentID=440 (accessed February 13, 2003).

35. "Ethical Statement," Social Audit, SocialAudit.org, www.socialaudit.org/pages/ethical.htm (accessed March 4, 2003).

36. Franklin Energy, http://www.franklinenergy.com/corevalues.html (accessed January 14, 2009).

37. "Verification," Business for Social Responsibility.

38. Ibid.

39. "Ethical Statement," Social Audit.

40. "Ethics, Compliance and Corporate Responsibility: Introduction," HCA Healthcare, http://ec.hcahealthcare.com (accessed February 17, 2003).

41. "Verification," Business for Social Responsibility.

42. Joseph B. White, "Ford President Faces Inquiry over Ad-Related Directive," *Wall Street Journal* online, March 10, 2003, http://online.wsj.com.

43. Buchholz, "Auditing Social Responsibility Reports," 15.

44. Mouton, "Chris Hani Baragwanath Hospital Ethics Audit."

45. "Verification," Business for Social Responsibility.

46. "Introduction to Corporate Social Responsibility," Business for Social Responsibility, www.bsr.org/BSRResources/WhitePaperDetail.cfm?DocumentID=138 (accessed March 5, 2003).

47. Mouton, "Chris Hani Baragwanath Hospital Ethics Audit."

48. "Introduction to Corporate Social Responsibility," Business for Social Responsibility.

49. Andrew Countryman, "SEC: HealthSouth Earnings Overstated by $1.4 Billion," *Austin American-Statesman* online, March 20, 2003, http://austin360.com/statesman/; Carrick Mollenkamp and Chad Terhune, "HealthSouth Says Its Auditor Has Found Big Misstatements," *Wall Street Journal* online, July 8, 2003, http://online.wsj.com.

50. "Accountability," Business for Social Responsibility.

51. Ibid.

52. Ethics and Compliance Officer Association, www.theecoa.org (accessed March 29, 2006).

53. "Accountability," Business for Social Responsibility.

54. "Verification," Business for Social Responsibility.

55. Ibid.

56. "Environmental and Social Report," British Petroleum.

57. Swift and Dando, "From Methods to Ideologies," 81.

58. Buchholz, "Auditing Social Responsibility Reports," 16–18.

59. Ibid., 19–20.

60. "Accountability," Business for Social Responsibility.

61. Buchholz, "Auditing Social Responsibility Reports," 19–20.

62. Mouton, "Chris Hani Baragwanath Hospital Ethics Audit."

63. "OCEG 2005 Benchmarking Study Key Findings," Open Compliance Ethics Group, www.oceg.org (accessed June 27, 2006).

64. *KPMG International Survey of Corporate Social Responsibility Reporting*, 2008, 28.

65. Sandra Waddock and Neil Smith, "Corporate Responsibility Audits: Doing Well by Doing Good," *Sloan Management Review* 41 (2000): 75–83.

66. Buchholz, "Auditing Social Responsibility Reports," 1.

67. Waddock and Smith, "Corporate Responsibility Audits."

68. Buchholz, "Auditing Social Responsibility Reports," 1.

69. Waddock and Smith, "Corporate Responsibility Audits."

70. J. C. Collins and J. I. Porras, *Built to Last: Successful Habits of Visionary Companies* (New York: HarperCollins, 1997).

71. Waddock and Smith, "Corporate Responsibility Audits."

Chapter 10

1. Alan K. Reichert, Marion S. Webb, and Edward G. Thomas, "Corporate Support for Ethical and Environmental Policies: A Financial Management Perspective," *Journal of Business Ethics* 25 (2000): 54.

2. Karen Birchard, "Britain Fines Drug and Chemical Companies for Vitamin Price Fixing," *Medical Post* 37, no. 41 (2001).

3. Neil King, Jr., "WTO Panel Rules Against Law on U.S. Punitive Import Duties," *Wall Street Journal*, June 18, 2002, A2.

4. "Dispute Settlement: WTO-Dispute Settlement Understanding (DSU)," Trade Negotiations and Agreements at http://www.dfait-maeci.gc.ca/tna-nac/disp/byrd-main-en.asp (accessed March 24, 2006).

5. Michael D. White, *Short Course in International Marketing Blunders* (Novato, CA: World Trade Press, 2002).

6. Ibid.

7. David A. Ricks, *Big Business Blunders: Mistakes in Multinational Marketing* (Homewood, IL: Dow-Jones Irwin, 1983), 83–84.

8. O. C. Ferrell and Geoffrey Hirt, *Business: A Changing World* (Burr Ridge, IL: Irwin/McGraw-Hill, 2000), 257.

9. Tibbett L. Speer, "Avoid Gift Blunders in Asian Locales," *USA Today* online, April 25, 2000, www.usatoday.com/life/travel/business/1999/t0316bt2.htm.

10. Jim Carlton, "Stymied in Alaska, Oil Producers Flock to a New Frontier," *Wall Street Journal,* September 4, 2002, A1, A15.

11. "Blow the Whistle—No Wait: Ethics Hotlines May Be Illegal in Europe," *Business Ethics* (Fall 2005): 10.

12. "Court Rules Parts of Wal-Mart Code Violate German Law," *Wall Street Journal* online, June 16, 2005, www.wsj.com.

13. Paul Burnham Finney, "The Perils of Bribery Meet the Open Palm," *New York Times,* May 17, 2005, via http://www.globalpolicy.org/nations/launder/general/2005/0517bribery.htm.

14. Michael Williams, "Many Japanese Banks Ran Amok While Led by Former Regulators," *Wall Street Journal,* January 19, 1996, A1, A9.

15. Andrew Singer, "General Motors: Ethics Increasingly Means Social Responsibility Too," *Ethikos,* May/June 2000, 9, 11–13.

16. Edward Alden, "Multinationals in Labour Pledge . . . ," *Financial Times,* July 28, 2000, via www.globalarchive.ft.com/search-components/index.jsp.

17. "Global Roundup," *International Business Ethics Review* (Spring/Summer 2005): 17.

18. O. C. Ferrell, Thomas N. Ingram, and Raymond W. LaForge, "Initiating Structure for Legal and Ethical Decisions in a Global Sales Organization," *Industrial Marketing Management,* November 2000, 1–10.

19. Peter Waldman, "Unocal to Face Trial over Link to Forced Labor," *Wall Street Journal,* June 13, 2002, B1, B3.

20. "Ethics in the Global Market," Texas Instruments, www.ti.com/corp/docs/company/citizen/ethics/market.shtml (accessed March 7, 2003).

21. Business for Social Responsibility, www.bsr.org (accessed March 7, 2003).

22. Stephen Power, "Update Needed for Tire Rules, Activists Argue," *Wall Street Journal,* September 8, 2000, B4; Tom Sharp, "Tiremaker Admits Mislabels," *Commercial Appeal,* August 29, 2000, B5, B10; Devone Spurgeon, "State Farm Researcher's Sleuthing Helped Prompt Firestone Recall," *Wall Street Journal,* September 1, 2000, B6; Joseph White and Stephen Power, "Federal Regulator Won't Probe Safety of Ford Explorer," *Wall Street Journal,* February 13, 2002, A4.

23. Rebecca Santana, "Women Entrepreneurs Take On Russia," MSNBC, September 4, 1999, www.msnbc.com/news/420132.asp.

24. "Bottom-Line Ethics," *Christian Science Monitor* online, April 3, 2000, www.csmonitor.com/durable/2000/04/03/p8sl.htm.

25. "IPEC Report on Child Labour," http://www.ilo.org/iloroot/docstore/ipec/prod/eng/200602_implementationreport_en.pdf (accessed January 2006).

26. Matthew L. Kish, "Human Rights and Business: Profiting from Observing Human Rights," *Ethics in Economics,* nos. 1 and 2, 1998.

27. Brandon Mitchener and Dan Bilefsky, "EU Fines Brewers, Other Companies for Price Fixing," *Wall Street Journal,* December 6, 2001, A17.

28. Karen Birchard, "Britain Fines Drug and Chemical Companies for Vitamin Price Fixing," *Medical Post* 37, no. 41 (2001).

29. David Fairlamb and Gail Edmondson, "Has the Euro Unleashed a Wave of Price-Gouging?" *BusinessWeek,* September 16, 2002, 4.

30. Peter Fritsch, "A Cement Titan in Mexico Thrives by Selling to Poor," *Wall Street Journal,* April 22, 2002, A1, A11.

31. Robert Read, "The EU-US WTO Steel Dispute: the Political Economy of Protection and the Efficacy of the WTO Dispute Settlement Understanding," http://www.lancs.ac.uk/staff/ecarar/steel.doc (accessed June 27, 2006).

32. Geoff Winestock and Neil King, Jr., "EU Aims at White House in Retaliation to Steel Tariffs," *Wall Street Journal,* March 22, 2002, A2.

33. Paul Burnham Finney, "The Perils of Bribery Meet the Open Palm," *New York Times,* May 17, 2005, via http://www.globalpolicy.org/nations/launder/general/2005/0517bribery.htm.

34. "Global Roundup" *International Business Ethics Review* (Spring/Summer 2005): 17.

35. Skip Kaltenhauser, "Bribery Is Being Outlawed Worldwide," *Business Ethics* (May–June 1998): 11.

36. "Transparency International Bribe Payer's Survey 1999," Transparency International, January 20, 2000, www.transparency.org/cpi/1999/bps.html.

37. "Genetic Engineering Hot New Topic in Shareholder Resolutions," *Business Ethics* (March–April 2000): 22.

38. Francesca Lyman, "Should Gene Foods Be Labeled?" MSNBC, September 15, 1999, www.msnbc.com/news/312001.asp.

39. Snapshot, "U.S. Cigarette Exports," *USA Today* online, www.usatoday.com/snapshot/money/msnap078.htm (accessed March 7, 2003).

40. Robert F. Hartley, ed., "Nestlé Infant Formula: The Consequences of Spurning the Public Image," in *Marketing Mistakes*, 3rd ed. (Columbus, OH: Grid, 1986), 47–61; "Nestlé and the Role of Infant Formula in Developing Countries: The Resolution of a Conflict," a series of reports, articles, and press releases provided by Nestlé Coordination Center for Nutrition, Inc., 1984.

41. Thomas M. Burton and Jill Carroll, "ConAgra Recalls Beef Products After at Least 16 People Become Ill," *Wall Street Journal*, July 22, 2002, B6.

42. Thomas M. Burton, "Baxter Devices Probed on Links with 10 Deaths," *Wall Street Journal*, September 4, 2001, B2.

43. Betsy McKay, "PepsiCo Challenges Itself to Concoct Healthier Snacks," *Wall Street Journal*, September 23, 2002, A1, A10.

44. *Delphi Automotive Systems Corporation 1999 Annual Report*, 17.

45. Aaron Bernstein, Michael Arndt, Wendy Zellner, and Peter Coy, "Too Much Corporate Power," *BusinessWeek*, September 11, 2000, 150.

46. "Mexico City Takes Action Against Polluters," Reuters Newswire, May 31, 1998, via America Online.

47. "Greenpeace Warns Israel to Stop Sea Dumping," Reuters Newswire, June 5, 1998, via America Online.

48. "Australia May Be Worst Air Polluter," Associated Press Newswire, June 1, 1998, via America Online.

49. Mylene Mangalindan, "Users Flame New Yahoo Privacy Plan," *Wall Street Journal*, April 8, 2002, A16.

50. Julia Angwin and Nichole Harris, "Order to Open Instant Messages May Not Matter," *Wall Street Journal*, September 18, 2000, A1, B8.

51. Google Milestones, http://www.google.com/corporate/history.html (accessed June 27, 2006).

52. "In the News—April 2000," Business for Social Responsibility, www.bsr.org/resourcecenter/news/news_output.asp?newsDT=2000-04&hTID=266 (accessed August 22, 2000).

53. Geri Smith, "Mexico: Zedillo Has to Sweep the Banks Clean," *BusinessWeek* online, June 1, 1998, www.businessweekonline.com.

54. Andrew Higgins, Alan S. Cullison, Michael Allen, and Paul Beckett, "Shell Games," *Wall Street Journal*, August 26, 1999, A1, A11; Andrew Higgins, Paul Beckett, and Ann Davis, "Off Duties," *Wall Street Journal*, September 15, 1999, A1, A17; Steve LeVine, Paul Beckett, and Andrew Higgins, "Moscow Bank Called Main Player in Russian Laundering Scheme," *Wall Street Journal*, September 15, 1999, B10; Erik Portanger, "Barclays Closing Some Russian Accounts," *Wall Street Journal*, September 16, 1999, A25; Glenn Simpson and Paul Beckett, "Money-Laundering Rules to Include Securities Firms," *Wall Street Journal*, November 21, 2001, A2.

55. Lola Nayar, "India Is Fighting 40 Basmati Patent Cases in 25 Countries," Rediff.com, August 24, 2001, www.rediff.com/money/2001/aug/24rice.htm.

56. Jefferson Graham, "Napster Ordered to Shut Down," *USA Today* online, July 2, 2000, www.usatoday.com/life/music/music208.htm; "Napster Brief Denies Wrongdoing," *USA Today* online, July 27, 2000, www.usatoday.com/life/cyber/tech/review/crh283.htm; "Napster Wins Respite from Shutdown Order," *USA Today* online, July 29, 2000, www.usatoday.com/life/cyber/tech/review/crh356.htm; "Napster Among Top 50 Web Sites," *USA Today* online, August 23, 2000, www.usatoday.com/life/cyber/tech/review/crh438.htm.

57. Greg Brosman, "Guatemalan Counterfeit Law Fuels Illegal Industry," Yahoo! Finance, July 28, 2000, http://biz.yahoo.com/rf/000728/n28384015.html.

58. Mrinalini Datta, "Unilever, Others Lose Millions in India to Copycats," Bloomberg.com, September 7, 2000, http://...fgcgi.cgi?ptitle=All%20Columns&touch =1&s1-blk&tp=ad_topright_bbco&T-markets =fgcgi_.

59. "'One World, One Forest'; The World Trade Organization," American Lands Alliance, www.americanlands.org/forestweb/world.htm (accessed March 7, 2003).

Index